Advanced Google AdWords™

Second Edition

Pete,
Good luck with Your
online Marketing

Advanced
Google AdWords™

Second Edition

Brad Geddes

John Wiley & Sons, Inc.

Senior Acquisitions Editor: WILLEM KNIBBE
Development Editor: AMY BRUEGET
Technical Editor: MATT VAN WAGNER
Production Editor: ELIZABETH CAMPBELL
Copy Editor: LIZ WELCH
Editorial Manager: PETE GAUGHAN
Production Manager: TIM TATE
Vice President and Executive Group Publisher: RICHARD SWADLEY
Vice President and Publisher: NEIL EDDE
Book Designer and Compositor: MAUREEN FORYS, HAPPENSTANCE TYPE-O-RAMA
Proofreader: JEN LARSEN, WORD ONE
Indexer: NANCY GUENTHER
Project Coordinator, Cover: KATHERINE CROCKER
Cover Design: RYAN SNEED

Dear Reader,

Thank you for choosing *Advanced Google AdWords, Second Edition.* This book is part of a family of premium-quality Sybex books, all of which are written by outstanding authors who combine practical experience with a gift for teaching.

Sybex was founded in 1976. More than 30 years later, we're still committed to producing consistently exceptional books. With each of our titles, we're working hard to set a new standard for the industry. From the paper we print on, to the authors we work with, our goal is to bring you the best books available.

I hope you see all that reflected in these pages. I'd be very interested to hear your comments and get your feedback on how we're doing. Feel free to let me know what you think about this or any other Sybex book by sending me an email at nedde@wiley.com. If you think you've found a technical error in this book, please visit http://sybex.custhelp.com. Customer feedback is critical to our efforts at Sybex.

Best regards,

Neil Edde
Vice President and Publisher
Sybex, an imprint of Wiley

To Sharon, my wife and best friend, who supports me in all my crazy endeavors.

Acknowledgments

Writing this book has been an amazing journey, and there are many who deserve a heartfelt thank you for contributing to this quest being completed.

At first, writing a second edition did not seem an overly difficult project as there were already more than 550 pages of content. I was wrong. It was amazing how much had changed in just a scant two years, and how much content needed to be created, updated, or completely rewritten.

Luckily, I had Matt Van Wagner, the technical editor who tirelessly checked every fact, calculation, and word. I've respected Matt for a number of years as we've spoken across the country together. After working with Matt on this book, not only do I have a higher respect for him, but the book is much better because of his dedication to this edition. Thank you, Matt.

I must always thank Sharon, my wife, who has supported my various adventures over the years no matter how insane they sounded. During the creation of the first edition, our daughter Lilith Rose was born. Two years later, Lilith still makes it difficult for me to tear myself away from her to finish the book, and many pages were written while she was giving her interpretation of marketing.

Thank you to my business partner, Leslie Clark, for keeping the company running while I was off writing and regularly ignoring the tasks at hand. It's been her support in growing the company that has made it possible for works like this to be created.

After three years, I am still impressed with the team at Wiley. Willem Knibbe had the idea to write a book on AdWords, and the foresight to keep me moving toward a second edition. He has provided input and assistance whenever necessary. Thank you Amy Brueget, Elizabeth Campbell, Liz Welch, and all the others who worked in the background for taking my thoughts and making them comprehensible and putting them to paper.

The teams at Google have not just given me support for the writing of this book, they have been giving me support for almost a decade, and for that I thank them. A special thank-you goes Fred Vallaeys, who is constantly striving to improve the product and is willing to listen to my rants and feedback about Google.

Finally, I must thank the Internet marketing community. I have been writing, speaking, and blogging about online marketing for many years. During that time, I have been an active participant in forums, blogs, and conferences. My interaction with the community, made up of significantly more people than I could ever acknowledge on paper, has helped to increase everyone's understanding and success with Google AdWords.

About the Author

Brad Geddes has been involved in online marketing for more than a decade. Over the years he has provided a variety of services, the most common being usability, SEO, PPC, product development, product positioning, agency consulting, and affiliate marketing.

One of his trademarks has been demystifying the more complicated aspects of SEO, PPC, and Internet advertising through writing, speaking, and training. Rather than keep secrets, Brad prefers to educate readers on the various aspects of crafting successful marketing campaigns to ensure the success for all parties involved.

Brad is not one to call himself an expert or guru. He prefers to educate marketers and let the results speak for themselves. Therefore, instead of writing paragraphs that use the words master, wizard, or thought-leader, and name-drop companies he has worked with such as Amazon, Yahoo!, and Google, he prefers presenting a simple bullet-point list of facts and letting intelligent readers make up their own minds based on what they learn.

As a speaker, Brad has spoken at:

- More than 50 conferences across the world
- Notable conferences such as AdWords Days (Germany), Afri-Tech (Kenya), Search Marketing Expo (SMX), Search Engine Strategies, and PubCon
- Events for both Google and Microsoft

As a trainer, Brad is the only Google-approved Advanced AdWords Seminar Leader and he has:

- Conducted more than 70 officially Google-sponsored, AdWords Seminars for Success that have been attended by more than 5,000 marketing professionals. AdWords Seminars for Success are two days of intensive training on Google AdWords.
- Worked with Google in implementing their reseller training program at R.H. Donnelley.
- Helped institute a training program for LocalLaunch that managed more than 40,000 PPC accounts.
- Conducted training days in multiple countries for conferences such as SEO Class, SMX, SES, Refined Labs, and PubCon.

As an Internet marketer, Brad:

- Built his first website in 1998.
- Started SEOing websites in 1998.
- Started affiliate marketing in 1999.
- Opened his first PPC account in 1999.

- Formed his first agency, iDjinni Consulting, in 2002, providing usability, PPC, SEO, and affiliate marketing services.
- Joined LocalLaunch in 2004. LocalLaunch began as a boutique agency. Then, it built a marketing platform that empowered sales forces to sell marketing products to their customer bases while the company did all of the product's management behind the scenes.
- Helped grow the LocalLaunch agency, providing PPC services to companies such as Red Lobster, Encyclopedia Britannica, YellowPages.com, and Yahoo!.
- Helped build marketing products that were used by more than 100,000 businesses.
- Helped build a system that managed more than 40,000 PPC accounts.
- Worked with companies such as Amazon, World Directories, DEX Media, and Local.com. While Brad managed vendor relations, R.H. Donnelley became one of the few Google and Yahoo! resellers in the world. LocalLaunch was sold to R.H. Donnelley in 2006.
- In 2008 formed bg Theory, a company dedicated to consulting, educating, and training businesses on Internet marketing theory and best practices.
- In 2010, formed Certified Knowledge, a training, tools, and community platform designed to teach companies Internet marketing and save them time managing accounts with robust tools.

Even more stuff:

- Author of *Advanced Google AdWords* (Sybex, 2010)
- Co-moderator of AdWords forum on Webmaster World since 2004
- *Search Engine Land* columnist since 2007
- Sits on the board for Boost Media
- Active blogger about PPC and marketing since 2001
- Technical editor for *Winning Results with AdWords* by Andrew Goodman (McGraw-Hill Osborne Media, 2005)
- One of the first Microsoft adCenter Excellence Members and participated in the beta
- One of the first 100 Google Advertising Professionals
- Worked with a range of companies that have spent as little as $17.50 to as much as millions per month

Contents

Foreword   *xix*

Introduction   *xxi*

Chapter 1   Understanding Search Theory   **1**

The Origins of Google AdWords. 2
Google Enters the Arena   5
Google AdWords Select Revolutionizes PPC   6

The Psychology of Search 7
Turning Concepts into Words   8
Understanding Search Results   10
The Purpose of Ad Copy   10
Landing Pages Lead to New Customers   12
Advertising Is Not Advertising When It Is Information   13

Goal Alignment: Google vs. You vs. the Searcher 15

Best Practices for Applying Search Theory 17

Chapter 2   Keyword Research   **19**

Understanding the Buying Funnel 20
Examining the Buying Funnel Phases   21
How Do Consumers Flow Through Your Buying Funnel?   22

Understanding Keywords 23
Types of Keywords   24
Finding Keyword Ideas   26
How Many Keywords Should You Have in Your Account?   29
Creating Keyword Lists   31
Using Long-Tail Keywords   33
Wide vs. Deep Keywords   35

Discerning Keyword Match Types. 36
Broad Match   36
Modified Broad Match   38
When Should You Use Broad Match?   40
Phrase Match   40
Exact Match   42
Which Match Type Is Best?   43

Using Negative Keywords 45
Implementing Negative Keywords   46
Negative Broad Match   47
Negative Phrase Match   48
Negative Exact Match   49

Putting Negative and Positive Keywords Together   50
Researching Negative Keywords   51

Advanced Organizational Techniques 52
Adding Multiple Match Types to the Same Ad Group   52
Restricting Match Types by Ad Group   53
Restricting Match Types by Campaign   53

Taking Control of Your Ad Display 54

Best Practices for Conducting Keyword Research 55

Chapter 3   Keyword Tools: Extracting Valuable Data from Google   57

AdWords Keyword Tool 58
Advanced Options and Filters   59
Generating Keyword Ideas   60
Keyword Suggestions by Category   64
Interpreting the Keyword Data   65
AdWords Keyword Tool vs. Third-Party Keyword Tools   71

Traffic Estimator 72

Google Trends 74

Google Insights for Search 76
What Services Should You Offer?   77
Determining Your Messaging   80
Determining Consumer Interest   81

Microsoft Advertising Intelligence 81

Best Practices for Using Keyword Tools 82

Chapter 4   Writing Compelling Ads   85

Do Your Ads Reflect the Search Query? 86

Writing Effective Ads 88
Calls-to-Action   89
Touching the Emotional Core   90

Following Google's Editorial Guidelines 91
Character Lengths   91
Editorial Requirements   92

Developing Unique Selling Propositions 93

Distinguishing Features and Benefits 94
Benefits, Features, and the Buying Funnel   96
When To Use a Feature vs. a Benefit   97

Employing Themes That Get Clicks 98
Utilizing Numbers in Ads   99
How Strong Is Your Call-to-Action?   102
Writing Informational Ad Copy   103
Utilizing Negative Ad Copy   105
Do Not Forget the Display URL   106

Spicing Up Your Ads with Ad Extensions 108
Sitelink Extensions   108
Product Extensions   110
Call Extensions   110
Social Extension   112
Lots of Limited Betas   113

Following the Law: Trademarks 113
Trademark Exceptions   115

The Quest for the Holy Grail of Advertising 116

Best Practices for Writing Compelling Ads 118

Chapter 5   Landing Pages That Convert Searchers into Buyers   119

Does Your Landing Page Answer the Searcher's Question? 120

Everything about Destination URLs 122
Using Destination URLs for Tracking   123
Complying with Destination URL Editorial Policies   130

Choosing Landing Pages That Increase Conversion Rates 131
Choosing Landing Pages Based on the Type of Query   132
Differentiating Local Business Queries   136
Using Segmentation Pages   138
Using Forms as Landing Pages   139
Thanking Your Customers   140
Crafting Perfect Landing Pages   142

Employing Usability, Trust, and Web Technology 142
Using Web Technology to Implement Usability and User Security   143
Psychological Factors That Increase Conversion Rates   151
Your Website's Usability Goals   157

Best Practices for Landing Pages 158

Chapter 6   Advanced Optimization Techniques   161

Optimizing for Traffic 162
Exploring Strategies That Display Your Ads More Often   162
Taking Advantage of Dynamic Keyword Insertion   166
Increasing Page Views   170

Optimizing for Conversions 174
Writing Ad Copy That Sells   174
Creating Landing Pages That Increase Conversions   176
Making Additional Conversions to Increase Your Profits   185

Best Practices for Advanced Optimization Techniques 188

Chapter 7   Demystifying Quality Score   191

What Is Quality Score? 192
How Quality Score Affects Ad Rank   194
Quality Score Factors for Search   195

Viewing Your Quality Score 199

Landing Page Quality: Making Your Pages Relevant 202
Spiderability   202
Relevance   202
Transparency   203
Navigation   204

Estimating Your First Page Bid 205

Understanding the Display Network Quality Score. 207
Quality Score for Managed Placements   208

Creating Highly Relevant Ad Groups 209

What to Do if Your Quality Score Drops 212
Increasing Your Quality Scores   214

Quality Score FAQs. 218

Best Practices for Optimizing Quality Scores 220

Chapter 8   Beyond Text: Image, Video, and Mobile Ads   223

Beyond the Desktop: Creating Mobile Ads 224
Reaching Smartphone Users   224
Call Extensions with Smart Phones   227
Reaching Other Mobile Users: Google Mobile Ads   228
Viewing Google Mobile Ads   230

Beyond Static Text: Creating Rich Media Ads 231
Creating Effective Image Ads   231
Developing Profitable Video Ads   236

Using Google's Display Ad Builder 239
Other Video Ad Formats   241

Best Practices for Employing Image, Video, and Mobile Ads 243

Chapter 9   Understanding the Display Network   245

What Is the Display Network? 246
Advantages of the Display Network   247
Explaining the Display Network   248

Creating a Successful Display Network Campaign 249
Creating Search- and Display-Only Campaigns   250
Ground Rules for Creating Effective Display Network
  Keyword-Based Ad Groups   251
Choosing the Correct Keywords for Your Display Network Ad Groups 252

Smart Pricing: Measure Success with Cost Per Conversion. 257

Learning How the Display Network Is Performing for You 259
Understanding the Network Reports   259
Stopping Google from Showing Your Ads on Sites That Do Not Convert 261
Managing Automatic Placements   265

Managed Placements: Choosing Which Display
Sites Show Your Ads 265
Placement Tool   266
Organizing Placements   269
Choosing CPM or CPC Bidding   269
Ongoing Management of Managed Placement Ad Groups   271

Best Practices for the Display Network 273

Chapter 10 Advanced Display Network Techniques   275

Enhancing Your Display Campaigns 276
Refining Your Display Exposure with Keywords   276
Controlling Your Placement Ad's Display   278
Optimizing Your Display Campaigns   280
Organizing Your Display Campaigns   282

Setting Different Bids by Demographics 287
Viewing Your Demographic Performance Stats   287
Setting Demographic Bids   289
Organizing Your Demographic Campaign   290

Remarketing 292
Defining An Audience   293
Custom Combinations   294
Place the Script on Your Site   295
Create a Remarketing Ad Group   296
The 500 Cookie Rule   297
Remarketing Strategies   298
Don't Creep Out Your Customers   304

Topic and Interest Targeting 305
Interest Targeting   305
Topic Targeting   307

Creating Scenarios to Understand and Reach Your Target Audience . . 308

Write Effective Display Ads 310

DoubleClick Ad Planner: Free Access to Expensive Data 312
Conducting Ad Planner Research   312
Adding Ad Planner Sites to AdWords   319

Best Practices for Advanced Display Network Usage 319

Chapter 11 Advanced Geographic Targeting   321

What Is Geographic Targeting? 322
The Technology Behind Location Targeting   322
How Accurate Is Location Targeting?   324

Reaching Users in Specific Locations 326
Finding Locations to Target   327
Radius Targeting   331
Advanced Location Targeting Options   332

Location Targeting Considerations 333
Targeting Multiple Countries   333
Reaching Users in an Area Smaller than a Country   335

Treating Locals and Nonlocals Differently in Your Ad Copy 340
Automatically Inserting Your Address into the Ad Copy   341
A Case Study into Local Belief Systems   345

Viewing Geographic Results 346

Geographic Performance Reports 348

Best Practices for Geographic Targeting 350

Chapter 12 Save Time and Scale Accounts with the AdWords Editor   353

AdWords Editor Overview 354
Choosing Your Viewpoint   354
Viewing Your Account in the AdWords Editor   358

How to Scale Your Account 362
Importing Keywords   362
Creating Thousands of Keywords and Ad Groups   364
Easily Creating Thousands of Ads   368

Optimizing Display with the AdWords Editor. 373

Best Practices for Using the AdWords Editor. 374

Chapter 13 Profitable Bid Strategies   377

Setting Your Marketing Goals. 378

Measuring Results with Google's Conversion Tracking Code. 379
AdWords Conversion Tracking Code   380
Accessing Valuable Conversion Data in AdWords Reports   384
Tracking Phone Calls   385

Exploring AdWords Bidding Options 386
Focus on Clicks, Option 1   386
Focus on Clicks, Option 2   387
Enhanced CPC   387
Conversion Optimizer   388
Focus on Impressions   390

Profitable Bidding Strategies 390
ROAS vs. Profit   391
Revenue per Click   392
Taking Margins into Account   395
How Can Publishers Determine Revenue per Click?   397
Tracking Long Sales Cycles with Conversion Funnels   399

Calculating Your Max CPC 401
Setting Bids Based on ROAS   402
Bidding for Exposure   403

Ad Scheduling: Automatically Changing Bids by Time Periods..... 406
Finding Conversion Information by Time Frames   408
Examples of Ad Scheduling Success   410
Creating Time-Sensitive Offers   415

Understanding Attribution Management...................... 416

Examining AdWords Reports to Make ROAS Bid Decisions 418

Best Practices for Utilizing Profitable Bid Strategies 421

Chapter 14 Successful Account Organization Strategies   423

What Is an AdWords Account?............................ 424
What Are the Limits of an AdWords Account?   424
Managing Multiple Accounts the Easy Way   425
Becoming a Google Advertising Professional   428

Developing a Successful Campaign Structure 429
Reasons to Create New Campaigns   430
Structuring Campaigns to Achieve Business Goals   431

Organizing an Ad Group to Increase CTR and Conversion Rates .. 445

Best Practices for Account Organization Strategies.............. 446

Chapter 15 Testing Techniques That Will Increase Profits   449

Testing Is Essential to Increasing Profits 450

Testing Ad Copy to Increase Conversions 450
Ad Copy Messages You Should Test   451

Ad Copy Themes to Spark Your Creativity 451
Test Discounts Instead of Prices   452
Creating the Ad Copy Test   455
General Guidelines for Statistical Significance   457
Measuring the Results of Your Ad Test   459

Testing Landing Pages to Increase Conversions................. 462
Testing Where to Send Traffic   462
Landing Page Testing Factors   468
Making Ads and Landing Pages Work Together   474
Essential Items to Test First   479
Creating a Landing Page Test   480

Testing Profit per Click and Profit per Impression.............. 484

AdWords Campaign Experiments........................... 486

Best Practices for Testing Techniques That Will Increase Profits.... 489

Chapter 16 AdWords Reports: Extracting Actionable Information   491

Choosing General AdWords Report Settings................... 492
Customizing the Interface   492
Downloading Your Data   495

Using Reports to Optimize Your Account.................... 497

Campaign Reports   497
Ad Group Performance Report   498
Ad Performance Report   499
Keyword Report   502
Network Reports   503
Dimension Reports   505

Custom Alerts 509

Best Practices for Using AdWords Reports 511

Chapter 17 Step by Step: Create and Monitor Your AdWords Account   513

Before You Create Your Account......................... 514

Creating Campaigns 516

Creating Search Campaigns   516
Creating Keyword-Based Display Campaigns   519
Creating Managed Placements Campaigns   521
Other Campaign Types   524

Optimizing Ongoing Campaigns.......................... 524

Optimizing Search Campaigns   524
Managing Budget Optimizer Campaigns   528
Optimizing Display Campaigns   530
Optimizing Managed Placements Campaigns   531
Optimizing CPM Campaigns   533
Optimizing Other Campaign Types   534
Creating an Optimization Schedule   535

Best Practices for Creating and Managing Your AdWords Account . . 539

Glossary   *541*
Index   *547*

Foreword

The need for businesses to find customers—and vice versa—is an age-old marketing conundrum. With varying degrees of effectiveness, solutions have included phone solicitation, email outreach, print advertising, and more—all designed to connect consumers and advertisers at the moment they're looking for each other. Today, with 97% of consumers researching purchases online, search engine marketing is a key component of any successful marketing campaign. I first got involved with pay-per-click advertising over a decade ago as a student at Stanford University. Using keyword buys on Goto .com, I started selling movies out of my dorm room, but my ads quickly lost effectiveness when I got outbid by advertisers with deeper pockets. There wasn't a book like this one to teach me the tricks of the trade and I soon gave up. Then a few years later in 2002, I started buying keywords for my photography business, but this time on Google's brand new AdWords system. AdWords was revolutionary because it rewarded relevance as much as the maximum cost per click, making it a great fit for those who took the time to create more targeted ads. Like many other advertisers, I saw great success with my campaigns and I was so excited by this revolutionary new way of advertising that when the opportunity presented itself, I signed on to join the AdWords team to work directly on this groundbreaking new product.

During my decade at Google, from 2002 through 2012, I was involved in countless product decisions for tools like the AdWords API, the AdWords Editor, Conversion Optimizer, Google Analytics, and many others that have helped shape AdWords into the advertising solution it is today. Nowadays, I help companies build online marketing strategies that incorporate all the latest proven techniques through my own company, Top Tier Inc.

"It's all about results..." That was the slogan of AdWords when I joined Google. My role has changed over the years but there's always been a focus on making sure AdWords delivers the best results for advertisers and users of Google. Building a system that works well for a wide range of advertisers meant adding many layers of sophisticated functionality, and while Place Pages, AdWords Express, and even AdWords are easy enough to use for novice advertisers, there are many advanced techniques for those who want more control to take their AdWords campaigns to the next level. This excellent book will help you make the transition from novice to expert AdWords user and will give you a leg up in discovering some of the best ways to use AdWords to its fullest. The beauty of this book is its comprehensiveness, covering everything from fundamental concepts like keywords to advanced topics like quality score, remarketing, and landing page optimization.

It is amazing how quickly search engine marketing has evolved into a key component of any successful marketing effort. This evolution continues today with more new ad formats that combine the simplicity and relevance of text ads with new formats that make information more useful. There are now also more metrics, more ways to segment data, and improved ways to use this data to drive improvements in ROI. And there's no slow-down in the growth of new places where advertisers can connect with their target audience such as through remarketing on the Google Content Network and with ads on the ever more ubiquitous smart phones and tablets. The one constant thread amongst these many changes is Google's focus on delivering relevance, measurability, and targetability. Regardless of where online advertising goes next, the expertise you gain in AdWords' advanced features today will help you become a savvier marketer in the future.

In the earliest days when AdWords became available as a self-service product, we were fortunate to have an active community of users who were ready to share their expertise with others. Brad was one of the very first community members who stood out as a trusted authority on all things related to AdWords; not an easy feat considering the rapid pace at which AdWords evolved. When I first heard about Brad, he was a top contributor in the AdWords forums, helping anyone who asked. To this day, he remains one of the leading experts on AdWords and I regularly see him continuing to share his knowledge and insight with others at industry conferences.

In this book, advertisers looking to get more out of AdWords will learn from one of the leading experts on the topic and someone who's used the system himself to build a very successful business. Once you get the basics of AdWords, there are a lot of sophisticated approaches to drive additional results—and this book will show you how.

Best of luck with your campaigns!

—FREDERICK VALLAEYS, FOUNDER OF TOP TIER INC.

@siliconvallaeys

+Frederick Vallaeys

Introduction

Who Should Read This Book

Advanced Google AdWords is written for people who have a solid understanding of AdWords and have opened and managed their own account. What you will not find is information on how to open an account, navigate through the interface, or introductory material on keywords. These basics can be found in the AdWords Learning Center for free.

This book begins where most blogs and training leave off—optimization for intermediate and expert users. There are so many options with AdWords that it can be difficult to determine where to start, or to understand what is possible. For instance, you could create an ad for a Google Android–powered phone that is only shown to a consumer if:

- The consumer is in the business section of *The New York Times*
- The article being read is about stock brokers
- The consumer is on an Android-powered phone
- The consumer is located in Minneapolis
- The day is Monday
- The time is between 6am and 8am

While rarely will you want and ad shown under such stringent conditions, choosing one or two of those options to constrain your ad serving to reach your ideal customer will help you save marketing dollars. And best yet, you will be putting the correct ad in front of your target market.

Of course, there is more to AdWords than image ads and the display network. We start with search and end with step-by-step instructions. We will dive into detailed ad copy and landing page testing, account organization, ad copywriting, and even multiple strategies for setting bids.

You will find one of the most comprehensive sections ever written on Quality Score. If you have been advertising with Google for a while and either do not know what quality score is, or have had issues with high first page bids or low quality scores—this book is definitely for you.

If you are an advanced user and wondering if you can learn from this book, just flip to the last chapter. There you will find a step-by-step guide for creating and optimizing AdWords accounts. Every single section in that chapter is the cumulation of what you will learn throughout this book.

This book's two mantra words are *creativity* and *profits*. To be creative with AdWords you need to understand your options and how various settings influence other settings. To increase profits you need to understand testing, conversions, and bidding strategies. When you combine creativity and profits, you will stop just advertising and spending money. Instead, you will put the correct ad in front of your ideal customer at the time when they are most likely to convert so that your company can increase their overall profits.

What You Will Learn

This book does not just tell you how a feature works, but gives you strategies into using that feature. For instance, most national companies ignore location targeting. This is a mistake. Did you know you can buy a diet beer in Japan? Try selling a diet beer to Americans. You cannot buy Coke Lite in the United States nor Diet Coke in Europe. Why? The words *diet* and *lite* invoke different feelings in different geographies. This book will give you strategies to determine your conversion rate and spend for different geographies, how to test different ads by geography, and how to maximize your returns in each geography where you are advertising.

Not everything is about location. This book examines how to find, measure, change, test, and implement strategies for a variety of topics including:

- Keywords
- Ad copy
- Quality Score
- Time of day targeting
- Testing ad copy
- Testing landing pages
- Profit by impression testing
- Account organization

We will go through the steps of helping you to learn where to best spend your time. With so many options it can be difficult to determine where to start. We will help by not just showing you where to spend your initial time, but also how to set up reporting schedules so that you can continue to grow and optimize your account.

By reading this book, you will learn step-by-step strategies that will increase your company's profits through using Google AdWords.

What Is Covered in This Book

Since Google AdWords is so complex, this book is intended to be used in two ways. First, read it straight through to learn how to use account strategies. Once you have read it once, then this book is intended to be a reference book that you can also refer back to as you are optimizing your account.

Each chapter ends with a best practice section that contains easy-to-comprehend points about the subject material to quickly refresh your memory. Secondly, the last chapter of this book is a step-by-step guide to getting things done. Refer to that chapter when you are opening or optimizing accounts and follow along. If there is a step where you need more information, simply refer back to the chapter where that topic is covered in detail.

By reading and then referring back to this book, implementing new AdWords strategies to optimize your account will save you time and money.

Chapter 1: Understanding Search Theory Learn the history of PPC advertising and the psychology of search.

Chapter 2: Keyword Research How the buying funnel and your keywords work together. Control when your ad is displayed through using a combination of both positive and negative keywords.

Chapter 3: Keyword Tools: Extracting Valuable Data from Google Learn how to combine Google's spiders with a dictionary to improve your keyword research. Learn how to use other Google and Microsoft free tools to improve your account.

Chapter 4: Writing Compelling Ads From benefits to features to trademarks to Unique Selling Propositions: Learn to write ads that connect with the searcher.

Chapter 5: Landing Pages that Convert Searchers into Buyers Learn how to choose the best page on your site for every keyword. Then ensure the proper elements of usability, trust, and options control exist on the page to convert the searcher into a buyer.

Chapter 6: Advanced Optimization Techniques Learn strategies for increasing conversion rates, click through rates, traffic, and ad impressions.

Chapter 7: Demystifying Quality Score Each quality score factor is torn apart, examined, and put back together so you can see exactly how your quality score is determined. Then, learn strategies for managing and increasing quality scores.

Chapter 8: Beyond Text: Image, Video, and Mobile Ads There is more to Google than text ads. Dive into the best uses of video, image, and mobile ads.

Chapter 9: Understanding the Display Network The display network may be the most misunderstood and least optimized section of AdWords. Understand how the display network really works and how to start taking advantage of it.

Chapter 10: Advanced Display Network Techniques The display network's reach is significantly larger than Google's search reach. These techniques will not only help you find new customers that have never searched for your products, but also show you ways of bringing lost conversions back to your site.

Chapter 11: Advanced Geographic Targeting Control exactly where your ad is shown. Understand the technology so you can avoid pitfalls and take advantage of displaying unique messages through location targeting.

Chapter 12: Save Time and Scale Accounts with the AdWords Editor When accounts include hundreds of thousands of keywords, and tens of thousands of ad copies, they can be difficult to create and optimize. This chapter will examine how to save you time in creating and managing small to enormous accounts through the AdWords Editor.

Chapter 13: Profitable Bid Strategies Examine your business model so that you can set and measure your marketing goals to ensure your company is profitable. Then, learn to how to set and manage bids by ROI, profit, day of the week, and time of day. Formulas and Excel walkthroughs are included so no one gets lost in the math and calculations.

Chapter 14: Successful Account Organization Strategies Success starts with account organization. Read tips, tricks, and strategies that will help you find the correct organization for your AdWords account.

Chapter 15: Testing Techniques That Will Increase Profits Testing ad copy and landing pages is essential to continuously increasing profits. Learn not just how to create and measure a test, but find out how to determine how much money you make every single time an ad is displayed.

Chapter 16: AdWords Reports: Extracting Actionable Information Learn how to create and use all the valuable data that your AdWords account accumulates. Create a reporting schedule so that you always have access to the data necessary to improve your account.

Chapter 17: Step-by-Step: Create and Monitor Your AdWords Account After sixteen chapters packed with information, it is time for a step-by-step walkthrough of how to create and optimize each campaign type based upon what you have learned. Refer back to this chapter every time you are working in AdWords to see what to do next.

Glossary If you do not recognize an acronym or piece of jargon, refer to this handy reference guide to look up the term.

The Companion Website

Google AdWords adds or tweaks features over time. Therefore, we have created a companion website with additional links and features which can help you through your AdWords optimization journey. The website can be accessed at: http://AdvancedAdWordsBook.com.

How to Contact the Author

I welcome feedback from you about this book or about books you'd like to see from me in the future. You can contact me at: http://certifiedknowledge.org /contact/. For more information about my work, please visit our sites:

http://AdvancedAdWordsBook.com

http://CertifiedKnowledge.org

Twitter: @bgTheory

Advanced
Google AdWords™

Second Edition

Understanding
Search Theory

The search process itself may seem simple: A searcher visits a search engine, enters a search query, and receives results. Every step of the search process, however, is accompanied by the searcher's thoughts and expectations. Understanding how your keywords and ads align themselves with the search process can help bring more visitors to your site and achieve more conversions from those visitors.

Pay-per-click (PPC) advertising is effective because it mirrors the search process, and the two work seamlessly with each other. Understanding the origins and evolution of PPC advertising will also give you a glimpse into its future, so you can continue to take advantage of this ever-expanding form of advertising.

1

Chapter Contents
The origins of Google AdWords
The psychology of search
Goal alignment: Google vs. you vs. the searcher
Best practices for applying search theory

The Origins of Google AdWords

In 1996, a small company was formed that would forever change the world of Internet marketing. This company was called Idealab. It took two years of hard work and creative ideas before Bill Gross's company would launch GoTo.com with a simple business model: Advertisers could choose to display their ads based on what a searcher was trying to find. A searcher would type a query into the search box (Figure 1.1), and if advertisers chose to advertise on that word, their ad would show in the search results. Four simple concepts made this business model revolutionary.

Figure 1.1 GoTo.com's search page, circa 1998

The first was relevance, a word later adopted by Google throughout their AdWords program. Showing ads based on what someone was actively seeking made these new search ads more relevant than anything previously displayed on the Internet.

 Note: AdWords is Google's pay-per-click program where an advertiser chooses words that will trigger their ad. The advertiser is charged only if their ad is displayed and clicked by a searcher. This unique pricing model not only ensures that an advertiser's message is seen but that the advertiser pays only when someone arrives at their website.

Advertisers would only choose to display their ads on keyword searches that were related to their products or services. Since their ads would then only be shown when someone was searching for related information, these ads would help the searchers find what they were seeking.

Before the days of PPC, the ads alongside a search results page were often banner ads that had nothing to do with the search query. While these ads did gather many impressions (an *impression* is when an ad is shown on a page), they were not relevant to the user and thus were rarely clicked. Advertisers were paying for exposure but were not receiving much traffic for their ad dollars.

In the early days of Google, before AdWords launched, the founders of Google had been questioned many times by their investors about how they would eventually monetize their search engine. At that time, the founders did not have an answer; however, they held steadfast to the belief that at the moment someone was shown a page of search results, Google had their undivided attention. It would be in that moment of someone scanning a page of search results that Google would make its money. It turned out to be an accurate observation by the early Googlers.

By displaying ads based on what someone was actively seeking, GoTo.com formed a synergy between searchers and advertisers that helped both reach their goals on a single search page. Advertisers would receive visitors who were actively seeking their products, and searchers would find products that were related to what they were seeking. This was a win for both searchers and advertisers.

The second concept was the pricing model. Previously, almost all advertisements were based on paying for impressions. A company would decide how many impressions they would like to buy for their banner ads, and then they would pay on a cost per thousand impressions (CPM) basis. This created a scenario where you had to have a large advertising budget to even sign an initial contract. In addition, you had no idea how many visitors or sales those ads would bring to your site. The world of Internet advertising was mostly formed by larger companies or companies with venture capital backing.

By changing to a PPC pricing model, advertisers paid only when they received traffic. This shift to performance-based advertising allowed companies to try out a fledgling business model with very little monetary commitment. The minimum monthly spend was roughly one dollar per day, a big change from minimums that were often several thousand dollars a month.

Because search engines were paid only when a click occurred, it also forced search engines to show only relevant ads. If an ad did not get clicked, the search engine did not make money. The pricing model helped reinforce that only relevant ads should be shown on a search results page. This forced advertisers and search engines to work together to create a better search page for the consumer.

The third concept—and how both Yahoo! and Google have built a base of hundreds of thousands of advertisers—was the signup process. GoTo.com removed the barrier of a salesperson between the advertiser and the inventory. Using a self-serve ad model, any advertiser could sign up for a PPC account and start selecting keywords and creating ad copy within minutes (Figure 1.2).

By choosing a self-serve model, a search engine did not have to pay commission to a salesperson. There were no contracts to sign, no insertion orders (IOs) to fax, and no phone calls to be made before you could start advertising on the Web. This straightforward approach allowed anyone from a small business to a Fortune 500 company to quickly experiment with Internet advertising.

Figure 1.2 The AdWords signup process is a simple wizard influenced by GoTo.com.

The Internet was still a new concept to most people, and both companies and consumers were unsure how widely adopted the Web would become. Thus, having the ability to commit a few dollars and experiment with the new medium was paramount to introducing thousands of new companies to the concept that they could make money on the Web.

It also enabled the search engines to scale their advertiser base quickly. People often slow down the advertising process, and allowing a self-serve model meant that the only barrier to advertising was a bit of time and a credit card.

The last concept is what has allowed Yahoo! and Google to make billions of dollars from their advertisers—the auction process. GoTo.com did not have a set price for what you needed to pay when a keyword was clicked in a search result. Advertisers set a price of what they were willing to pay, and the company willing to pay the most showed up highest in the search results.

If you were willing to pay more than your competitors, then your ad would show higher in the search results, which would gather more clicks and bring more visitors to your website. It is easy to see how the top positions were highly coveted.

Yahoo! vs. Google

In 2001, GoTo.com was awarded the patent entitled "System and method for influencing a position on a search result list generated by a computer network search engine." This patent is the heart of PPC advertising technology. In April 2002, Overture sued Google over patent infringement. The lawsuit dragged on for two years, during which Yahoo! acquired Overture, until it was time for Google to transform into a public company. Not wanting to go public with a major lawsuit that threatened its revenue, Google finally settled with Yahoo! by issuing 2.7 million shares of stock in exchange for a perpetual license to the patent.

The process has become much more complex over the years as search engines, users, and advertisers have become savvier.

In October 2001, GoTo.com, Inc., renamed itself Overture Services. In 2003, Overture was acquired by Yahoo! for $1.63 billion. In 2010, Microsoft and Yahoo! formed the Search Alliance. With this new deal, Yahoo! would now serve ads from Microsoft's adCenter platform and the original PPC engine would no longer be used by anyone.

Today, GoTo.com is an unknown name to most people; in fact GoTo.com is no longer owned or operated by Yahoo! and now redirects to a site unrelated to PPC advertising.

As described earlier, GoTo.com's four founding concepts were quite simple: relevance, pay-per-click pricing, self-service, and auction-based pricing. However, these principles were combined not only to quickly gain advertiser adoption, but also to reap the monetary benefits of advertiser competition for the top ad positions.

Google Enters the Arena

Back in 1998, when GoTo.com was first launching, Google's search engine was just renamed from BackRub and was running on Stanford University servers. Creators Larry Page and Sergey Brin were more concerned with moving their operations into Susan Wojcicki's garage than making money.

Note: Susan Wojcicki's garage served as Google's first workspace away from Stanford's campus. Wojcicki was instrumental in Google's growth when she became one of their early employees and is often referred to as the "Mother of AdSense." (AdSense is Google's contextual advertising program.)

Over the next two years, Google moved to Mountain View, accepted $25 million in funding, and hired key employees to help in their evolution. Their early hires revolved around scaling their search technology. Craig Silverstein was their very first employee and served as the director of technology. Much of his early work helped scale the IT operations that would allow Google to grow. The next step was finding a way to start making money.

Google's first offering was an uninspired CPM program. To advertise with Google, you had to talk to a sales rep and sign a contract for a fairly high minimum spend. Although advertisers could choose to show an ad based on a searcher's query, the four concepts that had made GoTo.com a success were not to be found.

The high barrier to advertising with Google was lowered in October 2000 when Google launched their first self-serve advertising program. The simply named Google AdWords started with 350 customers. However, AdWords was still bought on a CPM basis.

Google AdWords Select Revolutionizes PPC

February 2002 will always be remembered as the time when Google forever changed pay-per-click advertising. Google launched AdWords Select, which incorporated all of GoTo.com's founding principles; however, in typical Google fashion, they added their own twist to the auction model.

On GoTo.com, the more you paid, the higher your ad appeared in search results. That essentially made it so the company willing to pay the most had the highest visibility. Google's main advertising word was relevance, and they changed the PPC auction model both to increase relevance for a searcher and to maximize how much money Google made on a search results page.

Their twist was to incorporate click-through rates (CTR) in determining where an ad showed up in the results. They used a simple formula to determine ad position: Maximum CPC (cost per click) multiplied by CTR.

Note: Search engines protect their most important metric, revenue per search (RPS), from public consumption. However, with some rough math the numbers can be approximated. In 2004, Google made around $0.10 per search, which increased to $0.19 in 2006, and finally surpassed $0.25 in 2007. Conversely, Yahoo!'s revenue per visitor was roughly only $0.16 in 2007. As the economy dipped in 2009, so did Google's RPS, to approximately $0.095, which was still higher than Yahoo!'s at that time.

However, it is difficult to blame the entire dip on the economy. As more information is integrated into the search results, there is less of a need for the consumer to always leave the search results page. For instance, a search for "Chicago weather" will show the five-day forecast within the search results, which results in fewer people clicking away from the page to find the weather forecast.

Since 2009, Google's RPS has continued to decline; but that does not indicate poor performance for the search giant. Google's total revenues continue to increase year after year.

The logic was that if an ad was clicked more often, it was more relevant to the searcher, and the advertiser should be rewarded for showing an ad aligned with the searcher's query.

This simple formula also maximized the dollars Google made on every single search engine results page (SERP). In the PPC model, a search engine is paid only when a click occurs.

On GoTo.com, if advertisers were willing to bid more than everyone else for a click, their ads would show up at the top of the search pages. If those same ads did not receive clicks, the engines did not actually make money from displaying those ads.

Therefore, a search engine should not want to display the highest-bidded ads the most if they were not clicked. A search engine would make more money by displaying lower-bidded ads that gathered clicks than high-cost ads that received few clicks.

By incorporating a combination of both bid prices and how many clicks those ads received, Google managed to maximize how much they made on any single search results page. This simple change also created an environment where a small company with a more compelling offer could have its ad displayed higher in a SERP than a large national company that did not take the time to create relevant ads. Price no longer trumped relevancy. Having the most money did not ensure the most clicks or visibility. Advertisers had to choose keywords that were more relevant to their products and create ads to match.

This level playing field helped spur advertiser adoption to the point that Google eventually dropped their CPM program completely and renamed the AdWords Select program to the name used today: Google AdWords.

Over the years, Google has become much more sophisticated and has revamped their formulas for displaying ads on search pages. However, throughout the growing complexities of AdWords, Google has always kept their ad serving synergistic with the search process. To understand how to take advantage of aligning your advertising efforts with Google's ad serving, it is important to understand the psychology of search.

The Psychology of Search

One of the advantages of online advertising is transparency of data to the advertiser. It is easy to track click-through rates, conversion rates, cost per conversions, total conversions, bounce rates, and more data points than anyone could ever analyze. The numbers can be overwhelming. Between the reports you can run in AdWords, some simple Excel formulas, and your analytics program, you can get buried in meaningless data.

It is essential to look beyond the numbers and consider the individuals sitting at their anonymous keyboards conducting the searches. While numbers tell the story of your marketing, it is the actual people who can make your advertising profitable.

Since search marketing—and Google AdWords in particular—is based around people using search engines, you must also think about how search engines are used in everyday life. Understanding not only how people use search engines, but also how they decide to click on an ad from the search page will help align your marketing efforts with the searchers. Having someone arrive at your site is just one step in the equation. Your website must also be aligned with the searcher's interest so the searcher does not just browse your website but also becomes a new customer.

Search engines are not used to browse the Web. That is the domain of properties such as iGoogle, StumbleUpon, and Digg. There is more information on the Web than anyone could read in dozens of lifetimes, and most of that information is of no interest to the searcher. Therefore, people do not just read search engines attempting to absorb all the information that has been discovered around the Web. Search engines are used when people want to find a specific piece of information. More importantly, people use search engines to find answers to questions.

We all think differently. We all ask questions differently. Delving into the various ways that people think and ask questions can assist you in choosing keywords that will make sure your ad appears in front of someone searching with questions your site can answer.

Turning Concepts into Words

The majority of people do not think in words. Words are conventions to relay the thoughts that are present in our minds. Although words are how we communicate in daily life, they are just a vehicle to help us express the concept of our thoughts to others.

People are not mind readers. You cannot think at a person and have that person understand your thoughts. You have to take the concepts present in your brain and transform them into words so that another person can understand you. The translation that occurs from concept to word is different for each person. This is why you might readily understand one person and not understand another person who is trying to express the exact same idea.

This same process of putting our thoughts into words is also how we communicate with a search engine. Google has not yet developed the technology where you can telepathically receive your answer. Therefore, you need to express yourself in the typed word to receive a response.

 Note: While Google can't read your mind, they can interpret more inputs than just text. In 2007, Google launched a call-in search named Goog-411 that was only open a brief period of time. Then in 2009, Google incorporated speech to text on Android-powered phones. Then in 2011, Google's Chrome browser became capable of translating speech into search queries.

To further the process of examining how people translate their thoughts into words, we will use the following scenario and examine some of the ways in which this scenario can be typed into a search engine.

Chicago is brutally cold in the winter. Imagine sitting in your suburban house watching a movie on a Saturday evening. Suddenly, your spouse tells you that there is water flooding the basement. Upon examination, you discover that a pipe has frozen, causing it to break, and now you need a plumber to come out to your house to fix the problem.

This is a very common winter scenario in Chicago. However, the ways in which people will attempt to solve this problem are very different.

Some people are very direct in their thinking. They will go to Google and type in the actual question they need to find an answer to, such as "Where do I find a Chicago plumber?" Many people, instead of typing out the entire question, will shorten the query to just "Chicago plumber" or maybe more precisely "Schaumberg plumber," or "emergency plumbing services Schaumberg."

Others will have a preconceived notion about what they wish to find, and their query will be more aligned with the answer they wish to receive. For example, the query might be "A site about Chicago plumbers."

If you are the do-it-yourself type, you might first want to turn off the water to stop the initial problem before contacting a plumber. A search for "How to turn off the water in my basement" would be more appropriate.

What is the root cause of the problem? If you searched for the root cause, the site that held the answer could also help you fix the broken pipes. Queries such as "broken pipes" or "frozen pipes" could lead you to your answer. You could also search for the actual problem, such as "flooded basement."

It can be a useful exercise to walk into the office tomorrow and describe this scenario to your coworkers. Then ask each of them what they would type in the search box. If you ask them one by one, instead of in a group, you are sure to receive a slightly different answer from almost everyone you ask. There will be some repetition, but concentrate on the different types of answers.

In fact, there are thousands of ways that someone could search for the answer to this scenario. In later chapters, we will dive more into keyword research. Most queries usually fall into one of a few categories:

- The actual question, or a shortened version of the question
- The answer to the question
- A description of the problem
- A symptom of the problem
- A description of the cause
- Product parts or brand names

It is essential that you consider all the ways someone can search for your products. Search queries are thought processes. Understanding someone's query can give you insight into what question they want answered.

Understanding Search Results

Once the thought has been translated into words, it is time to find the answer to the question. You go to Google, type in your words, and before you click the Search button, something psychological happens—expectation setting.

As a human, every time you conduct any action, you have an expectation of results. When you first looked at the spine of this book on the shelf, you had a notion of what it contained. Before you bought the book, you had an expectation of what you would learn by reading it. Every event also changes and refines those expectations. As you read this chapter, you have a different expectation of what you will find later in the book than when you first bought it.

This series of ongoing expectation settings also affects how you view search engines. When you input a query, you expect to see certain ads and websites displayed that will help you find the answer to your question.

This same expectation setting happens for every person using a search engine. Everyone expects to find websites that will help them answer their question. Therefore, before you ever click the Search button, you have already built an idea of what the act of typing your query into a search box will bring to your computer screen.

Within the search process, your ad has a specific role. Having your ad appear on that search page is not your endgame. Your ad must be relevant to the search result. You do not want everyone who sees your ad to come to your website. You only want those who are going to engage your company to click on your ads and visit your website. Every click costs money, so you don't want all the clicks possible—you just want the clicks that are more likely to turn into customers.

The Purpose of Ad Copy

Once the Search button is clicked, Google displays a set of ads and websites (Figure 1.3). A quick scan of the page will tell the searcher if the results are in line with their expectations. If they are not, the searcher is likely to stop reading the results and change the search query.

As an advertiser, this brief moment is your chance to connect with the searcher. These few seconds can determine whether the searcher will visit your site, visit your competitor's site, or just search again for the answer and completely ignore your ad.

At this moment, your ad needs to stand up, jump around, wave its arms, grab the searcher's attention, and shout, "I have the answer to your question! Come click on me and I'll show you the answer."

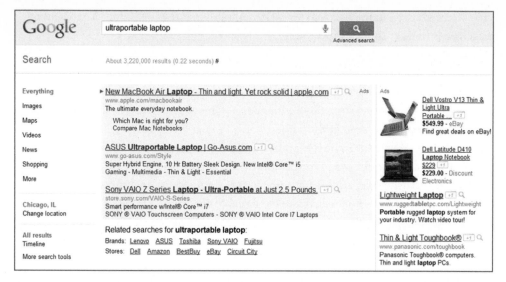

Figure 1.3 Google search result for "ultraportable laptop." Which ad answers the question?

Attempting to create ads that both stand out from the crowd to gain initial attention and are compelling enough to entice someone to click is a difficult proposition. As a marketer, your job is to write ads that meet the expectations of the searcher, and yet can communicate to that same person that your website can deliver the answer to their question.

AdWords ads are only 130 characters in length, and they have a tremendous amount to accomplish in just a few scant words.

An ad needs to have a headline that draws attention. It needs to stand out from other ads on a page that are clamoring for attention. The ad copy needs to tell a visitor why you have the answer to their question. And yet, the ad also needs to be faithful to your products or services. You can never lose sight of what makes your company money; otherwise, you will be paying for clicks that do not help you reach your goals.

Ads should not be written to please the advertiser. They should not be written to make the CEO smile. Ads should be written to convey to the searcher that you hold the key to their question, and they must first walk through your ad copy to your website before they can find out the answer. We will spend time in later chapters discussing how to create these ads and even how to test them against each other.

Hopefully your ad has caught the searcher's eye. The searcher thinks your ad can lead them to information that will help them complete their quest. And just before the searcher clicks on your ad, something else happens—another expectation is being set.

When a person does a search on Google, he or she has a preconceived notion of what they will see on a search results page based on what words they choose to search. Your ad copy is the only thing a user knows about your website; therefore, those few characters are setting the user's expectations about what they will find. Your landing page needs to meet those expectations.

Landing Pages Lead to New Customers

When someone clicks on your ad, they are taken to your website. Usually this is the first brand interaction someone has with your company. It's your first chance to showcase your offer to that searcher.

"Landing page" is industry jargon for the first page a searcher views after clicking on your ad. It should rarely be the home page of your site. It should be a page within your website that is most logically connected to the search query.

For instance, if someone conducted a search for "Sony digital cameras," that person would not want to be taken to Amazon.com's home page. The home page does not have information about Sony digital cameras. At best, the searcher will search again at Amazon's site. At worst, they will go back to the search results. A much better search experience would have the searcher taken to a page about Sony digital cameras within Amazon's website.

Remember, most searchers do not know your website. The searcher does not have prior knowledge about your company. They arrived at your site after clicking on just 130 characters of ad copy. That small amount of text is all the information they have about your site before first visiting it. In fact, your ad copy is the only thing within your entire AdWords account that a searcher can see. Therefore, that ad copy is crucial in setting the proper expectation for what the searcher will find after clicking on your ad.

To continue meeting the searcher's expectations, your landing page must be an extension of your ad copy. Since your ad copy informed the searcher about what they would find, the landing page should continue the conversation by assisting them to find their answer (see Figure 1.4).

If your landing page does not meet the searcher's expectation, they will use the most common navigational element on the entire Web—the dreaded Back button. You paid for the click; this is something you definitely want to avoid.

The landing page should show someone the answer to their question or instructions on how to get the answer to their question. For an e-commerce site, the answer is contained in the product someone will receive once they've checked out through your shopping cart. When they're looking for a plumber, the answer comes after they make a phone call. At other sites, the answer will come after the searcher fills out a form for more information. For most businesses, when the consumer receives the answer to their question, the business has a new customer.

The landing page is critical to your AdWords success. A bad landing page leads to wasted advertising dollars due to the searcher leaving your site without conducting any business with your company. A good landing page will turn shoppers into buyers.

Figure 1.4 This Bose landing page showcases a product and allows a searcher to either buy or get more information.

The process of someone searching and buying on the Web is much different from other forms of advertising. While many other types of advertising campaigns are structured to create emotional need within a consumer, the search advertising process is driven by giving someone the correct information at the correct time. This concept extends from choosing the correct keyword to creating your ad copy, and ultimately answering the searcher's question on your website.

Advertising Is Not Advertising When It Is Information

> Once upon a time I was riding on the top of a First Avenue bus, when I heard a mythical housewife say to another, "Molly, my dear, I would have bought that new brand of toilet soap if only they hadn't set the body copy in ten point Garamond." Don't you believe it. What really decides consumers to buy or not to buy is the content of your advertising, not its form.

> DAVID OGILVY

Often people are resistant to advertising. Ads are something you are bombarded with on a daily basis. You hear ads on the radio when you are driving to work. You see ads on TV when you are trying to relax in the evening. You see ads in the daily paper as you are trying to read the local weather forecast. You see ads in search results as you are trying to find information.

But ads do not have to be annoying or intrusive. Ads can be very helpful if they are created properly, because advertising is not actually advertising when it is information.

Ads Should Lead Searchers to Answers

If you performed the search, "plasma TV features," do you think clicking on this ad would help you find the information you are looking for?

Plasma TV. Massive new TV offerings. Visit us today to buy your new TV!

Unfortunately, ads that are not directly related to the search query and that do not mirror the search process are quite common.

Now consider this ad for the same search, "plasma TV features":

Compare plasma TV features. Find a new plasma TV that fits your lifestyle and budget.

Someone searching for features is most likely looking to compare products and is not ready to buy yet. They are still in the comparison shopping stage of the buying cycle. An ad focused on buying does not fit into their decision-making process.

Ad copy needs to both reflect the search query and recognize where a searcher is within the buying cycle; we will examine both of these elements in future chapters.

By aligning your ad copywriting, landing pages, and Google AdWords account with this concept, you are much more likely to see success in your search marketing efforts. This is a concept much better visualized than explained.

Imagine this weekend will be nice and sunny and you would like to spend it with your family at the beach. The drive will take several hours, but you manage to pack the kids and the spouse into the car and begin your journey.

You start driving down the interstate while the kids are glued to a DVD player in the backseat. Billboards whiz past on the side of the road, which you do not have to try to ignore; you have had the skill to tune out advertising for many years.

After a few hours, you start to get hungry and the kids start to get restless. It is time to find a restaurant for lunch. You have made the decision that you do not want to eat in the car as it is too messy with the kids, and you would like to get out of the car to stretch your legs.

Where do you start looking? Those ignored billboards. They are no longer advertisements cluttering up the roadside; they are now valuable pieces of information that will show you available lunch options.

You stop ignoring them and start reading them.

Why?

Because the advertisements are your source of information for finding the answer to your question. Your question is along the lines of "What are my lunch options?" Your answer will be found in the billboards alongside the interstate.

When ads become part of the information-gathering process, they cease to be ads. At this point in time, they are pieces of information that consumers are seeking. Wouldn't you like your ads to be sought after, not ignored? By aligning yourself with the search process, the quest for answers, not only will your ads help consumers find the answer to their questions, but they will also help your business make sales.

Stop thinking of ads as advertisements.

Start thinking of ads as pieces of information.

Goal Alignment: Google vs. You vs. the Searcher

Every search result has three different entities trying to reach their goals. Sometimes, these goals get in each other's way, leading to poor search results. Other times, they work in conjunction, leading everyone toward success. It is important to examine Google's goal, the advertiser's goal, and the searcher's goal for each search result.

All search results start with the same element, a searcher looking for the answer to a question. The searcher inputs a query, and SERPs appear.

Google's goal is to have that same searcher use Google for their next query. The more search queries that occur on Google properties, the more chances Google has to make money by people clicking on ads. Therefore, Google wants searchers to always find the answer to their question quickly, easily, and on a Google-owned property.

This is why Google also spends so much time and money on the natural results (also known as organic or free listings). Not all searches can be monetized, but if someone always finds their answer on Google, regardless of whether a particular search query is monetized or nonmonetized, that person is more likely to use Google for their next search. In addition, if someone finds their information on Google quicker and easier than on other properties, they will always return to Google to find information, which leads to more total queries per month for Google, which leads to more chances of Google making money.

> **Note:** Several studies in 2005–2008 have found that a user spends only 10 to 12 seconds on a search results page. Studies performed in 2010 and 2011 are finding that users are spending 12–17 seconds on search results. As more information is integrated into search pages, users are spending more time absorbing that information.

The advertiser's goal is to show an ad that is related to both their products and the searcher's query. The advertiser wants to control when their ad is shown, wants to choose which ad is shown, and then wants to take the searcher to the landing page of the advertiser's choice.

The advertiser wants to make money with their Google AdWords budget. That's the endgame—profitable advertising. Advertisers want control over how their money is being spent. They also want insight into the ad display process so they can expand their profitable advertising and stop their unprofitable ads.

Google's goal and the advertiser's goal are not the same. Since Google's goal is first and foremost to satisfy the searcher, not the advertiser, a conflict often arises between the two parties.

The advertiser will scream that it's their money and they should be able to display whatever they want in an ad and take someone to any page on their site they deem desirable. AdWords customer service reps will remind the advertiser about relevancy and attempt to help the advertiser make their keywords and ad copy more relevant. These relevancy rules are defined by Google.

Since Google is ruled internally by a quality control team—a team where relevancy trumps dollars—advertisers often feel like they are constantly trying to play catch-up in learning all the rules. Having an internal team that is more concerned about relevance than making money is beneficial to all parties, if everyone can align their goals.

It is critical to remember that the only person who makes Google or the advertiser any money is the actual searcher. Google does not make you money. You do not make Google money. Google is an intermediary between you and the searcher. You make money on AdWords because a searcher decided to do business with your company. You define a budget that you are willing to give to Google; however, if the searcher does not click your ads, you do not owe Google a penny.

Both you and Google make money from each other only if a searcher is involved. If there is no searcher, there is no search query, your ad is not displayed, and Google is not paid. Therefore, the person to actually align your goals with is the searcher. If you align yourself with the searcher, you help the searcher find information on your site. If they are finding information on your site, they are conducting business with your company, which helps you reach your end goal—a profitable business.

 Note: Google made more than $29 billion in 2010. More than half of their revenues were from countries other than the United States. Approximately 96 percent of Google's revenue comes from showing ads.

Because Google's goal is to assist the searcher in finding information, you will end up aligning yourself with Google as well. You will find that if you think of the searcher first, AdWords is much easier, and much more likely to be a successful advertising medium for your business.

After all, the searcher's only goal is to find the answer to their question.

Best Practices for Applying Search Theory

The basics of search are not difficult to understand; the principles have been the same ever since people started looking for information. By referring back to the fundamentals of search throughout your marketing, you keep your efforts aligned with the searcher, which can bring long-term success to your company.

- PPC marketing was created and revolutionized in less than a decade. As the industry is ever-changing, those who can continuously evolve their marketing can find great success.

- Search engines have transformed how people find their information. As more consumers use search engines as their starting point for finding information, more advertisers will find success with search marketing.

- The search process starts with a question. That question is translated into words by the searcher. Therefore, keywords are individual thought processes.

- Every time someone does an action, there is an expectation of results. Meeting these expectations with both ad copy and landing pages helps increase your PPC marketing returns.

- Advertising is not advertising when it is information. When your ads help a searcher find the answer to their question, your CTR and conversion rates often increase.

- On any search page there are three goals: the search engine's goal, the searcher's goal, and the advertiser's goal. Align your goal with your potential customer—the searcher—and success usually follows.

In future chapters, we will examine keyword research, ad copy writing, and multiple ways to target consumers. At each step, we are trying to enhance these fundamentals. If you can help the searcher find what they are looking for, you will continue to gain new customers.

Keyword Research

Keywords are the foundation of a successful AdWords campaign. If you have a keyword that matches a searcher's query, your ad could show. If you do not have a keyword that matches a searcher's query, your ad will not show. It is pretty simple: If you decide not to use a certain keyword, your company will not be visible to those searchers.

Keywords are so paramount to an AdWords campaign that PPC advertising is frequently called keyword *advertising or* keyword-driven *advertising.*

Not all keywords are created equal. Some keywords will have high search volume, whereas others will have small search volume. Some will have high conversion rates, and others will provide low-quality traffic.

Choosing the correct keywords is the first step to advertising with Google AdWords.

Chapter Contents

Understanding the buying funnel
Understanding keywords
Discerning keyword match types
Using negative keywords
Advanced organizational techniques
Taking control of your ad display
Best practices for conducting keyword research

Understanding the Buying Funnel

Before diving into all the various ways to research, group, and choose keywords, let's take a step back and examine how people buy products or services.

There are five stages to the buying funnel (Figure 2.1):

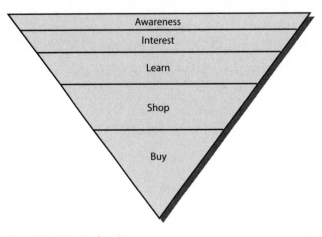

Figure 2.1 The buying funnel

- Awareness
- Interest
- Learn
- Shop
- Buy

Understanding where a keyword falls in the buying cycle can help signal where a consumer is within the buying process. That way, you can ensure that your ad and landing page match the consumer's shopping phase.

Although the buying funnel often refers to actual physical product sales, the same principles apply to B2B (business-to-business), service, retail, and other industries.

Note: The buying funnel is a subset of the broader known buying cycle. The entire buying cycle has two additional phases known as retention and advocacy. While customer loyalty and lifetime visitor values are important considerations for your entire marketing program, they can be distracting when we initially discuss keywords. Hence, we will work only with the initial aspect of the buying cycle, the sales funnel, during keywords and revisit the full buying cycle in later chapters.

The shopping cycle is illustrated as a funnel because many searchers will enter the beginning of your product's buying funnel. However, as consumers learn more information about your product as compared to others, fewer consumers will transition from one section to the next. One of your jobs as a marketer is to move as many prospects as possible through the funnel so they become customers.

Examining the Buying Funnel Phases

Awareness leads off the top of the funnel. If consumers do not know about your products, they can never buy from you. A marketer's first job is to make sure that consumers know that your products exist. If consumers are unaware of your product, they will not realize that your product can fix their problem, let alone understand that you offer a way to help them. At this stage of the buying funnel, your job is to shout from the rooftops that your product exists.

When we correlate this part of the buying funnel to keywords, the keywords are very general. Consumers do not yet know enough to do a search for the product's benefits, features, or part types. These keywords are often high-volume, low-converting words such as "TV," "plumber," "laptop memory," and "real estate."

Once a consumer knows that your product exists, your next function is to generate *interest* for your product or service. At this stage, you want consumers to think about your product and how it will make their lives better. We will discuss features and benefits more in Chapter 4, "Writing Compelling Ads," when we explore ad copy writing. At this stage of the buying funnel, you want to focus on benefits. Essentially, a benefit is what your product will do for consumers so they desire your product.

After consumers have become aware of and interested in your products, they need to *learn* more about the product so they have enough information to make informed purchasing decisions. This is known as the learning or information-gathering phase of the buying funnel.

This stage is where consumers start to delve into product specifications and features and begin to compare products. If a searcher were looking to buy a new HD TV, this is where they would start to examine the features and differences associated with plasma versus LCD vs. LED televisions. Consumers want to know about pixel burnout rates, what the magic mirrors are in LEDs, and what size TV they need for optimal viewing.

If you were an accounting firm, this is where you would showcase that you offer payroll services, are integrated with Intuit QuickBooks, and have a lawyer on staff for incorporation services.

It is in the learning stage where searchers first learn your industry jargon. The searcher's query is often more specific and commonly includes brand names and service specialties. Showcasing both benefits and features is useful for consumers during this phase.

Using these examples, you could easily put keywords such as "Chicago QuickBooks accounting firm," "Samsung LED TV," and "plasma TV pixel burnout rate" into your keyword list.

Once consumers understand enough about the industry or product that they can start looking at product specifications to make informed decisions, they will begin to compare similar products to each other. This is known as the *shopping* phase.

At this phase, a consumer might have decided they would like a plasma TV because it's light enough to hang on the wall and, based on how far their couch is from the wall, they want a 52-inch set. However, the consumer might not know if a Sony TV has certain features that a Samsung TV does not have. Therefore, while the consumer has decided on a 52-inch plasma TV, the brand and actual model are still in question. Or the consumer might have determined that they want a Sony, but there are multiple types of Sony plasma TVs, and therefore the consumer needs to compare the various model types.

Keywords at this phase are often quite specific and indicate a certain level of knowledge about the product. "Sony Vaio Z series laptop," "Sony plasma 52-inch TV," and "Chicago accounting services with lawyer on staff" are keyword searches that describe consumers in this aspect of the buying funnel.

Finally, a consumer has made up their mind on the actual product they are willing to purchase. At this point, the only question left to answer is where to *buy* the plasma TV or which accounting service can offer both a lawyer on staff and quick phone support.

These keywords are often product part numbers or company names: "Jim's accounting service" or "Samsung UN55D6000 55 1080P LED TV." A consumer will examine prices, warranties, shipping costs, service contracts, return policies, and similar items before finally making a decision on where to buy the specific product.

How Do Consumers Flow Through Your Buying Funnel?

The buying funnel is different for every business. It is important to examine your company to determine how people find their information, make their decisions, and finally engage companies within your industry.

There is no time limit to the buying funnel. A used book sale might consist of five minutes from initial query to buying. A B2B $100,000 software integration package may take six months or more.

Some consumers will jump directly into the learn or buy phase of the buying funnel. If you are shopping for a new book, and you already know an author you like because of a previous book you have read, you do not need to learn more about the author—you just want to see what other books that author has written and maybe take a quick look at customer reviews. If you are tasked with finding both a software package and an integration vendor to move your company's email to a lower total cost of ownership system, the search may take many twists and turns through many months of discussions and searches.

Always keep in mind that every single keyword you choose for your AdWords campaign will fall into at least one phase of the buying funnel. Some keywords may be somewhat ambiguous as to which exact phase of the buying funnel they fall into. In those cases, you may wish to test different landing pages for these keywords to see if the informational page or a product page has a higher return for your company.

It can be a useful exercise to examine your keywords and see in what aspect of the buying funnel you are reaching prospects. If all your keywords fall into the awareness and learn phases but you do not have any in the buy phase, you might help a consumer decide which product to buy but then not capitalize on their search when they are finally buying.

Conversely, if all your keywords fall into the buy phase, you might be generating very few sales. By using keywords further up in the buying funnel, you can generate more awareness and sales for your company.

Of course, having the keyword in your account just means your ad might show for the search result. Both your ad and landing page need to continue engaging the consumer so that you receive both the click and the conversion associated with that keyword. The first step is making sure you have the proper visibility.

Understanding Keywords

Keywords are thoughts put into words. We search to find the answer to a question. Always remember that when you choose a keyword, you are telling a consumer that you can help them find the answer to their question.

When doing keyword research, you should always keep the searcher in mind. It's their thoughts put into words that you want as keywords so your ad can be shown on a search results page.

Before we delve into the four main types of keywords, let's take a closer look at the scenario from Chapter 1, "Understanding Search Theory," to see how any scenario can utilize these types of words.

Our searcher is sitting in his Chicago suburban house in January watching TV on a Saturday afternoon. Suddenly, his spouse calls up from the basement that there is water everywhere. Upon investigation, our searcher determines that a pipe froze, causing the pipe to break and flood their basement. This happens every year in Chicago. What are the possible keywords?

First, keywords or thoughts are often segmented into four key areas:

- Explicit
- Problems
- Symptoms
- Product names or part numbers

We will examine each individually.

Types of Keywords

Explicit keywords are the easiest to research. These keywords often have the highest search volume of all the keyword types. They directly describe the product or service, and very little creativity is necessary to research these keywords. Here are some examples:

- Dermatologist
- Computer memory
- Plasma TV

In our example, if we were to list keywords for a plumber, we might have the following:

- Plumber
- North Chicago plumber
- Chicago plumbing services
- Emergency plumber
- Plumber phone number
- Saturday plumbing

Problem-based words are the second type of keywords. These keywords describe the conditions or problems that your product solves. These are also known as curing searches. Here are some examples:

- Acne
- How do I get rid of acne
- Can't run Excel
- Toothache
- What toothpaste will help cure a toothache?

If you examine your products and services and think of what you solve for a consumer, or how you make their life better, these are often problem-based keywords. In our plumber example, a "flooded basement" search would describe the root problem.

Symptoms make up the third type of keyword search. These keywords describe the symptoms of the actual problem. Here are some examples:

- Oily skin
- Slow computer

In our earlier example, symptom searches may include the following:

- Frozen pipes
- Burst pipe
- Broken pipes

The fourth type of keyword is *product names or part numbers*. These are common keywords late in the buying funnel. Here are some examples:

- P-10113/4 (a pipe number)
- Mint Soufflé Cleanser
- 512 MD DDR2-533 SODIMM (computer memory)

If we look closely at the keyword examples, we can devise our own story from them. We need a dermatologist because we have acne, which is caused by oily skin, but we could use the Mint Soufflé Cleanser to help care for our skin. Our slow Sony Vaio is causing large Excel files to fail to load because we don't have enough computer memory. After researching the problem, our choice for the best computer memory is two 512 MB DDR2-533 SODIMMs.

By not just looking at keywords but also by examining the scenarios that cause someone to need your product, you can quickly expand your keyword research into new, untapped areas.

There are other keyword types that might be more applicable for your industry. The next most common keyword search is an informational query. These are often harder keywords to monetize for those selling products or services—but with a bit of creative thought to both answering the question and engaging the searcher, you can find new keyword search volume.

Here are examples of informational queries:

- How to turn off the water in the basement
- How to install memory in a computer
- Computer memory installation
- Candle burning times
- Differences between plasma and LED TVs

These keyword searches may not have any commercial intent. However, they are excellent top-of-the-funnel keywords to create more awareness for your business and to engage a searcher to start them down the buying funnel.

Finding Keyword Ideas

When conducting keyword research, first consider your themes instead of actual keywords. A *theme* is a collection of closely related keywords. In AdWords accounts, they are also known as *ad groups*. By first concentrating on your themes, you will build a high-level list of how your products or services coordinate with the keyword types.

Often the navigation on a website is already broken down into themes, and much of your initial work is already conducted. However, these are only the direct keywords, and you will still need to do research on the other types of keywords for those direct keywords.

If your website does not have a good navigational structure then, as we walk through the following keyword research ideas, instead of thinking in individual keywords, first take a look at the high-level themes. Once those are established, come back to each theme and fill in the keywords.

For example, if you were a plumber, here's a list of some of the more popular themes:

- Plumber
- Broken pipes
- Fix shower
- Kitchen remodeling
- Bathroom remodeling
- Overflowing toilet
- Emergency plumbing
- Weekend plumbing
- Flooded basement

And the list goes on. You should be able to come up with more than 50 different themes for a plumber. With some work, you might even come up with a few hundred themes. Although you know your business well, your potential customers—the searchers—do not; your business is quite complex when you start researching every problem you can fix.

The Two-Word Rule

If you are having problems grouping your keywords, use the two-word rule. This is a simple rule where you pick two root words that will signify the theme of the ad group. Then, every keyword in that same ad group should have those same two words in them but may have additional modifiers before or after the root words.

Starting Your Keyword Research

Begin by analyzing your website: your website's navigation and the words used on your site. We will showcase the AdWords keyword research tool in Chapter 3, "Keyword Tools: Extracting Valuable Data from Google," which will help you take a deep look into your own website.

If you have offline marketing material, examine your print collateral. Often direct mail pieces are carefully optimized over years of time. Are there hot-button words in your materials?

Analyze your top competitors' sites. Do they have navigational elements that are different from yours? Why? Is it that they offer different services than you or that they have broken down their site differently? If their site is just broken down in different ways, make note of those themes and see how their organization might jumpstart new ways for you to consider additional themes.

Examine the natural search results. Search engines try to diversify their results by including both authority and hub sites. The authority sites are worth taking a closer look into as they are displayed on page one of the search results for some of your major keywords. Wikipedia.org or About.com are common authority sites.

Hub sites are places where consumers can find a variety of information and links to other similar sites. Follow what the search engines consider hubs to see what other keywords and navigational elements these sites use. Since a hub site is trying to link to the most relevant sites for a category, they often have refined navigation that can help you organize themes. Do not forget to take a look at whom they link to, as a good hub will showcase a large variety of information. DMOZ.org and DexKnows.com are good examples of hub sites.

Hopefully, you have a web analytics system in place. If not, Google offers a free system to get you started called Google Analytics. Your web analytics system will show you what keywords someone searched on various search engines to find your website. If you have goals or conversion tracking configured, you can even see which keywords led to higher conversion rates.

One of the best places to mine for new keywords and themes is your internal search engine. If your site has internal search, you should be tracking what keywords visitors are searching for within your site. This information will tell you exactly what someone was trying to find. It is also a good place to examine your landing page's effectiveness. If you have a page with a high search percentage, essentially the searcher did not find what they wanted on your landing page and had to do another search to find their information.

My absolute favorite tool will be the subject of Chapter 3: the AdWords Keyword tool.

When doing research for both your keywords and themes, there are two points to remember. First, always keep the searcher in mind. The searcher is who you are trying to reach. You are advertising on a keyword you think they will type into a search engine and click on a result afterward. The searcher is the one who will ultimately make you profitable.

Second, always keep your products in mind. Your products or services are the lifeblood of your company. It's by selling those items that you can satisfy a searcher. When choosing keywords, make sure they are an accurate reflection of your products and services.

Do You Know Your Keywords?

Who searches for the word "bleach"?

If you thought the most common searcher was a 20- to 50-year-old female, then you have joined a large group of people who do not watch Japanese anime. The most common searcher for the word "bleach" is a male under 24 years of age. The explanation? A few years ago a new Japanese anime program called *Bleach* launched. The show has completely changed the dynamic of that word.

There are words whose meanings have changed, and there are other words that describe multiple items. A search for the word "ceramic" could be for a $0.99 figurine or a $10,000 factory part.

A search for "buy pipe" could mean a nice meerschaum tobacco-smoking pipe or a replacement for the busted pipe in your basement.

Sometimes relatively few people searching on a particular keyword will fit your ideal customer profile, and you may want to avoid using that keyword altogether. For instance, if you sold Clorox and realized that the majority of people searching for the word bleach do not meet your website goals, you may wish to not advertise on that specific keyword. There are other times when the word is essential to your advertising campaign.

There are ways to write ad copy so you can showcase whether you are selling Clorox bleach or *Bleach* DVDs. This will help the searcher understand what products you offer. However, the first step is that you have to know it's a commonly confused word.

The best way to start understanding your words is to look at the natural search results. If you see sites or ads for seemingly unrelated industries, investigate further.

Another place to find these differences is in your keyword reporting, which we will discuss in later chapters. If you see words that seem highly targeted yet do not convert, it is worth your time to take a quick look and see if that word has multiple meanings.

Another fantastic tool is Yahoo! Clues. One of the various tools available attempts to predict the demographic characteristics (age and sex) of a keyword (Figure 2.2).

Figure 2.2 Yahoo! Clues demographic prediction

Understanding when your keywords might be confused with other products or services can help you be more specific with the words and themes you choose, to keep you from spending money on keywords that do not lead to sales.

How Many Keywords Should You Have in Your Account?

You have probably heard someone mention an AdWords account that has over a million keywords. Yet, by most estimates the English language contains only roughly one-quarter of a million words. How can an AdWords account have more than four times the number of words than exist in the entire English language?

The answer is simple: by creating keyword lists.

Before creating keyword lists and generating millions of keywords, consider what you are going to do with those keywords. Most companies do not need millions of keywords. There is no magic number for how many keywords you should have in your account. The answer to "How many keywords should I have in my account?" comes back to relevancy.

You should have only relevant keywords in your account. If the keywords you create help a searcher find the answer to their question, then these are good keywords. If your keywords start to become ambiguous and could have multiple meanings, you need to make a financial decision about whether it is worth it to your company to advertise on a word with marginal (or worse, negative) results.

For example, if you were to search for "TV," what would you expect to find?

- TV reviews
- TV guide
- TV repair
- TV celebrities
- Plasma TVs

These highly unrelated terms could all be shown for a keyword such as "TV." The keyword is not specific enough to have any definitive user intent. Here are some issues to consider:

Examining Your Keywords If you cannot determine the user intent of a keyword, it is probably not specific enough for your account. This is a general guideline, and there are definitely exceptions. It is useful to first test the more specific keywords, and then once you have an idea of cost per conversion and conversion rates on the more specific keywords, try some of the more general keywords to see if they are profitable for your advertising dollars.

Determining the Right Number of Keywords The next consideration in determining how many keywords you should use comes back to management time. If you have 100,000 keywords, you will need to find a scalable way to manage that many. Microsoft Excel files and database reports are highly time-consuming for organizing that much data and determining your profit on each keyword so that you can decide how much you would like to bid for each word. You may need a bid management system to handle that many words.

Understanding Google AdWords Account Limits The last consideration is Google AdWords account limits. If it has been a while since you examined your potential account limits, you need to look again. In 2011, Google raised the number of campaigns from 25 to 500. The number of keywords was raised from 50,000 to 3 million. With these new limits, most companies will never run into hard caps on how many keywords, ad groups, or campaigns can exist within their AdWords account.

If you do need more than 3 million keywords, or if you need to organize accounts by business units, Google can link accounts together on the back-end so they share some data and serve only one ad per search result. If you need multiple accounts, talk to an AdWords representative.

> **Note:** Google has designed their editorial system to maximize user choice and user transparency. Each Google account should be a single business. If a single business needs multiple accounts, all of your accounts should be linked together. A single business running multiple unlinked accounts can run into terms of service (TOS) issues with Google's editorial teams. The MCC (My Client Center) account, which can help manage multiple accounts at once, will be discussed in Chapter 14, "Successful Account Organization Strategies."

If you are wondering why Google has caps on keywords, you can examine it from their perspective. Every keyword entered into their system has to be stored in multiple databases. Every local database is examined for keyword matches every time someone conducts a search on Google. Google is trying to filter through millions of keywords to serve ads to a searcher in less than one second. The less total database space being used to house keywords, the easier it is to sort through the keywords to quickly serve results to the searcher.

Therefore, although you will learn techniques for creating millions of keywords, it is best to initially keep your list to far fewer words than Google allows, unless you have a system in place to manage that many keywords.

Creating Keyword Lists

Most words in the English language can be categorized as a noun, adverb, adjective, preposition, pronoun, or verb. The same can be said for products. Most products can be described by product types, product attributes, adjectives, and so on. By breaking down your products or services into their base elements and then recombining these words, you can easily create huge keyword lists.

For example, Table 2.1 is a chart for maternity clothing that is by no means exhaustive but can be used to illustrate this point.

▶ **Table 2.1** Maternity shirt example root words

Category adjectives	Product types	Product attributes 1	Product attributes 2	Example keywords
Pregnant	Shirt	Long sleeve	Cotton	Pregnancy shirt
Pregnancy	T-shirt	Short sleeve	Rayon	Pregnancy shirt long sleeve
Maternity	Dress blouse	Sleeveless	Silk	Pregnancy shirt cotton
	Tops		Stretchable	
	Polo shirt		Natural fibers	Pregnancy shirt long sleeve cotton
	Sweatshirt		Wool	

In the table, if we always used a word from both the Category Adjectives and Product Types column and then mixed and matched the rest of the words, the words in Table 2.1 would become 504 keywords.

If you were to make five lists of five root words and mix and match them all, that would create 6,026 keywords. As you can see, keyword listing is powerful but can easily grow out of control. Therefore, it is important to keep your account structure in mind when creating keyword lists. You should first diagram your final ad groups before creating the lists. If you create keyword lists first, you have to try to categorize them all into ad groups.

In Table 2.1, the minimum number of ad groups should be six, one for each product type. You could easily have a few hundred ad groups from this information.

For example, at the most granular level, each keyword generated could instead be an ad group. To fill in the keywords within the ad group, you could use plurals, misspellings, and similar words such as "t-shirt," "tshirt," and "tee shirt."

Creating word lists to generate thousands of keywords is useful. However, if done improperly, you could quickly end up with more keywords than you know how to organize, let alone manage. You can use the exact same techniques of creating lists to first diagram your ad groups, and then you can create lists within each ad group to generate the final keywords used within your account.

By first creating your ad groups and then filling in your keywords, it is much easier to organize your account and keep your keyword lists from spiraling out of control.

Keyword Mixer Tools

You do not have to do all this mixing and matching yourself. There are tools that will do the hard combination work for you. The following graphic shows one of the most popular.

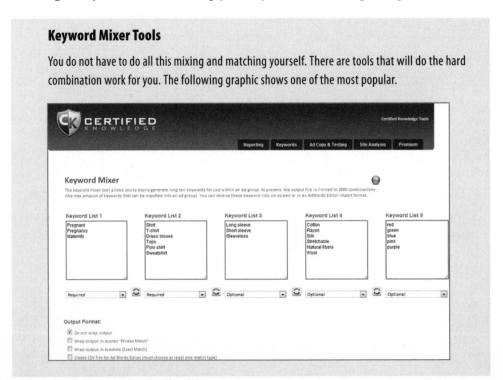

Using Long-Tail Keywords

The *long tail* is a term popularized by Chris Anderson in an article in *Wired* magazine (October 2004) to describe how niche markets can sell a large number of infrequently sold items that together create more total sales than the top-selling product lists.

For example, before the days of the Internet, bookstores had to keep physical inventory in their stores. There is a finite number of books that can be housed and displayed on shelves within a store. The top-selling books in each category were most prominently featured. A book had to constantly sell to continue to maintain space on the shelves; otherwise, it was regulated to the discount bin to make space for a book that was selling. Although some of these books might have sold a few copies each month, it was not worth the shelf space to try to keep them in stock.

Then came Amazon.com, which had no physical storage limit for its products. Suddenly, a book that sold only one copy a month, or only a hundred copies a year, could still be profitable for Amazon. When you combine the millions of books that only sell a few copies, those total sales can be equal to or even exceed the top best-selling books.

You can repeat the same logic for any niche-based business, such as Netflix. Netflix carries thousands of copies of the most rented titles. However, the power of Netflix comes from their ability to carry even a few copies of each low-demand title. It is a powerful value proposition to the Netflix customer that even these niche movies can be rented. The total rentals for the low-demand movies in aggregate numbers may be equal to the total rentals of the top hundred movies.

This same logic can be applied to keywords. Single-word keyword searches make up roughly 20 percent of the search volume in the United States. However, search queries that are five or more words in length make up nearly 20 percent of the search volume as well.

There are two main ways that marketers use the phrase "long-tail keyword" when discussing keywords:

- The first refers to keyword searches that are three or more words in length. Essentially, someone typing in three or more words in a search box is being specific in defining the information they are wishing to discover.

- The second refers to keywords with low search volume. Instead of focusing on how many words are in the search query, these marketers consider long-tail keywords to have low search volume. In this instance, even a one-word keyword with low search volume would be a long-tail word.

Each year, the number of words used in search queries grows (see Table 2.2). As the general search population starts to search with more words, the popularity of two- and three-word keywords will grow as well.

Therefore, when considering the long tail, I favor applying it to search volume. The principle of the long tail is to aggregate infrequent data points. In searches, this would be keywords with low search volume.

▶ **Table 2.2** U.S. clicks by number of keywords

Subject	February 2011	March 2011	Year-over-year percent change
1 word	23.86%	24.40%	2%
2 words	23.66%	23.76%	0%
3 words	19.91%	19.88%	0%
4 words	13.57%	13.45%	-1%
5 words	8.15%	8.00%	-2%
6 words	4.52%	4.41%	-2%
7 words	2.52%	2.44%	-3%
8+ words	3.80%	3.66%	-4%

Note: Data is based on four-week rolling periods (ending Feb. 26, 2011, April 2, 2011, and Jan. 31, 2009) from the Hitwise sample of 10 million U.S. Internet users.

Source: Hitwise, an Experian company

Please note that while it appears longer queries have fewer searches than in previous months, much of that is the result of direct navigation queries. Some of the most common searches on Google are Facebook, YouTube, Twitter, eBay, Yahoo!, and Gmail. These are single-word queries that make the search volume skew to the one-word queries, which are almost impossible for advertisers to monetize.

There are several advantages to using long-tail keywords and incorporating them into your keyword lists:

- There is often less competition on these search queries. It takes more keyword research and keyword creation discipline to have an encompassing keyword list. By expanding your keyword reach to these less frequently used search queries, you can often find gems that cost very little.

- The much more important reason is that many long-tail search queries are more specific, and it is easier to match the user intent with both the proper ad copy and the proper landing page.

Regarding the second reason, if someone searches for "long sleeve silk maternity shirts" and one ad copy talks about generic maternity shirts and another one talks about silk maternity shirts that have long sleeves, which do you think a consumer is more likely to click on?

Keyword advertising is about choosing keywords and ad copy that can answer a user's initial question. The closer you can associate the ad copy to the user intent, the higher the click-through rate. If you pair that ad copy with a landing page that also includes that same product or service, conversion rates are usually higher as well.

Utilizing the long tail for both ad group organization and keyword research will let you associate your marketing more closely with the user intent, which has benefits for both the searcher and the advertiser. The searcher finds the answer to their question, and the advertiser receives more conversions on their website.

Wide vs. Deep Keywords

When enacting keyword lists or using the long-tail approach, you must consider *wide* versus *deep* keywords. They are very different, and the wrong approach can send you spiraling down a path of tens of thousands of closely related keywords that do not accurately encompass the best keywords for your account.

Instead, consider the various ways people look for information about your product and services. Earlier in this chapter, we discussed explicit, problem, and symptom keywords. Each of those types of keywords represents different ways of finding the exact same product. You first need to aggregate the different keywords used before drilling down into the specific keywords.

For example, if you were advertising a spyware removal product, it would be easy to expand this list to create thousands of keywords from the simple root word list in Table 2.3. However, what you would end up with is a list of keywords that all include the root keyword "spyware." That does not represent all the ways people search for spyware removal.

▶ **Table 2.3**   Deep spyware root words

Adjectives	Brands or adjectives	Product	Program types
Free	Microsoft	Spyware	Removal
Cheap	Download		Scan
Discount	McAfee		Remover
Low cost	Norton		Programs
			Protection
			Detector

The list in Table 2.3 would be considered a deep keyword list. It only encompasses the way people search when they are using the root keyword "spyware." Before you start to go deep, you will first want to go wide with your keyword list.

A wider, more encompassing, keyword list would be built from a root word list that looks like Table 2.4.

Action words	Wide root words	Software type
Delete	Spyware	Software
Destroy	Adware	Program
Remove	W32	Download
Find	Virus	Freeware
Scan	Keylogger	Trial

Instead of relying on the root word "spyware" to be included throughout your keyword list and in the search query, this keyword list examines the different root words used in searching for spyware removal. If your product converted much higher for "adware" keywords, and you started with all "spyware" keywords, you would be missing your most profitable keywords.

This also makes it easier to concentrate on the correct keywords. Start with a very wide list. First, you should think of all the ways that someone can search for your product or services. From those thinking patterns, create a root word list. These are the major words used to describe your offerings.

Run these keywords (with their appropriate modifiers) for a while in your AdWords account. Once you start to see which wide keywords are receiving more clicks and conversions, you can focus on going deep within those root keywords.

By taking this two-step approach to both keyword and ad group creation, you will be spending your time more wisely building profitable keyword lists. It is easy to create massive amounts of keywords, but it makes more business sense to create profitable—and manageable—keyword lists.

Discerning Keyword Match Types

AdWords gives an advertiser a significant amount of control in determining when an ad will be shown. We will continue to discuss many of these additional options in later chapters. However, keep in mind that if you do not match your keywords appropriately, these additional controls will only have marginal increases in producing high-quality traffic.

There are four match types that AdWords uses to determine whether your ad should be displayed based on the user's search query: broad, modified broad, phrase, and exact match.

Broad Match

A word is considered *broad matched* when you enter a keyword into an ad group with no formatting around the word (Figure 2.3).

```
Settings    Ads    Keywords

All keywords ▼    Segment ▼    Filter ▼    Columns ▼    [⤴] [⬇]    [            ]    [ Search ]

These keywords determine which placements are good matches for your ads.

Add keywords

Add your keywords below, one per line.
To choose relevant keywords, try to imagine how your customers would describe your products or services.

Want to create keywords, bids, and URLs in bulk? Add keywords by spreadsheet

┌─────────────────────────────────────────────────────┐
│ coffee mugs                                           │
│ coffee mug                                            │
│ travel coffee mug                                     │
│ coffee cups                                           │
│ coffee cup                                            │
│ travel coffee cup                                     │
│                                                       │
│                                                       │
│                                                       │
│                                                       │
└─────────────────────────────────────────────────────┘
```

Figure 2.3 Broad match keywords in an ad group

Broad match keywords can trigger your ad to show if the searcher uses a query that is related to your keywords. Broad match keywords match to misspellings, plurals, and even similar words.

For example, if you had the broad match keyword "coffee cups," you could match to "coffee cup" (singular), "cofee cup" (misspelling), or "coffee mug" (similar word).

In addition, the order of the words does not matter. To continue our example, if you used the broad match "coffee cups," you could match to "cups coffee" or "mug coffee."

Lastly, you can be matched if the search query contains similar words to your keyword with additional parameters. For example, if your keyword was "coffee cups," you could match to "coffee red mug," "blue mugs coffee," or "coffee cup holder."

If you only sold coffee mugs, being matched to a keyword such as "coffee cup holder" is probably not a good match. In these cases, we will show you how to keep your ad from showing when we visit negative keywords later in the section "Using Negative Keywords."

The biggest problem with broad match is that you are matched to "similar" items and you don't get to define similar—Google does. This leads to a lot of queries triggering your broad match keywords that are not relevant to your business. In addition, the higher your CTR, the broader the search queries that could trigger your ads.

For instance, if you had a good CTR on the term "coffee mugs" in broad match, you might show for the search query "tea cups." If you did happen to also sell tea cups, you should have a different ad copy and landing page for that keyword than for the keyword "coffee mug." So while you will often match to these additional queries, sometimes these clicks will not turn into sales because of the irrelevant ads and landing pages.

However, there is an advantage to broad match: not having to find all the possible variations of keywords. In a November 2008 article, Google announced:

> *Did you know that 20% of the queries Google receives each day are ones we haven't seen in at least 90 days, if at all?*

HTTP://ADWORDS.BLOGSPOT.COM/2008/11/REACH-MORE-CUSTOMERS-WITH-BROAD-MATCH.HTML

Google restated this number privately in 2011, but it even went further: 20 percent of queries Google receives each day are ones they had not seen in the last six months, if at all. As more search queries occur, the number of possible keyword combinations is also growing.

When one-fifth of all searches on Google have not been seen by Google in the last six months, and that engine receives billions of queries each month, it is easy to see that it is impossible to have every single keyword related to your products or services within your account.

The problem of marketers wanting to use broad match to reach all of the possible queries and yet maintain some control finally manifested itself in a new match type: modified broad match.

Modified Broad Match

If you examine your keyword phrases, usually there are one to three words that really matter in the phrase, and the other words are modifiers that do not mean as much to your conversion rates. For instance, if you take the query "Size 9 Red Nike Shoes," the words "Nike" and "shoes" you would want to make sure are in the query, but the size or the color might not matter. With modified broad match you can signal to Google that only the words "Nike" and "shoes" are important and the search query should be closely related to those two words, but the rest of the words in your keyword phrase can be treated with more liberal matching.

To tell Google what words are important, you just put a plus (+) sign in front of the most important ones. The words with the plus sign can still match to plurals, misspellings, and very similar words, but they should not match to completely different types of words. With modified broad match, the ordering of the words does not matter, just as with broad match. Let's look at a few examples of modified broad match with a different main search query, "wedding cakes" (see Table 2.5).

Keyword in your account	Possible matched search queries
+wedding cake	Wedding cake
	Wedding cupcake
	Red velvet wedding cake
Wedding +cake	Cakes for weddings
	Anniversary cake recipes
	How to bake a birthday cake
+Wedding +cake	Weding (misspelled on purpose) cakes
	Cakes for Weddings
	Wedding cheesecake (only with a high CTR)
Chocolate +wedding +cake	Wedding cake with chocolate bride and groom
	Wedding cakes with vanilla
	Strawberry wedding cake

In each instance, a word very related to the keywords with the plus sign were in the search query—but plural, singular, or misspelled versions of the word did not matter.

Inside of Google's interface, you will still see modified broad match words listed as broad match. There is no modified broad match type in the interface. The fact that you have added a plus sign to the word makes it modified broad match (Figure 2.4).

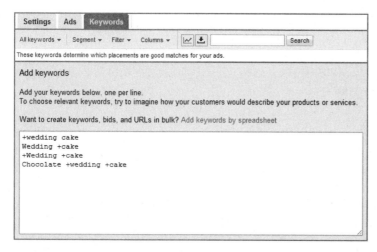

Figure 2.4 Modified broad match keywords in an ad group

If you want to maintain some control but do not want to have research every variation of possible words, modified broad match is an excellent place to start when you add keywords to your account.

When Should You Use Broad Match?

Because modified broad match gives you so much control, there are only a few reasons to use the standard broad match type.

One of the best uses of broad match is to buy research. With broad match, you can match to many queries, and search queries will give you excellent insight into search behavior. So, if you think of broad match as buying search data and not as keywords that you need to prove ROI, broad match can be very useful.

Another reason to try broad match is when there are very few queries for the account. If you are trying to serve ads into a very small geography or are in a very niche business, you might try using some broad match to increase your total impressions and clicks; just make sure they are helping you reach your overall marketing goals.

Phrase Match

A keyword is considered *phrase matched* when you enter the word in an ad group within quotation marks, as seen in Figure 2.5.

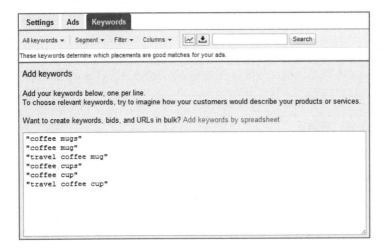

Figure 2.5 Phrase match keywords in an ad group

In order for your phrase match keyword to display your ad, the search query must contain your keyword in the same order you typed it into your ad group.

For example, if your keyword was "coffee cups" your keyword would match to phrases such as the following:

- Coffee cups
- Blue coffee cups
- Coffee cups blue
- Red coffee cups for traveling

In each of these instances, there could be words before, after, or before and after your keyword. It could also be the keyword phrase itself. However, your keyword was always included in the search query.

Phrase match keywords do not match to misspellings or plurals. Therefore, if you have the keyword "coffee cups," the following searches would not trigger your ad:

- Coffee cup (singular)
- Cofee cups (misspelling)
- Cups coffee (different word order)

Your ad would not trigger if someone entered a word in the middle of your keyword, between the words "coffee" and "cup." In the "coffee cups" example, if someone searched for "coffee blue cups," your ad would not show because the search query did not contain your phrase exactly.

Just to clarify, the user is not typing in quotes or adding formatting when entering their query into Google. The user is searching as usual; the quotes are only used to signal to Google that you would like your keyword to be triggered if it matched the search pattern. For example, in Figure 2.6, if you had the phrase match keyword "coffee cup," your ad would be displayed.

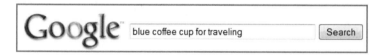

Figure 2.6 Google search query that will display an ad for coffee cup phrase match keyword

Phrase match used to be one of the best match types to use for new accounts since it gave you a lot of control. However, with the introduction of modified broad match, many advertisers have been using phrase match much less. If you are using an automated bid system where the number of keywords under management does not necessarily mean it takes you more hours to manage your account, you should use phrase match.

However, if you are managing accounts by hand, often using modified broad and exact match is a good way to start; then when you have instances where you cannot quite control the ad serving for modified broad match, use phrase match in those instances.

For example, if you are selling Pittsburgh Steelers (an NFL football team) gear and you add the keyword: "+Pittsburgh +Steelers Jerseys" in your account, you might show for search queries such as "the history of steel mining in Pittsburgh." Usually, NFL fans type in the name of their teams in the same phrase over and over but with different modifiers on the gear. In this instance, using "Pittsburgh Steelers Jerseys" in phrase match could be a better option than modified broad match.

Exact Match

Exact match is the most specific matching option that AdWords offers. First, you must enter the keywords into your ad group within brackets, as shown in Figure 2.7.

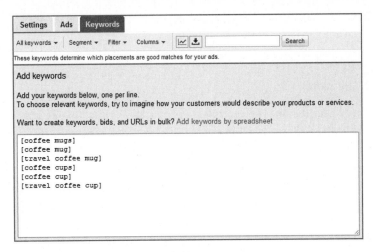

Figure 2.7 Exact match keywords in an ad group

Exact match works just how it sounds: a user must type into the search box a query that is identical to a keyword in your ad group for your ad to be displayed.

Exact match keywords do not match to misspellings, similar keywords, plurals, or singular forms of the words.

If you have the exact match keyword "[coffee cups]," your ad would not be shown if someone types in "coffee cup" (singular), "cofee cups" (misspelling), "blue coffee cups" (additional word), "coffee mugs" (similar word), or any other possible variation.

The biggest advantage of exact match is that you know exactly what someone is typing into the search box. You can examine your ad copy, landing page, and keyword to ensure that a perfectly formed synergistic chain has been established that will maximize your conversion rate.

In longer queries, exact match will also show user intent. A keyword such as "buy plasma TV" shows commercial intent. A keyword search such as "LCD vs. plasma TV" or "advantages of accountants over tax prep software" signals a comparison shopping intent. In this case, users need more information before they are ready to buy a product. A search such as "congressional term lengths" has an informational intent.

While we all use a search engine to find answers to questions, our intent upon finding those answers can vary quite significantly. The main intents online are commercial, informational, and navigational. However, just because you have a shopping site does not mean you should not use informational terms in your keyword list. It means you need to make sure you are engaging those users first with information and then have that information lead them to your products.

Which Match Type Is Best?

Now that you know the four match types, how should you use them within your AdWords account?

First, you should know you can use all four match types for the same keyword within the same AdWords account or campaign. You could have the same keyword exact, phrase, modified broad, and broad matched within the same ad group.

Second, when determining which match types to use, there are two major considerations: budget and reach.

If you are starting with a small budget and only want to increase your budget as you find profitable keywords, you will want to start with mostly exact match keywords, and maybe some modified broad match. Once you find keywords that are meeting your business goals, then you can add the phrase match or modified broad match versions of those keywords.

If you are starting with a large budget and are willing to throw everything at the wall to see what converts, you will want to start with mostly modified broad match or broad match keywords. If you have a large budget, but want some control, then start with mostly modified broad match. If you are want lots of data to work with, and are willing to pay for some clicks that will be irrelevant, then use broad match. As you find keywords that convert, add those words as exact and phrase match words over time.

You can also start with all four match types if you want. This is useful for adding the branded terms in mostly exact and phrase match, and then adding the two- to three-word keywords as modified broad and phrase match, and the four-word and longer keywords in modified and some broad match versions.

If you have multiple match types, make sure that you have exact match bid the highest, phrase match a little lower, modified broad even lower, and finally broad match at the lowest bid.

The reason why you want to set bids will become apparent in Chapter 7, "Demystifying Quality Score." Essentially, if all four keywords can be triggered in a search result, Google will show the one with the highest ad rank. Ad rank is a number derived from multiplying your Quality Score by your maximum CPC (cost per click). By bidding the most on exact match, you are forcing a higher ad rank for the exact match than the phrase or broad match keyword.

Another reason you would want to bid exact match the highest is that you know exactly the keywords used in the search query. It is much easier to determine user intent with exact match words than with the other match types. With phrase or broad match, the search query should be related to your keywords but it may not be your actual keywords.

You should find that exact match has the highest conversion rate, then phrase match, then broad match. If you find that broad match has a higher conversion rate than phrase or exact match, it is generally because you are being matched to some search queries where you do not have that corresponding keyword in your account, and those queries have higher conversion rates than your account's keywords—which then causes the broad match keywords to appear to have higher conversion rates This is another reason to use the search query report: to find those converting keywords you do not currently have in your AdWords account.

Lastly, if you use this bid technique, every time your phrase or broad match keyword is shown, it signals that you do not have that exact match keyword in your account.

Because of the number of unique queries seen on Google within a day, you will never have every exact match keyword in your account. It is just not possible to find every single variation. This brings us to the second point to consider when using multiple match types: reach.

Broad, modified broad, and phrase match will help you reach a larger user base. If you only have exact match keywords, you are considerably lowering the possible search queries that your keywords could be matched to, and thus, will not reach nearly as many users.

By examining both your budget and desired reach, you can determine how many different match types you wish to use when creating a new ad group (Figure 2.8).

Figure 2.8 Ad group using all four match types

Once an ad group starts to collect statistics, you can use the search query report to determine what keywords you wish to add to your ad group, and what keywords you do not wish to trigger your ad.

As a starting point guideline, bid phrase match 15 percent less than your exact match bid, and modified broad match another 15–25 percent less than your phrase match bid. If you want to buy some research or more impressions through the use of broad match, bid that another 15–25 percent lower than modified broad match.

Using Negative Keywords

Negative keywords are filtering words. This type of keyword stops your ad from being displayed on a search result. If you have phrase and broad match keywords in your account and some of the variations do not have good conversion rates, you could use a negative keyword to stop your ad from showing on a search result.

Before implementing negative keywords, you should have a way to measure your conversion rates and cost per conversion. In Chapter 15, "Testing Techniques That Will Increase Profits," we will discuss a free conversion tool that Google offers to measure your results.

The reason you need conversion tracking implemented into your account is that when you add negative keywords to your account, some specific things should happen:

- Your click-through rate should increase. Since you are now choosing to stop your ad from showing on irrelevant search queries, the times your ad is shown should be more relevant and thus gain a higher click-through rate.

- Your conversion rate should increase. Because you are now only showing your ad for queries relevant to your product or services and are not being matched to more obscure words that are not directly reflective of your offerings, you should see your conversion rate go up.

- Your cost per conversion should decrease. Since negative keywords keep your ad from displaying on less relevant results, when you do receive clicks, those clicks should be of higher quality and lower your overall cost per conversion.

If you do not see these three items happening, you need to revisit your negative keyword list to see if you added negative keywords that stopped your ads from showing on keyword searches that were driving sales. It is common for someone to know about negative keywords and automatically add the word "free." However, a search for "plasma TVs with free shipping" would not trigger your ad if you used the negative keyword "-free." If you happened to sell plasma TVs and offer free shipping, that is a wonderful query for you to show your ad. Therefore, you need to be careful when adding negative keywords.

Implementing Negative Keywords

There are a few places within your account where you can add negative keywords. The first is within an ad group. Navigate to an ad group, and when you enter a keyword, add the minus (-) sign in front of any words that you do not wish to trigger your ad.

For example, if you were using the broad match keyword "coffee cups," and you wanted to make sure you would never show for "tea cups," you would add the negative keyword "-tea" to your ad group, as shown in Figure 2.9.

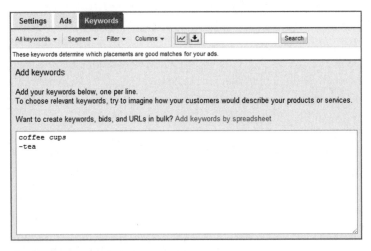

Figure 2.9 Negative keyword "-tea" in an ad group

You can also navigate to the bottom of the Keywords tab and enter negative keywords directly into the Negative Keywords area. When you add negatives here, you do not need to add the minus sign in front of the keywords as you add them.

When you add a negative keyword within an ad group, it only affects the keywords in that group. Therefore, in this example, you could have one ad group selling coffee mugs with the negative keyword "-tea," and another ad group selling tea cups with the negative keyword "-coffee." In this instance, you could now use some broad match words and ensure that the correct ad was displayed.

Please note that in this example, if you only had the just described two ad groups, a search for "tea and coffee mug set" would not display any ads. This is because both "tea" and "coffee" are within the query, and each ad group has a negative keyword that would keep your ad from showing on that query.

The second place you can use negative keywords is at the campaign level. You can manage campaign negative keywords from two places inside your account. The first is on the Keywords tab at the bottom of the page. To reach the other place where you can manage negative keywords, navigate to the Tools menu and click Edit Negative Campaign Keywords. From either place you can input negative keywords. In instances where you are adding campaign negative keywords, these negative keywords will affect every ad group within that specific campaign.

There is also a tool within the campaign negative interface that allows you to find other negative keywords in your account in case you wish to add them as campaign negatives. Be careful when using this tool as you may have negative keywords in specific ad groups that you do not wish to have affecting every single ad group. This approach is useful when used properly—just use with caution.

> **Note:** Google does not currently offer an account-wide negative keyword option. However, there is a Negative Keyword List option that lets you manage lists of negative keywords and then apply those lists to a campaign or multiple campaigns. Whenever you change the negative keywords in a list, your change will automatically be reflected for each campaign where the list has been applied.

As with positive keywords, there are also match types for negative keywords. These three match types are called broad, phrase, and exact negative keyword match. However, while the names are the same as positive keywords, the rules for how the match types work are different for negatives.

Negative Broad Match

When you navigate to your ad group and just type in a minus (-) sign and a keyword, you've created a *negative broad match*. Negative broad keywords stop your ad from showing if that word is anywhere within the search query. Negative broad keywords do not match to misspellings or plurals.

For example, if you had the negative keyword "cups" ("-cups"), a search for "coffee cups" or "tea cups" would not display your ad, as the search query contains the word "cups." However, a search for "coffee cup" (singular) or "coffee cps" (misspelled) would display your ad since the word "cups" was not explicitly stated within the search query.

You can also use multiple words in a negative broad keyword. In this instance, the order of the words does not matter, as long as all of the negative words are in the query. Once again, these do not match to plurals or misspellings.

If you added the negative keyword "coffee cups" ("-coffee cups") in your ad group, your ad would be displayed on a query such as "blue coffee cup" (singular) or "cofee cups" (misspelled). However, your ad would not be displayed for the following:

- Coffee cups
- Blue coffee cups
- Coffee blue cups
- Cups coffee blue
- Cups of coffee

This occurs because every example contains both the word "coffee" and the word "cups."

Negative Phrase Match

Negative phrase match keywords must be contained within the user query in the exact order you entered them. Additional words can be contained before or after the search query; however, if the search query contains your negative phrase in the same order, your ad will not be displayed.

As with broad match negative keywords and regular phrase match keywords, this match type does not match to singular or misspellings.

For example, if you had the negative phrase match -"coffee cups," your ad would not be shown for queries such as:

- Coffee cups
- Blue coffee cups
- Coffee cups and mugs

This is because every one of those examples contains the keyword "coffee cups" in the same order.

However, if you have the negative phrase match word -"coffee cups," your ad would be displayed for queries such as:

- Cups coffee (different order)
- Coffee cup (singular)
- Blue coffee cup (singular)

- Coffe cups (misspelling)
- Coffe cups and tea (misspelling)

When adding negative phrase match words, the formatting is straightforward. Add a minus sign and then the keyword in quotes: -"negative phrase match." If you are adding these negative keywords to the negative keyword text box, you do not need the negative sign (Figure 2.10).

Figure 2.10 Negative phrase match keywords used in an ad group

You can use negative phrase match words at either the ad group or campaign level.

Negative Exact Match

In the *negative exact match*, your ad is not displayed when the search query matches your negative keyword exactly.

For instance, if you had the negative exact match keyword -[coffee cups], your ad would only not be displayed if someone typed "coffee cups" into the search box.

If the search query was "coffee cup" (singular), "cup coffee" (different order), or "coffe cup" (misspelling), the negative exact match keyword would not stop your ad from displaying.

As with the regular exact match, the negative exact match does not match to plurals and misspellings.

The formatting is also the same as the exact match keyword, except you add a negative sign in front of the formatting brackets. The formatting is -[keyword].

Negative keyword	Search query
-mug (broad match single word)	~~coffee mug~~
	coffee mugs
	mugs blue coffee
	blue coffee mugs
- coffee mugs (broad match, multiple words)	coffee mug
	~~coffee mugs~~
	~~mugs blue coffee~~
	~~blue coffee mugs~~
-"coffee mugs"	coffee mug
	~~coffee mugs~~
	mugs blue coffee
	~~blue coffee mugs~~
-[coffee mugs]	coffee mug
	~~coffee mugs~~
	mugs blue coffee
	blue coffee mugs

Putting Negative and Positive Keywords Together

When discussing negative keywords, it can be useful to call regular keywords *positive keywords* to signify the difference between keywords that trigger your ad and their negative counterparts that keep your ad from showing.

When using both negative and positive keywords together, you should first determine when you want your ad to show and whether there are specific variations when you do not want your ad to be displayed. Once you have determined those conditions, it becomes easy to choose the proper negative and positive keywords and respective match types.

For example, let's create a fictional company that sells Disney videos. After running their ads for a while, they realize that when a searcher just types in "Disney video" their conversion rates are low and they are not profitable on those keywords. However, upon further investigation, the company realizes that if the searcher types in anything *with* the keyword "Disney video," they convert quite well. Therefore, they would not want their ad to show on the actual search "Disney video," but they do want it to show for variations such as "Little Mermaid Disney video," "Disney video for sale," and "newest Disney video."

This can be accomplished quite easily. The company would have an ad group with the negative exact match keyword [Disney video] and the positive keyword "Disney video," as seen in Figure 2.11.

Figure 2.11 Disney video negative exact match used with positive keywords

In this instance, the ad would be displayed only if someone searched for "Disney video" and any accompanying word. If someone just searched for "Disney video," the ad would not be triggered.

Often, you will want to use broad or phrase match words to capture a wide variety of search queries. However, this often results in your ad displaying on queries that do not accurately reflect your company's products. Using negative keywords to filter your ad from showing on these queries can allow you to maintain control over when your ad is shown and maximize your ad's reach.

Researching Negative Keywords

It is just as important to keep your ad from showing on irrelevant queries as to show your ad on the correct queries. That also means it's just as important to conduct negative keyword research as it is to research positive keywords.

The easiest place to find negative keywords is the search query report. If you navigate to the reporting section of your AdWords account, one of the reports is called a search query report. Run this report, and you will have an Excel file that looks like Figure 2.12.

	A	B	C	D
1	Ad Group	Search Query	Search Query Match Type	Cost/ Conversion
2	Coffee Cups	Blue coffee cup	phrase	$2.34
3	Coffee Cups	Red coffee cup	broad	$1.76
4	Coffee Cups	Starbucks coffee cup	broad	$4.55
5	Coffee Cups	coffee cups	exact	$2.34
6	Coffee Cups	coffee mugs for RVs	broad	$19.56

Figure 2.12 Search query report in Excel

If your business is selling coffee mugs and you must have a cost per conversion of fewer than $5 to be profitable, you can see that the actual search query that contains "RV" is not profitable.

Assuming that you had enough data to prove this was a trend, or you did not sell RV coffee mugs, you would want to stop your ad from showing when "RV" was used in the search query. By adding the negative keyword "-RV" to that particular ad group, you can stop your ad from showing when the word "RV" is used in the search query.

If you happen to sell RV coffee mugs and do not want to lose that traffic, you could create a new ad group with keywords and ad copy that specifically spoke to those searchers looking for RV coffee mugs. The search query report will give you a significant amount of insight into which actual queries are triggering your ads.

The other way of finding negative keywords is during your regular keyword research phase. In the next chapter, you will learn about Google's powerful keyword research tool. As you use the tool, if you see words that are unrelated to your business or words where you just do not want your ad to be displayed, make note of those potential negative keywords so you can add them to your account.

Advanced Organizational Techniques

When you have two or more keywords that can be triggered in your AdWords account from a search query, Google tries to show the most restrictive option. The constraints go beyond just match type to include geography, time of day, and so forth.

However, Google does not always show exact match over phrase match and phrase match over broad match. They also look at ad rank (max CPC × Quality Score), which we will cover in depth in Chapter 7. If you have an exact match term bid at $0.25 and the broad match bid at $1, Google will generally show the broad match term.

As an advertiser, you will likely find that your exact match converts higher than your phrase or broad match. You should control the ad serving so you know which ad copy and keyword will be displayed for any search query. You can control the ad serving through the use of bids or negative keywords.

There are several ways you can organize your match types within your paid search account. None of the strategies are better or worse than each other—they are just different. For each of these scenarios, we will assume you are using multiple match types for the same keyword and look at the pros and cons of each method.

Adding Multiple Match Types to the Same Ad Group

With this method, you add a keyword to an ad group multiple times, each with a different match type.

The pros of this method are that you have fewer total ad groups to create and optimize. This saves on both creation and management time. If you have a limited amount of time (and/or technology), this is by far the easiest method to use.

There are several cons to this method. With exact match, you can make a good guess to the user intent of the word, so your ad can be specific to the keyword. With broad match you know a lot less about the user intent, so you might write a more general ad copy that incorporates the keyword. This method does not allow you to write ads by match types.

The only way to control ad serving with this method is to make sure your exact match is the highest bid, your phrase match the second highest bid, and then modified broad match. If your ad rank for your broad match trumps your exact match, your conversion rates and other data by match types become compromised.

Restricting Match Types by Ad Group

With this method, each ad group will contain only one match type. If you want to advertise on both exact match and phrase match terms, you will have two different ad groups. In addition, for each of your ad groups you will use negative keywords to ensure the correct match type is being triggered. For instance, your phrase match ad group will contain exact match negatives of all the keywords.

There are a few advantages of this method. The first is that the proper keyword match type should be displayed in a search result. You do not have to ensure that your phrase match ad rank is higher than your exact match ad rank (however, it should be since the conversion rates for exact match should be higher than those for phrase match). This method also allows you to write ad copy by match type.

The biggest con is that your account can quickly be overwhelmed with too many ad groups to the point that you have to create new campaigns for all your ad groups because there are hard limits on how many ad groups can be within a single campaign. This method takes a lot longer to set up, and a little bit longer to manage than grouping all the match types in a single ad group.

It is common to see this method employed where the long-tail keywords are grouped by match type into a single ad group, and then the higher-priced keywords or higher-volume keywords are broken down by match type into different ad groups.

Restricting Match Types by Campaign

Brands that are successful with AdWords often have a campaign just for their branded terms. This campaign is often one of the higher-budget campaigns because it has the best conversion rates and lowest cost per acquisition (CPA), the amount you pay to acquire a customer or lead. A natural extension of that same logic is that exact match keywords have the second-highest conversion rates and second-lowest CPAs for most brands. However, there is a limit to how much you can spend on exact match each month based on search volume. Therefore, you can put all your exact match keywords in a campaign with a budget to capture all of that search volume.

The next highest conversion rates come from phrase match words. Group all your phrase match words into another campaign. Finally, have yet another campaign for modified broad match and broad match keywords. This last broad match campaign will use the last of the company's budget.

If the budget gets increased, the broad match campaign's budget is often increased. If the budget is being reached, lower the budget from the broad match campaign, which also has the lowest conversion rates of all the campaigns.

When you restrict match types by campaign, you also need to add negative keywords by match type at the campaign negative level (just like the method restricting match types by ad group) to ensure the proper keywords are being displayed.

The biggest pro to this account structure is that you can adjust both bids and budget by match types. This method also allows you to write ad copy for each match type and keyword organization.

The issue with this account structure is that you can quickly have too many campaigns. If you have multiple campaigns by match type, and each ad group only contains keywords of the same match type (which cause you to also need more campaigns), and you are doing geographic targeting or the content network, you can quickly become overwhelmed by too many campaigns.

Each campaign must also have a budget. If you slice your budget too thin, none of your campaigns will receive much traffic. In addition, this method takes more organizational and management time than the other structures. This method is not recommended for smaller budgets.

Taking Control of Your Ad Display

Positive keywords are the lifeblood of Google AdWords. If you do not have a keyword that will match to a searcher's query, your ad will not show. It's quite simple. It is crucial that you not only conduct keyword research, but that when you use these keywords in your account, you understand what search queries people can search for that will trigger your ad to show on a search result.

Conversely, when you find search queries that you do not want your ad to show for, block your ad from showing by using negative keywords. Negative keywords should raise your CTR, lower your CPA, and increase your conversion rate.

As you add negative keywords, keep an eye on total conversions. Even if the negative keywords are doing their job, if your total conversions drop significantly you may need to trim some of your negative keywords.

If keywords lead to conversions but at a higher cost per conversion than you are comfortable paying, you should lower the bids to a profitable level instead of just keeping your ad from showing by using negative keywords:

- Positive keywords trigger your ads.
- Negative keywords stop your ad from showing.

By using these two keyword types together, you can take control of your account to ensure you receive the maximum exposure and profit from your AdWords campaigns.

Best Practices for Conducting Keyword Research

Keywords are the foundation of your AdWords account. If you do not have a keyword that matches to the search query, your ad will not be shown. Comprehensive keyword research is essential to maximizing your account's exposure to potential customers.

- Every keyword falls into a section of the buying funnel. Understanding where your keyword falls in the funnel is important to ensure you are reaching consumers at different stages of their buying behavior.

- Keywords can be broken down into four major aspects: explicit, symptoms, problems, and product names or part numbers. Utilize each type of keyword to reach the maximum number of searchers.

- Start keyword research with your site, your competitors' sites, the natural search results, internal site search, and the dictionary.

- Make sure you know your own keywords. If your keywords describe one or more different products or ideas, use ad copy to tell the consumer which keyword variation is related to your company.

- A good way to start expanding your keywords is to create keyword lists. By creating lists for both ad group and keyword organization, you can create larger, yet more focused, lists.

- When starting long-tail keyword research, do not use deep keywords. Deep keywords describe only a single aspect of how someone searches. Instead, start with wide keywords, and when you find keywords that are converting, do deep keyword research on those particular keywords.

- There are four different match types: broad, modified broad, phrase, and exact. Use a combination of these various match types based on your budget and marketing objectives.

- Negative keywords stop your ads from showing. It is just as important to conduct negative keyword research as it is to find new positive keywords.

- The search query report will show you what someone actually searched for that triggered your ad to show. Use this report to find new positive and negative keywords.

Keyword research can be time consuming, but it is necessary for maximum exposure. Many tools are available that will help you along in your keyword research efforts to help save you time and give you ideas you may have overlooked. In the next chapter, we will examine one of these tools: the AdWords Keyword tool.

Keyword Tools: Extracting Valuable Data from Google

Understanding where keywords fall into the buying funnel is critical. Choosing your keywords wisely and then measuring results will ensure the best chance of success for your campaigns. By starting with wide keywords and then moving to deep keywords, you can ensure that you are directing your keyword research time into the proper areas.

After examining your site, competitors' sites, search results, and internal site search, where do you go next to look for keywords?

A variety of tools are available online that will help you discover new keywords.

3

Chapter Contents

AdWords Keyword Tool

Traffic Estimator

Google Trends

Google Insights for Search

Microsoft Advertising Intelligence

Best practices for using keyword tools

AdWords Keyword Tool

Google has a tremendous amount of search data. Between its organic and paid search listings across its web properties such as news, Google.com, Google sites in various countries, images, and even products, Google has compiled a massive amount of data about search queries.

One of the most powerful tools you can use to start your keyword research process is Google's own AdWords Keyword Tool. This tool can examine the information collected across all of these various properties.

You can access the AdWords Keyword Tool from a few different places:

- Access the tool directly: `https://adwords.google.com/select/KeywordToolExternal` (this will redirect you to the actual tool URL)
- From the Tools menu in your AdWords account
- From an individual ad group

There a difference in how you can use the tool if you are logged into your account or using the tool anonymously. If you access the AdWords Keyword Tool from the URL (or any other way that is not clicking into the tool from within your AdWords account), you will not see all the data points. This is because Google does not know which AdWords account to associate this data with and therefore cannot show you data items from within your AdWords account.

If you click the Sign In link in the upper-right corner (Figure 3.1), you will be able to log in and take advantage of the tool's full power.

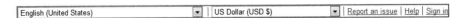

Figure 3.1 Logging into the AdWords Keyword Tool

There are three ways you can use the tool to find new keywords (see Figure 3.2):

- Word Or Phrase—similar to a thesaurus tool
- Website—find keywords from a web page
- Category—find keywords based on category association

You can use one of more of these options at the same time. If you are doing broad-based keyword research to find ad group ideas, then just use one option so you receive more results. As you start drilling down into specific keywords or ad groups, using words and categories at the same time is useful so that you see the data related to the combination of inputs.

For example, if you were doing keyword research for "bleach," the results would show both searches for laundry detergent and anime. If instead you input the keyword "bleach" and chose the category Anime, you would see only the search volume for the bleach type words that are related to anime because the laundry words would be filtered out of the results.

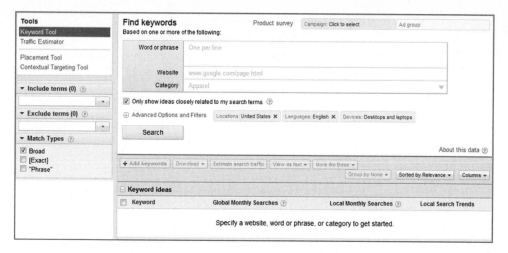

Figure 3.2 AdWords Keyword Tool main screen

After you specify how you want to find keywords, the next step is to specify the type of data you wish to see based on the advanced options and filters.

Advanced Options and Filters

Expand the Advanced Options and Filters section to select the type of data you wish to see (Figure 3.3).

Figure 3.3 Advanced Options and Filters

The first option lets you specify the country and language that you are researching. Even if your company is global, it is useful to estimate to a single country at a time so that you can obtain a better estimate of search volume and costs per click (CPCs) for each country. It is common for CPCs to vary dramatically by country, and when possible, you should limit your campaigns to showing in a single country (location targeting will be discussed in Chapter 11, "Advanced Geographic Targeting"). You can hold down the Shift or Ctrl key to select multiple languages if you wish to see data from multiple languages from a single country.

If you are estimating adult content, you must select the Include Adult Ideas check box. Google does not show adult keywords by default.

The next option, Show Ideas And Statistics For, lets you choose the devices you are estimating for. Click the drop-down arrow to reveal your choices:

- Desktop And Laptop Devices
- All Mobile Devices
- Mobile WAP Devices
- Mobile Devices With Full Internet Browsers

We will discuss mobile devices fully in Chapter 8, "Beyond Text: Image, Video, and Mobile Ads"; however, mobile search queries are shorter than desktop search queries, so if you are estimating for mobile devices, you should do keyword research for mobile devices independently of research on desktop devices.

Finally, you can choose to filter the data based on the following:

- Competition
- Google Search Network
- Global Monthly Searches
- Local Monthly Searches
- Ad Share
- Search Share
- Approximate CPC

These filters can be quite powerful once you understand the definitions for all of the data points, which we'll cover shortly. One of my favorite filters is to see only keywords for which you have low ad share (how often your ad is displayed) and have at least a minimum number of impressions (see Figure 3.3 earlier). This filter ensures that you are not seeing keywords for which you already have strong coverage, and will find the higher volume keywords when you start your research.

Once you decide what data you wish to view, it is time to start finding the keywords you want to use.

Generating Keyword Ideas

When using tools to generate ideas, keep in mind that they are just tools run by computers. These tools do not know your business, they do not think, and they do not understand your customers. While a tremendous amount of data is available from these tools, *you* are the one responsible for choosing your keywords.

Ensure that the keywords you choose accurately describe your products or services, the problems they solve, and the conditions someone may be in when they need your business. Remember, keywords are thought processes.

You should start by finding wide keywords—those keywords that describe the vast ways people search for words that are not closely related (for example, spyware, adware, virus, keylogger)—before diving deep into one specific keyword (for instance, spyware, spyware remover, spyware program).

We will first look at the three main ways of conducting keyword research.

Word or Phrase

The first way to use the AdWords Keyword Tool is to input words or phrases and ask Google to show you similar keywords (Figure 3.4).

Keyword	Global Monthly Searches	Local Monthly Searches	Approximate CPC
Search terms (1)			
spyware	4,090,000	1,220,000	$2.60
Keyword ideas (752)			
free **spyware** removal	74,000	49,500	$2.69
spyware removal	246,000	135,000	$3.74
free **spyware** software	33,100	18,100	$2.87
spyware protection removal	12,100	6,600	$3.56
spyware removal free	74,000	49,500	$2.68

Figure 3.4 Viewing words or phrases in the AdWords Keyword Tool

Use this tool when you are first starting your keyword research to identify the synonyms and ideas related to your major keywords. When you find different wide keywords, note them in a separate list from your keyword research. Doing so will help you keep tabs on the wide keywords and sort them from the thousands of keywords you might normally add to your ad groups.

However, when you check the option Only Show Ideas Closely Related To My Search Items (see Figure 3.5) the results will be more targeted to your original inputs. Using this option is a good way to find deep keywords because the wide words will often be eliminated.

After advertising for a period of time so that you have enough data to examine your conversion rates and costs per conversion, you may realize that a few sets of wide keywords are driving most of your sales. You'll find this tool valuable because it allows you to dive into all the variations of those keywords.

Website: Jumpstarting Your Keyword List

Since you already have a website, and most likely you spent quality time writing your content, wouldn't it be useful if you could just receive suggestions based on each of your website's pages?

That is exactly what the Website option accomplishes. You can enter a landing page in the Website field, and the Keyword Tool will suggest keywords based on what it finds on those landing pages (Figure 3.5).

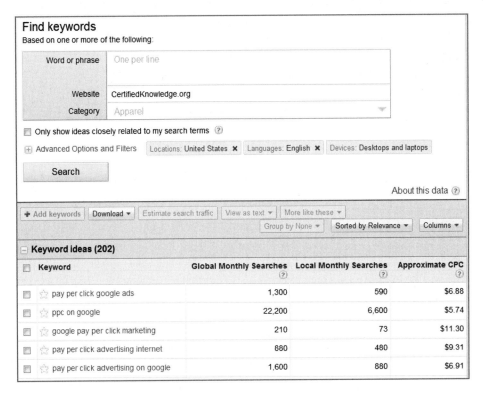

Figure 3.5 Entering a landing page in the Website field

Using this option is an excellent way to start finding your wide keywords. Take a look at your landing page, and then enter the URL into the search box. AdWords will crawl your page, attempting to decipher what keywords that page describes.

Most Adobe Flash pages have problems being crawled and understood by search engines. However, Google and others have made great strides in attempting to crawl sites designed in Adobe Flash. You can enter an Adobe Flash website in the tool to see if AdWords has any understanding of the website. Often, Adobe Flash sites have a difficult time achieving relevancy in AdWords because Google's crawlers cannot understand their pages. Just because the Keyword Tool brings back information about your page does not always mean it can be crawled well. In any case, it is good directional information if Google has some understanding of your website.

Understanding a Spider's Role in the Web

When a search engine wants to index the Web, it uses a program called a *spider* or *robot* (often also called a *webbot*, or just *bot*). The search engine sends out its spider to crawl the Web to find new pages to index so it can build a database from the information it discovers. The spider indexes content such as HTML, images, PDF files, or any other file found on the Web. The terms *spider*, *spidering*, *crawl*, or *crawling* are commonly used to describe the process of the spider discovering and indexing the content it finds.

Note: We will discuss quality score in Chapter 7, "Demystifying Quality Score." In the meantime, keep in mind that entering your landing page in AdWords also helps you see if Google thinks your page is about what you think it is about. If the two of you disagree, you may see much lower quality scores.

There is no restriction on what sites you can enter—you can attempt to crawl any page on the Web. If someone has amended their `robots.txt` file to not allow crawlers to access the page, the tool should respect the `robots.txt` file.

Note: A `robots.txt` file is an instruction manual for your website that tells a spider what pages they can crawl and index. It is found at `yoursite.com/robots.txt`. If you do not have a `robots.txt` file, a spider assumes it can index any page of your website. To learn more about `robots.txt` files, see `www.robotstxt.org`.

You can spider competitor pages, industry pages, search results, and so on to help build your wide keyword list. Here is a list of sites to spider when you are first starting your wide keyword research:

- Your website
- Your competitors' websites
- DMOZ.org category for your site
- Thesaurus.reference.com
- Dictionary.reference.com
- MetaGlossary.com (one of my favorites)
- Wikipedia.org
- Ask.com (related results are very useful)
- Google or Yahoo! news
- The top authority magazine or journal for your industry
- Sites where you receive your industry news

- Any sites or blogs where you regularly receive your industry information
- Any directory related to your industry

Note that you may want to do a search on some of these sites for your keyword first. For example, spidering the homepage of Thesaurus.com is not useful, whereas spidering the search result page for your keywords at `http://thesaurus.reference.com/browse/YourKeyword` will be more relevant to your company.

Every time you see a page on the Web that is highly related to your business, make note of the page so you can spider it when you do keyword research. This simple exercise will help you expand your keyword list over time.

The Keyword Tool can also help with your search engine optimization (SEO) efforts. With SEO, you do not get to pick keyword match types—you have to choose exact keywords. More advanced versions of SEO are available that examine traffic more than individual keyword rankings, but you have to start somewhere. When using this tool for SEO research, make sure you only look at the exact match of a keyword when trying to predict keyword volume.

Even beyond SEO and pay-per-click advertising, if you are looking for related keywords, or for thesaurus, competitor, trend, and other data, the Keyword Tool has uses within social media as well as competitor research. It is a powerful resource for conducting keyword research about your specific website and almost every other website on the entire Internet. Always keep this tool in mind when you are trying to find new wide keywords or when you come across an authority site related to your industry.

Keyword Suggestions by Category

The other way to use the Keyword Tool tool is by browsing through the categories. When you click on the category section, a large drill-down of various categories and subcategories will appear that you can select (Figure 3.6).

Most of the keyword suggestions will be wide keywords. In many cases, the keywords will be so general you might not even want to use them in your AdWords account.

One of the best uses of the categories is to find other keyword themes you may have missed. This is good information for not only your AdWords keywords, but also for your natural search rankings. You may see better ways to structure your site navigation based on some of the category information. In addition, this information can be useful for determining how to structure your ad groups.

However, never select all the keywords and dump them into your ad groups. These keywords are selected by automated programs that do not always understand the intent of a word, and you will see some poor suggestions that you should not use. For instance, in the Jobs & Education category, you will see "worksheets" (Figure 3.7) as a keyword. Because the word "work" is in the keyword, Google automatically assumes it's a work-related keyword.

Figure 3.6 Keyword drill-down by category

Figure 3.7 Jobs & Education category keywords

Browsing categories is useful for finding ideas on keywords you might have missed or for gaining insight into Google's association of keywords within a category. However, never build your AdWords account just using the category tool. There are too many poor suggestions, and missing keywords per category, to rely solely on this tool.

Now that you've seen how to generate keyword data, let's examine the data you can view for each of those words.

Interpreting the Keyword Data

Before you start looking into the data, choose the match types you wish to view. By default, Google only shows broad match information. Never do estimates in broad match unless they are long-tail keywords. Usually phrase match is a good match type if you are looking to do quick estimates. If you want a good idea on any single keyword, examine the data in exact match. You can select the match types you wish to see by selecting the check box next to each match type (Figure 3.8).

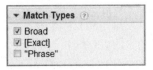

Figure 3.8 Choosing your match types

The reason you never want to do estimates on broad match is that broad match can show for a large variety of queries—including ones that you do not even want to show your ads.

In addition, if you were to choose broad match and add that keyword to your account, often the broad match keywords will not actually receive the total impressions that the Keyword Tool suggests because so many possible variations of broad match words exist. There is often a large difference between exact, phrase, and broad match estimates (Figure 3.9).

Search terms (6)	
Keyword	**Local Monthly Searches** ?
☆ mortgage	11,100,000
☆ "mortgage"	9,140,000
☆ mortgages	673,000
☆ "mortgages"	246,000
☆ [mortgage]	49,500
☆ [mortgages]	9,900

Figure 3.9 Estimating match types

In this scenario, the keyword "mortgage" in phrase match has 9.1 million impressions and the same keyword in broad match has 11.1 million impressions. That means there are 2 million impressions for which broad match would be displayed that don't even have the actual word "mortgage" in it. While some of those impressions would go to the plural "mortgages," even the volume of both the singular and the plural in phrase match do not come close to adding up to all of the broad match impressions.

The exact match keyword "mortgage" only has 49,500 impressions. That's a far cry from broad match's 11.1 million impressions.

Estimating Modified Broad Match

There is no way to estimate modified broad match with the AdWords Keyword tool. Here are some general guidelines to get closer to estimating modified broad match.

For keywords three words in length with a common term that has decent search volume (cheap web hosting, inexpensive web hosting, etc.; *web hosting* is the common term), estimate the two-word term at phrase match if you are planning on adding most of these various terms as keywords across multiple ad groups. You will know that in aggregate you will probably capture one-third to one-half of the traffic across all the ad groups—although you will not know exactly what ad group will end up with what traffic. This is a rough estimate at best.

For keywords of four words that do not have high search volume, estimate at broad match and you will probably capture 50–75 percent of that search volume.

It is easy to give guidelines for estimating based on how many words are in a keyword, but you should also keep in mind how concrete or abstract the idea of the keyword is. For instance, "Los Angeles Lakers Uniform" is one overall idea even though it contains four words, whereas "paternity testing" is also one idea at just two words.

Treat these as overall guidelines, but remember they are not perfect since the number of ideas in a keyword is just as important as the number of words in that keyword.

Once you use one of the previous methods to find keywords, you will also see a variety of data about each of the possible keywords. Not all the data is displayed by default. If you examine the Columns drop-down selections (see Figure 3.10), you can choose which data you wish to examine.

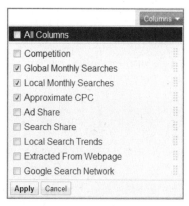

Figure 3.10 Customizing columns in the AdWords Keyword Tool

First we will look at the columns for traffic estimates that are available for any keyword. Next we will examine data that is available only if you use the website tool suggestions.

Competition, Local and Global Searches, Approximate CPC, and Local Search Trends

The first column, as you can see in Figure 3.11, shows a relative competition level. Google never discloses how many competitors there are for any keyword. You just get a relative idea (Low, Medium, or High) of how competitive the word is among advertisers.

Keyword	Competition	Global Monthly Searches	Local Monthly Searches	Local Search Trends
current mortgage rates	High	165,000	135,000	
home mortgage rates	High	201,000	90,500	
mortgage rates today	High	135,000	110,000	
compare mortgage rates	High	33,100	12,100	
mortgage rate trends	High	27,100	27,100	
second mortgage	Medium	90,500	90,500	
adjustable rate mortgage	High	49,500	33,100	
private mortgage insurance	Low	33,100	33,100	
lowest mortgage rates	High	74,000	40,500	

Keyword ideas (800)

Figure 3.11 Viewing competition, search data, Approximate CPC, and trends in the Keyword Tool

You should only look at competitive data by match types. In this example, the competition is vastly different based on the match type. Because broad match can trigger a large variety of keyword queries, some will be competitive and others less so. Therefore, it is common to see the exact match versions of words more competitive than the broad match versions.

The next two columns are approximate search data. Global Monthly Searches shows the number of times that keyword was searched in the entire world for the language you chose, averaged for the past 12 months. Local Monthly Searches shows the approximate number of times that keyword was searched for in the country and language you are estimating, averaged for the past 12 months.

 Note: This is a change from how Google used to display these results. For years, local monthly searches were for the previous month. They now represent an average for the past year.

Because these are rolling yearly averages, estimating monthly search volume from these numbers is difficult when the word has large changes in trend data. You can see trend data (Figure 3.12) in the Keyword Tool.

Search terms (2)			
Keyword	Global Monthly Searches ②	Local Monthly Searches ②	Local Search Trends
☆ [suntrust mortgage]	49,500	49,500	
☆ [mortgages]	74,000	9,900	

Figure 3.12 Trend data from the AdWords Keyword Tool

When the keyword trend data is very flat, as it is for "Suntrust Mortgage," you can be more confident in your monthly estimates because the volume does not change significantly. When you see that the trend data changes significantly, such as for "flowers," you will want to take a closer look at the data when you do your estimates.

If you have Trend Data selected and then click the Download button, you can download a file that shows you the estimated search volume by month (Figure 3.13) so you can be more confident in your monthly estimates.

Keyword	Sep-11	Aug-11	Jul-11	Jun-11	May-11	Apr-11	Mar-11	Feb-11	Jan-11	Dec-10	Nov-10	Oct-10
[suntrust mortgage]	49500	60500	49500	49500	49500	49500	49500	49500	49500	49500	49500	49500
[mortgages]	8100	9900	6600	8100	8100	8100	9900	9900	9900	8100	9900	12100

Figure 3.13 Downloaded trend data

Trend data is very powerful. It shows you how the keyword has changed in search volume over the past year. This information is so useful that we will discuss Google Trends information later in this chapter and you'll learn how to use trending data.

The final piece of information to examine is the approximate CPC. The Keyword Tool is not hooked up to the quality score in your account, and if you have never used a keyword before, your account does not even have that information available for the tool. Therefore, the average CPC data is a rough estimate.

Since so many factors go into average CPC—such as other advertisers changing their bids, advertisers within a specific geography, and a plethora of other variables—the suggested CPC should be used as a guide and not as a definite number. Use your common sense and the historical information you have learned about your industry to determine how useful the estimated CPC is for your account. Google has made a lot of strides in helping average CPC to be more useful and accurate, but consider the information a rough guideline at best.

Ad Share, Search Share, and Landing Pages

The final sets of columns (see Figure 3.14) are useful for learning more about your current visibility. To see these columns populated with data, you must enter a URL in the Website field and you must be sending traffic to that website from within your AdWords account.

Keyword ideas (800)			
Keyword	Ad Share	Search Share	Extracted From Webpage
☆ learning french with	30.28%	100%	
☆ learn mandarin chinese quickly	91.89%	100%	
☆ learning to speak cantonese	93.33%	100%	
☆ learn japanese in 10 days	100%	100%	
☆ learn japanese course	92.64%	100%	

Figure 3.14 Ad Share, Search Share, and Extracted From Webpage data

Ad Share is the percentage of times your ad was displayed for that keyword. While you can see overall impression data in your account (as discussed in Chapter 16, "AdWords Reports: How to Extract Actionable Information"), this is the only place where you can see exact percentages of how often any one keyword was displayed. The data is only for Google search, so search partners or the display network is not included.

Search Share is the percentage of times your website was displayed on the first page of organic results. This is the most valuable data that search engine optimizers (SEOs) do not use nearly enough. You can run reports on a regular basis and see if your major keywords are increasing or decreasing in organic impressions.

Extracted From Webpage (blurred out in Figure 3.14 to protect the advertiser) is the page that Google believes is the best result on your site for that keyword. If you are making pages dedicated to search queries that you are only using for paid search, this data is of minimal value. However, if you are trying to build a large account quickly, having Google spider your site for keywords and suggested landing pages can give you a jumpstart on building or expanding your account.

For instance, if you enter your website and then choose the filters for only showing keywords with less than 25 percent search share and at least 100 impressions per month (see Figure 3.15), Google will show you a list of keywords and landing pages that you can easily add to your account.

Filter keywords ⑦				
Ad Share	▼	< ▼	25	%
Local Monthly Searches	▼	>= ▼	100	

Figure 3.15 Using filters to find new keywords

Once you find keywords that you wish to advertise on, you must decide what to do next with those keywords.

Where to Save Your Keyword Data

Next to each keyword is a box. You can click on this box to select the keyword. Once you have found a list of keywords that you like, you have to decide what you want to do with those selected keywords (see Figure 3.16).

Figure 3.16 Selected keyword options

You can click the Add Keywords button to add the keywords to your account. You will be able to save those keywords to any ad group in your account.

> ## Negative Keywords
>
> To add negative keywords to your account from the tool, hover over a word and you will see a down arrow. Click that arrow to open a list of options of negative keywords and match types that you can add to the keyword list.

If you use the Category or Website option, be careful with the check box that lets you select every keyword at once—you most likely will have keywords in the list that are not related to your products. For instance, if you spider "Google news," you will get keywords related to breaking news in your keyword list.

You can click the Download button to download the keywords. If you have done extensive keyword research and have to organize the keywords into different ad groups, download the data and organize it in a spreadsheet program. In Chapter 12, "Save Time and Scale Accounts with the AdWords Editor," we will examine the AdWords Editor, which has a feature that lets you quickly add lots of keywords to different ad groups and campaigns. Using the AdWords Editor to build your ad groups and keyword lists is much faster than using the AdWords interface.

You can view the keywords as text, which brings up a list of the keywords that you can easily copy. Clicking the More Like These button does another keyword search for your selected terms.

Finally, you can estimate traffic for the keywords. With this option, Google will attempt to determine not just the search volume, but how many possible clicks you will receive for those keywords. This is another tool that does not know your quality score or your click-through rate (CTR). If you write fantastic ads that have very high CTRs, you could receive significantly more clicks than what is estimated. Conversely, if your ads have low CTRs, or you have a daily budget that is lower than what is required to capture all of the clicks, you may receive fewer clicks than what is estimated. We will examine the Traffic Estimator Tool later in the "Traffic Estimator" section.

AdWords Keyword Tool vs. Third-Party Keyword Tools

Several keyword tools are available that can help you learn more about your keywords. The most popular, and one of the original keyword tools, is Wordtracker.

Wordtracker draws its data from a few meta–search engines, such as Dogpile .com. These meta-engines did have decent search volume years ago when pay-per-click (PPC) was new. However, they make up a miniscule amount of the search volume. Wordtracker takes the data it receives from these engines and extrapolates the numbers to determine search volume. Estimating search volume from such a small data set often creates a significant difference in the suggested search volume versus the impression you receive when you advertise on those same keywords.

Another tool is WordStream. This tool draws data from a variety of sources and attempts to estimate search volume.

Because Google accounts for roughly 70 percent of all search volume in the United States (and higher in many European countries), it is often best to rely on Google's numbers to estimate traffic. If you are doing some advanced calculations, you can use all three data sets together to attempt to determine search numbers.

However, that does not mean that Wordtracker and WordStream are useless. Quite the contrary—when you are doing specific research into wide and deep keywords, they both have some nice features that help you dig into your keyword lists. They are useful for keyword research and both are tools I use regularly—just be careful of the search volume numbers.

In addition, Wordtracker and WordStream both have free trials. This makes it easy to test their keyword research capabilities to see if they work for you before committing any money.

Traffic Estimator

The Traffic Estimator is another Google tool you can access from the AdWords Tools menu. It allows you to estimate the traffic you will receive from a keyword. To generate estimates, you must enter three starting variables (see Figure 3.17):

- Word Or Phrase
- Max CPC $
- Daily Budget $

Figure 3.17 Traffic Estimator inputs

In the Word Or Phrase entry, you must wrap the keywords in the appropriate formatting to see traffic levels by match types.

- [Brackets] means exact match.
- "Quotation marks" is phrase match.
- No Formatting is broad match.

Optionally, you can open the Advanced options and estimate the keywords for one specific match type. But you cannot mix and match keywords and match types with that format option.

In the Advanced options, you can also estimate traffic at a city, state, province, country, or multiple country level. The wizard for selecting locations (shown in Figure 3.18) is the same interface used for choosing your location settings (which will be discussed in Chapter 11).

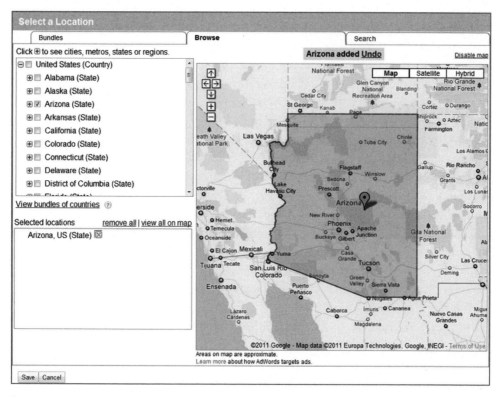

Figure 3.18 Selecting location regions

When you choose an area smaller than a country, you will usually not see Local Monthly Search Volume. This is because Google is not good at giving search estimates or trend data for locations smaller than a country, but you will have an idea of what you can actually spend and the clicks you will receive from that region (Figure 3.19).

	Keyword	Local Monthly Searches ⑦	Estimated Avg. CPC	Estimated Ad Position	Estimated Daily Clicks	Estimated Daily Cost	Local Search Trends
☐ ☆	[mortgage]	-	$2.64	1.1	0.95	$2.52	-
☐ ☆	"mortgage"	-	$2.04	1.26	91.84	$187.24	-
☐ ☆	mortgage	-	$1.99	1.76	24.2	$48.29	-

Figure 3.19 Traffic estimates for Arizona

Just like the AdWords Keyword too, this tool does not access your real Quality Score data; and therefore average CPC and position are only rough estimates. You should use your common sense and the historical information you have learned about your industry to determine how useful those two numbers are to your specific account.

Google Trends

Google Trends (www.google.com/trends) is a tool that lets you see how search queries have risen and fallen over time. You can gain many insights by examining the trends of search queries. In an online world, it is easy to forget the lessons taught through hundreds of years of data from the offline world.

A brick-and-mortar store has a limited amount of inventory. Each month they have to consider the goods that will need to be stocked in the upcoming months based on what will sell in the store. If a store stocks goods that are not sold, that wasted space can lead to a loss of profits. The inventory specialist examines what goods were sold in the previous years in order to predict the inventory they need in the store in any given month.

Almost every business has some seasonality. Seasonality in the flower industry is one of the most obvious. Valentine's Day, Mother's Day, Easter, and similar holidays have correlations with spikes in searches, sales, and even conversion rates. Even an office supply store will see trends in their sales. During various holidays, spikes will occur in the number of searches for holiday stationery and printable cards. At Father's Day, it is common to see a spike for Cross pens, a popular Father's Day gift. During Christmas, high-end pens such as Waterman or Montblanc see search spikes (see Figure 3.20), even though overall trends for buying luxury pens has decreased significantly in the past several years.

Not all seasonality is driven by holidays. An office supply store will want to stock low-cost laptops and computer desks in the fall when the college semester starts. It is always important to keep in mind the daily factors of life that drive search and buying behavior.

When you examine AdWords reports, which we will cover throughout this book, you are always looking back in time at data. If you are making bid or budget decisions by only utilizing the past month or two of data, you are missing possible changes in conversion rates and search behavior that are driven by trends that may only occur a few times a year. If you sell computer desks, it can be useful to make changes to your inventory and ad copy based on the fall back-to-school season versus the spring, when both people and businesses move and need new furniture. Instead of making changes based on your account's past history, examine the history to project changes to conversion rates, sales, bids, and budgets.

Figure 3.20 Trend data for Cross, Waterman, and Montblanc pens

This is where Google Trends shines. It is a free tool that will display changes in keyword search volume or even in visitors to a website. You can segment this data by various time frames and by regions. Once you have the data, you can click into a region to drill down into states and cities.

The most important thing to note when examining the region, city, and language data is that it is normalized by population (see Figure 3.21). The data shows the likelihood of that search term being used in that language or region. In the chart shown in Figure 3.21, the data does not mean that Singapore and the United Kingdom conduct more searches for Waterman pens than the United States. It means there is a higher chance of a user in one of those countries searching for a Waterman pen than in the United States.

Rank by	waterman pen ▼		
Regions	**Cities**	**Languages**
1. Singapore	1. Singapore, Singapore	1. English
2. United Kingdom	2. Thames Ditton, United Kingdom	2. Dutch
3. United States	3. Birmingham, United Kingdom	3. Polish
4. Netherlands	4. New York, NY, USA	4. Italian
5. Australia	5. Chicago, IL, USA	5. French
6. New Zealand	6. Brentford, United Kingdom	6. Chinese
7. Canada	7. Houston, TX, USA	7. German
8. India	8. Boston, MA, USA	8. Portuguese
9. Belgium	9. Pleasanton, CA, USA	9. Spanish
10. Poland	10. Philadelphia, PA, USA	

Figure 3.21 Search trend information normalized by population

You can also view trending data by individual websites. If you are using placement targeting campaigns (discussed in later chapters), it is useful to see changes to website traffic.

With trending data for websites, you can see which geographies are more likely to visit a website, other websites visited, and even other websites also searched for (see Figure 3.22). These sets of data can give you ideas about placing ads on various sites, keyword ideas, or just some competitive research information.

Figure 3.22 Trend data for Walmart.com and Target.com

Google Trends is an easy tool to use to gain insight into changes in search behavior for either specific words or websites. You can export the data to easily see changes in the search behavior on a weekly basis. Doing so makes it easier to visualize what weeks lead to higher or lower search volume.

One exercise that can be useful for visualizing all of your keywords and trend information is to export the data into Microsoft Excel and then cross-reference the Excel file with a calendar. This can help you build a reference source for your business so that you can quickly look at a week or month to anticipate the changes to search volume.

Google Insights for Search

One of the more complex tools that Google offers is Google Insights for Search. This tool lets you compare groups of search terms, view terms by locations or time frames, and then segment the entire data set by industry.

You can obtain this tool by hovering over a word in the AdWords Keyword Tool and clicking the magnifying glass icon, or you can navigate to www.google.com/insights/search/. You can gain a tremendous amount of insight from Google Insights for Search. It can be useful to first consider your goals when using this tool to stay focused on the information that will help you make actionable decisions.

There are three major ways by which you can search for information:

Search Term You can compare up to five different groups of up to 25 keywords (see Figure 3.23).

Figure 3.23 Multiple items compared to view search volume

Location See which locations have higher search volume.

Time Frame Compare search volume by different time frames.

You can filter the data by several items depending on how you are searching for information. The most common filters (seen in Figure 3.23) are as follows:

Search Type You can see just image, product, news, or general web search information. This is useful if you specialize in a specific type of search.

Location For search terms and time frames, you can either view a specific country or worldwide. If you are comparing by location, you can specify a particular metro or state. In addition, you can drill down into more granular locations, which we will explore in the "What Services Should You Offer?" section.

Time Frame There are several options for viewing different time frames.

Category Category drill-down is very useful. If you have a word, such as "bleach," that falls into many categories, understanding the search volume for that keyword in a specific category can give you a better understanding of the search volume available.

There are more possible uses for Google Insights for Search than we could possibly cover in a chapter, so let's take a look at some of the most useful comparisons.

What Services Should You Offer?

If you have several services, it would be useful to know which ones have higher search volumes and how those volumes change so you know where to focus your online marketing efforts.

With Google Insights for Search, it is easy to compare several items to see which has a higher search volume and if there are definitive trends. If you are a plumber who specializes in kitchen and bathroom remodeling, where should you spend more time optimizing your search marketing (see Figure 3.24)?

Figure 3.24 Kitchen remodeling vs. bathroom remodeling search information

In Figure 3.24, you can clearly see that the trends for kitchen remodeling and bathroom remodeling are similar. Before 2008, kitchen remodeling had a higher search volume. Starting in 2008, bathroom remodeling took over the higher search volume of the two options. By examining trend data, you can see that you should have switched your focus from kitchens to bathrooms in 2008.

What happened with the collapse of the real estate market is that people wanted to remodel to sell their homes. However, bathrooms are much cheaper to remodel than kitchens. Therefore, advice from real estate agents became "redo the bathroom" instead of the older advice of "redo the kitchen" in order to get the house ready to sell. Although it is useful to bid on both of these terms, there is a higher possible payoff when you focus more attention on bathroom remodeling because the search volume is higher.

More drill-downs are available on the page. Below the search volume chart is a chart that shows regions and a heat map based on the search volume in various regions. You can view this information at a country, region (state), or city level.

If you tailor your search campaigns for geographic regions (which will be covered in depth in Chapter 11) you can gain more insight by drilling down into various regions. For instance, if you were a Washington, DC, plumber, it would be useful to know that Washington is one of the few regions where there is more search volume for kitchen remodeling than bathroom remodeling (see Figure 3.25). Therefore, a Washington plumber might focus his campaign differently than a Dallas plumber, who sees the exact opposite in terms of top searches.

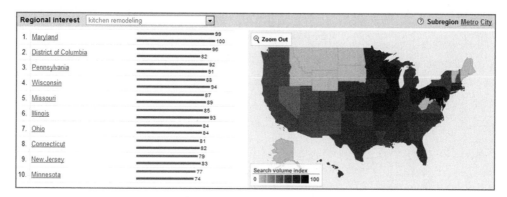

Figure 3.25 Kitchen remodeling search volume

Lastly, at the bottom of the Google Insights for Search page, you can find information about top searches and raising searches. The top searches are just what they sound like—the top searched keywords related to the keywords you chose and the geographic region. If you choose different regions, you may see the top related searches change as well.

The top gaining searches are words that have gained in popularity based on the time frame you chose. It is useful to select the past year, or even the past 90 days in a quick-changing industry, to see what additional words are gaining in search volume. This can be useful to determine whether there are new products you should offer (see Figure 3.26). Occasionally you may see a word labeled "breakout." This means the search volume has changed by more than 5,000 percent. If it is related to your business, it is a trend you want to make sure your company is aware of and possibly testing.

Search terms	bathroom remodeling		
Top searches		**Rising searches**	
1. bathroom ideas	100	1. remodeling small bathroom	+300%
2. bathroom remodeling ideas	100	2. remodeling bathroom ideas	+250%
3. remodeling ideas	95	3. bathroom ideas	+200%
4. remodeling small bathroom	40	4. bathroom remodeling pictures	+200%
5. remodeling a bathroom	35	5. remodeling ideas	+180%
6. kitchen remodeling	35	6. bathroom remodel	+170%
7. bathroom remodel	30	7. bathrooms	+150%
8. kitchen bathroom remodeling	30	8. remodeling bathrooms	+140%
9. bathroom pictures	30	9. bathroom pictures	+130%
10. remodeling bathroom pictures	30	10. remodeling a bathroom	+120%

Figure 3.26 Top searches and raising searches for kitchen remodeling

In this case, you see that the top raising search for bathroom remodeling is "remodeling small bathrooms." Small bathrooms are less expensive to remodel than large ones, so you might want to focus on a few ideas for remodeling small bathrooms and ensure that "small bathroom remodeling" is in your keyword list.

Determining Your Messaging

If you were selling cars, should you promote a family car or a luxury car? What about car safety versus fuel efficiency versus financing? If you could compare the search volume for these different aspects of a product, it could help you decide how to position your product, as shown in Figure 3.27.

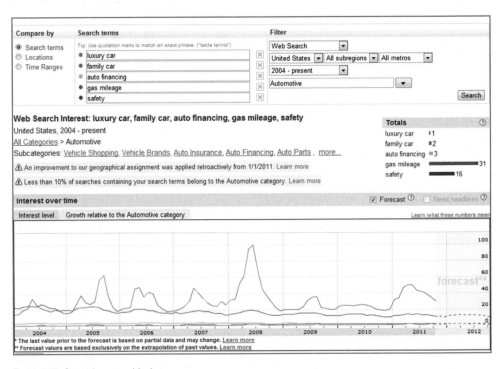

Figure 3.27 Comparing car positioning

In Figure 3.27, you can see that the search volume changes slightly for family versus luxury cars, with family cars having a slight edge. This might not be enough of a difference for you to change your product positioning.

However, it becomes easy to see that gas mileage is much more important than either safety or auto financing. Several years ago, car safety was the most important aspect of buying a car. In 2004, safety and gas mileage vied back and forth for the top searches. Starting in 2005, gas mileage has consistently beaten other aspects of car buying.

By comparing features of your products, you can see which features have higher search volume and are often a larger consumer concern. This knowledge can help shape your ad copy and landing pages to address the consumer's greatest questions.

Determining Consumer Interest

If you are expanding your market, knowing which areas have a greater interest in your product can help you create test markets and determine where your expansions will have the best chance for success.

For example, if you created an add-on for the popular Microsoft Xbox game console, where should you market your product? You could attempt to look at market interest by individual city or by country. How much do you want to expand your marketplace?

By comparing searches for Xbox across different geographies (see Figure 3.28), you can determine a list of regions where the interest for Xbox is high. Because Google Insights for Search shows interest, and not total search volume, you will need to reference this information with the actual population size, but Google Insights for Search creates a much easier starting place for your additional research.

Figure 3.28 Search interest for Xbox

There are many other creative ways you can use Google Insights for Search. Whenever you are conducting research that involves keywords, locations, or trends, keep it in mind to see how you can use this tool to help with your research.

Microsoft Advertising Intelligence

Google sunsetted their labs products in 2011, and many useful products were removed. However, Microsoft has come to the rescue with a great suite of products known as Microsoft Advertising Intelligence.

Microsoft Advertising Intelligence is an Excel plug-in tool, so you must own a copy of Excel to use it. In addition, you must have a Microsoft adCenter account (it does not have to spend money, but you must have an account). If you own Excel and have an adCenter account, you can download the plug-in from `http://advertising.microsoft`
`.com/small-business/adcenter-downloads/microsoft-advertising-intelligence`.

There are many useful data points you can see within the tool, and most are self-explanatory. I also suggest taking a look at the demographics for your keywords just to make sure you are reaching the correct audience. For instance, Figure 3.29 shows the demographic data for the word "bleach."

Keyword	Age0_12	Age13_17	Age18_24	Age25_34	Age35_49	Age50_64	Age65Plus	Female	Male
bleach	0.42%	9.37%	27.79%	26.61%	23.80%	9.67%	2.33%	35.77%	64.23%

Figure 3.29 Microsoft Advertising Intelligence data for the word "bleach"

By looking at this data, you can see that the major demographics for the word "bleach" are young males and not what most people think, which is Clorox bleach. When you see outliers in demographic associations for your keywords, you should view that as a signal to learn more about that keyword.

I suggest downloading the tool and playing with the features. We could spend another 100 pages talking about how to use all the options of this tool. Suffice it to say, if you are advertising in a region where Microsoft has decent search volume, this tool will help you gain more insight into keywords for any PPC campaign.

The most important point to remember about tools is that they are only as good as their inputs and interpretations. If you put bad data into a tool, you will see bad data come out of the tool. If you do not understand the information being presented, or the business rules behind how the data is calculated, you may not be able to interpret the data to come to the correct conclusions.

Understanding what the tool does and how it calculates and presents the data is crucial in extracting valuable, actionable data from any toolset.

Best Practices for Using Keyword Tools

Keyword tools do not tell you what keywords you should use; they give you keyword suggestions that you can choose to either use or bypass. Using keyword tools is essential to researching the full breadth of keyword possibilities for your account. Keywords are thought processes, and everyone thinks differently.

- The AdWords Keyword Tool should be one of the first tools you utilize when you are conducting keyword research.

- Use the Word Or Phrase section of the AdWords Keyword Tool when you have a list of words and would like suggestions based on that list.

- Use the Website section of the AdWords tool when you wish to extract data from a website. Try entering your website, your competitor's website, search results, or the dictionary to find new keywords. Whenever you see a page on the Web and think that page is highly related to your products, enter the page into the tool to see if there are new keywords that are relevant to your account.

- Once you find keywords with the AdWords Keyword Tool, you can either save those keywords to an ad group or export them for organization and later use.

- The AdWords Keyword Tool can not only help you find new keywords but also suggest the most relevant corresponding landing pages on your website.

- The Traffic Estimator can help determine the click and pricing volume for a keyword. One of its best uses is estimating traffic in small geographic regions.

- Google Trends is useful for looking backward in time to help you project changes in keywords search volume.

- Always remember with Google Trends that the data is not absolute but is relative to the geography's population size and the propensity of its inhabitants to search for a keyword or visit a particular site.

- Google Insights for Search is a powerful tool that can help you in many unique ways, such as by crafting marketing messages or seeing the differences between multiple locations.

Finding keywords is not difficult, although it can be time consuming. It's important that you understand the search intent behind the keyword; that way, you can show the searcher compelling ad copy so they will visit your website. In the next chapter, we will discuss how to write effective ads based on the keywords you have found.

Writing Compelling Ads

Ad copy is the only part of your AdWords account a consumer will ever see. When a searcher sees your ad, the ad needs to stand up, wave its arms, jump up and down, and shout, "I have the answer to your question!"

However, there are many subtleties to writing ad copy. The messaging, value proposition, editorial requirements, and information need to be tightly wrapped into just a few characters. Accomplishing this type of writing can be quite tricky.

Chapter Contents

Do your ads reflect the search query?
Writing effective ads
Following Google's editorial guidelines
Developing unique selling propositions
Distinguishing features and benefits
Employing themes that get clicks
Spicing up your ads with ad extensions
Following the law: trademarks
The quest for the Holy Grail of advertising
Best practices for writing compelling ads

Do Your Ads Reflect the Search Query?

Ads serve as a bridge between the search query and your landing page. Your goal is to have enticing ad copy that causes a user to "cross the bridge" from a search result and arrive at your website.

AdWords ads do not need to be gimmicky. The ads need to quickly convey to the consumer that the answer to their search can be found on your website. If your ad has enticed someone to cross the bridge, the ad copy has done its job.

Of course, it's not quite that simple. There are many types of bridges. Some ads emphasize conversions, and others focus on clicks. Your job is to build an ad that produces results for your company, based on your company's goals, by bringing the correct prospects to your website.

The ad should reflect both the keywords in your account and the user's search query. If the ad is not highly relevant to both of those items, it will be less effective (Figure 4.1). Ad copy that does not cover both the search query and your keywords is like a bridge that leads to nowhere. Either your ad leads someone to the answer to their question, or it leads off in an irrelevant direction. Make sure you are always bringing the consumer closer to the answer to their question, assuming the answer is a conversion on your website.

The VIERA from Panasonic
Gather Your Friends and Family.
It's Time for Some VIERA® Time.
Panasonic.com/VIERA

Panasonic **tv** sale
Low Prices on LCD & **Plasma** HDTVs.
Fast Shipping And Secure Checkout!
www.BuyDig.com/PanasonicHDTVs

Samsung **Tv** Sale
Enhance Your HD Experience
Shop Dell For HD TVs By Samsung!
www.Dell.com

LCD Monitors
Save on LCD Monitors at Staples.
Guaranteed Low Prices & In Stock.
www.Staples.com

Figure 4.1 For the highly commercial search "buy plasma TV," these ads do not speak to the user's query.

About Ad Copy Screenshots

Most of the ad copy screenshots are taken from within the AdWords interface. Therefore, they will not look identical to what you see on the Web. For instance, on the Web Google puts the display URL just below the headline. Within the interface, they still have the display URL in the old slot, which is just below the description line 2. Google is often tweaking how ads are displayed within search results, so the ads may not mirror exactly how Google displays them. However, the concepts we will discuss throughout this book for writing ad copy remain the same regardless of a few minor changes to the ad's display.

Therefore, it is imperative that you go through the exercise of ensuring that your ad copy will be reflective of your keywords and the search query. Since you know your keywords, and what type of related queries should trigger them (refer to the search query report in Chapter 16), one of the most important exercises to undertake before writing ads is to ensure you have *granular account organization*. I will mention this concept several times throughout this book because this organization can determine the effectiveness of your account.

Granular account organization means that the keywords in an ad group are highly related and you do not see additional ways to separate out the keywords. In addition, your ad copy should reflect every single keyword in your ad group. For example, let's say your ad group is about HDTVs and contains these keywords:

- LED TV
- Plasma TV
- HDTV
- Hi-def TV

With these keywords, your ad group is not granular enough. The keywords could be in several different ad groups: one for plasma TVs, one for LED TVs, and so on.

First, write an ad with one explicit meaning. Imagine that if someone saw this ad, they could only assume you do this one particular thing, such as you only offer weekend plumbing services, small business accounting solutions, or used books under $5. Now, look at your keywords. Does the ad copy reflect the keywords? If yes, the keywords are in the correct place. If no, move the keywords to a new ad group.

Consider someone who searches for "buy plasma tv" and sees the two ads shown in Figure 4.2.

Buy a Plasma TV
Compare features of all Plasma TV:
TVs for your budget & lifestyle
example.com

Hi-Def TV
Compare features of all Hi-Def TVs
TVs for your budget & lifestyle
example.com

Figure 4.2 "Buy plasma TV" ad copy

Which one would you click? While a plasma TV is a hi-def TV, there are other types of hi-def TVs, such as LED or DLPs. The use of the word "buy" in the query informs us that this is a commercial query with a high purchase intent. This searcher is not likely to change their TV choice from a plasma TV. Therefore, you would want to show this searcher a plasma TV ad.

The exercise of breaking down your ad groups into specific keyword and ad copy combinations will take a while, but it will assist greatly in ad copy writing. Because you now only have to reflect one specific theme in your ad copy, you only need to write ads for one explicit meaning.

Note: It is much better to have 100 ad groups of 10 keywords than to have one ad group of 1,000 keywords. When it comes to searching, there is no magical number of keywords that belong in an ad group. When you go to organize your ad groups, it is vital that you make sure the keywords and ad copy are closely related.

Writing Effective Ads

Once your granular ad group organization is completed, it is time to think about the content of the ad copy. There are many ways of writing ad copy, some of which we will revisit in Chapter 15, "Testing Techniques That Will Increase Profits," when we discuss ways of testing different ad copy messages to see which are more effective.

Note: If you have a dozen ideas for ad copy, which one is best? There is no way to know without running a test to find out which ad has a higher conversion rate or click-through rate (CTR). Split testing is essentially testing multiple elements (such as ad copy or landing pages) to find out which is the best for your business.

Ad copy must promote your goals for success. Before you begin advertising, it is important to determine the goals for your campaigns (which will be discussed in depth in Chapter 13, "Profitable Bid Strategies"). Once you have established the goals, your ads should reflect those goals.

Your ad should display your products' features and benefits. This is so important that an upcoming section ("Distinguishing Features and Benefits") focuses on this aspect of your ad.

You want to make sure that the consumer identifies with your ad copy. Marketing is about identifying and connecting with consumers. Using your consumers' language is important. If you use terms that your consumers do not understand or terms they do not often see, it can cause them to not identify with your ad copy and click on a competitor's ad instead of yours (Figure 4.3).

Deep Vein Thrombosis
Do You Suffer From **DVT**? Learn Abou
Diagnosis, Treatment Options & More
www.vdf.org

Deep Vein Thrombosis
Info for HCPs about **DVT**, the most
common form of VTE. View Videos
www.VTEConsultant.com

Defective BARD IVC Filter
G2 and Recovery IVC Filters
Aggressive Representation
www.filterlaw.com

PPT Vision
Compact Intelligent Cameras for
Machine Vision & Vision Inspection
www.ONExia.com
1220 American Blvd, West Chester

Deep Vein Thrombosis- DVT
Symptoms, Diagnosis and Current
Treatment Options for **DVT**.
www.dvtanswers.com

Figure 4.3 How many ads do you understand?

Using Words Consumers Understand

It is useful to read writers and columnists who write about your local area and industry. If you are advertising in a specific location, the local newspaper columnists usually try to make interesting points about that particular area within their column. If you see words that are not typically used in your location, these could be words that are common to another area (which could be state, city, or country). By reading the local columnists, you can find words your audience understands and finds familiar. This is a fantastic place to find some unusual adjectives to test in ad copy.

Each industry can get lost in its own jargon, but consumers often do not know these industry words. Read magazine reviews of your products and services that are written for the general populace and not just your industry. When you find places where you feel words or concepts are not quite accurate, the wrong word is being used, or a common word is used instead of a specific one (denoting jargon), note that these words might be used because the general populace does not understand the jargon. If you are using this jargon, do you think consumers can understand your ad?

Calls-to-Action

Direct a consumer to take action. What do you want someone to do once they arrive at your site? When you tell someone what to do within the ad copy, it is going to predispose them to look for that action on the landing page. Some generic examples of calls-to-action are:

- Call us today
- Subscribe to our newsletter
- Download our whitepaper

Those who do not wish to take such action may not even click on your ad. If you are looking to increase CTR and views to a new product page (regardless of who buys the product), you may not want to add a purchasing or prequalifying call-to-action within the ad copy as it could lower CTR. This will be discussed in more depth in Chapter 6, "Advanced Optimization Techniques," when we examine optimizing your account for conversions.

Often in search advertising, a straightforward marketing message connects cerebrally with visitors. By using logic and informational ad copy, you are trusting that the consumers can make decisions if they are presented with all the facts. This is very useful in ad copy writing—the purpose is to answer a searcher's question, and an answer is made up of facts. This is also useful when you are trying to reach consumers who do intensive research before making a decision, which is common in B2B and technical fields. However, you will see higher CTRs and conversion rates if you also connect emotionally with a visitor.

Touching the Emotional Core

It is possible to connect both informationally and emotionally with a searcher. There are some common assumptions about what any person wants and what one would most likely try to avoid:

What people want:

- More control
- Independence
- Freedom
- More time
- More money
- Better health
- Better appearance
- Promotions at work
- To feel included
- Social advancement
- To be appreciated
- Security
- Confidence
- Enjoyment

And what people try to avoid:

- More work
- Unacceptable risk
- Doubt
- Criticism
- Guilt
- Embarrassment
- Pain
- Feeling stupid
- Being ignored

By combining emotional and informational factors (Figure 4.4), you can create ads that elicit emotional responses in your visitors while still directing them to find their necessary information on your website.

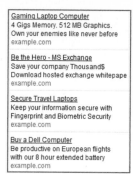

Figure 4.4 Ads that combine emotion and information

Following Google's Editorial Guidelines

Before we continue examining different aspects of ad copy writing and creating effective ads, let's examine the editorial policies. If an ad will not be approved by Google to show on a search result, there is no need to waste your time writing that type of ad.

Google has gone to great lengths to ensure that ads meet a certain standard before being shown to their visitors. Because one of Google's major success metrics is a returning visitor, they want to ensure that the ads are just as relevant as the natural search results.

Character Lengths

The first consideration is character length. There are stringent requirements for how many characters can appear in an ad, as shown in Table 4.1.

▶ **Table 4.1** Character lengths

Ad copy section	Character length
Headline	25
Description line 1	35
Description line 2	35
Display URL	35
Destination URL	1,024

It is commonly said that the best headline is 26 characters. Attempting to write creative marketing messages using 95 characters is difficult and takes some time to master. This is why it is important to test different messages.

Even though description lines 1 and 2 appear as different lines when ads are created, it can also be useful to test writing one 70-character sentence to see if the ad reads better as a single sentence than as two distinctive messages on separate lines. This is especially true if your ad regularly appears at the top of the page, where the two description lines are run together.

Note: If your ad is shown above the organic results and your description line 1 ends in a punctuation mark (period, question mark, exclamation mark), Google may combine your headline and description line 1 into a long 60-character headline.

These headlines stand out on search results and many times increase CTRs. This is one of the easiest ways to increase your ad's CTR.

Editorial Requirements

The most ambiguous of the editorial rules is "accurate ad text." While Google explains this requirement as ensuring that your ad reflects what the consumer will find on your landing page, it is also a rule they can fall back on if they want to disapprove ad copy for various reasons.

Following this rule is important for conversion rates. If your ad copy claims the user will find something on your landing page and that item is not there, the user will hit the Back button and you have just wasted the price of the click. Following this rule can also help your Quality Score (discussed in depth in future chapters) since "relevancy" is a word Google uses repeatedly to describe their AdWords program.

The second rule is accurate capitalization. Although you can capitalize the first letter of each individual word, you cannot have a word in all caps: exceptions include acronyms or words that naturally always appear in all caps. For instance, if you wrote the ad copy "FREE Software," the ad would be disapproved because "FREE" is not a word that should appear in all caps. However, if your ad copy was "Learn PPC Marketing," this would be approved, as the acronym PPC should be in all caps.

You must back up all competitor claims on the landing page. If you claim that your product is better than another product, you need supporting evidence on that page. This could be an accurate comparison chart or a third party who has verified that information.

All ads must use proper grammar and spelling. You cannot use misspellings in ad copy, with the exception of some common misspellings or words that have alternate spellings. For instance, the words "optimize" and "optimise" are both acceptable because they are alternate spellings of the same word (optimise is the British spelling, optimize is the American spelling).

Ads cannot have offensive or inappropriate language. This is another ambiguous rule that helps to keep out of search results hate-based ads, some adult ads, and other offensive items.

If you make a claim of a price, discount, or special offer, you must show the consumer that offer within a couple of clicks from your landing page. If you make the claim that DVDs are 60 percent off and that offer is not on your site, the ad should be disapproved. Following this rule will also help conversion rates. If you make a claim of free shipping and a searcher navigates throughout your site and is about to check out but has yet to determine if they will receive free shipping, odds are they will not enter their credit card.

You must use proper punctuation marks and symbols. This means you cannot bullet-point each line of your ads to make them look different on a search result. In addition, an ad copy can only have one exclamation point, and that exclamation point cannot be in the headline. We will discuss trademarks and copyrights later in this chapter; however, since there are so few symbols used in ad copy, adding the ®, ©, or ™ symbol (assuming you have the right to use it) can help make your ad copy stand out from the other ads.

You cannot repeat the same word multiple times in a row in ad copy. For instance, "Free Free Free" ads would be disapproved for gimmicky repetition.

In general, superlatives such as "best" are disapproved in ad copy. The exception is if you can prove it. If you claim to be the best at something, you will need third-party verification. If you do have third-party verification, it can be useful to use a word such as "best" in your ad copy, since very few other ads will make superlative claims.

You also cannot imply a Google affiliation or relationship that does not exist. Making the claim of "Recommended by Google" will be disapproved in almost all cases.

There are specific policies by industry as well. You can see Google's industry-specific policies on their Help section: http://adwords.google.com/support/aw/bin/static.py?hl=en&topic=1310883&guide=1308252&page=guide.cs.

Although some of the editorial restrictions can be annoying, in general they foster an environment of fair play between advertisers and help consumers find their information. Following the relevancy aspects of the editorial guidelines often leads to higher conversion rates and more profit for your company. Knowing the editorial restrictions will help you create ads that will be approved by editorial so you do not have to keep trying new ads in hopes of them becoming approved. Too many companies spend time trying to work around the restrictions, which just creates short-term work that does not give long-term results. The goal of writing ads within the editorial guidelines is to find unique ways to differentiate your ads regardless of any restrictions.

Developing Unique Selling Propositions

Why should someone buy from you instead of your competitor? That is one of the fundamental questions you need to answer about your business, as it should permeate your marketing efforts.

To visualize different unique selling propositions, it is easy to turn to the car industry. What is the first thought that pops into your mind as you read this list of cars?

- Porsche
- BMW
- Ferrari
- Lexus

- Subaru

- Volvo

Lexus, BMW, Porsche, and Ferrari are all luxury cars that will make a serious dent in your wallet. However, even among these cars differences exist in their unique selling propositions (USPs). A Porsche can be driven off a lot and raced that same day. A Ferrari is a status symbol that stands out wherever it is seen. A BMW is a German-engineered luxury driving machine. Lexus is the pursuit of driving perfection.

Volvos often tout their safety record, while a Subaru is great for all-weather driving. That does not mean a Subaru is not a safe car or that a Volvo cannot drive well in the snow. These are marketing statements that are top-of-mind to consumers when they consider which cars to purchase.

These are extreme scenarios dealing with companies who have many years and millions of dollars behind their marketing efforts, but any business can come up with something unique about their particular company. You can find anything at eBay. You can compare insurance quotes from competitors at Progressive. Customize your new computer at Dell. Zappos is powered by service.

If you are unsure of what your USP should be, you can test this through AdWords ads. Create several different ads with different USPs and see which ones gather the highest CTR and conversion rates on your website. (For full details on testing ad copy, please refer to Chapter 15.)

If you are a local company that advertises against national companies, your USP may include the fact that your business is local and someone can walk into your office or easily call and talk to a human.

By choosing a USP that is core to your business, it is easier to make decisions about how to position yourself in the marketplace. The USP also makes for a good line of ad copy because it showcases why someone wants to do business with your company. Do not blend into the crowd. Stand apart by showcasing your company's uniqueness.

Distinguishing Features and Benefits

Features and benefits are often misunderstood. They are very different, and each has its own place within the buying funnel.

A *feature* is a component or function of your products and services. This is often the big list of details found on the outside of a product's box or included in the PDF description of a product. Features are facts about the product or services. Features are easy to list—just create a bullet point list about the product.

For instance, this book is being written on a Sony Z laptop with these features:

- 13.1-inch wide screen display

- 8 GB of memory

- 512 GB solid-state drive

- 1 GB graphics card
- 8-hour battery life
- Carbon fiber casing
- Built-in webcam
- Weight: 2.57 pounds

This list could go on for hundreds of bullet points. Look at any product or service, and start writing down its components. Features are easy to determine.

A *benefit* is something the product or service will do for you. How will the service make your life better? Why should you spend your hard-earned money on a particular product? Essentially, if you can answer "What's in it for me?" you've come up with the product's benefits. Benefits are based on evoking emotional responses.

It is easy to turn a feature into a benefit by adding a "so," "to," or "will" to the end of the feature and completing the sentence.

- The laptop has an 8-hour battery life so you can be productive on an international flight.
- The Sony Z weighs less than three pounds to save your back from excessive strain.
- Having 8 GB of memory will easily let you analyze a million rows of Excel files to find the most profitable keywords.
- You can use the built-in webcam to see your family when you are traveling.
- The carbon fiber casing will protect your investment if you accidently drop your laptop.

Always keep your customer in mind when creating your benefits. If your customer does not travel, a 9-hour battery life might not be a benefit. However, if your customer is constantly examining large Excel files to optimize keyword lists, being able to manipulate a million rows in Excel could save them both time and money.

You can take the extra step of segmenting your customers into different demographics and then examining what features and benefits are most important to each segment. For instance, if you sold the Sony Z laptop I just described, which features and benefits would be most beneficial to these groups?

- Frequent travelers
- Gamers
- PPC marketers

By segmenting your audience into groups, you can send custom messages to those users. This can sometimes be difficult with keywords on the search network; however, across the content network (discussed in Chapter 9, "Understanding the Content Network"), you can examine the demographics of individual websites and then write appropriate ads based on the website's visitor demographics.

What do your customers want? Your benefit list can be paired with the lists earlier in the chapter about what people want and what they avoid. By creating emotionally beneficial statements about your product, you can move past the features of a product to showcase how buying your product will improve someone's life in a particular way.

Benefits, Features, and the Buying Funnel

When writing ad copy, you need to keep the buying funnel in mind (we covered the buying funnel in Chapter 2, "Keyword Research"). Users have different concerns and questions throughout the buying funnel, and adjusting your ads appropriately can help engage users to click on your ads and eventually do business with your company.

The buying funnel starts with the awareness and interest phases. At this point in time, searchers do not know much about your products or services. Using jargon confuses consumers because they do not yet know enough about the products to understand what the jargon means.

At this phase of the buying funnel, you need to emphasize why your products will make someone's life better. Why should they want the product or want to learn more about your services? Using benefit-driven ad copy that tells a story of how you will improve their life will help to engage users.

The next step of the buying funnel is the learn phase. It is in this phase that a consumer's research transitions from just understanding the benefits to also learning about the features. Mixing both benefit and features within your ad copy is useful. This will help transition users to understanding why they need the product, and then start them down the next path of the buying funnel into feature comparison.

If you do not know where a keyword lives in the buying funnel, it can be useful to first treat the keyword as part of the learn phase since your ad copy showcases both benefits and features. Once you write your initial ad copy, you should test these keywords with different ad messages to see which resonates better with the consumer to determine where the keyword lives within the buying funnel. These are excellent keywords to start some of your testing (discussed later).

In addition, often the search buying funnel starts at the learn phase. As a consumer cannot search for something they have no knowledge of, the content network is more useful in reaching users at the top of the buying funnel (more on the content network in Chapter 9).

Once a consumer has learned more about a product and has decided they want to buy a product, or engage a company's services, the consumer moves into the shopping comparison phase.

When someone is comparing products, they already understand why a product will enhance their life (which is a benefit of your product). At this stage of the buying funnel, it is important to showcase features. However, while you want to start emphasizing features during this phase, never forget benefits. Consumers eventually buy because of benefits; don't lose sight of this fact.

It is easy for a customer to compare products side by side to see which product has which feature. It is usually more beneficial for you to make a comparison chart for the customer so you can highlight your best features.

You may test some ad copy (more on testing in Chapter 15) that shows features, and then list the benefits of those features on the landing page. Other ideas for ad copy are all features that tell a story about why your product is superior to the other products in the marketplace. You can always fall back on the standard ad copy to test one feature and the major benefit of that feature.

In the shopping comparison phase, you can also make an assumption that the consumer has a basic understanding of the jargon associated with the products. It is now okay to use some jargon in your ads. Price-conscious shoppers will compare both features and prices. When the economy is in a downturn, often you will see consumers buy "good enough" products that are less expensive as opposed to the "best" product in the market.

When To Use a Feature vs. a Benefit

Finally, it is time for the shopper to make a purchase. While we comparison shop on features, we buy because of benefits. When your keywords fall into the buying stage of the buying funnel, you should include benefits in your ad copy. These are also excellent ads to test. In some cases, you may find an all-benefit ad copy works best. In other cases, a benefit-and-feature ad copy may work best. In many industries, the feature may not be about the product, but instead about the final cost of the product. Therefore, items like shipping, prices, and discounts can serve to enhance your ads.

Ad Copy Format to Start Utilizing Features and Benefits

There will be times when a keyword does not fit neatly into one aspect of the buying funnel. In this instance, since you might be unsure of what type of ad to write, start with one of the standard ad formats:

- Captivating headline
- Product or service feature
- Product or service benefit
- Display URL

This is an excellent starting ad. It might not be the best ad in the long run, but you have to start somewhere. Once you have created this standard ad type, you can test it against other ads that focus more on user benefits and product features to see which ad type consumers respond to for those particular keywords.

While ads should be written that reflect the keywords that trigger the ad to be shown, the content of the ads should change based on searcher behavior and knowledge. Do not just write all-benefit or all-feature ads regardless of where someone is in the buying funnel. Determine where someone is in their decision-making process and then write ads appropriate to their current mind-set.

If you are certain where the searcher is within the buying funnel, emphasize the benefits or features of your products; doing so can serve to increase your CTR, conversion rates, and ultimately, your company's profits.

Employing Themes That Get Clicks

An ad copy has three lines where you can be creative: the headline and the two description lines. (You can be creative with display URLs, but there's a limited amount of creativity possible.)

Headline This is generally used to captivate the audience. The headline should draw the consumer's eye so they read your two description lines. You can use the headline as a benefit or feature line as well; it does not always have to be a line to draw the eye.

Two Description Lines These are your chances to show off two different aspects of your products or services. These description lines could be benefits, features, prices, USPs, and so forth.

No matter how you choose to use these three lines, there exists a maximum number of themes or different thoughts you can include in a single ad. Themes are the high-level classifications of different types of ad writing styles, such as the following:

- Ads that include prices or discounts
- Ads focused on testimonials
- Ads that convey information
- Ads that include negative information

We will focus on themes with concrete examples in the next section.

Because of character restrictions, you must pick and choose which messages you are going to use to create these haiku-like ads to bring a searcher from viewing your ad to your website. If you decide to showcase two product-specific benefits, you probably do not have room to also talk about pricing and shipping and customer service within the same ad copy. There just is not enough room in these brief lines to add every marketing message you desire.

You can utilize various themes in your ad copy. Each theme emphasizes a different message. No one theme is better or worse than any other. Your goal is to test different themes to see which one performs best for your marketing goals.

Every time you include a theme in an ad, you are also excluding another theme. This goes for your competition as well. Your goal is to make your ad stand out, show the searchers you can answer their questions, and make them desire to view your website. If your competition is using just one theme, you may decide to test some completely different themes to see if that can make your ad stand apart from the other text on a page.

Utilizing Numbers in Ads

You can use psychology to help determine how searchers view different types of ads. You will see two prevalent themes when utilizing numbers in your ads: number ranges and exact numbers.

People often focus on the number that is most beneficial to their current situation. In ad copy writing, you can use this type of psychology to test single numbers versus ranges for numbers in your ad copy (Figure 4.5).

Figure 4.5 Prices in ad copy

Among these three ads, there is already a probable loser you can spot logically even before you start testing. The first ad says up to $199. $199 is more than $89 or $99, and is therefore the worst ad in many cases. If the third ad was from $99 and up (so the same price as the middle ad), then the middle ad would usually be the winner. While it says "from $99," it does not explicitly state that more expensive products are available.

There will be times when the competition's prices are similar or you do not want to include the actual price in the ad—you may want to showcase a discount offer instead of an actual price point. You can apply the same principles of using numerals in ad copy to discount ranges (Figure 4.6).

Figure 4.6 Discounts in ad copy

In these two ads, there is also a winner in the majority of tests. The first ad copy states 25 percent off. The second one states 25–60 percent off. Sixty percent is bigger than 25 percent, so usually the 60 percent off ad will get the higher CTR. The merchant might have only one item at 60 percent off and the others all at 25 percent off. That doesn't matter. Bigger is usually better as far as CTRs go.

With discounts, your conversion rate will often go up along with the CTR. However, you will also make less per sale than without a discount. Therefore, you need to perform another level of math to determine the effectiveness of any discounts you might offer.

For instance, take a look at Table 4.2 and determine your best discount point to maximize profits. The clicks are varied in the table because often adding a discount to the ad copy will increase the CTR.

▶ **Table 4.2** Should you offer a discount?

Test	Impressions	Clicks	Spend	Conversion rate	Conversions	Average order value	Discount	ROAS
Baseline	6,000	600	$600	2%	12	$125	0%	$900
Offer A	6,000	600	$600	2%	12	$125	10%	$750
Offer B	6,000	700	$700	2.1%	14.7	$125	10%	$1,285
Offer C	6,000	600	$600	2.3%	13.8	$125	20%	$780
Offer D	6,000	700	$700	2.4%	16.8	$125	20%	$980

Return on ad spend (ROAS) in Table 4.2 is:

(((Conversions × Average Order Value × (1-Discount)) – Spend)

In this case, Offer B with a lower discount and a slight bump in conversion rates creates a better return than D, which has a larger increase in conversion rates and CTR but also utilizes a much steeper discount. Bigger isn't always better.

If one of your goals is to get the most customers possible because you have a nice lifetime visitor value program, then offer D might be best overall. In that case, do not use your average order value in the match—use your lifetime visitor value instead.

In e-commerce scenarios, sometimes you will also see your average order value change with discounts (see Table 4.3).

In Table 4.3, Offer D with the large discount would be best on both a profit and customer basis. However, just by building a simple spreadsheet—one that lists your discounts and offers some projections about how much higher your conversion rate would have to be in order to make up the sale discounts in your total profits—you can start to visualize what type of impact your ad copy discounts and landing page offers have to have on both CTR and conversion rates in order to be successful.

► **Table 4.3** Discounts can change the average order value

Test	Impressions	Clicks	Spend	Conversion rate	Conversions	Average order value	Discount	ROAS
Baseline	6,000	600	$600	2%	12	$125	0%	$900
Offer A	6,000	600	$600	2%	12	$150	10%	$1,020
Offer B	6,000	700	$700	2.1%	14.7	$150	10%	$1,285
Offer C	6,000	600	$600	2.3%	13.8	$160	20%	$1,166
Offer D	6,000	700	$700	2.4%	16.8	$175	20%	$1,652

The last number to try in ad copy is a very exact number: "I saved $241.56 last year by using Tax Software." These exact numbers draw consumers' eyes as they do not look like standard pricing and discount numbers. Using exact numbers in ad copy is best in the following cases:

- Your ad shows how much of something you can save someone:
  - Learn how I saved 37 hours using the Getting Things Done methodology for managing my email.
  - Our IT department cut costs by $238,021 by instituting Google Apps for domains.
  - Our customers can lose 26.5 lbs in just 3 months.
  - Reduce your calorie intake by 354 calories a day.
- Your ad shows how much money you made:
  - Learn how I made $328,282 selling real estate.
  - Our staffing agency increased salaries by $23,055.

Using prices and discounts in ad copy is useful to test when:

- Consumers are very price conscious.
- You are advertising in highly competitive product industries.
- There are large price ranges for the same type of products.
- You are using shopping comparison keywords.

There are times when you might have an opportunity to change the pricing rules. If a customer sees two ads with the prices $10 and $50, usually they will assume these two products are quite different even if they are the same. If you were to create an ad with a $40 price point, then the $10 ad looks cheap, and the $50 and $40 ads look similar. In this case, the $40 price point might win out. However, in that same scenario, if you were to create an ad that listed a $15 price point (so the ads would be $10, $15, and $50), the $50 looks quite expensive and the $10 ad might turn out to be the winner.

Two price points do not give consumers a good comparison if there is a significant difference in prices. Three prices on a page are enough data points that consumers can start to compare products from just the ad copy.

You should always take into consideration your competitors' ads. If all of your competitors are using prices in their ads, you may want to test an ad that showcases features and benefits of the product instead of pricing. This is especially true in industries where everyone is trying to showcase the lowest price. If you lower your price to a point where you no longer make money on the sale, then why buy that keyword? In those cases, you may want to forego showing a price at all and instead focus on the other customer benefits.

How Strong Is Your Call-to-Action?

A *call-to-action* is a statement in your ad copy that informs customers what you want them to do once they arrive at your website. Some calls-to-action are straightforward:

- Subscribe to our newsletter
- Call for an appointment
- Buy a new TV today!

You can mix and match ad types and lines. You could have a call-to-action that is also a benefit. You can use a USP that is also a company feature.

Consider the ads shown in Figure 4.7. Which one would you click?

Figure 4.7 Different calls-to-action

"Sign up for our newsletter today!" is a generic call-to-action. It does not add any additional benefit for the searcher.

"Receive Your Secrets Today!" is not necessarily a call-to-action. It is showcasing a benefit to the customer. When these three ads were run in a test, this one did receive the highest CTR of the three ad types. That often has to do with the words "free" and "secret." Secret is an interesting word to use in ad copy because it makes people feel included in a little-known club. However, this ad did not have the highest conversion rate of the three ads.

"Sign Up for Powerful Marketing Tips" had the second-highest CTR but the highest conversion rate, and when you combine the actual numbers, this ad was the most profitable of the three. This line still includes a call-to-action but also tells consumers they are going to receive "powerful tips." Who does not want powerful information?

In this example, there are many other calls-to-action you could test:

- Using the word "inbox" reminds consumers it will go to their email.

- The word "inbox" could also be associated with spam, so showcasing multiple delivery options, such as RSS feeds, could be tested.

- Using the word "daily" or "weekly" would let someone know how often they would see this information.

- Is "powerful" overused? Try different adjectives such as "effective" or "persuasive." A thesaurus is one bookmark that should always be at your fingertips.

Once you find an effective message, it does not mean your job is complete. It means you have a nice starting place from which you can continue to refine your ads and increase your profits.

Writing Informational Ad Copy

The reason someone uses a search engine is to find the answer to a question. That answer is a piece of information. Showcasing informational statements in ad copy (Figure 4.8) can be a useful way to connect with the searcher.

Figure 4.8 Informational ad copy

These informational ads can also showcase pieces of information that might not be part of the product but, when included with the product, help increase its usefulness.

How much exercise equipment is bought, used for a month, relegated to the garage for the next six months, and put up for sale on eBay the following year? Since this is a common aspect of buying exercise equipment, including bonus information that showcases ways to help someone continue to use a treadmill could be highly effective.

When they are buying headsets, some of the biggest consumer questions revolve around clarity, background noise, and volume. By addressing one of the important issues about a product within the ad copy, you show that you do not just sell the product but that a searcher can also learn about the products on your site.

Examine the top questions, issues, complaints, and user behaviors that exist with your services. What additional information can you include in the ad copy that helps a consumer make a decision on which product to buy?

Reflecting the Consumer's Question

You have a question for which you would like to know the answer. Therefore, you go to a search engine to find that answer. If you see an ad that reflects your original question, it is easy to assume that website has relevant information to help you find the information you seek.

It is worthwhile testing questions in ad copy. Since your ad will be reflecting the reason why someone originally went to a search engine and the question that user is currently trying to answer, you may see some nice increases in CTR by utilizing questions in your ad copy (Figure 4.9).

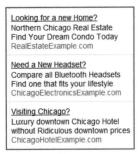

Figure 4.9 Questions in ad copy

When writing questions in ads, it is more important to have the question mark (?) in the ad copy than to write a properly structured sentence. By just adding the question mark to your current headline, you may see a difference in CTR, and searchers will automatically add the understood "Are you..." to the ad copy with the question mark.

Including Testimonials or Reviews in Ad Copy

Often we sit isolated behind a computer when making online purchasing decisions, without another person to ask what they think about a product. We understand that we are not experts in every field. Therefore, reading testimonials others have left, or expert reviews about a product, can help us feel more confident in making a decision (Figure 4.10).

```
Need a New Headset?
Read Thoughtful Headset Reviews
Left by Experts and Bluetooth Users
CertifiedKnowledge.org/Reviews

Need a New Headset?
Users prefer the Jawbone 3 to 1
Read Customer Reviews
CertifiedKnowledge.org/Testimonials

Need a New Headset?
See what others have found is
their favorite Bluetooth Headset
CertifiedKnowledge.org/Favorites
```

Figure 4.10 Ad copy testimonials and reviews

The actual testimonial or review does not have to be included in the ad copy, although a short review can be useful. Your ad copy just needs to let the consumer know that upon visiting your site, they can read the opinions of others.

The actual testimonial information can even change based on the buying funnel. If someone is in the comparison shopping phase, they are most likely looking for product reviews. However, if someone has decided on the actual product and they are now looking for which site they are going to buy the product from, testimonials about your company could be more useful.

Expert reviews about different types of products (LED versus plasma TVs) are more aligned with the buying funnel if the consumer is in the learn phase.

Even with different ad themes, these various types of ads should consider which phase of the buying funnel the consumer is in to ensure your ad is resonating with the searcher.

Utilizing Negative Ad Copy

When you read the newspaper, view TV headlines, or watch political campaigns, a common theme emerges: negative information.

Negative information stops many people from looking elsewhere and immediately draws their attention. If you consider what people want and don't want (the lists earlier in this chapter), often negative information reflects those types of conditions. Many people are drawn to negative information. This includes search ads (Figure 4.11).

```
Be Careful of Bluetooth
Think Bluetooth Headsets are Safe?
Get the Real Information Here!
CertifiedKnowledge.org/Caution

Do Not Buy A Headset
Without Reading the Secret Shoppers
Guide to Bluetooth Headset Reviews
CertifiedKnowledge.org/Shoppers

Headsets Waste Money
Don't buy non-compatible headsets
Free Bluetooth Compatibility Info
CertifiedKnowledge.org/SaveMoney
```

Figure 4.11 Negative information advertisements

Although negative ads often stand out in a search result, especially if none of the other ads is negative, it is important to consider your company positioning before utilizing negative ads. Negative ads are read by consumers. Not only does your ad copy contain your website's URL, it also directs consumers to your website. The information contained within an ad is a reflection of your company. Therefore, before running a negative ad, please make sure that it is in line with your company positioning:

- If your company wants to be known as a friendly company, you may not want to run negative ads.
- If your company is about consumer warnings and recalled product information, for example, then negative ads may be in line with your company's image.

If you are an agency or part of a marketing department within a larger company, before creating and testing negative ads, first check with the CEO or the department that runs brand management and company positioning to make sure that negative ads are okay to run and test.

Do Not Forget the Display URL

The display URL tells consumers where they are going after they click. However, the display URL can also help signal a user where on the site they will be directed.

Google has more than 5 million pages indexed from IBM.com. Knowing you are going to IBM.com is not necessarily useful. If the display URL is IBM.com/BladeServer, suddenly you know that you are not just going to one of the 5 million pages on IBM.com, but that you will end up on a page about blade servers. If you are in the market for a new server, that is a much more useful page than the homepage of IBM.com.

Google does have two editorial rules that you must follow in regard to display and destination URLs:

- The display URL must be the site where the user ends up. In other words, if you were Dell, you could not have IBM.com as your display URL and then direct someone to Dell.com.
- All of the destination URLs within an ad group must go to the same website. In other words, you could not have one ad that goes to IBM.com and a second ad within the same ad group that goes to Dell.com.

The other thing you need to consider when using display URLs is that you make sure how your consumer will read it. For instance, take a look at this URL, presented in three ways:

- commentsexchange.com
- CommentSexChange.com
- CommentsExchange.com

There are two completely different interpretations for these same letters. Google automatically lowercases the display URLs in text ads; therefore, even if you capitalize the letters in your ad copy, it will not be displayed that way on a search result. However, Google does capitalize the characters after a slash in the display URL. In this case, you might want to pick a different site to use with AdWords since it will be difficult to overcome the various ways in which the URL can be interpreted.

This concept extends to not just single words within a display URL but to other ways of interpreting your URL. Always take a look at your URL to see how many ways it can be interpreted.

With the display URL, that exact URL does not have to exist within your website. It also does not have to be the same as the destination URL. The root domain must be the same for your destination and display URL, but the URLs themselves do not have to be the same. For instance, you could have the following display and destination URLs:

- Display URL: `CertifiedKnowledge.org/Seminars`
- Destination URL: `http://certifiedknowledge.org/adwords-seminars/`

In this case, the root domain, CertifiedKnowledge.org, is the same for both URLs and therefore the ad would be approved.

The two most common display URLs are either the root domain of the website or a folder containing the product name. However, there are other ways to write display URLs (Figure 4.12).

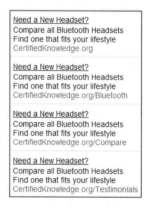

Figure 4.12 Display URLs

If you have a narrow theme site, just including the domain name and no additional information can be useful. If a searcher sees AdWords.com and is familiar with AdWords, this domain name signals they will arrive at the AdWords program's website. No additional information is necessary in that case.

Adding a folder, such as `/ProductInfo`, can help you show a user where on the website they will arrive. Folders are useful to test on larger websites.

However, when you add a folder, it does not just have to be about the product or service. You can also create synergies with the ad copy that reinforce the ad's message. In the examples in Figure 4.12, the ads speak to comparing headsets. Therefore, using /Compare in the display URL reinforces to the user that they will arrive at a site that is comparing products. If someone is comparison-shopping products, this synergy of reinforcing the ad copy can help your company attract the searcher's click.

The display URL is a line of ad copy. Since you only have four lines that you can control, do not forget to test this particular line of ad copy. The display URL CTR is also a Quality Score factor (more about Quality Score in later chapters). Testing display URLs is useful not just to examine click-through and conversion rates, but to test for ways to improve your overall Quality Score.

Spicing Up Your Ads with Ad Extensions

Ad extensions allow you to append additional information to your text ads. Not only do these extensions help your ads stand out from other ads on the page, but they can also direct visitors into different sections of your site or even perform actions on the search page. All of your text ads should be using ad extensions.

To create new extensions, navigate to the Ad Extensions tab (Figure 4.13) and create a new extension.

| Campaigns | Ad groups | Settings | Ads | Keywords | Networks | Ad extensions | Dimensions | ▾ |

View: **Location Extensions** ▾   All but deleted ▾   Segment ▾   Columns ▾

Location Extensions
Call Extensions
Product Extensions
Sitelinks Extensions

Figure 4.13 Ad Extensions tab

Ad extensions are associated to all ads within a campaign. Therefore, you can have different extensions for different campaigns. If you want to use the same extension across multiple campaigns, you will have to create the extension multiple times. A campaign can have multiple extension types associated with it.

Sitelink Extensions

Sitelinks allow you to add additional links to your ad. When that ad is displayed above the organic results, these additional links can be added to your ad copy (Figure 4.14).

Figure 4.14 Sitelink example for Hilton Hotels

To create sitelinks, navigate to the Ad Extensions tab and choose to create a new sitelink extension. You can add several links that will appear with your ad (Figure 4.15).

Figure 4.15 Adding sitelinks to a campaign

Google does not report metrics for each sitelink. If you want to see how each sitelink performs, you will want to add tracking parameters to the URL. Tracking links will be covered in Chapter 5, "Landing Pages That Convert Searchers into Buyers."

The main rule about sitelinks is that each link must go to a different URL. You cannot send all of the links to the same page. This is where you should start to think about your overall messaging to see where you want to send the additional traffic on your site.

If you have various goals across your account—for instance, you have both an ROI and sales goal—and you have a newsletter subscription goal, adding sitelinks that help you reach these additional goals is a good idea. If you have sales pages, pages you wish more people knew about, or special messaging you want to test, direct one or more of your sitelinks to these pages to see how they perform.

We will cover location extensions in Chapter 11, "Advanced Geographic Targeting," but for now note that when you see directions in ads, this is due to the location extension being used by the advertiser. The sitelink extension is the only extension that can be displayed with other extensions (Figure 4.16).

Figure 4.16 Sitelink and location extension displayed at the same time

Because sitelink extensions will work with other extension types, every account should be using sitelinks.

Product Extensions

Product extensions allow you to add data from Google Merchant Center directly to your ads (Figure 4.17). When this extension functions, there will be a plus box with additional links to your products. This extension is primarily intended for e-commerce sites.

Figure 4.17 Product extension ads

To take advantage of product extensions, you first need to create a Google Merchant Account. Next you need to populate your merchant account with a feed of your products. Most e-commerce sites have a way to export a feed for Google Merchant Center in them, so this should not be difficult work for most shopping carts.

Google Merchant Center has had a few names over the years. If you see an export to Froogle, Google Base, Google Shopping, Google Products, or Google Merchant Center, then you have the basic file to start with. Depending on when the export function was created, you may need to tweak the file to upload it properly to the Merchant Center.

Once your feed is uploaded to your Merchant Center account, go back to your AdWords account and create a product extension. All you need to do is link the Google Merchant Center account to your AdWords account and Google will automatically start showing products with the ads when they deem the query fits one of your products.

Google is okay at matching search queries to products, but they are not fantastic at it. If you want another level of control, you can add additional targets inside AdWords. It is a time-consuming process to add these targets, and many e-commerce sites say Google is "good enough" in their matching that adding all of the targets is not worth the time involved. However, if you want additional levels of control, check out Google's help file at `http://adwords.google.com/support/aw/bin/answer.py?hl=en&answer=186299` on product targets.

Call Extensions

Call extensions add your phone number to ads when shown on desktop computers. When they are displayed on mobile devices, the number is also clickable and can initiate a click-to-call scenario. If your primary goal is phone calls, you should use the call extension.

To enable the call extension, go to the Ad Extensions tab and create a new extension. The biggest choice you have is if this phone number will be displayed on only mobile devices or on desktops and mobile devices (Figure 4.18).

Add call extension

Extend my ads with a phone number ⑦

| Country or territory | United States ▾ |
| Phone number | |

☐ Call-only format: Only the phone number is clickable when ad is shown on mobile devices capable of making phone calls. ⑦
☐ Call metrics: use Google forwarding number to track calls from my ads ⑦

This ad extension works with location extensions. Learn more

Figure 4.18 Choose all ads or mobile only for call extensions

Use the Call-only Format when your ads are only on mobile devices. If you want to receive as many calls as possible regardless of the device type, then use the Call Metrics option.

When this ad is displayed on a desktop computer, Google will not use the phone number you input into the extension. Google will display a Google number that will forward to your number.

When someone clicks on the phone number on a mobile device, you will be charged a typical click cost. When someone calls you from a desktop, you will be charged your typical click price or $1, whichever is higher. There is always a minimum fee for calls on a desktop.

If you receive quite a few phone calls, you may be eligible for bid per call, a process Google calls CPP bidding. CPP bidding allows you to set another bid at the ad group level for what you are willing to pay on a call basis, and Google will factor in your CPP bid for determining your ad's position.

To see how many calls you are receiving, you can run a call report in the Dimensions tab (Figure 4.19).

This report will show you how many calls you are receiving, as well as the duration of those calls at the ad group level. With this data you can see if the call extension is working for you, and then adjust bids as necessary.

The one caution I will offer before looking at call duration is that you should determine the length of a quality call before examining the data. I know of plenty of sites that can have a 60- to 90-second call and end up with a new customer. Often advertisers see a 60-second call and think it was so short it could not have been a quality call. Measure a few calls that come into your office and see how long a call has to be before you can book a new patient, take a reservation, or give someone directions to your store before you look at the call durations and are shocked (or surprised) at how short or long the calls actually are.

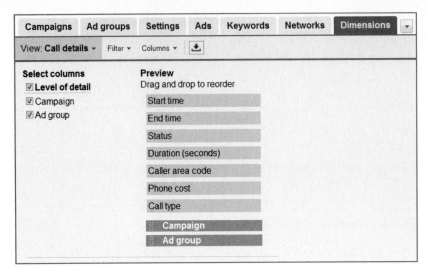

Figure 4.19 Creating a call metrics report

Another option you have is to keep a phone log and measure when a call came into your office and if you booked a new customer at that time. In the reports, you can see the time that the call started. By examining your own logs and the AdWords reports, you can determine which ad groups are leading to quality calls.

Social Extension

Google shows the +1 button next to ads. For someone to see the +1 button lit up on the ad copy, this scenario has to happen:

- The searcher must be logged into a Google account and have some social data associated with the account (such as a Google+ account)
- The searcher must have someone in their social circle who hit the +1 on a particular page
- The ad copy's destination URL must be the same page that received the +1 button

If one of your friends +1s a page but the ad you are seeing goes to a different page, then the +1 will not be displayed for you. This creates few scenarios where the +1 will actually be displayed.

This extension aggregates +1s at the domain level instead of the page level. With the social extension, if anyone in your circle +1ed any page on the entire domain, the +1 button will be lit up on the ad copy.

Before you enable this extension, you need a Google+ page that has been verified and you should have had the +1 button on your site for a while so that you do receive +1s.

The advantage of this extension is that it will show social proof on your ads. The disadvantage is that right now (and Google has said this will change eventually) if your ad is above the organic results, the sitelinks extension does not function with the social extension. Therefore, you need to decide if you want sitelinks or social proof.

If you have a lot of +1s for your domain, social proof is usually better than sitelinks. If you do not have many +1s, sitelinks are generally better to use.

Lots of Limited Betas

A few years ago, Google was making new ad types, such as Local Business Ads. This was causing a major issue since not only did they have to support all these ads, the formatting for all of them were slightly different.

With ad extensions, you write a typical text ad as normal, and then information gets appended to the ad—which means the ads are consistent and Google can easily scale the number of extensions that exist.

There are a significant number of extension betas happening right now, such as:

- Ratings
- Videos
- Contact
- Leads

Some of these betas will be graduated to use by all, and some will be retired. If you have a Google rep, it is useful to discuss the beta extensions with them to see if there is a type that fits your business model.

Following the Law: Trademarks

Google's editorial policies regarding trademarks vary by country. In most countries, an advertiser can choose any keyword they desire. According to Google's trademark policy, regardless of whether the word is trademarked, you can use it as a keyword to trigger your ad copy. However, in those countries, if the trademark holder has filed an exception request with Google, the keyword can still be used to trigger an ad but that trademark cannot be used in ad copy. In general, in the other countries, a trademarked word cannot be used as either a keyword or in ad copy. To view a list of the editorial policies regarding trademarks, please visit www.google.com/tm_complaint_adwords/complaint.html.

If you are a trademark holder and want to protect your trademark from being used, you can visit that site to view the exception process, which is straightforward:

1. Fill out and fax paperwork to Google.
2. Google will investigate if you own the trademark.
3. If you do, Google will disapprove other ads within the same industry that are using your trademark.

"Within the same industry" is an important caveat when it comes to trademarks. For example, there are over 3,000 records at the U.S. Patent and Trademark Office (www.uspto.gov) for the search word "apple" in their database. While the word "apple" is trademarked in many industries, an orchard farmer can use the word "apple" in his ad copy. If you submit an ad and a form pops up that tells you a word is trademarked but it is not trademarked for your industry, just put that information on the exception request form ("not trademarked for my industry").

Note: Since trademarks are held at the country level, it is also important to consider in which countries your campaign will be displayed. If you choose to have your campaign shown to two different countries that each have different trademark laws, your ads and keywords will then have to follow the laws of both countries. There are many reasons to limit your campaigns to only show in one country, and one of them is based on trademark laws.

There are a few different ways that brands can think about their trademark utilization within ad copy. Let's walk through a few scenarios that show why a company may have various feelings about the enforcement of their trademarks. I will use Nike in this example since they sell both directly and through other outlet channels. However, please note that this may not be Nike's current policy.

Many stores sell Nike shoes. Regardless of whether a consumer buys shoes from Nike.com, Zappos.com, or yet another store that sells Nike shoes, Nike will sell a pair of shoes. Therefore, they might not file an exception request with Google and may allow other companies to use the Nike trademark in ad copy, because Nike can gain additional sales through their distribution partners.

Nike could take another approach and decide to selectively give accounts permission to use their trademark. They may decide there are certain retailers they have a special relationship with and only allow those retailers to use the Nike trademarks in ad copy. Therefore, Nike would first file an exception request with Google. Once it was granted, Nike would file some more paperwork that gives permission for specific accounts to use the Nike trademark.

This practice is common in franchise companies. If the corporate office holds the trademark, they may want their actual franchises to be allowed to use the trademark. This means the corporate office would need the AdWords account ID numbers for each franchisee account. However, you cannot selectively give permission until Google has completed their initial trademark investigation.

The most restrictive approach Nike could take is to not allow anyone but Nike.com to use their trademarks. Nike could decide that since they sell shoes online, they do not want additional competition for their trademarked words. In this instance, in the United States, consumers could see a wide variety of ads on a search for the word "Nike," but only the Nike.com ad would actually display the word "Nike."

Currently, Nike has not taken a restrictive approach. I'm not attempting to call out Nike specifically but to walk you through the conversations that should occur within your organization about the use of trademarks.

In addition, just because Google may allow you to use a trademark in your ad copy does not mean the trademark holder could not sue you anyway. While Google's editorial policies may be introduced into the court case, a company can sue another company regardless of Google's policies.

This is especially true of company names. In these case, there is a good reason for other companies to use Nike's trademarks in ad copy. However, if you use a competitor's name in your ad copy, regardless of the word being trademarked, you could end up in a lawsuit. A competitor could also sue you for using their name as a keyword even if it does not appear in the ad copy. Your competitor may or may not win, but you will still have to pay to defend your keyword usage.

It is a worthwhile exercise to sit down with your marketing and legal departments to create rules about your use of trademarks and competitors' names. If you use a third party to manage your AdWords account, make sure that party understands your policies on these items.

Trademark Exceptions

In certain countries, Google will allow the use of trademarks in ad copy—even if the company has filed an exception request—as long as you meet certain conditions, such as:

- You sell a product
- You fix a product
- You are an information site

To be approved for use of a trademark in the ad copy, your landing page must be about that trademark. You will not be allowed to use the words "Dell computers" in your ad copy and send the visitor to a page that sells Apple computers.

In these instances, you can fill out an exception form and tell Google that you are allowed to use this term because you fit one of the criteria. Google will take a look at your ads, keywords, and landing pages and if you meet the criteria, Google will approve the ads on a limited basis (Figure 4.20).

These ads will not go live on non-Google-owned properties. Therefore, you will want to create another ad in the ad group that can go live on search partner sites.

Figure 4.20 Limited ad approval status

The Quest for the Holy Grail of Advertising

Wouldn't it be nice to be given a magical formula where an ad always received a click and a conversion? Unfortunately, there is no magic formula for writing ads. Writing the perfect ad copy is like the search for the Holy Grail. It is a never-ending search of examining where you have been, ascertaining where others have gone, and plotting new paths to see where they lead.

Ad copy changes depending on not only your industry but on your company's specific customer base as well. Consider two different accounting software companies, one specializing in Quicken and the other in Peachtree. Quicken is generally used for personal finance; Peachtree is generally used for business bookkeeping. Although these are technically both accounting software firms, their customers are different. Therefore, their ad copy should also be different to showcase why they are distinct from each other.

Just because an ad works for your competition does not mean it will work for your company. Sometimes a company will start advertising, choose an ad that has been running for a competitor, and just duplicate that ad copy in their account. Ignoring the ethics of such tactics for a moment, you should know that this tactic will often fail. Each business has a different website, different sales pitches, and various benefits and features. These differences often cause an ad for one company not to work for another.

Each ad will have different CTR and conversion rates when paired with different keywords. Let's say you wrote ad copy about high-definition televisions and used these keywords to trigger that ad copy:

- Plasma TV
- Buy a plasma TV
- LED TV

- Compare LED to plasma TVs
- HDTV

Each of those keywords will have vastly different conversion rates and CTRs. The user intent, commercial intent, keyword specificity, landing page, and ad copy all come together to form different metrics for keyword and ad copy pairs.

These are important points to keep in mind when looking at ads used by other companies. Just because a company has used an ad for several years does not mean it's effective. You do not know how much another company is testing ads, what their success metrics are, or how well those ads blend with your landing pages.

You do need to examine your competitors' ads to make sure your ads stand out on a search page. If all the ads showcase pricing, try a different message. If all the ads only speak of benefits, try using a question in your ad copy.

If you need a formula to start with, I have found the following are good starting places. Through solid testing you may find they are not the best ads after testing, but they will get you started.

- Ad Copy 1:
  - Compelling Headline
  - Customer Benefit
  - Call-to-Action
- Ad Copy 2:
  - Compelling Headline (use a different one than in ad copy 1)
  - Product/Service Feature
  - Customer Benefit

PPC success is measured with hard numbers. You should know statistics such as CTR, conversion rate, average sale amount, lifetime visitor values, and profit per sale. These numbers will show you which ad copy and keyword combination is most successful based on your metrics.

When you are ad copy writing, it is one of the few times you can escape from numbers and use the right side of your brain for a while. Ad copy writing can be a fun exercise in utilizing different adjectives, marketing messages, unique selling propositions, features, and benefits. Let your creative juices flow. The numbers will eventually tell you which ad is the most successful for your company. However, until that time, be creative, test, and find new messages that resonate with searchers.

If you do not test various messages, you will never know what messages resonate best with your customers. Knowing which ads drive the most profit will not only make you more successful but will also shift you from chasing your competitors to being a market leader.

Best Practices for Writing Compelling Ads

Writing, refining, and testing ad copy is an ongoing process that can lead to higher CTRs, higher conversion rates, and ultimately higher profits for your company. The following is a checklist of items to continuously keep in mind as you strive to find that perfect ad copy:

- Ensure that your ads reflect the search query. When a consumer conducts a search, they are seeking specific pieces of information. Make sure that your ads can speak to the consumer's search query and show them how you can assist in helping them find their answers.

- Develop granular ad groups to create a scenario where your ads are appropriate to both your keywords and the search query.

- Ensure that your ads are understandable. Jargon is only acceptable if the consumer knows the jargon. Do not use jargon for keywords that fall into the beginning stages of the buying funnel, because the searcher may not know the lexicon in their early research phases.

- Create a unique selling proposition for your business. This will differentiate your business from the other ads on the page.

- Features are facts about your product or service. Showcase features when someone is comparing products or services.

- Utilize benefits to connect emotionally with the searcher. Benefits inform someone why your product will make their life better.

- Direct a consumer to take action. If you inform the searcher what you want them to do after the click, they are more predisposed to seek and conduct that action.

- Test different types of ad copy.

- Use the display URL to clarify to a searcher where they will arrive after they click.

- Use ad extensions; at a minimum, use the Sitelinks extensions.

- Never be satisfied with your ad copy. Journey down the never-ending quest to find the perfect ad copy.

These best practices should help guide you in creating effective ads that will connect with searchers and lead them to your website where you can continue to engage them and show them how your company can fulfill their needs.

Once you have ads written, those ads need to go to landing pages that reflect the keywords and the ad copy. In the next chapter, we will examine what makes a landing page effective in turning a visitor into a customer.

Landing Pages That Convert Searchers into Buyers

Where should you send a searcher after they click your ad? The homepage is rarely the best place. You have several options, and choosing the correct one will ensure that the visitor does not just view your website but becomes engaged with it as well.

First impressions last a lifetime, and that fact is just as true for websites as it is for people. If your website is trustworthy, friendly, and easy to use, it makes a good first impression.

Chapter Contents

Does your landing page answer the searcher's question?
Everything about destination URLs
Choosing landing pages that increase conversion rates
Employing usability, trust, and web technology to increase your conversion rates
Best practices for landing pages

Does Your Landing Page Answer the Searcher's Question?

You advertised on a keyword. Your ad copy was compelling enough for someone to click on it. You paid for a click, you received a visitor. Now it's time for your website to convert that visitor into a customer.

The term *landing page* is industry jargon for the first page of your site someone visits after clicking on an ad. It might not be the homepage of your website. It could be any page within your site or a page built specifically for your ad campaign.

Often, the only information the searcher has about your website is what was contained in your ad copy. A searcher only has a maximum of 130 characters of knowledge about what they are about to find after the click. Most searchers will spend just a few seconds looking at your landing page before deciding to continue interacting with your website—or to click the back button. Therefore, the first thing your landing page must do is answer several questions that are going through the searcher's mind. These questions are not all related to their initial search query; they are related to the quality of your website and a searcher's ability to extract information from the web page:

Am I in the correct place? This is the first question your website must quickly answer. Someone did a search attempting to find an answer to a question. If you look at your landing page for three to five seconds, does the page appear to lead someone down the path to finding their answer?

Is this what I expected? Is your landing page an extension of your ad copy? Is the information contained in your ad showcased on the landing page? If your ad mentioned product comparisons and your landing page only shows a single product review, you are not setting the expectations properly in the ad copy, and a visitor is likely to leave your website. Ensure that your ads are not just the same theme as the keyword but that they are setting the proper expectations for what someone will see after the click.

Do I trust this site? Trust is a major concern for many searchers. It is common for demographics that are not overly familiar with the Web to need additional reassurance that their credit card or personal information will be safe. Conversely, those who are more familiar with the Web know how to quickly look for SSL certificates, whether a site has HTTPS (secure pages) components, and if there's a privacy policy. I will cover more on trust elements later in this book.

How long will this take? People value their time. Before committing to any action, many people unconsciously calculate how long it will take to accomplish that action. If the landing page consists of a long, intimidating form, the perception will be that there will be a high time commitment to complete the action on the site. Make sure that process seems quick. If your landing page is a form, just tell how long it will take (such as "This is a three-page form that will take five minutes of your time").

What should I do next? Does your landing page have a clear call-to-action? Once someone sees your landing page and has been satisfied that the preceding questions have been answered, what do you want them to do? Though people can be resistant to being told what to do, when they are unsure of the next action they are more open to being informed about what their next action should be. Tell your visitors what the next step is for them to obtain their answer.

Where should I go next? This aspect is closely related to "What should I do next?" If someone knows what to do next, do they know *how* to do it? Does your site have a clear path to action? The human mind can hold five to seven thoughts in short-term memory. If your website has 20 links on the landing page all going to different places, you can confuse the visitor. Your main button or image on the landing page should be where you want the visitor to go next. The button could be a subscription, add-to-cart button, or "contact us" form. Make sure that your primary action for a landing page stands out from the rest of the page's content.

Should I click the back button? One of the most common navigational elements on the Web, and the one that loses websites the most visitors, is the dreaded back button.

Regardless of how you code your site, choose your design, and lay out information, there will be visitors who click the back button. You cannot be all things to all people. You can try to minimize how often the back button is clicked by making sure all these questions are quickly and easily answered. If any of these questions are not quickly answered, you risk losing a visitor.

You're a Bad Judge of Your Website

Unfortunately, this is a true statement for almost all marketers and designers. You know that the big red button is a link that takes someone to the subscription page. You know that the images are not linked and that clicking on them will not let you see a larger image or take you to that product page. You know that your phone number is buried in your banner-like header.

Ask a colleague, spouse, customer, or someone else not familiar with your website to complete an action on your site. Give them a specific direction such as "contact us," "buy this product," or "subscribe to our newsletter." Now watch how they navigate through your website.

Even better, take five to seven people and ask them to do the same action. If you ask ten people to complete an action, you may see five to seven different ways that the exact same action was completed. Do not just watch how they completed the action; look for signs when they are lost, such as clicking on a non-hyperlinked image.

Many analytics programs have a reverse goal path report. This report shows you the different pages that someone visited before completing an action. By examining the reverse goal path report, you can gain insight into how visitors are navigating your website.

The first question echoing through someone's mind when they visit your landing page is, "Am I in the correct place?" Does your landing page reflect the ad copy? Choosing which page you send the traffic to is an important decision since it is the first step in engaging visitors. You have several options about where to send the traffic depending on if you use keyword -level, placement-level, or ad copy–level destination URLs. First let's focus on how and where to create destination URLs; then I'll discuss where to send the traffic.

Everything about Destination URLs

There are three ways within AdWords to choose where you send traffic for a particular click.

The first is at the ad level. In this instance, every click from that ad goes to the same landing page. An ad group can have several different ads (or even different ad types, as discussed in Chapter 8, "Beyond Text: Image, Video, and Mobile Ads"). Each ad can have a different destination URL (Figure 5.1). You must assign each ad a destination URL.

Figure 5.1 The destination URL is the last entry in your ad.

You can also set a destination URL at the individual keyword level. Doing so is optional. If you create keyword-level URLs, these URLs are used instead of the ad destination URL (Figure 5.2).

Figure 5.2 Editing a destination URL for a keyword

If you set keyword-level destination URLs, for automatic placements on the display network (you'll find a detailed explanation in Chapter 9, "Understanding the Display Network"), Google will attempt to determine which keyword best matches the content of that page and use that keyword's URL. If the keyword that best matches the landing page does not have a keyword-level URL, the destination URL of the ad will be used for the display network.

With placement targeting (again, see Chapter 9 for more details), you have the option of setting a destination URL for each placement. If you specify a placement-level destination URL, that URL is used when someone clicks on your ad. If you do not specify a placement-level destination URL, and you also have keywords in that ad group, Google looks to see what the best matching keyword is for the content. If that keyword has its own destination URL, it is used; if it does not, destination URL of the ad is used to determine where to send the visitor.

The search hierarchy for destination URLs is:

- Keyword destination URL
- Ad destination URL

The content network hierarchy for destination URLs is:

- Placement destination URL
- Keyword destination URL
- Ad destination URL

Building destination URLs for accurate tracking can be tricky, as you need to consider the wildcard variables that Google will fill in for you (such as the keyword) and what your analytics system can understand. In the next sections, I will walk you through examples of how to build destination URLs so you can gain insight into visitors' behavior once they have reached your website.

Using Destination URLs for Tracking

For tracking purposes, you might want to add additional parameters to your destination URLs. Some may be dictated by your tracking system, and there are some variables that Google supports. This is why a destination URL can be 1,024 characters—when you start adding tracking parameters to a URL, they can grow quite long.

These additional parameters are not for visitors. They should not affect where a visitor goes on your site. These additional variables are for your tracking purposes, whether you are parsing them out in log files or in a separate analytics system.

URL Parameters: Understanding the Basics

In a URL, the question mark is a delimiter that signals the beginning of the query string portion of your URL. The query string is what contains parameters, also known as variables. The ampersand (&) is used to separate multiple parameters/variables in the query string. The question mark comes right after the URL of your landing page, and it is followed by the tracking variables separated by ampersands. In certain server environments, you may also need to add a forward slash directly preceding the question mark (?) character.

In addition, do not leave spaces in destination URLs. Some systems interpret spaces as %20 or %2B, some leave them as spaces, and some add a plus (+) sign. By using a space, you could break the URL for some visitors, causing them to see a 404 (error) page on your website.

You should always test to make sure your destination URLs work properly before putting them live. For instance, if you wanted to send a visitor to `http://www` `.certifiedknowledge.org` for the search term "AdWords seminars," and you wanted to add source and keyword parameters to the destination URL for tracking purposes, your final destination URL would be:

`http://www.certifiedknowledge.org?src=AdWords&keyword=adwords+seminars`

The most common tracking parameters to add to an AdWords URL are as follows:

- Source
- Medium (what type of traffic—in this instance, PPC)
- Campaign
- Ad group
- Ad ID
- Keyword
- Keyword match type
- Network (search or content source)
- Mobile
- Ad position
- Placement

Some of these inputs are supported by Google with variable replacements, meaning you can input a variable into your URL and Google will fill in that variable with the actual information. This is useful if you want to track at the ad level.

Adding Custom Parameters to Destination URLs

Some of the earlier information (such as ad group) is not supported by Google. If you wanted to track that set of information, you would need to build keyword-level destination URLs.

The variables that Google supports are shown in Table 5.1.

Inserted data	URL formatting
Keyword	`{keyword}`
Match type	`{matchtype}`
Ad ID	`{creative}`
If click came from search	`{ifsearch:YourName}`
If click came from display	`{ifcontent:YourName}`
Network	`{network}`
Domain name where ad was clicked	`{placement}`
Placement categories	`{target}`
Mobile	`{ifmobile:YourName}`
Ad position	`{adposition}`
Control or experiment ID from AdWords Campaign Experiments (Chapter 15)	`{aceid}`
Sitelink and product extension tracking	`{copy:YourName}`

When you see *YourName* inside one of the parameters, you should replace it with your own information. For instance, when I am tracking search, I will use `{ifsearch:Search}`. If you are using your own tracking system or a customizable analytics system, you should match the variables in your destination URLs to how your analytics system needs to read and interpret the data.

The keyword parameter will pick up the keyword that caused your ad to be triggered. The ad ID is unique to every ad in your AdWords account. The easiest way to associate an ad with the ad ID is to either use the API (a back-end program that lets your database communicate with the AdWords database) or run an ad report and include the ad ID data point in the report.

The two interesting variables are `ifsearch` and `ifcontent`. All clicks come from either search or display. AdWords will automatically include which network sent you traffic. If your click originated from a placement, the placement information will be included in the URL.

Some of these variables represent features of AdWords that will be discussed in later chapters, such as the display network and placement categories.

There are a few other variables that can only be used through the API, such as `{param1}`, which are variable replacements for specific aspects of ad copy. If you are an API user who is often changing the prices or discounts in ads, I recommend looking more into the param variables.

For the majority of users, the variables in Table 5.1 are enough to be able to track the data necessary to understand the user behavior inside your analytics program.

I will illustrate how to build destination URLs at the ad level. As one of the variables is placement, you can use this same URL at the placement level as well.

Although I am not going to dive deep into Google Analytics, it is important to incorporate your tracking system's variables into your destination URLs. Therefore, in these examples you will use the main variables of Google Analytics. However, please examine your own analytics system first to understand the parameters necessary for your own system.

Google Analytics has a URL Builder tool (Figure 5.3), which can be found at www.google.com/support/googleanalytics/bin/answer.py?hl=en&answer=55578 (or you can search for "Google Analytics URL Builder").

Figure 5.3 Google Analytics URL Builder

Google Analytics uses the main variables shown in Table 5.2. When you see *YourName*, this means you can input anything you desire to help you understand what data point is being referenced.

Google Analytics name	Google Analytics formatting
Campaign Source (traffic source)	`utm_source=YourName`
Campaign Medium (marketing type)	`utm_medium=YourName`
Campaign Term (keyword, optional input)	`utm_term= YourName`
Campaign Content (ad types, optional input)	`utm_content= YourName`
Campaign Name	`utm_campaign= YourName`

Note that you can link your AdWords account with your Google Analytics account and see much of this data without having to code all of these URLs in AdWords. In some cases, you can combine both the analytics and the AdWords inputs, which will pass large amounts of information to your analytics program.

In addition, you do not have to code all these URLs one at a time. You can use formulas in Microsoft Excel or a tool such as the Certified Knowledge Google Analytics URL Builder, which will create all these URLs very quickly.

If you are building ad-level URLs, the one piece of data that is missing from the Table 5.2 variables is the ad group. Therefore, you will have to code that information directly into the URL.

The following URL contains information for Google Analytics data, Google AdWords variable replacements, and the manual coding of the source ad group. This would be your final ad URL:

```
http://certifiedknowledge.org /?utm_source=AdWords&utm_medium=PPC&utm_term=
{keyword}&utm_content={creative}&utm_campaign=AdWordsSeminars&Network=
{ifContent:Display}{ifSearch:Search}&SiteTarget={placement}&AdGroup=
ChicagoSeminar
```

While this would be your ad destination URL, it is not what the URL will look like when someone makes it to your website. To illustrate the final URL, let's assume that these are the variables that triggered your ad:

- Keyword: AdWords
- Ad Group Name: Chicago Seminars
- Campaign Name: AdWords Seminars
- User clicked on a search click

Here is the final destination URL once the variables are replaced by actual values:

```
http:// certifiedknowledge.org /?utm_source=AdWords&utm_medium=PPC&utm_term=
AdWords&utm_content=123456&utm_campaign=AdWordsSeminars&Network=
Search&SiteTarget=&AdGroup=ChicagoSeminars
```

You will rarely look at these URLs after you build them. What is important is to know how to build the URLs so that your tracking system can parse the information from the URL and store it appropriately in a system where the data is easily understandable.

The same URL can also be used at the keyword level. There are a few reasons to have destination URLs at the keyword level—for example, if your keywords are going to different pages. If this is the case, be careful that the keywords in your ad groups are tightly themed. Rarely will you send different keywords to different pages. It's most common in very large accounts that are supporting hundreds of thousands of keywords.

Another reason to do keyword-level tracking is that some tracking systems need keyword-level destination URLs as they use different variables for tracking keywords, or they may add additional parameters to the URL for other purposes. This is a system-by-system consideration, and your vendor should be able to help you format these URLs (or they may do it automatically for you).

Some systems grab the keyword from the URL and do a site search or add keyword-specific information to the landing page. In these cases, the systems will want to ensure they know the exact keyword being clicked by coding it into the URL.

Note: If you are using Google Analytics, and this seems like a huge amount of work, do not despair. There is an easy way to pass most of this data from AdWords to Google Analytics. The data that is not passed can easily be accessed from AdWords reports, which will be covered in depth in Chapter 16, "AdWords Reports: How to Extract Actionable Information."

When you first set up your Google Analytics account, do so from within your AdWords account. During the setup process, Google Analytics will recommend that you auto-tag your links so that information can be passed from AdWords to Analytics. Just answer yes to this question.

If you have already set up a Google Analytics account and you are unsure whether the data is being passed, there are two things to check:

1. Navigate to Google Analytics from within your AdWords account (Tools & Analysis > Google Analytics). You will either see the Google Analytics interface (in which case you should move to step 2) or you will see a setup wizard. In the setup wizard, there is an option to link an existing Analytics account to AdWords. Just follow those instructions to link them together.

2. Navigate to My Account > Preferences. Under Tracking (see Figure 5.4), make sure Auto-tagging is marked Yes.

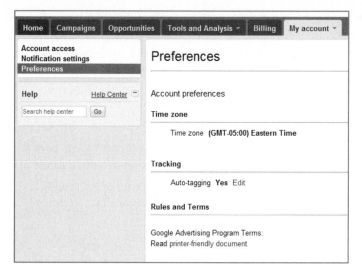

Figure 5.4 Auto-tagging AdWords data for Google Analytics

If you turn on auto-tagging, you will not want to manually code destination URLs with UTM data, as Google Analytics will become confused and will often double-count your traffic or misappropriate the data. Auto-tagging inserts a tag called gclid into the destination URL, which is click data from AdWords that Google Analytics uses to automatically track your Google AdWords data.

The last tag you can use is the no override tag. This tag tells Google Analytics not to overwrite the cookie data for the user if there is already a Google Analytics cookie for your domain on their computer. This tag is useful if you find that many people first search for a product name and come to your site, and then search again for your brand term and come to your site and buy. In that scenario, Google Analytics will show you that the brand name is leading to many conversions and that the initial terms have zero conversions. Since the no override tag will not cause the cookie to be overwritten, if the user check outs at a later visit the originally referring data, such as the keyword, will be attributed to the conversion.

Destination URLs most commonly occur at the ad, keyword, ad extension, or placement level within your AdWords account. They do exist in other areas, such as remarketing (discussed in Chapter 10, "Advanced Display Network Techniques"); however, unless your tracking system requires additional data, you do not have to set destination levels for every possible feature within AdWords. You can add additional parameters however you want to the URL, as long as the final URL renders to an actual page in the browser.

By using custom destination URLs, you can pass certain pieces of information to your tracking, lead generation, e-commerce, or custom database that will help you understand what keywords, ad copy, placements, and so forth are sending you high-quality traffic.

There are a few editorial policies that your destination URL must meet before it will be approved by Google. First I will cover these policies, and then move on to where on your website you should send the traffic.

Complying with Destination URL Editorial Policies

There are a few editorial policies that your destination URLs must follow. The first is quite simple: The URL must be 1,024 or fewer characters and resolve to an actual page. Second, the destination URL must go to the same root domain as the display URL of the ad. Table 5.3 shows examples of display and destination URLs and how they comply with the editorial guidelines.

▶ **Table 5.3** Display and destination URL editorial examples

Display URL	Destination URL	Editorial
CertifiedKnowledge.org	`http:// Certifiedknowledge.org/ article name`	Approved: Both root domains are the same.
CertifiedKnowledge.org/ AdWords	`http:// CertifiedKnowledge.org/ Google-AdWords`	Approved: Both root domains are the same.
CertifiedKnowledge.org	`http://google.com`	Disapproved: Root domains (`CertifiedKnowledge.org` and `google.com`) are different.
Google. CertifiedKnowledge.org	`http://www.google.com`	Disapproved: Root domains (`CertifiedKnowledge.org` and `google.com`) are different.

The one exception occurs if your domain name is over 35 characters in length. Because the display URL can only be 35 characters, you cannot enter a 36-character domain into the display URL.

In this case, you can work with the AdWords team to use a shorter display URL for your ad, and then the destination URLs will still have to go to your full domain name. When working with the AdWords team to choose a shorter domain name, the main consideration is that the chosen display URL does not cause confusion with another website.

If you have to choose a shorter domain name for your display URL, it is best if you purchase the domain so that another site will not spring up using your shortened URL. You do not have to use the new domain, but redirecting the shorter domain to your primary site will ensure that you do not lose any branding traffic from using a different display URL and that another site will not purchase your display URL, causing confusion between the two sites.

The third editorial policy also influences your display URL: All ads within the same ad group must go to the same root domain. This means that you cannot send traffic from one ad (or keyword) to a different root domain from any other ad (or keyword) within the same ad group.

If you owned two domains, such as CertifiedKnowledge.org and ewhisper.net, even if the content on both sites is the same, you could not send traffic within the same ad group to those two separate domains.

Since this editorial rule is for each individual ad group, you can send traffic from one ad group to one domain (such as CertifiedKnowledge.org) and then have the traffic from a second ad group sent to a different domain (such as ewhisper.net). Therefore, if you want to test two different domains, you can accomplish this by using two different ad groups.

The final policy is a restriction in the AdWords system. You cannot use umlauts in URLs. Umlauts are special characters such as ø, or ï that are used in some non-English languages. If your URL contains umlauts, you can use an Internationalized Domain Name (IDN) converter to transcribe your URL into a string usable by the AdWords system.

Many of the display URL and destination URL policies revolve around where to send the visitor and are intertwined with each other. Therefore, always keep the policies of both these ad copy aspects in mind when writing destination and display URLs.

Choosing Landing Pages That Increase Conversion Rates

You can send traffic to any page on your website (assuming it conforms to editorial policies), but you will see drastic differences in conversion rates depending on where on your site you are sending your paid search traffic.

The best page is the one that answers the advertiser's question. Where on your site can they receive the answer to their original search question? Another way of thinking about this concept is to send traffic to the page that is the furthest logical page in your website that starts the conversion process for each keyword.

> **Note:** Please remember that the searcher might have to buy a product, fill out a lead-generation or contact form, or place a phone call to receive their answer. On your website, you are answering the question or showing the consumer how to receive the answer.

In most cases, this page will be the same for all keywords in an ad group. If you have done the hard part of organizing your keywords granularly, the keywords will often share the same landing page. There are exceptions to this rule based on account organization, but in most cases this rule should hold true.

Consider these three points:

- People enjoy being lazy.

- People do not want more work.

- You are the expert on your website.

Why would you not choose the exact page on your site the visitor should see first? If you do not send someone to the best page on your site for the query, visitors will start to wander around your website, which will take them off the conversion path, or they will just hit the back button and visit the next site on the list.

Taking the extra time to link your keywords or ad groups with the most specific page on your website will help keep visitors focused and moving down the buying funnel toward becoming a customer.

Choosing Landing Pages Based on the Type of Query

To best determine a landing page, you need to understand the three main types of keyword queries:

Transactional Query Transactional queries are those in which there is an intent to buy. These are often called commercial searches.

Informational Query Informational queries, or noncommercial queries, are those in which the searcher is looking for a specific piece of information, or is trying to learn more about a specific item or concept.

Navigational Query Navigational queries are those in which the searcher is just trying to navigate to a specific website or web page. There is often only one satisfactory result for the user. This type of query might be "Amazon.com Prime shipping information." In this case, the user wants to find one specific page on Amazon.com, and the other results hold little interest for the searcher.

These query types are described in detail in the following sections.

Leveraging Transactional Queries

The easiest examples to use when deciding where to send traffic are commercial-based queries. Most shopping carts have a homepage that provides navigation into categories and from the category to the product page. Category pages showcase all of a product type (for instance, all Samsung or all DLP TVs), and finally, a product page highlights a single product. Although many shopping carts contain many more types of pages, almost all have these three types of pages (home, category, and product).

When examining where to send traffic, imagine, for example, someone is doing a search for Samsung HL61A650 (which is the part number for a Samsung DLP TV) and you send the searcher to the homepage of your site. In this instance, the visitor has to search again (or attempt to browse through your website) using the same query they just performed on Google. This additional action of searching again is redundant and akin to giving the searcher more work. The more tasks you assign your visitors, the more visitors are going to refuse your tasks and go back to Google and look at your competitors' ads.

If you send the searcher to the Samsung DLP category page, the searcher then needs to look through the available selections and try to find the same TV. If your category pages do not have part numbers listed, or if the searcher knows your product under a different name than the one listed, the visitor has no idea where to go next and will often click the back button.

If you send the searcher directly to the Samsung HL61A650 product information page, you have done the hard work of finding the best page for them. The searcher will spend less time trying to find the information and more time engaged with the information on your website. This example of a good search experience should lead to higher conversion rates.

If you know where on your website you should send traffic, why make the searcher take the time to find the information? The more freedom you give someone to wander around your site and make decisions, the lower the conversion rates you will see.

There is a balance between giving someone enough information and options to make a decision and maximizing conversion rates. Always make sure you answer the searcher's question. That and any offer made within the ad copy (such as free shipping) is the minimum amount of information you should present on your landing page.

While product searches are common on the Web, and an easy first example, let's examine some different classifications of search queries to see where conventional wisdom would suggest sending the traffic.

Getting Conversions from Informational Queries

A 2007 Pennsylvania State University study, "Determining the Informational, Navigational, and Transactional Intent of Web Queries," by Bernard Jansen, Danielle Booth, and Amanda Spink (http://ist.psu.edu/faculty_pages/jjansen/academic/pubs/jansen_user_intent.pdf) concluded that over 80 percent of all queries are informational, whereas the remaining 20 percent are about half navigational and half transactional. Often this information is misinterpreted to assume that only 10 percent of queries can lead to a purchase.

If we keep the buying funnel in mind, we are reminded that purchase decisions are usually based on research and learning before buying. While there are informational queries that cannot be monetized, often informational queries are under-monetized, and one of the most common reasons is choosing an incorrect landing page.

If a searcher does not have enough information to make a decision, even a perfectly designed sales page will not convert most visitors. In some cases, the information may be on the product page, and sending a user to the product page is the best course of action.

It is important to look at your keywords and think like the searcher. If a searcher input a particular keyword, what scenario going on in their life might have caused that search? It is that scenario that your landing page needs to address. By addressing those scenarios, you can include additional information on the landing page to help you monetize informational queries.

For instance, the query "candle burning times" is an informational query. Often the ads for this type of query end up sending the user to a specific candle type or maybe a candle product page. Those pages do not have an easy way for the user to see the burning times of all the candles.

Why would someone want to know how long different candles burn? Here are a few reasons:

- Romantic dinner
- Religious service
- Emergency lighting
- Meditation
- Halloween haunted house
- Relaxing bath
- Wedding

The list could continue with hundreds of examples. In each of those instances, you could imagine wanting to know how long a candle will burn. For example, a host would not want his candles to burn down halfway through a dinner party.

Instead of sending those searchers to a candle product page or category page, send them to a page that lists the types of candles (votive, taper, etc.) and how long those different candle models will burn. Then you can link the candle type, a call to action, or a buy-now button to the product pages so the visitor can buy the candle that best meets their needs.

Any Business Can Leverage Informational Queries

Informational queries and shopping carts are easy examples. However, the concept of answering the question and then showing a way for a searcher to do business with your company can be accomplished regardless of your business model.

In April 2008, at the height of the tax season, a search for "sales tax deduction" in Washington, DC yielded zero ads for accounting firms (and only four total ads, all going to search result pages of various search engines). Yet a search for "sales tax deduction" was conducted over 50,000 times in the United States that same month.

During April, bids for tax-based keywords skyrocket, and many of the direct keywords such as "tax," "tax return," "tax accountant," etc. become too expensive for accounting firms or software companies to bid high enough to be displayed on page one. In January 2010, that same search query in Chicago yielded zero ads for accounting software or firms even though the query continues to yield over 1,000 queries a month outside of tax season. This is another example of an informational keyword being under-monetized year over year.

What about Publishers?

If you are a publisher, such as a newspaper, most of your traffic will come from informational queries. Publishers often make money by selling ads to their advertiser base. Usually publishers are paid on an impression basis (often called CPM, cost per thousand impressions). Then the publisher buys traffic from a search engine. The difference between what they make on a page view from the ads they sold and the cost of the click they paid to the search engine is their profit (profit = income from displayed ad − cost per click.) If a searcher visits several pages, the publisher makes money on each page view. One of the key success metrics, and often a conversion action, for publishers is page views per visit. If publishers can double their page views per visit, they've increased their profits significantly.

Publishers generally have secondary conversions, such as subscriptions. It is important for publishers to measure both page views and any secondary conversions that result from informational queries, so they can determine the true value of paid search clicks on informational queries, and to continue to optimize their pages to encourage more paid subscriptions.

There is often less competition on informational queries (and cheaper clicks) because they are harder for product companies to monetize, and so they don't always advertise on them. For publishers, however, this can create a big opportunity to buy more cost-effective traffic on review or breaking news queries, to give searchers the information they are seeking and also to sell them subscriptions.

If your accounting firm can create a page that explains what a sales tax deduction is and how your firm can help someone decide to use sales tax or income tax as their deduction, this can help your company monetize an informational query.

In this case, even if the informational query has a lower conversion rate than more commercial queries, the lack of advertisers will most likely cause this keyword to be an inexpensive click. Lower-converting, inexpensive clicks can often result in a lower cost per acquisition than a high-converting, expensive click.

Informational queries make up a large percentage of total web searches. If you treat these types of searches like transactional searches where you just send visitors to shopping cart pages or form-fills, you will not find a lot of success with informational queries.

If you answer the searcher's question first and then try to monetize the searcher based on the information you presented to them, you will have much more success advertising on information-based keywords. Never forget to answer the searcher's question. That's the searcher's primary objective for conducting a search.

Once you have answered the question and the searcher has engaged with your website, you should introduce commercial actions. Selling is not just about the best sales pitch. You need to wait for the proper moment to introduce the pitch.

Getting the Most from Navigational Queries

Navigational queries are difficult to monetize as the user is often looking for a specific company or web page and only that result will satisfy their search. For most companies, monetizing navigational queries for other companies is difficult. For example, a search for "barnes and noble" usually means someone wants to go to the Barnes & Noble website and does not want to go to Amazon.

You can attempt to buy some navigational queries to see how they work for your company, but they are keywords you should put in separate ad groups and watch the traffic. If these keywords are not providing clicks or conversions, feel free to delete them.

If your business is not easily found for your brand terms, website name, or business name, you will want to make sure you are buying those terms so searchers can find your website. If your product page is listed number one in the organic results for a navigational query, you should test sending AdWords traffic to a different page. As ranking organically takes time and effort, and changing a page could jeopardize your rankings, testing dedicated PPC landing pages that are built for conversions can lead to higher profits.

In addition, if you are considering a site redesign, buy the navigational keywords for the new design to see if the new design will have a positive effect on the page's profitability.

Differentiating Local Business Queries

The term "local business" is often misunderstood. A local business is one with a physical address or that serves only a specific geographic area. This means that while the plumber down the street is a local business, so are Best Buy and JCPenney.

With local businesses, you first need to ask a few basic questions:

- Who is your target audience?
    - Locals
    - Nonlocals (travelers)

- Who travels to whom?
  - Customer travels to business (Best Buy, lawyer)
  - Business travels to customer (plumber, lawn care)
- Where are the products sold?
  - Online
  - In store

Until you answer these questions, it is impossible to determine where to send a user.

If you have both a physical store and sell online, the rules of sending traffic are similar to the commercial query information just listed. Adding conversion options, such as in-store pickup or the benefits of viewing a product in person, to your landing page gives consumers more reasons to do business with your company. If you do not sell online, the very first question to answer about local business marketing is with your target audience. Are they locals or nonlocals?

Locals know the area. They understand your specific use of geography. They want to know if you serve their area or they want directions to your business. Only after the user is satisfied with the geographic issues will they examine whether they should do business with your company. I will focus on some of these distinguishing factors of why someone should do business with you instead of your competitors later in this chapter.

Nonlocals are often business or leisure travelers. They do not immediately need to know that a hotel is located at a specific address, for example. Travelers want to know how close the hotel is to the airport, shopping districts, or major attractions. Your landing page should show what is around your location and why your hotel should be chosen over the competition.

You should not market to local and nonlocals in the same way. These two groups have different knowledge sets about the area and different questions that need to be answered by your website. A local wants to know specific information right away. A nonlocal first needs to be reassured that they are in the correct place before moving to the next stage of evaluating your business.

These differences extend to the ad copy as well. Consider these two description lines for our example hotel:

- Located in the Water Tower
- 5 blocks from shopping district

Both refer to major shopping areas in downtown Chicago. A local already knows where the shopping districts are located; therefore, telling them your hotel is five blocks away does not give them additional information. Informing a local that you are in the Water Tower gives them precise information to make a decision about traveling to the business.

Conversely, telling a nonlocal about the Water Tower is a waste of ad copy characters. If someone does not know where the Water Tower is located, why tell them your business location? Informing a nonlocal that your hotel is walking distance from the shopping district gives them the general information they need to know in planning for their trip.

With local advertising, you need to break down the messages based on the user's knowledge of your area and by who is traveling, the customer or the business. Once a searcher is confident that your business serves their area, or they can easily travel to your business, only then should you move the visitor into the conversion funnel.

Using Segmentation Pages

There will be many times when you do not know the consumer intent of a keyword. It could be that the keyword is ambiguous or that the word could describe multiple aspects of your business. In these instances, using segmentation pages can help the consumer pick the option that describes their question. A segmentation page is where a user can self-select which aspect of your business they are interested in learning more about.

Consider a search for hotels or plane travel; is the searcher a business traveler or a leisure traveler? They each have different concerns, yet they will use the same keywords when searching for information.

The keyword "accounting jobs" could either mean a company is looking to hire an employee or that a searcher is looking for a job. By using a segmentation page (Figure 5.5), you can help the user find the correct information when the query is ambiguous.

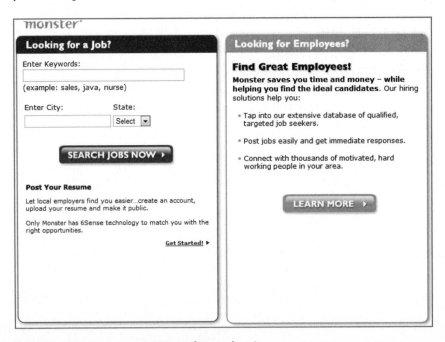

Figure 5.5 A Monster.com segmentation page for general queries

Segmentation pages are most commonly used with narrow theme sites, but they can also be useful even within a larger site to help narrow down choices. Consider the TV buying process. You ask the consumer to select an answer from each of these bullet points:

- TV Type (LED, plasma, LCD)
- TV Size (63, 61, 55, 51, 43, or 28 inch)
- Price (Over $2,000, $1000–2000, under $1,000)

Once you know those three answers, you will be able to narrow down which products are most relevant to the consumer. While this is usually referred to as a category search or product refinement, the resulting page is a segmentation page, because it *segments* the products that are being presented to the user so the user can self-select which avenue to explore.

The downfall of a segmentation page is that it adds another page view and customer decision between the search query and the final conversion. The more pages in your conversion process and the more decisions you force someone to make, the higher your abandonment rate will be.

For most of your keywords, you will probably not need a segmentation page. If you have keywords that have multiple meanings or speak to different audiences, or if your website has multiple audience types, testing segmentation pages can allow you to successfully advertise on a larger set of keywords by presenting the consumer with an option for where to go next.

Using Forms as Landing Pages

The primary focus of your landing page can be a form. This approach is common if you are collecting contact information for lead generation or generating online quotes (such as insurance and mortgage quotes).

While a form can be a good landing page, be sure you are also answering the searcher's question. It is common to see a scenario where a user searched for "merchant accounts," made it to the second page of the form, and then encountered a question such as, "What type of merchant account do you want?"

If the consumer has not learned about the various merchant accounts you offer, this question may cause them to abandon the form and start searching for different merchant account types. Make sure that product, company, or personal information you are asking for can be easily accessed from the form (Figure 5.6).

While the AdWords signup process is not perfect, it does contain important form elements:

- Easy-to-follow steps
- Short process that shows progression (top-left side)
- Ability to easily find additional information without abandoning the form
- Phone number support if you need more assistance

Figure 5.6 The Google AdWords signup form contains FAQs on the left side.

A good example of adding information to a form is the CVV (card verification value) information from your credit card. Most credit cards have a three-digit code on the back of the card that is the security information for that card. It has become a common practice to show a picture of where to find that information on the card. However, American Express is different from most cards. The security number on an American Express card is a four-digit number on the front. For some time, American Express card holders had a difficult time checking out on websites that either validated a three-digit CVV or did not show where to find the number on an American Express card.

An e-commerce checkout is also a form. While it will not be your landing page, ensuring the information a consumer needs can be accessed from your form is important regardless of where the form is on your website.

In addition, a page that is just a form is often not a good landing page because the consumer may not have enough information about your company or the products to make a decision. Your form landing pages should include benefits and calls-to-action within the text of the page.

In the English language, we read left to right, so it is usually best to put your text on the left and your form on the right so that searchers' eyes keep ending up at the form after reading your content.

Because forms are such a common element of websites, I will discuss forms again in the next chapter.

Thanking Your Customers

Thank-you pages are not landing pages, but they are an essential part of your website that your converting traffic will see. If someone converts on your website, they trusted your company enough to give you a credit card number, email address, or phone number. This is the start of your relationship with a customer. A properly framed landing page can turn a simple inquiry into a relationship.

Some of the more common thank-you pages are:

- Thank you for shopping with us.
- Thank you for contacting us.
- Thank you for downloading our whitepaper.

While these thank-you pages are essential, they may be the least effectively utilized pages on the entire Web. Thank-you pages are essential because they communicate to the customer that an action has been completed. But what does your thank-you page really say to the visitor?

- Thank you for shopping with us. You will receive an email with your shipping confirmation. Now go away.
- Thank you for contacting us. We will get back to you within 24 hours. We're done with you until we have time to call you back.
- Thank you for downloading our whitepaper. Enjoy reading our hard work. We hope you come back one day.

One of the hardest and most expensive goals to accomplish in marketing is to acquire a new customer. It is generally cheaper to maintain a customer than to gain a new customer. Thank-you pages can be the starting place of maintaining that relationship.

Instead of making your thank-you page a place where the visitor stops interacting with your website, give the visitor additional options:

- Thank you for shopping with us. Would you like to join our loyalty program and gain 10 percent off your next purchase?
- Thank you for contacting us. We will call you back within 24 hours. Here's a whitepaper about our company and products for you to read while we find the answer to your inquiry.
- Thank you for downloading our whitepaper. Would you like to subscribe to our newsletter to stay on top of industry trends?

You can have multiple conversion funnels on your website. If your first conversion funnel is an e-commerce checkout, your next conversion funnel should be for the user to either subscribe to your newsletter or join your loyalty program.

It is also useful to cross-sell or upsell from within your website. Adding a subscription form to a "thank you for shopping" page, or driving a consumer into an e-commerce experience after downloading a whitepaper, is acceptable as long as the consumer is finding their information and trusting your website. You rarely want to surprise a user, but adding some twists here and there can be useful if the customer is having a good experience on your site. Of course, to find out if they are having a good experience, you need a solid analytics platform in place to make sure they are continuing on your website after seeing some of these options.

If you are a B2B company with a six-month sales cycle, do not waste the opportunity to keep communicating with a potential client. Do not just let them download a whitepaper and walk away. Let the customer download the whitepaper and then subscribe to your newsletter or request a product demonstration.

The thank-you page is a great place to test:

- Loyalty programs
- Customer satisfaction surveys
- Downloads such as whitepapers or catalogs
- Offers to tell a friend or other social media options such as "join our Facebook page"

Changing the messaging on your thank-you pages from being an ending point to a continuation point so you can keep moving visitors through your conversion funnels is essential to increasing the profitability of your company.

Crafting Perfect Landing Pages

The perfect landing page is one that answers the searcher's question and accomplishes your marketing goal. In this scenario, the searcher is satisfied with what they have learned (which could be a new accounting firm to handle their taxes, a purchase, or a new subscription) and you have accomplished your marketing goal, which is usually what keeps your company open and in business.

There will be many times when you are not sure where to send the traffic. In these cases, you can test different landing pages and different layouts for those pages. Testing your landing pages is essential to refining your marketing efforts and receiving the highest return for your marketing investment dollars. Chapter 15, "Testing Techniques That Will Increase Profits," shows you how to test ad copy, landing pages, and traffic.

Choosing a landing page is the first step to sending visitors to your website. The next step is making sure visitors can easily find the information on your landing page. This means that the web page should contain the answer *and* that the web page is coded in such a way that users can both find and read your information so they can continue to interact with your website.

Employing Usability, Trust, and Web Technology

Usability is a catchall word used to describe how well users can navigate, find information, and accomplish their goals on your website. Usability is often associated with users. However, usability should also be associated with conversion rates. If users cannot find information on your website, they cannot complete an action.

If users do not trust your website, they will click the back button. With the increasing number of phishing attacks, security concerns, and worms and viruses, users are becoming more concerned with protecting their computer and personal information. If your site does not appear trustworthy, you will see visitors quickly leave.

The purpose of providing a good experience on your website is not just so users have a better experience and will return; it also ensures they can convert and your business can make money with your online marketing efforts.

Usability is so important that entire books are devoted to the subject. In this section, I will highlight some of the most essential usability elements to ensure your website has embraced the basics.

There are two main aspects to usability and conversion analysis: technical and psychological. Technical aspects stem from the technology being used by both the visitor and the website to render the information. Different browsers, operating systems, servers, plug-ins, and your website's code can completely change how a visitor sees and interacts with your information.

The second major factor that affects your usability is psychological: how a visitor sees, understands, trusts, and is persuaded by your website. There are subtle ways of using images, color, and testimonials that can help increase your website's profit.

Using Web Technology to Implement Usability and User Security

The foundation of any website is the actual code. There are different ways you can code your website so it has the exact same look and feel. However, while your website might appear the same on the surface, there are other technical issues (such as browsers or operating systems) that might render your website differently.

The browser market is diverse, offering Internet Explorer, Firefox, Safari, Opera, Chrome, and several others. Some are aimed at special market segments, such as social network users. There are three different browsers with over 20 percent of the market share each. Four operating systems (Windows XP, Windows Vista, Windows 7, and Mac OS), combined with various browsers and dozens of ways to code your website, create almost infinite variations of ways your website could be viewed.

Luckily, there are only a few major factors that you need to be concerned with when examining the technical aspects of usability on your website, as explained in the following sections.

Accessible Information

The text on a website can be coded in a few ways. There are usually two outcomes to the coding:

- Font size is absolute—that is, it is not rendered smaller or larger in a browser.
- Font size is relative; it can be rendered smaller or larger in a browser.

If your website that sells eyeglasses is coded in absolute font and a searcher has their browser set to show larger text (Figure 5.7), the searcher will still see your small text. If someone cannot read your website, they cannot convert on your website.

Figure 5.7 Resizing text in Chrome

It is important to take a look at your demographics. If your website caters to groups that use screen readers or surf your website while viewing a larger font size, ensure they can view your information in their preferred font size. Do not take away someone's ability to read your site.

Browser Compatibility

Different browsers render sites in different ways. Your site could look one way in Firefox and another way in Internet Explorer. You should surf your website, check out, test your contact forms, and so forth in the browsers used by your visitors to ensure they can convert on your website regardless of their browser choice.

w3schools.com maintains global statistics on browser, JavaScript, screen resolution, and many other web stats. As of November 2011, w3schools.com reports browser market share as follows:

1. Chrome (33.4%)
2. Firefox (38.1%)
3. Internet Explorer (21.2%)
4. Safari (4.2%)
5. Opera (2.4%)

You can view the updated information at this URL: www.w3schools.com/browsers/
browsers_stats.asp.

Combined, Firefox and Chrome have a 71.5 percent market share. If your website worked in both browsers, could you assume that 71 percent of all traffic could view your website?

The answer is an absolute no. These numbers are global statistics and may not apply to your site at all.

For instance, my blog's (CertifiedKnowledge.org/blog) statistics (Figure 5.8) show a very different picture of Chrome and Internet Explorer browser usage.

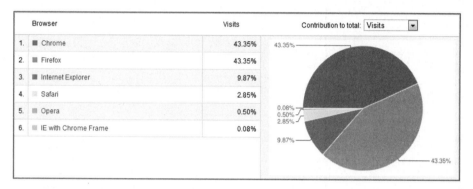

Figure 5.8 Google Chrome is 43.35 percent of my blog traffic.

In fact, when Chrome had less than 10 percent market share, my blog was almost 35 percent Chrome usage, and Firefox was about half. I have not seen Internet Explorer higher than 15 percent market share for more than two years on my blog. I work with one site that sees almost 70 percent of its traffic from Opera and Safari.

If you examined the global browser usage statistics, you might not even test your site in some browsers. This is why you should look at your analytics system to determine what browsers your visitors are using.

> **Note:** Never rely on global statistics to show you the entire picture of your site. Use actual data to determine how your site needs to be coded for your visitors.

When testing your website in different browsers, install just the default version of the browser, since many people do not change the default settings. Here's how to do so in Internet Explorer: Choose Tools > Internet Options > Advanced Options. There you can reset the browser to its default conditions (Figure 5.9).

There are many errors you can tell your browser not to display to you again. If you choose not to see these errors, you cannot find them when surfing your website.

Figure 5.9 Advanced Internet Explorer options

In general, look to see which browsers contribute more than 5 percent of your traffic (if you see a browser with a small percentage of traffic but a high conversion rate, you should also include it) and keep a default installation of those browsers on your computer. For Firefox, you can add a new profile that contains the default settings.

When you make changes to your site, load up each browser and surf through your site. Are there navigational elements that are not loading? Check out on your site (or complete all conversion activities); are there some actions you cannot accomplish?

There are also services, such as AnyBrowser.com (`http://anybrowser.com/site-viewer.html`), that help you see your site in different browsers. There is no substitute to having someone check your site in an actual browser, but sometimes these services are useful if you do not have multiple operating systems or computer types (such as a Mac) in your office.

In addition, often a developer browser version is launched before the final public version. Your design team can test your website in new versions—before your customers think your site is broken.

Enhancing Browser Functionality: Flash, Java, and Plug-Ins

Most plug-ins are optional. Installing Firefox does not mean your computer suddenly has PDF support. Adobe Flash, for example, is essential for seeing graphics on particular websites (Figure 5.10). But ask yourself: Do your visitors want to see the graphics enough to install something unknown on their computer?

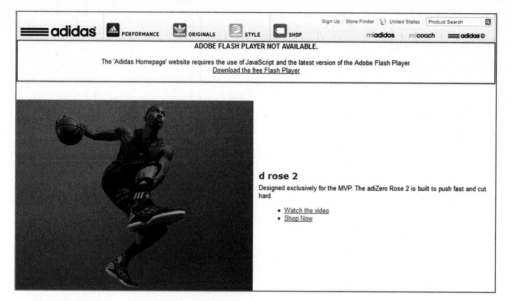

Figure 5.10 Adidas homepage without Flash installed

Most users will not install additional software to view a page. In some cases, it could be that their browser does not support particular plug-ins (especially on a mobile device or iPad). Other users do not trust plug-ins because they don't know what side effects they might encounter with their computer or browser. Rather than extend the functionality of their browsers, these users are cautious and no amount of cajoling will ever get them to install a plug-in. It is just as easy for these users to find similar products or services on a different site. This is where your analytics system can let you know how many of your visitors do not have Flash, Java, or other plug-ins installed. If your website uses plug-ins, and even 10 percent of your users do not have support for those plug-ins, you are immediately lowering the number of possible conversions on your website.

It is also important to note that robots (programs that search engines use to index the Web) have a rudimentary understanding of Flash and other scripts. If your navigation is in all Flash or all JavaScript, a robot might not be able to index your entire website.

> **Note:** There are two plug-ins for Firefox that make it easy to view your website without certain features (such as Java or CSS) enabled. The first is a powerful plug-in called the Web Developer toolbar. The second is FlashBlock, which simply turns Flash on or off.

I'm not saying that you should not use Flash or other plug-ins across your website. Just be aware of your users' browser capabilities to ensure they can navigate and convert on your website based on how your website is coded.

Is Your Website Fast for Everyone?

The numbers for U.S. broadband penetration rates vary significantly. Some studies say that more than 77 percent of users have broadband at home. Others claim that more than 50 percent of the country still does not have broadband. The issues that come into play that create such a wide span of statistics are broadband type (DSL, FiOS, cable), ISP traffic throttling, and how fast a connection has to be before it's considered high speed.

Regardless of the numbers involved, the United States and Canada have a large number of users who are on slow networks. Typically, rural areas have slower connections than urban areas, but even in urban centers, there are plenty of users on slow connections.

Impatience is a common human trait. People with slow connections are not granted more patience than those on a broadband connection. Therefore, you should consider how long it takes your site to load on all connections. Are you losing visitors because all your images are high resolution? They may only take a few seconds to load on your connection but five minutes to load on a dial-up connection.

Examine your analytics to see if you have a large percentage of visitors on slow connections. If 99 percent of your visitors are using broadband, it might not make financial sense to add another version of your website.

Securing the User's Data: SSL Certificates

Users are becoming increasingly aware of and concerned about the security of their data online. If you accept personal information, especially credit cards, having an SSL certificate is a necessity.

Secure Sockets Layer (SSL) and the newer Transport Layer Security (TLS) encrypt data sent from a browser to a website so the data is harder to intercept and provide greater security for the users' information. Most host providers can help you set up a security layer for your website. VeriSign and GeoTrust are two of the leaders in providing security for websites.

It is useful to not just have a security layer for your website, but to also let users know their data is secure. This can increase users' trust of your website and help increase conversion rates.

When adding secure layers, look through your website for one of the most common errors on the Web: The browser message that some content on the page is not secure (Figure 5.11). The error shown in Figure 5.11 is for Internet Explorer; each browser displays security error messages differently.

Figure 5.11 Security error warning

Usually—but by no means always—this is not a nefarious error. It commonly occurs when a logo or script is being rendered on a secure page from a nonsecure server. To fix this error, view the source of your web page (either by right-clicking and choosing View Page Source or navigating to the View menu and choosing Page Source), and look for images, scripts, and other files where the source is http instead of https.

The worst error is when the browser interrupts the process of loading a website, informs the searcher that there is an issue with the website's security certificate, and asks if they want to continue (Figure 5.12). This keeps any part of the page from loading until the user has made a choice. If a user sees this screen instead of your website after clicking on an AdWords ad, their most likely action will be to leave the website immediately.

Figure 5.12 Problem with a website's security certificate

Data security is going to continue to be a growing concern. Do not let this easy-to-fix technical issue lower your conversion rates. Keep your customers' data safe and let them know that the information they send you is secure.

Is Your Information Above the Fold?

What a consumer first sees in their browser when your website loads is known as *above the fold*. This is information the visitor sees without having to scroll down. It is your website's first impression.

The most complex issue with the above-the-fold concept is that monitors come in all shapes and sizes. Some laptops have only nine-inch monitors, while some widescreen monitors are more than two feet wide. This creates a scenario where there is no definite above the fold that you can code into your website.

This is another place where your analytics system can tell you about your visitors (Figure 5.13). While w3schools.com does publish statistics about the most common browser resolutions, those stats do not necessarily apply to you. If your target audience is business travelers, you may see some very small browser resolutions with the advancement of ultraportable laptops. If your audience is web developers, you may see some extremely large browser resolution sizes.

Figure 5.13 Google Analytics showing visitor browser resolutions

Harald Weinreich, Hartmut Obendorf, Eelco Herder, and Matthias Mayer in 2006 published a paper titled *Off the Beaten Tracks: Exploring Three Aspects of Web Navigation*, in which they examined where people clicked after arriving at a website. Table 5.4 highlights why showcasing your most important information—especially the actions you want someone to take—at the top of your website can dramatically increase conversion rates.

▶ **Table 5.4** Where users click

TableHeadCol1	Visible area	Right of visible area
Visible area	76.5%	0.3%
Below visible area	23.1%	0.1%

As more than three-fourths of all clicks occur in the area that loads above the fold, you always want your call-to-action, major benefits, and conversion actions above the fold. Users do not scroll right. If you have a website where a user has to scroll horizontally to see more of your website, most visitors will never see that information.

 Note: The Firefox add-on Firesizer or the Chrome plug-in Resolution Test allows you to see your website in different resolutions. These are useful plug-ins to quickly view how your website looks in different browser sizes.

The concept of above the fold is both a technical concept—it concerns your website's coding—and a psychological one—it showcases human behavior and where consumers look for information. The proper coding and security of your website can increase your website's usability and trust. These concepts can be enhanced by examining additional psychological factors that help your website convert browsers into buyers.

Psychological Factors That Increase Conversion Rates

It is easy to get caught up in a world of statistics that make you blind to the person sitting behind the computer. Stats do not pull out their credit card and buy from your website. You need to convince the human who is referenced in those statistics to pick up the phone and call your business.

Next you will see several ways your website can convey trust and usefulness to the user.

Testimonials and Reviews Lead to Sociability

There are two truths about humans that have been proven over and over again in studies:

- People act differently when they are alone than in a group.
- People conform to those around them.

Often the word "conform" is taken harshly, but try these two experiments and see what happens:

- During a face-to-face conversation, keep looking over someone's shoulder at something in the distance.
- Stand in the middle of your office (or on a street corner) and stare up.

How long did it take for someone to stop and try to determine where you were looking? Humans are social creatures, and we want to feel included within the group around us.

Browsing the Web is an isolated activity. Rarely do searchers sit on the couch with a group of friends and search for information. Rarely do searchers have someone sitting next to them telling them where to click next or to scroll down the page. Therefore, you need to find ways to make the solitary activity of browsing the Web more social and instill a sense of being included in a group; doing so can change the way people feel about your site. The most common example of this is the use of testimonials and reviews. These items are closely related as they are the words of actual people who have used a product or a company's services.

When reading reviews or testimonials, people are no longer alone. They no longer have to form an opinion about a website by themselves. Now a searcher can incorporate the opinions of others in forming their decision about a product or service that your company offers.

Featuring testimonials or reviews on your landing pages or the page where someone is making a decision about using your service (or buying your product) often leads to higher conversion rates.

Testimonials are usually positive, but allowing some testimonials that contain both positive and negative information shows that you are human like everyone else. This is something to test, not just blindly incorporate. For example, a testimonial might say, "Phil's Accounting Service did our taxes quickly and saved us a couple thousand dollars, but they are slow to respond on the phone and prefer communicating via email or in person." There will be some people who do not care that Phil is slow on the phone, as they prefer email communication. In this case, the negative information that made the review seem honest is actually positive for some people. Other searchers will just like the fact that Phil saved people some money and will want to see how Phil can help them.

You can also incorporate social media elements such as Facebook likes and shares, Google +1s, and tweets. However, there is no substitute for actual testimonials on a page no matter how many people "liked" your company.

Just remember, your primary goal is to ensure that your visitor feels part of a group and to raise your conversion rates. If your reviews and testimonials are not changing conversion rates, you need to examine why that is happening. We all like to feel included. Utilizing testimonials, reviews, or other social aspects in your website can help turn a solitary decision into an easier one as the searcher joins a group that has already enjoyed using your company.

Associations: What Company Do You Keep?

Many industries have governing bodies, associations, and networks that are well recognized within that particular industry. Showing which associations you are a member of is another way to instill trust in your visitors. You may be able to go beyond just showing your associations to why you are a market leader. Include any awards received within your field, speaking engagements, press clippings, and other demonstrations of authority to your visitors.

For example, at this point you have read almost five entire chapters of this book, yet you know little about the author. If I were to show just a small sample of associations and statements that I have been able to use over the past few years for myself or companies I have worked for, the list would look something like this:

- Google AdWords Seminar Leader
- Google AdWords Professional

- Google AdWords Qualified Company
- Google AdWords reseller
- Microsoft adExcellence member
- SEO class speaker
- 2008, 2010 SEMMY runner-up
- 2009 SEMMY nominee
- Member of the American Marketing Association
- Member of the eMarketing Association
- Member of Search Engine Marketing Professional Organization (SEMPO)
- Speaker at SES Latino
- Speaker at ad:tech Latino
- Speaker at Search Engine Strategies Chicago, New York, San Jose, San Francisco, and London
- Speaker at Search Engine Strategies Local
- Speaker at Search Marketing Expo (SMX) Local, Advanced, New York, and San Jose
- Speaker at Pubcon Boston, Vegas, and New Orleans
- Speaker at Afri-Tech in KenyaSpeaker at AdWords Days in Germany
- Local Search Ranking Factors contributor
- Search Engine Land columnist
- Spent more than 400 hours speaking in front of groups in 2010 and 2011 across 3 different continents in a few dozen cities

By now, most readers will have a different opinion of the material they are reading based on the author's authority. This is due to our ever-changing expectations based on the information we have with which to make decisions. While I listed many associations, there is no mention of any business I've worked with or worked for; it is only a list that helps to gain trust.

It can be useful to also show your partnerships and featured clients. Most people will assume that if a company chose to work with you, that company did their due diligence in researching your company before engaging your services. This statement is even truer if the featured client is a well-known business. Most people assume that Amazon does more research than Joe's Used Books in choosing a partner. Essentially, there is a transference of trust from the featured client or partner to your business.

People are also visual, and images can quickly show your authority instead of just bullet points (Figure 5.14). If you can use association seals or images, they can help break up the text on the page with subtle reminders of your authority.

Figure 5.14 Brad Geddes's associations

The goal is for visitors to be able to examine your company and quickly find reasons why you are a better company to engage with than your competitors. If you have symbols of authority, or memberships in organizations such as the Better Business Bureau or Chamber of Commerce, test using them on your website.

Using Coupons or Discounts

A common marketing tactic is to offer coupons or discounts. If you use either of these items in the ad copy, make sure you also show the same offers on your landing page.

It is common to see a discount code listed in an ad. The user clicks to the landing page and does not see the discount code. They navigate through the site, add items to the shopping cart, and go to checkout. If they cannot remember the code, they often go back to the search engine to try and find the code. If the searcher cannot find the same ad again, they can become frustrated and may abandon the cart completely.

Reinforcing the discount code on the landing page, or even adding the code to a navigational frame so that it stays with the user throughout that visit, can help increase conversion rates. The visitor will not have to abandon the shopping cart to find the coupon.

Using coupons is also a way to track in-store shopping. If you have both a physical store and an online store, it can be difficult to see your marketing effectiveness. By tracking in-store coupon redemption from your AdWords visitors, you can start to see if your AdWords campaigns are driving visitors into your store.

The end of 2008 saw a higher increase in searches for coupons and discount codes than previous months, and that trend has continued for several years due to both the economy and the ease of finding coupons on the Web. In a down economy, consumers become more price conscious. By not only advertising discounts but buying those keywords on your products ("discount TV," "TV coupon"), you can bring additional visitors to your website.

Using coupons is also a way to increase customer loyalty. If you have an email marketing list, make sure you showcase your coupons in your newsletters. Consumers like deals. The deals could be for a coupon, free newsletter, free consultation, or special discount. Find unique ways to give your customers a deal and they will reward you with more orders.

Using Images to Direct a Consumer's Focus

People are drawn to images of other people—that is a well-known fact. We are compelled to not just look at images of people, but to look closely at their faces. Earlier in this chapter, you saw how if you look behind someone while talking to them, the person will turn and look at where you are looking. The same thing happens on the Web with images of people. If you have a face on your website, searchers will follow the eyes in the picture to see where they are looking.

If your image is at the bottom-right corner of the page, often consumers will skip your text content to look at the image. If the image is then looking down and to the right—where if you drew a line from the eyes they would be looking off the monitor onto the desk—the searchers' eyes will no longer be on your website, but distracted by elements on their desk.

Make sure that if you use faces on your website that the image is looking back into your content at either your major benefits or the Submit button where you want them to take action. Images are excellent to use on websites because they break up the monotony of text. However, you must make sure that the image is enhancing your conversion rates and not distracting your visitors.

Coding for Color Blindness

Approximately 8–10 percent of males have problems distinguishing between red and green colors. Another 1–2 percent of the population have problems perceiving the difference between blue and yellow. Less than 1 percent of women suffer from any form of color blindness.

Examining your site in grayscale can allow you to determine whether your text can be read against your background. If you use red text and a green background, some might only see a gray page with no visible text.

Additionally, never rely on just color-based instructions, such as "click the red button to proceed." Always label website elements.

What Color Is Your Website?

The subtle use of color is another way to subconsciously influence your visitors. Here are some common color associations:

- Green conveys trust or money.
- Red conveys aggressiveness.
- Blue is calming.
- Black and white are neutral colors.

However, even within colors there are variations of meaning. Deep purple is associated with royalty and riches whereas light purple is romantic. Experimenting with color on your website can lead to combinations that are highly effective; just be careful with your meanings.

Red might seem like a good color for a DUI attorney as they need to go in and fight. Red is probably not a good color for a family planning attorney. Green conveys both trust and money, which is a good color if you are a nonprofit trying to attract donations, but it might make you seem expensive if you are selling stocks.

You must also be careful with overuse of a color. Looking at blue for too long can cause one to go from a calm state to almost a depressed state (that's why it's called "the blues").

White works well with any other color, and it is easy to read black text on a white background. In general, you do not want to overdo background colors where someone must spend a lot of time reading. A poorly chosen color scheme can doom your website to failure. In the United States, Canada, and Western Europe, most users prefer light background colors, with other colors used to denote different aspects of a website (such as sidebars, navigation bars, and headers). Most websites should not be bold and sparkly, but that is not always true if you are trying to reach a younger demographic, for example. This is why it's important to test different color schemes (more about testing in Chapter 15).

Beyond just your website's navigation bar and sidebars, experiment with the color of your Submit button. A red Submit button on a white and blue page stands out from all other elements. If your page only has one or two conversion activities, using a different color for those actions can help those items draw visitors' eyes.

Buttons vs. Text Links for Conversion Activities

Most websites have several links on any one page. If your call-to-action is also a link, it can get lost in the myriad of other links and text on the page. A button stands out from the rest of a page, making it more effective than a text link, and it invites the visitor to take action.

Consider the three possible links shown in Figure 5.15. Which stands out the most to you?

Figure 5.15 Button and text links

If you use buttons, use only one or two on a page. You do not want to overuse them so they no longer stand out. Changing your main actions (such as add to cart, check out, subscribe, download, etc.) from a link to a button should have an effect on conversion rates.

Privacy Policies

Privacy policies are at a crossroads in several countries. In the United States, a privacy policy is not required, but if you have a privacy policy it becomes a legal document that you must follow. This is a general statement, and not necessarily true for all industries and company types, such as public, private, and governmental, within the United States.

Adding a privacy policy can be a difficult choice for a company to make. There will be users who look for a privacy policy before submitting their information. If you wish to maximize your conversion rates, adding a privacy policy should help. In addition, one of Google's mantras for websites is transparency to the user. Google suggests that websites have privacy policies. They require them for AdSense publishers, but not for advertisers. Falling in line with Google's guidelines often leads to higher quality scores.

Your privacy policy could state, "We will sell your data to anyone who is willing to buy it." Now, that might not increase conversion rates for those who read it, but if you are trying to be transparent to the user, at least they know what will happen if they give you their email address.

Everyone is concerned about spam these days. Most searchers want empathy and reassurance more than they want to read through an entire privacy policy. Just by adding a small message to your Submit button (Figure 5.16), you can help reassure your visitors that they will not end up with spam from your company.

Receive Your Powerful Marketing Tips
(We hate spam as much as you do)

Figure 5.16 Add empathy and a benefit to your Submit button.

Your Website's Usability Goals

Many books are available that are devoted to website usability. There is no way to cover all of the possible tricks and elements in just one chapter. I have also examined conversion elements such as associations (and you will learn more about increasing conversions in the next chapter). What you should take away is that your website should accomplish these tasks:

- Allow the customer to find the answer to their question
- Allow the searcher to easily find information about your products and services
- Allow the customer to be able to access that information regardless of their browser, operating system, or eyesight
- Instill a sense of trust
- Showcase your authority
- Protect the privacy and data of your customers
- Make the conversion process easy

If your website can accomplish these goals, you can engage the customer and hold their attention. This is the first step to increasing conversion rates: making sure your website is accessible, readable, and trustworthy. If you cannot accomplish these three actions, the quality of your services and products do not matter, because searchers will not stay on your website long enough to learn more about your offerings.

Your landing page is the first impression a visitor has about your website. Therefore, you should closely examine the usability and conversion paths of your landing page. Most websites are not a single page, so incorporating these elements over your entire website is also a must for increasing your website's effectiveness.

Best Practices for Landing Pages

Devising the right landing pages is a crucial technique for converting searchers into buyers. A misstep here can send potential customers back to square one or to rival sites. The following are issues that you must address to enhance your potential for success:

- Make sure that your landing page answers the searcher's questions—not the search query itself, but the searcher's need to know whether your site can fulfill their needs.
- Craft the destination URL to comply with Google's editorial policy and to add additional tracking information that you can utilize to see how AdWords visitors navigate and convert on your website.
- Send the user to a page on your site that is the furthest logical page within the buying funnel for your website or a page dedicated to the search query.
- Correctly directing AdWords traffic is crucial. To do so, you need to understand the different types of user queries: transactional, informational, and navigational.

- Your site must be user friendly and trustworthy in the mind of your potential customer. You can accomplish these goals by understanding web technologies and using those technologies to your advantage.
- Use testimonials, reviews, and certifications to show that not only can your website be trusted but that your business can be trusted as well.

By using the techniques in this chapter, you will be able to achieve a good conversion rate. In the next chapter, I will examine techniques for bringing more visitors to your site and ways of increasing the conversions of those who view your landing pages and interact with your website.

Advanced Optimization Techniques

Once you have done the difficult part of choosing keywords and writing ad copy, you will start to see some results from your campaigns. Based on these results, you can optimize your account in a few ways.

The first optimization technique increases traffic to your website. This chapter shows you how to gain more impressions and more clicks from them. Then, once you have visitors, you'll learn how to gain more page views from them.

The second optimization technique increases conversion rates. You'll learn how to increase these rates and explore additional conversion types that help move your visitors through the buying funnel.

6

Chapter Contents
Optimizing for traffic
Optimizing for conversions
Best practices for advanced optimization techniques

Optimizing for Traffic

The most common analytics metrics to examine for any website are total page views and unique visitors. How many different people visited your website? How many page views did those visitors generate? These metrics are useful because they give a high-level picture of your website's exposure.

Although these are common metrics for website measurement, they can also be applied to any AdWords advertising campaign. How often were your ads shown (ad impressions), how often were they clicked, and how engaged were those visitors with your website (page views or conversion rates)?

These numbers are important because they will direct you to the type of traffic optimization you need. If you have a good click-through rate (CTR)—clicks divided by impressions—you need more impressions. If you have plenty of impressions but very few clicks, you need to raise your CTR.

Often publishers are paid per page view by selling cost per thousand impressions (CPM) ads. In that case, a conversion can be counted for each page view, and increasing page views per visitor has a direct influence on the site's profitability.

You might find increasing page views useful if you have an e-commerce or a local business website, especially if you have one customer recruit another to visit your website, or if you want more total visitors to see your offerings. These viral characteristics help you receive multiple customers from a single click.

First, we will look at techniques for increasing traffic to the website. Then we will examine various methods designed to help you receive multiple visitors from a single click.

Exploring Strategies That Display Your Ads More Often

Before you can determine how to receive more impressions for your ad, you need to know why your ad is not being shown in the first place.

The first setting to examine is your daily budget. If you are spending your daily budget every single day, odds are you are capping your impressions due to budget limitations. In this case, you have two options:

Raise Your Daily Budget If you raise your daily budget, your ads should be shown more often. Your CPCs (cost per click) and cost per conversion should remain stable.

Lower Your Bids If you lower your bids, your ads may receive more impressions and clicks for the same budget. This is not a guarantee, since some of your keywords may not have a high enough CPC to be displayed on page 1, which will end up lowering your total impressions.

If your average position is 5 or higher, it is usually best to lower CPCs. If your average position is below 5, lowering your CPCs may or may not gather more impressions. This average position is a rough guideline, because sometimes there are 12 ads on a page, and other times there may be a maximum of 8 depending on how many ads are shown above the organic results (more about the premium ad slots when we discuss Quality Score in Chapter 7, "Demystifying Quality Score").

> **Note:** The two most common ways your ad exposure becomes limited are ad scheduling (Chapter 13, "Profitable Bid Strategies") and geography (Chapter 11, "Advanced Geographic Targeting"). If you have chosen to only show your ads between 1:00 a.m. and 2:00 a.m. in Fargo, North Dakota, for example, you will not see many impressions.

When you lower bids, there is no guarantee that your conversion rate or cost per conversion will stay the same. If you do not want to spend more but want to receive more clicks, then lowering bids is useful. However, daily budget is the most common reason your ad is not being shown. If you are not reaching your daily budget, or would like more information about why your ads are not being shown even if you are reaching your daily budget, the first step is to run the impression share report.

Creating and Reading an Impression Share Report

The *impression share report* is the name the industry has adopted for one of the AdWords reports. This report tells you the percentage of times your ad was shown when it was eligible to be shown and the reasons it was not displayed. For instance, if you set your ad to be shown only between 1:00 p.m. to 2:00 p.m., and the user searched at 4:00 p.m., your ad was not eligible to be shown.

To create this report, navigate to the Campaigns tab and customize your columns (Figure 6.1). Then, in the Competitive Metrics category select these fields:

- Impr. Share
- Exact Match IS
- Lost IS (Budget)
- Lost IS (Rank)
- Relative CTR

Once you select these columns and click Save, you will see the impression share of your campaigns along with the reasons you did not receive impressions (Figure 6.2).

You will have your typical interface and other data columns along with the impression share statistics. Each row represents a different campaign. Impr. (Impression) Share (IS) represents the percentage of time your ads were shown. In this instance, the ads were only shown 12–78 percent of the time when they were eligible to be shown. *Eligible to be shown* means the number of times the searcher could have seen your ad, based on your campaign's ad scheduling choices, network options, keyword choices, and geography.

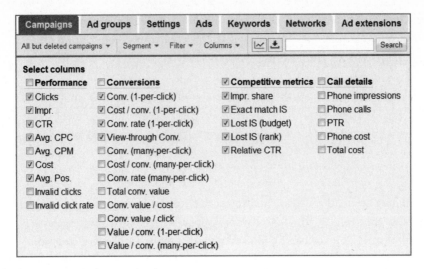

Figure 6.1 Creating an impression share report

Impr. share (?)	Exact match IS (?)	Lost IS (budget) (?)	Lost IS (rank) (?)
21.66%	**75.59%**	**28.24%**	**50.11%**
21.30%	--	54.12%	24.58%
12.01%	--	16.76%	71.23%
55.89%	62.08%	2.32%	41.79%
49.15%	36.89%	25.90%	24.94%
32.00%	47.09%	6.40%	61.61%
14.49%	--	59.94%	25.57%
27.76%	62.70%	0.00%	72.24%
33.30%	--	47.96%	18.75%
30.18%	50.00%	59.01%	10.81%
78.80%	71.14%	0.00%	21.20%

Figure 6.2 Reading the impression share report results

When your impression share is 85 to 95 percent or above, depending on how many advertisers are in your industry it is difficult—sometimes impossible—to raise your impression share. This is due to the sheer number of ads and advertisers Google is trying to serve.

Lost IS (Rank) shows the percentage of times your ads were not shown because of your rank—your ad's position. If your ad position was too low to be shown on page 1 and the user did not go to page 2, your ad lost its impression due to its rank being too low. In this case, raising your Quality Score (see Chapter 7) or your bids is one of the few ways to receive these impressions. There are situations where you might always lose some impressions due to rank.

To illustrate a situation in which you might lose impression share even if your average position is number one, consider this scenario:

- Your search partner only shows two ads.
- The keyword is ultra-competitive only in Miami.
- Companies in Miami bid 500 percent normal cost price for this keyword.

Micro-situations like this exist, and trying to track down areas where you are only losing a few percentage points of rank might not be worth your time—even if you found where you were losing impressions, you still might not raise your bid to a profitable level.

The Lost IS (Budget) column shows the percentage of time that your ads were not shown because your daily budget was too low. Once your daily budget is exhausted, your ad no longer shows for that day. If you are consistently reaching your daily budget, consider raising it to receive more impressions.

If you cannot raise your budget, and you mostly lose impressions due to budget issues, you are overbidding. Consider this scenario: Your lost impression share due to budget was more than 30, your daily budget is $100, and you are receiving 100 clicks a day. Therefore, your average CPC is $1. If you were to lower your average CPC to 0.75, you could potentially receive 133 clicks for the same budget. There comes a point where lowering your CPC will not get you more clicks because your rank will fall too low. However, if you are capped by budget, you should first remove your least profitable keywords. Assuming you still can spend your entire budget on the keywords that are left, you will want to start lowering your CPCs to the point where you can get the most clicks possible for your budget.

If you have a high daily budget that is rarely reached, and you see that you are losing impressions due to budget, there are a couple other common possibilities:

- The keyword was in the news and created an unusually high search activity for that keyword.
- Your keyword's search volume changes based on day of the week or month, and that's the only time you are losing impressions.

In these scenarios, try running the impression share report over different time periods and then comparing the reports. You may see some days or months where your ad is shown much more often than other periods of time.

The Lost IS (Budget), Lost IS (Rank), and Impr. Share (IS) columns should equal 100 percent.

Exact Match IS is a bit tricky to work with as it might not be overly actionable. It is only useful within the context of your keywords, match types, and goals. Exact match impression share is how often your ads show if all your keywords are set to exact match. The higher this number, the more impressions you would receive if you added phrase or broad match variations of your keywords.

When examining your share of voice, or online visibility, the first place to start is learning how often your ads are not being shown due to the limitations you have put on your account. If your ads are not being shown due to rank or budget, those are easy fixes. If your impression share report shows that your ads are being shown most of the time, the only way to increase your impressions is to add new keywords.

The impression share report only measures impressions for search. There are often new impressions available from the display network, which we will discuss in Chapter 9, "Understanding the Content Network," and Chapter 10, "Advanced Content Network Campaigns."

But what if your ad is being shown and you want more of those clicks? The second way to optimize for more clicks is not to get more impressions but to make better use of the impressions you are receiving by increasing your CTR.

Taking Advantage of Dynamic Keyword Insertion

When someone does a search on Google, their search query is bolded in both ad copy and organic results on the search results page. In general, if the keyword is in the ad copy (and therefore bolded), the ad copy receives a higher CTR. Wouldn't it be fantastic to be able to automatically insert the searcher's keyword into your ad copy? This is almost what dynamic keyword insertion accomplishes.

When your ad is shown, it's because a keyword in your account triggered that ad to be displayed. With dynamic insertion, you can automatically insert the keyword that caused your ad to be displayed in the ad copy. For example:

- Your account has the broad matched keyword "computer memory."
- Your account does not have the keyword "laptop computer memory."
- Someone searches for "laptop computer memory."
- This search triggers your keyword "computer memory" to display an ad.
- Since the keyword "computer memory" was what triggered the ad, that keyword would be inserted into your ad copy.
- If your account had the keyword "laptop computer memory" in it, the searcher would have seen their keyword query inserted into the ad copy.

What's in a Name?

Google did not publicly acknowledge dynamic keyword insertion when the feature was first released, since it was meant for internal use. Because it was not recognized by Google, the community ended up choosing the name *dynamic keyword insertion* (which was influenced by some Googlers who privately talked about the feature).

Both Yahoo! and Microsoft released public information about this feature on their systems before Google finally acknowledged the feature existed. Google chose to name the feature *keyword insertion*; however, by that time the term *dynamic keyword insertion* (commonly referred to as DKI) was so ingrained that the official label is rarely used. Suffice it to say, DKI is keyword insertion, which is also called dynamic keyword insertion, and whenever you hear someone mention any of these names, they all refer to the same feature.

If all of your keywords are exact match, you are inserting the searcher's keyword into every single ad. Since you will most likely be using different match types, you are inserting the closest match in your account.

There are a few restrictions to using dynamic keyword insertion. The first is that the ad copy must still follow editorial rules. If the keyword is trademarked and cannot be shown in an ad copy for legal reasons, dynamic keyword insertion will fail. This is also true for capitalization and misspellings.

Several options are available for how to display your ad, and understanding the capitalization is essential to creating effective keyword insertion ads.

How to Create Keyword Insertion Ads

To create a keyword insertion ad, you replace part of the ad copy with a special syntax that denotes that the keyword should be inserted into a specific section of the ad copy. Along with denoting where the keyword will be inserted, you need to define what will show if the keyword cannot be inserted (such as trademarks, misspellings, or exceptionally long keywords).

For instance, if you allocate the entire headline to keyword insertion but the keyword is 30 characters long, the keyword cannot be inserted into the ad copy since the headline is limited to 25 characters. Therefore, you also specify text that shows if the keyword cannot be inserted into the ad copy.

The syntax is very straightforward: insert {**keyword:***Backup Text}* into any part of your ad copy, replacing *Backup Text* with what you would like to see in your ad copy if the keyword could not be inserted. Figure 6.3 shows several examples of keyword insertion in ad copy. With keyword insertion, you can accomplish the following:

- Allocate an entire line to keyword insertion
- Allocate only part of a line to keyword insertion

- Add keyword insertion into any line of ad copy
- Use keyword insertion in multiple lines

Figure 6.3 Examples of dynamic keyword insertion

When a keyword is inserted into the ad copy, the words *Backup Text* will not appear, having been replaced by the inserted keyword.

The secret to keyword insertion is the way the word "keyword" in the ad copy is capitalized (see Table 6.1). This only applies for the way you write "keyword" in the ad copy—the way you capitalize your actual keywords in each ad group does not matter for keyword insertion.

▶ **Table 6.1** Keyword insertion examples for the keyword "Chicago AdWords seminar"

Your ad copy	What a searcher sees	Notes
{keyword:marketing seminar}	chicago adwords seminar	All lowercase
{Keyword:marketing seminar}	Chicago adwords seminar	Sentence case
{KeyWord:marketing seminar}	Chicago Adwords Seminar	Title case
{KEYWORD:marketing seminar}	Chicago Adwords Seminar	Title case

A Note on Keyword Insertion

Be careful when using keyword insertion: often companies become lazy and either forget the rules of successful organization or write some very poor ads. If you ever seen ads where the capitalization seems incorrect (acronyms such as TV spelled Tv or ROI spelled Roi) or the word order seems wrong (such as TV Sony), this is often due to lazy use of keyword insertion.

There is a nice tool (created by the technical editor for this book, Matt Van Wagner) called the DEKE, the Dynamic Keyword Insertion Simulator, that will allow you to see 1) how your keywords will look within your ads and 2) fail rates for DKI insertion based on keyword lengths and other variables. You can find the tool at `http://dki-ads.com`.

Keyword insertion is one of the few times when the order of the words in your account matters (excluding match type, where it is very important). If you are creating keyword lists and have the keyword "TV Sony" in your ad group, "TV Sony" will appear in your keyword insertion ad and not the more commonly stated "Sony TV." Poorly formed keyword insertion ads can lower your CTR.

When using dynamic keyword insertion, keep a second ad in the same ad group that does not use the feature to see which one receives the higher CTR. It is useful to test keyword insertion versus non–keyword insertion ads, because it is common to see search results where all the ads start to look the same (Figure 6.4).

Plumber Chicago
All Types of Plumbing Repair.
Service is Just One Step Away.
www.RotoRooter.com

Plumber Chicago
Find licensed plumbers in your area
Get free multiple plumbing quotes
www.plumbingnetworks.com

Chicago Plumber
Compare Free Quotes From Licensed
Plumbers in Chicago, IL
www.123ContractorQuotes.com

Quality, On Time
Right The First Time!
Schedule Online Now
www.plumbintime.com
Chicago, IL

Plumber
Find Chicago Area Plumbers &
Plumbing Contractors at SuperPages
www.SuperPages.com
Chicago, IL

Chicago Plumber
Searching for Chicago plumbers?
Visit our Chicago plumbers guide.
ChicagoPlumberDirectory.com

Figure 6.4 Does your ad stand out from the crowd?

The use of keyword insertion in this search result is not the issue. The larger problem is that the ads blend together as the headlines are so similar. In this case, writing a different ad that stands out can dramatically increase the CTR.

If your ad was among those in Figure 6.4 and you wanted to use keyword insertion, you could move the feature to the second or third line of ad copy. This way the word is still bolded in the ad copy, but you could write a headline that stands out from the crowd and increases your CTR.

Keyword insertion is fantastic if you have thousands of part numbers and do not want to create thousands of ad copy versions to show the actual part number. However, keyword insertion is not always the best ad feature for your account. While keyword insertion might increase the CTR, do not forget the conversion rate. If you are a publisher being paid per page view, dynamic keyword insertion will probably work well. If you are selling a product, you need to measure if your keyword insertion ads have different conversion rates than your other ads. More visitors are not useful if it leads to fewer conversions.

Please note that the use of keyword insertion does not automatically increase your Quality Score. (We will discuss Quality Score in the next chapter.) The ad (after keyword insertion) is used in determining a keyword's Quality Score so it might have a slight effect on increasing your Quality Score, but the larger effect on Quality Score is usually from an increase in CTR. CTR is the largest component of Quality Score, and if your keyword insertion ad receives a higher CTR, this will help your Quality Score.

Keyword insertion works on both the search and display networks. For the search network, the keyword inserted is straightforward; it's the one that triggered your ad to show.

On the display network, keyword insertion is more ambiguous. On the display network, the keyword that is inserted into your ad is the one that Google determines is the most likely to trigger your ad for that particular page. For example, say your ad group contained these keywords:

- Plumber
- Kitchen remodeling
- Fixing showers

If a user were reading a news article about the increase in home owners remodeling their kitchens and bathrooms for resale, the most likely match for that article would be the keyword "kitchen remodeling." Therefore, your keyword insertion ad would use the keyword "kitchen remodeling" in your ad copy for that particular page. If your keyword list contained both the keywords "kitchen remodeling" and "bathroom remodeling," either of those could be inserted into the ad copy.

On a content page, your keyword may or may not be contained within the article. Therefore, it is common to see very different response rates for the keyword insertion feature across display and search. We will cover the display network in Chapter 9, "Understanding the Content Network," but this is another example of why you should always separate out search and display reporting.

Keyword insertion can be a powerful tool when used correctly. The ability to automatically add keywords into the ad copy can help increase your ad's relevance to the consumer. However, when used poorly, a keyword insertion ad can lower your CTR.

Keyword insertion can help make better use of your current impressions. Instead of finding new keywords, if you increase your CTR on your existing keywords, you will receive more visitors to your website. Once someone has clicked on your ad and visited your site, how do you increase the number of pages each searcher visits?

Increasing Page Views

With Google AdWords, you pay every time someone visits your website. Although this can be a very profitable endeavor, finding ways of increasing the page views from each visitor or even having a visitor bring someone else to your site for free can increase your profits and site visibility.

E-commerce companies are often focused on return on investment (ROI) and not page views. This focus can lead to creating landing pages dedicated to a single product where the page does not offer any navigation except to add an item to a shopping cart. If you only have one product on the landing page and the searcher does not want that product, their only option is to click the Back button and leave your site. When optimizing for page views, always consider the options—or lack of options—that you present to searchers.

The other consideration is that when surfing the Web, searchers often do not know what to do next. They have read a page of content, or looked at a product and decided they do not want it, so what is the next thing they should do on your website?

There are two main ways to increase page views:

- Give the reader additional or related information.
- Have the reader send information to a friend that there is content they will enjoy on the website.

These two ways can be broken down into several techniques:

Related Articles If someone reads an entire article on your website, they are generally interested in that topic. Give the reader related articles where they can continue learning more. If your site is a news site, usually you want your related articles based on the same overall story or a top story section. If it is an informational article, the timeliness of the articles generally does not matter as long as the information is related.

Related and Supporting Products In the grocery store, as you are waiting to check out, there are many last-minute impulse items you can add to your shopping cart. On the Web, there is no last-minute aisle that features candy, gum, and magazines. Each page of your website can be customized with impulse items and last-minute related products.

Showcase your related and ancillary products across your product pages. You can also use this tactic to engage a user who is in the learning phase of the buying funnel. If someone is interested in purchasing an iPod, they may not know if they want an iPod Touch, 80 GB iPod, or a Nano. Help the user easily navigate between the related products or show a comparison of all the products on a single page.

This is also true for supporting products. If the iPod is being purchased as a gift, many users will also want to give an iTunes gift card along with the iPod. By showing additional products, you can increase not only your page views, but often your average order amount as well.

Recommended Articles Have you created an authoritative set of informational articles? Do you have some articles that readers absolutely love? Put these articles in a recommended article section. This not only helps increase the page views on your website, but also showcases your best writing so that users will have a higher level of trust for your content.

Recommended Products You are the authority on your website. Searchers look to a website to guide them. If they are unsure about what to buy, a recommended product section can help put them on track toward a checkout. Often gift buyers have no idea what to purchase for another person. By organizing your products by age, price, gender, and so on, you can create a recommended buying section to help a user narrow down their gift options.

Buying Guides Have you ever bought a camcorder, laptop, or high-definition TV? The different types of technologies, displays, recording devices, and acronyms associated with buying these products are staggering. Creating a how-to buying guide, or recommendation wizard, can not only increase page views, but can also help your site become an authority in a specific area. If you have the best resources for determining how to buy a particular product, showcase these resources so others will find them and tell their friends.

Top-Read Articles and Top-Selling Products It is commonly noted that we live in a world of fads. From choosing a watch because a celebrity is wearing it to reading a news article that everyone is discussing in the break room, people want to be included. One way you can incorporate these desires on your website is to show the top-read articles and top-selling products.

Highest Reviewed Articles and Products Do you let users rate your articles or products? Do you allow users to write reviews that you show on your pages? If so, take advantage of that content by showcasing the highest reviewed pages or products of your site.

Breaking Long Articles into Multiple Pages If your goal is page views and you write very long articles, break the content into multiple pages. This is especially useful if you sell CPM ads on your site and are looking to maximize page views.

Search Box If you have been online for more than 10 years, you remember the days when the best navigation was drilling down through the Yahoo! directory to find the proper category and then finally a website. Today, there is an entire generation that does not even look for navigation but starts the browsing behavior within the search box.

Regardless of how your site is designed, incorporating a search box into your website will increase not only page views but functionality and user satisfaction as well. When you incorporate your search box, remember to track the words being used to search. These are not only good keywords for your search campaign, but if you see frequent searches from particular pages, it can be a sign that the page is lacking some critical information.

Bookmark or Save This on Social Media Sites Just about every user knows that you can bookmark a web page, but it is often forgotten. Adding subtle reminders, such as "bookmark this" or "save to Delicious.com" can help get more page views from return visitors.

Social media sites (such as Digg, Facebook, Google Plus, and Twitter) can drive a massive amount of traffic to your website. Incorporating social media tactics so that your content is easy to share on these sites can help you find new avenues of traffic.

Send to a Friend The oldest of the sharing tactics is send to a friend. If someone likes your site's content, is there an easy way for them to email it to someone they think will also like it?

Print This Page One thing that has amazed me over the years is how often people print pages and either call a business at a later date, read the story on the train, or pass the pages on to someone else they think would enjoy the information. As much as we live in a digital world, paper is still greatly used. Creating printer-friendly pages is useful because you can customize your site's logo and URL on those pages so the searcher can always remember how to get in touch with your business or where the information originated.

None of the above examples are exclusive. On a site like www.nytimes.com, for example, you will see "print," "email," "search," and "save" functionalities. On a site like Amazon.com, you will see "recommended," "top rated," and "top reviewed" products. Incorporating social and related information can help increase page views across your site.

Increasing the number of page views per visitor on your website is not just about selling more CPM ads. It also ensures that your visitors are finding the information they seek so they have a positive experience with your site and return, recommend it to another person, or buy from your company.

The information could be a product or an article. Incorporating some of these ideas on your website should not just increase page views—it should also increase conversion rates as consumers find exactly what they are seeking and maybe a bit more (in the case of related products).

Techniques are available that are specifically geared toward increasing the conversion rate. These techniques do not rely on making sure the consumer can wander around your site to find the specific information. Instead, they try to sell one product per keyword and do everything possible to have the consumer take one specific action.

Too Many Options Lead to Confusion

The more information you give to someone at a single time, the more mental processing it takes to absorb all the information. In psychology circles, this is known as *cognitive load*. Giving your visitor too many options can lead to *cognitive overload*, in which your visitor no longer has enough mental processing left to make a decision.

This phenomenon is often coupled with short-term memory capacity. Most people can only hold five to nine concepts in short-term memory. If you give someone too many options, they could forget the original reason for coming to your website, or decide to wait until later to make a decision. Your site requires too much mental processing and memory capacity for the user.

Most users already have part of their short-term memory occupied with other tasks, such as why they visited your website or the fact that they have a meeting in 15 minutes. They only have a percentage of their cognitive load and short-term memory to dedicate to your website. Therefore, provide the user with options that are most beneficial for your company. If you are an e-commerce site, your primary option would be a sale. Your secondary option might be to create an account or subscribe to a newsletter. Your tertiary option might be social network sharing. You can test adding additional options, but your test should not just examine whether users are taking advantage of secondary or tertiary options, but whether the percentage of users engaging in your primary options is decreasing.

Optimizing for Conversions

Instead of focusing on traffic, you could put your efforts into increasing conversion rates. These two optimization techniques are generally at odds with each other. With traffic, you are looking to entice someone to come to your website regardless of their intent. When trying to increase conversion rates, you are only trying to bring people to your website who may perform some action.

A 100 percent conversion rate is not useful with one visitor a month. Conversely, a million visitors a day with zero conversions is a quick way to go out of business. Therefore, you generally want to use a combination of both conversion and traffic optimization when fully optimizing your AdWords campaign.

There are two aspects of increasing conversions: the ad copy and the landing page. We will start with techniques for writing high-converting ad copy, and then move to additional landing page options you can implement to increase conversion rates.

Writing Ad Copy That Sells

Ad copy is the bridge between the search query and your website. If the bridge is inviting to all, then all the cars will cross if the bridge leads in the generally correct direction. Conversely, if you hang a warning sign that says the bridge can only support up to certain weight and height limits, those who do not fit will not cross the bridge.

The sign serves as a filter to keep those who do not fit into your criteria away from your website, saving you money on those potential clicks. When trying to increase conversion rates, your ad copy should only be inviting to those whom you determine wish to perform an action on your website.

Usually, the ad copy's job is to stand up and shout, "You can find the answer to your question here." For increased conversion rates, the ad copy should instead be saying, "We have the answer to your question if you want to perform this one action. If you do not want to perform that action, do not cross the bridge." That action could be one of the following:

- Call us to schedule a visit
- Buy an HD TV
- Subscribe to our newsletter
- Fill out a form to receive free quotes

The second line of your ad copy should be a specific item you want the user to complete on your website (Figure 6.5).

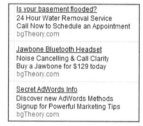

Figure 6.5 Use calls-to-action in your ad copy.

By letting visitors know exactly what you want them to do, you are accomplishing two goals:

- Those who do not wish to complete that action are less likely to click on the ad.
- Those who do click are more predisposed to both perform the action and to seek ways to conduct that action on your website.

As discussed in Chapter 4, "Writing Compelling Ads," a call-to-action can still contain a benefit. Testing benefit-laden call-to-action ads is one of the most important tests you should run to keep unqualified searchers from clicking.

Your CTR will decrease when you use ad copy that discourages unqualified searchers from clicking your ads. Since CTR is one of the most important Quality Score factors, you could see a drop in Quality Score. This is why it is crucial to test your ads. You have to balance your AdWords account between Quality Score, traffic, and conversions. This is a difficult balance to find, and only through trial and error will you find the correct combination for you.

When your ad does receive a click, it should be from a prequalified searcher who is ready to continue down the conversion path. The next step is making sure that your landing page can keep the searcher on the path toward reaching your goal of conversion.

Creating Landing Pages That Increase Conversions

When designing landing pages to increase conversions, before you move to the next step you must decide whether to use:

- A dedicated landing page designed only for conversions and single actions
- A page of your existing website

If you use a page in your existing website, you most likely have additional navigational and other elements on the page. You can still use some techniques to increase conversions, but some users will wander off your primary conversion path. Most e-commerce sites send traffic to pages in their existing website. You may choose a few of your top-selling products or late sales cycle keywords to send to dedicated landing pages with a different layout than your usual site. However, it is rarely cost effective to design a dedicated landing page for every product.

If you use a dedicated landing page for the search query, you can control every option a user has, which can help increase conversion rates. However, be careful of limiting someone's options too much if the keyword falls into the early buying cycle phases. Someone who is researching a product is not yet ready to purchase and will want some additional options to learn more about the product or service.

Using Dedicated Landing Pages

Dedicated landing pages are excellent for form actions, such as receiving quotes, filling out a contact form, or subscribing to a newsletter. With dedicated landing pages, you need to choose only one or two actions you want someone to complete. If you don't overwhelm users with choices, you have made the conversion choice for them. Now your page needs to move them from viewing the page to taking action.

When limiting a user's options, it is also important to keep in mind Google's landing page criteria:

- Relevance
- Navigation
- Transparency about the business and personal information collection

"One-page wonders"—single-page websites that often contained 100 paragraphs of scrolling sales copy with only one option on the page, usually an email signup—were saddled with very low Quality Scores a few years ago. This was due to the fact that the user had no options, rarely was there a privacy policy, and there was little business transparency.

You can be creative with dedicated landing pages as long as you keep the major AdWords landing page criteria in mind.

Keep Your Dedicated Landing Pages from Hurting Your SEO Efforts

If you spend time on search engine optimization (SEO), you want to make sure that your dedicated landing pages are not hurting your SEO efforts. If Google finds the same content on multiple pages, they will choose which one to rank; this is called the *duplicate content penalty*. Usually dedicated landing pages are not built for ranking; they are only built for conversions. Therefore, you do not want them included in the regular Google index.

The easiest way to keep these pages from being spidered by Google is to put them in their own folder (such as yoursite.com/landingpages). Then in your robots.txt file, exclude Googlebot from indexing that folder. You can also exclude all bots from indexing the folder. If Adsbot-Google, the bot that spiders your page for AdWords, sees a global disallow in your robots.txt folder, it will ignore the instructions, since Google assumes that if you are buying traffic to a page you want that page spidered for Quality Score purposes. If you accidentally block Adsbot-Google, then Google cannot spider your page and you will see poor Quality Scores.

You can also make microsites that are only used for PPC and conversion purposes. We have several dedicated pages at our AdWords training site at CertifiedKnowledge.org, and a few microsites. One microsite that has been particularly effective at conversions for general keywords (Figure 6.6) includes the major benefits of our program and quick calls-to-action to learn more or start a trial. There is some navigation on the microsite; however, this microsite is only about 10 pages, whereas our entire site is a few thousand. If you need to explain more about your product, show demos, and so forth, you might need more than a single page. In that case, feel free to design a small site whose only purpose is conversions.

When designing dedicated landing pages or microsites, make sure that your primary action is above the fold and the page centers around that one particular action. The action could be a form fill, add-to-cart button, or any other action you desire. The most important aspect is to make sure that there is a very clear call-to-action that is the first thing your visitors notice.

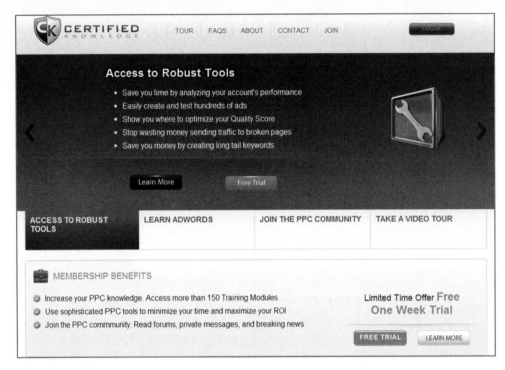

Figure 6.6 Certified Knowledge microsite designed for conversions

Increasing E-commerce Conversion Rates

Add-to-cart buttons are essential for e-commerce websites and should appear anyplace the product appears. This means users should be able to add a product to the shopping cart from the product page, category page, specials page, and even search results pages.

Detailed product information should be available within one click of the landing page. Even if you have a dedicated landing page for a product, detailed information should be easily accessible. Although people ready to purchase may ignore it, you will engage those who are still learning about a product before they are ready to buy.

Bose has an excellent example of an e-commerce landing page (Figure 6.7). The major actions on the page are "Buy Now" or "Learn More." The information above the fold for most monitors ends at the "Learn More" link. In addition, you can mouse over aspects of the headset to see its benefits.

Keeping with Google's policies, there is also navigation at the bottom of the page for those who wish to view other Bose products or headsets.

Whereas Bose went with limited navigation, Amazon did something quite different. Once you enter the shopping cart, all your options change. You still have navigational options, but those options are items like change shipping address, add a credit card, and so forth—all options that only keep you moving toward finishing your purchase.

Figure 6.7 Bose headset landing page

Shipping prices should be easily accessible. Consumers are very conscious about shipping prices. If you offer free shipping, make sure your landing page reinforces that message. If you ship to multiple countries, also make that obvious.

Make sure the shopping cart is easy to find. On some sites, you cannot view the cart unless you have just added a new product, which means that if someone adds a product, then starts shopping around, they cannot check out until they add another product. On other sites, the shopping cart is difficult to find. Use a highly visible shopping cart icon.

Do not put a registration barrier between the shopping cart and the final checkout. Registration requirements only serve to increase the number of abandoned carts on your site. If you would like users to register, give them the option to do so, and a reason why it will benefit them, after you have processed their credit card.

The shopping process should be no more than three pages. The longer the checkout process takes, the higher the chance of shopping cart abandonment.

The Easiest Way to Increase Profits

Rarely are there simple ways of increasing profits dramatically; however, not forcing account creation is one of them. I was working with an advertiser who had a mandatory account creation process before you could buy. I asked them to simply uncheck the account creation button in their site for a few days to see what would happen. They agreed, and the next day their revenue went up 40 percent. There are not too many things than can increase revenue by 40 percent in a single day; however, not forcing account creation is one of the few items that can have dramatic changes in overall revenue. This dramatic change might not happen for everyone, but even a 10–20 percent change in revenue is worth unchecking a simple box and moving account creation to after you have processed the credit card.

Increasing Form-Fill Conversion Rates

Web-based forms are used to collect email addresses and other contact information, check out at an e-commerce site, or register for a download. They are heavily used, but may be the least optimized pages across the entire Web. How intimidating do your forms look?

Even if you only want to collect name, email address, physical address, phone number, and credit card information, it still is common to see a form with at least these fields:

- First name
- Last name
- Email address
- Confirm email address
- Address line 1
- Street type
- Address line 2
- City
- State
- Zip code
- Area code
- 3-digit phone exchange
- Last 4 phone digits

For our purposes, we are going to keep the form simpler to illustrate a point and assume that your billing address is same as the shipping address. If these fields are just tossed on a webpage, it looks like it will take a while to fill out (Figure 6.8).

Figure 6.8 Poor form collection layout

While this form is not that long in comparison to many forms on the Web, compare the form in Figure 6.8 to another form that collects the exact same data (Figure 6.9).

Figure 6.9 A simple form that collects a lot of data

In the second form, Figure 6.9, the title field (Mr., Mrs., etc.) is used to determine the gender. The zip code field will let the merchant know the user's city and state. The credit card number denotes the card type. Consumers type first name and then last name. There is little need to make someone fill out separate fields. Your development team can parse out this information.

These simple form design principles work very well in most areas outside of e-commerce. If you have shipped to rural areas, or have dealt with individuals who have hyphenated last names, then you have come across exceptions where you might need the first name field or where someone's zip code does not match their city shipping address.

> ## Credit Card vs. Non–Credit Card Forms
>
> Occasionally, the approach of asking for first name, then last name in separate fields works better for credit card collection because consumers are trained to input credit card data in specific ways. However, for non–credit card forms, the fewer fields, the better. You can have your developers parse the information into your CRM or follow-up system as necessary to match the fields between the two systems.

In cases where you need to ensure the information is exactly correct, you have three options:

- Ask more explicit questions, but try to keep to as few fields as possible.
- Collect basic information with simple fields on the first form page. Save that information (especially basic contact information), and then present users with specific fields on page 2 of the form.
- Show a final review page before submitting the order, which is common with shipping carts, where you present your full information to users and then let them edit any mistakes.

In most cases, users will not need to edit their information. However, there will be some exceptions, and using a final review page will allow those few users to edit their information, while the majority of users who have standard addresses and names will quickly go through the entire form process.

Note: Did you know that all American Express cards start with a 3? All Visa credit cards start with a 4, MasterCards start with a 5, and Discover with a 6. Asking for both the credit card type and the credit card number is redundant.

The following are a few crucial considerations when designing forms:

The Value of Your Information When users are filling out a form, they are getting something of value in return. If you ask for more valuable information than they are receiving, your form abandonment rate will increase.

Sales vs. Marketing Many companies have a fight between marketing and sales. Marketing tells sales that if they only ask for a name, phone number, and email address, then sales can contact the prospective customer. Sales wants to know the contact's cell phone, best time to call, industry, how much money they make, the total income of the company, and the person's title. This is enough to make many customers abandon a form.

A compromise can take place between marketing and sales. On the first page of a form, ask for basic information that sales needs to contact the customer. On page 2, inform the customer that you would like to personalize their phone call, but to do so you need to collect some additional information about their company. This second page is where you can ask some of the more intrusive questions such as cell phone and gross sales numbers. Sales will not receive everyone's full information, but they can still put their calls in a queue based on the information they do receive.

Making Buying Easy Have you ever filled out a credit card form where your information was rejected because you did not use spaces? Or received the error that the form will not accept spaces or dashes in the credit card field? If someone is trying to give you a credit card number, take it. Your developers can parse out spaces and dashes on the back-end and accept the customer's data regardless of their personal preference for typing out their card information.

Respecting the Customer's Time Setting proper expectations is important for any business, especially when it comes to respecting someone's time. If you have a very long form, just tell the customer how long it will take to complete. If someone fills out page 1 and then sees page 2, then page 3, that prospective customer will start worrying about their time investment and may abandon the form. Tell the customer, "This is a three-page form and will take five minutes of your time. If you need assistance, do not hesitate to call us and we will walk you through the form." That small message sets the expectation of how long it will take, respects the customer's time, and gives them additional conversion options.

Many customers feel reassured of their progress by seeing a graphical navigation bar at the top of the page showing their progress. Let's say your checkout process is:

1. Review cart
2. Choose shipping method and address
3. Enter credit card billing
4. Review everything one last time
5. Check out

Showing those steps at the top of the page—and which page the customer is currently on—can help people understand the process, see if they have a chance to review their information, and know when they will be finished.

An Informed Searcher Is a Happy Searcher Make sure the searcher has the necessary information to complete a form before they start filling in the form's fields. Many landing pages are simply forms with limited information. Many of these forms contain detailed questions that require some knowledge about the industry. If your form contains a field for which a searcher does not know the answer, they will have to abandon your form to do some research. Whenever you ask a specific question that the consumer might not know the answer to, make sure that information can be easily found on your website.

For example, say someone searched for "merchant accounts" and came to a form page on your site. They happily fill out the first page of the application. Then, the second page of the application asks a required question, "What type of merchant account do you want?" If the searcher does not know that different types of merchant accounts exist, they have to abandon your form to do this additional research.

 Note: One of the best ways to optimize forms is to track where the forms are being abandoned and then investigate for potential causes. If you find there are two or three fields where abandonment consistently happens, add information to the page or change those particular fields.

Some Questions Should Never Be Asked It is common to see the question, "How did you hear about us?" on a form. The data received is usually very poor. I worked with a company that spent millions each year in marketing on many channels except TV. Every time the company surveyed customer how they heard about the company, TV was always number one. They could move the TV option anywhere in the list, but consumers still picked TV. Your analytics system will tell people how they found you.

A poorly designed form can drastically lower conversion rates. A well-optimized form can significantly raise conversion rates. Take a look at your forms, see how intimidating they seem, and find ways of making them friendly and easy to complete.

What If the Consumer Is Not Yet Ready to Buy?

Not everyone is ready to conduct an action when they visit your website. It is important to consider what is happening in the searcher's life that would cause that person not to convert so that you can engage these potential customers.

- Many office workers hide in their cubicles and shop online. However, while they may surf at work, they might not be ready to pull out the credit card while still in the office.

- Administrative assistants are often asked to conduct research on a topic and compile a list of resources and papers. This information is then handed to a second person to evaluate and make a decision.

- A shopper spends the afternoon on a site configuring options for the next computer they wish to purchase. Before they buy, they need to wait for the next payday and get the spouse's opinion.

In all three of these scenarios, someone may give your company money, but it will not be today. What options do you give those who are not ready to purchase immediately?

Empowering the customer to be able to print pages, download whitepapers, save items in a cart, send a configuration in email, and so forth can help entice users to come back to your site when they are ready to purchase. This is especially important in industries with long sales cycles. It is common for business-to-business companies to have six months pass between initial contact and final purchase.

One of the reasons to ask for an email address in up-front fields is to send reminders when forms are abandoned on your website. If a consumer adds products to their shopping cart, makes it through two steps of the cart, and suddenly abandons your site, you can increase conversions by sending them a reminder email that their shopping cart is about to expire. You can do the same for whitepapers or any form that captures an email address. There are times when the phone rings or someone walks into the office and disrupts the conversion process. Please note that, when sending emails such as this, you must follow any applicable laws, such as the CAN-SPAM Act.

In many of these cases, you might need to add additional conversion types so you can track the initial conversion and keep in touch with your prospective customer as you move them through the analysis of your products to finally purchase.

Allowing Consumers to Contact You Their Way

Do you force searchers to email you? Do you only list a phone number? Do you offer live chat? Different types of consumers have their favorite ways of contacting a business. If that choice is not available, they may not contact you at all.

You might want to offer more conversions than necessary for a while, see which ones are being used, and then remove the rest. If your customers do not use live chat, there is no reason to support it.

If you only offer phone support, and you only answer the phone during business hours during the week, what do you expect customers to do when they click on your ads during the weekend or at night? You should offer them a different course of action, and maybe even a different landing page, to make sure you are not alienating those searchers.

Many businesses find that by offering both email and phone support their conversion rate increases due to additional consumer choice.

Making Additional Conversions to Increase Your Profits

In Chapter 2, "Keyword Research," we discussed the consumer decision-making process, known as the buying funnel. Many companies can benefit by adding conversion actions to different segments of this process to keep in touch with the consumer and to keep moving the consumer through the buying funnel toward a final purchase.

If you have a long sales cycle, what does your conversion funnel look like?

Too many conversion funnels look like this:

1. Offer a free whitepaper download.
2. Hope the customer calls you (or add the customer to your email list).
3. If the customer calls you, try to sell them something.

This type of conversion funnel relies on the customer reading your whitepaper, doing their research, understanding your business, and then deciding to contact you.

Consider a conversion funnel such as this:

1. Searcher downloads a whitepaper to learn more about the product.
2. Searcher is sent an email to attend a free webinar to learn more about your company and how the product will benefit them.
3. Searcher attends free webinar and becomes more confident about your company.
4. Salesperson calls customer to offer free demo.
5. Salesperson conducts personalized demonstration with customer.
6. Customer makes a decision.

The second conversion funnel allows for more customer contact, more hand-holding, more interaction, a better customer relationship, and usually more sales.

Even if the customer's decision is to not buy from you, often the effort you put into the second conversion funnel is the same or less than the first one, as you do not have salespeople constantly calling or emailing to reach a bad prospect—the prospect has made up their mind. In addition, in this second conversion funnel, the prospect knows more about your company and may feel confident in recommending you to someone else as an option, or they might call you back when their situation changes.

When sales teams call customers after they have only attended a webinar or read a whitepaper, customers are usually resistant because they do not have enough information to make a decision. When there are multiple touch points, the customers naturally move through the conversion cycle into having enough information to make a decision.

By adding additional conversion options and tracking them all, you can see what patterns lead to higher conversion rates. In the previous scenario, you might find that the free demo does not increase conversion rates, so you could remove it. Or you could find that when someone attends your webinar, your contact ratio increases significantly, so you push that conversion option to more consumers.

Understanding Your Conversion Options

A conversion is anything you want to define on your website. Often conversions lead to your company becoming profitable, such as contacts, purchases, or subscriptions. You do not necessarily have to be paid on each conversion for it to be useful. A conversion can be someone entering your conversion funnel or viewing a key page of your website.

Here are some common conversion types that are worthy of tracking:

Contact Us Use this conversion action to track how often someone is contacting your business.

Any Form Fill Every time a form is filled out on your site, you gain some information or a searcher has taken an action.

vCard Download A vCard or "save to contacts" option allows you to be part of someone's Outlook or other email program.

Whitepaper Download Whitepapers are often PDF files that cover details about a product or idea. Offering whitepapers is critical in business-to-business selling where the person doing the research is not the decision maker.

Webinar A webinar is an online presentation.

Subscription When someone subscribes to your newsletter, RSS feed, or protected section of your website, you have a chance to continue the conversation.

Save to Cart and Add to Wish List These are various ways to let someone save a product to buy at a later date. Allowing people to publish their wish lists can also help your website's visibility and conversion rate.

E-commerce Checkout Someone gave you money—track it!

Send to Friend (or Self) via Email Allow someone to send product or article information to another person, or even to themselves to investigate at a later date.

Send to SMS or Mobile Phone This is useful to allow customers to send your contact information or driving directions to their phone.

Driving Directions If you have a physical store, track how often people are getting directions to visit you in-store.

Phone Call Phone call tracking takes some work, but it allows you to understand how many calls and sales your marketing is generating. With more sophisticated systems, you can even correlate phone calls to keywords, ad groups, landing pages, and ad copy.

Bookmark While this does not lead to direct revenue, it shows some interaction with your site.

Social Network Share There is no direct revenue in a social network share; however, it can lead to other traffic that does convert. Examining both the sharing of content, and then the profit from social traffic sources is very useful.

Print Page Offering a printer-friendly page and Print button can allow you to see how often your information is being printed. It is not uncommon for searchers to print a website and call a business at a later date.

Coupon Print If you have a physical store, track both how often coupons are printed and how often they are redeemed in the store. With proper coding, coupon redemption can be traced back to a keyword, landing page, and ad copy.

While offering too many conversion options can cause consumers to be overwhelmed and unsure which is correct for them, offering too few can cause you to lose consumers either on the initial visit or by not being able to move them through the shopping and conversion funnels.

Best Practices for Advanced Optimization Techniques

The first step to any pay-per-click campaign is to send traffic to your website by bidding on relevant keywords. There will be many times when you want to increase the traffic your website receives. In those cases, these practices can help bring more visitors from the search engine to your site.

- The impression share report will help you identify why your ad is not being shown, and then you can take action to improve the situation:
  - If you are already hitting your daily budget, then either raising your budget or lowering your maximum CPCs can increase the number of clicks you receive without adding new keywords.
  - If you are not reaching your daily budget, and you have a high impression share, the next step is to either increase your ad's CTR or add more general keywords.
- One technique for raising CTRs is to use dynamic keyword insertion to automatically insert keywords into your ad copy.
  - The trick to proper use of dynamic keyword insertion is to correctly use your ad copy capitalization syntax, because this will determine how your keywords are displayed in the ads.
  - When using dynamic keyword insertion, make sure your ad stands out from the other ads on the page.

It does not matter whether you send traffic to a dedicated landing page or an existing page of your website. Here are some best practices you should follow to increase conversion rates:

- The visitor should feel that the landing page is what the ad was describing—that is, it should be an extension of the ad copy.
  - The call-to-action that appears in the ad copy should be on the landing page.
  - Any claims, pricing, or special discounts should be echoed on the landing page.
- Create a synergy between the ads and the landing page so that visitors feel they have arrived at the correct site.
  - When using media-rich ads, echo the same images in the ads on the landing page to avoid confusing the visitors by a landing page that has a very different look and feel. The graphics can be different sizes and shapes, but the same basic images.
  - Make sure visitors see the same offer so they can continue converting on your website without wondering whether they have arrived at the correct place.

- Leverage the few simple principles of increasing conversion rates:
  - Have a clear call-to-action.
  - Have a clear path-to-action.
  - Offer a compelling benefit and message.
  - Ensure your information is accessible to all.
  - Ensure the user has the correct information to make a decision.
  - Make the conversion process painless.

The principles are easy to grasp. The execution of those principles is difficult.

Furthermore, testing ad copy and landing page layouts is essential to maximizing both traffic and conversions. Once you test, you need to let both the results of those tests and your analytics systems tell you the story of what combination provides the best response rates to turn searchers into customers.

Demystifying Quality Score

Quality Score is the most important number in your Google AdWords account, because it has far-reaching effects on your AdWords success. This number can decide the fate of your account. Low Quality Scores can doom your account to failure. High Quality Scores can place your ad above your competitors while you pay less per click than they do. It is also the hardest number to quantify and try to improve across your entire account.

This chapter examines what Quality Score affects within your account and the factors that influence your Quality Scores. You will also learn how to improve your Quality Score to gain a strategic advantage over your competitors.

7

Chapter Contents

What is Quality Score?
Viewing your Quality Score
Landing page quality: making your pages relevant
Estimating your first page bid
Understanding the display network quality score
Creating highly relevant ad groups
What to do if your Quality Score drops
Quality Score FAQs
Best practices for optimizing Quality Scores

What Is Quality Score?

Quality Score is the single most confusing number in your entire AdWords account. It is often considered an ambiguous number that is almost impossible to directly change, and yet it has more impact on your account's performance than any other number, and that includes your bid. So what is this Quality Score, anyway?

Quality Score is a metric that Google uses to help keep the paid search results relevant to searchers. Quality Score is used by Google to determine the ranked order of ads that appear for any given search result and is meant to balance the desire of advertisers to always have their ads above everyone else's ads as long as they are willing to pay for it, and the needs of searchers who are looking for relevant search results both for paid ads and organic search results.

Ads that are more relevant to searchers' intent are assigned higher Quality Scores. Google has many factors it considers for relevancy, which I will discuss in this chapter. By far, the most heavily weighted factor is click-through rate (CTR). The more people tend to click on your ad, the more relevant the ad must be.

Without a Quality Score factor, the highest bidder would always show first for any search result, and you can imagine the types of ads you would see over and over again that have nothing to do with your search query. If Google were to allow totally irrelevant ads to appear for search queries, users would soon stop clicking on paid ads and even abandon Google in favor of other search engines. That's not good for Google or advertisers, and certainly not for people conducting searches.

By using a relevancy metric in its calculation, Google helps balance the common needs of Google, its advertisers, and people who rely on it to deliver great search results.

The reason this number is especially important to advertisers is that Quality Score influences so many aspects of your AdWords campaigns, such as the following:

Your First Page Bid The first page bid is an estimate given to you by Google for each of your keywords that is an approximation of what you need to bid for your ad to show up on page 1 of the search results.

Ad Rank for the Search Network Ad rank is the number that Google calculates for all ads that qualify to show in any particular auction. Google then uses ad rank to determine the order of ads on a search results page. The ad with the highest ad rank score displays on the page, the next highest is second, and so on.

The formula Google uses for calculating ad rank is:

$$\text{Quality Score} \times \text{maximum CPC} = \text{Ad Rank}$$

Eligibility to Appear on Specific Display Sites Display network ads appear on nonsearch pages. In search, Google looks to see if the search query is related to your keywords. On the display network, Google looks to see if the article's contents are related to your keywords. For example, if someone is reading an article about airline travel on the *New York Times* site, the display ads will also be related to airline travel. Your Quality Score, along with several other factors, is used to determine whether or not your ad can appear on one of these sites when the site content matches your display campaign keywords.

Whether a Placement Targeted Ad Will Appear With Google's managed placements option, you can select individual websites across the display network where you would like your ad to appear. Your Quality Score will help determine whether your ad can appear on the sites you select.

Essentially, if you can increase your Quality Score, you can pay less for clicks and increase your ad's visibility by having it shown higher in the search results. Every keyword in your account is assigned a Quality Score, which Google reports as a metric at the keyword level.

Quality Score is an important metric that you can manage and optimize as long as you understand what factors go into it and how it impacts various elements within your account, such as ads, keywords, and landing pages. By breaking down Quality Score and examining its associated factors, you can understand how to improve your Quality Scores and the performance of your whole account in the process.

Some Essential Terminology

Here are definitions of the various types of networks covered in this and other chapters:

Search Partners Sites where you conduct a search but that are not owned by Google, such as AOL.com and Ask.com.

Google Search Network Sites that are owned by Google, such as Google.com and Google.co.uk.

Google Display Network Sites owned by Google where ads are shown based on the content of the page, rather than based on someone conducting a search; examples include YouTube.com and Gmail.com.

Google Network Both search and display sites that are owned by Google.

Display Network Sites that may or may not be a part of the Google display network where an ad is displayed based on the article's contents, such as NYTimes.com and Gmail.com. For instance, the *New York Times* shows AdWords ads on their article pages based on the article's content, yet the *New York Times* is not owned by Google.

To make matters confusing, Google considers some of their own search sites, such as maps.google.com, as *search partner* sites and not as Google search sites.

How Quality Score Affects Ad Rank

Every time your ad is shown, the keyword is given an ad rank score. The higher your ad rank, the higher the position in which your ad will appear. At the same time, Google determines the ad rank for all the other ads that could be shown. The ad with the highest ad rank is shown in the first position, the second ad rank is shown in the second position, and so on.

Ad rank is calculated by a very simple formula:

(Maximum Bid) × (Quality Score)

To increase your ad rank, you can either increase your Quality Score or increase your bid. You will encounter many instances when working with your AdWords account when you should not raise bids but instead attempt to increase your Quality Score.

It is also possible to pay less than a competitor for a higher position. Consider the scenario shown in Table 7.1.

▶ **Table 7.1** How Quality Score calculates ad position

	Advertiser A	Advertiser B
Max CPC	$0.75	$2
Quality Score	8.5	3
Ad Rank	6.375	6

In this scenario, advertiser A's ad will show higher in the search results than advertiser B's because advertiser A's ad rank is higher. Advertiser B is already bidding 266 percent higher than advertiser A. Just because you are willing to pay more than your competitors does not mean your ad will be displayed higher in the results.

If advertiser B wanted to leapfrog advertiser A and have their ad appear higher, they could continue to increase their bids. However, paying a significantly larger amount for each click than your competitor is not a good long-term strategy. It makes more sense to raise your Quality Score so you save on advertising costs. Or you can put that money to good use in gaining more clicks by increasing your budget or developing new ads and adding new marketing channels. In this scenario, advertiser B should not focus on increasing their bid. Instead, they should attempt to raise their Quality Score.

Determining Actual CPC from Quality Score

There is usually a difference between your maximum CPC and your actual CPC. For example, even though you may bid $2, you may end up paying $1.57. This is because of the way the Google auction works, which effectively discounts your CPC bid down to pay $0.01 more than is required for your ad to appear just above your competitor.

The formula that determines actual CPC is:

Actual CPC = Ad Rank to Beat ÷ (Your Quality Score + $0.01)

If you plug in the numbers from Table 7.1, you will arrive at this formula:

$0.72 = 6 ÷ (8.5 + $0.01)

Therefore, even though advertiser A is bidding $0.75, they are actually only paying $0.72 per click. If there were more than two advertisers, the ad ranks and actual CPCs would be calculated for every single advertiser.

Because AdWords is a blind auction system, it is impossible to know what your competitors are bidding. The AdWords system is built on setting bids based on your advertising profits. To profitably increase bids, you may need to increase your website's conversion rates, change match types, or try different ad copy. If you increase conversion rates, you are increasing the searcher's satisfaction with your website, which again aligns your advertising with Google's goal: Make the best search experience possible for the searcher.

Quality Score Factors for Search

There are a few Quality Score factors that are used in your AdWords account. The most transparent of all these scores is the one used for search, because you can see this number in both your account and your AdWords reports.

One of the confusing aspects of Quality Score is that you have one number displayed in your account that is determined by one set of factors, and a different set of factors is used to calculate your first page bid and ad rank. First let's examine all of the factors used to determine the Quality Score that is shown in your AdWords account, and then I'll show you some of the exceptions. The Quality Score factors are as follows:

Click-Through Rate on Google The single most important factor in determining your Quality Score is your click-through rate (CTR). The higher your CTR, the higher your Quality Score can be for each keyword.

The CTR is normalized by position. This means that your ad is not penalized for showing in a lower position and conversely you don't automatically get a boost when your ad is in higher positions that are expected to always have higher CTR. Google does not directly compare the CTR of an ad in position 5 with the ad in position 1, because Google understands that position 5 generally receives a lower CTR than position 1; therefore, before CTR is used in the Quality Score calculation, Google normalizes the CTR across positions based on projected click-through rates at those positions to determine how effective your ad is at gathering clicks.

When ads are shown on the Google search network, only the CTR of the Google search network is used. Your display network CTR and search partner CTR do not matter whatsoever for determining your Quality Score for search when your ad is shown on a Google search network site.

When your ad is shown on a search partner, such as Ask.com or AOL.com, the CTR of your ad on that partner site is used along with your CTR on non-Google search partners.

Click-Through Rate of Display URLs within an Ad Group Google tracks the display URLs used within your ad group separately from your text ads. The higher your display URL CTR, the higher your Quality Score can become. This is another reason to vary your display URLs and test to see which ones lead to higher CTRs.

Relevance of the Keywords to the Ad Copy within an Ad Group Relevance is one of Google's mantra words, and one of the places where this word takes on a special significance is in your ad copy. How closely does your ad copy describe and reflect your keyword? You do not have to use the actual keyword in the ad copy, but they should be closely related.

For example, the words "flowers" and "roses" are closely related. If the keyword is "flowers" and it triggers an ad copy about buying rose bouquets, these are closely related terms, since roses are a type of flower. A searcher may search for the word "flowers" but really want to buy roses.

However, the keywords "real estate" and "mortgage" are very different. When looking for real estate, the location, price, and number of bedrooms are pieces of the same puzzle. While most people who are looking to buy a house will need a mortgage, the search process is very different. A user looking for a mortgage is more interested in financial information than the number of bedrooms a house contains. In this instance, the ad copy will have a low relevance score as it is not helping someone arrive at the answers to their search query.

Google does not do semantic analysis for determining Quality Scores. Google uses a different set of CTR analysis formulas for determining relevance. However, as an advertiser, you should think about relevance semantically so that you write compelling ads for searchers based on what they are trying to find.

Relevance of the Keyword and Ad Copy to the Search Query Google made a change in October 2008 when they moved to a real-time Quality Score analysis. In real time, Google examines the relevance of your keyword and the ad copy that will be shown in the search result and then compares your keyword and ad copy to the actual search query. Therefore, if you are using dynamic keyword insertion, it can help improve this one factor.

Since this factor is in real time, it does not influence the Quality Score shown in your account, but it does affect the Quality Score used when determining your ad's position in a search result.

Landing Page Quality This factor is very similar to the relevance of ad copy to the keyword. How relevant are your landing pages to the keyword? You do not have to have the actual keyword on the landing page; the landing page must be thematically related to the keyword.

I will go into greater detail on landing pages in the section "Landing Page Quality: Making Your Pages Relevant," later in this chapter. In addition, since several factors make up landing page relevance, I will also examine those factors in depth in the section "Landing Page Quality: Making Your Pages Relevant."

Landing Page Load Time The speed at which your landing page loads for the user is also a factor in determining Quality Score. If you pass the threshold, there is nothing more to optimize. In the following section, "Viewing Your Quality Score," you can see how to determine whether or not your landing page load time is acceptable.

The AdWords system follows all keyword-level destination URLs (or ad level if you do not use keyword-level URLs) to determine the final page to analyze.

When Google determines if your page loads fast enough to be considered acceptable to the user, it is just looking to see if the HTML of your page loads as fast as the other pages hosted in that same geography. Since Google only looks at the HTML—not image sizes, scripts, etc.—this should never be an issue for most accounts.

If you are having landing page load time issues and are not using redirects, you have a larger problem than your AdWords account. You need to evaluate your host and website to find out why your site is loading so slowly.

If you are using redirects, make sure your redirects are not slowing down the searcher before they reach the final landing page. In the case of redirects, your site could load quickly, but if the redirects are slow, you may see issues with landing page load time.

Account Performance in Geographic Region Where Your Ad Will Be Shown This is another factor that has more influence on your ad's actual position than the displayed number in your account. Google examines the different geographies where your keyword and ad are being shown. If a pattern emerges where your ad receives a higher CTR in one geography over another, your ad will be shown more in the geography with the higher CTR and usually have a higher position in that geography (assuming the completion and other bids are relatively similar).

This Quality Score factor could be at odds with your conversion rates. You may find that you have a higher conversion rate in one geography, but in a completely different area you have a higher CTR. In this instance, Google will show your ad more in the area with the higher CTR and you could lose out on conversions.

There is a geographic performance report that will give you insight into different statistics by geography, which I will cover in depth in Chapter 11, "Advanced Geographic Targeting."

Account History Google examines the entire account, both the keywords and the ad copy, to determine how the account has done overall. Your overall account history is used when determining Quality Score.

With most AdWords statistics, such as account history and keyword CTR, the most recent history matters more than the overall history. Think of it as "What have you done for me lately?" Since most recent matters more than overall, accounts and keywords can almost always be saved when the proper techniques are applied.

Quality Score Is Only Calculated by Precise Matches

When examining the Quality Score factors, do not worry about the click-through rate or related queries for your phrase and broad match keywords. If you add the same keyword as an exact match, phrase match, and broad match keyword, all three versions will have the same Quality Score. That Quality Score will be derived from the exact match version. If you have a broad match keyword that does not have the exact match equivalent in your ad group, Google will calculate the Quality Score for that keyword based on the times when the search query matched your keyword precisely.

Therefore, it is useful to either use an exact match version of all your keywords or run the search query report to see the actual CTR of your phrase and broad match words when attempting to optimize for Quality Score.

Other Relevancy Factors Google uses many other relevancy factors that only occasionally apply. Most of these factors are fairly minor, are extremely difficult to optimize, and do not always come into play. Therefore, they are not disclosed by Google. However, they tend to be so minor they are not worth worrying about, and you can instead focus on the other factors described earlier.

For example, let's assume two advertisers are using the broad match keyword "teeth whitening." One of the advertisers is a dentist located in Chicago. The other advertiser is an e-commerce site that sells a teeth-whitening product. Now consider a searcher sitting in Chicago doing a search for teeth whitening. Most dental queries are inherently local and the Chicago dentist is geo-targeting the Chicago area. In this instance, odds are that the Chicago dentist is a bit more relevant. Now let's say the searcher changes their query to "online teeth whitening." While the user is still sitting in Chicago, their search query has turned more product oriented than local oriented, and in this case the online e-commerce store might see a slight bump.

This scenario may not be used by Google, but it is intended to give insight into one of many reasons why Google might have these other relevancy factors that only sometimes come into play.

Most of these factors are used when determining the displayed Quality Score in your account (with the exception of the factors that vary by user, such as the relevance of the keyword and ad copy to the actual search query). However, the weighting of the various factors can change based on many other factors, such as a user being on a computer versus a mobile device. Although it is useful to know the factors involved in determining Quality Score, it is equally useful to be able to see the actual Quality Score by keyword to understand how your keywords are doing.

Viewing Your Quality Score

Quality Score is listed as a number from 1 to 10. The higher the number, the better your Quality Score. Technically, Google keeps a different number strung out to many decimal places that is used in their calculations; however, they display only whole numbers to advertisers.

You can view your Quality Scores in the AdWords Editor or in the interface when you examine the Keywords tab (Figure 7.1).

The Quality Score column is hidden by default. If you do not see your Quality Score listed at the ad group or campaign level when viewing Keywords, then you will have to customize the columns.

Click on the columns link, then click Customize Columns. You will be presented with options for specifying statistics you would like to view (Figure 7.2).

Figure 7.1 Viewing your Quality Score

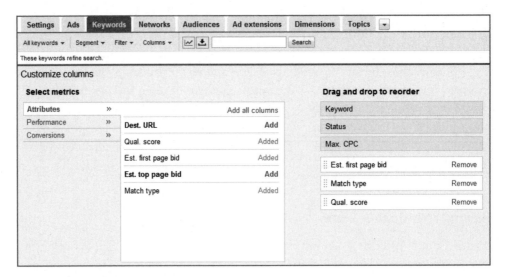

Figure 7.2 Customizing the keyword columns

Once the Quality Score is shown for your account, you can click on the conversation box icon in the Status column to view more specific information about that keyword (Figure 7.3).

When you see a low Quality Score in your account, this is the first step you should undertake to diagnose problems. Often if there is a reason why your ads are not showing, it will also be shown in this dialog box. Please note that "landing page performance" is the same factor as "landing page load time."

Figure 7.3 Detailed Quality Score information

The second place to view your Quality Score is in the AdWords Editor (Figure 7.4). The AdWords Editor is free software from Google that enables you to manage your account on your desktop (or when you are offline). I will discuss it in detail in Chapter 12, "Save Time and Scale Accounts with the AdWords Editor"; for now, please note that this is another place where you can view your Quality Score.

Keyword	Type		First page bid...	Max. CPC (USD)	Quality Score
	Phrase	‖	0.01	Auto	10
	Broad	●	0.02	0.31	10
	Broad	●	0.02	0.31	10
	Broad	●	0.01	0.31	10
	Broad	●	0.02	0.31	10
	Broad	●	0.25	0.31	10
	Broad	●	0.35	0.78	10
	Broad	●	0.30	0.60	10
	Broad	●	0.35	0.45	10
	Broad	●	0.20	1.08	10
	Broad	●	0.09	0.53	10
	Phrase	●	0.15	1.00	10
	Phrase	●	0.01	0.35	10
	Broad	●	0.02	1.00	10
	Phrase	●	0.01	0.31	10
	Phrase	●	0.01	0.55	10
	Exact	●	0.01	0.55	10
	Phrase	●	0.01	0.55	10
	Exact	●	0.01	0.55	10
	Phrase	●	0.01	0.85	10
	Exact	●	0.01	0.85	10
	Phrase	●	0.01	0.85	10

Figure 7.4 Viewing Quality Score in the AdWords Editor

One of the easiest ways to work with Quality Score is to export the data from your account into an AdWords report. This will give you a list of your keywords, Quality Scores, and other data that you can manipulate to find the areas of improvement. I will revisit some ways to utilize this data in the section "Increasing Your Quality Scores," later in this chapter.

Not only is your choice of landing pages important for increasing conversions, it is also essential to maintaining high Quality Scores. Later in this chapter, I will discuss ad group organization that will make it easy to choose the appropriate landing page. However, you also need to ensure that your landing page meets Google's guidelines.

Landing Page Quality: Making Your Pages Relevant

Google has developed landing page guidelines for AdWords based on giving the searcher the best possible experience after the click when they leave Google's property and enter your website.

Luckily, most of these guidelines help with conversions and your website's usability. By following these guidelines, you can make your page relevant for the consumer and for Google's Quality Score formula.

Spiderability

The first step to creating a relevant landing page is making sure that Google can read the page with their spiders (programs that index websites). If Google does not understand your landing page, it cannot ascertain whether your landing page is relevant.

Google uses two robots to spider your site for AdWords:

- Adsbot-Google, or Adsbot-Google-Mobile
- Googlebot

A `robots.txt` file is an instruction manual that tells a robot what it can or cannot crawl on your website. If you use disallow all robots from crawling a page, then Adsbot-Google will ignore your `robots.txt` instructions. Adsbot-Google ignores these global disallows because it assumes since you are buying traffic to that page, you want the page to be indexed so a Quality Score can be created.

There are times when Googlebot may index your site instead of Adsbot-Google. If Googlebot has recently visited your site, Adsbot-Google may ignore your website since AdWords will use the information from the Googlebot crawl to determine your Quality Scores. However, if you block Googlebot in your `robots.txt` file, then Adsbot-Google will crawl your site so your account can be assigned Quality Scores.

If you are unsure how Adsbot-Google is treating your site, you can create a free Google Webmaster Central account (`google.com/webmasters/`) and use their tools to analyze your `robots.txt` file and make sure the site can be crawled.

Once you know that your site can be crawled, the next step is creating relevant pages.

Relevance

The destination URL should lead the searcher to a page on your website that answers the searcher's question or shows them how to receive their answer. This relevance is very similar to the ad copy relevance, because you do not need to have the actual keywords on the landing page. The page needs to be topically related.

If you are unsure what Google thinks your page is about, use the AdWords Keyword Tool discussed in Chapter 3, "Keyword Tools: Extracting Valuable Data from Google." Input your landing page and let Google crawl your site. Now examine the keywords. If the keywords are similar to the keywords in your ad group and what *you* think the page is about, your page should be relevant to the search query.

If the Keyword Tool thinks your page is about something completely different, you need to revisit the content on your page and possible rewrite some paragraphs. If you have a page that is mostly images and Flash, you may just wish to add some HTML content.

The content should also be unique to your site. You can have the content on multiple pages of your site, but you do not want the content to appear on other pages across the Web.

> **Note:** For paid search, it is acceptable to have the same content on multiple pages of your website. However, for organic search engine optimization, having the same content across your website can lead to either a duplicate content penalty or to Google ranking one page of your website when you would rather have a different page rank for that term. Use the `robots.txt` file to make sure only one version of your content is crawled and indexed by Googlebot. To learn about `robots.txt` files, visit www.robotstxt.org.

Sites that utilize manufacturer descriptions in their content can run into problems with this guideline. If there are a hundred sites with the same content, why should the searcher read it on your website? Mixing in some additional content, or writing some original content for your top-selling products, can help increase the originality of your website.

The same concept holds true for *affiliates*. Affiliates are companies that refer consumers to another company to buy a product and in return receive some sort of compensation. An easy example is travel agents who are affiliates for airlines and cruise ships. Often affiliates feel that Google dislikes them. This is not true. There are many affiliate sites that have fantastic user experiences within them. The question affiliates should ask themselves is:

- Should the user have gone directly to the merchant instead of to my site first?
- What did I include on my site to enhance the search experience?

Your landing page should contain unique and relevant content that can be read by Google's bots. However, that is not quite enough to satisfy all of Google's landing page requirements. Transparency to the user about your business and website is also considered.

Transparency

Consumers are increasingly becoming aware of scams, phishing attempts, and privacy issues online. Being transparent with your offers and business information goes a long way toward meeting Google's editorial guidelines and landing page quality, and often increases conversion rates because searchers have a better understanding of your company. For example, if you make a claim in your ad copy, such as free shipping, discounts, or a third-party authorization, put that information on your landing page.

Respect the searcher's computer. Do not alter their browser settings, disable the back button, or attempt to autoinstall software. Violating any of these three rules usually results in your ads quickly becoming disapproved. In addition, autoinstalling software may result in your website being marked as untrusted in some privacy software.

In the United States, privacy policies can be tricky. In unregulated industries, privacy policies are not legally required. However, if you have one, it becomes a legal document. Please note that the other countries have different laws regarding privacy policies and whether they are required.

If you collect personal information, such as email addresses, credit cards, or phone numbers, you must disclose how you use that information. You can either include information on the page or link to your privacy policy. If you collect credit card, bank information, or other sensitive data, the page must be secure.

In addition, do not automatically sign up users for your newsletters if you collect their email address for other purposes, such as sending an e-commerce receipt. Allow a user to choose to receive your newsletter.

If you require registration to view the content on your site, allow someone to see a preview of the information before they are required to register on your website.

Navigation

If the searcher does not find the information they are looking for on the landing page, do they have additional options? In Chapter 6, "Advanced Optimization Techniques," you learned best practices for dedicated landing pages and reasons to include additional navigation to your site from your landing page.

Another reason to add navigational elements is that navigation is a factor in determining landing page quality. Your landing page does not have to have your typical full navigation; however, if the consumer does not find what they are looking for on your landing page, or if they want to learn more about your company, offers, and so forth, can they easily find that information on your website?

Generally, if you have the following links on your landing page, you will meet Google's navigational requirements:

- Homepage
- About us page
- Contact us page
- More about the product or service
- Privacy policy

You should avoid pop-ups on the landing page. Hover items that do not open new windows are currently acceptable. However, adding pop-ups on load or exit often results in disapproved ads or low landing page Quality Scores.

Landing page quality is generally considered to have less weighting in the Quality Score formula compared to some of the other factors such as CTR. However, a low landing page Quality Score can hurt your Quality Score more than any other factor. A low landing page Quality Score may result in your ad not even showing.

Once your landing page has been deemed relevant by Google (which you can see earlier in Figure 7.3), your work is usually done. In 2011, Google started adding additional weight to landing pages in regard to how ads are ranked; however, it is currently a fairly low consideration if the page is deemed relevant. If your page is deemed not relevant, you must work on your landing pages.

There are a few times you will want to work on your landing pages even when Google has deemed your landing pages relevant:

- You have a high average position, other ads are above the organic result, and your ad is never placed there.

- You have a healthy CTR, no other problems are listed in the quality score details, and you cannot improve your ad position.

- You are in high-priced industry (average CPCs above $50) and want to try everything to increase your Quality Scores

Because landing pages take much more work than organization or ad copy writing and testing, you will probably wait until you have exhausted other means of increasing your Quality Score before attempting to change your landing page for Quality Score purposes. You should test your landing pages and layouts to increase your conversion rates, but there is no need to test landing pages in attempts to increase your Quality Score.

Estimating Your First Page Bid

The first page bid is an approximation of what you need to bid for your ad to be shown on page 1. If your bid is below this number, your ad will rarely be shown on page 1. If your bid is above this number, your ad will usually be shown on page 1.

This approximation is based on the exact match version of the keyword. You may find that phrase match and especially broad match may be shown in much higher or lower positions than the exact match version. The search query report, discussed in Chapter 16, "AdWords Reports: How to Extract Actionable Information," will provide insight into these broad and phrase match keywords. The first page bid is more accurate when your campaign is set to only show in one country.

Because each region has different advertisers, each with their own daily budgets that affect how often their ads are shown, even if you bid above the first page bid there may be times when your ad is not displayed on page 1. However, it is a decent number to work from when you are looking to ensure that your ads are receiving exposure.

You can see your estimated top page bid within AdWords as well. This is the approximate CPC it will take for your ads to be displayed above the organic results. You can customize the columns to see both of these numbers within your account or the AdWords Editor (Figure 7.5).

▽ Quality Score	First page bid...	Top of page bid est. (USD)
7	0.15	0.50
7	0.15	0.40
7	0.15	0.60
7	0.08	0.35
5	0.85	2.00
7	2.25	4.00
3	1.75	3.25
5	0.30	0.50
6	0.20	0.80
6	0.20	0.70
3	1.00	1.50
4	0.40	1.25
4	0.40	0.55
7	0.15	0.45
7	1.25	4.25
4	0.45	1.75
5	0.65	1.50
7	0.30	0.85

Figure 7.5 Viewing first page bids in the AdWords Editor

It can be time consuming to look for instances of first page bids within each ad group. The easiest way to determine whether your bids are below the first page bid is to create a keyword report that includes the current bid and first page bid attributes and then download it into Excel. Next, use conditional formatting to locate instances where your maximum CPC is lower than your first page or top of page CPCs.

Note: Excel has a feature called *conditional formatting*, which lets you change the formatting of a cell or column based on particular criteria in that Excel file. One use of conditional formatting is to highlight the current bid column in red if the current bid number is below the first page bid number. This will allow you to quickly find which keyword bids are below the first page bids.

By viewing current bid and first page bids side by side in either Excel or the AdWords reports, you can easily determine where your ad is not receiving page 1 placement.

Just because your current bid is below page 1 does not mean you should raise your bid to the page 1 bid amount. You may have keywords that are not profitable on page 1 and you may therefore be willing to have them not appear on page 1.

When Google determines page 1 bids, they use most of the Quality Score factors listed in the earlier section, "Quality Score Factors for Search." The factors that are not used are the ones that require real-time analysis, such as relevance of actual search query to the ad copy and keyword.

Understanding the Display Network Quality Score

The display network will be analyzed in Chapter 9, "Understanding the Display Network," but there is one detail about the display network that you must understand when you are examining Quality Scores. For the automatic placements that just use keywords to determine where your ads are displayed, Google examines all the keywords within an ad group to determine the ad group's theme. Google then tries to show your ad on websites that match based on that particular theme.

For instance, if you are reading an article on the *New York Times* website about airline travel, you will see a list of travel-based ads that are marked "AdChoices." These ads are served based on the article's content and are not triggered by a user conducting a search.

This means there are two considerations when you are thinking about your display network Quality Score:

- The ad group's theme matters more than individual keywords.
- Your display performance statistics are shown at the ad group level (and ad level), not at the keyword level.

Your display network Quality Score is not shown within your account. There is generally a correlation between good search Quality Scores and strong network placement. However, this is not always true because display advertising is quite different from search advertising.

Your display network Quality Score determines:

- If an ad will be shown on a particular site
- The ad's position on that site

The factors that determine your display network Quality Score are as follows:

The Ad's CTR on That Exact Site and Similar Types of Sites Google examines how an ad performs on specific sites with similar themes to determine if they will show an ad on a site. There are many thousands of sites in the display network, and often your ad has not been shown on a site previously. Therefore, Google uses a combination of how an ad has performed on similar-themed sites and the site where your ad will be displayed to determine whether your ad should be shown on any specific site.

The CTR utilized for the display network will not affect your search CTR or search Quality Score. Often, display network CTRs are much lower than search CTRs. Therefore, the CTRs from these two different networks do not affect each other.

The Relevance of the Ads and Keywords in Each Ad Group to a Particular Website Google examines the keywords within an ad group to determine the ad group's theme. Google also examines the relevance of the ad copy to the website where your ad might be shown. The closer these two items are to the website's theme, the more likely your ad will be shown on that site.

Landing Page Quality The landing page quality used for the display network is the exact same as for the search network described earlier. We examined what makes a quality landing page in the section "Landing Page Quality: Making Your Pages Relevant" earlier in this chapter.

Other Factors The other factors are a catchall of various data points that are similar to the ones for search.

These factors are all you need to use to determine your display network Quality Score. As this Quality Score can be thought of as being kept at the ad group level, when you want to optimize this Quality Score you will either need to reorganize the keywords or write some new ad copy.

These factors are used to determine if an ad is shown across the display network when you have not chosen specific sites to place your ad, an approach known as managed placements. However, when you have chosen specific sites where you want your ad displayed, different factors are used to determine whether your ad will be shown, and where it will be shown, on those sites.

Quality Score for Managed Placements

With managed placements, you choose exactly the sites where you want your ad to be displayed. Since you have chosen these sites, Google does not have to spend as much computing power determining the ad group's theme and whether an ad is appropriate to be shown on a particular site. Therefore, the factors used in Quality Score are different.

If you are bidding CPC (cost per click) on a placement, the two factors used in determining if your ad is shown are:

• The ad's CTR on that exact site and similar types of sites

• Landing page quality

The description of these two factors is the exact same as for the content Quality Score factors described earlier.

When managing placements across the display network, you have an option to pay by CPM (cost per thousand impressions) instead of the usual cost per click. With CPM bidding, Google knows exactly how much they will make when your ad is shown because you are paying for each impression; therefore, they do not need to determine how likely your ad is to be clicked so they can get paid. This means that most of the relevancy factors do not come into play.

For CPM bidding on the display network, the only factor that is used to determine the Quality Score is landing page quality.

Since there are so many places where Google stores and utilizes data to determine if, when, and where your ad should be shown, the first step to optimizing Quality Score is to identify where you want to increase your exposure (and decrease click prices). Once you have figured out where you want to increase exposure, examine the factors that make up the Quality Score for that specific exposure type and work within those variables. (See Chapter 9 for more on managed placements.)

If you are in doubt about working with Quality Scores for search or for display, default to search. Quality Scores play a pivotal role in your placement for search. Quality Scores are used for display, but display optimization can often reach far beyond Quality Scores.

Now that we have looked at how Quality Score is determined for different aspects of your account, let's dig deeper into Google's mantra—relevance.

Creating Highly Relevant Ad Groups

Relevance is a subjective word, and yet being relevant determines much about your account's success. There are four main places where Google attempts to ascertain relevance:

- Keyword to ad copy
- Ad copy to landing page
- Keyword to landing page
- Ad copy and keyword to display network sites

In these four instances, you might not be able to quantify relevance; however, you can conduct exercises and research to help ensure you are coming close to meeting Google's relevance guidelines.

The most time-consuming exercise, and the one that will give your account the best chance of long-term success, is successful account organization. Make no mistake, this organization will take time, but the rewards are worth the effort. Not only will creating tightly themed ad groups where the ad copy is closely related to the keywords lead to a higher Quality Score due to Google's relevancy algorithms, but it will also lead to higher click-through rates, which is the major component in your Quality Score.

To begin, write one highly targeted ad—an ad that does not have to be used within your account but that if a searcher reads it, they could only assume that it describes exactly one service or product. After you write this ad, examine the keywords within that ad group. If the ad copy describes those keywords, that means the keyword is in the correct ad group. If the ad copy does not describe the keyword, the keyword needs to be in a new ad group.

The best organization possible would be to write one ad for one keyword. This way, the keyword and the ad copy are always closely related. However, that is not usually possible due to the restrictions on how many ad groups can be in a campaign and the fact that it would take significantly more time than the vast majority of people have. Therefore, it is much better to have 10 ad groups of 10 keywords that are closely related than one ad group of 100 keywords that are only marginally related.

It is common to see an ad such as:

John's Plumbing Service

Servicing the Chicago area

Call for an appointment today!

to be shown for an ad group with these keywords within it:

- Chicago plumbing
- Plumbing service
- Broken pipes
- Emergency plumbing
- 24-hour plumbing
- Fix shower
- Overflowing toilet
- Saturday plumbing
- Weekend plumbing
- Flooded basement

The common argument is that plumbers offer all of these services; therefore, you need to write only one ad to describe all these keywords. The truth is that while you might have some keywords that are fairly generic (such as plumbing) where this ad copy would serve, the account would be much better served to break this copy into more targeted ad groups.

An emergency plumber is one who is willing to come to a house at 3:00 a.m. on Tuesday. You might want to hire a weekend plumber who will not charge double time for the visit to your house. Instead of using a single ad, consider the ads and keywords shown in Table 7.2.

▶ **Table 7.2** Ads vs. keywords

Ad group	Ad	Keywords
Emergency plumbing	Emergency Plumbing Service	Emergency plumbing
Emergency plumbing	Call 24/7 for immediate service	24-hour plumbing
Emergency plumbing	We will be there in an hour or less	Midnight plumber
Weekend plumbing	Weekend plumbing service	Saturday plumbing
Weekend plumbing	Don't pay high weekend rates	Weekend plumbing
Weekend plumbing	We work all day, every day	Sunday Chicago plumber

This granular grouping of keywords and ad copy will allow you to write ads that truly reflect your keywords. In addition, because your ad groups now contain only a single theme, it is easier to pick (or create) the landing page on your website that best reflects your keywords. Almost every ad group will use a different landing page.

Using the Tilde Search Command to Find Relevant Keywords

There are several advanced search operators that you can string together to find related keywords on a Google search result.

- When you do a search on Google, your keyword is bolded in both ad copy and the natural results.

- When the tilde (~) character prefixes a search on Google, it signals that you want information related to that search query.

- When you use a negative sign in a search query, it signals to Google that you do not want to see that word in the search results.

Therefore, the search query "~roses -roses" tells Google that you want information related to roses but that you do not want to see the word "roses" in your search results. The search results will then bold the next most related keywords, as shown in the following illustration, which in this case are "flowers," "florist," "flower," and "rose."

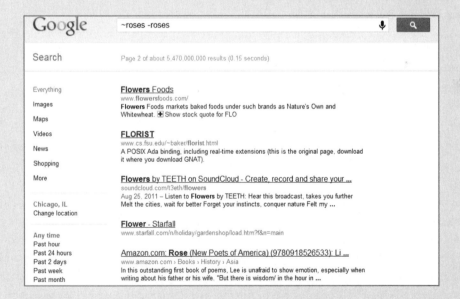

You can continue this search string and continue to add negative search queries to the search to find all of the related keywords. In this example, your next search would be "~roses -roses -flowers -flower -rose."

While not a factor in Quality Score, you may often see higher conversion rates when you use ad copy and landing pages that are closely related to the original search query.

By organizing your account in this manner, it is common to see:

- Higher click-through rates
- Higher relevancy
- Higher Quality Scores
- Higher conversion rates
- Lower cost per lead
- Lower cost per click

Compared to accounts that are organized in the original manner described that contain one ad and a handful of semi-related keywords, this might take some time, but it is some of the best time investment you can make with your account.

What to Do if Your Quality Score Drops

There will be times when your Quality Score may suddenly drop. In these cases, there are some steps you can follow to find the problem and try to fix it.

The very first step is to look at the Quality Score pop-up (refer back to Figure 7.3) to see if Google will let you know what the problem is. However, the problem will not always be listed.

A good corporate practice is to make sure your company has a communication system between your IT and marketing departments. It's possible that IT has launched a new version of the website and has broken your URLs. In this case, you are sending traffic to error pages. If you also have an SEO (search engine optimization) department, make sure there is communication with this department as they might institute mod rewrites, modify a robots.txt file, or make other changes to your website that could affect your Quality Score. Having a record of website changes, and preparing for website changes, can save you many headaches at a later date.

Keep track of and archive your Quality Score data. When you run a report in Google, the Quality Score listed is the number at that exact moment in time. You cannot see previous Quality Scores. You can schedule a report to be automatically run (Figure 7.6). Set up a keyword report that includes your Quality Score to be created on a regular basis (usually weekly) so that you have an archive of your keywords and Quality Scores. Google does not email these reports, but they will email you a notification that the report has been created. You can always navigate to the reports section and download these reports.

Figure 7.6 Schedule reports to be sent to you automatically.

When you find that a Quality Score has dropped, look through your reports to find the time frame where the drop occurred. Once you have isolated the time frame, use the My Change History tool (Figure 7.7) to see what changes were made in your account during that time. You will find times when new destination URLs, ad changes, or campaign changes affected your Quality Score.

Figure 7.7 My Change History tool

If you have yet to turn up a reason for the lower Quality Score, examine the natural search results. Has the keyword changed in search intent? In Chapter 2, "Keyword Research," you saw an example of the word "bleach" having a higher search volume for the anime show than for the cleaning product. There are many examples of news stories, new products, and new services changing the meaning of a word, which could result in changes to that keyword's Quality Score.

The AdWords Editor (featured in Chapter 12) allows you to keep notes associated with data points in your account. Using the AdWords Editor notes helps you keep track of your changes, reasons, and investigations into Quality Score changes.

There will be times when none of these investigations turns up a reason for that change. If the Quality Score box does not list a reason for the low Quality Score, your landing page, keyword, and ad copy should be relevant. In these situations, the best steps to take are the ones you take to improve Quality Score in the first place:

- Check your ad group organization. Can it be more granularly organized?

- Does your CTR vary widely by geography? You can determine this by looking at geographic performance reports (covered in Chapter 11). If so, use geo-targeted campaigns to write more effective ad copy.

- Does your CTR vary widely by time of day, day of week, or even days of the month? If so, try utilizing ad scheduling (see Chapter 13, "Profitable Bid Strategies").

- Test new ads. Determine if a different ad has either a higher CTR or higher relevancy, which will raise Quality Score.

If Google does not give you a reason for the lower Quality Score, that almost always means you need to increase relevancy or CTR. Focus on those two items to see what combinations of ad delivery, ad copy, and keyword usage increase your Quality Score. However, never forget your profit. There may be times when a campaign is highly profitable and you make a business decision that working with lower Quality Scores is acceptable for your account.

Increasing Your Quality Scores

Spending all day looking for low Quality Scores, clicking on the text box to see the detailed Quality Score information, and then trying to reorganize your ad groups or write new ad copy can be a daunting task. There is a more efficient way to spend your time by isolating the problem areas:

1. Run a keyword report that includes at least these six columns:
   - Campaign
   - Ad group
   - Keyword
   - Cost
   - Quality Score
   - Impressions
2. Once you become familiar with this method, you may wish to add conversion data to the process.
3. After you have run the report, export the data into Excel.
4. Create a pivot table using your keyword report as the data source.

With pivot tables, you can choose to see the average Quality Score of an ad group. However, when you look at the average Quality Score by ad group, each keyword is given the same weight regardless of clicks and impressions. For instance, if your ad group contained these statistics:

Keyword	Impressions	Quality Score
Keyword 1	1000	4
Keyword 2	10	7
Keyword 3	1	10

the average Quality Score of this ad group would be 7—that is, $(4 + 7 + 10) \div 3$.

However, if you weighted the Quality Score of this ad group by impressions, you would have a much different picture. If you take a keyword's impressions multiplied by its Quality Score, add these numbers together for all keywords within the ad group, and then divide by the ad group's total impressions:

$$(1000 \times 4) + (10 \times 7) + (1 \times 10) \div 1011$$

you would see that this ad group really has a Quality Score of 4.03, not 7.

The reason to work with the weighted average is that you are going to create a pivot table that will let you find places where you have low Quality Scores and high spends. Therefore, once you have your keyword report imported into Excel, add one more column labeled QS * Impressions. To populate this column, create a formula that multiplies the keyword's Quality Score by its impressions.

Note: Tools are available that will do all of this analysis for you, and even go a step beyond and put these ad groups in order of importance. One I created, called the Quality Score Analyzer (`http://certifiedknowledge.org/membership-information/ppc-tools/quality-score-analyzer/`), uses algorithms to find the best places to optimize your Quality Scores based on impression, normalized Quality Score, and spend data.

Now create the pivot table. Once the pivot table is created, use ad groups as the rows, and Sum of Impressions, Sum of QS * Impressions, and Sum of Cost as the columns.

Finally, create a column for real Quality Score where you look at the weighted average. All you need to do is divide the Sum of QS * Impressions by Sum of Impressions. This will create a column that shows you your real Quality Score. When you are done, you should have a pivot table that looks like Figure 7.8. In some Excel configurations, you cannot create a formula that utilizes pivot table data. Therefore, copy and paste the pivot table columns you want to work with (such as Sum of QS * Impressions and Sum of Impressions) and paste them as values only; then use these values-only columns when you write the real Quality Score column's formula.

Figure 7.8 Pivot table with real Quality Score and cost data

What you want to look for is ad groups with both high spends and low Quality Scores. In Figure 7.8, Ad Group 9 has the highest spend and the lowest Quality Score. That is the best ad group for you to spend your time optimizing. As you become more familiar with pivot tables, you can add additional data points such as conversions or ROAS (return on ad spend) to the table. This table will not tell you what to do. It will present summary information that should be easy to analyze to find a starting place for your optimization. Looking at ad group data is easier than looking at tens of thousands of keyword Quality Scores.

Once you have found ad groups with high spends and low Quality Scores, navigate to these ad groups in your AdWords account and click on the dialog boxes (Figure 7.3) to see what the problems are with those keywords.

Healthy Quality Score Accounts

When you have so many keywords, some with low-quality scores, some with high-quality scores, others with high CPAs, and others that are barely making money—how do you determine the Quality Score of your overall account?

There is another way of using pivot table data to see a quick snapshot of an account. Instead of examining ad groups, look at the number of impressions by each Quality Score number (Figure 7.9).

Quality Score	Sum of Impressions	Count of Keyword	Percentage Impressions	CTR
1	2767	2	0.07%	0.9%
2	119895	194	3.15%	0.8%
3	415980	1360	10.92%	1.1%
4	742971	10714	19.51%	1.8%
5	529640	21919	13.91%	2.9%
6	759986	41011	19.95%	4.2%
7	1212056	130020	31.82%	8.1%
8	1416	3071	0.04%	6.2%
9	1567	1907	0.04%	17.4%
10	22407	8897	0.59%	22.9%
Total	3808685	219095	100.00%	

Figure 7.9 Quality Score impressions for an account

You want roughly 70 percent of your impressions to be Quality Score 7 or higher. Google makes money based on impressions, not keywords, so the impressions are more important than the number of keywords. In the case of this account, the percentage of keywords that are Quality Score 7 or higher is under 33 percent; therefore, they need to be more aggressive in trying to increase their Quality Scores.

If this account had 80 percent of their impressions at Quality Score 7 or higher, they could easily keep some low Quality Score keywords in their account without worrying about how that keyword would affect their account.

It is also common to see a trend between CTR and Quality Score. In Figure 7.9, with the exception of the Quality Score 8 keywords (that only have 0.04 percent of the account's impressions), there is a clear correlation between CTR and Quality Score.

If in doubt about Quality Score optimization—assuming it's not the landing page—try to increase your CTR.

Pivot tables are so useful that you will use them in other chapters when there are too many data points to find meaning. Instead, you can summarize the data, find the weaknesses, and then investigate and optimize the ad groups.

Quality Score FAQs

There are a handful of questions that always present themselves when Quality Score is being discussed.

What happens if a keyword or ad is paused or deleted? When a keyword or ad copy is paused or deleted, it does not accrue impressions. If no data is being collected, this ad copy or keyword does not currently affect your Quality Score.

Can I save this keyword? If you have a keyword that has not done well for you but you believe in it and want to run it, then, yes, you can save it. Most recent history matters more than all-time history. If you have a problem keyword, do this:

1. Delete it everywhere in your account. This will help you isolate its appearance.
2. Create a new ad group with just that keyword.
3. Write a few highly targeted ads for just that keyword, and send the traffic to a relevant landing page.

It will take some work, but if the keyword is relevant to your business, you should be able to make it work.

When reorganizing my account, what keywords should I move? If a keyword is performing in your account, do not move it. When you move a keyword, it needs to build up a new history in the new ad group. Instead, always move low-performing keywords to new ad groups.

Can't I just buy my way out of trouble? Relevancy trumps money at Google. There are times when you can buy your way to the top with enough money if your landing page and ad copy are somewhat relevant. If they are completely irrelevant, your dollars will not help you. Spend your money on creating a more relevant experience on your website and writing appropriate ads. You will find much better success in this manner.

I resumed a paused keyword and it dropped in position and Quality Score; what happened? Pausing and resuming keywords or ad copy does not affect your Quality Score. Pausing campaigns will not affect your Quality Score. It is not uncommon to see new competitors enter the market, changes in keyword meanings that change searcher intent, and changes in Quality Score formulas occur over time. When you resume a keyword, it may drop in position due to the new competitors driving up the keyword price or a new Quality Score formula being released.

How do I get my ad above the natural search results? Sometimes you will see no ads above the search results, and other times you may see several ads (Figure 7.10) in that same spot. There are two things that need to happen for your ads to show in the top spot:

1. Google examines a keyword for commercial intent and how often that keyword results in clicks (and some other secret sauces), and determines how many ads they might show in these premium positions.

2. Assuming Google has decided to show at least one ad in the premium position, they look at your Max CPC and Quality Score.

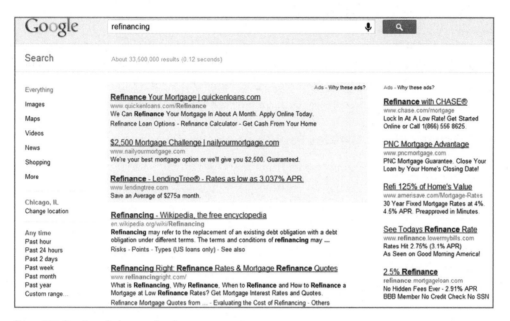

Figure 7.10 Premium ads shown on Google

Your Quality Score is held to a higher standard than normal and must meet certain minimum guidelines for your ad to be shown in these top positions. If your keyword meets the minimum Quality Score guidelines, Google examines your Max CPC. If the combination of your Max CPC and Quality Score are high enough, your ad can be shown in the top spot.

If your Quality Score and CPC do not meet their minimum requirements to be shown in the top position, and your competitor's ad in a lower position does meet those requirements, Google may leapfrog your competitor's ad over yours and display it in the premium position.

How often is Quality Score updated? Google currently updates Quality Score in regard to click-through rate every day. Google updates Quality Score in regard to relevancy about once per week. Google updates landing page data even less frequently.

Google crawls landing pages on occasion; the more traffic you receive, the more often your site is crawled. When your landing page changes have been processed, the changes should be reflected within your account the next time Quality Score is updated.

Google updates the Quality Score algorithm about once per month. These are slight tweaks to the algorithm that may or may not affect your account.

Quality Score was created to ensure that Google shows searchers relevant ads and sends those searchers to websites that help them find the answers to their search queries. While there are some factors and rules that can be quantified to help you optimize your keywords for higher Quality Scores, always keep the searcher in mind when making changes to your ad copy and landing pages.

Google tries to show the most appropriate ads to each searcher, but the searchers also vote by clicking on your ads. As click-through rate is the highest weighted factor in determining Quality Score, those clicks ultimately decide if your keywords will receive high Quality Scores.

Best Practices for Optimizing Quality Scores

Quality Score is one of the most important numbers you can understand and optimize in your account. While the number can seem ambiguous to work with, once you understand these principles, it is a number that can be quantified and improved.

- To increase your ad rank, you either need to raise your bid or increase your Quality Score.
  - If you have a low Quality Score, you should optimize your Quality Score instead of raising bids.
  - If your Quality Score is high, you need to raise your maximum CPC. When raising your maximum CPC, always make sure the new bid does not make your keyword unprofitable.
- It is essential that you create granular ad groups with closely related keywords and ad copy.
- To make your landing page relevant, make sure it possesses the following four attributes:

  Spiderability Ensure that Google's bots can find and read your landing pages.

  Relevance Your landing page must reflect the keyword or its general theme.

  Transparency Tell the searcher what you will do with their private information.

  Navigation Enable the searcher to navigate to other sections of your website if they do not find what they are looking for on the landing page.
- It is useful to always have your Quality Score displayed in your account and the AdWords Editor so you can easily notice Quality Score changes.
- Look for areas where your first page bid is higher than your maximum CPC. These words receive little exposure, and raising the maximum CPC or optimizing their Quality Score will help raise their ad rank so they appear on page 1.

- Your Quality Score will change over time. This is due to your keywords and ad copy accruing more data from clicks or from Google updating their Quality Score algorithm. Use the My Change History tool, AdWords Editor notes, and report scheduling to keep historical data about your account.

- When trying to increase Quality Scores for search, there are three main steps:

  1. Examine the detailed Quality Score information inside your AdWords account. If you identify a problem there, fix that problem first.

  2. If no problems are listed, examine your ad group's ad copy and keyword organization. Move any unrelated words to a new ad group.

  3. If keywords in the ad group are already closely related, write new ad copy to examine its relevance and click-through rate.

- Your display network Quality Score is not shown by Google. However, you can still optimize your display network Quality Score by keeping these two points in mind:

  - The theme of your keywords should match the theme of your landing page and ad copy. Individual keywords on the display network do not matter as much as keywords on the search network. The theme of the keywords within your ad group is the most important factor to consider for content placement.

  - The click-through rate of your ads on a single site or similar types of sites is used in determining whether your ad will show on a site. Do not focus on overall display network CTR—focus on the CTR of sites bringing you valuable traffic (discussed in Chapter 9).

- Use pivot tables to save time in identifying Quality Score problem areas.

By following these principles, you should be able to track your Quality Scores and changes over time. Then, when you find areas that can be improved, you can improve your Quality Score, which will lead to higher ad position or a decrease in cost per click.

Up to this point in the book, I have primarily focused on text ads and the search network. In the next chapter, I will cover some of the additional ad types found in Google AdWords, such as video and image ads, which are shown not on search but across the display network.

Beyond Text: Image, Video, and Mobile Ads

Mobile usage has been on the rise for several years and is a significant challenge for all web developers. You can use available techniques to reach and engage this mobile audience. Google AdWords also supports several types of ads that enable you to reach desktop users in new ways. You can use rich media (such as video, interactive, or image) to boost your campaign and increase clicks to your site and brand recall.

Building image or video ads can be costly and time consuming. This chapter examines the Google tool that allows you to build rich media ads within the AdWords interface, saving you time and money.

This chapter focuses on building additional ad types, and then the following two chapters discuss places to utilize these ads in your AdWords display campaigns.

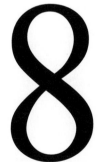

Chapter Contents

Beyond the desktop: creating mobile ads
Beyond static text: creating rich media ads
Using Google's Display Ad Builder
Best practices for employing image, video, and mobile ads

Beyond the Desktop: Creating Mobile Ads

Mobile users have different needs than people on a desktop computer. They often want different information when they are out in the community than when they are at home or in the office. For example, if someone searches for the brand Best Buy while on the computer, they may be looking for an actual location, to purchase an item, or for some price comparison. If that same user is looking up Best Buy on a mobile phone, the searcher is most likely not looking to buy an item over the phone (e-commerce activity on mobile devices is still quite low compared to desktops, and much of it occurs in apps and not via browsers). On a phone, it is more likely that the user is either comparing prices or trying to find the nearest location. In this case, the landing pages could be completely different for the mobile search versus the desktop search.

The desktop search will take someone to Best Buy's main website, where the user can decide where to go on the site. For a mobile phone user, waiting for a site to load and then trying to search throughout a website can be a frustrating experience. Sending the mobile user to a landing page that has driving directions or location lookups for the nearest locations as a primary action, and then viewing products as a secondary action, can lead to a higher user engagement for that mobile site.

As another example, someone searching for a locksmith on a desktop computer might want to know more about locks, pricing options, redoing the locks on their front door, or maybe adding an alarm system to their house. You do not know the intent of such a general search. However, if someone is on the phone searching for locksmiths, that user is probably locked out of their car or house. Those two experiences should be met with two different landing pages.

For many businesses, mobile advertising is highly effective. Before starting mobile advertising, first think about the reasons someone might search for your products or services from a mobile phone. Once you have those pieces of information, some of the later decisions you will make in setting up mobile campaigns will be easier.

There are a few ways to reach mobile users with Google AdWords, depending on the user's mobile technology. The sophistication of the user's phone will determine what type of ads they can see and what type of ad you need to create to reach them.

Reaching Smartphone Users

Two types of browsers come installed on mobile phones:

- A full Internet browser, also called a full HTML browser
- A basic browser that does not display entire websites (these browsers rarely support scripts)

The full HTML browser is the type that an iPhone or Android device has. These browsers can support scripts that enable websites to render similarly to what you would see in a desktop browser.

However, cell phone speeds are slower than broadband speeds. Therefore, web elements such as large images, scripts, and so on can take a long time to load. When designing landing pages for smartphone users, keep in mind the total time it will take for your page to load on a mobile device. Most users understand that it takes a few more seconds, but if the page takes too long, these users will navigate back to the search results and visit someone else's website instead of yours.

In addition, not all full HTML browsers support Flash or all web elements. Be careful not to add too many design parameters to mobile landing pages even if the user has a full HTML browser.

Reaching a user on a full Internet browser can be done quite easily. Navigate to your campaign settings screen, where you can specify the networks on which you wish to display your ads. One of the options is Devices (Figure 8.1), where you can choose to display your ad on any of the following:

- Desktop and laptop computers
- Mobile devices with full internet browser
- Tablets with full browsers

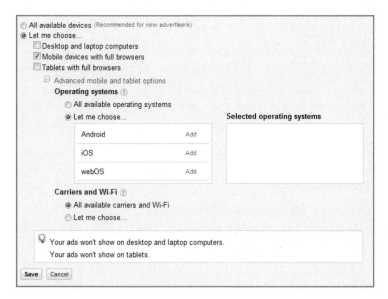

Figure 8.1 AdWords campaign Device settings

You can choose one or multiple options. If you select all the options, your search text ads will be shown to users of any of these devices. Be careful about using that method. If you want to show a different landing page to mobile versus computer users, you will want two campaigns.

Targeting Tablets

You can target tablets independently of mobile devices and computers. If you have a tablet-optimized site, you should create another campaign just for tablet users. If you do not have a tablet-optimized site, then it is usually okay to bundle tablet targeting with laptop and desktop computers. While tablet usage is on the rise, the devices are used much more like laptops than phones.

The first campaign will be your existing campaign that reaches computer users. Duplicate that campaign (when you use the AdWords Editor discussed in Chapter 12, "Save Time and Scale Accounts with the AdWords Editor," duplicating a campaign will take only a few seconds), and then set the new campaign to only be shown on mobile devices. The next step will be to change the landing pages of your ads and keywords in the new mobile campaign to send the users to your mobile landing pages.

Finally, you may wish to do some additional keyword research. Keyword lengths are shorter on mobile devices than on laptops. In the AdWords Keyword Tool (discussed in Chapter 3, "Keyword Tools: Extracting Valuable Data from Google"), you can see keyword data for only mobile devices.

You can target mobile users based on the phone's operating system or the carrier. If you are selling iPhone applications in the United States, you will only want your ad shown to iPhones. If you are selling Android applications, you will want to show your ad on all carriers, but choose to only show your ad on Android devices. A local store using mobile ads to send searchers to driving direction pages should not filter ads by device or carrier and choose all carriers and all devices.

Viewing Your Site's Mobile Usage

You can view your site's current mobile usage in some analytics systems. If you use Google Analytics, navigate to the Advanced Segments of your Google Analytics account. There you can choose to only view mobile visitors, as shown here:

Call Extensions with Smart Phones

If you have enabled the call extension, discussed in Chapter 4, "Writing Compelling Ads," for your smartphone ads, the phone number can also be displayed within the ad copy.

The easiest way to see these ads is with the AdWords preview tool (Figure 8.2), which you can find at https://adwords.google.com/d/AdPreview/.

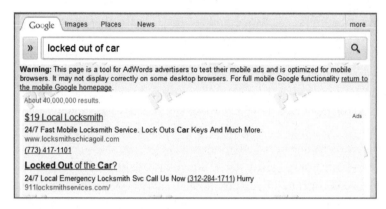

Figure 8.2 Phone numbers on mobile devices

In the top ad, the phone number is displayed just below the ad copy. This is the call extension at work. The searcher can click on the phone number and the phone can initiate a call.

In the second ad, the advertiser placed their phone number within the ad. When you do this on mobile devices, the phone number becomes hyperlinked and if someone clicks on the phone number, you will be charged for the call like normal on a mobile phone.

Mobile Image Ads

I will discuss image ads in-depth later in this chapter, and you will learn how to manage the display network in future chapters. Please note that mobile devices can support image ads as well. The most common image ad sizes for smartphones:

- Small square (200 × 200)
- Square (250 × 250)
- Medium rectangle (300 × 250)

The biggest difference between image ads for smartphones and image ads for desktops (besides the sizes) is that image ads for phones cannot be in Flash. Many high-end phones do not support Flash, so that technology is not allowed for mobile image ads.

Since Google automatically hyperlinks phone numbers in mobile devices, do not waste your precious ad copy space by putting the phone number in the ad copy. Use the call extension to display your phone number, and then use the ad as a call-to-action so the searcher will initiate a call.

Not all users have sophisticated phones with full Internet browsers. To reach these users, you need to utilize Google's mobile ads.

Reaching Other Mobile Users: Google Mobile Ads

Many phones do not have full Internet browsers. These are often called *featured* phones. Featured phones can access the Internet, but they can only view pages that are designed to be rendered on a mobile device.

Because featured phones need specifically created pages, their users do not see the typical text ads on a Google search page. These users only see Google mobile ads on their search pages.

Google mobile ads are created at the ad group level. They are shown only if your keywords within that ad group are triggered. These ads follow all of your typical campaign settings such as location or time-of-day targeting. To create a Google mobile ad, follow these steps:

1. Navigate to the ad group where you wish to create the ad.
2. Click on the Ads tab.
3. Click New Ad.
4. Choose WAP Mobile Ad (Figure 8.3).

Figure 8.3 Choose Mobile Ad to create a new mobile ad.

You should be presented with an ad creation screen (Figure 8.4). Your new ad can be either text or an image. Since mobile screens are smaller than computer monitors, so are the mobile ads.

If you choose to create a text ad, your new ad will only contain two 18-character lines along with a display URL. Mobile text ads must still meet all of the editorial requirements of typical ads, as discussed in Chapter 4.

Mobile image ads are smaller in size than normal image ads. If you click the WAP Image Ad button (as seen in Figure 8.4), you will be presented with an upload button and the image size requirements. Mobile image ads must meet image ad editorial requirements (discussed later in this chapter in the section "Technical and Editorial Requirements for Image Ads").

Figure 8.4 Mobile ad creation wizard

Once you have created the ad, the next step is deciding what options you will present to a user who clicks on your ad. You have three options:

- Send the user to your website

- Initiate a call to your phone number

- Give the user both choices

If you want to send users to your website, your website must be mobile compatible. You cannot send users who click on a mobile ad to a typical HTML-coded website.

An Easy Way to Create Mobile-Compatible Sites

If you want to test out mobile advertising but do not want to pay to have a full website developed, there is an easy way to create a small mobile site to test the traffic.

First, install WordPress, an open source content management system that takes only a few minutes to set up on a server that supports PHP and MySQL.

WordPress supports a large variety of plug-ins that expand the functionality of the content management system (CMS). One of these is WordPress Mobile Edition. Information for the plug-in can be found at `http://certifiedknowledge.org/blog/adwords-retiring-google-mobile-business-pages-quick-mobile-site-creation-guide/`. Install the plug-in.

Lastly, create your landing pages based on what you want a visitor to see, such as phone number or driving directions.

If you are technically minded, you can set up WordPress, install the plug-in, and create some new pages within an hour. And best of all, since it is open source, the entire system is free outside of your hosting fees.

If you do not have a mobile compatible site, or you want users to call you instead of visiting the site, you can choose only to allow visitors to call your business. This is often the best choice for locksmiths, towing companies, and other service-based businesses that prefer phone calls to website visits.

You can give the user the choice of calling or clicking. In this case, the ad will be clickable and there will be a call feature next to the ad for someone to initiate a call to your company.

The last option is to have your ad show across all carriers or only specific carriers. For most companies, you will want to choose all carriers. However, if you are offering services that only certain types of phones can install, you might want to limit your ads to the carriers that support that phone.

Tracking Mobile Conversions

AdWords conversion tracking (covered in Chapter 13, "Profitable Bid Strategies") works with mobile ads; put your conversion tracking script on your mobile site's thank-you pages. However, not all phones support all scripts, so although conversion tracking is supported, the numbers will not be 100 percent accurate.

If you allow users to call you from your mobile ads, it is beneficial to use a separate phone number from your website so you can track how often you receive calls and the quality of those phone calls.

Viewing Google Mobile Ads

If your customers search for your services, products, or business while away from their computers, it can be worth your time to test mobile ads. Seeing what your ads look like if you do not own a phone on each carrier can be difficult, however. The easiest way to view mobile ads is to use Google's mobile ad preview tool (Figure 8.2), which you can access at `https://adwords.google.com/d/AdPreview/`.

While you can do a search on Google Mobile (`www.google.com/m`) in an attempt to see mobile ads, Google rarely shows mobile ads to desktop users, and odds are you will not see your ad at that property.

The other option is to use Firefox plug-ins, such as wmlbrowser (`https://addons.mozilla.org/en-US/firefox/addon/62/`), that make your browser appear to be a mobile device. This is useful for previewing both ads and mobile web pages.

The total inventory for mobile ads is still low. The number of searches on phones is smaller than what occurs on the desktop, but it is steadily increasing. However, often the buy intent is higher on a mobile device. You might comparison shop different locksmiths from a desktop computer, but if you are searching for a locksmith on a mobile device, you probably need a locksmith quickly.

While mobile ads allow you to reach those not on a desktop, Google offers many ad types besides text ads to reach users who are still on their computers. In the next section, you will learn about additional ad types that will increase your company's visibility across the Internet.

Beyond Static Text: Creating Rich Media Ads

AdWords support different ad formats beyond text ads. The simplest of these are *image ads*. Image ads look like your standard banner ads. The second ad format is known as *rich media ads*. Rich media ads are ad formats with which a user can interact, such as video ads.

These additional ad formats only show up on the display network (which will be discussed in depth in the following two chapters). Image and rich media ads are not shown on Google or search partners.

Image and rich media ads are typically paid for the same way you pay for text ads: cost per click. There is an additional feature of AdWords where you can bid cost per thousand impressions (CPM) for the image types, which will be discussed in Chapter 9, "Understanding the Content Network." Although the bidding methodology and setting bids are the exact same for these additional ad formats, it is not uncommon to see slightly higher prices for image ads due to the fact that you need to win the entire ad block for your ad to be shown.

Here are some of the benefits of using image and rich media ads:

- Creating product awareness
- Establishing higher brand recall value
- Associating your brand with a product line
- Introducing new products or services
- Educating consumers on the product
- Creating higher display network CTR
- Increasing search CTR due to brand recognition
- Increasing product awareness
- Moving consumers into the buying funnel

Creating Effective Image Ads

Image ads serve two main purposes. The first use of image ads is to direct traffic to your website. These ads are measured in total clicks, conversions from those clicks, and cost per click.

The second reason to use image ads is to increase awareness of your products or services. These images should match other advertising efforts you are conducting, such as TV, print, or banner ads. Matching online and offline images can help increase your brand's awareness by connecting the consumer's awareness of your brand across channels.

Often the success of image ads is measured in brand lift, as measured by increased searches for your branded keywords or increased CTRs of your search ads. It is not uncommon to see your search CTR rise while your image or banner ads are being displayed across the Web as your brand becomes more recognizable and your site increases in authority.

There is a reason the old adage "A picture is worth a thousand words" has stood the test of time—it is true and can be applied to display ads. Text ads have very little recall. After a consumer sees your text ad, there is little chance they will remember the benefits the product promised. Image ads have much higher recall values. Often a consumer can recall the benefit of an ad that included images. If one of your advertising goals is not just to click but to increase your brand presence or align your company with a product, image ads are much more effective at accomplishing these goals.

The Tenets of Effective Image Ads

Follow these commandments when creating image ads:

Image ads should command attention. Most banner-type ads can be camouflaged in the page. If your ad blends in with the rest of the page, it will be easy for users to ignore the image. Use visuals that stand out from the page and illustrate your point (Figure 8.5).

Figure 8.5 While this ad does many things correctly, the highlighted spine enhances this ad's point of living pain free.

Image ads should be easy to comprehend. Although image ads should contain some text that lets the reader know what you offer, if you have too much text in a small ad your main points will be lost. You should be able to glance at your image ad and know exactly what is being advertised without having to study it.

The first ad's offer (Figure 8.6) is less expensive than the second ad (Figure 8.7). However, the text in Figure 8.6 makes it difficult to quickly comprehend all the information in the ad. Most users will not study your ads before clicking. The information should be clear and concise.

Figure 8.6 Ads that contain too much text are difficult to comprehend.

Figure 8.7 An ad that lacks a call-to-action

Image ads should clearly offer consumers a benefit. Search ads are shown to individuals who are researching your market and are learning the features and benefits of different products and services. Image or banner ads are shown to an individual regardless of their purchase intent. Therefore, showing a clear benefit is essential. In addition, since these individuals may not even be in the buying funnel yet, offering free information or a compelling reason to click is also essential (Figure 8.8). This approach can help you move someone who is unaware of your product into the buying funnel.

Figure 8.8 Offering free information can entice someone into the buying funnel.

Image ads should contain a call-to-action. There is a difference between someone reading your ad and someone clicking on your ad. Without a clear call-to-action, a user will often read the ad, understand the information, but without further instructions will wander back to the content on the page. Make sure there is a clear call-to-action, such as a button that stands out from the rest of the ad. In addition, your callout buttons should contain benefits or call-to-action statements that go beyond just "click here." See Figure 8.9.

Figure 8.9 "Reclaim Your Time" is an orange button that stands out from the mostly blue and silver ad.

If you know the website where your ad will be displayed, you can also direct your message differently to the consumer. For instance, an image ad that displays across various networks needs to have a general offer, such as a free download, free trial, or compelling benefit for the user to visit your website. The biggest reason for these offers is that the user may not be in the buying funnel for your products, and you need to use the image ad to entice them into the buying funnel so you can eventually do business with them.

If the user is on a website that indicates they have entered the buying funnel, you could show them an ad that does not offer a free or low-cost entry point to your services, but instead directs them further into the buying funnel (Figure 8.10).

Figure 8.10 If someone is on a site that contains LCD TV reviews, this is a perfect ad to show them so they enter the buying funnel on your website.

If you know additional information about a user, utilize that information within your ads as well. This ad from Ford (Figure 8.11) shows the user's location and how far a single gallon of gas will take them by incorporating a map program into the ad. This type of ad helps the user visualize exactly the benefit of buying this car.

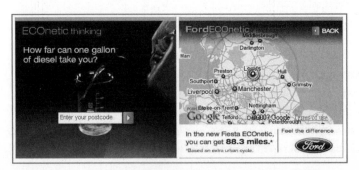

Figure 8.11 A Ford ad that incorporates a map to illustrate a vehicle's gas mileage

These same tenets of effective ads apply to both static and dynamic (such as Flash) image ads. With dynamic ads, the user may not watch the entire ad; therefore the opening and ending images should follow the exact same rules as static ads. However, while any additional animations are being displayed within the ad, feel free to be creative as long as you can keep the user's attention. Do not let an image animate for too long (more than a few seconds) without showing a benefit to the user. Long-running animations might be fun for the graphics department to create, but a user's attention will start to wane after a few seconds.

Technical and Editorial Requirements for Image Ads

Although these guidelines will help you make more effective image ads, there are certain standards your ad must meet before Google will approve your images:

- Image ads must meet all of the standard editorial guidelines for text ads that were covered in Chapter 4.
- Image ads can be in any of these formats:
  - JPG or JPEG
  - GIF
  - SWF (Flash)
  - PNG
- Image and animated ads must be one of the standard Internet Advertising Bureau (IAB) sizes:
  - Mobile leaderboard: 300 × 50
  - Banner: 468 × 60
  - Square: 250 × 250
  - Small square: 200 × 200
  - Leaderboard: 728 × 90
  - Medium rectangle: 300 × 250
  - Large rectangle: 336 × 280
  - Skyscraper: 120 × 600
  - Wide skyscraper: 160 × 600
- All ads can be no larger than 50k in size regardless of the file format.
- Animated ads cannot be longer than 30 seconds.
- Animated GIFs cannot be faster than 5 frames per second.
- Animated flash ads cannot be faster than 20 frames per second.

Note: Google will add a small overlay to your image ad. This overlay will contain a line stating "ads by Google" or "AdChoices" that will link to more information about online advertising. Do not submit ads that have been resized for this overlay—those ads will either be rejected or will have additional whitespace in them.

While your ad must meet all of the editorial requirements for standard ads, there are some additional requirements for image ads. Most of these requirements follow the four tenets of landing pages:

Respect the user's privacy. For instance, you cannot use click tracking in Flash ads.

Do not be obnoxious. An animated ad cannot expand beyond its frame. You cannot use strobing or Flash effects.

Do not trick the user. You cannot mimic computer functions, computer error warnings, etc.

All image ads must be family friendly. Google does not allow adult image ads.

If you would like to see the full details and editorial policies for image ads, please visit Google's editorial policy page at `http://adwords.google.com/support/aw/bin/answer.py?hl=en&answer=176108`.

Image ads can effectively increase the recall rate of your brand, drive traffic to your website, and increase the search volume for your business. However, image ads contain a limited amount of information. If you wish to convey more information to Internet users or tell them a story about your products, video ads are a more effective communication tool.

Developing Profitable Video Ads

The massive increase in broadband penetration and Internet bandwidth around the world has given rise to an increase of video usage, from sites that contain user-generated videos such as YouTube to entire TV programs on Hulu.com.

The rise of video usage has not escaped marketers. Video allows you to both visually and audibly communicate a message to consumers. This increased interaction allows markets to show how their products are used, utilize video testimonials, or create a more traditional message similar to a TV commercial. (An actual TV commercial is rarely useful for video ads unless it is complementary to the TV commercial and you are creating a cross-medium message.)

Here are the three major ways to measure the effectiveness of your video ads:

- The first is by examining how many people clicked on your video ad and then visited your website and conducted business with your company.

- The second is similar to image ads, where you examine the increased searches and CTR of your search campaign on branded terms.

- The third is a combination of the two, where you examine your play rates (the number of people who saw the video ad compared to the number who watched the video) and optimize your account to increase your play rate. Play rate is a useful metric if you are launching a new product or service that currently does not have search volume. The use of video can increase the awareness and benefits of a service.

When you create video ads, you will have access to additional reports that include:

Play Rate The percentage of people who play your video

Average Percent Played The percentage of your video that is being watched

Cost per View How much it costs you each time your video is watched

Frequency How often users are being exposed to your ads

Reach Estimated number of different individuals who have seen your ad

Click-Through Rate The percentage of people who clicked on your ad

Cost per Click The average cost you pay when someone clicks on your ad

You can choose to pay either CPC or CPM with video ads. You are not charged when someone watches the video—you are only charged for the impression or the actual click. I will discuss these two options in Chapter 9.

Video ads look very similar to image ads (Figure 8.12), with the exception that they each contain a play button and video bar at the bottom.

Figure 8.12 A perfect pairing of medium and subject

How to Create Videos That Are Actually Watched

These guidelines will help you get the most out of your video ads:

Utilize a compelling opening image. AdWords video ads do not autoplay. A user has to click the play button to start playing the video. Therefore, the opening image (an image that you choose and upload along with your video ad) must be compelling so that someone will want to watch the video. Using a combination of testing opening images (testing will be discussed in Chapter 15, "Testing Techniques That Will Increase Profits") with the guidelines for creating image ads can help increase your play rates.

With image ads, you want a commercial feel to them. With opening images for video ads, noncommercial images tend to increase play rates. Use a compelling image that is easy to comprehend and that contains a user benefit or call-to-action. Keep commercial items such as prices or shipping out of the image.

Keep videos to the point. A video ad can be up to 2 minutes in length. However, after roughly 30 seconds, a user's attention starts to decrease and you may see a lower percentage of your video being viewed. Try to keep your videos on the shorter side.

Utilize a strong call-to-action. Since a user can stop watching your video at any time, make sure you have a strong call-to-action at multiple points within your video so that the viewer will want to click on the ad to visit your website. Do not have your only call-to-action at the end of the video. If you do, and no one finishes watching the video, your call-to-action will never be seen.

The video is a story, not an ad. Videos that do well usually do not look like advertisements. These videos tell a story, educate the consumer, entertain the watcher, and give them a reason why they need to learn more about your business. Remember, the user can stop watching the video at any time. If your storyline is boring or appears to be a commercial, you will see fewer visitors continuing to interact with your ads. Educate, inform, and entertain your viewers.

Technical and Editorial Requirements for Video Ads

The editorial requirements for video ads are quite simple: Follow the editorial requirements for both text and image ads. To view the latest information about video ad requirements, please see the AdWords page at `http://adwords.google.com/support/aw/bin/static.py?hl=en&topic=1310862&guide=1308145&page=guide.cs&answer=176114`. The technical requirements for video ads are also straightforward:

- The audio cannot be louder than 12 dB.
- The maximum length of the video is 4 minutes.
- Only 300 × 250 and 336 × 280 sizes are supported.
- The opening image cannot be larger than 50k (you can upload this separately from the video).
- The supported formats are:
  - AVI
  - ASF
  - QuickTime
  - Windows Media
  - MP4
  - MPEG
- The suggested frames per second is around 30; however, the minimum is 14.

- A 4:3 aspect ratio is preferred for best viewing. Other aspects may be accepted, but the video may be shown in letterbox format.

- The maximum file size is 75 MB.

Video ads allow you to tell your company's story to its viewers. They can take a viewer who is not in your buying funnel and show them how your business can help them fill a need in their lives. As soon as a viewer thinks you can assist them with a need, they have entered the first steps of the buying funnel: awareness and interest.

The keys to effective AdWords video ads are the opening image that induces someone to watch the video, and then the story itself.

Video ads are a challenge to create. They take time, money, and technical resources. If you want to create video or image ads but do not have the resources to start yet, there is another tool Google offers that can help you get started. The Display Ad Builder is a free tool that lets you create image and interactive ads within Google's interface.

Using Google's Display Ad Builder

Display Ad Builder is a tool that allows you to quickly create image, rich media, and interactive ads. Google has designed a significant number of ad templates. All you need to do is fill in the template's blanks to customize those ads for your own business.

To access Display Ad Builder, navigate to an ad group where you would like to create the ad. Click the Ads tab, and then click New Ad. In the drop-down list, choose Display Ad Builder (Figure 8.13).

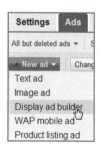

Figure 8.13 Accessing the Display Ad Builder

Once you've chosen to create a new Display Ad Builder ad, you can examine the various templates to find one that fits your needs (Figure 8.14).

One useful feature of the Display Ad Builder is that you can build multiple ad sizes at once. Below the ad template image you will see the available sizes. You do not have to build a different ad for each size. If you build one ad, the same ad can then be saved as all the different image sizes. This is a huge timesaver when you are testing various formats and sizes.

Figure 8.14 Use the Display Ad Builder screen to select an ad design.

After you have chosen an ad size, it is time to build the ad. Building the ad is a straightforward process (see Figure 8.15). Here's all you need to do:

- Fill in the text boxes.
- Choose the colors of that text.
- Choose the font for the text.
- Upload images or logos where applicable.
- Choose your background colors (if you wish to change them from the defaults).
- Choose the display and destination URLs.

Before you save your image, preview the image in all the possible sizes. It is common for the Display Ad Builder to build most of the sizes well, but usually you see one or two sizes that just do not look correct. If you do not like how the tool built the image in certain sizes, uncheck those sizes so that you will not create ads that you do not like.

Note: AdWords launches new templates on a regular basis, and often there are seasonal templates (such as Valentine's Day or Halloween) released before each new holiday. Using the holiday templates can keep your ads fresh and relevant to the current seasons.

Figure 8.15 The Display Ad Builder ad creation screen

Depending on the amount of customization you add to an ad, it can take as little as 5 minutes to build an ad from scratch using this tool. It can be useful to first test different types of images, layouts, color schemes, and sizes before hiring a more expensive designer to perfect your images. First find out what works for your company, and then move to a more polished design step. Of course, you do not have to hire a designer; you can exclusively use the Display Ad Builder templates and still find advertising success.

Other Video Ad Formats

Google offers a few additional video ad formats. The standard video ad format previously discussed is the click to play video ad. If you navigate to the video section of the Display Ad Builder (Figure 8.16), you will see other ad formats that Google supports:

YouTube Video Ads YouTube video ads are displayed on YouTube.com. You can run these ads from either the YouTube ads page (https://ads.youtube.com) or from within your AdWords account. The biggest difference between the two is that if you run them from your YouTube account, your only targeting is by country. If you run these ads from within your AdWords account, the rest of your campaign settings apply.

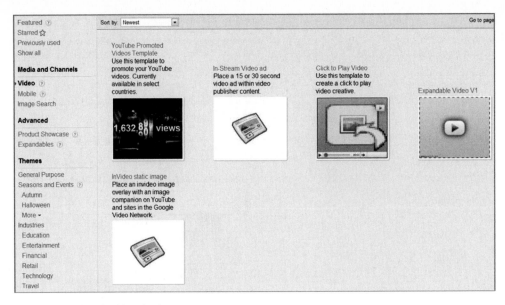

Figure 8.16 Display Ad Builder video formats

YouTube-promoted ads show in the ad results for YouTube. With these ads you will bid on a cost per view (CPV) instead of a cost per click. Therefore, you can receive many views that you will be charged for, but you might not receive traffic to your site.

Your YouTube-promoted videos can be longer than your standard click-to-play video ads; however, all of the other best practices related to building video ads apply to YouTube-promoted video ads.

In-Stream Video Ads In-stream video ads are short videos (maximum of 60 seconds, although 15 is often best since publishers can limit the length of your ads) that are played during someone else's video.

For instance, a publisher may publish their TV news content to the Web. To monetize that content, they will include in-stream video ads within the content. Often these are preroll, but can be included in other parts of the video.

With in-stream video ads, you are only charged when the user clicks on your ad and is taken to your website.

Expandable Video Ads Video content is only served in very specific sizes; however, there are a lot of other ad sizes that publishers employ. To serve video on any ad size, you can use expandable video ads.

These ads look like the standard ad sizes; however, they can be expanded by the user so that your standard video ad can be watched regardless of the initial ad size.

With expandable video ads, you will upload standard banners called *poster images*. These are the images that someone will initially see. You will then upload your video.

If someone expands the poster, they can play your video ad. The best way to think about these ads is to follow the best practices for building video ads, only instead of your opening image being just on the ad, you will also create it in multiple sizes that convinces someone to expand the ad to learn more and watch your video.

In-Video Static Image These ads are small (480 × 70 max) static image ads that are overlaid on top of videos. When someone watches a video, your ad can appear on top of the video while they are watching it. Usually these ads have a close button or are only displayed for 15 seconds of video watching; however, they can be displayed for longer.

With in-video ads, you can also upload a companion banner that may show alongside the video. Not all publishers support companion banners. YouTube does support these banners, so we recommend that you upload a banner that can accompany your in-video images.

Best Practices for Employing Image, Video, and Mobile Ads

Image and rich media ads allow you to target the display network in new and interesting ways. These ads usually have response rates higher than you can receive from text ads. However, mobile users and the display network can be tricky to effectively target and reach your goals.

- When utilizing mobile ads, always consider whether the searcher has different needs than when they are on a desktop so that you send the searcher to the proper place on your website.

- Watch your mobile device usage statistics in Google Analytics to determine whether you need to create a mobile website for your current users.

- If you want to reach all mobile users regardless of their mobile browser type, you need to create mobile ads and ensure your campaigns are set to be shown on mobile devices with full Internet browsers.

- If you do not have a tablet site, you can send these users to your typical desktop site assuming it does not use Flash.

- Use image ads to increase the recall of your brands and to increase the CTR of your display campaigns.

- When using video ads, always test opening images to see which image increases play rate, CTR, and conversion rates.

- Measure the changes to your branded search volume, search CTR, and conversion rates when using rich media ads. Image and video ads can not only increase branded search volume, but they can also improve your search performance metrics.

- Use the Display Ad Builder seasonal templates to take advantage of the changes in search behaviors during holidays.

Image and video ads are only shown on the display network. The display network is significantly different from search. The next two chapters will dive into exactly what the display network is and how to effectively use the network to increase your advertising reach with text, image, and/or video ads.

Understanding the Display Network

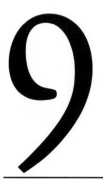

The display network is an often misunderstood aspect of Google AdWords. The display network will show your ads on nonsearch pages, such as news articles. Because search page views are a small percentage of the Web, using the display network can increase your advertising reach tremendously.

However, the display network uses different rules to display your ads—users are in a different mind-set when reading articles compared to when they are searching. Therefore, understanding how the display network works and how to reach your prospects is essential to creating successful display campaigns.

Chapter Contents
What is the display network?
Creating a successful display network campaign
Smart Pricing: Measure Success with Cost Per Conversion
Learning how the display network is performing for you
Managed placements: choosing which display sites display your ads
Best practices for the display network

What Is the Display Network?

When you think of Google, you naturally think of search. After all, it's the premiere search engine on the Web. If someone has to conduct a search before they can view your ad, then your ad is being displayed on Google search or Google search partners.

However, there are many times when someone does not have to conduct a search to see your ads. In these circumstances, your ads are displayed based on the content of the page.

If a person is reading an article on a newspaper site, would it not make sense to show ads based on what the article is about? Unrelated ads are easy to ignore, but when the ad is related to the article, it can help a consumer understand their choices or products and services related to that article.

For instance, if you are on the *New York Times* website reading an article entitled "With New Smartphone, High Hopes for Nokia and Microsoft Union" (Figure 9.1), and the article talks about smartphones and cell networks, would it not make sense to also show ads related to cell phones?

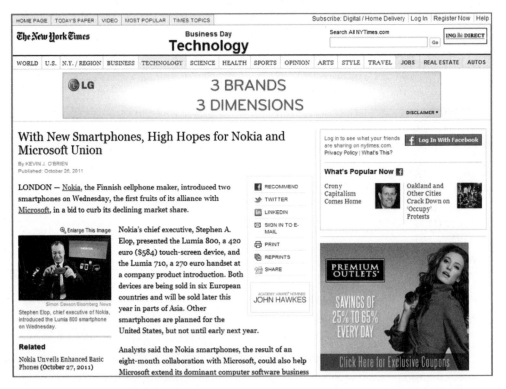

Figure 9.1 *New York Times* article about cellphones

Below this *New York Times* article are ads, like the one shown in Figure 9.2. In general, most ads on content sites likes these are well matched to the article's content.

Figure 9.2 Cell phone–related ads

If you have ever seen "Ads by Google" around the Web, you have seen Google's display ads.

Advantages of the Display Network

There are a finite number of searches conducted every month. That number continues to grow, but search page views are still a small percentage of all web activity. According to numerous studies, by Pew Internet, Nielsen (`http://blog.nielsen.com/nielsenwire/online_mobile/what-americans-do-online-social-media-and-games-dominate-activity/`) and others, search page views make up approximately 3–5 percent of all page views on the Web. Other studies have stated that search page views make up approximately 3–5 percent of consumers' time online.

If a page view is not a search result, it is a content page view. For instance, do you go directly to a news site every morning to read the news? If so, you could be making 20 or 30 content page views and no search page views. Those who go directly to Amazon to read product reviews often make 10 or 20 content page views and no searches. Of course, there are those who combine searches and page views. However, when you want to expand your advertising efforts, there is no larger network than *display advertising*.

Google's display network has a massive reach:

- 4.3 billion daily page views
- Over 1 million content partners
- Reaches 80 percent of Internet users

Individuals who search for a product already have a need in mind. They are conducting a search to find the answer to their need. These individuals are a small percentage of everyone online who could benefit by your product. Generally, these searchers are in the learning or later stages of the buying funnel (Figure 9.3), which is described in detail in Chapter 2, "Keyword Research."

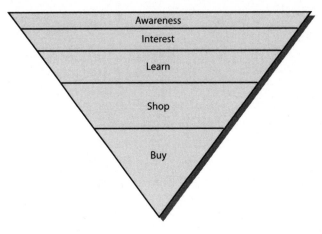

Figure 9.3 The buying funnel

The buying funnel starts with awareness and interest. If no one is aware of your products or services, they do not know enough to search for them. As the display network reaches those who may have a need for your product or service but who are unaware of your offerings, it can introduce many new prospects into the buying funnel.

Another advantage of utilizing Google's display network is that you can use the alternate ad formats covered in Chapter 8, "Beyond Text: Image, Video, and Mobile Ads." Image and video ads are highly visual; combining rich media ads with the display network is a good technique for introducing your company to new prospects who otherwise wouldn't have become aware of what you offer.

Explaining the Display Network

There are numerous ways that your ads can be triggered across the display network. First I will walk through the more common ways in which your ad can be displayed and the jargon.

The most common use of the display network is when you choose keywords and Google matches your ads based on those keywords. You can also just choose a topic that you wish to advertise on, and Google will automatically place your ads on sites that match your topics. When your ad is placed on a site, the site is known as a *placement*.

Another way to use the display network is to pick the individual sites where you want your ads to be displayed. This is known as *placement targeting*.

This topic can be a bit confusing as in one instance you are choosing keywords or topics, and Google is automatically matching you to sites, which is known as placements—or you can choose the site you are on, which is also known as a placement. There are two types of placement jargon that you should be aware of:

Automatic Placements When Google automatically matches you to a placement—you do not explicitly choose it

Managed Placements When you pick the actual site where you want your ad to appear

There are additional ways in which your ads can be shown as well. For instance, you can mix keywords and placements together, an approach known as enhanced targeting. Remarketing allows you to show your ad based on someone's behavior on your website.

Because the display network can be quite complex, I will first examine the basic way of showing your ads, which is based on keywords, and introduce Google's matching technology for automatic placements. Then I will move into managed placements. These two types of targeting set the foundation for how Google matches your ads. The next chapter explores additional ways you can show ads across the display network.

Creating a Successful Display Network Campaign

The way Google matches your display ads with pages in its display network is a three-step process:

1. Google scans a page within their display network (such as the NYTimes.com page displayed earlier) and they assign a theme to that page. There are times when they might only scan a section of a page, because items such as links or other ads do not always help determine the theme of a page.

2. Google scans your ad groups, and based on the keywords or other targeting options set for each ad group, they assign a theme for that ad group.

3. When the content page and your ad group contain the same theme, your ad can be displayed.

This is a simple look at how Google displays content ads; for organization and optimization purposes, there is no need to dive further into the nuances of this ad serving. Instead, I will show you some tools and tips to help refine your organization.

It is important to note that the display network obeys all of your campaign settings, such as location, time of day, or daily budget. Therefore, you can have your display ads only shown to a specific city or only shown at certain times of the day.

Another important note is that Google does not look at any individual keyword within your ad group to determine whether your ad should be shown. In fact, Google does not even look at the match types (other than negative) of your keywords. Google looks at all the keywords combined to create a theme for that ad group. You can only set a display bid at the ad group level.

Display placement is much different from search. With search, each individual keyword and its associated match type is used to determine whether your ad should be shown. In addition, you can set a different bid for each keyword and match type intersection.

Since these two networks (search and display) are so different in how the ads are displayed and bid, it is best to have different search and display campaigns.

Creating Search- and Display-Only Campaigns

To set a campaign to only show on search or on display, navigate to the Settings tab. Under Networks and Devices, click the Edit button and you will be presented with your network and device options (Figure 9.4).

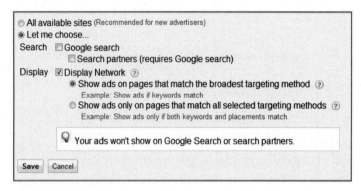

Figure 9.4 Adjust the network settings so your ads only show on search or the display network.

Choose to have your ads shown only on search or only on display and then click the Save button. Now you have a campaign running only on search or display. This will make creating ad groups and setting bids and budgets much easier.

Once you make these changes, it can be useful to include the network type in your campaign name so you know which campaigns are shown on different networks (Figure 9.5).

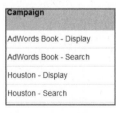

Figure 9.5 Campaign names can help with organization.

> **Note:** You can also make these changes by using the AdWords Editor, which will be addressed in Chapter 12, "Save Time and Scale Accounts with the AdWords Editor." In addition, if you already have existing campaigns and want to change your account structure so that you have both search and display campaigns, there is an easy way to accomplish this with the AdWords Editor.

Ground Rules for Creating Effective Display Network Keyword-Based Ad Groups

Google examines the keywords within an ad group to try to establish the theme of that ad group in order to show it on appropriate pages. There are a few rules when creating keyword-based display ad groups:

Only 50 keywords are examined. Google only looks at 50 keywords within an ad group when determining the theme of that ad group. Never use more than 50 keywords in any display ad group. If you use more than 50, you may not know which 50 Google is using in determining your theme. While you can have up to 50 keywords, often 3–10 is plenty. Google recommends 5–20, but I often find that 20 words are too many and can be confusing to Google's matching technology. I try to limit myself to 12 at the most. It is even okay to have one-word display ad groups.

Match types do not matter. Google does not give more weight to exact match keywords over broad match keywords in determining your ad group's theme. Match types are ignored. Therefore, if you have a keyword with all three match types in a display campaign, you are just wasting your time in adding these additional match types. Ignore match types.

Google takes negative keywords into account. While Google ignores whether a keyword is a broad, phrase, or exact match, they do take into account negative keywords when trying to determine your theme. If there are words that when used in an article signal to you that the article is not being read by your desired audience, you should add them as negative keywords.

For example, let's assume you are marketing an iPhone application. You regularly check the pages that are sending you traffic but are not converting. Over time, you find a pattern that when the words "jailbreak" and "jailbreaking" appear on the page, the traffic does not convert. As jailbreaking an iPhone is a method of unlocking the iPhone that makes the phone incompatible with other features, it turns out these "jailbroken" iPhones can't take advantage of your app; therefore, these clicks do not convert. In this case, you would then add "jailbreak" and "jailbreaking" as negative keywords in the ad group so your ads no longer show up on those pages.

The use of general keywords is acceptable. There are many keywords that are so general you would never want to use them for search. For example, the word "wi-fi" has no stand-alone meaning. That search could refer to wi-fi hotspots, routers, phones, cards, and so forth. However, if general words are paired with other words to define a theme, they are okay to use for display campaigns.

Choosing the Correct Keywords for Your Display Network Ad Groups

A successful display network ad group should contain keywords that together create a theme—words that appear often on types of page(s) where you want your ads to show.

If you are trying to sell TVs, this first example will usually give poor results. Consider an ad group with these keywords:

- TV
- Plasma TV
- Hi-def TV
- Samsung TV
- LED TV
- Television

The preceding ad group could be displayed on a wide variety of sites, such as:

- TV reviews
- TV repair
- TV listings

Those three types of content are quite different, and running the same ad across that variety of sites will usually yield poor results.

Consider an ad group with these keywords:

- Cell phone
- App store
- Wi-Fi
- Bluetooth
- Apple
- iPhone

When you examine any page about the iPhone, these words usually appear on the page. One way to organize your display campaigns is to play the game Taboo with your products. In this game, the "giver" is presented with a card with a primary word on it. The object of the game is to have the giver describe the word on the card so that the other players can guess the word. In addition, there are taboo words on the card that the giver cannot use in trying to describe the product, because they will easily give away the primary word.

> ## Never Use Your Display Campaigns for Search
>
> A common mistake is taking your search campaigns and making them display campaigns, or vice versa. This rarely works because the way AdWords examines your keywords to determine if an ad will be displayed is very different in each network. For instance, say a display ad group has the keyword "apple" in it. This word can help create the theme for the display campaign. However, what does "apple" mean as a keyword? The broad-matched keyword "apple" could show for "pear" (apples and pears are fruits) or "how to grow an orange tree." If you were selling iPhones, being matched to fruit is not going to help your account bring in new customers.

Display organization is similar to the game Taboo. You will have words that if someone sees them they will automatically guess the product (the taboo words). You will have other words that help to describe the product but are not taboo (the words the giver chooses to say).

In the earlier ad group on the iPhone, if you read the words one by one, how long would it take you to guess that an iPhone is being described?

Because the display network works on themes, and there is automated technology involved that does not make qualitative decisions, it can be useful to create several variations of ad groups to see which ones give you the better placements. Let's return to the TV example, where you might have several ad groups to describe the products being sold.

If you specialize in DLP TVs, you would know there are two major types of DLP TVs. One is a projector, and the other is a more typical thin TV set. Projector brightness is measured in lumens. A typical TV review would not use the word "lumens." Therefore, you might start with these ad groups to determine which works best for you:

- DLP TV Ad Group 1:
  - -Projector (negative keyword)
  - DLP TV
  - Digital light processing
  - HDTV
  - 1080p
  - Rear projection
- DLP TV Ad Group 2:
  - DLP TV
  - Digital light processing

- HDTV
- HDMI
- 1080p
- Rear projection
- Rear projector
- -Lumens (negative keyword)
- DLP TV Projector Ad Group:
  - DLP projector
  - Digital light processing
  - HDTV
  - Lumens
  - -Rear (negative keyword)
- DLP TV Projector Ad Group 2:
  - DLP projector
  - HDTV
  - Lumens
  - Distance

The reasons for duplicating the same themes in multiple ad groups is to see which one Google places better based on the keywords being used. It can be useful to try several different word combinations. In the second DLP projector example, the word "distance" is used. That is because many reviews look at the distance a projector can be from a wall and still receive an accurate picture. However, some review sites use the term "lens and throw distance" as one of their standard terms for reviewing all projection devices. Therefore, you could even have another ad group that uses the more specific set of words on that review than just the single word "distance."

The ad groups just listed might receive nice placements on product review pages, which are viewed by someone further along in the buying funnel. Many new hi-def TV buyers research the different types of TVs before deciding which to buy. Therefore, if you wanted your ad to show on pages dedicated to comparing rear projection DLP TVs to DLP projector TVs, you might want a third ad group with these keywords:

- DLP TV
- Projector DLP TV
- Rear projection DLP TV
- Lumens
- Digital light processing
- Distance
- 1080p

Other consumers have decided they want to buy a projector and compare LCD and DLP projectors to see which one they prefer. If you wanted to be on such pages, utilizing a different set of keywords could gather placement on those pages. The LCD vs. DLP Projector ad group might contain the following:

- DLP projector
- LCD projector
- Rainbow effect
- Contrast
- Home theater projectors
- Lens
- Zoom

If you sell all types of TVs, all of these ad groups would be useful to try so you can find which combinations of keywords lead to the best placements and ultimately the highest ROI for the display network. Because different type of sites use their own terminology, it is useful to test multiple combinations of words and even leave all of the ad groups running at once, since they may be shown on different types of pages.

Keyword Density Analysis

Another way to try to find the correct words to use in an ad group is to use a keyword density analyzer (Figure 9.6).

phrase	frequency	words	dispersion
DLP	76	1	6383.5
LCD	55	1	4394.1
TV	44	1	5436.7
color	29	1	6073.8
will	24	1	3247.6
TVS	23	1	6480.1
have	22	1	5364.1
you	21	1	5076.6
DLP TV	21	2	5050.4
can	18	1	6939.1
light	18	1	7579.8
image	17	1	7055.7
than	17	1	6274.2
projection	17	1	5323.6

Tabs: Phrase frequency | Concordance | Wordforms | Summary | Options

Filter

Figure 9.6 Keyword density analyzer by Textanz

Note: A *keyword density analyzer* is a program that examines a page, or set of pages, and tells you the frequency at which words and phrases appear on the pages.

When using a keyword density analyzer, there are a few rules to keep in mind:

Choose the types of pages where you want your ad to be shown. If you want your ads to be shown on review sites, examine the density of the review page. Different words are used in describing a product review versus an editorial page versus a news article. By using words in your ad group that show up on these pages, your ad is more likely to be placed correctly.

Analyze several pages and combine the data before choosing your keywords. Authors vary in writing styles. Different types of sites have different editorial guidelines. If you were to analyze only a single page, your results would be skewed and your placements could suffer. Choose several different pages across multiple websites when you are analyzing the top keywords.

Always use common sense. When you use a density analyzer, you will find instances of common words (you, submit, can, have, etc.) and ad copy from poorly targeted text ads that do not describe your services or goods. Just because a word has a high frequency of occurrences does not mean it is a good word to use in your ad group. Always use common sense in choosing words that create a cohesive theme.

Contextual Targeting Tool

Google has a tool for suggesting display network keywords, known as the Contextual Targeting tool (Figure 9.7).

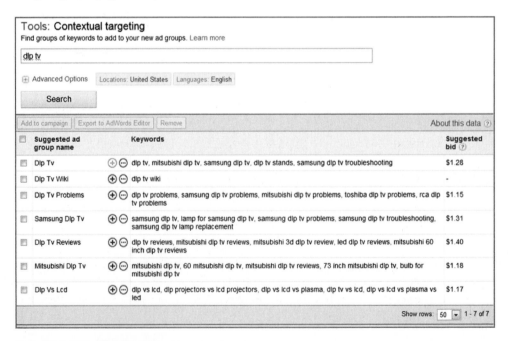

Figure 9.7 Contextual Targeting tool

With this tool you can input a word and Google will give you suggested key-words, groupings, and bids. The quality of the suggestions varies greatly by key-word. Sometimes the tool does a good job of suggesting keywords, but other times its suggested list is fairly poor. As with any tool, use your common sense before using its data.

The best feature of this tool is the suggested bid. It is difficult to determine starting bids across the display network, and this is one of the few tools that can give a fairly accurate (but not absolute) picture of what a click will cost across the entire display network.

The other nice feature of the tool is the suggestion of various keyword groupings that create themes you might wish to advertise on or to use as potential negative keywords. In Figure 9.7, one of the main ad groups suggested is "Dlp Tv Problems." If you are trying to sell DLP TVs, you probably do not want your ads showing next to articles that contain the details of any problems with these TV sets. Therefore, the words "problem" and "problems" are good candidates for negative keywords.

Go through the exercises described to choose keywords for each theme. As each ad group should be a complete theme, no single keyword matters as much as the over-all theme. Therefore, while you rarely want to use the same word in different ad groups for search, it is okay for different ad groups to contain some of the same keywords for the display network. For instance, if you sell iPods and iPhones, these two products will not be two different ad groups, but you may have the same keywords (such as "Apple," "MP3," "video," etc.) in different ad groups.

Once you have created a display campaign with tightly themed ad groups, the next step is refining your ad exposure to make sure your ads are only shown on sites where you feel comfortable showing your ads.

Before we jump into reporting, let's first examine success metrics for the display network. The display network is priced differently than search, which means there are different metrics to focus on when optimizing for display campaigns.

Smart Pricing: Measure Success with Cost Per Conversion

In search, Google uses a feature called the AdWords Discounter so that you only pay a penny more than necessary to appear just above the ad below yours. Google uses a dif-ferent set of pricing rules, called *smart pricing*, for the display network.

With smart pricing, Google looks to see if a page is more or less likely to end in a conversion action. If a page is less likely to end with a conversion, Google may dis-count the price of that click. If a click is more likely to turn into a conversion, they may charge more for that click (up to your maximum CPC).

Note: While Google may discount your click prices for the display network, you should set different bids for the display network based on the return of ad spend or what it will cost to reach your marketing goals. You may have ad groups where you are willing to bid more per click than on search. Conversely, you will have ad groups where you are willing to bid less than on search. Do not use the same bid for both networks. If in doubt, using a display bid of 75 percent of your search bid will get you started. For example, if you were willing to pay $1 for a click on search, set your display bid at $0.75.

The smart pricing feature creates a scenario where your conversion rates are not nearly as important as your cost per conversion.

Let's assume for a moment that you sell digital cameras and that your maximum CPC is set to $1. The first site where your ad is shown is an authoritative review site where your ad is shown alongside an article that reviewed the digital camera you are selling. This type of site is far along in the shopping cycle and the traffic is more likely to convert on your website than traffic from other display sites; therefore, you are also going to pay a higher CPC than a less authoritative website. Let's also say that your ad was shown on Johnny's blog alongside a story where he talks about how he used his new digital camera on a trip to Aruba. This site is less commercial in nature and therefore less likely to convert for your products. However, that does not mean you do not want your ad to show on Johnny's blog. The numbers should tell you the story of your ad's effectiveness on each of these two sites (see Table 9.1).

▶ **Table 9.1** Comparison of two sites

Metrics	Authoritative review site	Johnny's blog
Clicks	100	100
CPC	$1	$0.25
Total Cost	$100	$25
Conversions	10	5
Conversion Rate	10%	5%
Cost per Conversion	$10	$5

In this scenario, Johnny's blog has half the conversion rate of the review site (5 percent vs. 10 percent). However, because you are paying significantly less per click ($0.25 vs. $1), Johnny's blog has a better cost per conversion ($5 vs. $10). You make more profit from a visitor to Johnny's blog instead of a visitor to the review site.

Each site has different types of users and will therefore send different types of traffic. You may see large differences in CPC and conversion rate for each website where your ad is shown. However, conversion rates and CPC are not nearly as important as cost per conversion when examining success for the display network.

Once your ads have some exposure across the display network, you should examine the websites where your ad is being shown to determine where you are receiving both good and bad returns.

After your ads have run for a while and accrued enough data for you to make sound decisions, it is time to run AdWords reports and fine-tune your display campaigns based on success metrics.

Learning How the Display Network Is Performing for You

Once you have created a display campaign, Google will start to show your ads across the display network. The AdWords display network reaches approximately 80 percent of all Internet users, which means your ads can be placed on a multitude of sites.

While the first step in successful display campaigns is account organization, the second step is measuring what types of sites and categories are sending you traffic so you can refine where your ads are shown.

In this section, I'll assume that you are using the Google AdWords conversion tracker (a system of tracking conversions in your AdWords account that will be discussed in depth in Chapter 13, "Profitable Bid Strategies").

Understanding the Network Reports

Several years ago, it was difficult to optimize for the display network since Google did not show advertisers a list of sites, or metrics, about where their ads were placed. This led to many companies abandoning the display network because the network was so opaque. However, Google has made great strides in the past couple of years to provide marketers with enough metrics to extract value from the display network.

To start finding data about the display network, navigate to the Networks tab inside of your AdWords account (Figure 9.8). Here you can see overall data about the various places where your ads are being shown: search, search partners, and display.

	Clicks	Impr.	CTR	Avg. CPC	Cost	Conv. (1-per-click)	Cost / conv. (1-per-click)	Conv. rate (1-per-click)
Search	4,986,783	282,359,219	1.77%	$0.75	$3,735,721.27	72,709	$42.14	2.46%
Google search	4,000,738	179,267,435	2.23%	$0.74	$2,965,138.30	52,810	$44.82	2.39%
Search partners ⑦	986,045	103,091,784	0.96%	$0.78	$770,582.97	19,899	$35.02	2.66%
Display Network	1,688,449	3,164,800,498	0.05%	$0.76	$1,287,383.66	34,568	$36.72	2.12%
▦ Managed placements ⑦ hide details	133,179	251,587,179	0.05%	$0.86	$114,783.06	2,357	$48.70	1.77%
▦ Automatic placements ⑦ show details	1,555,270	2,913,213,319	0.05%	$0.75	$1,172,600.60	32,211	$35.84	2.15%
Total - All networks	6,675,232	3,447,159,717	0.19%	$0.75	$5,023,104.93	107,277	$40.39	2.34%

Tabs: Campaigns | Ad groups | Settings | Ads | Keywords | **Networks** | Audiences | Ad extensions | Auto targets | Dimensions | Topics | ▾

All but deleted managed placements ▾   Filter ▾   Columns ▾   ⬇

Figure 9.8 The Networks tab gives you an overview of your traffic by source.

In the Display Network section of the Networks tab, you will see both managed and automatic placements. Let's concentrate on the automatic section for now, and we will discuss managed placements later in this chapter. Automatic placements are the sites where Google is automatically showing your ads based on your chosen settings, such as keywords.

On the Networks tab, click Show Details next to the Automatic Placements option to see a list of all the sites where Google has placed your ads (Figure 9.9).

Domain	Campaign	Ad group	Clicks ⑦	Impr. ⑦	CTR ⑦	Avg. CPC ⑦	Cost	Conv. (1-per-click) ⑦	Cost / conv. (1-per-click) ⑦	Conv. rate (1-per-click) ⑦
Total - all automatic placements			1,555,270	2,913,213,319	0.05%	$0.75	$1,172,600.60	32,211	$35.84	2.15%
aralifestyle.com			11,136	1,486,288	0.75%	$1.66	$18,432.01	1,087	$16.95	9.76%
youtube.com			159,790	52,176,944	0.31%	$0.38	$60,853.30	569	$106.91	0.36%
howlifeworks.com			4,747	1,030,732	0.46%	$1.97	$9,343.21	439	$21.28	9.25%
myjewishlearning.com			3,639	3,742,835	0.10%	$1.26	$4,596.07	307	$14.97	8.44%
mail.google.com			13,103	31,253,503	0.04%	$1.07	$14,006.38	303	$46.22	2.31%
chinese-tools.com			3,888	2,024,012	0.19%	$1.05	$4,093.12	227	$18.03	5.84%
mail.google.com			16,571	56,410,432	0.03%	$0.55	$9,181.25	224	$40.99	1.35%
israelnationalnews.com			3,089	6,238,386	0.05%	$1.88	$5,804.56	221	$26.26	7.15%
about.com			5,111	14,370,953	0.04%	$0.75	$3,831.68	218	$17.58	4.27%
gmail.com			6,106	24,950,114	0.02%	$0.69	$4,212.71	171	$24.64	2.80%
about.com			2,240	3,671,468	0.06%	$0.79	$1,763.14	162	$10.89	7.23%

Figure 9.9 Viewing automatic placement data

You can click See URL List at the top to view a full list of the URLs where your ad was placed.

Placement Performance Report

The screens that allow you to see your display network data are often called the placement performance reports. This is the old AdWords report name where you could see the data for all the sites sending you traffic. Because the new interface does not have specific names for the screen views, often the old report names are still used to explain the data you are viewing.

The first step is to look at the URLs and click a few of them to see if they are appropriate pages for your ads. If you look at the pages and they are not appropriate for your ads, you need to refine your keyword list or adjust other targeting options to prevent your ads from showing. If you look at the URLs and they are appropriate for what you are selling, it is time to move to the next step of controlling your display campaigns.

Once you see each site's cost per conversion, you can start to control your ad's exposure based on actual metrics. You can change the CPCs by ad group based on your target CPA (cost per action) goals.

In addition, you can either block sites so your ads never show on them again, or add the sites as managed placements so you can set different bids for each site depending on how that individual site converts for you.

First, let's look at how to block your ads from being shown on certain sites or types of content, and then I'll explain how to target a specific site.

Stopping Google from Showing Your Ads on Sites That Do Not Convert

Once you run a placement performance report (the Networks tab data showing where your ads have been shown across the display network), you will have data about what sites are not performing for your campaigns. If you want to block your ad from being shown on certain sites, doing so is a straightforward process.

There are two ways of blocking sites and content with AdWords. The first is within the interface, on the Networks tab. The second is by using the Site and Category Exclusion tool that is available from the Tools menu.

From within the interface, you can click the box next to the site, and then click the Exclude Placements button. This gives you the option to exclude that placement at the ad group or campaign level and put an excluded graphic next to the placement (Figure 9.10).

	Domain	Campaign	Ad group	Clicks
	Manage placement and bid	**Exclude placements**	**See URL list ▾**	**Download**
	Total - all automatic placements			946
☑	gmap-pedometer.com Excluded	San Diego	AdWords	196
☐	google.com	Houston - Display	Help	30
☐	mail.google.com	San Diego	PPC	30

Figure 9.10 Excluding placements using the Networks tab

In addition, you can click the Add Exclusions link under the campaign data and exclude categories. Excluding categories using the Networks tab is faster than using the tool. However, the Networks tab is a unwieldy screen that does not allow for an easy segmentation of the types of information for illustration purposes.

The second way to block placements, and other types of content, is to navigate to the Tools menu in your AdWords account. One of the tools is called Site and Category Exclusion. This tool has several different ways to block traffic from seeing your ad.

When using this tool or choosing to block sites and categories using the Networks tab, you will first choose the campaign where these settings will apply. If you want to block traffic in several campaigns, you will need to enter the information in the tool for each campaign.

Being able to block traffic at the campaign level creates a scenario where you might have one campaign where you are not filtering traffic and another one where you are, so that you can have even greater control in displaying your ads. I will explore this concept further in Chapter 10, "Advanced Display Network Techniques."

Blocking Domains from Showing Your Ads

The first way to control your ad display is by blocking domains from seeing your ads (Figure 9.11). Enter the domains you want to block, and your ad will no longer be shown on those domains.

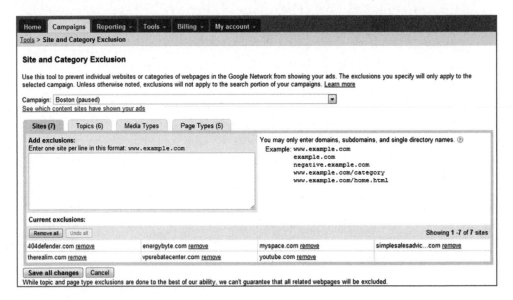

Figure 9.11 Blocking domains from showing your ads

You can block traffic at three levels within a domain:

- Top-level domain name: `example.com`
- First-level subdomain: `widget.example.com`
- Single directory name: `example.com/widget/`

If you block a top-level domain name, your ad could still be shown on a subdomain. Google does not currently support wildcards for blocking subdomains; therefore, if you want to keep your ad from showing on a site and all of its subdomains, you need to enter all the subdomains into the tool.

If you choose to block a single directory, such as `example.com/widget/`, then your ad could be shown on `example.com` or `example.com/redwidgets/`, as those pages do not fall into that exact directory.

Blocking Your Ad from Being Shown Next to Undesirable Content

The second use of this tool is to inform AdWords that you do not want your ad to appear on certain types of content pages. AdWords will attempt to discern the type of content on a page and, if you choose not to have your ads shown on that content, will keep your ad from appearing on those pages.

You can block six types of content (Figure 9.12):

- Crime, policy, and emergency
- Death and tragedy
- Military and international conflict
- Juvenile, gross, and bizarre content
- Profanity and rough language
- Sexually suggestive content

Sites (131)	**Topics**	Media Types	Page Types								

Check one or more of the following topics to exclude related webpages. ⑦

Exclude	Impr.	Clicks	CTR	Cost	Avg. CPC	Avg. CPM	Conversions	Conv. Rate	Cost/Conv.
Conflict & tragedy ⑦									
☐ Crime, police & emergency	0	0	0.00%	$0.00	$0.00	$0.00	0	0.00%	$0.00
☐ Death & tragedy	1	1	100.00%	$0.47	$0.47	$470.00	0	0.00%	$0.00
☐ Military & international conflict	600	2	0.33%	$2.08	$1.04	$3.47	0	0.00%	$0.00
Edgy content ⑦									
☐ Juvenile, gross & bizarre content	687	6	0.87%	$4.83	$0.81	$7.03	0	0.00%	$0.00
☐ Profanity & rough language	2	2	100.00%	$3.59	$1.80	$1,795.00	0	0.00%	$0.00
☐ Sexually suggestive content	529	4	0.76%	$5.33	$1.33	$10.08	0	0.00%	$0.00

Data from the last 48 hours may not be available

◉ Last 7 days ▼
○ Oct ▼ 20 ▼ 2011 ▼ - Oct ▼ 26 ▼ 2011 ▼ [Go]

Figure 9.12 Blocking your ad from showing on specific types of content pages

This is a useful tool for brand protection. If you sell vacation packages, for example, you might not want your ad to be displayed on a news article describing an airline crash. While Google does a good job of classifying these pages and keeping your ad from showing, it is not 100 percent accurate. You might find pages that are misclassified where your ad is not showing or is showing improperly.

Google will display your performance statistics for each of these content sites for the currently selected campaign to help you decide what returns you are receiving on each of the content types that you can block.

Keeping Your Ad Off Video Sites

A publisher can design video ads that show content ads within that video. In addition, users can embed those videos on their own websites; for instance, they might embed a YouTube video on a blog. You can control whether you want to keep your ads from being displayed within this type of content (Figure 9.10):

- If you exclude video, your ad will not be shown within any video.

- If you exclude embedded video, your ad can be shown within the video on a publisher's site, but if users embed the video on their own site, the ad will not be displayed.

Sites (239)	Topics	**Media Types**	Page Types							
Your ads can also appear with online video content to help you reach a vast audience of video viewers. You have the option of excluding this media type by checking one or both boxes below.										
Video content types ⑦										
Exclude	Impr.	Clicks	CTR	Cost	Avg. CPC	Avg. CPM	Conversions	Conv. Rate	Cost/Conv.
☐ Video	77,837	1,118	1.44%	$511.17	$0.46	$6.57	16	1.43%	$31.95
☐ Embedded video	177	1	0.56%	$0.30	$0.30	$1.70	0	0.00%	$0.00

Figure 9.13 Keeping your ad from being displayed within video

Blocking Various Types of Pages from Displaying Your Ad

Lastly, you can block certain types of pages from showing your ad:

- Error pages
- Parked domains
- User-generated content sites

An *error page* is a page that is displayed when a page does not exist. This is a common tactic for Internet service providers (ISPs) to employ. If you attempt to navigate to a domain that does not exist or do a search from your address bar that leads to an error page, the ISP will show a page of ads based on the mistyped URL or search query instead of a 404 (Not Found) error page.

Parked domains are domains that have been purchased, but the content is never developed; instead, all you see is ads when you navigate to these pages. Most of the traffic from parked pages comes from a user mistyping URLs in their browser or typing a domain name into their browser's address bar that does not exist. You can block parked domains or error pages from displaying your ads (Figure 9.14).

Sites (239)	Topics	Media Types	**Page Types**							
There are several page types that can show your ads. You can choose to opt out by checking one or more of the following options. ⑦										
Network types										
Exclude	Impr.	Clicks	CTR	Cost	Avg. CPC	Avg. CPM	Conversions	Conv. Rate	Cost/Conv.
☐ Error pages ⑦	0	0	0.00%	$0.00	$0.00	$0.00	0	0.00%	$0.00
☐ Parked domains ⑦	0	0	0.00%	$0.00	$0.00	$0.00	0	0.00%	$0.00
User-generated content ⑦										
Exclude	Impr.	Clicks	CTR	Cost	Avg. CPC	Avg. CPM	Conversions	Conv. Rate	Cost/Conv.
☐ Forums	0	0	0.00%	$0.00	$0.00	$0.00	0	0.00%	$0.00
☐ Image-sharing pages	29	5	17.24%	$3.20	$0.64	$110.35	0	0.00%	$0.00
☐ Social networks	6,877	102	1.48%	$38.10	$0.37	$5.54	0	0.00%	$0.00
☐ Video-sharing pages	598,052	15,285	2.56%	$5,344.54	$0.35	$8.94	85	0.56%	$62.88
Data from the last 48 hours may not be available				⦿ Last 7 days						
				○ Oct ▾ 20 ▾ 2011 ▾ - Oct ▾ 26 ▾ 2011 ▾ Go						

Figure 9.14 Placement report showing statistics for parked domains and error pages

Finally, you can block your ads from being shown on certain types of *user-generated content sites*. You can keep your ad from being shown on pages such as the following:

Forums Sites where users discuss topics, such as webmasterworld.com

Image-Sharing Pages Pages where users can submit, browse, or download images, such as zooomr.com or Google's Picasa

Social Networks Sites where users can interact with friends, such as Orkut or Facebook

Video-Sharing Pages Pages where users can upload, watch, or download video, such as YouTube

To block page types, check the box next to the type of page where you do not want your ad to be displayed and then save your settings.

Managing Automatic Placements

Follow these steps to create and manage a profitable display network campaign:

1. Create tightly themed ad groups.

2. Collect the data.

3. Examine where Google has placed your ads; click the actual URLs.

4. If you are not happy with the pages where your ads are being placed, choose different sets of keywords within an ad group.

5. Once your ads are being placed on the appropriate pages, set your bids based on your target cost per conversion.

6. When you see your ad on sites that are not converting, block them with the excluded placements feature.

7. If you see categories of content where you do not wish to have your ads placed, use exclusions to block entire types of content or sites from showing your ads.

These steps allow you to advertise on keywords successfully across the display network. However, the display network is vast. There is no way to know in advance all of the pages where your ads can be shown. If you want to have your ads placed only on websites that you choose, or if you want to set a separate bid for various websites, Google has another feature that gives you absolute control, and you can pick and choose exactly which sites will display your ad. This process is known as *managed placement targeting*.

Managed Placements: Choosing Which Display Sites Show Your Ads

The display network contains a vast number of websites where your ad can be shown. Automatic placements are useful for finding websites that are sending you excellent traffic and maximizing your ad's exposure. With managed placements (often called *placement targeting*), you can choose which websites you want to display your ads. If you only use placement targeting, your ads will be shown only on sites that you approve. Chapter 10 explores ways of using a combination of both automatic and managed placements to maximize your exposure.

With placement targeting, you do not need to choose any keywords. Since you are explicitly informing Google where you want your ads to be displayed, Google does not need to match the themes of your keywords to the content of the web page to find matches where your ads will be displayed. There is an advanced method (discussed in Chapter 10) of using keywords with managed placements to further refine your ad targeting.

Placement Tool

The first step in creating managed placements is to find websites where you want your ads to be displayed. The easiest way to find these websites is with Google's Placement tool. You can access this tool by clicking the Add Placements button in the Managed Placement section on the Networks tab, or by clicking the Tools & Analysis tab and choosing the Placement tool (Figure 9.15).

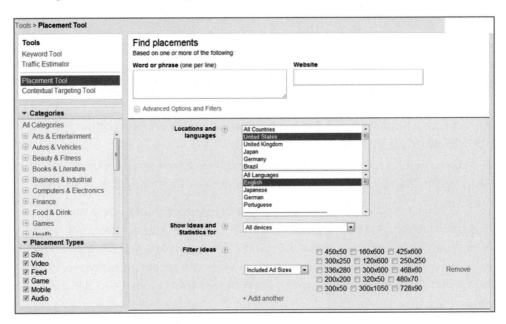

Figure 9.15 Clicking the Placement tool link at the top left shows you the Placement tool.

The goal of the Placement tool is to help you find websites where you want your ad to be displayed. There are several ways to find placements through this tool. The most basic way is to input a set of keywords or websites and then view the results.

You can filter the data based on several criteria:

- Location

- Languages

- Device types (mobile, desktop, etc.)

- Ad sizes

- Ad types (image, text, video, etc.)

- Age demographics

- Gender demographics

- Household education

- Household income

When you filter by demographic items, the majority of visitors on that site will likely match that demographic. However, the demographic targeting is not exact; the sites presented will have people outside your chosen demographic.

Publishers have final control over their site. Some publishers only allow text ads, some allow any ad format, others only have certain sizes available, and others are only on desktops and not mobile devices. It is useful to filter by specific criteria if you are looking for placements that will accept your 250 × 250 video ad.

You can also use the Category selector on the left side of the screen to view sites. With the Category filter, you do not have to use keywords or websites. You can just click through the category and view sites that fit that category (Figure 9.16).

Figure 9.16 Viewing sites by category

Choosing categories is very useful when your keywords can describe multiple ideas.

Placements may not just be on websites. They can also be included in feeds, mobile devices, games, and other places. The Placement Types filter (Figure 9.17) will allow you to filter by placement type.

Figure 9.17 Filtering by placement type

Once you choose your criteria, you will see a list of sites that meet your criteria, along with the placement type, ad specs, and daily impressions. You can hover over any of the icons to see the ad sizes and formats that are accepted (Figure 9.18).

Note: Some websites publish *Really Simple Syndication (RSS)* feeds. RSS feeds are a standard content format that can be displayed within a feed reader (such as reader.google.com). Feed readers provide an easy way to keep up with news content, and many use them to read articles instead of having the articles delivered via email or visiting websites to read them. Publishers can place ads within feeds. When browsing through websites to show your ads, you may occasionally see *feed placements*. If you choose a feed placement for your ad, your ad will be placed in that publisher's RSS feed.

Placement	Placement Type	Ad Types	Impressions Per Day
nytimes.com	Site		500,000+
nytimes.com	Mobile		100,000 - 500,000
nytimes.com	Feed		10,000 - 100,000
nytimes.com » U.S. & World News Pages,Bottom right	Site		
nytimes.com » Sports Pages,Bottom right	Site		100,000 - 500,000

Image Ads
300x250 (Medium Rectangle)
300x50 (Mobile Leaderboard)
468x60 (Banner)

Figure 9.18 List of sites that fit the search criteria

Some sites have multiple placements. *The New York Times* has more than 100 different placements. This is why it is called managed placement targeting and not website targeting. You are targeting actual ad placements within a site and not necessarily the entire site.

Just like with the AdWords Keyword Tool, when you find a site that you want to advertise on, click the check box next to the site. When you are done collecting sites, save them to an ad group.

If you find a significant number of websites and do not want to add them all to the same ad group, you can export your list to a CSV file. You can then organize the placements in Microsoft Excel, and use the AdWords Editor (discussed in Chapter 12) to import all those placements back into your account.

You may not want to save all your placements to a single ad group. There are ways of organizing placements and ad groups to achieve better results with your placement efforts.

Organizing Placements

When you are creating search keyword ad groups, the ads should be closely related to the keywords. Granular ad groups usually lead to higher click-through and conversion rates.

The same organization can be applied to placement ad groups. Examine the placements where your ads will be shown to create themes for these placements. Then group these different themes into ad groups.

This organization will make your ads more relevant when they appear on placement targeted sites, which should increase both click-through and conversion rates. For instance, if you sold wedding supplies you could start with ad groups such as these:

- Wedding dresses
- Wedding cakes
- Wedding favors
- Wedding flowers
- Wedding pictures

With this organization, you no longer have to write generic ad copy about how your company handles everything related to weddings. You can now tailor your ads to each type of website where your ads will be shown. This strategy will create higher relevancy between your ad, placement, and landing page, which will in turn make your marketing more effective.

By taking this extra step in organizing your placement campaigns, you will find it easier to see not only what sites are converting for you, but which ad groups (or themes) are bringing in revenue.

Choosing CPM or CPC Bidding

With the display network, placements, or keywords, there are several ways you can choose to pay for your ads. The typical method is cost per click or CPA bidding (discussed in Chapter 13). However, if your ad is only shown on the display network, you can choose to pay per impression instead of by click.

Cost per thousand impressions (CPM) is the way most banner ads are purchased on the Web. With CPM bidding, you are informing Google how much you want to pay for a thousand impressions. As with CPC bidding, you could pay less than your bid amount, but you will not pay more.

With CPM bidding, your goal is not just traffic to your website—your goal is also to increase the recognition of your brand, products, and services. It is not uncommon to see a company buy banner ads and then see an increase in search volume for their company's name or products.

Since you are paying for an impression, you need to make sure each impression is worth your marketing dollars. Therefore, always use a visual ad when bidding CPM. Text ads have little recall value, and bidding CPM on a text ad is a waste of money. If you decide to bid CPM, make sure that you are using image or video ads.

Every time your ad shows, you pay for an impression. It does not matter if a user sees your ad or not—if the ad appears, you pay. So be careful about buying CPM ads on sites where users are highly engaged in the content, or where the site generates many page views but very little time on each page. Here are some examples:

- Forum sites
- Image-sharing sites
- Social networks
- Ads below the fold

Blocking Below-the-Fold Inventory

You can access a single large list of all possible content type exclusions using the Networks tab, from the campaign exclusion list. This will list all possible exclusions but in an uncategorized list, so using the Site and Category Exclusion tool is often easier.

However, there are two additional exclusions that are only found in this list and not in the regular blocking tools: Non-Ad Planner 1000 (the Ad Planner will be covered in Chapter 10) and below-the-fold inventory. If you are going to buy CPM at a premium bid level, block below-the-fold inventory. If you are going to bid less for below the fold inventory, then do not block it.

This does not mean you should not buy CPM ads below the fold or on a social network site. What you should take away is that those impressions may be worth less to you, and therefore, you may want to bid lower on those individual websites. CPM bids start at $0.25 for 1,000 impressions.

Before you can bid CPM, the campaign must be set to only appear on the display network. Once you have enabled a campaign to be shown on display only, when you examine your bidding options in your campaign settings you will now have an additional option to bid CPM (Figure 9.19).

 Note: A campaign can have only one bidding type associated with it. You cannot have one ad group in a campaign that bids based on impressions and another ad group within the same campaign that uses cost per click bidding.

Figure 9.19 Enabling CPM bidding in the campaign settings

With CPM bids, you will first set a bid at the ad group level. This is the default bid that all new placements will receive. You can adjust this bid either higher or lower for each placement.

When using CPM ads, you are generally trying to raise the awareness of your products, services, or brand. Therefore, your ads should not contain specifics, such as prices. They should be memorable and easy to recall. If you want to add a call-to-action, do not make it commercial in nature. Instead, use a call-to-action that lets consumers know that you will teach them valuable information.

CPC bidding gives you more control of your spending each time someone visits your website. If you want to examine the cost per conversion for an ad group or placement and then set a bid based on those metrics, you should use CPC or CPA bidding. If you are using text ads, do not use CPM bidding. In cases where you are unsure of which bidding type to use, start with CPC bidding, since you should have more experience with it because that is the primary method that AdWords utilizes.

In general, if you want to control costs, use CPC or CPA bidding. If you want to maximize your exposure, CPM bidding is more effective. Once you have created a placement ad group and chosen the bidding type for the campaign where that ad group resides, it is time to manage the bids for each of those placements.

Ongoing Management of Managed Placement Ad Groups

Once you have created a managed placement ad group, you can manage bids, pause, resume, or delete each individual placement. Your ad group will show the same statistics you can view in keyword ad groups, except that the data will be for each placement (Figure 9.20). In the ad group or campaign, navigate to the Networks tab, and click Show Details next to Managed Placements.

Begin by viewing the conversion statistics next to the placement within the interface, or run a placement report. Once you have the data, set bids based on your goals (I will discuss bidding in Chapter 13) for each placement.

If your goal is to bid by ROI for each placement, which is a similar goal to keyword bidding, use the same techniques for determining and setting these bids. Your goal might be to maximize video plays. In that case, you can run a report to examine the play rate for various placements and adjust your bids appropriately.

Content: managed placements				
+ Add placements	Edit	Change status... ▾	See URL list... ▾	More actions
		Placement	Ad group	Status	Max. CPM
☐	◉	washingtontimes.com	DC Placements	Eligible	$10.00
☐	◉	wsj.com	DC Placements	Eligible	$8.00
☐	‖	linkedin.com	DC Placements	Paused	$9.37
☐	‖	manta.com::Company Porofiles,Middle right	DC Placements	Paused	$0.25
☐	◉	nytimes.com::U.S. & World News Pages,Bottom right	DC Placements	Eligible	$8.23
☐	◉	nytimes.com::Technolog Pages,Bottom right	DC Placements	Eligible	$7.35
☐	◉	businessweek.com::Tec locations	DC Placements	Eligible	$9.21
☐	◉	cnn.com::technology article,Bottom right	DC Placements	Eligible	$6.54

Figure 9.20 Managing CPM placement bids

If your goal is to maximize the total number of people who are seeing your ads, it can be useful to limit the number of times any single user can see your ad. You can accomplish this by frequency capping.

Using Frequency Capping to Limit the Number of Times a User Sees Your Ads

There are times you might want to limit the number of times a unique user views your ads. If you are trying to reach the most users possible, especially if you are bidding by CPM, you might only want to pay for a single person to see your ad a few times. This is called *frequency capping.* If you limit the number of times a single user sees your CPM ads, you will not use your budget on only a handful of users but instead spread out your budget among many users.

Frequency capping only works to control the exposure of your display ads. However, it applies to both keyword and placement display exposure.

You cap impressions by both a time frame (day, week, or month) and at an ad group or ad copy level. To enable frequency capping, navigate to the Campaign Settings tab and click Edit next to the frequency capping text. You will be presented with a screen where you can select the maximum number of impressions, a time frame, and the data (ad group or ad copy) where you want to cap impressions (Figure 9.21).

Figure 9.21 Frequency capping interface in your campaign settings

For CPC bidding, frequency capping is usually not necessary, as you are only paying on a per-click basis. The only reasons to worry about frequency capping with CPC ads is if you are having display quality score issues, or you just want to make sure you are not annoying people with showing your ad too often. Frequency capping is most commonly used in CPM campaigns or in remarketing (discussed in Chapter 10). Why pay for one person to see your ad a thousand times? Instead, pay for someone to see it a few times and then use the rest of your budget to reach more total users.

Best Practices for the Display Network

Running your ads across the display network can help increase exposure for your business by increasing your reach, reaching nonsearchers, and introducing your product and services to start someone down the buying funnel. In other words, the reach of the display network is so vast that you can find many new customers on websites who will never search for your products. By implementing display campaigns, you can introduce your products to a significant number of web surfers who have never heard of your business. The following is a recap of critical points to remember when utilizing the display network:

- You should always run a campaign that is either based on display or search. Never combine search and display in a single campaign.

- Choose groups of keywords that create a theme. Use 3–12 keywords for most of your ad groups. One-word ad groups are okay, but never use more than 50 keywords per ad group. Although match types are ignored, negative keywords are used by Google in determining your theme.

- It is okay to use general keywords on the display network. It is also okay to have the same keyword in multiple ad groups in a display-only campaign.

- Focus on cost per conversion. With smart pricing, the click price and conversion rates are not nearly as important as cost per conversion.

- Become familiar with the Networks tab. This information will give you insight into your metrics for every site where your ad is displayed.

- When you find sites that do not meet your performance goals, exclude them from your ad groups or campaigns. Alternatively, you could add that site as a managed placement site and then write ad copy specific to that site or set a bid for that site.

- Use managed placements to reach users on specific websites.

- Use CPM bidding only with rich media or image ads. Usually, you want to use CPM bidding when you are trying to increase awareness of your products and you want someone to see your ad.

- Use CPC or CPA bidding when you want to focus on bidding by cost per conversion or you are only utilizing text ads.
- Break down managed placement ad groups by themes so you can write targeted ads for each site where your ad is displayed.

This chapter only outlined the basics of creating display campaigns. There are ways of structuring your account that can help you take greater advantage of the display network. You can change bids based on the demographics of users viewing your ads, and only serve an ad to those who visited your website but did not convert. In the next chapter, you will dive even further into additional features, placement research, and structure that will help make your display campaigns a success.

Advanced Display Network Techniques

The display network has a dizzying array of options.

You will learn how to target very small audiences and exceptionally large ones. With so many options available, the display network can become unwieldy. You will learn a strategy for managing and organizing the display network.

Remarketing allows you to bring lost customers back to your site. This chapter explores several remarketing techniques that have proven effective.

This chapter wraps up by examining the Doubleclick Ad Planner tool, a free research tool that gives you valuable insight into the users of individual websites.

10

Chapter Contents

Enhancing your display campaigns
Setting different bids by demographics
Remarketing
Topic and interest targeting
Creating scenarios to understand and reach your targeted audience
How to write effective display ads
DoubleClick Ad Planner: free access to expensive data
Best practices for advanced display network usage

Enhancing Your Display Campaigns

In the previous chapter, we showed how you can use placement targeting to put your ad on just a single website. You can also be more specific with larger sites, such as the *New York Times*, and have your placement ad only shown in the business section, for example. However, the specific sections of the *New York Times* can still result in hundreds of thousands of page views per day (Figure 10.1), according to the AdWords Placement tool.

	Placement		Placement Type	Ad Types	Impressions Per Day
☐	☆	nytimes.com	Site		500,000+
☐	☆	nytimes.com	Mobile		100,000 - 500,000
☐	☆	nytimes.com	Feed		10,000 - 100,000
☐	☆	nytimes.com » U.S. & World News Pages,Bottom right	Site		100,000 - 500,000
☐	☆	nytimes.com » Sports Pages,Bottom right	Site		100,000 - 500,000
☐	☆	nytimes.com » NY Region ,Bottom right	Site		10,000 - 100,000
☐	☆	nytimes.com » Art, Dance, TV & Music,Bottom right	Site		10,000 - 100,000

Figure 10.1 *New York Times* estimated daily page views

Although placement targeting is fantastic for sites with a small number of page views, when reaching a large site that has millions of daily page views, your ad could be seen by those outside of your target audience. Enhanced display campaigns allow you to further refine your ad exposure by using both keywords and placements to signal to Google where you would like your ad placed.

Refining Your Display Exposure with Keywords

Each ad group has the ability to house automatic placements, managed placements, and keywords. You control exactly what level of targeting you would like for each ad group.

When you combine both placements and keywords within an ad group, your ad will only be shown to users on the website (or website section) you specify and when the article is related to the keywords you have chosen.

For example, let's assume your company sells a product that helps stockbrokers track breaking news related to their portfolio. In this instance, showing a placement ad in the *New York Times* business section seems like a good idea since many stockbrokers visit those pages each day. However, the business section of the *New York Times* is estimated to have over half a million page views every day (refer back to Figure 10.1).

Instead of showing your ad to anyone reading the business section, you could add keywords to your ad group that are related to stockbrokers. Now someone would have to be in the *New York Times* business section, reading an article that matched your stockbroker keywords, and only then would your ad be displayed.

You can start with either placements or keywords in your ad group. When targeting large numbers of smaller sites, it does not matter which you add first. If you are targeting larger sites, however, first add the placements, and then examine articles on those placement websites so you can add keywords based on the word choices their writers utilize.

For example, let's assume you sell cell phones. Some review sites will use "mobile phone" to describe the product, whereas others may use "cell phone," and yet others will use "cellular phone." By examining a larger site's lexicon, you can use more targeted keywords to make sure your ads are placed correctly.

> **Note:** When choosing keywords so your ad will be displayed correctly on a single site, use a keyword density analyzer, as discussed in Chapter 9, "Understanding the Display Network." However, instead of examining many different pages across the Web, find a handful of articles on the site where you want to see your ad displayed, and only look through the keyword density of those articles when selecting your content keywords.

For our purposes, you will first create an ad group that contains managed placements (Figure 10.2) in the Networks tab of an ad group.

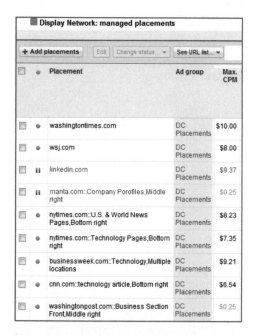

Figure 10.2 Managed placements in an ad group

Next, in the same ad group, click the Keywords tab and create a keyword list (Figure 10.3) using the information from Chapter 9 in the section "Choosing the Correct Keywords for Your Display Network Ad Group."

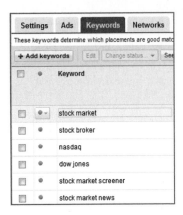

Figure 10.3 Keywords in an ad group

Using both keywords and placements in conjunction with each other can help refine your exposure across the display network so that your ad is only shown to visitors who are on the website you targeted and reading an article related to your keywords.

It is simple to use a combination of keywords and placements, but an additional campaign setting is crucial to understand when you are using placement targeting so that your ad is only displayed on the websites you have selected.

Controlling Your Placement Ad's Display

In your campaign settings, you can define whether you want your ads to only be displayed on sites you choose or the entire display network (Figure 10.4).

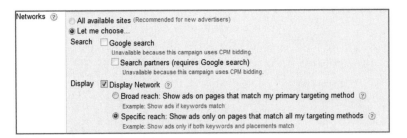

Figure 10.4 Defining where your placement ads are shown

Broad Reach: Show Ads On Pages That Match My Primary Targeting Method

If you choose the first option, Broad Reach: Show Ads On Pages That Match My Primary Targeting Method, your ad can be shown on any site in the display network that matches your keywords, but you can set separate bids for each placement you have chosen (Figure 10.5).

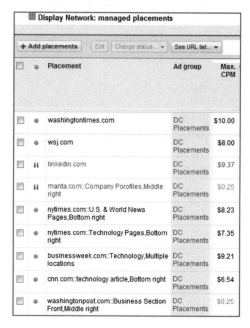

Figure 10.5 Different bids by placement site

When using the option Show Ads On Pages That Match The Broadest Targeting Method, you can set a display network bid for each ad group (Figure 10.6). Within each ad group, you can choose to have placements where you set separate bids.

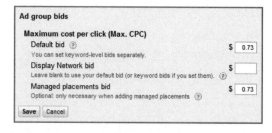

Figure 10.6 Setting the ad group bids

Bidding Types for Display

These screenshots assume you are using max CPC or CPM bidding. However, if you are using one of the other bid methods (discussed in Chapter 13, "Profitable Bid Strategies"), you may see different bid options.

If you have a placement level bid, Google uses that bid. If you have not set one, Google uses the ad group display bid. Google tries to bid at the most specific level based on where you have defined your bids.

If you do not want to manage an entire placement campaign where you might have anywhere from one to thousands of placements, using the display bidding technique can be useful. It will provide you with both display exposure and the ability to set different bids by sites based on their returns.

If you want to have one campaign that is only shown across the display network, and then another campaign where you choose exactly where your ad is shown, the second campaign setting can help you control your ad's exposure.

Specific Reach: Show Ads Only On Pages That Match All My Targeting Methods

The second option in your campaign settings is Specific Reach: Show Ads Only On Pages That Match All My Targeting Methods (refer back to Figure 10.4). When you select this option, your ad is only shown on pages on sites you have chosen and that match your keywords. If you are looking to control your ad exposure to only certain sites, this is a better option. In addition, if you have a display campaign where you are trying to find new sites but once you find them, you want to write specific ads for those sites, then this option gives you more control. You can read more about this in the section "Organizing Your Display Campaigns," later in this chapter.

With Specific Reach: Show Ads Only On Pages That Match All My Targeting Methods, the same bid hierarchy system we discussed earlier will be used in determining your maximum CPC.

Knowing the difference between the two options and selecting the correct one based on your display campaign's organization is crucial to understanding the breadth of your display advertising. Since these options are set at the campaign level, you could have one campaign that uses option 1 and another campaign that uses option 2. We will discuss using both of these options in different campaigns to maximize your content exposure and control later in this chapter.

Optimizing Your Display Campaigns

In the previous chapter, we showed how to block a site from showing your ads. While this is a crucial step in display optimization, it is best to first know if your offer is converting and if your ad is being placed appropriately, before blocking traffic.

The first step to display optimization is ensuring that your ad is being placed on the proper sites. Examine the Networks tab data for placements, and include individual URLs where your ad was shown (Figure 10.7).

Then click some of the URLs to look at the actual pages where your ad has been shown. If these pages are related to your ad group's theme, there is nothing else to do at this step. If the pages do not look relevant to your ad group's theme, you need to change the keywords in the ad group so that your ad is shown on more appropriate pages. Once you change the keywords in an ad group, let the display network accrue some more impressions, and then repeat this step until you are seeing your ads on relevant sites.

Figure 10.7 Examining the Networks tab data for placements

Once your ad is being shown on the proper pages, the second step is to find high-quality sites where your ad has been shown. Look for newspaper sites or sites you recognize by name without having to look them up. These types of sites should be sending you high-quality traffic. If the traffic from these sites is converting, then again, you are done and can move to the next section about display campaign organization.

Understanding Site Quality

Personally, I like to place websites into one of four categories: low-quality, low-traffic, medium-quality, and high-quality sites. I define them as follows:

Low-Quality Sites These are sites that you look at and you just do not want your ad on the site. Often this is automatically generated content, scraper sites, or sites that have more ads than content on them. Feel free to block these immediately, as often they will not convert or do not fit your brand message.

Low-Traffic Sites Usually these are small sites that do not have much traffic and therefore do not send enough traffic to make it worth your time to create specific offers for them.

Medium-Quality Sites These could be local newspapers, for example, or sites in your niche that you are familiar with, but they are not the authority sites in your industry.

High-Quality Sites These sites are either the authority in your niche or sites that everyone knows. These sites have the potential to send large amounts of high-converting traffic.

If the traffic is not converting, your ad copy and landing pages may not be in proper alignment with your keywords. If you find that it's not only high-quality sites that are not converting but that most sites are not converting as well, you need to improve your ad copy, landing pages, or both before it is worthwhile to spend money on the display network or refine your exposure by blocking these sites.

In the case of low-converting traffic, instead of having your ad shown all over the display network and trying to find where you are receiving high-quality traffic, only use placement targeting until you perfect your offer.

Note: A publisher can choose to block an individual advertiser or to not allow placement targeting on their website. If you find sites where you cannot seem to have your ad displayed, it might not be your marketing efforts. There is no way to know if a publisher has blocked your ad from showing.

Choose a handful of high-quality sites in your niche, and only have your ads shown on those sites. You can also run some ad copy and landing pages tests (discussed in Chapter 15, "Testing Techniques That Will Increase Profits") to find what combination of ad copy and landing page converts. Once you have found a combination that works well, it is time to turn on the entire display network again and use the following organizational techniques to refine your exposure over time.

There will also be times when you find that a category of websites is not working for you. For instance, if you are doing well on high-quality sites but local newspapers are not converting, rather than just blocking these sites, you can use an enhanced campaign (the keywords in your ad group and the placements in the local papers) to test different ad copy and landing pages to discover whether some different combination works well on just those types of sites.

You may often see that social networking sites (such as Facebook) perform quite differently than local newspaper sites or forum sites. Therefore, even testing different types of websites together can help you determine whether you are more or less likely to convert the traffic on those sites. The same user is in a different mind-set when on Facebook as opposed to a newspaper site, and that difference in mind-set can make a difference in conversion rates.

Whenever you find good traffic from an individual website or a combination of similar websites that is not converting, your first thought should not be to block these websites from sending you traffic. Your first thought should instead be to try to optimize the ad copy and landing page for that traffic. The more traffic you block, the fewer potential customers your company can have. By trying to convert the traffic with different offers first, and then blocking second, you will constantly be improving your campaigns and finding more total customers.

Organizing Your Display Campaigns

There are two main ways to use the display network to reach your audience:

- List keywords in an ad group and let Google place your ads across sites in the display network that have themes similar to your keywords.

- Target individual websites where you want your ad to be placed with placement targeting (placement also includes keywords plus placements in enhanced campaigns).

The easiest way to block your ad from being shown on a specific website is at the campaign level. Therefore, you can have one campaign where your ad is shown on a website and another campaign where your ad is not shown on that same website. Please note you can block an individual website at the ad group level as well.

By using each of these targeting options—specific managed placements and the more broadly targeted automatic placements—in conjunction with each other, you can start to control the display network so that your ads will meet your company's goals.

Before using this technique, make sure that your offer is converting using the criteria from the previous section, "Optimizing Your Display Campaigns."

The first step is to create two campaigns:

Discovery Campaign The first campaign will contain targeted keywords in each ad group. In your campaign settings, select only the display network for placement with the option Broad Reach: Show Ads On Pages That Match My Primary Targeting Method. Do not have this campaign shown on search. Google will then automatically place your ads across the display network when the theme of your ad group matches the theme of the web page. For our purposes, let's call this a *discovery campaign*. Note that in the AdWords interface, Google refers to these as automatic placements. The goal of this campaign is to use automatic placements to discover sites that are meeting your performance goals.

You will set a daily budget for this account lower than your search campaigns or the next campaign type, the managed placements campaign. You may see limited returns from this campaign (and you might see nice returns); however, as the goal is discovery, your ads will be shown on both sites that do well for you and sites that do not.

Managed Placements Campaign Next, create a second campaign, which we will call a *managed placements campaign*. This campaign is for websites that are meeting your campaign goals. This campaign will also only be targeted to the display network but will use the reach setting Show Ads On Pages That Match The Broadest Targeting Method. When you find a site that does well, move it into the placement campaign. Since these websites are performing, you always want your ad to be shown on these placements.

When you move the site to your managed placements campaign, examine your placement report and set a bid for that specific placement based on the ROI it is bringing your company. Then block this placement from being shown in your discovery campaign. Because you have targeted this site explicitly in your managed placements campaign, you want to utilize your discovery campaign to find new sites that are performing.

This campaign will have a higher budget than the discovery campaign since it only contains websites that have proven they will send your company traffic that meets your goals. You always want your ads to be shown on these websites, and setting a higher daily budget than the discovery campaign can help you sustain this converting traffic.

How Much Data Should I Have Before Blocking Websites?

In Chapter 15, we will discuss statistical significance in performing tests. However, many companies do not wait to acquire statistically significant data before deciding to block websites—and with good reason. There are more websites across the display network than most companies could ever find to place their ads. Thus, it can be easier to quickly block low-performing websites, because your ad will just be shown on another site.

Make sure that you are receiving conversions from high-quality sites. If you are not, you will not be blocking sites appropriately. In addition, if you find categories of websites that are not performing well, use the enhanced campaign techniques described earlier to help convert traffic before you block it.

Low-Traffic Sites If I receive 50 to 100 clicks and no conversions, I usually block these sites. There are enough sites floating around the display network to fill the traffic from these sites. If you look at a site and it does not seem highly related to your offer, feel free to block it with much less data.

Medium-Quality Sites If you have received 200 or more clicks and no conversions, then feel free to block this traffic, assuming you do not see a nonconverting theme, such as newspapers you should test before blocking.

High-Quality Sites If one of these sites is not converting after a few hundred clicks, I like to create an enhanced ad group (keyword plus placement) first to test a different offer. If the site just cannot convert even with offers, feel free to block it. Just remember that blocking high-quality sites can remove many potential customers, so you are better off trying to convert this traffic before blocking it.

The second step is to run a placement performance report (examine the Networks tab's placement data). When you first start using this organization technique, you will not have any websites listed in your placement campaign; therefore, start by examining data from your discovery campaign. Use the data in this report to segment sites into three categories:

- Sites that are not meeting your goals
- Sites where you do not have enough data to make a decision
- Sites that are meeting your goals

When you find sites that are not performing for you, block them in your campaign settings. If you are not receiving the proper returns from a website, you no longer want your ad to be shown on that website.

Using Google Analytics to Find Sites to Block

If you are using Google Analytics, you can see additional data such as bounce rates, conversion rates, and time on site for your placements. I find it is useful to create interaction goals (see the following graphic) and block placements without much data based on how those visitors are interacting with your site. If a site has a 100 percent bounce rate after 20 visitors, either your landing page needs serious work, or the placement will probably will not convert in the future as the traffic is not relevant for you.

If you do not have enough data to make a decision for some sites, do nothing. Let these sites accumulate more data before you decide what to do with them.

When you find sites that are doing well for you, you will want to add them as placements in your managed placements campaign. Since these sites are doing well, ensure that your ad will continue to be shown on these websites.

Before you add a site to your managed placements campaign, first use the Placement tool (Figure 10.8; also discussed in Chapter 9) and type in the URL of the website to see if there is more than one placement available on that website. Smaller websites, or websites that are not easily broken down into categories, may only have single-placement options. In the case of single-placement options, choose that placement. However, if it's a larger site that can be broken down into sections (for instance, the *New York Times* has more than 50 different placement options), you may want to choose only a few of the available placements.

Figure 10.8 Listing URLs in the Placement tool

If you want to be shown on every placement of a site that has multiple-placement opportunities, rather than selecting the entire site choose each individual placement. The reason to add all the smaller placements is that you can set a different bid for each placement even within a website. For instance, you could set a bid of $0.50 for the *New York Times* travel section, a $0.75 bid for the *New York Times* business section, and $1 for the *New York Times* technology section (Figure 10.9).

Figure 10.9 Different bids for different sections of the *New York Times*

In addition, you will want to block these sites from being shown in your discovery campaign. The discovery campaign's purpose is to find new sites to place your ads. If you do not block a site from being shown in an automatic placements discovery campaign, your ad could still be shown on a site that is also listed in the managed placements campaign and it will slow down the process of finding new sites that are performing for you.

Since each placement in the managed placement campaign can have its own bid, calculate the bid based on the returns that site is sending you (more about calculating bids in Chapter 13), and set that as the starting bid. Next, run a placement performance report for the placement campaign and continue to refine bids based on each placement's performance.

Repeat this process to find sites doing well and sites not performing, and then block and add them as necessary. You can use the flowchart diagram in Figure 10.10 to follow the steps just outlined.

By using the process of first making sure your offer converts, and then placing your ad around the display network and refining your exposure based on individual websites, you can achieve excellent results from the display network.

Figure 10.10 Display network organization flowchart

Our bidding process so far has only encompassed setting a bid at the ad group level with respect to keywords or at the placement level. These bids are static regardless of who is seeing the ad. There is another level of complexity you can add to the display campaigns: automatically changing your bid based on the gender or age group of the person viewing your ad. This is known as *demographic bidding*.

Setting Different Bids by Demographics

When a user creates a MySpace profile, they enter additional information about themselves such as their gender and age. There are a number of social networking sites, such as Orkut, YouTube, and hi5.com, that partner with Google (or are owned by Google), and send anonymous demographic data about people who are viewing your ads. You can then use this data to set different bids by both gender and age.

> **Note:** Demographic targeting and bidding apply only to the display network. Each of these partners is a display network partner.

Because users don't log in on every site they access, and not all sites know their users' demographics, demographic bidding only applies to certain sites in Google's display network. To see the entire list of websites where demographic bidding is available, go to http://adwords.google.com/support/bin/answer.py?answer=88168&topic=13665.

Viewing Your Demographic Performance Stats

The first step in creating demographic bids is to see if you have any demographic data. Navigate to the Dimensions tab and select Demographics from the View menu to create a demographic report (Figure 10.11).

Figure 10.11 Demographic performance statistics

The reports allow you to drill down into the performance stats of every single domain, age, and gender combination, but when first getting started it can seem like a huge amount of data. As with most AdWords reports, a plethora of data is available. One data point that can cause the demographic report to be unwieldy is Domain. You cannot unselect Domain inside AdWords and see a roll-up of conversion data by just age and gender information. However, you can do this quite easily in a Microsoft Excel pivot table (Figure 10.12).

Row Labels	Sum of Clicks	Sum of Impressions	Sum of Conv. (1-per-click)	Average of Cost / conv. (1-per-click)
⊟ --	357	752649	5	$55.25
--	357	752649	5	$55.25
⊟ 18-24	152	335375	0	$0.00
female	146	322280	0	$0.00
unknown	6	13095	0	$0.00
⊟ 25-34	87	170640	1	$12.38
female	82	162870	1	$16.50
unknown	5	7770	0	$0.00
⊟ 35-44	43	100180	1	$3.89
female	40	97137	1	$6.49
male	0	13	0	$0.00
unknown	3	3030	0	$0.00
⊟ 45-54	39	64173	1	$2.24
female	36	62502	1	$2.99
unknown	3	1671	0	$0.00
⊟ 55-64	16	21708	0	$0.00
female	15	20952	0	$0.00
unknown	1	756	0	$0.00
⊟ 65+	8	11544	2	$0.91
female	8	11224	2	$1.21
unknown	0	320	0	$0.00
⊟ unknown	12	49029	0	$0.00
female	12	41880	0	$0.00
male	0	2	0	$0.00
unknown	0	7147	0	$0.00

Figure 10.12 Examining demographic data with pivot tables

If you do not see much demographic data, that means your ads are probably not displaying on social sites very often and you do not need to worry about demographic bidding options. If you see a lot of demographic data, and vastly different conversion rates by demographics, you might want to use demographic bidding.

Setting Demographic Bids

In your campaign settings, click Edit in the Demographic section (Figure 10.13).

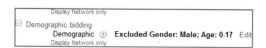

Figure 10.13 Viewing demographic bidding information

Doing so opens a page where you can see the last seven days of performance statistics by demographic as well as specify different bids by demographic (Figure 10.14).

Demographic bidding

This summary shows how your ads have performed on sites that offer demographic data. Use the exclude checkboxes to hide your ad from that group.

0.00% of total impressions are from sites with demographic data. ⑦

Traffic Reports by Gender and Age (for last 7 days)

Gender	Exclude	Clicks	Impr.	CTR	Avg. CPC	Cost	Conv. (1-per-click)	Cost / conv. (1-per-click)	Conv. rate (1-per-click)	View-through Conv.
Male	☑	0	0	0.00%	$0.00	$0.00	0	$0.00	0.00%	
Female	☐	22	47,087	0.05%	$0.81	$17.92	0	$0.00	0.00%	
Unspecified		6	8,482	0.07%	$0.88	$5.29	0	$0.00	0.00%	
Total		**28**	**55,569**	**0.05%**	**$0.83**	**$23.21**	**0**	**$0.00**	**0.00%**	

Age	Exclude	Clicks	Impr.	CTR ⑦	Avg. CPC ⑦	Cost	Conv. (1-per-click) ⑦	Cost / conv. (1-per-click) ⑦	Conv. rate (1-per-click) ⑦	View-through Conv. ⑦
0-17	☑	0	0	0.00%	$0.00	$0.00	0	$0.00	0.00%	
18-24	☐	13	28,137	0.05%	$0.73	$9.45	0	$0.00	0.00%	
25-34	☐	7	14,091	0.05%	$1.02	$7.17	0	$0.00	0.00%	
35-44	☐	2	6,233	0.03%	$0.50	$1.01	0	$0.00	0.00%	
45-54	☐	5	3,788	0.13%	$0.96	$4.80	0	$0.00	0.00%	
55-64	☐	0	1,577	0.00%	$0.00	$0.00	0	$0.00	0.00%	
65+	☐	0	918	0.00%	$0.00	$0.00	0	$0.00	0.00%	
Unspecified		1	825	0.12%	$0.78	$0.78	0	$0.00	0.00%	
Total		**28**	**55,569**	**0.05%**	**$0.83**	**$23.21**	**0**	**$0.00**	**0.00%**	

Figure 10.14 Setting demographic bids for a campaign

In this screen, you can exclude demographics from viewing your ads by clicking the Exclude box next to the age or gender information. You can also set different bid boosts by age or gender. Please note that Google plans to remove the age 0–17 targeting, and it may be unavailable by the time you read this. This is the percentage you want your maximum CPC to be multiplied by in determining your bid for that gender or age range.

It is important to note these percentages are additive. For instance, if this is your bid information:

- Ad group maximum CPC $1
- +25% if the viewer is male
- +35% if the viewer is 18–24

then your maximum CPC used by Google would be:

- $1 if gender and age is unknown
- $1.25 if the viewer was male, but between the ages of 45 and 54
- $1.60 if the viewer is an 18–24-year-old male

Since these numbers are additive, it can be useful to set low-maximum CPCs at the ad group or placement level and then use demographic bid boosts to increase your bids when your target market is viewing your ads. This lower-maximum CPC will be the maximum CPC of your ad groups for nondemographics seeing them. Therefore, it can be useful to create demographic-only campaigns.

Organizing Your Demographic Campaign

There are two major ways to organize your demographic campaigns based on your objectives. If you find that you receive enough returns from the sites that allow demographic targeting that you are willing to set a different budget for demographic targeting, and you are willing to write ads for each site, or category of sites, creating a demographic campaign with site placements can be worth your time.

If you do not want to set a different budget for a demographic campaign, or you are still experimenting with demographic targeting, setting demographic bids in current display campaigns is probably your better option.

Creating a Demographic Campaign with Managed Placements

If you want to set a different budget for demographic targeting versus your regular display network reach, or you find that demographic optimization is leading to good returns, you can create a demographic-only campaign.

The first step is to create a display-only campaign as normal (in your campaign settings, set this campaign to only be shown on the display network). Next, choose to only allow this campaign to be shown on Specific Reach: Show Ads Only On Pages That Match All My Targeting Methods in your display settings. Then you can add each of the demographic targeted sites as placements. This will ensure that your ad is only shown on sites that allow demographic bidding.

In this way, you have the option to write specific ads for each demographic site by adding just one placement per ad group and then creating corresponding ads in that same ad group.

But suppose writing a different ad per website is more work than you are willing to undertake. In that case, you can add all the placements into a single ad group, or break the placements into like-minded sites and write ads for only the ad groups you create.

Using this method, since you have set a different budget for the demographic sites and are writing custom ads for these sites, you need to block these sites from being shown on your discovery display campaign (which uses automatic placements). If you do not block these sites from that campaign, Google could use your display bids and budget from the discovery campaign instead of your demographic bid and budget when showing your ads on those sites.

Setting Demographic Bids in Your Current Display Campaigns

Demographic bidding only applies if someone is on one of the websites that passes demographic information to Google. The bid changes do not apply to any other display network sites. Therefore, you could add the list of demographic sites as placements in your current display campaigns.

As with the previous method, you can add all of the demographics to a single ad group or break up the list of demographic sites into different ad groups. It all depends on how you want to organize the ad copy.

If you add these sites to a placements-only campaign, like the one discussed earlier in display organization, add the demographic targeted sites to your blocked sites list in your discovery campaign settings.

With either method, if you do not like the returns of a single site, you can remove that site from your list of managed placements, and then ensure that site is also blocked in any general display campaigns.

Why You Should Add the Demographic Sites as Placements

With both methods, you used placement targeting instead of setting demographic bids for that display campaign and let Google adjust your bids based on where the searcher is viewing your ad. The reason for this is that demographic bids can only increase your CPC—they cannot lower it.

If you set low bids for an individual placement, and then use demographic bidding where you are increasing your bids based on the demographics of someone seeing your ad, you can be highly accurate in determining what you are willing to pay based on both the site where your ad is being displayed and the demographics of the visitor. If you just set demographic bids and do not use placements, you lose some ad serving control. Since you should set bids at the ad group level based on returns (although in some discovery campaigns, you might bid higher because you want the exposure on various websites so you can find good placements), you might only have the option of bidding even higher than your returns when specific demographics see your ads.

If there are only a couple of age ranges or a single gender where you see higher conversion rates, this is acceptable. But suppose you see widely different conversion rates, or cost per conversion by demographics, especially on the demographic targeted sites. In such cases, you will run into scenarios where you cannot set your desired bid without using managed placements.

For example, say you have this scenario:

- Want to bid $0.50 if someone is between 18 and 24
- Want to bid $0.30 if someone is 55–64
- Want to bid $0.40 if someone sees your ad from a random display network site

In this scenario, because you wish to pay less for the 55–64 age group than your standard bid, there is no way to set appropriate display bids without the use of managed placements.

With demographic bidding, since you can only raise your bid, you should set the bid for that placement at the minimum you are willing to pay when someone clicks on your ad from that placement, which would be $0.30 in this scenario. Then use the bid boost to bring your bid price up to the point you are willing to pay when someone from a specific demographic clicks on your ad.

Remarketing

Remarketing campaigns (called retargeting in many non-AdWords circles) allow you to serve ads based on visitor behavior on your website. This is an excellent way of reaching visitors who came to your site, showed some interest in your company, but left before completing an action.

The beauty of remarketing is that you are targeting the user. You do not have to use placements or keywords to target individuals. The other part of remarketing that is useful to know is these do not have to be AdWords visits. You can target anyone who visits your sites. This is a great way of combining both SEO (search engine optimization) efforts with AdWords.

First we will walk through conceptually how remarketing works so you have a basic idea of the execution, and then we will dive into the specifics.

At a conceptual level, this is the remarketing process:

- You define an audience in AdWords.
- For each audience, you will have a script that you place on your site (the entire site, or just specific pages).
- You will make an ad group that only targets an audience.
- When someone visits the pages where your remarketing script is placed, a cookie is added to their browser.
- The visitor leaves your site, but the cookie is still on the browser.

- That person then visits a site that is in the display network.

- You can serve an ad to that person based on the cookie being placed on their browser regardless of the site they are currently on (assuming the site is in the display network).

- Hopefully, the user clicks on the ad and returns to your site and performs your desired action.

Defining An Audience

The first step to remarketing is to create an audience. To do that, you can either navigate to the Audiences section in your navigational tabs list, or go to the shared library and click the Audiences tab.

Once there, it is time to define your first remarketing list (Figure 10.15).

Important

Please review the Remarketing program policy to learn more about what you need to include in your site's privacy policy, and which sensitive categories of sites cannot use this feature.

New remarketing list

Remarketing list name	
Description *Optional*	
Membership duration ⑦	30 days
Tags ⑦	⦿ Create new remarketing tag

Figure 10.15 Defining your audience

When defining your audience, you need to define a few pieces of information:

Remarketing List Name This is what you want the list called. Usually calling it something obvious based on where the code will be placed is the best way to define your lists. Naming conventions such as *checkout*, *visited women's apparel*, and *in shopping cart* can help you to remember exactly where this code is being placed.

Description This is an optional description for you. If you are using some complex remarketing lists (which will be discussed later in this chapter), it can be useful to put a small reminder to yourself about the purpose of the list.

Membership Duration You can define your own cookie length. This is how long the cookie will stay active on the visitor's browser. The default is 30 days. However, there are many reasons to create longer or shorter cookies, which will be discussed later in the chapter.

Tags A remarketing tag is the code you are placing on your site. When you first create a list, also create a new tag. As you make more lists, you can use existing tags instead of constantly creating new ones.

Custom Combinations

Once you have a few lists created, you do not always have to create a new list; you can use custom combinations. With a custom combination (Figure 10.16), you can make simple rules that tell Google that if someone is in list A or list B, you want to add that user to the combination. Or, you can tell AdWords to include someone from list A but exclude anyone in list B.

New custom combination

Combination name	Market to Non-Converters
Description	
Optional	

Users included or
interested in... (?)

all these audiences ▾ : select audiences ▾

remove   AdWords Seminar Visits

and

none of these audiences ▾ : select audiences ▾

remove   Seminar Registration Complete

and

Add another

Figure 10.16 Custom combination example

I'll walk you through executional strategies shortly, but first I want to show you an example of why you would want to use a custom combination list. I work directly with Google to give in-person seminars about AdWords. When someone comes to our seminar page, we place one cookie on their browser (called AdWords Seminar Visits in the custom combination list). When someone checks out and buys a ticket, we place a second cookie on their browser, Seminar Registration Complete.

In our custom combination example, if someone visited the Seminar page but did not convert, they are in the list. If someone visited that page and then did convert, they are not in the list. In this fashion, we can then selectively serve ads to nonconverters and not spend money advertising to those who already bought a ticket to our AdWords Seminar.

You can always see how many active cookies exist at any time on the remarketing screen in the shared library (Figure 10.17).

Type	Name	Description	Open / Closed ⑦	Membership duration ⑦	Tags / Rules ⑦	Number of users ⑦
Remarking	All Site Visitors		Open	30 days	All Site Visitors [Tag]	610,000
Remarking	Visitors Who Converted		Open	30 days	Visitors Who Converted [Tag]	35,000
Combination	Visitors Who Did Not Convert		Open	–	all of (All Site Visitors) and none of (Visitors Who Converted)	570,000

Figure 10.17 Remarketing lists and active cookies

Place the Script on Your Site

Once you define a list, you will need to put the tag on your site. When you receive the tag (Figure 10.18), you have the option of choosing HTTP (nonsecure) or HTTPS (secure). Do not put an HTTP script on an HTTPS page. The opposite (HTTPS scripts on HTTP pages) is fine. If in doubt, always choose HTTPS.

Figure 10.18 The tag code

This tag goes on every page of your site where you wish to place the cookie. In the previous example, one tag was on the seminar informational page and that page only. Another tag was on the Thank You For Registering page and that page only. You can place the tag on one or more pages. A page can have one or more tags on it.

When you put the tag on your site, you must also adjust your privacy policy page to tell visitors you are using remarketing. This is a Google terms of service rule. The policy adjustment must also let consumers know how to opt out of remarketing. To learn more about creating a good privacy policy, see Google's privacy policy at `http://certifiedknowledge.org/terms-of-service/#privacy`. Before you just copy and paste that policy, make sure you talk to your lawyer about what you may need in your policy or the policy implications.

Create a Remarketing Ad Group

It is useful to create a new campaign for just remarketing. If you add a remarketing list to an ad group that only contains placements and has the campaign settings set to Most Restrictive Match, the user has to be on a placement you choose and in that remarketing list before they can see your ad. As you create more targeting options in ad groups, you can inadvertently create very small targeting segments.

With remarketing campaigns, you can target based on just audiences. You do not need keywords or placements. Therefore, for your first remarketing campaign (and as you play with them, feel free to refine this targeting), you will set the campaign to Display Only, and have the campaign set to Most Restrictive Targeting (more on this shortly). Then, you will only use remarketing lists to target your ads.

Create a new ad group. In the Audiences tab, choose the lists or custom combination lists you wish to target (Figure 10.19). Essentially, these are your positive keywords.

Audience	Status	Clicks	Impr.	CTR	Avg. CPC	Avg. CPM	Cost	Conv. (1-per-click)	Cost / conv. (1-per-click)	Conv. rate (1-per-click)
CK Visitors	Eligible	59	20,565	0.29%	$1.73	$4.96	$102.08	35	$2.92	59.32%
bg Visitor List	Eligible	160	178,785	0.09%	$1.39	$1.25	$222.93	32	$6.97	20.00%

Figure 10.19 Positive audiences

An ad group can also have negative lists (Figure 10.20). These are the same as your negative keywords. Negative ad group audiences only affect the targeting of that ad group. Negative campaign audiences affect the entire campaigns.

Your ads will now only be displayed based on these lists. The next step is to navigate to the Ads tab and create ad copy that is associated to the list.

Figure 10.20 Negative audiences

The 500 Cookie Rule

Until a list has 500 active cookies, the list will not go live. This is akin to keywords that are not active due to low search volume. The word *active* is very important here. When you create the remarketing list, you will define a cookie duration. If your site receives 300 visitors a month and you went with the standard 30-day cookie, you will never have 300 cookies placed. If you change the cookie duration to 60 days, you will break 500 active cookies.

When planning your remarketing campaigns, you will find it useful to have your analytics program open and examine the number of unique visitors a page, or website section, receives in various time durations to ensure you can make a list go active by hitting 500 active cookies.

Once you have written your ads and have audiences listed, and those audiences have 500 cookies, you are remarketing and trying to bring back visitors to your site. Those are the basics of remarketing. Next, let's examine ways of organizing your remarketing campaigns based on your website.

Remarketing Strategies

With remarketing, you have four main variables that allow you to create custom marketing lists:

- Cookie duration
- Pages the cookies are placed
- Positive lists
- Negative lists

Let's look at a few common ways to set up remarketing campaigns.

Basic: Visitors and Converters

The most basic way of remarketing is to create two lists:

- Nonconverters
- Converters

The nonconverter cookie will be from 7 days to 60 days in length for most sites. To determine this cookie duration, examine your analytics to see how many unique visitors you receive a month and the average time between first visit and purchase.

Be careful of placing the nonconverter cookie on the homepage, or pages of blogs and forums. Often someone who just visits your homepage or your blog is not a very engaged visitor and in many instances you may not wish to remarket back to this visitor.

The converter cookie will be a year long, and only go on the Thank You page that appears after a visitor has completed some action.

Your positive list will be nonconverters. Your negative list will be converters. Now, you will only show ads to those who visited your website and did not convert.

Intermediate: Visitors, Abandons, and Nonconverters

With this setup, you will start with the same framework as the Basic version you just saw. However, you will add one more cookie: Abandoned Cart Shoppers.

The Abandoned Cart Shoppers code will only be placed inside your shopping cart, or on the middle pages of a multipage form. Because these visitors are more valuable than those who just visited your site (they almost converted), this cookie duration will be longer than for your basic visitors.

Next, add the Abandoned Cart Shoppers list to the Audiences tab. Someone who almost converted is worth more than someone who just visited your site. Therefore, your Abandoned Cart Shoppers CPC will be set higher than your website visitor audience. You should be willing to pay more to bring back an abandoned shopper to your site than just a typical visitor.

Advanced: Targeting by Interest

You can take your remarketing efforts to fairly granular levels if you have enough traffic. For our AdWords training and tool site, we have several types of visitors. So before even setting up the cookies, I made a simple table of what our lists would be, where we were going to place the codes, and how long each cookie would be enabled (Table 10.1).

► **Table 10.1** Certified Knowledge remarketing codes

List name	Purpose	Placed	Cookie duration
All Visitors	To reach everyone who examined the offer	Global footer	30 days
PPC Tools	To reach those who examined the Tools section	PPC Tools pages	60 days
AdWords Tutorials	To reach those who entered the tutorial section	AdWords Video page	60 days
PPC Community	To reach those looking for community engagement	PPC Community page	60 days
Pricing	To reach price-conscious shoppers	Visited price page	60 days
Shopping Cart Abandoners	To reach consumers who showed intent to buy but did not finish	All cart pages except Order Confirmation	90 days
Converted Free Email Training	Free 5 email training message for sneak peek; to reach those consumers who showed high interest in the system	Thank You For Subscribing email confirmation page	90 days
Converted Subscription	If someone subscribed, to make sure we don't serve them ads	Thank You For Subscribing page after billing information entered	360 days

And before we started, I laid out the execution strategy in a simple document so that the entire company could see how the site worked and view our customer acquisition strategy for remarketing. Our initial remarketing strategy with comments follows.

Ad Group 1: Nonengaged Users

This ad group is for users who visited the site but did not enter a specific section of the site. Therefore, they are the absolutely least qualified of all the visitors. This is the reason the cookie duration for this list is only 30 days, the shortest of all the lists.

- The positive list: All Visitors.
- The negative lists: All the other lists. If someone is on any other list, we don't want them seeing our general ad; we want a more specific ad served to that user.
- The ad: Showcasing all benefits.
- Bid: Lowest of all the remarketing lists. These visitors went to at least the homepage, and possibly an interior page, but not one of the specific pages useful for tailoring a separate ad for that user.

Ad Group 2: Price Shoppers

This ad group is for users who visited the pricing section.

- The positive list: Pricing.
- The negative lists: All others except Nonengaged Users list.
- The ad: Showcasing that your time is worth money, and then showing how Certified Knowledge can save you time.
- Bid: Second lowest of all the remarketing lists. Price-conscious users can be difficult to convince. In addition, I'd rather the more specific ad (the ad groups below) be shown to consumers instead of this ad. If someone happens to be on both the Nonengaged Users list and the Price Shoppers list, they should see this ad because its bid will be higher than the Nonengaged Users list.

Ad Group 3: PPC Community

This ad group is for people who visited the PPC community page. I expect that most people who visit this page will also visit other pages across the site. Therefore, while this will be an ad we show, we're going to put less importance on what I expect the stronger benefits to be: Tools and Training. However, if someone did visit this page, we're willing to show them this ad (in addition to other ads they may see from the more specific ad groups).

- The positive list: PPC Community.
- The negative list: All others except Price Shoppers and Nonengaged Users.
- The ad: Showcasing the benefits of having access to an active forum, email, and news system.
- Bid: Third lowest. Higher than Price Shoppers; lower than PPC Tools and AdWords Tutorials.

Ad Group 4: AdWords Tutorials

This ad group is targeting consumers who examined our tutorials. Because we're going to have many pages explaining the tutorials, we can break this down into two lists over time: the Main Tutorials page and the All Training subpages. Doing so will help us identify those who just glanced at the tutorials versus those who looked at our videos and read more about the AdWords lessons.

- The positive list: AdWords Tutorials.
- The negative list: Converted Subscription, Converted Email Training, Shopping Cart Abandoners. If someone converted, or was closer to converting than just visiting the features pages, I want them to see the more specific ad.

- The ad: Showcasing what Certified Knowledge can teach users about AdWords with more than 50 lessons, and more than 100 coming by the end of the year.
- Bid: Higher than PPC Community and lower than the three lists used here as negatives.

Ad Group 5: PPC Tools

This ad group is targeting consumers who examined our toolset. Because we're going to have several pages explaining the tools, we can break this down into two lists over time: the Main Tools page and the All Tools subpages. Doing so will help us identify those who just glanced at the tools versus those who looked at our videos and read more about the tools.

- The positive list: PPC Tools.
- The negative list: Converted Subscription, Converted Email Training, Shopping Cart Abandoners. If someone converted, or was closer to converting than just visiting the features pages, I want them to see the more specific ad.
- The ad: Showcasing the benefits of the PPC tools we have developed, which will save users time in creating ad copies, geographic keywords and keywords. They will help users bid, find quality score issues, find broken links, and analyze their site. While most of the ad groups will contain two or three image ads to start (by themes, each theme will have different sizes); I expect this ad group will have more test ads to see what messages resonate better.
- Bid: Same as the AdWords Tutorials. I expect it will become slightly higher than the tutorials over time as tutorials are one to three time views for most consumers, and many repeat views will help refresh your knowledge. The tools will be used daily, weekly, or monthly depending on what users are trying to accomplish inside their account, and will grow more valuable over time.

Ad Group 6: Converted Free Email Training

This ad group is for targeting those who signed up for a free lessons training via email. Many people who sign up for free training do not have an intent to buy—they just want the free stuff. Others want a trial of what you are offering and have a high chance of converting. However, email open rates can be sporadic on free training offers. Therefore, these ads will both remind users about Certified Knowledge and serve as a reminder about the emails delivered to them.

- The positive list: Converted Free Email Training.
- The negative lists: Converted Subscription, Shopping Cart Abandoners
- The ad: Showcase the Certified Knowledge tutorials with messages to remind users about their email subscription. I'm not sure if the messages will be

something like: "Did you enjoy your free email training from Certified Knowledge? Learn how you can access all of our training" because that might seem a bit strange to people that we know have the email—or if the messages will contain images more aligned with the training aspects of Certified Knowledge.

- Bid: To start, a bit higher than AdWords Tutorials and Tools lists since these users were willing to give us a name and email address to receive the information. Over time, the bidding for this list might change significantly up or down.

Ad Group 7: Shopping Cart Abandoners

This ad group is for targeting those who entered the shopping cart but did not convert.

- The positive list: Shopping Cart Abandoners
- The negative list: Converted Subscription, Converted Free Email Training
- I'm making an assumption here that I might change in the future: I'm considering these users more valuable than the Converted Free Email Training list because these shoppers were within a submit button of entering their credit card information and becoming customers. I might be wrong; therefore, I might test this same ad group minus Converted Free Email Training as a negative list in the future.
- The ad: One ad will showcase the Certified Knowledge benefits. One will show a phone number with the benefits that talks about support for any problems. As we start to map out sign-up objections, we will base the ads around the most common ones.
- Bid: The highest of all the lists.

It's this type of organization where you have to start balancing time and possibilities. If you examine a site such as Lands' End (Figure 10.21), there are several ways you could organize the remarketing campaigns.

A simple approach is to set a remarketing cookie in each major section (women, men, girls, boys, etc.) with an ad that examines that type of apparel. In addition, there should be a converters and abandoned shopping cart list.

You could segment each subsection, so you would have a girls outerwear, girls shorts, girls pants, girls sleepwear, and so forth. That quickly becomes more than a hundred lists.

When considering how to break up your remarketing lists based on interest, you need to balance your time and your unique visitors (500 cookies minimum to be active).

Figure 10.21 Lands' End

Remarketing by Trends

Your current customers do not have to be negative lists. It can be just as useful remarketing to your current customers. You should be careful, though; you do not want to overwhelm visitors with your offers.

Many industries have trends in how their products are sold, or peak times, that occur the same way on a yearly basis. Take the flower industry; two of the biggest days are Mother's Day and Valentine's Day. These two holidays are roughly 90 days apart. You should count this out for yourself, but for ease of illustration, we will assume they are exactly 90 days apart.

If someone bought from you on Valentine's Day, they are obviously someone who purchases flowers. One of the most common Mother's Day gifts is also flowers. So in this case, you would want to show a Mother's Day ad copy to anyone who bought from you around Valentine's Day in hopes of enticing them back to your site to buy their Mother's Day flowers.

In this case, you can make two lists:

- Valentine's Day Buyers: 80-day cookie
- Mother's Day Offer: 100-day cookie

You set these cookies on the Thank You For Shopping page for the seven days preceding Valentine's Day, Valentine's Day itself, and the next two days after Valentine's Day for those who forgot and need that last-minute (late) gift.

Next, go to your ad group and add these lists. The Mother's Day Offer will be your positive list. The Valentine's Day Buyers will be your negative list. For the next 80 days, the person will be in the negative list and therefore not see your Valentine's Day ad. After 80 days, the cookie will expire and the user will see your Mother's Day ads for the week or so leading up to Mother's Day.

You can be creative with remarketing once you understand your website, your customers, and how your products are researched, purchased, and hopefully purchased again. The biggest problem with remarketing is that you can start to scare your customers if you don't control your ad serving. You need to ensure that your remarketing efforts do not give the appearance of stalking people.

Don't Creep Out Your Customers

Remarketing is fantastic when it is done properly. When it is done poorly, you can "creep out" your potential customers so they can come to despise your ads.

The major culprit for causing this emotional state is often an advertiser not controlling their ads. You should always set a frequency cap when running remarketing ads. This is not an AdWords policy, but it is a good marketing policy. A frequency cap limits the number of times someone can see your ads. Go to your campaign settings of your remarketing campaign, and set a frequency cap.

The second way to combat ad fatigue is to use multiple ads within your remarketing campaign. It is common to see companies use different sizes of the same ad (for image or video ads) for your remarketing campaigns; however, that is just the same ad that has been resized.

If someone has seen the offer fifty times, the fifty-first impression is not going to be magical. Create a few different ads with different offers, using completely different themes (look and feel of the ads) and place them in the same ad group. Now when you show your ad to the same person a few times, you are rotating in new themes and offers. If offer 1 does not convert them, then maybe offer 2 will.

It is common to see what is known as search sessions or research sessions. Someone will start researching one product or service, and then later they will start researching a completely unrelated product or service. For instance, they were sitting with their spouse looking at cruise specials and getaway vacation packages on a Saturday afternoon. On Sunday, the husband is watching a football game and decides the TV is too small. So, he goes to the computer and starts researching new TVs. At this point in time, the remarketing ads for the cruise vacation are useless. He is no longer researching cruises—he is researching TVs.

In the travel industry it is common for someone to take a few weeks between initial research and purchase. During those few weeks, the user is not always interested in vacations. Interests and research vary depending on other life factors. There are two ways that you can take even more control over your remarketing campaigns so that someone only sees the ad when they are more likely to be in the proper research mode for your products and services.

The first method is to refine the ad group with keywords. When you first set up the remarketing campaign, if you choose Most Restrictive Ad Serving in the campaign settings and also add keywords to the ad group where you have your remarketing lists, your ad will only be served when the person is both in your remarketing list and on a page where the topic is about your keywords. In this case where you are only trying to refine your lists by keywords, feel free to use general keywords such as "vacation" or "cruises." You do not need to go into the depth of detail for these keyword lists (of course, you can if you want to, but that does make a lot more ad groups to manage) that you normally would go to in creating display campaigns.

When you refine your ad group by keywords, you will often see quite a few less impressions. If your offer is very general (credit cards, cell phones, etc.), you may decide not to refine your ad groups with keywords. If you are afraid you will lose too many impressions, just do a test of the same remarketing list, but in one ad group there are keywords and the other one there are no keywords, and see how they each perform. The best way to do this testing is with AdWords Campaign Experiments, which we will discuss in Chapter 15.

The other way of refining your remarketing lists is through topic targeting, which lets you serve ads to users based on overall topics and not keywords.

Topic and Interest Targeting

Topic and interest targeting allow you to target users based on their interests or the page's topics. These are the two broadest versions of reach that exist.

These two options can give you a lot of reach, but you will often see much lower CTRs with these options than with more specific targeting such as keywords or remarketing.

These two types of targeting can also be combined with placements or keywords to help filter where your ads are being displayed.

Interest Targeting

With interest targeting, you are targeting a user based on their interests regardless of the site they are currently on. This is the absolute broadest form of targeting that Google offers.

If you are looking for massive reach, interest targeting is for you. Just remember, marketing is about connecting with customers. The more targeted the ad is to the customer, the higher the CTR and conversion rates usually are. As the targeting becomes more ambiguous, the CTRs and conversion rates often decline.

With interest targeting, you are targeting users who are interested in that topic regardless of what page they are on. So if someone is interested in cars, they can see your ads even while trying to learn more about AdWords.

Note: Google tracks a lot of data on the Web. If you are using certain Google technologies, or their search engine, they can start to infer what type of information you are interested in based on the sites you visit, your search queries, and other signals. This is how they determine someone's interests. As a user, you can always opt to see what categories Google thinks you are interested in on the Ads Preferences page (https://www.google.com/settings/ads/onweb/), you can add your own interests, or you can completely opt out of all interest ads.

To set up interest targeting, navigate to the Audiences tab and select Interests (see Figure 10.22). The process is very similar to setting up remarketing campaigns.

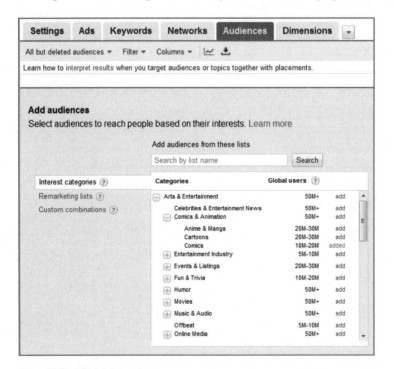

Figure 10.22 Selecting Interests

The one advantage of interest targeting is that because you are not always selecting sites based on their quality, the CPCs are generally lower than you would receive from highly targeted placements.

The real work with interest targeting is testing ad copy. You need to make sure that your ad copy is explicit to the interest you are targeting and test what types of offers and messages will bring the most qualified users to your site. You can also exclude users based on their interest. If there are certain types of users you do not want on your site, feel free to exclude them.

For a large reach, interest targeting can be good. If you are looking for more control, consider using topic targeting.

Topic Targeting

Topic targeting allows you to select various topics, and then your ad will only be displayed on pages that match your topics. Topic targeting has a large reach, but it is a slightly more targeted reach than interest targeting.

To set up topic targeting, navigate to the Topics tab (Figure 10.23) inside your AdWords account and add the topics of pages where you want your ads to show.

Figure 10.23 Topic targeting selection

If you have general offers such as car insurance or credit card offers, topic targeting is excellent. If you are looking to expand the reach of your site and make sure more people know about you, topic targeting is for you. If you are bidding just based on ROI, you might want to use topic targeting as a filter for the various ways Google displays your ads.

For example, we looked at the query "bleach" in an earlier chapter. Bleach could either be a household cleaning supply or it could be an anime show. The same word has very different intents. In that case, you could use "bleach" and "bleach dvd" as your keywords across the display network, but then also select the topic "anime."

If in the campaign settings you had chosen Match All Selected Targeting Methods, the ad would only be displayed if the user was on a page about bleach and the topic of that page was categorized as anime.

Another good use of topic targeting is for remarketing. Set up your remarketing campaign as normal, and then add the topic for your products or services. This way, the user will not see your ads when they have switched search sessions and they are researching a completely different idea than what your products and services address.

You can use topic targeting all by itself without any other refinements to the display of the ad, and that will get you quite a few semi-targeted impressions. If you only show ads based on topics, make sure you are doing ad copy testing to ensure your ad has a general enough appeal for the entire topic.

If you are refining keywords, placements, or remarketing lists with topics, you will probably relate your ad to a specific message you wish to promote as opposed to a more general offer.

It is easy to confuse topic targeting and interest targeting. The easiest way to remember is that topics are triggered based on the page's content and interests are targeted based on the person's interest. Topics are pages and interests are people.

Creating Scenarios to Understand and Reach Your Target Audience

Using automatic placements for discovery, managed placements, and potentially demographic campaigns, interest, topic, and remarketing campaigns will lead to a scenario where you can start to control and refine your targeting based on returns. However, if you have a smaller budget, or you only want to reach a specific user, having a general display campaign might not be cost effective or financially possible for you.

If you have a smaller budget, starting with managed placements and remarketing, determining what type of placements are doing well for you (news, social, forums, etc.), and then finding additional placements that meet that criteria can help you grow your content advertising in a more returns-oriented environment.

As you start to layer on more targeting options, it can become confusing to determine how to reach your target market. Instead of focusing on all the options, focus on creating real-life scenarios and then see what options apply to your audience.

Here's a list of the ways you can target a display ad:

•   Time of day (discussed in Chapter 13)

•   Day of the week (discussed in Chapter 13)

•   Location (discussed in Chapter 11)

- Individual website or section of a website (managed placement targeting)
- Page topic
- Audience interest
- Person's previous behavior on your website (remarketing)
- Keywords (automatic placements targeting) or keywords plus managed placements (enhanced campaigns)

For general display reach that has some control, beginning with either keywords or managed placements is a good starting place—it is a nice balance between both reach and control. You can use all or none of the additional targeting options. Instead of trying to think through all the options, create a scenario for reaching your target market.

Even though someone is viewing your ad online, they still have a physical presence in the world where their life is dictated by offline factors and daily routine. Examine the life of your customer, and the targeting options can become apparent.

For instance, let's expand on the earlier scenario that your company has just developed a product that allows stockbrokers to get real-time U.S. news results based on their portfolio. And let's also assume that you are doing a limited test to view the response rate and have chosen Minneapolis as your target market. In addition, you do not have a limitless budget, so you want to refine your targeting as much as possible.

Therefore, the question is how do you reach stockbrokers who live in Minneapolis? Let's begin by building a profile of how they receive their current news, since that is what your product addresses.

Because your company only wants to reach users in Minneapolis, the first setting is quite easy: only show the ad in Minneapolis.

Next, a stockbroker has to be ready for the New York Stock Exchange to open at 9:30 a.m. EST. However, Minneapolis is on Central time; therefore, the stockbroker has to be ready for work at 8:30 a.m. Some will read the news at home, others at work, so let's run the ad from only 5:00 a.m. until 10:30 a.m.

Most people behave differently on weekends than on weekdays. The weekends are for relaxing; the weekdays are about work. Therefore, we'll only run the ad from Monday to Friday.

Where do stockbrokers read their morning financial news? Use the placement tool (and the Google Ad Planner, discussed later in this chapter) to research financial news sites. For our purposes, choose a starting place of:

- Bloomberg.com, only one placement available
- *New York Times*, business pages placement
- *Business Week*, all placements except Asia and Europe

These three websites have a tremendous amount of daily page views, even when only that handful of sections is chosen. Therefore, also choose some keywords such as "stock market," "NASDAQ," "Dow Jones," and "NYSE."

Now, when you add all those components together, the ad will only be shown to those who meet all these criteria at once:

- Located in Minneapolis
- Viewing the *New York Times*, Bloomberg.com, or *Business Week* in one of the chosen placement sections
- During a weekday
- In the morning from 5:00 a.m. until 10:30 a.m.
- The article matches your keyword list

It is important to note that the more you segment your audience, the smaller the potential audience is, because they have to meet all the criteria.

If you have ads that are already running, when you start to refine your ad's exposure, always track total conversions and conversion rate to make sure you did not remove your ads from being seen by converting customers.

If you feel overwhelmed by the possibilities of the display network and all the options, step away from Google's options and start thinking about the user:

- Who is your ideal customer?
- How do they live their life?
- When during their daily routine are they more open to reading your ad and viewing your offer?

By examining those three simple questions, you can learn how to reach your customers.

Write Effective Display Ads

Writing ads for the display network is different than writing search ads. With search ads, someone has conducted an actual search, which shows they are aware of the product and service. The fact that a searcher has conducted a search means they are somewhere in the buying funnel.

When reaching individuals with the display network, many users may not be in the buying funnel at all. Your ads are shown based on the article's contents, not the user's intent of actively seeking information. Therefore, you should be writing display ads to reach users who are not in the buying funnel so that they will enter your buying funnel.

Although some people who are in the buying funnel will see your display ads, they are often not your primary audience for such ads. You will reach those individuals when they are searching for your products. Your display ads will help reinforce your message for those who are in the buying funnel, and you may see conversions from these individuals. However, as those already in the buying funnel usually make up a small percentage of those who see your display ads, they should rarely be your primary audience (with placement targeting being the common exception).

When examining these ad copy writing rules, we are making the assumption that you are using the display network to introduce your existing product or service to consumers to start them down the buying funnel. There are many other reasons to use the display network, such as CPM image ad buys to create awareness for a new product. If you are using the display network for some of these specific reasons, borrow what makes sense from the ad writing sections (here and in Chapter 8, "Beyond Text: Image, Video, and Mobile Ads") to create your own ads that meet your company's goals.

Showcase Relevancy The more relevant an ad is to the consumer, the more interest it will attract. Relevancy is attained by your keyword, placement, topic, or interest selection. Make sure your ad is relevant to the website it is being shown on. This point is as much about choosing the proper placements and keywords as it is about the ad's design or chosen text. Ads that seem to underperform might be very effective ads, but are underperforming because they are being seen by the wrong audience. Always check to make sure your ads are being placed on the proper pages.

Showcase Benefits The reason people move further into the buying funnel is that the product or service has made some promise about how it will make their life better. We become interested in products because of benefits. As consumers who are reading related articles might be aware of similar products or services—and in someone else's buying funnel—if your product or similar products are well known, you should test adding a feature or two in the ad along with your primary benefit.

What Will They Learn After the Click? This is not necessary in every ad copy, but it is worthwhile testing. Tell consumers what they will receive when they click on your ad. By letting them know what they will learn, you might give those who have entered the incentive they need to click on the ad to view your landing page.

Call-to-Action All ads should have a call-to-action. Tell a customer why they should click on your ad and what they should do on the landing page. Phrases like "begin your free trial" are calls-to-action that let customers know the next page will be a free trial sign-up.

Use General Offers Too specific an offer can confuse a visitor who is not yet in the buying funnel and does not know about your products. General offers, such as "download a whitepaper," "free trial," and "calculate your savings," create a compelling message for a general audience.

While these rules generally apply to all display network ads, you can be more specific with managed placement ads. For instance, if you sell server monitoring software and your ad is being placed on a site that caters to advanced IT individuals, you are reaching an audience that understands the benefits of server monitoring. In this case, your general consumer benefit may not be that compelling to an audience who already understands the entire monitoring process and knows they need it. They are interested in new features that will make their lives easier that are not typical in other software. Therefore, you might need more specific benefits in your ad copy, such as why this monitoring software is easier to use, that it is less resource intensive, or that it can send text messages when servers go down when most software just sends email notifications.

As a general rule, the more you know about your audience and the more specific the audience, the more your ads can be tailored to meet their needs. Conversely, the more general the audience, the more you should test specific versus general the ads. Often specific ads will still outperform general ones even when broadly targeted, but it is not always true. Therefore, when targeting large audiences, your first round of tests should be specific versus general messaging.

DoubleClick Ad Planner: Free Access to Expensive Data

Data is expensive. The more data you desire, the more it will cost your company. While many large companies use comScore or Hitwise for market intelligence, their price points often preclude small and medium enterprise businesses that do not have the data research budgets to pay for such information.

Luckily, Google has introduced DoubleClick Ad Planner, which gives some information about websites for free. Although this data is by no means as comprehensive as comScore or Hitwise, it is excellent data to use when researching information about various websites.

Because there is more data available in Google DoubleClick Ad Planner than I could cover in an entire chapter, I'm going to concentrate on how to use it to find effective placement targeted websites.

To start using DoubleClick Ad Planner, visit `www.google.com/adplanner/` and sign in with your Google account.

The first step in using Ad Planner is to create a media plan (see Figure 10.24). This is a collection of websites you have added to your plan from research you have conducted. You can have as many plans as you wish; therefore, name it something descriptive so you can easily find your research at a later date.

Once you have created a media plan, select the plan and then it is time to start researching websites.

Conducting Ad Planner Research

With Ad Planner, you can navigate to the Research tab and input a single website. This will give you a quick snapshot of that website's data.

Figure 10.24 Create and access your media plans.

As your goal for this chapter is to find new websites to use in your managed placements, I'll walk you through a few different methods of using your AdWords data to find these sites. Please note, while you'll go through some of these options individually, in most cases you can combine the methods. The more you segment the data, the fewer websites will meet your criteria.

DoubleClick Ad Planner shows details for the following:

- Sites that accept advertising
- Sites that are in Google's display network
- All sites regardless of the previous two criteria (if you uncheck both boxes, you can see information from most websites regardless of what ads are shown on a site)

For our research purposes, the first step will be to only view details of sites that are in the Google display network (Figure 10.25).

Figure 10.25 View information for sites only in the Google display network.

Along the top of the Ad Planner research page is a filtering bar (see Figure 10.26). In the next few sections, you will see this bar several times but with only one item selected. Each of the filtering options is available somewhere along this main filter bar.

To understand the filtering options, let's first examine what data is available for any website.

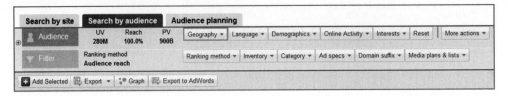

Figure 10.26 Ad Planner filtering bar

Detailed Website Information

As you filter your audience, the bottom of the screen will refine the websites listed based on those filters. You can click on any of the websites to find detailed information (Figure 10.27) that contains some of these data points:

- Categories
- Traffic statistics
- Daily unique visitors
- Gender
- Education
- Age
- Household income
- Children in household
- Sites also visited
- Keywords search for
- Ad specifications

Please note that Figure 10.27 contains only half of the available data points that are shown when you actually use the Ad Planner tool.

Demographic Research

One of the options for Google Ad Planner is to segment the audience by demographic characteristics. If you run a demographic performance report in your AdWords account and have data that shows what gender and age range are converting on your site, you can only view sites that have a high composite of that specific audience.

However, Google Ad Planner allows more demographic inputs (Figure 10.28) than you can achieve from your AdWords reports. You can filter by:

- Gender
- Age
- Education
- Household income
- Children in household

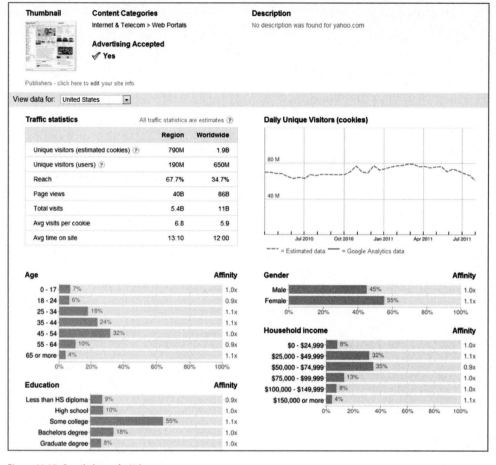

Figure 10.27 Detailed stats for Yahoo.com

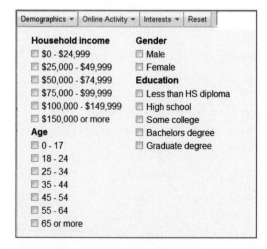

Figure 10.28 Demographic filtering in Ad Planner

Therefore, it can be useful to build an ideal customer profile. Determining additional statistics such as income and education can help you find more specific placements.

If your AdWords reports do not give you demographic data because your ads have not been placed on those sites, examine the demographic statistics discussed in the next section to see if you find a pattern.

Finding Related Websites

When you run a placement performance report, you can see which sites are sending you traffic that meets your advertising goals. Take those sites and input them into Google Ad Planner. This will give you detailed statistics about each of those websites.

The goal is not to examine each website individually. With composite data (high-level data mixed together), there are always anomalies because the data comes from multiple sources and is mixed together. Therefore, instead of looking at all the stats of each website that has performed well for you, look for patterns among the data.

For example, if you do not have a clear demographic picture yet, look for commonalties of gender, age, income, and education levels among all the sites that are performing for you across the display network. Make note of any patterns and see if you can start to build a demographic profile.

When examining the data items, look for the following:

- Sites also visited (Figure 10.29)
- Categories
- Keywords searched for

Sites also visited	
Site	**Affinity** ?
searchenginewatch.com	218.5x
searchengineland.com	164.2x
seomoz.org	135.7x
mashable.com	29.6x
techcrunch.com	26.8x
t.co	12.5x
mozilla.org	5.3x
twitter.com	3.3x
linkedin.com	3.3x
wordpress.com	3.3x

Figure 10.29 Sites also visited for CertifiedKnowledge.org (the author's blog)

You can copy and paste them into an Excel sheet. Repeat that process for your top-performing display network websites. As you copy and paste, you will start to form a list that contains some sites listed multiple times as they are related to other high-performing websites. Once you have compiled a list of websites, use a pivot table in your spreadsheet program to create a single list of websites where column 1 is the website name and column 2 is the number of times it appeared in the sheet. Repeat this step for keywords searched for, related websites, and categories. You will use this data in the next few research techniques.

Sites Also Visited

Another way you can filter websites in the Ad Planner tool is by other sites your audience has visited (Figure 10.30). Either use the top-performing sites from your placement performance report, or use the most common sites also visited from the previous research step that you created in a spreadsheet.

Figure 10.30 Filtering based on related websites

If you have a defined demographic, you can leave those items selected so that the related sites will be included if they also reach your demographic.

In this filtering list, click on a website and view its detailed information. If there is a website where you want to place your ads, click the box next to the website from the Research pane and it will be added to your media plan.

Each time you add a site to your media plan, the top of the Research pane will be updated with the number of placements in that media plan and its overall reach.

Keywords Searched For

You can also view sites based on what keywords people search for that lead to that website. You can run a keyword performance report and see what keywords are your highest-converting keywords. Then you can input those keywords into the Ad Planner

(Figure 10.30) to see what other sites these searchers are visiting. If they accept advertising, you can place your ads on those websites.

By placing your ads on related sites, you get a second chance with the user who conducted a search for one of your keywords yet chose to go to another site instead of yours. You can visit the detailed profiles of several related websites and copy the list of keywords for each site into Excel. Then, you can create an Excel pivot table from the keyword list to see the most common words used to navigate to those sites. Examine the most commonly used words to see if they should be added to your display network keywords.

You can also use demographic filtering, related site filtering, and the other filtering options along with the keyword filter. However, if you filter by too many data points, you will eventually end up with a message that no websites can be found.

Filtering the Information by Category

If you only want to see what sites fall into predefined categories, you can use the category filtering option (Figure 10.31) to either view all the websites within a category or use some other filtering items (such as demographics) to only see sites within a category that match your audience characteristics.

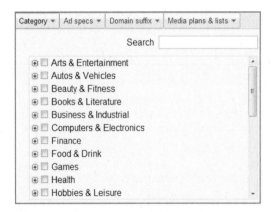

Figure 10.31 Filtering Ad Planner data by categories

If you saved all of the previous research in Excel with the categories listed per website, you can utilize a pivot table to see which categories are already performing for your ads.

Filtering the Information by Ad Size and Type

Not all websites, even in the Google display network, accept all ad formats. You can view websites based on the ad types and sizes that they accept. For example, if you are beginning to analyze image ads to see if they are performing for your company but you have only created a 250 × 250 image for testing purposes, you could choose to only see sites that show image ads of that size format.

After you have conducted your research, added sites to your plan, and saved your plan, it is time to move those sites into your AdWords account.

Adding Ad Planner Sites to AdWords

When you have finished conducting research, you can save your media plan for further use and study in the future, export the data into a spreadsheet program, or export the data directly to AdWords.

Just click the Export To AdWords button and you will walk through a wizard that asks you which ad group you want to save the placements to inside your AdWords account.

DoubleClick Ad Planner gives you access to a tremendous amount of data. However, you need to combine it with an advertising outlet, such as Google AdWords, before you can find the full value in the research for advertising purposes.

Best Practices for Advanced Display Network Usage

The display network has multiple layers of complexity you can use to display your ads, from using keywords to placements to keywords plus placements to demographic targeting. In addition, all of your typical campaign settings such as geography, time of day, and budget also apply to display campaigns. With so many options available, it is often simpler to create scenarios for reaching your target audience and then examine the list of possible targeting options to best reach that audience.

- If you are placing your ads on either very large sites or a large number of small sites, refine your ad exposure by adding keywords in the same ad group as your managed placements. This way, your ad will only show on the sites you want when the article also matches your keywords.

- If you are new to display targeting, start with just managed placements (or managed placements and keywords together). This gives you the most control over your ad serving.

- The most important setting for the entire display network is how you choose Google to show your ads: use the broadest targeting method, or match all selected targeting methods.

- You need to be familiar with the Networks tab data, often called the placement performance reports, to accomplish any display campaign optimization.

- Run the placement performance report. If a site is not performing for you, either take action to improve performance or block your ad from being shown on that site. If a website is performing for you, block it from the discovery campaign and add it to a placements-only campaign.

- Become familiar with the demographics of customers who convert on your website so you can set demographic bids and use that information to find new sites to place your ads.
- Remarketing will help you bring back potential customers so you can try to sell to them again.
- Interest and topic targeting will allow you to have a large reach, but at the cost of highly refined targeting.
- When writing ads for interest targeting or very general display advertising display network, test general versus specific offers that are laden with benefits.
- DoubleClick Ad Planner can give you free insight into many statistics about most websites on the Internet. Use the Ad Planner to find new sites where you want to place your ads.

The display network is about reach. There are more possible impressions and clicks on the display network than on search. Therefore, understanding your audience and writing ads to reach that audience will help you get not just clicks from the display network but conversions as well.

In the next chapter, we will discuss another way of reaching your target audience based on their location. With location targeting, you can make sure that only users in specific locations can view your search or display ads.

Advanced Geographic Targeting

Location targeting allows you to show your ads to consumers in specific geographic regions, whether it is multiple countries or five miles around a single zip code. The first part of this chapter focuses on how to show your ads to specific locations and some pitfalls that you should understand.

The second half of the chapter focuses on writing ads for different geographies and on using methods to engage users based on their knowledge of your target area and what they consider credible.

Finally, the chapter closes with a geographic report where you can find opportunities to optimize your account based on your performance in specific geographies.

Chapter Contents

What is geographic targeting?

Reaching users in specific locations

Location targeting considerations

Treating locals and nonlocals differently in your ad copy

Viewing geographic results

Geographic performance reports

Best practices for geographic targeting

What Is Geographic Targeting?

AdWords allows you to choose where your ads will be displayed. This is useful if you want to show a different message in different locations, set different budgets by location, or optimize your spending based on returns from different geographies.

The benefit for a location-based business, such as a New York dentist or a Best Buy in Fargo, is fairly obvious: You reach only consumers who will travel to your business location. Therefore, a plumber in San Francisco or a pizza delivery company in Dallas only needs to show their ads to those who are in their business area.

However, e-commerce and national companies often overlook the advantages of using location-specific online ads. If you examine the marketing of a company like Coca-Cola, you will notice different billboards and commercials in San Francisco as opposed to those that appear in New York or London. This is because consumers react differently to various messages based on their location norms.

All campaigns must choose in which geographies the ads in each campaign will appear. The default option is usually a country or bundle of countries. However, regardless of the reach you want your ads to have, it is a setting you should be aware of so that you know exactly where Google is displaying your ads.

Before exploring the location targeting options and how local, national, and multinational companies can take advantage of them, you must understand how the technology that is used to identify a user's location works.

The Technology Behind Location Targeting

Google identifies a user's location in four main ways:

- By looking at the Google property used for the query
- By examining the explicit geographic keywords used in a search query
- By inspecting the previous geographic keywords used in searches
- By determining the searcher's location based on their IP address

For our purposes, I will simplify these as much as possible and leave out some of the technology so these concepts are easy to grasp in the framework of a single chapter.

The first factor used to determine a user's location is based on the extension of the Google search engine being used. For instance, users in France go to Google.fr and users in Canada go to Google.ca. The country extension tells Google from which country a searcher wishes to see information.

The second is when a searcher uses an explicit geographic qualifier in their search query, such as "Austin plumber." When a geographic qualifier is used, Google must feel confident that they understand the area in which the searcher is seeking information.

In the Austin plumber example, there are a few locations in the United States that use the word "Austin." However, the vast majority of them are looking for Austin,

Texas, information; therefore, Google may be fairly confident that the user is looking for that information and might therefore serve ads for Austin, Texas.

If you consider a query such as "Washington plumber," the query could refer to Washington, DC; Washington state; Washington, Utah; or any of the other Washington-named cities or counties. In another example, there are two large cities named Kansas City. In both of these cases, Google will show fewer (or no) ads because they are not highly confident that they understand the user's location.

The third method that Google uses to show ads is based on a person's previous search history. If you use explicit geographic qualifiers in the search query, which is the second method, Google has an idea of the location where you want to find information and may use that information to target ads for other queries. If you do a search for "Washington DC plumber," and then follow that query with "Washington kitchen remodeling," you may see geographic ads, as Google now has some idea that you have defined Washington, DC, as your target location. In addition, if you search for "Washington DC plumber" and follow that query with "kitchen remodeling," you might also see location-based ads even without a geographic qualifier in the search query, as Google remembers previous searches.

The fourth way Google shows location-based ads is based on your IP address. When a computer logs on to the Web, it is assigned an IP address. This could be considered your computer's location on the Web. Many IP addresses are mapped to physical locations so that Google understands where you are located.

However, the IP address for your computer is not always your computer's actual location: it's your ISP's location, otherwise known as your host provider. Therefore, the fourth method looks at ISP locations and attempts to discern your location with the assumption that most people live close to their ISP provider.

This leads to the following scenario: When you do any form of location targeting, whether it's for a country or a city, three things are going to happen:

- A searcher inside your target location will see your ad.
- A searcher outside your target location will see your ad.
- A searcher inside your target location will not see your ad.

If you only want to show your ads in Chicago, these are the three scenarios (Figure 11.1) that will occur:

- Searcher 1 is inside your target area. The host provider is in your target area. This is a perfect match.
- Searcher 2 is outside your target area. The host provider is in your target area. Though this searcher is outside your target location, they will still see your geographic ad.
- Searcher 3 is inside your target area. The host provider is outside your target area. Though this searcher is in your target area, they will still not see your geographic ad.

Figure 11.1 Location targeting examines host provider locations.

Location targeting will help you reach an audience with a unique message, give you the ability to raise your CTR and conversion rates in different locations, and make better use of your budget. Understanding the basics of how location targeting works will help you troubleshoot why certain groups of people are or are not seeing your ads.

How Accurate Is Location Targeting?

The first step in location targeting is to choose a location. This is a required setting for every campaign. Even if you used a geographic keyword, such as "Chicago dentist," you must still set the United States as the location targeting option in that same campaign.

Since you are often not targeting a consumer's location but their host provider location, how accurate is location targeting? Before we get into the numbers, let's look at a few exceptions that adversely affect location targeting:

The AOL Conundrum AOL dial-up users all appear to come from Reston, Virginia. This means that Google cannot always show ads to AOL users based on their IP addresses; they must use other forms of technology or dissect geographic search queries to discern AOL dial-up user's locations. As of November 2011, AOL dial-up has more than 3.5 million subscribers in the United States and still has European customers as well. To reach AOL dial-up users, it is best to use geographic keywords in a campaign targeted at the country level, which will be fully explained in the section "Reaching Users in an Area Smaller than a Country." While this is AOL specific, other dial-up and satellite providers have the same issue.

Corporate VPNs When a user logs into their corporate virtual private network (VPN) and then accesses the Web, their location is often shown as their VPN's location, which is commonly the corporate headquarters, not their actual location.

Data Cards These are often called air cards or cell cards. They are connection devices you can attach to your computer so that your computer can access the Web via a cell connection. Often these cards show completely different locations than your cell phone on the same network. Although cell phones can use cell tower triangulation to determine location (and a few other methods, such as GPS), these additional data points are not always used in determining a computer's location when accessing the Web from a data card. The search engine may not realize you are using a data card to access the Web. Therefore, a data card user may be assigned an IP address from the cell company, which might be in the exact same location or in a completely different state.

Cities That Cross State Lines The Chicago metro area is primarily in Illinois, but it also encompasses areas in Indiana and Wisconsin. The Washington, DC, metro area crosses into Maryland and Virginia. In these cases, you may see IP addresses assigned from an incorrect state. It is not a common occurrence, but it does happen.

The following unofficial numbers were calculated by talking with people at the search engine companies and by my own testing. The accuracy of these numbers is thrown off by the above factors, as well as some other technological idiosyncrasies. Therefore, this is a rough compilation of all geographic areas; some areas will have higher degrees of accuracy and others lower. Here are the unofficial numbers for the United States:

99.9999 Percent for Determining a Country The country of origin is easy for a search engine to determine. More than just IP data is used to establishing country of origin, and the search engines are highly accurate at determining country information. The most common issue that throws off country-level targeting is corporate VPNs.

90 to 95 Percent at the State or Region Level That is a global U.S. average. There are some states, such as California, where most of the population does not border another state. Therefore, most of the ISPs are in that state and the accuracy of state-based targeting is exceptionally high. Illinois has cities that border and spill over into other states: There's Chicago in the North, which flows into both Indiana and Wisconsin, and in the southern tip of the state, there's the St. Louis, Missouri metro area. These two areas cause some users in both the north and the south to potentially see ads from other states. However, the users in the middle of Illinois will mostly see Illinois-based ads. Each country has widely different accuracy levels at the state or regional level. Canada's numbers are fairly similar to the United States'. However, the accuracy of regional targeting in the United Kingdom is quite poor.

85 to 90 Percent at the Metropolitan Level A metropolis is a city that influences adjacent neighborhoods or cities. For instance, San Francisco is a city with a population around 800,000 people. San Francisco influences San Jose and Oakland. Therefore, the San Francisco metropolitan (often called metro) area is considered the entire region around San Francisco, Oakland, and San Jose with a population nearing 8 million people.

Another overall U.S. average is 85 to 90 percent. There are some cities where user location is easy to determine due to lack of ISP competition and rural areas outside of the city. Fargo, North Dakota, borders Morehead, Minnesota. The same metro area has two different names based on which state you live in. The areas outside Fargo are very rural. If you want to reach users in the Fargo metro area (users in Fargo and Morehead), your accuracy will be fairly high. However, if you only want to reach users in Fargo and not Morehead, your accuracy will be lower as some of the same ISPs service both areas.

75 to 80 Percent at the City Level Reaching only users in a city can be challenging at times because although a city is a predefined geographic area most ISPs create their infrastructure based on the wider metropolitan area.

If you are targeting a city that is not in a metro area and is surrounded by rural areas, the accuracy increases. If you are trying to target a city in a metro area, the accuracy decreases.

For instance, if you are attempting to reach only users in Chicago city proper, your accuracy is high for the middle of the city, as the middle of the city does not border any other cities. Many users on the north side of the city of Chicago see ads from Evanston, a city just north of Chicago. Therefore, your accuracy when targeting the city of Chicago is high in the middle of the city and will decline for users in the north. Since Evanston is still in the Chicago metro area, if you are targeting the entire metro of Chicago, the north-side residents would see your ads. This is why metro targeting is often more accurate than city targeting.

Google has tried to make location targeting more accurate by showing the location within search results and allowing users to adjust their location to show more accurate results. These numbers only reflect Google search data. For Google Maps, searchers must use some location identifier and, therefore, the maps properties are highly accurate.

These numbers are rough guidelines, since there are many exceptions where the numbers could be higher or lower. None of these numbers should scare you away from trying geographic targeting. Targeting a specific location with ads written for that location is one of the more powerful combinations you will find in AdWords, regardless of whether you are a national company or a local company that serves only a single region.

Marketing is about connecting with users. People love and defend their local areas. Reaching consumers based on their geography allows you to connect with searcher not just by their search query, but by their location as well.

Reaching Users in Specific Locations

Location targeting is set at the campaign level. To access these settings, navigate to the campaign Settings tab. In the Location And Languages section you will see your current settings (Figure 11.2). To change your location settings, click the Edit link near your current location list to choose where you want your ad to be displayed.

Figure 11.2 Viewing and changing your location settings

Once you choose to edit your locations you will be presented with a list of your current locations and a box where you can search for locations (Figure 11.3), or you can view a map. To ensure that you are targeting the correct locations, using the map is useful. For the purposes of limiting the number of images, we will only look at the map listings; just note that you can do these same searches directly from the campaign Settings tab.

Locations		
Targeted locations	**Reach**	
All countries and territories - add a location to refine your targeting		
Enter a location such as a city, region, or country	Show map | Send feedback	
Save Cancel		

Figure 11.3 Editing your location options

When you click the map option, you can start to search for any geographic areas.

Finding Locations to Target

Once you have navigated to the maps section, you can search for locations that you wish to include. As you type, Google will present a list of locations that match your search result (Figure 11.4).

The first items to examine are the matches. These are the locations that match the search query you are performing. Depending on the search query, you may see matches that include your terms, matches that include your location, or related locations. For each match you have several options. Next to each location you will also see the geographic area: country, state, province, metro, city, and so forth.

You will not see every possible geographic area. Google does not allow you to target counties and neighborhoods. The most common results you will see are:

- Country
- State / Province
- Metro
- City

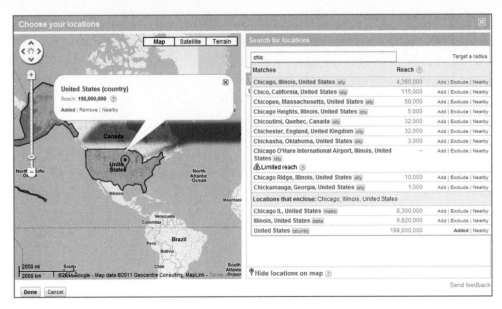

Figure 11.4 Searching for locations

For each geographic area, you will also see an estimated reach. This may differ significantly from the actual population as this is the unique cookie estimate for any region. This estimate can also be skewed by multiple cookies for the same user. For instance, if the same person has a desktop, laptop, tablet, and phone, Google sees this as four unique cookies even though it is one person.

Within the search results you have several options that we will examine individually.

Add the Location

If you click on the location or click the Add link, that location will be added to your list of targeted locations, and a map will be displayed highlighting your target area. You can add multiple locations to a single campaign in this fashion (Figure 11.5).

Exclude the Location

There are times you do not want to show an ad to a geographic area. This is common if you do not serve an area, ship to a location, or have underperformance within a region.

If you click the Exclude link, your ad will not be displayed to a region and that region will be called out within the interface.

You can only exclude regions in the area you have chosen. For instance, if you are only showing your ads to the United States, you cannot exclude Russia, because your ads are not being shown there anyway. However, if you are an e-commerce site and want to reach everyone in the United States but you do not ship to Alaska and Hawaii, you could include the entire United States and exclude Alaska and Hawaii (Figure 11.6).

Figure 11.5 Choosing locations

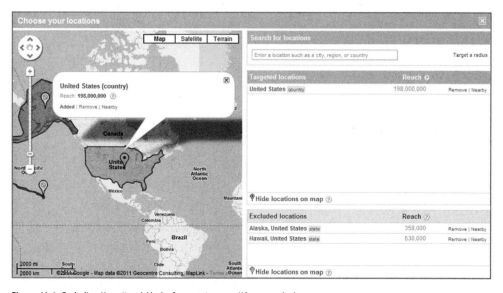

Figure 11.6 Excluding Hawaii and Alaska from seeing your US-targeted ads

There are times you may want to use this feature for organizational purposes so you can showcase different ads based on a user location. For instance, if you sell renter's insurance, you might want to have three different campaigns based on the benefits in the ad copy and the landing page you want to send visitors to on your website. Let's assume these are the goals of your benefit messages in ad copy:

- Showcase fire insurance benefits in San Diego

- Showcase earthquake benefits in San Francisco and Los Angeles
- Showcase a general benefit to the rest of California

In this instance, you would have one campaign that was targeted to California and excluded San Diego, Los Angeles, and San Francisco. Then you would create a campaign that was shown to just users in San Diego, and another one that targeted San Francisco and Los Angeles.

By utilizing a combination of location targeting and excluded regions, you can narrow down exactly who will see your ad copy. This strategy is also useful for showing different offers, messages, and benefits in different sections of the same country.

However, one of the most important aspects of writing ads for specific locations is to determine if the user is local or nonlocal. Each of those groups has different concerns and knowledge about your area, and therefore you need to engage them in different manners.

Search Nearby

Sometimes you will be targeting locations when you are unfamiliar with the geographic regions near your location. When you want to find other locations near your target area, click the Nearby link and you will see additional locations near the location you are searching (Figure 11.7).

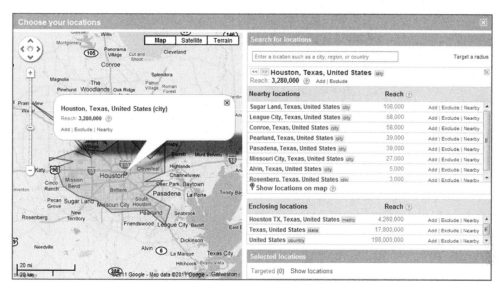

Figure 11.7 Locations nearby Houston

From this interface, you have the typical options to include, exclude, or find even more nearby location data.

Radius Targeting

If you would rather reach users around a central point instead of targeting specific locations, you can use radius targeting. With radius targeting you can enter an address, zip code, or other map point and then choose how far you wish to target around that location (Figure 11.8). To specify a radius, click the link Target A Radius, and you'll see the screen shown in Figure 11.8.

By default, the radius is set to 20 miles, and often Google recommends a minimum 10-mile radius. Keep two factors in mind as you choose a radius:

- How far will people travel to visit your business?
- How far are you willing to travel?

In State College, Pennsylvania, for example, it is not uncommon for searchers to drive over an hour to one of the major cities from the rural center of Pennsylvania. Choosing a large radius could be a good choice for your business if you were targeting a rural area. However, even a five-mile radius could be over an hour drive during rush hour in Washington, DC. Therefore, examine how far you travel to your customers, or how far your customers travel to you when selecting your target radius.

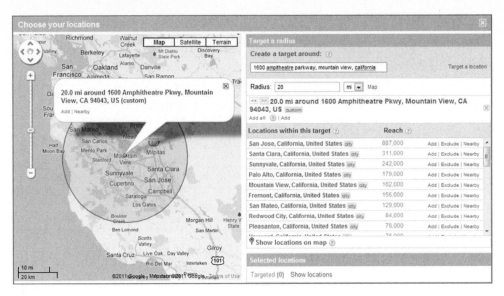

Figure 11.8 Radius targeting an address

The second factor to keep in mind is that you are often targeting *ISPs* and not always someone's physical location. For instance, Rogers Park is a neighborhood in Chicago consisting of over 60,000 residents. Yet, almost everyone in Rogers Park sees ads from either Evanston or downtown Chicago. If you were to target your ads to only Rogers Park, your ad impressions would be much smaller than actual searches for your company from people who live in Rogers Park.

Radius targeting is rarely accurate when you are targeting only a few miles, unless the searcher is on a maps property where they had to enter a specific address. In that case, radius targeting is highly accurate.

Advanced Location Targeting Options

The restaurant Chicago Pizza is my favorite place to order Chicago-style pizza. While their pizza is great, they suffer from a large problem when trying to advertise with AdWords. Google sees someone from Seattle searching for "Chicago Pizza" and assumes the user wants to see pizza restaurants in Chicago. In fact, that user probably wants to learn how to make Chicago-style pizzas or what that pizza type even is; however, "Chicago Pizza" ads appear by default because the geography is part of the company name.

The advanced location targeting options can solve these issues. By default Google examines location by:

- Physical location (IP address and other signals)
- Search Query Intent (Chicago pizza)

The advanced options allow you to adjust these default settings. To adjust the default options, open the Advanced Location Options (Figure 11.9) and change the default settings.

Figure 11.9 Changing the location targeting method

If you are a hotel in Seattle, you might not want someone in Seattle who types in "hotel" to see your ad—you want nonlocals to see your ads. Therefore, you can exclude users based on physical location or search intent as well (Figure 11.10).

Figure 11.10 Excluding users based on location or search intent

In the case of a hotel, what you might do is create two campaigns. One campaign excludes users based on search intent so that your ads will only be seen by people in your local region. Since these ads are targeting locals, you can run ads that are targeted to locals looking for a getaway, hosting a meeting, or wanting to rent the ballroom for a prom. The second campaign will exclude based on physical location and only target travelers looking to book a room in your hotel.

If you are having problems reaching the correct people based on location or search query signals, the advanced options can help you ensure that only the correct audience is seeing your ads.

So far, you have learned how to target or exclude users. Beyond just targeting users, there are some specific items you should think about when targeting various regions.

Location Targeting Considerations

Although you can reach users from an area as small as one mile around an address to almost every country in the world, there are some things you should consider before choosing your location targeting options.

Targeting Multiple Countries

You can easily add multiple countries at once with the search and add functionality of the location targeting tool. However, it is rarely a good choice to show the same ad to multiple countries at the same time for a variety of reasons, which I will explain in some detail.

It is common to see advertisers choose United Kingdom, New Zealand, Australia, Canada, and United States in a single campaign because all these countries speak English. However, that thinking can lead to problems down the road.

For example, if you choose these five countries, how do you spell a word such as *color*? It is spelled *colour* in some countries and *color* in others. While the basics of English are the same in most English-speaking countries, there are many colloquialisms, slang, and local customs that can cause a breakdown in communication even though the "correct" words are being used.

There are many words that not only have different spellings by country but have different meanings as well. For instance, the word *currar* is a Spanish word that means "to work" when used in Spain. However, in Argentina that same word means "defraud."

Country-Based Optimization

If you group all your countries into a single campaign, what is the next step to optimization? If you learn that the stats for your countries look like those in Table 11.1, what would you do next?

▶ **Table 11.1** Statistics for multiple countries

Country	Click-through rate	Conversion rate
United States	10%	1%
United Kingdom	1%	10%
Australia	3%	5%

In this case, you are receiving traffic in the United States, but the ad and landing page are not converting; therefore, you would want to choose a different combination to show to your visitors. However, in the United Kingdom you are converting quite well but your ad is not being clicked on very often, so you might want to test different ad copy to increase the click-through rate.

Since you have chosen all of your ads to be shown in these different countries in the same campaign, you would not be able to accomplish these changes in the same campaign. Therefore, the first step would be to duplicate the entire campaign and change the location targeting options for each campaign to show to the appropriate countries. If you advertise in only a handful of countries, it is useful to limit yourself to one country per campaign.

When to Ignore the One Country per Campaign Rule

Multinational companies may want to disregard this rule due to the number of countries they have to run ads for with limited staff or time to manage the campaigns. You always have to balance best practices with time and staff management.

Even if you are a multinational company that can serve multiple countries at once, if you do not have a large budget to effectively penetrate every single country you serve, it can be better to concentrate your budget on a small list of countries.

If your multinational company's goal is to advertise to searchers who have a high chance of converting, choose a handful of countries you do well in and limit your ads to show only in those few countries. Once you have effectively penetrated the marketplace and are seeing returns on your ad spend, expand your list of countries.

If your multinational company's goal is to penetrate new markets, selectively choose those new markets, reach your goals in those markets, and then move on to the next set of countries you want to learn more about your products.

For multinational companies, if you have a small budget and try to reach every single country, you will often fail at your objectives—you cannot be everything to everybody. Therefore, choose your country list wisely based on your marketing goals. Once you reach those goals, you should have higher revenues and can increase your budget as you expand your reach to new countries.

For most accounts, limiting yourself to one country per campaign will help you write better ad copy and allow you to send your visitors to country-specific pages in your website. This combination will lead to a better user experience, and higher conversion rates usually follow good user experiences.

Reaching Users in an Area Smaller than a Country

If you choose to advertise in an area smaller than a country, there are a few considerations for both your keywords and your campaign setup.

First, do not use geographic keywords in a campaign targeted to an area smaller than a country. When you choose to show your ads to users in a specific location, such as Chicago, you should not use nongeographic qualified keywords. For instance, if you are a plumber, your campaign is targeted to Chicago, and you use the keyword "Chicago plumber," your ad will only be shown to those identified as being in Chicago or explicitly looking for plumbers in Chicago, and those who search for "Chicago plumber." This double qualification of both keyword and location targeting is unnecessary. Since the campaign is already targeted to Chicago, you can use the keyword "plumber" and those users who search for "plumber" and are identified as looking for Chicago information will see your ad. Therefore, you can use nongeographic keywords such as plumber, kitchen remodeling, and so on, in location targeted campaigns.

If you were to use the keyword "Chicago plumber" in a campaign targeted to only Chicago, someone would have to be identified as being in Chicago and using "Chicago plumber" as their search query for your ad to be displayed.

As many users do not search with geographic queries, using a geographic qualified keyword in a campaign targeted only to Chicago would result in far fewer impressions than using a nongeographic keyword in the same campaign.

The one exception to this rule is when you have a small budget. It is common to see that search queries containing geographic terms have higher conversion rates than queries that do not contain geographic terms, assuming your business is based on location, such as a plumber or dentist. A searcher using a geographic area in the search query is looking for a local company. A search who does not specify a geography may not be looking for a local company or even services in the area where they are located.

Second, you need to decide if you want to reach most users in a location, or everyone in a location. If you want to reach everyone, you need to use two campaigns.

Using Multiple Campaigns to Reach All Searchers

Google is excellent at detecting the searcher's country of origin. However, there are many times when a searcher's location cannot be discerned, such as those listed in the earlier section "How Accurate Is Location Targeting?" In these cases, your geographic ads will not be displayed to these users. Therefore, if you want to make sure every searcher looking for your services sees your ad, use two campaigns.

The benefits of using a second campaign vary by location. When you are reaching a large area where there is less ISP confusion by location, the benefits may be minimal. If you are reaching areas where IP targeting is not very accurate—which is much more common outside of the United States—using two campaigns can be quite useful. To reach everyone possible, you will want both an IP and a GEO campaign:

IP Campaign This campaign is named after the IP detection technology used to detect a user's location. In this campaign, choose the location targeting of the area where you want to show your ads and do not use geographic keywords.

GEO Campaign This campaign will contain all geographically qualified keywords. In this campaign, choose your ads to be shown to the entire country, and then every keyword you use will have a geographic qualifier attached to it.

For instance, if you were an accounting service that was trying to reach searchers in Dallas, you would use the campaign structure shown in Table 11.2 to make sure the maximum number of searchers could find your ad.

▶ Table 11.2 Campaign structure to maximize geographic reach

Campaign name	IP campaign	GEO campaign
Target Geography	Dallas	United States
Example Keywords	Accounting services	Dallas accounting services
	Tax preparation	Dallas tax preparation
	Bookkeeping services	Dallas bookkeeping services

If you are constrained by time or budget and only want to use one campaign, keep in mind that most accounts will have more total impressions from an IP campaign than from a GEO campaign. However, many accounts find that their conversion rates are higher in their GEO campaign. Therefore, if you can only have one campaign to reach geography, choose based on your goals: more total searches or a higher conversion rate. When you want to reach all the searchers possible, using a combination of both GEO and IP campaigns will maximize your exposure.

Are Your Visitors Traveling Long Distances to Reach Your Business?

If your customers search with geographically qualified queries to find your business, do not rely on IP campaigns to reach your customers. For instance, searchers looking for hotels are rarely in the local area. Most searchers looking for hotels are searching for a city name and a hotel-based keyword, such as "San Francisco hotel." While Google attempts to discern if there is a local intent in the search query to show IP targeted ads, you should take greater control of your ad serving by using geographically qualified queries as keywords in your account.

You can still run two different campaigns to reach all the users searching for your hotel; however, in this case if you only wanted to run a single campaign, you would reach more qualified users by using a GEO campaign instead of an IP campaign.

The Most Popular Geographic Keywords

In GEO campaigns, you will want to use geographic qualified keywords. Most accounts will not use every possible geographic keyword. Based on the area you want to reach, choose the ones most applicable to your campaign's geo-targeting goals.

State Names When reaching all users in a state, use the state name as a keyword qualifier. Some common examples are "California car insurance" and "Alabama BMW dealership."

State Abbreviations The longer the state name, the more common it is to see searchers use the state abbreviation instead of the full state name. Keywords such as "NJ car insurance quote" or "AZ golf courses" are common searches. However, be careful when automating these abbreviations. Oregon's abbreviation is OR, which is such a common word that Google often ignores it and often does not consider it a state-based search. It is common to see ads for "plumber MD." While plumber doctors are not common businesses, MD is the abbreviation for Maryland. Maine is such a short state name that the residents rarely search for "plumber ME," which is a good thing, as their abbreviation ME could be mistaken as the common use of the word and not as a state abbreviation.

County Names Some states, such as Ohio, identify greatly with their local counties. Other states see very little search volume for county names. If you are licensed in a county or see a decent search volume for your local county, then use it as a keyword, such as "Orange County contractor."

There are times when a geographic name is used in many locations. For instance, Orange County, California, is near Los Angeles and home to Disneyland. Visitors to Disney World have passed through Orange County, Florida. There are several Orange Counties in the United States. When your geographic area's name, whether it be a county, city, or other area, is the same in multiple locations, then use your ad copy to identify which location you serve.

While the electrician in Orange County, California, and the electrician in Orange County, Texas, are competing for impressions on the keyword "Orange Country electrician," they are not competing for the clicks. The electrician in California does not want the users from Texas clicking on his ad. By adding the state abbreviation or some other geographic qualified keyword, such as the city name, the ad will inform the users of the actual area you serve. Santa Ana is the country seat of Orange Country, California. In this example, the ad copy "Orange County TX plumber," or "Santa Ana plumber" will help differentiate your ad from the other ads targeting Orange Counties in other states.

City or Metro Names Some of the most common geographic keywords are city and metro names. "Los Angeles museums," "Orlando resorts," and "Seattle travel agents" are good examples of using a city name as a keyword. There are also a handful of cities where the city abbreviations are worth considering; NYC for New York City and LA for Los Angeles are the most common U.S. examples.

Zip Codes and Area Codes "72113 plumber" is searched for by those looking for a plumber in Maumelle, Arkansas. Zip codes are hyper-local queries that generally have low search volume but highly targeted consumers. Area codes can also be used to designate a very specific local search.

When using area codes or zip codes as keyword qualifiers, do not utilize broad match. Google does not always realize that 60606 is different than 60406, yet anyone who lives in Chicago will tell you that one is in south Chicago and the other in north Chicago. Plumbers rarely serve both of those areas as it can take well over an hour, depending on traffic, to go from one zip code to another.

Neighborhoods Some larger cities, such as Chicago, have many residents who identify with their neighborhood and use their neighborhood names as geographic qualifiers in their search results. The search "Rogers Park apartments" was conducted an average of 1,300 times a month throughout 2009. While that is not a high search volume, the search query has an explicit geographic intent. If you rent apartments in Rogers Park, it is a keyword you should use. Searching by neighborhood names is not common in smaller cities; however, it is always worth examining the areas you are reaching to see if the consumers in your target market search with their neighborhood terms.

Airport Codes Many frequent travelers have been stuck in a city overnight due to the weather. Their first search is usually for the airport code and the word hotel followed by the airport code or restaurant. For instance, LAX is the abbreviation for the Los Angeles Airport. The search query "LAX hotel" is often searched more than 74,000 times a month.

There are instances where searchers have used SFO iPod headphones and gone shopping during a long layover. If you are near an airport, test using the airport codes as qualifiers. For example, if you were at the Hilton hotel located in the Chicago O'Hare airport, "ORD Hilton" and "ORD hotel" would be excellent keywords. In the LAX example, the query "LAX sushi" is searched a few hundred times each month. While the search volume is small, that is an explicit query. The more explicit the query, the higher the likelihood that conversion rates will be high.

If you serve the airport in some unique fashion, such as a taxi or limousine company, for instance, you should use airport codes as geo-qualifiers to your usual keywords.

Regional Lingo Every area has ways they describe themselves that are not official designations. Some of these words have high search volume, as that is how the locals think about their geographic area.

For instance, downtown Chicago is called the Loop. The query "loop restaurant" frequently breaks 15,000 searches a month, while "loop hotel" often breaks 27,000 monthly searches on Google. Since the word "loop" could describe multiple places, such as the Loop Restaurant in Minneapolis, adding ad copy such as "Serving Chicago's West Loop" can help weed out searchers looking for a different service.

While regional lingo can provide good geographic keywords, it is also excellent to use in ad copy. Using the local lexicon in your ad copy helps identify your company as understanding the local area and can often increase your click-through rate. Ad copy such as "Sushi Delivery in the Loop" or "Located in the Water Tower" instantly tells the searcher your location or delivery area, and it can help prequalify searchers who click on your ads.

However, always be careful when using regional lingo. Chicago is known as the Windy City. That term refers to Chicago politics, not the wind blowing off Lake Michigan. When a local hears someone refer to Chicago as the Windy City, they usually assume the person is not from Chicago.

Beyond targeting users with keywords or putting geographies in the ad copy is to think back to the actual person. Are they a local or a nonlocal? One of the most important aspects of writing ads for specific locations is to key in on the user's knowledge of the area. Each of these groups has different concerns and informational needs about your area, and therefore you must engage them in different manners.

Treating Locals and Nonlocals Differently in Your Ad Copy

A *local* is someone familiar with the location you are targeting. They have an understanding of the region, landmarks, and culture. A nonlocal is someone who has limited knowledge about your location, and therefore needs a different set of information than a local. Let's examine a few ways to treat these two audiences differently:

Geographic Descriptions A local searcher knows the area you serve. They want to know if you serve their actual location. Therefore, when a local searches for "Chicago plumber" they want to know if the plumber will come to their house. Using descriptors such as "Serving North Chicago" or "Located in the heart of the Triangle" tells a local exactly where you are or where you service.

A nonlocal may not have enough information about the area to understand the locations in the preceding ad copy. They are looking for blunt descriptors such as "New York City hotel" or "Downtown Pittsburgh hotel." When using geographic descriptors in ad copy for nonlocals, rarely should you use regional lingo. Reassure the searcher that you serve the location where they are searching for information.

Where Are You Located? A local will look for precise information. What building is your office located in? How long does it take to drive to your store? Using ad copy such as "Near Rush Street," "Located in the Water Tower," or "Rogers Park Real Estate Specialists" gives a local exact information.

However, a nonlocal will be confused by much of that language. A nonlocal wants to know if you can even serve their needs. A traveler wants to know general information such as how far you are from shopping, if you are near the airport, or if you are close to downtown.

Rush Street and Michigan Avenue are both in the heart of the Chicago shopping district. A local knows that fact. Therefore, "On Rush Street" tells a local more precise information than "In the Shopping District." However, a nonlocal may not know that fact about Rush Street; therefore, the more general ad copy "Located in the Shopping District," is better nonlocal ad copy.

Engaging the Searcher Once someone has clicked on your ad, your landing page needs to continue to engage the searcher based on their knowledge of the local area. A local will look for driving directions, phone numbers, maps, and detailed business information on your website. If you are a delivery company, show a map that highlights the areas you deliver to so the person can quickly see if you serve their area.

Conversely, if you are a hotel catering to nonlocals, showing a map of the area with your location, the airport, the shopping district, or the nearest amusement park will let them understand how far you are from those various items that maybe related to the purpose of their trip.

Conversion Activities Since locals know precise information about your area, they often jump to items such as driving directions, online delivery ordering, or in-store pickup once they realize you can serve their needs.

However, nonlocals rarely have enough information to make that quick of a decision. It is common for a nonlocal to make a phone call or send an email looking for a specific piece of information before finishing any conversion processes you have. Take note of the most common questions you receive as you can put those as pieces of information on your landing page to help a nonlocal make a quicker decision.

Rarely are locals and nonlocals looking for the same information. Think through what someone who knows your local area would want to find. If you are an actual store, it's most likely driving directions or a phone number. If you are a pizza delivery company, it is most likely delivery area and online ordering, or a phone number to order over the phone.

For nonlocals, you may need to give out as much information about the local area, such as shopping opportunities or the local amusement park, as you do about your actual business. By thinking through the differences between these two groups of individuals, you can write better ads and send the searcher to appropriate landing pages that can answer their questions so they can take the next step of doing business with your company.

If you use regional targeting, your ad could show a fifth line of ad text denoting the region your ads are targeted to. This is good for locals and excellent for nonlocals. However, there is a way to put an actual address below your ad copy using location extensions.

Automatically Inserting Your Address into the Ad Copy

The location extension allows you to add additional information about your business location to your ad copy. This is another ad extension similar to those discussed in

Chapter 4, "Writing Compelling Ads," except this extension is only available if you want to showcase your business location to a user.

To access the location extension, navigate to the Ad Extensions tab and choose the Location Extension options (Figure 11.11).

Figure 11.11 Location Extension options

From this interface, you can view all your location extensions or add new ones. There are two ways of adding location extensions. The easiest way to accomplish this is to link your AdWords account with your Local Business Center account. Expand the section under Addresses From Google Places and enter your account credentials. This will automatically link your AdWords account to your Google Places account so that your locations can show in your ad copy (Figure 11.12).

Figure 11.12 Connecting your Google Places account

As with all extensions, they are enabled at the campaign level, so if you wish to use the location extension in multiple campaigns you need to create a new extension for each campaign. You can use the same Google Places account for all your campaigns.

> ## Google Places Account
>
> All businesses should claim their Google Places account. This lets you control your business information that is displayed on Google maps and ensures the information is accurate. Navigate to www.google.com/local/add/ and walk through Google's wizard to create your account and enter or edit your business information. If you have several locations, use the bulk upload feature to add all your businesses at once. After you have created an account, you will be able to see statistics on how often your information was viewed and the number of actions that occurred with your listings.

When entering your information, you can choose from Google's icons or upload your own icon that will show on Google maps. The default icons on Google Maps are red. Therefore, it can help your listing stand out on the map by utilizing yellow or blue in your icons. At a minimum, use your website's favicon (the icon that shows up in most browsers next to the site's URL in the location box) so that you can extend your branding to multiple properties.

If you do not want to link your Google Local Business Center account, you can enter addresses manually (Figure 11.13). This is very useful when you are advertising for a location you do not own. For instance, if you are holding an event at a conference center or hotel, you may not own the venue but you still want to advertise the location. Therefore, adding addresses manually can be useful to promote the location of the event.

Figure 11.13 Manually adding addresses

Once you have saved addresses in your campaign settings, Google will display your address in the text ads on Google.com (Figure 11.14) when Google determines that your address will help the searcher find the information they are seeking. Your address will almost always show on Google Local properties like maps.google.com.

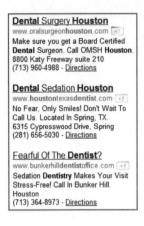

Figure 11.14 Address shown in text ads on Google.com

If you have multiple addresses in the same campaign, each ad could be shown with any of your addresses. Generally, Google will display the address that is nearest the searcher. If you want to limit an ad to only display one address with an ad, you need to use the filtering option for the location extension (Figure 11.15) and only use one address per campaign.

Figure 11.15 Location extension filtering options

Using location extensions will help your business connect with searchers on Google.com by showing the additional address and giving the consumer more information about your business. However, location extensions really shine when your ads are shown on Google Maps. Utilizing custom icons and creating a robust Google Places page will help your business stand out from the competition and can dramatically increase your presence on local properties.

A Case Study into Local Belief Systems

Local residents usually respect and defend their cities. One does not walk on stage in Boston and disparage the legacy of the Boston Celtics. Each area also has different beliefs and uses different criteria to determine whether information is credible.

These beliefs carry over into response rates for advertising. It is not uncommon to show the same ad in two different geographies and find two very different click-through rates or conversion rates. I'm going to walk through a study I did with a company that serves ads in the northeast United States.

This company has several locations throughout multiple states. As they were trying to drive awareness of their new locations and attempting to drive foot traffic into their buildings, the main goal was to bring qualified visitors to their website so they could showcase how easy it was for anyone in the northeast to find one of their locations. They wanted to show that same ease in the ad copy as well as create a synergy between the ad copy and the landing page.

The headline, description line 1, and display URL of these ads were identical. The only difference was description line 2. The two lines were:

- Locations throughout the state
- Convenient locations near you

Both of those lines of ad copy talk about multiple locations, but the difference in response rates between Pennsylvania and New Jersey (two states that border each other) was stunning (Table 11.3).

▶ **Table 11.3** Click-through rate by ad copy and geography

	Convenient locations near you	Locations throughout the state
New Jersey	13.6%	2.1%
Pennsylvania (All)	5.6%	11.3%
Philadelphia	8%	5.5%
Rest of state	2.3%	16.4%

New Jersey is a state where most people, except for commuters, do not drive from the north side to the south side of the state on a regular basis, even though it takes less than three hours to do so. Therefore, the ad copy "Locations throughout the state" did not do well. New Jersey is a state of convenience. The adage "if it's more than 15 minutes away, it doesn't exist" can be used to explain much of the state's behavior. Hence, the ad copy that used the word "convenient" did well in the state.

The middle of Pennsylvania is rural. Consumers often drive an hour or more to shop at the outlet malls. It is not uncommon to see someone from State College, which is in the middle of the state, drive to Philadelphia, Pittsburgh, or the Poconos to do their shopping. All of those options take more than an hour of driving time. Overall, people in the middle of the state do not believe the word "convenient" applies to them. Therefore, outside of Philadelphia, the ad copy using the word "convenient" did poorly. However, telling people in Pennsylvania the truth—we're not close, but we are all over the state—increased response rates.

Philadelphia, one of the largest cities in the United States, was the exception in Pennsylvania. It is common to see residents of large cities behave differently from people who live in rural areas. The CTR difference between Philadelphia and the rest of Pennsylvania highlights these differences.

If this were your account, you would want to divide your targeting into four campaigns:

- The first campaign would target only New Jersey with the "convenient" ad copy.
- The second campaign would target Pennsylvania and use the excluded regions feature so consumers in Philadelphia do not see the ad. This campaign would use the "Locations throughout the state" ad copy.
- The third campaign would only target Philadelphia with the "convenient" ad copy, and test a few other variations of ads to see what else resonated in this city.
- The fourth campaign would utilize geographic keywords. This campaign would have a large number of ad groups that all use the geographic modifiers, such as New Jersey, Pittsburgh, Pennsylvania, Allentown, Trenton, and Philadelphia.

The difference in belief systems by geography is one of the reasons you see different billboards and TV commercials from national companies in different locations. Each area has different cultural norms. If no one believes your ads, the ads will not get clicked and you will not receive conversions from those searchers.

Viewing Geographic Results

When you start adding multiple addresses or showing your ads in a variety of geographies, it can be difficult to see your ads and the local competition as you might not live in all of your target markets. Google provides a nice tool that allows you to see ads in various locations.

Navigate to `https://adwords.google.com/d/AdPreview/`. At the top of the page you can enter specific criteria to preview ads (as shown in Figure 11.16):

- Searcher information:
  - Keyword
  - Google domain (Google.com, Google.co.uk)
  - Language
  - Location
  - Device type

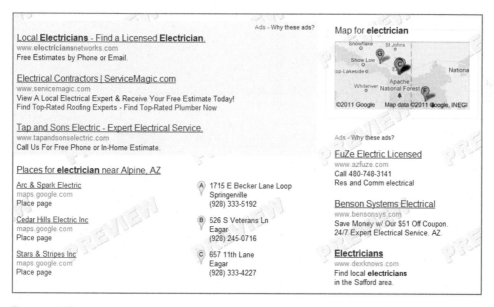

Figure 11.16 Ad Preview Tool

Once you fill out the information, you can preview what a user who is conducting a search at that moment in time would see in that target geography. This is an important caveat: *at that moment in time*. If your daily budget is exhausted for the day, your ad will not show up on Google.com, and therefore, it will also not show up in the Ad Preview Tool.

If you want to see what someone who lives in Alpine, Arizona, would see when conducting a search for "electrician" on Google.com in English, enter the information into the tool. The bottom of the preview page will reload with your search results (Figure 11.17).

Figure 11.17 Electrician preview results for Alpine, AZ

You should always use this tool when searching for your own ads, because if you conduct searches on Google for your ad and then never click on them, it appears to Google that your ads are not relevant to you as a searcher. When this happens, Google may stop showing your ads to you when you conduct searches, or you may see the ad in different positions than one-time searchers. When your ad is displayed on the ad preview page, it does not count as an impression or affect the statistics in your account in any manner.

Geographic Performance Reports

AdWords offers geographic performance data, which will give you statistics broken down by geographic region. For instance, you can see the cost per click, click-through rate, conversion rate, and cost per conversion by geographic region (Figure 11.18).

In Chapter 16, "AdWords Reports: How to Extract Actionable Information," I will take a detailed look at reports and extracting data out of AdWords in order to optimize accounts. Please note that with the geographic data, you can customize this data by country, region (state or province), metro area, and city (Figure 11.19).

Page 348 · CHAPTER 11: ADVANCED GEOGRAPHIC TARGETING

Country/Territory	Clicks	Avg. CPC	Cost	Avg. Pos.	Conv. (1-per-click)	Cost / conv. (1-per-click)	Conv. rate (1-per-click)	Region
United States	6,574	$8.90	$58,485.20	1.7	72	$800.28	1.10%	California
United States	5,157	$8.42	$43,447.03	1.7	57	$756.93	1.11%	New York
United States	8,399	$2.81	$23,592.93	1.5	45	$512.73	0.54%	Targeted areas with low traffic
United States	3,033	$10.65	$32,291.53	1.8	42	$759.48	1.40%	Texas
United States	2,528	$9.37	$23,692.53	1.9	26	$901.31	1.03%	Florida
United States	868	$10.67	$9,262.08	2	19	$486.38	2.20%	Washington
United States	563	$11.93	$6,717.44	1.8	17	$385.01	3.06%	Alabama
United States	1,138	$10.26	$11,672.14	1.9	17	$674.92	1.51%	Michigan
United States	1,629	$9.81	$15,978.08	1.7	17	$935.92	1.05%	Pennsylvania

Figure 11.18 Geographic performance data

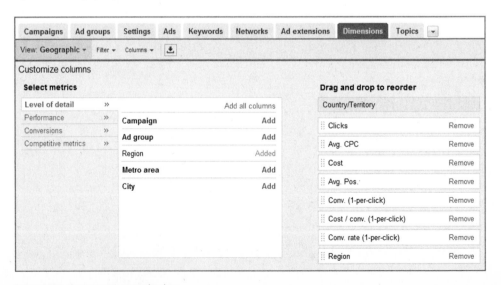

Figure 11.19 Customizing geographic data

One good use of this report is to find areas where you are not performing well. If you are targeting the entire United States and find that only 1 percent of your conversions are coming from New York City, yet that metro area is roughly 16.5 percent of the entire U.S. population, then you are not fully taking advantage of the region.

You may find there is more competition in New York City for your services and that your ads are on page 2 or 3, and to receive more exposure you need to raise your bids in just that area. Or you may find that you are receiving the visitors, but your conversion rate there is much lower than in other areas.

In this case, you might want to create a new campaign that is targeted to just New York City, where you can showcase a different offer and bid separately from the rest of the United States. You should also exclude New York City from showing ads in your original campaign that is targeted to the entire country.

An easy way of working with this report is to use Excel pivot tables, as discussed in Chapter 7, "Demystifying Quality Score." If you examine your data by geographic region, you can see conversions, conversion rate, and other data points by individual region (Figure 11.20).

Figure 11.20 Geographic data in a pivot table

One of the quality score factors for search is your click-through rate in a geographic region. If your ads have a high CTR in Seattle and a low CTR in Phoenix, your ads will be shown more in Seattle due to a higher CTR in that region. The geographic performance report will allow you to see CTR by geographic area (Figure 11.21).

It is useful to layer other statistics with CTR to see where you want to spend your time optimizing an account. For instance, this account has only spent $0.60 in Arta. Regardless of CTR, this probably is not a place to spend your time, especially when combined with the knowledge that Arta is a city in Greece with a population of

23,000. This account's overall CTR is 14.62 percent. However, in Baja, California, the CTR is 3.11 percent. In Attiki, Greece, the CTR is only 1.54 percent. As both of those locations have more than 3 million residents, and have higher spends than many other locations, optimizing the ads for those locations would be a more appropriate place to spend your time.

Figure 11.21 Examining CTR and spend by region

When optimizing local ads, the first step is to use Google's Ad Preview Tool and see if the ad is blending into the others in that region. If the ad does stand out, it could be that the locals just do not respond to your current ad copy. If you wanted to reach Attiki differently than the other regions where the ad is shown, you could create a different campaign for just Attiki.

The geographic performance report allows you to examine your statistics for each region where your ad has been shown. When combined with location targeting, you can optimize your account by geographies to make sure searchers are responding to your ads in every area where you want to reach consumers.

Best Practices for Geographic Targeting

The first step in location targeting is to understand where your target market lives and then make sure you are targeting those users appropriately. The second step is to ensure that your ads are being received properly in the various geographic regions and to then adjust your ads and location targeting properly. By following the best practices in this chapter, you should be able to accomplish those two concepts in an effective manner.

- Define where your users are located. Then ensure that your ads are only being shown to the appropriate users.

- You should try to limit your exposure to a maximum of one country per campaign. This will allow you to create more targeted ads and send users to more specific landing pages.

- Use a combination of location targeting and excluded regions to organize your campaigns and to make sure you are reaching your target locations.

- As much of the technology behind geo-targeting is based on a user's host provider's address, the smaller the area you target, the more people you will miss. It can be useful to target a larger area than you serve to reach more potential prospects and then use ad copy descriptors to let searchers know exactly the areas you serve.

- Geo-qualifiers are useful as both keywords and in ad copy. Here are a few guidelines:

  - Be careful when using state abbreviations as keywords. Some state's abbreviations, such as Maine (ME), Oregon (OR), and Maryland (MD), have alternate meanings.

  - When two areas share the same name, use a metro, state, or regional qualifier in the ad copy to let the searchers know which area you serve.

  - When using zip codes, do not use broad match; always use phrase or exact match.

  - Using regional lingo both as keywords and in ad copy will help you connect with local searchers.

- Understand whether your target market is comprised of locals or nonlocals so you can write ads and use landing pages based on their knowledge of your area.

  - Nonlocals need to be reassured that you can serve their needs and that you are in the area where they are searching for information.

  - Locals want precise information such as address and driving directions.

  - Examine the local belief systems to make sure consumers consider your offers credible.

- If you have a physical business or are advertising a specific location, the location extension will let customers know exactly where you are located.

- Always use the Google Ad Preview Tool when searching for your own ads as it will not count in your account's statistics. The Ad Preview Tool should be your first step when researching local competition for your ads.

- Geographic data will give you performance insights in the various locations where your ads were shown. Use these metrics to optimize your account.

By following these best practices, you should be able to target your ads to the locations that house your target market. Then write ad copy that engages users based on their knowledge of the area. Finally, run reports that will show you if you are being successful and reveal areas where you can improve.

These past few chapters have been about reaching your audience through location targeting and the content network. Many of these best practices can be time consuming when you use the AdWords online interface. In the next chapter, I will introduce the AdWords Editor, which will speed up how quickly you can make account changes. I will also walk through methods to scale your account in a quick yet efficient manner.

Save Time and Scale Accounts with the AdWords Editor

The AdWords Editor is a free downloadable desktop program offered by Google that allows you to manage your AdWords account on your computer instead of using Google's online interface. Learning how to use the AdWords Editor can save you tremendous amounts of time.

The AdWords Editor also supports the bulk importing of ad copy and keywords. Combining the editor with Microsoft Excel can help you scale your account to house thousands of pieces of ad copy with tens of thousands of keywords.

In this chapter you will learn how to define and organize your ad groups offline so that you can still use best practice management even with extremely large accounts.

12

Chapter Contents
AdWords Editor Overview
How to Scale Your Account
Optimizing Display with the AdWords Editor
Best Practices for Using the AdWords Editor

AdWords Editor Overview

Google's AdWords Editor makes it easy to manage your account. You can add, remove, or pause keywords, ad copy, ad groups, or campaigns from a single interface. You can see your statistics, Quality Score, first page bids, and other metrics within this program. You can make the vast majority of changes to your account within this editor. This should be the program you use to optimize your account. Since the editor sits on your computer, and not on the Web, you can work on your account quickly instead of waiting for the AdWords interface to load.

Once you download your account into the editor and start making changes, those changes do not go live immediately—they remain offline until you decide to upload them. You can make any number of changes to your campaigns and then post them online when you are satisfied with the adjustments. Once you post the changes, they will go live within your AdWords account instantly.

Although most of the options available through the AdWords online interface are also in the editor, a handful of more advanced options are not available there. However, the AdWords Editor does have capabilities, such as import and export, that are not available in the online interface. Whenever you need to make bulk changes to your account, you can save yourself a significant amount of time by using the editor instead of the online interface.

I will walk through the interface and basic functionalities of the editor and then look at some tricks to save you time and headaches.

To download the editor, you can go to www.google.com/intl/en/adwordseditor/. Or choose the Tools menu in your AdWords account and click on the AdWords Editor link, which will take you to this web page.

When new features are added to the interface that can easily be added to the editor, they usually appear in the next release of the editor. When you open the AdWords Editor, it will automatically check for new versions and prompt you to download a newer version if one exists. The editor is available for both Windows and Mac computers.

Choosing Your Viewpoint

The layout of the AdWords Editor is similar to the interface that Google launched in the summer 2009. You can choose how much data and the type of data you want to view and have access to several tools. Figure 12.1 shows what the editor looks like in its entirety.

Please note that the editor shows so much data about an account that I cannot use a client's account to show the information. The information being displayed is from my demo account, so examine the screenshots from a functionality view and not from the data or organization standpoint.

In the left column (Figure 12.2), you select how much data you want to view. You can see all data points in your account, a campaign, or an individual ad group.

Figure 12.1 The AdWords Editor Interface

Figure 12.2 Account
navigation column

Along the middle horizontal bar, you can choose what data points you want to see: keywords, placements, audiences, ads, ad groups, extensions, or campaigns (Figure 12.3). In addition, you can filter the data by unposted changes, errors, warnings, or all the data available. Some tabs, such as Keywords, have multiple view options, including positives and negatives for keywords.

Figure 12.3 Choosing the data you want to view

In the top navigation column, you can right-click to choose exactly what types of data you want to view (Figure 12.4). Depending on the data you are viewing, you will see different customization options. For instance, on the Ads tab you will see items such as Headline, Description Line 1, and so on, whereas on the Keywords tab you will see items such as Match Type and Bids.

Figure 12.4 Customizing the Keyword column

The combination of the navigation and data columns allows you to work with any type and amount of data you wish to view. You can see all ads in your account or just negative keywords in a single ad group. How you want to view the data is entirely up to you.

AdWords Editor Shortcuts

Since this is a desktop application, your standard desktop shortcuts also work. For instance, for Windows users, Ctrl+C lets you copy the data point you are working on and Ctrl+V lets you paste that same data point into another area. For Mac users, the keyword shortcuts Cmd+C and Cmd+V do the same. Becoming familiar with the available shortcuts will allow you to quickly navigate through the interface and make bulk changes. Table 12.1 lists the shortcuts you've probably been using for years in various Windows applications. Similar shortcuts are also available for Mac users, too. Table 12.2 deserves special attention, as it provides the special AdWords Editor shortcuts.

▶ **Table 12.1** Common keyboard shortcuts

Command	Windows shortcut	Mac shortcut
Open account	Ctrl+O	Cmd+O
Search	Ctrl+F	Cmd+F
Replace text in selected items	Ctrl+H	Cmd+Shift+R
Copy selected items	Ctrl+C	Cmd+C
Cut selected items	Ctrl+X	Cmd+X
Paste items	Ctrl+V	Cmd+V
Delete selected items	Delete key	
Post changes (the standard Save command)	Ctrl+S	Cmd+S
Exit AdWords Editor	Ctrl+W	

▶ **Table 12.2** AdWords Editor Windows keyboard shortcuts

Command	Shortcut
Get recent account changes	Ctrl+R
Check changes	Ctrl+P
Check changes in selected campaigns	Ctrl+Alt+P
Post changes in selected campaigns	Ctrl+Alt+S
Open advanced search	Ctrl+Shift+F
Select all items in data view	Ctrl+A
Revert selected changes	Ctrl+Z

Besides the common shortcuts, there are a few that everyone should know even if you decide not to become a shortcut wizard with the AdWords Editor.

Many more shortcuts are supported by the AdWords Editor ranging from complex ones such as adding deleting multiple campaign keywords to creating a new ad group. Additional shortcuts for Windows and Mac users are available on Google's AdWords Editor website here:

Windows:

`http://support.google.com/adwords/editor/bin/answer.py?hl=en&answer=54654`

Mac:

`http://support.google.com/adwords/editor/bin/answer.py?hl=en&answer=57767`

Using Visual Cues

As you add and remove data from the editor, visual symbols appear:

- Plus (+): Added item.

- Delta (Δ): Edited item.

- Minus (−): Deleted item.

- Red-colored circle: Item may violate AdWords policies, and an exception request will need to be filed before you can make the change.

- Yellow-colored circle: Item may violate AdWords policies, but you can still upload the changes.

- Green-colored circle: Item passed AdWords policy checks.

- Comment Icon: A comment is associated with that data point (Figure 12.5).

Figure 12.5 There is a comment associated with the keyword "AdWords learning center."

The comments feature in the AdWords Editor is extremely useful for keeping notes on why you made a change or why you added or removed a data item. It's also nice for keeping track of something you need to check on in the future.

These are the basics of how the editor functions. You will discover many more options when using the editor. It's an intuitive interface, so you'll find it easy to learn its functionality once you understand the basics.

Viewing Your Account in the AdWords Editor

When you first install the editor, it will not be associated with any AdWords accounts. The first step is to open your AdWords account in the editor. Either use the shortcut Ctrl+O or navigate to the File menu and click Open Account (Figure 12.6).

A dialog box opens where you can enter your AdWords login email address and the password. Once you enter the information, your account is downloaded into the editor.

Figure 12.6 Opening your AdWords account in the editor

You can enter the credentials of several different accounts in the AdWords Editor for quick access to all those accounts. If you enter a My Client Center (MCC) email address, you will be able to see every account that is linked to that MCC.

In the editor, you can perform typical account management items such as the following:

- Change bids

- Add or remove keywords

- Add or remove text ads

- Create or delete ad groups

- Create or delete campaigns

- Change campaign settings

When you first start, your AdWords Editor file and your AdWords online interface will contain the same data. As you make changes within the AdWords Editor, those changes are not automatically made to your online account. To post changes online, click the Post changes (or Post Selected Campaigns) button (Ctrl+Alt+S), and you will be presented with a box listing your changes (Figure 12.7). If your current view is not the entire account but either an ad group or a campaign, then you will have the option to post changes either for the entire account or for just a single campaign.

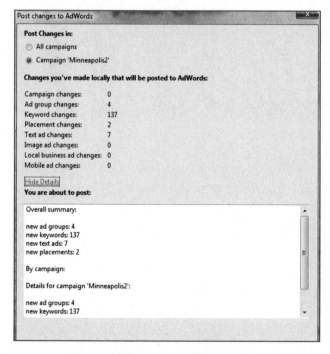

Figure 12.7 Reviewing and then posting your changes

If you are posting a handful of changes, you can post them for your entire account at once. If you are posting more than 10,000 keywords, or more than 1,000 pieces of ad copy, you may run into problems. It is not uncommon for the AdWords Editor to appear to be working but actually to have timed out on the back-end. Therefore, if you are making large bulk changes, only upload the changes to a single campaign at once. If you are making a few keyword changes or adding a dozen text ads, it will take the editor seconds to make the changes. It could take a few hours to do large bulk changes.

While the AdWords Editor is posting changes, do not change those same campaigns in the online interface. The AdWords system could become confused as to which changes should be in effect.

It is a good idea to make sure that no one else on your team is working on the same account, or the same campaigns within an account, while you are making changes offline in AdWords Editor. If you, or anyone else on your team, makes changes online, your AdWords Editor file will not be synced with your AdWords account. Additionally, if someone else has downloaded the same account into the editor and then posts their own sets of changes to the same items while you are still working on your edits, you will overwrite their changes when you post yours. It is a good idea to sync your AdWords Editor file with your Google AdWords account before you begin a new round of edits offline in the AdWords Editor. To do that, use the Get Recent Account Changes button to download your account. If you want to download your entire account and overwrite any local changes you made in the editor, use the Get Full Account feature (Figure 12.8).

Figure 12.8 Downloading new changes to your AdWords Editor file

Giving Multiple People Access to Your AdWords Account

In either your AdWords account or your MCC, you can create a user login for each person who has access to your account (Figure 12.9).

This ability is useful from both security and tracking standpoints. If someone leaves your company, you can disable a single login and not worry about having to change all of your access passwords. When someone makes changes in your account, the change shows up in the My Change History tool with the associated login that made each change.

Figure 12.9 Giving account access to additional people

When someone first opens your account in the AdWords Editor, they can download your account with their login credentials. When that person posts changes to your account from the AdWords Editor, the account used to post those changes will show up in the My Change History tool as well, so you can track which login is making changes to your account. The Change History report can help you fix things up when one person inadvertently overwrites another person's changes. However, it is never any fun to make the same changes twice, so the best bet is to make sure that only one person is working on a campaign at a time.

However, if you would like even more control over who can make changes to your account, the AdWords Editor has an additional feature called Export Changes for Sharing (AES) (Figure 12.10). The AdWords Editor file extension is .aes.

Figure 12.10 Exporting your editor changes for sharing

You can export your editor file and send it to another person who can open your account in their AdWords Editor program. That person can then make changes to your account, and instead of uploading the changes, they can send the file back to you. Then you can see what their proposed changes are and have the capability to accept or reject changes (Figure 12.11).

Figure 12.11 Accepting or rejecting changes

Once you have accepted the changes you would like to go live in your account, you can post those changes. If you have several people who work on your account, having a central gatekeeper who understands all of the changes and their implications can be useful in maintaining control over what is happening inside your AdWords account.

How to Scale Your Account

Most of the best practices for PPC account management you read about recommend creating small ad groups of tightly themed keywords and handwriting ad copy that can be tested for those keywords.

While these are best practices for small and medium-size accounts, it is not always practical when you are managing thousands of ad groups, tens of thousands of keywords, and thousands of pieces of ad copy. However, there are ways of mass-creating keywords and ad copy inside a spreadsheet program and then using the AdWords Editor to import that information into your account.

First you will learn how to import anywhere from a single keyword to thousands of keywords into your account. Then you will examine how to import ad copy for those keywords.

Importing Keywords

One of the AdWords Editor functions lets you copy and paste data from a spreadsheet into the AdWords Editor. This allows you to use a spreadsheet program, such as Excel, to create and organize your keywords, and then you can copy that data and paste it into the AdWords Editor. Just follow these steps:

1. To access this function, navigate to the Keywords tab, click Make Multiple Changes, and choose Add/Update Multiple Keywords (Figure 12.12).

Figure 12.12 Mass importing keywords into the AdWords Editor

This will bring you to a screen where you can paste large amounts of data. There are a couple of ways that you can import the data; for now, we are going to focus on importing everything so that you can automatically create new campaigns, ad groups, and add keywords all at once.

2. Create an Excel file where each column, in this order, contains these data points (Figure 12.13):

	A	B	C	D	E	F	G
1		Required (or Strongly Suggested)				Optional	
2	Campaign	Ad Group	Keyword	Keyword Type	Max CPC	Destination URL	Keyword Status
3	Austin	Seminars	advanced marketing seminar	Exact			
4	Charlotte	Seminars	advanced marketing seminar	Exact			
5	Austin	Seminars	advanced marketing seminars	Exact			
6	Charlotte	Seminars	advanced marketing seminars	Exact			
7	Austin	AdWords	adwords class	Exact			
8	Charlotte	AdWords	adwords class	Exact			
9	Austin	AdWords	adwords classes	Exact			

Figure 12.13 Excel file with the proper headers

- Campaign name
- Ad group name
- Keyword
- Keyword type (same as match type; this is optional, but strongly recommended)
- Max CPC (optional)
- Bid (optional)
- Destination URL (optional)
- Keyword status (optional)

3. In Excel, you can then create all the data you want to add to your AdWords account. If you conducted research with the AdWords Keyword Tool (from Chapter 3, "Keyword Tools: Extracting Valuable Data from Google") and have hundreds or thousands of keywords, you would not want to go through the AdWords online interface to add all of those keywords to various ad groups. Instead, put your keywords in column 3, and then add the campaign name, ad group name, and so on for the data you want to import.

When you import the data, if there is no campaign or ad group name within a campaign that you are adding, the AdWords Editor will automatically create those campaigns and ad groups for you.

4. Once you have organized the data, copy and paste it into the AdWords Editor. At the top of the screen, check the option "My keyword information below includes columns for campaigns and ad group names."

5.   Click the Preview button. This will bring you to a wizard that asks you to define the columns. Define the columns based upon the Excel organization and then choose "Remember the order of my column headers for future imports" (Figure 12.14). This will ensure you can skip this step in the future.

Figure 12.14 Defining the import columns

6.   Click the Process button and the editor will add your new keywords to your account.

If you created new ad groups or campaigns, navigate to those items in the editor to set your bids, daily budget, and other campaign or ad group settings.

Creating Thousands of Keywords and Ad Groups

You can also use Excel to create hundreds of thousands of keywords, although when doing so, it is suggested that you just create one campaign at a time.

Let's reexamine the keyword methodology chart from Chapter 2, "Keyword Research." In the keyword listing methodology, you will create several lists of several keywords. Table 12.3 is the maternity shirt example from Chapter 2.

Category adjectives	Product types	Product attributes 1	Product attributes 2	Example keywords
Pregnant	Shirt	Long sleeve	Cotton	Pregnancy shirt Pregnancy shirt long sleeve
Pregnancy	T-shirt	Short sleeve	Rayon	Pregnancy shirt cotton
Maternity	Dress blouse Tops Polo shirt Sweatshirt	Sleeveless	Silk Stretchable Natural fibers Wool	Pregnancy shirt long sleeve cotton

The first thing to do when scaling your accounts is to determine your campaigns and ad groups. For ease of explanation, in this example we are going to assume it is a national retailer who is just getting started, and therefore they only need national search campaigns.

In addition, make the assumption that the lists in Table 12.3 are much longer. For instance, there are many more product types, attributes, brands, and so forth that could be included in the lists in Table 12.3.

Since for this example you are using a single campaign, the next step is to decide on the ad groups. In the earlier list, the words are not yet defined as ad groups or keywords. For instance, you could have the ad group Maternity Cotton Shirts with keywords such as "xl maternity cotton shirts." Or you could have the ad group Maternity Shirts with the keyword "cotton maternity shirts." There are many possibilities. Therefore, determine how many ad groups you want to devote to your current list.

If this company sold men's, women's, children's, and other clothing, you might not want to use thousands of ad groups for just maternity clothing. As you would also have hundreds or thousands of ad groups for each of men's, women's, and children's clothing categories, it would not make sense to start with thousands of ad groups for a specific clothing type, such as maternity, shoes, or outerwear. An account might get there after learning what is converting and optimizing the account, but let's start more simply.

If the company only sold maternity clothing, and therefore all your ad groups were going to be related to maternity, you could be more liberal in your ad group selection and have thousands of maternity ad groups.

Organizing Your Account

Account organization is so important to long-term success that it can be useful to create a document that covers how you are going to reach your audience, how that audience searches, and how you are going to break down your ad groups and campaigns into a manageable account structure before even opening your AdWords account. Chapter 14, "Successful Account Organization Strategies," takes an in-depth look at successful account organization.

Let's assume that after you did research you found out these points (and these are made up, so please do not use them for your organization):

- The words "maternity" and "pregnancy" are used interchangeably, and user intent did not vary based on the word being searched.

- "Cotton" and "stretchable" are the most common attributes searched, and the search volume for the other materials is much smaller.

- There is a large search volume for branded terms, and the branded terms can be used in the ad copy as they will be compliant with the trademark policies and laws.

- It is summertime, and while the search volume for "swimsuits" and "sundresses" is high, those words do not combine well with the list in Table 12.3, and you will need a second list for sundresses and swimsuits.

This is a short list of points for illustration purposes only. Your research should uncover more information about the searchers.

Armed with this information, it is now time to create the ad groups. The information leads you to making these assumptions about our organization:

- The words "maternity" and "pregnancy" are used interchangeably, and user intent did not vary based on the word being searched.

  You are going to use the words "maternity" and "pregnancy" as keyword modifiers and not as different ad groups. Therefore, whenever a keyword is added, it will be added twice, once with the "pregnancy" modifier and once with the "maternity" modifier. For instance, your keywords would be "maternity cotton shirt" and "pregnancy cotton shirt."

- "Cotton" and "stretchable" are the most common attributes searched; the search volume for the other materials is much smaller.

  For each product type, there will be three ad groups: Cotton, Stretchable, and Other. Therefore, you will have Cotton Suits, Stretchable Suits, and Other Suits as ad groups.

  In the Other Suits ad group, you will use all of the additional product attribute modifiers as keyword modifiers. For instance, "pregnancy wool suit," "maternity wool suit," "pregnancy rayon suit," and "maternity rayon suit" would be some of the keywords in that ad group.

- There is a large search volume for branded terms, and the branded terms can be used in the ad copy as they will be compliant with the trademark policies and laws.

  Since there is such high brand search volume, and you want to use the branded terms in the ad copy, you need to create brand-specific ad groups.

  Therefore, you will make a list of all the brands and what ad groups contain keywords that each brand sells. For instance, if Chiarakruza only sold shirts, pants, and sundresses, then you would "clone" the nonbranded ad groups that contain those items and make new, brand-specific ad groups from them by adding Chiarakruza as another product attribute to those ad groups.

  However, if you have one ad group that is Chiarakruza Maternity Shirts and another one that is Maternity Shirts with some broad match keywords, Google could choose which keyword to trigger and which ad to serve. Therefore, in the nonbranded ad group, Maternity Shirts, you would add the negative keyword "Chiarakruza."

- It is summertime, and while the search volume for "swimsuits" and "sundresses" is high, those words do not combine well with the list from Table 12.3, and you will need a second list for sundresses and swimsuits.

This information will start our next action list. You will have to do more research on sundresses and bathing suits and create new lists before adding these ad groups.

With this information, you would then re-create your lists to first create ad groups, as shown in Table 12.4.

▶ **Table 12.4** Maternity clothing ad groups

Brand	Attributes	Product type	Ad groups
Chiarakruza	Cotton	Shirts	Cotton shirts
Belabumbum	Stretchable	Pants	Stretchable shirts
	Other	Suits	Other shirts
			Belabumbum shirts
			Chiarakruza shirts

Once you have listed all of your ad groups, you can use your keyword list information to create the keywords that fit into each of these ad groups. By going through this exercise in a spreadsheet, you can use formulas to create thousands of ad groups and tens of thousands of keywords fairly easily. The hard part is the initial research into the keyword lists and laying out your account structure. For larger accounts, the actual keyword creation can be easier than the planning stages.

Importing Keywords and Ad Groups into the AdWords Editor

Once you have this organized, it is a simple copy and paste from your spreadsheet into the bulk import function of the AdWords Editor to get them into your editor file. If you have created new ad group or campaigns, make sure you set the appropriate bids, budget, and other settings.

If you are creating a campaign that will have more than 10,000 keywords or 1,000 pieces of ad copy, before creating text ads upload the data to your AdWords account. These ad groups will show a warning because there is no associated ad copy. However, when you are selectively uploading from an AdWords Editor file, the smallest amount of data you can upload is a single campaign. The AdWords Editor can time out when uploading huge amounts of data; therefore, by selectively uploading the keywords first, you are uploading less total data at once and mitigating the chances of the data not being uploaded into your account. After you have created the ads from the next section, upload just the ads as the second step to create whole ad groups.

Now that you have created potentially hundreds of ad groups with tens of thousands of keywords, it is time to create ad copy for those ad groups.

Easily Creating Thousands of Ads

A search ad group is not complete until it contains both keywords and ad copy. After determining your ad groups and populating those ad groups with keywords, the next step is to write associated ad copy.

The AdWords Editor also supports the bulk importing of ad copy. In the editor:

1. Navigate to the Ads tab and click Make Multiple Changes.

2. Select Add/Update Multiple Text Ads (Figure 12.15).

Figure 12.15 Finding the ad copy import tool

This will bring you to a screen similar to when you were importing text ads (Figure 12.16).

3. In your spreadsheet program, create a sheet with these column headers (Figure 12.17):

    •   Campaign
    •   Ad Group

- Headline
- Description line 1
- Description line 2
- Display URL
- Destination URL
- Status (optional)

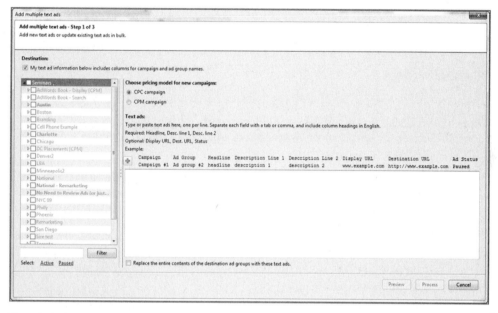

Figure 12.16 Importing multiple ads

	A	B	C	D	E	F	G	H
1				**Required**				**Optional**
2	Campaign	Ad Group	Headline	Description 1	Description 2	Display URL	Destination URL	Ad Status
3	Austin	Marketing	AdWords Cla:	AdWords Succes	Limited Seats. Reser	bgTheory.com/AdWord	http://www.bgtheory.com/ad
4	Charlotte	Marketing	AdWords Cla:	AdWords Succes	Limited Seats. Reser	bgTheory.com/AdWord	http://www.bgtheory.com/ad
5	Austin	AdWords	In Person Ad\	Two Days Only -	Limited Seats. Reser	bgTheory.com/AdWord	http://www.bgtheory.com/ad
6	Austin	Seminars	In Person Ad\	Coming to Austii	Limited Seats. Reser	bgTheory.com/AdWord	http://www.bgtheory.com/ad
7	Charlotte	AdWords	In Person Ad\	Two Days Only -	Limited Seats. Reser	bgTheory.com/AdWord	http://www.bgtheory.com/ad
8	Charlotte	Seminars	In Person Ad\	Limited Seats. R	AdWords Seminars fc	bgTheory.com/AdWord	http://www.bgtheory.com/ad
9	Austin	AdWords	Learn AdWor	Two Day, In-Per:	Learn AdWords Succe	bgTheory.com/AdWord	http://www.bgtheory.com/ad
10	Austin	AdWords	Learn AdWor	Two Day, In-Per:	Limited Seats. Reser	bgTheory.com/AdWord	http://www.bgtheory.com/ad
11	Austin	AdWords	Learn AdWor	Learn AdWords !	Max your AdWords R	bgTheory.com/AdWord	http://www.bgtheory.com/ad
12	Austin	PPC	Learn AdWor	AdWords Succes	Limited Seats. Reser	bgTheory.com/AdWord	http://www.bgtheory.com/ad
13	Charlotte	AdWords	Learn AdWor	Two Day, In-Per:	AdWords Seminars fc	bgTheory.com/AdWord	http://www.bgtheory.com/ad
14	Charlotte	AdWords	Learn AdWor	Two Day, In-Per:	Limited Seats. Reser	bgTheory.com/AdWord	http://www.bgtheory.com/ad
15	Charlotte	AdWords	Learn AdWor	Learn AdWords !	Max your AdWords R	bgTheory.com/AdWord	http://www.bgtheory.com/ad
16	Charlotte	PPC	Learn AdWor	AdWords Succes	Limited Seats. Reser	bgTheory.com/AdWord	http://www.bgtheory.com/ad

Figure 12.17 Creating ad copy in a spreadsheet

When creating the ad groups and campaign names for your ad copy, make sure that you use the exact same names from your keyword import sheet. If you use different campaign names, you will have one campaign with ad copy and a different campaign with only keywords. There are simple tricks you can use that will help you write multiple ads at once to save you precious time.

Writing Multiple Ads

If you are only writing a handful of ads, write them customized by hand with the best practices from Chapter 4, "Writing Compelling Ads." However, if you are creating thousands of ads for hundreds or thousands of ad groups, you will need to write formulas to create this many ads.

The first step in writing multiple ads with formulas is to break down your ad groups into similar product lines where formulaic ads will still be relevant to the searcher. For instance, if you sell maternity and men's clothing, a tagline such as "Maternity Wear for Fashionable Moms" would not resonate with the men searching for clothes.

Once these are broken down into various ad groups, write some calls-to-action, headlines, and taglines for those ad groups.

For instance, let's say these are some of the initial ad copy lines you want to try:

- Headlines:
  - Ad Group Name (in this case, you are assuming the ad group name is closely associated to the keywords in the ad group and that it would make a good headline)
  - Fashionable Maternity Clothing
  - Shop at Company Name
- Taglines:
  - Shop today, wear it tomorrow.
  - Free shipping on all orders!
- Destination URL:
  - Company URL
  - Company URL/AdGroupName
  - Company URL/Shop

Next, you will write a set of formulas where you will insert this information (see Table 12.5). The more traffic you are going to buy, the more ads you can write. Because you are writing formulas that will be used across multiple ad groups, you can also run reports where you are looking at which formulaic writing is leading to clicks and conversions, so you do not have to rely on testing at the ad group level.

▶ **Table 12.5** Example ad copy formulas

Headline	Description line 1	Description line 2	Display URL
Ad Group Name	Headline1	Tagline1	Display URL 1
{Keyword:Ad Group name}	Shop at Company Name	Tagline2	Display URL 2
Headline1	Buy {Keyword:Ad Group Name}	Tagline1	Display URL 3
Headline2	Tagline1	Tagline2	Display URL 2

Mass Ad Copy-Writing Tools

While this section will give you an idea of how large companies create thousands of ads, it can be time consuming and difficult to create different benefit lines by both ad group and across a campaign. You can use a tool like the Mass Ad Copy Creator from CertifiedKnowledge.org (http://certifiedknowledge.org/membership-information/ppc-tools/mass-ad-copy-creator-tool/) to create thousands of ads quite easily.

Once you have the formulas written, plug in the ad copy variables. You can easily do this in Excel by calling information from different cells within the spreadsheet. For instance, if your headline was Ad Group Name and the ad group is located in column B of your spreadsheet, you could enter **=B3** and the cell would be replaced by the content of cell B3. Since Excel automatically adjusts formulas as you copy, paste, and drag them, it is simple to write the formulas for one ad group, and then copy and paste the selection multiple times or drag the cells down across multiple ad groups. If your ad group was Chiarakruza Maternity Shirts, then your final ad copy would look like Table 12.6.

▶ **Table 12.6** Maternity clothing ads

Headline	Description line 1	Description line 2	Display URL
Chiarakruza Maternity Shirts	Fashionable Maternity Clothing	Shop today, wear it tomorrow.	*CompanyName*.com
{Keyword: Chiarakruza Maternity Shirts }	Shop at Company Name	Free shipping on all orders!	*CompanyName*.com/ ChiarakruzaMaternityShirts
Fashionable Maternity Clothing	Buy {Keyword: Chiarakruza Maternity Shirts }	Shop today, wear it tomorrow.	*CompanyName*.com/Shop
Shop at Company Name	Shop today, wear it tomorrow.	Free shipping on all orders!	*CompanyName*.com/ ChiarakruzaMaternityShirts
Chiarakruza Maternity Shirts	Our friendly return policy means	Guilt Free Shopping	*CompanyName*.com/ Chiarakruza

The last ad copy is just one we added to test what a multiple line ad copy would do. Feel free to add additional ad copy as it makes sense to your goals. In this example, you would replace *CompanyName* with your actual company, and the same with the display URL.

In addition, you will have a destination URL based on where you are sending traffic to on your website; however, you would not use a formula to create the destination URL. You want to make sure the destination URL resolves to the correct page on your website.

Character Limits and Naming Conventions

When you write formula-based ads, some of them will be outside of character limit policies. If you are writing these ads in Excel, use the conditional formatting to highlight instances where you have gone over character limits. Then you will need to adjust the ads appropriately.

For instance, in the previous example, the word "Chiarakruza" contains so many characters that a few of the ad copy lines have exceeded their character limits, such as the display URL *CompanyName*.com/ChiarakruzaMaternityShirts. In this instance, you would remove the MaternityShirts aspect, leaving the *CompanyName*.com/ Chiarakruza, which might be within the 35 allocated display URL characters depending on how long the company's URL is.

When you create the ad copy to match your existing keyword ad groups, make sure the naming conventions for your campaigns and ad groups are identical. If they are not the same, you will have one ad group with keywords and another ad group with just ad copy.

Once you have finished writing your ad copy, copy the new ads and paste them into the AdWords Editor. The AdWords Editor will inform you of how many ads you are adding and if any new ad groups or campaigns will be created. If you have already imported the keywords, you should not be creating new ad groups or campaigns. Hence, if the editor informs you that new campaigns or ad groups will be created, check your naming conventions.

Advantages of Using Excel with AdWords Editor

Using a spreadsheet and the AdWords Editor together allows you to easily import large amounts of information into your AdWords account in a quick and scalable manner. The hard work of scaling your accounts should no longer be the AdWords front-end interface. The hard work should be in mapping your ad groups, keywords, and ad copy together so that you can still use many of the best practices from those who create ad groups by hand, yet in a scalable manner.

Once you have larger accounts, especially ones written through formulas, you can use the best practice optimization techniques discussed in Chapter 17, "Step by Step: Create and Monitor Your AdWords Account," to find your strengths and weaknesses, and be able to find ad groups that need to be further broken down based on returns. Even if you have smaller accounts, the exact same optimization techniques apply, only you will have a smaller number of ad groups to analyze.

Optimizing Display with the AdWords Editor

In the previous two chapters, you saw examples of why it is best to have your campaigns only set to search or to display. If your campaigns are currently set to both, do not fret—with the AdWords Editor, it will take you only a minute to duplicate your campaigns and change the appropriate settings.

First, navigate to the campaign that you want to duplicate. Then use the copy (Ctrl+C) and paste (Ctrl+V) functions to duplicate that campaign. With those two simple keystrokes, you now have two identical campaigns.

The campaign you just created will have an error associated with it because it has the same name as another campaign (Figure 12.19). Rename the first campaign as **Current Campaign Name - Search**. Then rename the second campaign as **Current Campaign Name - Display**. This will not only fix the error but let you quickly tell if you are working on a display or a search campaign.

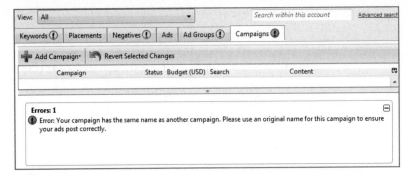

Figure 12.19 Campaign name error in the AdWords Editor

Once the campaigns are renamed, it is time to change the settings so that the first campaign is only displayed on search and the second campaign is only shown on the display network (Figure 12.20).

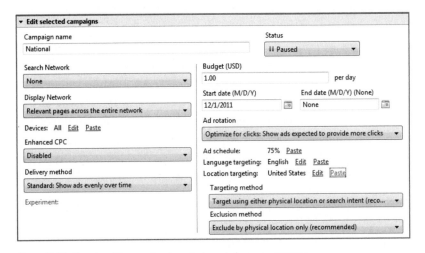

Figure 12.20 Choosing either search only or display only for your campaigns

Next, you will want to go through the typical display organization techniques discussed to choose your display keywords and placements. However, because your new campaign is only targeted to the display network, you can use more general keywords to help create a theme for your ad group and not have to worry about those keywords triggering your search ads.

Best Practices for Using the AdWords Editor

Whenever you are hesitant to start working on your AdWords account because of the front-end interface, it is time to use the AdWords Editor.

While there are a few features that are available within the AdWords online interface that are not in the editor, they are generally settings that are not commonly used. In addition, they are usually features that are not changed often; hence, they are not always necessary to have in the editor.

- Your view in the editor is determined by settings. To get started, use the left navigation column to select the amount of data you want to view (account, campaign, or specific ad group), and the middle horizontal bar to select the data points (ad copy, keywords, ad groups, or campaigns).

- Look for visual cues in the editor. The red or yellow warning labels let you find problems. The plus sign or minus sign shows what is being added or deleted.

- Use the comments feature in the AdWords Editor, designated by a conversation icon. This will allow you to keep track of why you made certain changes for future analysis.

- At a minimum, you should give everyone who has access to your account their own login. If you have a large team, make sure that only one person at a time is editing the same account elements at one time to avoid overwriting someone else's changes. One way to ensure that is to use the export your account for sharing feature, and then have all changes come through one person.

- The AdWords Editor allows the bulk creation of keywords, ad copy, campaigns, or ad groups. When you bulk create items, always adjust any bids, geographic targets, or other ad group and campaign settings before you push the changes live.

- When creating large numbers of keywords, follow these steps:
  1. Determine your ad groups.
  2. Populate those ad groups with the proper keywords.

- When creating large amounts of ad copy, use formula writing, but ensure that the ads are still relevant to the user and fall within the editorial requirements before posting the ads.

- Learn the keyboard shortcuts. Although it is easy to duplicate a campaign for display and search targeting purposes, you can also use shortcut keys to select all ad copy that requires an exception request and fill out a single exception request at a time.

The AdWords Editor is a powerful tool to help you quickly add data, remove data, or change existing data, such as bids. Using the AdWords Editor import functions along with Excel can not only save you time, but also allow you to use best practice account management in both small and large accounts.

However, it is not enough to create thousands of ads or tens of thousands of keywords if they do not fit within the goals of your business. In the next chapter, you will learn various bid strategies so you can set bids that increase your company's profits.

Profitable Bid Strategies

Is your AdWords account making money or costing money? The only way to know is to first understand the goals that your marketing initiatives must accomplish for your company to be profitable. Once you have determined your goals, you then need to find a way to measure them. Only after these two steps have been completed can you begin to decide how much you should bid.

Various bidding techniques are available that you can use to set bids, control costs, and reach searchers by time of day and day of the week. Learn how to extract the proper data from AdWords so you can take the necessary actions to develop a successful AdWords account.

13

Chapter Contents

Setting Your Marketing Goals
Measuring Results with Google's Conversion Tracking Code
Exploring AdWords Bidding Options
Profitable Bidding Strategies
Calculating Your Max CPC
Ad Scheduling: Automatically Changing Bids by Time Periods
Understanding Attribution Management
Examining AdWords Reports to Make ROAS Bid Decisions
Best Practices for Utilizing Profitable Bid Strategies

Setting Your Marketing Goals

The first thing you should do in any advertising campaign, before you spend a single penny, is to set the goals your advertising campaign needs to accomplish. It does not matter if your advertising outlet is Google AdWords, yellow pages ads, newspaper ads, radio, TV, or any other medium. If you do not have goals set for the campaign, you cannot define success and optimize the campaigns to increase performance.

Many companies will have multiple goals. You may also need to refine your goals over time. Let's examine the steps a plumber may take in setting and refining goals.

Before the advertising campaign starts, the plumber examines his phone records and realizes that he receives 50 calls per month. Of those calls, he closes five jobs a month. Therefore, his conversion rate is 10 percent. His average job nets him $1,000, and it takes about 20 hours to accomplish each job. Since he only works 160 hours per month, he figures out he needs to close eight jobs per month. Because he has a 10 percent conversion rate, he needs to receive 80 calls per month. However, each job is worth $1,000, so he can do some math and realize that when he pays $100 per phone call his advertising costs are equal to his revenue and he has nothing left over after closing the jobs. Therefore, he wants make double what a call costs him to get and is willing to pay $50 per phone call.

In the first month of advertising, he manages to receive 50 additional calls to a dedicated phone number exclusively for this campaign. However, all of these calls come from keywords for fixing pipes and broken showers. His conversion rate is much higher, 20 percent, but these smaller pipe repair jobs only take 3 hours each. Even though he exceeded his goal of 30 additional phone calls, he only ended up working 30 additional hours that month. Therefore, he needs to refine his goals.

After further examination of the phone call records, the plumber realizes that he closes one in five calls for small jobs, such as fixing pipes and repairing showers. However, his close rate for large jobs such as kitchen remodeling is only 1 in 20, or 5 percent. After doing some math, he realizes that he wants to do three kitchen remodeling jobs each month, and then fill in the rest of his time with small jobs. Therefore, his final goals are 60 phone calls for kitchen remodeling each month and 134 calls for small jobs. In addition, he is willing to pay $50 for the kitchen remodeling calls, but only $25 for the smaller job phone calls.

An e-commerce company might take a different approach. The company might look at their finances and realize that based on their margins, they need a 200 percent ROI for all products sold. However, they also have a newsletter and they find that if someone subscribes to their newsletter, they make at least two sales a year to those subscribers, at an average of $50 per sale. Therefore, after doing some calculations on the returns they want from their email marketing, they are willing to pay $10 per newsletter subscriber. But since they need to pay overhead and monthly bills each month, and the newsletters are long-term investments, they must have at least 1,000 e-commerce sales per month.

Many times a company will need to dig back into its business model to understand how the business makes money and what is required to not just hit payroll each week, but to also grow as a company. This is often harder than setting bids for ad groups or keywords. Consider a drop-shipper who realized that if they could sell 7 percent more goods, they could switch suppliers and receive a 10 percent discount on the wholesale price of the goods they purchase. If this is the case, that drop-shipper could run an additional campaign at a breakeven number just to hit the new sales numbers so they could save on the total cost of goods they buy—which would put more dollars back into their bank account without changing a single bid price.

Many companies do not know their internal numbers well enough to set goals that improve their supply chain. However, setting goals is essential.

Some of the more common goals are as follows:

- Set percentage ROI on goods sold
- List a minimum number of sales per month
- Determine your minimum revenue per month
- Number of phone calls per month per product
- Define your cost per phone calls by product
- Set a cost per acquisition of a new customer, newsletter subscription, or RSS feed subscription
- Choose how many new visitors you want per day
- List the number of total visitors per day (this is a common goal for publishers who make money by selling CPM ads on their website)
- Determine your target number of leads per month
- Set a cost per lead

Once the company examines itself and understands how it makes money, set the goals for what the marketing campaigns need to accomplish. Once these goals are set, they need to be measured.

Measuring Results with Google's Conversion Tracking Code

Optimizing Google AdWords campaigns can only be done with proper metrics. If you do not have the numbers to examine, there is no way to know if you are hitting your goals, or even what keywords and ad copy are helping you reach those goals.

Therefore, for every goal you set, you need to find a way to measure it. This may lead you to institute phone call tracking, FeedBurner for RSS tracking, Google Analytics for page views per visits, or other software as necessary.

Google offers a conversion tracking script you can implement that will add conversion metrics to your AdWords account. Once you install the conversion tracking code, you will be able to see cost per action (CPA), total conversions, and ROI numbers by keyword, ad copy, and landing page in both the AdWords interface and your AdWords reports.

Clarifying the CPA vs. CPC Confusion

CPC, or cost per click, is a standard acronym across AdWords and generally when you see CPC you assume cost per click. However, many reports show cost per conversion as CPC as well, which leads to confusion. When CPC refers to conversions, often the acronym is changed to CPA or cost per action even though the reported metric is conversions and not actions. Whenever you see the term CPA, it could mean cost per action or cost per conversion—both of which are how much you pay for a conversion or action to occur on your site.

AdWords Conversion Tracking Code

The AdWords conversion tracking code is powerful and easy to install. The first step is to navigate to the Conversions page under the Tools tab within your account (Figure 13.1). This screen will show you all the currently defined conversion actions.

		Conversion	Conversion location	Category	Tracking Status	Conversions (many-per-click)	Value
☐	●	Purchase/Sale	Webpage	Other	Reporting	124317	$124,352.75
☐	●	Views of a key page	Webpage	View of a key page	Unverified	2	$2.00
☐	●	Lead	Webpage	Lead	Unverified	1	$1.00
☐	●	Other	Webpage	Other	Reporting	14	$13.00
					Totals - all conversions	124,334	$124,368.75

Figure 13.1 AdWords conversion tracking overview

Click New Conversion and you will be presented with a screen where you can set up tracking for either phone calls or web pages. First, choose a name for the conversion type that describes the type of conversion you want to track. If you are tracking online conversions, then choose Webpages and continue.

Next you will see a screen where you define information about the conversion type you are tracking (see Figure 13.2). The items are as follows:

Conversion Category Choose the type of conversion you wish to track such as a lead, sale, signup, page view, or other. This will allow you to create reports that segment your reports by a select set of categories.

Figure 13.2 Conversion tracking script wizard

Page Security Level This is an important setting to note so you do not cause trust errors with your customers. Choose whether your conversion page is a secure (HTTPS) or nonsecure (HTTP) page. If you put a nonsecure script on a secure page, most browsers show an error like, "This page contains secure and nonsecure items. Do you want to view the nonsecure information?" You do not want users to see this message, because it can lower the trust they have in your company. It is OK to call a secure script from a nonsecure page. Therefore, if you are in doubt about the security level of your website, choose the secure (HTTPS) script.

Markup Language Choose the coding language of your website. Please note that extensions such as .php or .aspx are still HTML pages. The other options are for mobile extensions such as .xhtml. If this is your standard website, choose HTML. If you are placing the code on a mobile site, examine the options to make sure you are calling the appropriate language code.

Conversion Value This field will populate your AdWords reports with the actual revenue you gained from an action. In your AdWords reports, you will be able to see that keyword 1 led to $15 in revenue, and keyword 2 led to $25 in revenue. There are three ways of defining this field.

The first is to leave it blank or use the number 1 as the field number. In this case, you will not see revenue in your AdWords reports; you will only see the total number of conversions.

The second is to do some math and then put in the estimated revenue for that action. For instance, if the e-commerce company from the previous example were using this method to track their newsletter subscriptions, they would enter 50, since that is what they calculated a newsletter subscription was worth to their company.

The third way to use this field is to enter a variable from your shopping cart. Most shopping carts have three variables on the checkout page: total cost of goods, cost of shipping, and total cost to consumer. Most companies do not make money on shipping, so by entering the variable for total cost of goods, you will be able to see the actual revenue that each keyword or ad copy led to on your website. To find the variable, ask your shopping cart provider or web developer. They should be able to assist you.

Tracking Indicator When a user clicks on your AdWords ad, a cookie is placed on their browser. If that cookie is on a user's browser when they get to a page where you are using this conversion code, Google will display a piece of text to the user. You can customize this text to fit the look and feel of your website, or you can update your privacy policy to inform users that you are using a tracking script and not display any text to the user.

View-Through Conversion Window When someone sees your ad and does not convert right away but they convert at a later time, they are considered a view-through conversion. These users see the ads but do not click on them. The view-through conversion window is how long you wish to track users who saw an ad and later converted. Please note that view-through conversion tracking only applies to image or rich media ads.

View-Through Conversion Search De-Duplication If someone views your image or rich media ad and also clicks on a search ad and then converts, they can be considered both a view-through conversion and a click-through conversion. If you enable this setting, you will not be counting these conversions twice and the user will only be a click-through conversion.

How browsers load web pages

A browser loads a web page in the order in which it receives the web page code. If after the open body tag (<body>) your website has several scripts, the browser must load all the scripts before the text of your website can be loaded. If a script is slow to load—or worse, it times out—the user will stare at a blank page for a while until the scripts finish loading or time out. Therefore, it is best to add all scripts at the bottom of your web pages before the close body tag (</body>). When you add scripts to the bottom of a page, the user may still leave the page before the script loads, which will cause you to lose some tracking data; however, all users will be able to see the text of your site first and not think there is a problem if the page loads slowly. It is better to lose some tracking and keep the user's trust than to track everything and lose consumer confidence.

If you have many scripts on a page, such as a Facebook like, Tweet This, and a conversion code, place the scripts in the order of importance—any single slow script can make it so the others never get a chance to load.

Once you have filled out all the options, click the save button on the page. The next page displays the code you need to install on your website (Figure 13.3).

Figure 13.3 AdWords conversion tracking code

Copy this code and paste it in the thank-you page or other type of page that signifies a conversion on your website, such as a store locator results page. This code only goes on the page that the user sees after they have completed an action, such as the "Thank you for shopping" or "Thank you for contacting us" page. If you install this code in a global footer, you will be tracking page views.

If you have multiple conversion actions, such as a newsletter and e-commerce conversion, use a different code for each action. If you use the same code for all actions, you will not be able to see which keywords, ad copy, or landing pages lead to the different types of actions on your website. Utilize the conversion tracking wizard once per action you want to track, and then install the code on the various thank-you pages associated with those actions.

Accessing Valuable Conversion Data in AdWords Reports

Once you have conversion tracking, you will have access to valuable conversion data. In most of the interface screens, you can customize the columns. Under the Conversions section, you can add conversion data to your view (Figure 13.4).

Figure 13.4 Customizing columns to include conversion data

After you have selected the conversion columns, you can see your conversion rates (see Figure 13.5). You can view conversions, revenue, cost per conversion, and conversion rate by many data points, including (but not limited to) the following:

Keyword	Ad group	Status	Avg. CPC	Cost	Conv. (1-per-click)	Clicks	Conv. rate (1-per-click)	Cost / conv. (1-per-click)
Total - all keywords			$1.93	$912,878.98	20,984	473,210	4.43%	$43.50
		Eligible	$2.22	$236,644.60	3,393	106,760	3.18%	$69.74
		Eligible	$2.26	$141,612.71	3,657	62,793	5.82%	$38.72
		Eligible	$1.57	$44,139.33	720	28,118	2.56%	$61.30
		Eligible	$2.20	$47,943.36	1,079	21,827	4.94%	$44.43
		Eligible	$2.01	$41,455.01	796	20,580	3.87%	$52.08
		Eligible	$2.23	$32,233.22	976	14,435	6.76%	$33.02
		Eligible	$2.20	$21,163.40	445	9,619	4.63%	$47.56

Figure 13.5 Conversion data for each keyword

- Keyword
- Ad landing page
- Ad group
- Campaign

- Placement
- Geography
- Search query
- Audience

> ## Google Analytics Goal Tracking
>
> An alternate way of tracking conversions is to combine Google Analytics with your AdWords account so that you can use Google Analytics goals with AdWords. This is useful when you have a slow IT department or you wish a central interface to see all of your data.
>
> To use Google Analytics goal tracking, you must have your analytics account connected to your AdWords account. Once these two are connected, when you navigate to the conversion tracking screen, you will have the option to import your goals from Google Analytics.
>
> The AdWords to Analytics connection can sometimes not function correctly and you may not have the option to import the goals. This commonly occurs if your AdWords login email address does not have access rights to your analytics profile or if you have changed email addresses in either Analytics or AdWords. If this has happened, the only way to correct it is to contact AdWords support.

As you explore bidding techniques in this chapter and examine reports in future chapters, I will assume you have installed the AdWords conversion tracking script. If you are using another tool to track revenue, you can still use all these techniques, but you will have to combine the AdWords reports with your own metrics system.

Tracking Phone Calls

You can use the AdWords call extension to track phone calls from your ads. Often you will want to track calls that originate from your site as well.

There are several ways to track phone calls, including using AdWords' conversion tracking code. Many vendors will let you buy one or more tracking phone numbers. Some vendors will help you track phone calls by keyword, ad copy, or landing page. The more phone numbers you want, the more expensive the solutions become. There are a few ways that you can track calls that occur on your website:

Unique Phone Number per Data Point This solution tracks search engine, ad group, keyword, and so on. It's the most accurate but the most expensive.

Unique Extension per Data Point This solution can be cheaper to institute with a sophisticated in-house call system. However, you will need to correlate extensions with data points.

MEASURING RESULTS WITH GOOGLE'S CONVERSION TRACKING CODE

Code Identifiers You can generate a code underneath the phone number on your site that is associated with AdWords data points. Then have the sales reps collect the identifiers from callers and correlate sales to data points. This is not a hard method to implement, but it does require retraining sales reps.

Estimate Using Confidence Factors If you have a high call volume, instead of having unique phone numbers or extensions by data points, you can create confidence factors so that when a certain keyword is clicked, on average the phone rings 2 percent of the time.

AdWords Conversion Tracking Code If you can get someone back to your website after the call, you can use the AdWords conversion tracking code. You may have to be creative—generating online receipts, for example—to consistently get people back to your website to trigger the code. This method is the cheapest to implement and will allow you to see phone call conversion data inside your AdWords account.

Exploring AdWords Bidding Options

AdWords supports several methods of setting bids. Setting max CPCs, also known as manual bidding for clicks, is the default method; however, depending on your goals, the other methods may work better for you.

These options are at the campaign level in your account. Hence, you can have one campaign that uses one method and another campaign that uses a different method. However, all ad groups in the same campaign will utilize the same bidding methodology.

Navigate to the campaign Settings tab. Under the Bidding And Budget options (Figure 13.6), there are up to four methods listed that you can use to determine your bids.

Bidding and budget

Bidding option ⓘ
- ⦿ Focus on **clicks** - use maximum CPC bids
  - ⦿ I'll manually set my bids for clicks
  - ○ AdWords will set my bids to help maximize clicks within my target budget

  Enhanced CPC ⓘ
  - ☐ Use my conversion tracking data and bids to optimize for conversions
    Enhanced CPC will adjust your Max CPC bid up or down for each auction in an effort to improve your return on investment.
- ○ Focus on **conversions** (Conversion Optimizer) - use CPA bids
  Unavailable because this campaign doesn't have enough conversion data.

[Save] [Cancel]

Figure 13.6 Campaign bidding methods

Focus on Clicks, Option 1

The first option under Focus On Clicks is "I'll manually set my bids for clicks." This is the default method of bidding. You will set a maximum (max) CPC, and you will pay up to that max CPC. The advantage of this option is that it is compatible with all the advanced options in AdWords. For instance, if you want to use advanced ad scheduling where you change your maximum bid by time of day, you must use this bidding method.

Focus on Clicks, Option 2

The second option under Focus On Clicks is "AdWords will set my bids to help maximize clicks within my target budget," also known as the Budget Optimizer. With the Budget Optimizer, Google will attempt to maximize the number of clicks your campaign receives. You can choose to set a maximum bid cap or let AdWords take full control of the bidding. I recommend that you set a bid cap; otherwise, you could end up paying a significant amount per click, since Google will attempt to spend your budget.

If you consider your keywords to have different values for your company, you should not use the Budget Optimizer. For instance, if you are willing to pay $4 per click for the keyword "Samsung 63 DLP TV" but only $2 for the keyword "DLP TV," you should not use the Budget Optimizer. If you are looking to maximize traffic, however, it can be useful.

There's another reason to use the Budget Optimizer. Suppose you have keywords that are good words for your industry and you want to have some exposure on searches that use them. However, those words are so early in the buying funnel that you do not see returns on searches that use them. In this case, you can put the early buying funnel keywords in a Budget Optimizer campaign with a branding budget, and then let AdWords maximize your traffic. For the other keywords for which you are receiving conversions and want to control the bids, leave them in a max CPC or Conversion Optimizer campaign.

If you use both a Budget Optimizer and a max CPC campaign to separate keywords based on where they are in the buying funnel, make sure that the max CPC set for the Budget Optimizer campaign is lower than the max CPCs you are setting in your max CPC–based campaign. If your Budget Optimizer campaign uses broad-matched keywords and has higher bids than your ROI-based campaign, a Budget Optimizer ad could be shown instead of your ROI-based ad. Since the Budget Optimizer ad is meant to get someone to enter your funnel, its value is less for someone who is already in the buying funnel who searches for a keyword in your max CPC campaign. Hence, you should never want to pay more for a Budget Optimizer keyword to show instead of a max CPC keyword where you are bidding on an ROI or profit basis.

Enhanced CPC

Enhanced CPC bidding is not a standalone bid type. It is an optional setting when you are using either of the Focus On Clicks bid methods. With Enhanced CPC, Google will adjust your bids based on the likelihood of a conversion. Google may raise your CPC by 30 percent above your max CPC, or lower your CPC by up to 100 percent. Because Google can raise your CPC by up to 30 percent above your max CPC, it is possible that your average CPC will be higher than your max CPC.

If your overall goal is conversions and you wish to bid manually, this setting should help you increase your overall conversion rates. I have seen Enhanced CPC do very good things for accounts, and I've also see it fail on occasion. Do not just turn on this setting blindly and walk away. If you wish to try it out, turn it on for a couple weeks and see if your overall profits are being increased. If they are, leave the setting on. If your profits are not increasing, turn this setting back off.

Conversion Optimizer

Focus On Conversions is known as the Conversion Optimizer. To enable the Conversion Optimizer, the campaign must be using the AdWords conversion tracking script and must have at least 15 conversions in the past 30 days.

If you meet the criteria and want to use the Conversion Optimizer, you will enter a cost per action (CPA) for each ad group. AdWords will adjust the bids for your keywords in attempting to meet your cost per action. You will still be charged on a cost-per-click basis. You will not just pay for actions. However, AdWords has access to many data points that you don't, and they will use this information, along with other information gathered, to manipulate your bids to try to maximize the conversions you receive for your target CPA.

Unfortunately, you cannot enter different CPAs for different conversions you have defined. For instance, in the earlier plumber example, the plumber was willing to pay different prices for a phone call that led to a small job versus a kitchen remodeling job. However, with the Conversion Optimizer, you can only define a single CPA. Therefore, you might have to separate keywords into different campaigns based on your goals. For instance, the plumber could put the kitchen remodeling keywords in one campaign with a CPA of $100 and the pipe repair keywords in another campaign with a CPA of $25.

Target vs. Max CPA

You can choose a target or a max CPA. Max CPA is the most you want to pay for any single conversion. Target CPA is the average you with to pay for the average of all your conversions. For example, let's assume you have six possible conversions and that you want to pay $17 for a conversion. Check Table 13.1 to determine whether you will receive that conversion based on the chosen CPA method.

In this example, the average $17 (target CPA) collected more conversions than the max CPA, which will commonly be the case. However, average CPA could not collect all the conversions because all the conversions combined averaged a $22.50 CPA. Therefore, you may not get the $50 conversion (number 6) as that would have brought the average from the desired $17 to $23.

Conversions	Cost of conversion	Running avg CPA	Avg CPA ($17)	Max CPA ($17)
1st	$10	$10	Yes	Yes
2nd	$20	$15	Yes	No
3rd	$15	$15	Yes	Yes
4th	$5	$12.50	Yes	Yes
5th	$35	$17	Yes	No
6th	$50	$22.50	No	No
Total Cost	$135			
Total Possible Conversions	6		5	3
Average CPA, All Conversions	$22.50			

The max CPA did not receive several conversions because this method does not want any single conversion that is above $17. Therefore, if Google thinks a conversion will cost $20 (such as number 2), it will not try to get that conversion. In other words, it will not show your ads and keywords when it believes that ad and keyword combination will not bring in a conversion within your specified limit.

If you run a lead-generation site and are getting paid on each individual lead, max CPA is generally a better option. If you have a sales force and just want to keep every rep busy (and your average order value varies dramatically by sale), average CPA is generally a better bid method.

Although companies have found great success with the Conversion Optimizer, the biggest drawback some companies find is that while Conversion Optimizer hits their target CPA, their total conversions dropped. Therefore, if you want to test the Conversion Optimizer but do not want to turn over your entire budget to it, follow these steps:

1. Use the AdWords Editor to duplicate the campaign you want to test.
2. Split your budget among the two campaigns. If you are an aggressive tester, give the new campaign half your budget. If you are a conservative tester, give it a quarter or less of your budget.
3. In the new campaign, set max CPC bids and try to maximize your conversions.
4. In the old campaign, turn on the Conversion Optimizer and let Google take over your bidding.
5. After a few weeks, see which has the better results.

If you have a campaign that is doing very well right now, instead of turning on the Conversion Optimizer in your established campaign, wait for the new campaign to reach at least 15 conversions and then test the optimizer in the new campaign. This strategy will help mitigate the risk of putting your current profits in jeopardy if the Conversion Optimizer does not perform well for your campaigns.

This is one of the few times when it is OK to compete with yourself. Rarely do you want to let Google choose which keyword they should show from your account. Much of optimizing AdWords is taking control from Google so you know that when someone does a search they will see the exact combination of a keyword, ad copy, and destination URL you choose. In this case, you are testing bidding methods that can only be set at the campaign level. Therefore, it is OK to compete with yourself for a few weeks until you can determine which bidding methodology will work best.

> ### Automated Rules
>
> AdWords supports some automated bid rules so that you do not have to keep making the same changes over and over again. For instance, you can set up a rule to change your bid by +10 percent if your CPA is below $20 and to change your bid downward by −10 percent if your CPA is above $30.
>
> You can change ad group or keywords bids; pause or enable campaigns, keywords, or ads; and even change daily budgets with the automated rules.

Focus on Impressions

The first three bidding methodologies can be used on both the search and the display networks. However, this option will be available only if your campaign is set to the display network. When you choose Focus On Impressions, you are setting cost per thousand impressions (CPM) bids. Please refer to the "Choosing CPM or CPC Bidding" section in Chapter 9, "Understanding the Display Network," to learn more about CPM bidding methods.

When using Budget Optimizer or Conversion Optimizer, you should always measure profit and determine if those methods are helping your reach your goals. If you are using max CPC bidding, by far the most common method, you need a strategy to set your bids based on your goals.

Profitable Bidding Strategies

If you are using max CPC bidding, you need to set your own bids. We will walk through some strategies for setting bids. There are a few different places in your account where you should set bids:

- Ad group default
- Ad group for display
- Keyword for search
- Placement for display
- Audiences
- Topics

The ad group–level bids are the default bids. You can override these bids by also bidding by keyword for search, or by audience, topic, or placement for display. Google will use the most specific bid.

For instance, if you have both a keyword-level bid and an ad group–level bid, the keyword is more specific, so Google will use that one. If you have an ad group display bid and a placement bid, Google will use the placement bid if someone is on that placement because it is more specific. If you have placements but you have not set bids for each placement, Google will use the default ad group bid when there is no placement bid.

To maximize your bidding control, use specific bids at the keyword, placement, audience, and topic levels. If you have a number of ad groups, you can just set ad group–level bids and not keyword–level bids. However, you might find that similar keywords in the same ad group lead to different returns for your ad spend. While you can take the shortcut of setting ad group bids instead of keyword bids, if you want to maximize your bidding strategies, you should use keyword-level bids.

Regardless of where you decide to set bids, these strategies apply to any of the four places you want to set bids.

ROAS vs. Profit

In several of your bidding strategies, to set bids you will use a return on investment calculation specific to the advertising industry called return on ad spend (ROAS). However, keep in mind that maximizing your ROAS does not always maximize your profits.

ROAS vs. ROI

Return on investment (ROI) has been long misused in search. The true formula for ROI is ROI = (revenue − cost) / (cost).

This formula has been warped by many marketers into ROI = (revenue) / (cost). They choose to use this incorrect formula because ROI can be a negative number, and negative numbers make bid calculations more complex. A 100 percent ROI in the incorrect formula is your breakeven point, so calculations become easy. The simple explanation for this is that since you are calculating marketing costs, you just removed those same costs from the formula to calculate ROI.

When search marketing was primarily conducted by nonmarketing people in the early years when the web designer or IT department often ran paid search, this slight change in definition often did not matter to the company. However, as search has grown into a multibillion-dollar business and is being taught in college marketing classes, an effort must be made to correct the use of these terms so that it is consistent between company departments.

The ROAS formula is ROAS = (revenue / cost). The ROAS formula is the same as the warped or incorrect ROI formula used in search. Therefore, in this chapter you will use ROAS in your calculations to determine bids.

ROAS is easy to calculate. The formula is ROAS = revenue / cost.

A 100 percent ROAS is breaking even. A 200 percent ROAS means for every dollar you spend, you make two dollars. A 50 percent ROAS means for every dollar you spend, you bring in only 50 cents. In other words, a 50 percent ROAS means you are losing money.

For example, let's examine a company that sells both chocolates and flowers. Chocolates are less competitive than flowers, and therefore the CPC is less. However, flowers have a higher average sale than chocolates, and therefore, the potential for more profits exists. As Table 13.2 illustrates, higher ROAS does not always mean more profits.

▶ **Table 13.2** Profit vs. ROAS

Campaign	Average CPC	Conversion rate	Cost per conversion (average CPC / conversion rate)	Profit per conversion	ROAS (profit / spend)	Profit per sale (profit – cost per conversion)
Chocolate	$1	10%	$10	$20	200%	$10
Flowers	$3	10%	$30	$50	166%	$20

In this example, the chocolate campaign has a higher ROAS than flowers. Many companies would consider this the more successful campaign. However, the flowers campaign brings in more total profits each time it makes a sale. Other companies would consider this to be the more successful campaign. The success metrics can be correlated with your original goals, which can be modified whenever you learn more about your business or change your business direction.

ROAS is an easy number to work with, and you will use it in several of your calculations this chapter. However, never forget to calculate profit. I will show you a bidding strategy that focuses purely on profit.

Revenue per Click

Each time you attain a final business goal, there is revenue associated with the goal. With AdWords, you also pay each time someone clicks on your ad. Each click usually does not lead to revenue. It is a bundle of clicks that finally results in a conversion that leads to company revenues. When thinking about how much you should bid on a click, first calculate your breakeven point, which you can easily determine by the metric revenue per click.

Determining Revenue per Click

To calculate revenue per click, simply divide the revenue that a keyword, placement, or ad group brought to your company by the number of clicks that same ad group, keyword, or placement received.

If a keyword received 100 clicks that led to $1,000 of revenue, then the revenue per click is $10 ($1,000 / 100 = $10).

If you are using AdWords conversion tracking and have associated revenue numbers with conversions, you can easily gather this data from AdWords. When you customize columns, add the column Conv. Value/Click (Figure 13.7).

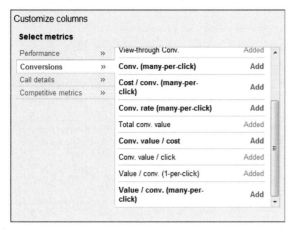

Customize columns		
Select metrics		
Performance »	View-through Conv.	Added
Conversions »	Conv. (many-per-click)	Add
Call details »	Cost / conv. (many-per-click)	Add
Competitive metrics »	Conv. rate (many-per-click)	Add
	Total conv. value	Added
	Conv. value / cost	Add
	Conv. value / click	Added
	Value / conv. (1-per-click)	Added
	Value / conv. (many-per-click)	Add

Figure 13.7 Include Conv. Value/Click when running AdWords reports.

Google will then divide how much revenue a data point received (for AdWords, this could be ad copy, ad group, keyword, campaign, placements, etc.) by the number of clicks that same data point received. Understanding your value per click will help you gain insight into your marketing effectiveness. It is one of the best metrics to work with inside your account.

To simplify the explanations, you will look only at keywords throughout the next several reports and mathematical calculations. However, please note that instead of keywords, these reports could be showing you data at the placement, ad group, landing page, and other levels.

Once you download the keyword report including the value per click information, you should have an Excel file that shows your keywords, the number of clicks, conversions, total value, and value per click for those items (Figure 13.8).

	C	H	M	N	R	U	W
1	Keyword	Max CPC	Avg CPC	Clicks	Conversions	Total Value	Value / Click
2	Keyword 1	$0.35	$0.32	8716	195	$14,625.00	$1.68
3	Keyword 2	$0.75	$0.65	8270	194	$14,550.00	$1.76
4	Keyword 3	$0.29	$0.27	6955	131	$9,825.00	$1.41
5	Keyword 4	$1.12	$0.95	3852	111	$8,325.00	$2.16
6	Keyword 5	$0.35	$0.27	3522	75	$5,625.00	$1.60
7	Keyword 6	$0.50	$0.53	1658	49	$156.00	$0.09
8	Keyword 7	$0.20	$0.08	4589	39	$2,925.00	$0.64
9	Keyword 8	$3.00	$1.05	676	36	$1,903.00	$2.82
10	Keyword 9	$0.30	$0.22	4222	35	$1,001.00	$0.24
11	Keyword 10	$0.35	$0.21	2098	34	$2,550.00	$1.22
12	Keyword 11	$0.25	$0.16	2957	34	$335.00	$0.11
13	Keyword 12	$0.68	$0.57	1852	33	$2,475.00	$1.34
14	Keyword 13	$0.68	$0.59	1628	32	$2,400.00	$1.47

Figure 13.8 Excel report showing keyword value per click data

Clarifying Data with Conditional Formatting

If you have a large account, this is the point where you can easily become overwhelmed by data. There is another Excel function, called conditional formatting, that can turn large spreadsheets into visual references.

The basic use of conditional formatting allows you to highlight cells if they meet certain conditions. To use conditional formatting in Excel 2007 or 2010, on the Home ribbon tab, click Conditional Formatting and choose the type of rule you want to create (Figure 13.9). Then select the cells and the formatting you want to apply to those cells.

Figure 13.9 Creating conditional formatting rules

Use these conditional formatting rules to create a visual reference to see how various keywords, ad groups, and placements are performing:

Red *The value per click is lower than the average CPC.* The first rule you should create is to determine where you are losing money. Since value per click is your breakeven point, if your average cost per click is higher than your value per click, every time you receive a click, you lose money.

Orange *The estimated first page bid is higher than the value per click.* To receive first page exposure across all geographies where you are advertising, your maximum cost per click needs to be higher than the first page bid. When the value per click is lower than your first page bid estimate, these keywords can never be on page 1 profitably. This is a good place to do some testing to see if you can raise the value of those keywords.

Yellow *The value per click is higher than the average CPC but lower than the max CPC.* When your value per click is higher than your average CPC, you make money on each click. However, if your value per click is also lower than your max CPC, you could start to lose money on this keyword without changing the bid. These keywords need to be watched to see if they start losing you money. They are also good keywords to test to see if you can raise the value per click by testing different ad copy and landing pages.

Brown *The value per click is higher than the average CPC and first page bid estimate, but the max CPC is below the first page bid estimate.* These are words that are profitable as the value per click is higher than the average CPC. These words would also be profitable on page 1 since the value per click is higher than the first page bid. However, because the max CPC is below the first page bid, these words are not receiving first page exposure. These are good words on which to bid so that they receive page 1 exposure since they will be profitable at those positions.

Green *The value per click is higher than the max CPC, and the max CPC is higher than the first page bid.* These keywords are on page 1 and are making you money. Although you might adjust the bids so they receive more exposure or set bids based on ROAS, they are not words that are currently losing you money.

By using these conditional formatting rules, you can transform large spreadsheets into visual reference charts that allow you to understand how your keywords, ad copy, landing pages, ad groups, or placements are performing.

Taking Margins into Account

Value per click only takes total revenue into account. This metric does not take margins into account. If you have hard costs, such as an e-commerce company that has to buy the products they are selling, you need to move beyond value per click to look at profit per click.

If you run a lead-generation company without hard costs of goods, your value per click is usually your profit per click. That means you do not need to perform any additional calculations.

There are a few ways to take margins into account so that you are setting bids based on actual profits. The most accurate method is to use Google's API or a third-party vendor to incorporate your back-end system with AdWords so that you can see exactly which keywords are selling which products and then determine the margins automatically. This is a costly solution, although it's the most accurate. But next I'll show you a lower-tech approach that any company, regardless of budget, can incorporate.

First make sure that your ad groups consist of closely related keywords. Create ad groups that only promote a specific product or closely related products with similar margins. For instance, let's assume you sell the products shown in Table 13.3.

Keyword	Margin
iPod nano	25%
iPod touch	35%
Coby Video Player	30%
SanDisk Sansa	20%
Sony Walkman	20%

Your best organization would be to group each of these keywords and their closely related variations (such as "pink iPod nano," "8GB iPod nano") together to form ad groups. However, if you have a tremendous number of items, that organization is not always possible. In that case, the only two items you should combine into a single ad group would be the SanDisk Sansa and the Sony Walkman because they have the same margins.

 Note: From a conversion rate standpoint, this is not a good organization; you would want different ad copy and landing pages for these products. This example is for illustration purposes only, so you can see how to incorporate margins into your reports.

To create reports that include margin data, follow these steps:

1. Make a list of all your ad groups in Excel. The easiest way to get such a list is to run an ad group report or export your account from the AdWords Editor.

2. In another column, list your margins for the product that the ad group should sell, just like in Table 13.3.

3. When you run a report from AdWords, add a new column for margins. Then incorporate your margin data into the AdWords report using the VLookUp function.

4. Create an additional column called Profit per Click, and populate this column by multiplying your value per click by your margin (Figure 13.10).

5. Finally, use the conditional formatting rules on the Profit per Click column instead of the Value/Click column. This will give you a visual reference of your actual profits.

Instead of applying margins at the ad group level, you could incorporate margins at the keyword level. However, determining your margins for each keyword could consume so many hours of work that it might be cheaper to incorporate your back-end system into a third-party vendor or use the AdWords API.

Figure 13.10 Taking margins into account when examining performance

This low-tech approach should be directionally accurate. However, what you will find is that some of your sales are for completely unrelated items. You will find that someone searches for an iPod and buys a plasma TV—or someone searches for a plasma TV and buys a 10-cent pencil. Using this margin approach is better than not understanding how your profits are derived whatsoever, but the results will be inaccurate at times.

How Can Publishers Determine Revenue per Click?

The metric that publishers, such as newspapers, should track is revenue per visitor (RPV). Sometimes RPV is calculated by individual user, and other times by 1,000 visitors, similar to CPM.

Most publishers have two main revenue opportunities. One is to sell ads on their site and the second is to sell subscriptions. To calculate your revenue per visitor, you first need to find how much you make on any page view.

For instance, if a publisher sells $50 CPM ads (meaning an advertiser is willing to pay $50 for 1,000 page views), then each individual page view is worth $0.05 ($50 / 1,000). If a publisher has three ad display units on a page, the page view is actually worth $0.15.

Once you understand how much you make on any single page view, the second step is to calculate average page views per visit. For our analysis, let's assume the average visitor sees three pages. By multiplying the average page views (3) by the RPV ($0.15), you can see that by getting a visitor to the site, the publisher makes $0.45. Average page views will vary by traffic source and by keyword.

The second metric publishers track is subscriptions. For ease of analysis, let's assume that one out of every 100 visitors buys a subscription for $10 per month. A subscription is not a one-time purchase. A publisher should then track how long someone is paying for a subscription. Our example newspaper finds that when someone buys a subscription, that user pays the newspaper for 10 months. Therefore, a one-time sale is actually a $100 lifetime value. At a 1 percent conversion rate, that means the publisher makes $1 per visitor ($100 purchase × 1 percent conversion rate) when tracking subscription revenue.

Combining RPV and Subscription Revenue

You can take this approach even further and look at the number of page views per subscriber per month. For ease of calculation, let's say our newspaper finds that subscribers see 100 page views per month. When you calculate RPV ($0.15) times page views per month (100) times the number of months someone is a subscriber (10), you find that the actual subscriber is worth $150 over their lifetime. This is the *lifetime RPV*.

Adding the lifetime RPV ($150) to the lifetime subscription value ($100), you end up with a $250 product. Since only 1 percent of searchers buy a subscription, the actual value per click for subscription conversions is $2.50: $250 (product value) × 1 percent (conversion rate) = $2.50.

When you add the original RPV ($0.45) and the lifetime subscription price value per click ($2.50) of each visitor, you see that the newspaper on average makes $2.95 per visitor. Therefore, $2.95 is their actual lifetime value per click of a nonsubscriber. The value per click of a current subscriber is only the RPV ($0.45) since you cannot sell them a product they already own (the subscription). Within AdWords you cannot target nonsubscribers, so the best the publisher can do is to use a blended average for their profit per click.

That value per click number represents all keywords and traffic sources combined. A publisher might find that one keyword leads to 10 page views per visit but no subscriptions. Another keyword might lead to a 10 percent subscription rate but only three page views. To set bids at the ad group, keyword, display, and placement level, you will want to be able to calculate those values for each data point.

Tracking Conversions in AdWords

The easiest way to view this data in AdWords so that you can see value per click by keyword, landing page, and ad copy is to use the AdWords conversion tracker. In the AdWords conversion tracker, set up one script that tracks page views. In the value column, enter $0.15 (the value per page view). Put this script on each page of your website. Then set up a second script that goes on the "Thank you for subscribing" page. In the subscription script, for the total value enter $250, the lifetime value of a subscriber.

Technically, the most accurate number would come from tracking average subscription length and page views per subscriber by traffic source to adjust that $250 lifetime value appropriately based on actual data. To get to that level of tracking, you will need to incorporate your own tracking system—that information cannot be gathered from AdWords alone. However, this is a good place to start to examine how profitable each keyword or placement is to your bottom line.

Once you have incorporated these tracking scripts, when you run an AdWords report you can see the revenue associated with each keyword as a publisher. In the section "Calculating Your Max CPC," later in this chapter, you will use this revenue per click number to set appropriate bids for each keyword, ad group, or placement based on actual revenue.

Tracking Long Sales Cycles with Conversion Funnels

Many companies do not make a final sale off their first conversion activity. If you are in a business-to-business environment, or selling high-end products, you may find that it takes several contacts with a user before you finally sell a product. In cases of multiple touch points, you need to build a conversion funnel to understand what each keyword and lead is worth to your company.

Let's look at a fictional company called RSI, which integrates BlackBerry mobile devices with Microsoft Exchange and a company's internal instant messaging desktop applications. This is a complex procedure, and their service is expensive; their average enterprise customer spends $100,000 per integration. RSI finds that they never make a sale from a single phone call. They need multiple touch points to move a corporation through the buying funnel before the customer finally signs a contract and writes them a check.

After some analysis, RSI builds a conversion funnel with five steps:

1. Buy clicks to their website from AdWords.
2. Offer those searchers a free whitepaper download. To receive the download, users must enter their contact information.
3. Invite everyone who downloads their whitepaper to a free webinar that showcases their product.
4. Call each person who attended their webinar to attempt to sell them a product.
5. Make a final sale for $100,000.

RSI exists for illustration purposes only; you may find that you need to add more steps to your own conversion funnel, such as in-person demos.

RSI tracks the conversion rates from clicks to whitepaper downloads. As that action occurs on the Web, they can easily use the AdWords conversion tracking to see the percentage of downloads by keyword or placement to determine how much they are paying for a download. However, a download does not lead to revenues for the company; it just introduces a searcher to their buying funnel. Therefore, RSI needs to do some math and offline tracking to determine what an actual click is worth.

Buy clicks to their website from AdWords. RSI finds that they are currently paying an average of $10 a click from AdWords. They can do this entire analysis at the keyword, landing page, or placement level. For now, let's keep it simple to illustrate how to analyze a conversion funnel. RSI buys 1,000 clicks at $10 a click, so their initial investment is $10,000.

Offer those searchers a free whitepaper download. RSI's whitepaper download conversion rate is a fantastic 25 percent. Of those 1,000 clicks, they have received 250 downloads. Therefore, they have paid $40 per download ($10,000 / 250 = $40).

Invite everyone who downloads their whitepaper to a free webinar. It seems those who like a free download also like free webinars. Forty percent of those who download the whitepaper attend RSI's webinar. They receive 100 viewers of their webinar (250 downloads × 40% conversion rate). They have essentially paid $100 to have someone attend their webinar ($10,000 in clicks / 100 attendees).

Call each person who attended their webinar to attempt to sell them a product. The sales team manages to get 10 percent of the webinar attendees on the phone. The cost per phone call contact is $1,000 ($10,000 in clicks / 10 phone calls = $1,000).

Make a final sale for $100,000. Of those 10 phone calls, the sales team makes one sale for $100,000. Now that they have a sale, they can finally calculate the ROI of that sale and the value per click. ROI is profit / spend: in this case, $100,000 profit / $10,000 spend = 1,000 percent ROI. Although most e-commerce companies would love a 1,000 percent ROI, often in a B2B environment that ROI is necessary, because you have a large team making a single sale based on the customer touch points.

RSI is a savvy company, so they do not automatically assume that their ROAS is actually 1,000 percent. They do some math and realize that, based on the time invested in paying sales reps, emailing customers, and conducting webinars, as well as building, installing, and supporting the RSI system, the fully loaded cost of the sale was $50,000. Therefore, their net profit is $40,000: $100,000 (revenue) − $10,000 (ad spend) − $50,000 (all other product, sales, and overhead) = $40,000.

By dividing the net profit ($40,000) by the number of clicks (1,000), they come to realize that their value per click is $40.

It can be useful to put these steps into a visual reference chart (Figure 13.11) so you can see the chain of events.

If RSI wanted to optimize their ability to sell their product, their first step should not be examining their AdWords account. Before a salesperson attempts to contact a business, the business has opted into two steps (whitepaper download and webinar attendance) with RSI. A 10 percent phone call contact rate to a company that has gone through only two steps of engagement is quite low.

Clicks	• 10,000 Clicks • $1 per Click • $10,000 Ad Cost
Whitepaper Download	• 250 Downloads • 25% Conversion Rate from Clicks • $40 Cost Per Download
Attended Webinar	• 100 Attendees • 40% Conversion Rate from Downloads • $100 Cost Per Conversion
Sales Rep Contact	• 10 Phone Call Contacts • 10% Conversion Rate from Webinar Attendee • $1000 Cost Per Phone Call
Sales	• 1 Sales • 10% Conversion Rate from Sales Call • $100,000 Revenue

Figure 13.11 RSI conversion funnel

RSI should observe how their sales reps are contacting companies and also study the sales scripts. If their contact rate went to 20 percent, the company would have made another sale, leading to much higher profits than testing ad copy that led to another 5 percent of visitors. That does not mean RSI should not test ad copy—it just means if you have a full picture of your conversion funnel, you can spend your time making the biggest impact for your company. Once the phone call contact rate has been fixed, RSI should work on optimizing their AdWords account.

Calculating Your Max CPC

There are two main ways to perform calculations to determine your bids. One is to bid based on your ROAS. Setting ROAS bids is preferred by many companies because it lets them build in a buffer of a higher ROAS so they do not have to calculate such items as payroll, rent, and so forth.

The second method is to set bids by profits. When I show you this bid method, I will simplify the calculations, so I won't take into account your lighting bill. You are going to try to maximize the profit that your account generates as if it operated in a vacuum apart from your typical operating costs. Once you see how the simple calculations are done, you can and should develop your own profit calculations that account for all appropriate product and sales costs.

Setting Bids Based on ROAS

The difficult part of bidding is not setting bids. The difficult part in determining bids is understanding your revenue. Once you have determined the revenue for each keyword, ad group, or placement, setting a bid based on ROAS is quite easy. There are a few formulas you can use based on the information you have available to you.

In this section, you will use value per click, revenue per click, and profit per conversion, which is information you can glean from your AdWords reports (as discussed in the earlier section "Revenue per Click").

If you know your profit and conversion rates, you can use this method. For the keyword "chocolate," here are the metrics:

- Profit per conversion: $25
- Desired ROAS: 200%
- Conversion rate: 10%

The basic formula for setting bids based on profits is as follows:

- (Profit per conversion / desired ROAS) × (conversion rate) = max CPC
- ($25 / 200%) × 10% = $1.25
- This can also be expressed by: ($25 / 2) × 0.1 = $1.25

If you know your value or revenue per click and do not have a margin, you can use this information to set a bid:

- Value or revenue per click: $2.50
- Desired ROAS: 200%

In this case, you can use the following formula:

- Value per click / desired ROAS = max CPC
- 2.50 / 200% = $1.25 is the max CPC

If you know your value or revenue per click but you have a margin, you need to go through two steps to calculate your max CPC. In this example, the metrics are

- Value per click: $2
- Margin: 50%
- Desired ROAS: 200%

The first step is to calculate the breakeven point:

- Value per click × margin = breakeven CPC
- $2.00 × 50% = $1.00

The second step is to calculate the bid from the breakeven CPC:

- Breakeven CPC / desired ROAS = max CPC
- $1 / 200% = $0.50

Easily Make Multiple Bid Changes

Since setting bids by ROAS is a simple calculation, you can build the formula in an Excel spreadsheet and calculate a bid by placement, keyword, or ad group. Once you have a spreadsheet that contains your bids, use the bulk import feature in the AdWords Editor to quickly make all your bid changes. After you import your existing keywords, ad groups, or placements with your new CPCs, post those changes to your AdWords account. Making bulk bid changes with Excel and the AdWords Editor will save you a tremendous amount of time.

The preceding formulas work for setting keyword bids, placement bids, and ad group bids. If you want to bid by ROAS, regardless of where you want to set those bids, the same formulas apply. ROAS is a very simple metric to use for setting bids, and one of the powerful bid methods available if you are going to manually bid by hand. If you are looking to gain more exposure, you can see bid suggestions directly from AdWords.

Bidding for Exposure

You can receive recommended bids from Google for your ad to be placed on the first page of results or at the top of the results. Just remember, this is the bid to be on the first or top of the page most often—it does not guarantee you will get clicks or that those clicks will convert.

Bidding just to receive exposure and clicks with no other goal in mind is often called *ego bidding*, because it satisfies the CEO's ego to be at the top of Google. However, if you do not make any money, you might not be at the top very long.

You can customize the columns on the Keywords tab to see the estimated first page and estimated top page bids (Figure 13.12).

Most industries do not have click prices this high; however, if you ever delve into the realm of class action lawsuits, expect to see many bids in the $75–100 range, or even higher. The first page bid estimate is the approximate cost to be on page one for that keyword when the query is the same as your keyword. There are three main reasons your CPC may be below the first page bid and you are displayed on the first page.

Avg. CPC ⓘ	Est. first page bid	Est. top page bid ⓘ
$89.25	--	--
$137.74	$56.00	$100.00
$135.41	$100.00	$100.00
$121.28	$46.00	$100.00
$121.26	$17.00	$61.00
$120.02	$25.00	$100.00
$119.90	$60.00	$100.00
$117.60	$12.00	$100.00
$117.41	$13.00	$100.00
$116.00	$11.00	$39.00
$114.05	$54.00	$100.00
$113.76	$17.00	$75.00

Figure 13.12 First page and top page bids

The first is the most common: geographic reach. The first page bid takes into account all the geographies where you are advertising. It is common to see hyper-competitive areas, where bids are much higher than average. In this case, you might be on page one for the majority of your region with a bid below the first page bid estimate—you just aren't on page one in every region.

The second most common reason is that this bid is based on when the search query is the same as your keyword. If you are using any match type except for exact match, other queries can trigger your ads to show. Your CPC could be below the first page bid, but for certain queries you still show on page one.

The third reason is related to budgets. Many advertisers do not have the budget to be displayed the entire day for an entire month. It is common to see budgets deplete near the end of the month or later in the day. As other budgets are depleted, your ads may show since there is less competition.

The estimated top page is the estimate required to be above the organic results. Often you will see many more impressions and clicks if your ads are above the organic results as opposed to being displayed in the right rail. To see the difference in side versus top impressions, you can use the AdWords Bid Simulator.

Bid Simulator

The Bid Simulator shows you a projection of the number of impressions you would see if you raised or lowered your bid for a particular keyword.

To access the Bid Simulator, navigate to the keywords in your account and look for the graph icon next to the max CPC (Figure 13.13).

Figure 13.13 Accessing the Bid Simulator

Not all keywords will show the graph icon. If Google does not have enough data to project how many impressions and clicks you will receive at different max CPCs, you will not see a graph. If you have a campaign that constantly hits its daily budget, you may not see the icon. Raising the CPC of one keyword might not get more impressions since other words are also using a percentage of your daily budget. You may not see it inside Conversion Optimizer, Budget Optimizer, or display-only campaigns because you cannot bid by keyword in these instances.

Once you find a keyword where the graph exists, click on the graph and you will be able to see projected clicks, cost, and impressions by different max CPCs (Figure 13.14).

These estimates do not guarantee similar results in the future. Learn more

Max. CPC	Estimated Impr.	Estimated Top Impr. (?)
○ $121.00	753	399
○ $97.00	712	321
◉ $80.00 (current)	661	251
○ $60.80	625	143
○ $45.20	561	63
○ $33.60	454	25
○ $23.30	331	4
○ Use a different bid: $		

Impressions
753

$23.30 $47.73 $72.15 $96.58 $121.00
331
Max. CPC

Figure 13.14 Projected changes by max CPC

Google refreshes this data daily, but changes in Quality Score, competitors' bids, or search behavior can cause these numbers to become inaccurate. In addition, this information is only based on the last seven days of data. Therefore, it is inaccurate around seasonal peaks since the bids are volatile during those periods.

You should use them for guidance purposes only and not rely on the information as absolute. However, these numbers can help you get an idea of the available impressions as you raise and lower your bids.

Ad Scheduling: Automatically Changing Bids by Time Periods

Ad scheduling allows you to control what days of the week and times of the day your ads are shown. In addition, you can automatically change bids by a percentage higher or lower depending on the time of day or the day of the week. This feature is also called *day parting* in many circles.

You enable ad scheduling at the campaign level, and therefore it affects every ad group in your campaign. To enable ad scheduling, navigate to your campaign settings, and under Advanced Settings, click the Edit button next to Ad Scheduling (Figure 13.15).

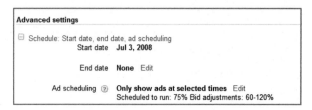

Figure 13.15 Enabling ad scheduling

Clicking the Edit button will bring up an interface where you can set exactly when you want your ads to show (Figure 13.16). The basic version of ad scheduling allows you to turn your ads on or off by time of day or day of the week.

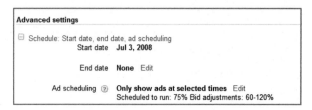

Figure 13.16 You can turn ads on or off by day of the week or time of day.

The most important thing to note about ad scheduling is that the ads are shown based on your account's time zone—not the user's time zone. If you have an older account and have not adjusted the settings, your account is most likely in GMT–8 or Pacific Standard Time (PST). In the bottom-right corner of Figure 13.16 you can see your account's time zone.

If your account and target geography are not in the same time zone, you need to manually adjust the times when your ad is displayed. There is a three-hour time difference between PST and EST. If your account is in PST, and you want ads to be displayed from 8 a.m. to 5 p.m. in an EST location, such as New York City, you would change your ad display by three hours. In this case, you would turn your ads on at 5 a.m. and turn them back off at 2 p.m.

The advanced use of ad scheduling is to adjust your bids by a percentage by time of day or day of the week. If you were a catering company, you might find that:

- Between midnight and 6:15 a.m., you receive few phone calls, yet some people are looking for your service; therefore, set your bids to 60 percent of normal.
- Between 6:15 a.m. and 9:00 a.m., those who hire you for the day are starting to filter into the office, and therefore you want to run your bids at a normal rate.
- Between 9:00 a.m. and 11:00 a.m., your calls skyrocket for businesspeople who want their lunch catered. In this case, you set your bids to 120 percent of normal. This will cause all the bids in your campaign to be increased by 20 percent.
- Between 11:00 a.m. and 1:00 p.m., you are delivering orders and do not have time to answer the phone. Therefore, you turn off your account during these hours.
- Between 1:00 p.m. and 5:00 p.m., some companies order catering for the next day, and therefore you set your bids to 100 percent of normal. These are the standard bids you set for your account.
- Between 5:00 p.m. to 8:00 p.m., you receive some orders, but the call volume is lower; therefore you set your bids to 80 percent of normal.
- Between 8:00 p.m. and midnight, call volume drops significantly, and therefore you only want to pay 60 percent of your normal click price.

If this is your scenario, in the ad scheduling interface you would first create this scenario for a single day (Figure 13.17).

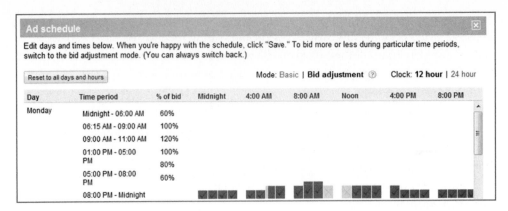

Figure 13.17 Catering company ad scheduling

After going through this exercise for a single day, you can use the interface to copy the schedule to the rest of the weekdays (Figure 13.18).

Figure 13.18 Copying ad scheduling data from one day to another

If you are trying to control costs, only run your ads when your conversion rates are highest. To maximize returns, examine when you receive conversions and change your bids based on that conversion activity.

Finding Conversion Information by Time Frames

There are a few methods you can use to extract conversion information by day or hour from Google products. You will need to use a combination of Google Analytics and AdWords reporting to see all the possible trend data.

Finding Day-of-the-Week Conversion Information in AdWords Reports

Google AdWords allows you to see conversion information and most of your metrics by day of the week (Figure 13.19). In the Dimensions tab, examine the unit of time in the drop-down list.

The second step is to export the report to Excel and put the information into a pivot table (Figure 13.20). For ease of illustration, this information is not broken down into ad groups. However, you should study this information on an ad group, keyword, or placement level.

Figure 13.19 Viewing day of the week

Figure 13.20 Day of the week pivot table

This account's conversion rate and cost per conversion are much better on the weekend than the weekdays. While their CTR is fairly static during the entire week, their average position drops slightly during the weekends. In addition, they are currently losing money during several weekdays (cost is higher than revenue), yet they are highly profitable on the weekends. In this case, they may want to try lowering their bids during the week and raising them on the weekends.

Whenever you start changing bids by the time of day or the day of the week, or you turn off your account completely, track total conversion changes. You may find that someone is looking for you on a Sunday but calling you on Monday morning.

You can also see hourly information in the AdWords reports (Figure 13.21), which can be useful to see how conversions change based on the course of days. It is common to see conversion rates higher for travel companies during lunch hour, dating sites after 10 p.m., and retail throughout the daylight hours.

Hour of day	Clicks ⑦	Avg. CPC ⑦	Cost	Conv. (1-per-click) ⑦	Cost / conv. (1-per-click) ⑦	Conv. rate (1-per-click) ⑦
0	8,085	$1.20	$9,739.38	64	$54.33	4.78%
1	6,150	$1.22	$7,478.47	49	$56.75	4.85%
2	4,281	$1.21	$5,172.02	37	$50.81	5.47%
3	2,148	$1.33	$2,866.46	21	$53.61	5.56%
4	1,787	$1.37	$2,444.39	9	$116.94	2.55%
5	1,540	$1.57	$2,412.88	11	$115.31	2.71%
6	1,987	$1.63	$3,244.84	24	$76.60	3.98%
7	3,277	$1.55	$5,091.40	61	$44.68	6.19%
8	5,365	$1.57	$8,426.65	105	$44.89	6.31%
9	7,656	$1.56	$11,951.18	141	$46.13	6.15%
10	9,599	$1.53	$14,690.36	203	$37.99	7.42%
11	10,862	$1.49	$16,156.25	202	$40.65	6.83%
12	11,361	$1.51	$17,183.41	198	$44.62	6.45%

Figure 13.21 Viewing conversion rates by hour

Once you have chosen the information you want to see, export it to Excel and create charts so you can view the information and see if there are clear trends. Some businesses will not see conversion rates change by time of day or by hour; others will see drastic changes.

Often the differences can be explained by typical user behavior. Marketing is about reaching people. People's behaviors change based on the factors in their lives. Therefore, you need to ask the question, How do your customers go about their daily lives?

Examples of Ad Scheduling Success

Microsoft's Atlas Solutions published an interesting paper on conversion rates by industry titled "Search Conversion Rates by Day Part," by Esco Strong (available at www.atlassolutions.com/institute_marketinginsights.aspx). In this paper, Atlas Solutions published several charts that showed conversion rates by time of day. Upon examining each of these charts, you can see conversion rates change based on what is going on in someone's life. The first chart (Figure 13.22) shows conversion rates for consumer finance.

Conversion rates are low in the morning; many people are sleeping, and those who are surfing the Web are often not buying. Once consumers awaken, they may be more concerned with getting to work and earning money than they are about their personal finances. However, lunch hour is their own time. The conversion rates over the lunch hour spike. After lunch, consumers go back to work, and then commute home. This is no longer their personal time, and conversion rates go down. Just before and after dinner time, the conversion rates again increase. As the evening wanes on, conversion rates steadily decline as consumers go to sleep. The chart looks interesting. When paired with a consumer's daily routine, it tells you the best time to reach these consumers.

Figure 13.22 Atlas One Point conversion rates by hour for finance industry

Examining your consumer's routine, and finding the times when the consumer is searching for you so you can adjust your targeting, applies to both consumer and business searchers.

Business-to-Business Case Study

When deciding to change bids by the day of the week or the time of day, it is essential that you have enough information to make solid decisions. This is a case study for a business-to-business company. Their goal was to offer an IT whitepaper download to bring consumers into their conversion funnel. The first step was to graph conversion rates by hour (Figure 13.23).

Figure 13.23 Conversion rates by hour for a whitepaper download

At first glance it appears that conversion rates are higher during work hours. The second step is to graph conversion rates by day of the week (Figure 13.24).

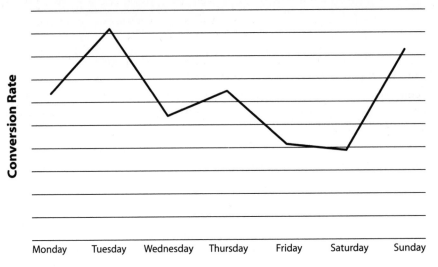

Figure 13.24 Conversion rates by day of the week for a whitepaper download

Now we have some interesting information. While the conversion rates seemed higher during working hours, it turns out that Sunday is their second highest converting day. If you stopped here and decided to make bid decisions, you would be making a mistake. Because Tuesday and Sunday are their highest converting days, let's see the conversion rates by hour for those two days (Figure 13.25).

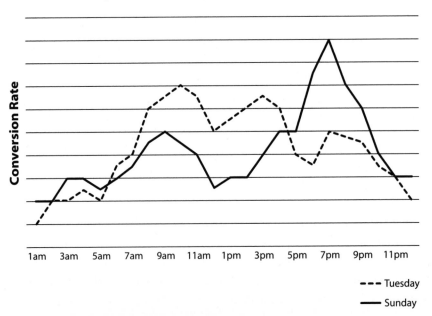

Figure 13.25 Conversion rates by hour for Tuesday and Sunday for a whitepaper download

Although on Tuesday conversion rates are higher during work hours, the opposite is true of Sunday. Sunday night is a common business-to-business search evening for people who left work early on Friday evening or did not finish all the work assigned to them the previous week. Only after this last chart is completed does this company have enough information to set bids by time of day and day of the week. Please note that these are the results for one company. You may not find the same results and should conduct your own research into your conversion rates by hour.

This company's goal was a whitepaper download. But what if you have multiple goals? Let's look at a company that needed to change their conversion actions based on user behavior throughout a month.

High-End Electronics Case Study

This study is for a company that sells expensive electronics. Their average order size is in excess of $2,000. Instead of graphing conversion rates by day and hour, they graph them by day of the month. Figure 13.26 shows a chart of their average conversion rates by day of the month for a three-month time frame.

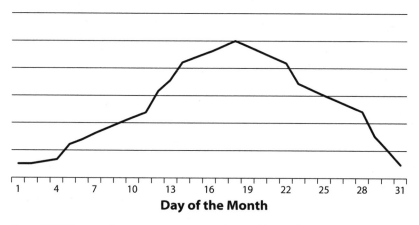

Figure 13.26 Three-month average of conversion rates by day of the month

It appears that conversion rates go up in the middle of the month, and at the beginning and end of the month their conversion rates are lower. However, if we graph their conversion rates by those three months individually, and not as an average, we see a much different picture (Figure 13.27).

This chart does not seem to make any sense. There does not initially appear to be any consistency to conversion rates. However, you must always take into consideration the lives of your consumers. When do they get paid? Many people in the United States get paid on the first and fifteenth of the month, or every two weeks. If we examine the data from the middle of the months, and then look at the weekends after the weekend paycheck, this data starts to make sense (Figure 13.28).

Figure 13.27 Three months of conversion data graphed against each other

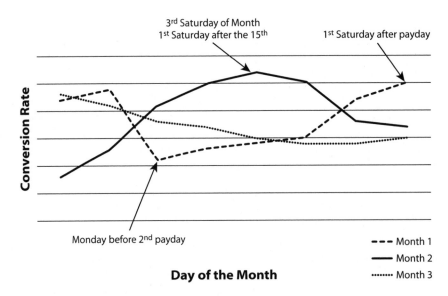

3rd Saturday of Month
1st Saturday after the 15th

1st Saturday after payday

Monday before 2nd payday

Month 1
Month 2
Month 3

Day of the Month

Figure 13.28 Graphing paychecks against conversion rates

The first paycheck of the month usually goes to mortgages, rent, gas, and utility bills. The second paycheck of the month is generally more disposable income. When consumers spend, their disposable income is directly reflected in this company's conversion rates.

After going through extensive analysis of their conversion rates, this company did something unique with their marketing. At the beginning and end of the month, their conversion goal was for consumers to sign up for their sales newsletter. Just before paychecks are distributed, the company sends out their sales newsletter and then sends their paid traffic to their e-commerce pages.

You do not need to be this sophisticated to take advantage of ad scheduling. There are simpler approaches that can help you engage customers.

Creating Time-Sensitive Offers

Marketing is about connecting with consumers. With AdWords, the first connection is based on keywords. The second connection is often location targeting. You could make the next connection to the display network by writing ads specific to a site or type of website where your ads appear. And finally, you can use day of the week or time of day in the ad copy.

Most restaurants have daily specials. You could create a campaign for every day of the week. In your ad copy, add the daily special (Figure 13.29). Your keywords will be the same for each campaign. The keywords will not compete with each other—one campaign will only run on Monday, another only on Tuesday, and so on.

Monday's Sushi Special
Free edamame on orders over $10
Order before noon for Free Delivery

Figure 13.29 Time-sensitive offer for restaurant

Are there times when your business is slow? On Friday afternoons, most people in the office are more concerned with their evening plans than fixing a leaky pipe. However, you can write an ad that speaks to both the day of the week and the time of the day to help engage those who are searching (Figure 13.30).

25% Off Plumbing Services
If you call between 12-5p on Friday
Serving the Greater Chicago Area.

Figure 13.30 Time-sensitive offer using
day of the week and time of day in the ad copy

In this example, there would be two campaigns. One campaign would run from noon until 5:00 p.m. on a Friday. The other campaign would run from 5:00 p.m. on a Friday until noon the following Friday.

Once you understand all the possibilities of how ads are displayed, you can be highly creative in engaging your audience in unique methods beyond just changing bids and conversion actions.

So far, we have examined ways of bidding based on ROAS or profit metrics, and then ways of engaging the audience or manipulating bids based on ROAS or profit metrics. But should you always bid based on ROAS? A look into attribution management may tell you there are times when you do not want to set bids based purely on ROAS.

Understanding Attribution Management

Each of the bidding techniques we examined set bids based on the conversion rate of a keyword or ad group. The AdWords conversion tracker only applies a conversion value to the last keyword, ad group, ad copy, and landing page clicked from your AdWords account.

For example, if someone clicked on your ad yesterday for the keyword "MP3 player," looked at your website but did not convert, and then that same user saw your ad today for the keyword "16GB iPod touch," clicked it, and then converted on your website, what metrics would show in your AdWords account?

Both keywords would show that they received a click and incurred costs. However, only the last keyword clicked, "16GB iPod touch," would show a conversion in your AdWords account. Each time a user clicks on your ad, Google overwrites the conversion tracking code cookie. Therefore, the conversion tracker is known as a last-keyword-clicked attribution management system.

To make matters more complicated, Google Analytics associates goals with the last entrance to the website. Therefore, if someone clicks on your ad today, then comes back to your site directly tomorrow and converts, Google Analytics will show that a direct traffic entrance received the conversion, and yet Google AdWords will show the last keyword clicked in your account received the conversion.

It is common for searchers to start out with general phrases to learn more about a product. As they learn more, their search becomes more specific in their keyword selection. The search behavior mirrors the buying funnel. Let's assume that you sell MP3 players and that a searcher did the searches shown in Figure 13.31; each time they clicked on your ad before finally purchasing from your company.

Figure 13.31 Search process before making a purchase

If you only bid by ROAS or by profits, technically only the last keyword, "16GB iPod touch," would have a bid higher than zero. Because the other keywords did not have a conversion associated with them, they did not bring ROI to your account and therefore are costing you money. However, are they *really* costing you money? Or is it that the searcher first became engaged with your company after searching for "MP3 Player" and the only reason they kept clicking on your ads before finally purchasing was that you helped them learn more about MP3 players after their very first click?

In this scenario, if you deleted all of the words except for "16GB iPod touch" you might find that your total conversions drop significantly. Although your ROAS would probably go up—ROAS is only a percentage—your total revenue and profits would most likely drop. In these cases, what do you do? You have two options.

The first is to use an attribution management system. There are third-party vendors that will track each of these clicks and tell you which keywords did not convert but originally brought a searcher to your site who converted at a later time. You could also build such a system in-house, but if you do, be prepared to invest some time and money. Even using a sophisticated third-party system is not cheap. If you do not have the money to invest right now, there is a second solution you can employ: You can use Google's Search Funnel report.

When you navigate to the Conversions section from the Tools And Analysis tab, you can click the link Search Funnels on the left. Doing so will bring you to an area where you can see additional information about your conversions (Figure 13.32).

Click-Assisted Conversions	Impression-Assisted Conversions				Views:
Last Click Conversions (?)	**Last Click Conversion Value** (?)	**Assisted Conversions** (?)	**Assisted Conversion Value** (?)	**Assisted Conversions / Last Click Conversions** (?)	
2,957	**2,957.00**	**688**	**688.00**	**0.23**	
% of Total: 100.00%	% of Total: 100.00%	% of Total: 100.00%	% of Total: 100.00%	% of Total: 100.00%	

	Dimension: Campaign ⌄	Last Click Conversions ↓	Last Click Conversion Value	Assisted Conversions	Assisted Conversion Value	Assisted Conversions / Last Click Conversions
1.		786	786.00	196	196.00	0.25
2.		691	691.00	137	137.00	0.20
3.		468	468.00	152	152.00	0.32
4.		350	350.00	105	105.00	0.30
5.		247	247.00	52	52.00	0.21
6.		210	210.00	42	42.00	0.20
7.		128	128.00	36	36.00	0.28
8.		75	75.00	29	29.00	0.39

Figure 13.32 Additional conversion reports

The simplest one to use is Click-Assisted Conversions (Figure 13.33). Assisted conversions will show you how many conversions a keyword both assisted on and received via last-click attribution.

If you see keywords that are assisting in conversions but do not have many conversions themselves, you may not want to just remove them from your account. You can instead either set bids on them based on the additional value they are bringing to your company, or you can use them in a Budget Optimizer campaign as discussed earlier in the section "Exploring AdWords Bidding Options."

Figure 13.33 Assisted conversions

If you would like to use metrics to determine what keywords should be placed into a Budget Optimizer account, examine bounce rates, average page views, and goal conversions in Google Analytics for each keyword. If you see keywords that are leading to high interaction on your website but those keywords are not converting and are early buying funnel keywords, then add the words to the Budget Optimizer campaign. If those keywords start to convert and you wish to bid on them based on their value, move them into a max CPC or Conversion Optimizer campaign.

Attribution management is a buzz phrase that will receive more exposure in the future. If you buy banner ads and they seem to not lead to conversions, your wallet will tell you that you should stop buying those ads. However, if you have data that shows you that when someone sees your banner ad your conversion rate for search increases for those individuals, you might have a different opinion on those banner ads. Multiple marketing channels do affect each other. Cross-channel attribution management will only continue to increase in sophistication over the coming years.

Examining AdWords Reports to Make ROAS Bid Decisions

When you download AdWords information, you are often buried in data. The first step to analyzing the information is to use conditional formatting to put the data into a visual reference, as discussed earlier in the section "Revenue per Click." It can also be useful to put your ad groups into various buckets so that you can analyze similar ad groups together. Let's examine an ad group report (Figure 13.34) and sort the ad groups into a meaningful organization.

You can do this analysis at the keyword, ad copy, landing page, or placement level. We will walk through it at an ad group level, but there are times you will want to go through this same exercise with different data points.

It is useful to add two columns to the AdWords reports. The first, Column F, is ROAS. It is a percentage of how high the returns are for any ad group regardless of total dollars spent. The second data point is profit. Subtract cost from revenue to arrive at profit. This profit metrics is profit for the account only; it does not take into account hard costs or other overhead. In this case, we are assuming there are no margins involved. If there are, first calculate margins, then profit. Once we have those data points calculated, let's group these ad groups.

A	B	C	D	E	F	G
Ad Groups	Revenue	Spend	Average CPC	Value / Click	ROI	Profit (revenue - cost)
Ad Group #1	$0.00	$1.49	$0.17	$0.00	0%	-$1.49
Ad Group #2	$0.00	$31.47	$0.20	$0.00	0%	-$31.47
Ad Group #3	$0.00	$3.87	$0.10	$0.00	0%	-$3.87
Ad Group #4	$0.00	$20.84	$0.14	$0.00	0%	-$20.84
Ad Group #6	$325.00	$495.92	$0.77	$0.66	66%	-$170.92
Ad Group #7	$260.00	$354.64	$1.13	$0.73	73%	-$94.64
Ad Group #8	$455.00	$159.71	$1.44	$2.85	285%	$295.29
Ad Group #9	$8,775.00	$4,719.88	$1.11	$1.86	186%	$4,055.12
Ad Group #10	$4,745.00	$3,596.16	$0.85	$1.32	132%	$1,148.84
Ad Group #11	$5,980.00	$5,140.16	$0.20	$1.16	116%	$839.84
Ad Group #12	$88,595.00	$26,869.74	$0.41	$3.30	330%	$61,725.26
Ad Group #13	$22,165.00	$11,292.96	$0.25	$1.96	196%	$10,872.04
Ad Group #14	$21,580.00	$19,046.49	$0.95	$1.13	113%	$2,533.51
Ad Group #15	$5,005.00	$885.81	$0.45	$5.65	565%	$4,119.19
Ad Group #16	$715.00	$127.29	$0.64	$5.62	562%	$587.71

Figure 13.34 Ad group report

Low-Cost, Low-Return Ad Groups Ad groups 1 to 4 have zero conversions associated with them. They also have not spent much money. If you set a bid based on profits or ROI, these ad groups would have to be turned off, as the bids would be $0.00. First analyze if they are good keywords. Are they keywords that you tested and they failed? If so, delete them. Are they keywords that appear early in the buying cycle, and you like them, but they do not receive returns? If so, move them to a Budget Optimizer account.

Medium-Cost, Solid-Return Ad Groups Ad groups 6 to 11 have all spent some money and have decent revenue. A few of them have negative revenue numbers. For these ad groups, set bids based on profits or ROI. You should do some testing and tweaking of these ad groups over time, but they are not going to be top-priority ad groups.

High-Spend, High-Return Ad Groups Ad groups 12 and 13 have high spends and excellent returns. While you might be tempted to significantly increase the bids on these ad groups based on profits, especially ad group 12, be careful about making dramatic changes in your profit centers. These two ad groups bring in more revenue than all of the other ad groups combined. It is not uncommon to find a handful of keywords or ad groups that are a large percentage of your overall revenue.

The AdWords system can be temperamental at times. In ad groups like these, change the bids by 10 percent or 20 percent and make sure your returns are the same at the higher bid prices. If the returns stay profitable, then raise the bids again by 10 or 20 percent. Do not make dramatic changes in these ad groups. In addition, on the home screen of your AdWords account you can set a watch list of items you want to keep a close eye on. Add these ad groups to the watch list. These are ad groups you should check on daily, as a slight change can cause a dramatic change in your profits.

High-Spend, High-Traffic, Medium- or Low-Return Ad Groups Sometimes the hardest part of AdWords is finding keywords with high search volume or keywords where you can drive a lot of traffic to your website. Ad group 14 has spent $19,046 and has only made $21,580. This ad group has a lot of traffic, but it barely makes money. However, it has potential to be a high-revenue ad group. This is an ad group that you want to keep a close eye on because a slight change could cause you to start losing a lot of money instead of barely making money. Add this ad group to your watch list as well.

The best optimization you can take with an ad group like this is to start testing. In Chapter 15, "Testing Techniques That Will Increase Profits," you will learn how to test ad copy and landing pages to increase conversion rates. This ad group is a perfect candidate for testing.

High ROI Ad Groups The ROI of the first 14 ad groups does not break 330 percent. However, ad groups 15 and 16 both have over a 560 percent ROI. That is a significant difference from all the other ad groups. While these ad groups are not at the top in spend or profits, there is some combination that is leading to a fantastic customer experience. When you see ad groups like these, learn from them. Examine the keywords, ad copy, and landing pages to see if there are aspects of this search combination that you can utilize in other ad groups. With these ad groups, you can set bids based on profits or ROAS; however, when you have outliers, examine and learn from the data.

Once you determine your ad group types, you can label them in AdWords for easy reference. The number of labels you use will vary by account size; however, here are some easy ones (Figure 13.35):

- HCHC: high conversion and high clicks
- HCLC: high conversions and low clicks
- MCMC: medium conversions and medium clicks
- LCHC: low conversions and high clicks

Repeat for your own segmentation.

Figure 13.35 Ad group labels

Once you have labeled your ad groups, you can easily create filters in the interface to see only a certain type of ad group (Figure 13.36).

Figure 13.36 Ad group filters

Working on long-tail ad groups, where you will bid at the ad group level is much different than working with ad groups, where the keywords have so much data you want to do keyword level bidding. By filtering by various types of ad groups, you can easily group your ad group work so that you do not have to switch mind-sets as you progress through your day.

Setting bids, controlling your marketing costs, and examining your profits are essential to making money with AdWords. However, it is equally important to understand how your customers buy from you so that you do not suddenly stop buying keywords that were indirectly leading to conversion or start making dramatic changes in your profit centers.

It is easy to end up in a paralysis-by-analysis scenario with AdWords because you have so much data available to you. Put your ad groups into meaningful groups so you can work on similar items together and continue to refine and improve your campaigns.

Best Practices for Utilizing Profitable Bid Strategies

Every ad group must have a bid associated with it. You can set bids at the keyword, ad group, ad group display, placement, and other levels. However, a bid must exist for your ad to be shown. What is important is not just bidding to the top position, but bidding based on the profit your AdWords account is making your company. By following these best practices, you should be able to set bids based on conversion metrics:

- Do not spend a penny on marketing until you understand your company's goals.

- After you have written down your marketing goals, find a way to measure those goals. Use the AdWords conversion tracker to track goals that occur online. Use phone call tracking to track offline conversions.

- If you want to maximize conversions, test the Conversion Optimizer bid system.

- If you want to maximize traffic, put keywords into a Budget Optimizer campaign. If you have keywords you like that do not lead to conversions, put them in a Budget Optimizer campaign.

- If you want to change your bids by time of day or day of the week, or maintain tight control of your marketing costs, then use the default bidding option, setting max CPCs.

- Calculate the ROAS for each keyword, ad group, placement, and the display network in your account.

- Once you have determined the profit by taking margins and other factors into account when necessary, set bids based on profit or ROAS.

- When examining large spreadsheets, use conditional formatting to give yourself a visual reference of the data.

- Learn when your customers are most receptive to your marketing messages based on how they live their lives, and then use ad scheduling to set bids based on your returns at those various times.

- Put ad groups into like-minded buckets so that you can work on similar types of ad groups at once.

- Do not always set ROAS bids if they make dramatic changes in your most profitable ad groups. Be careful with your profit centers and make incremental changes.

- The more traffic an ad group receives, the higher the chance it has to bring profit to your company. If these ad groups are barely profitable, test both their ad copy and landing pages.

- Be creative; the more you learn about AdWords possibilities, the more creative you can become in reaching users in unique ways.

Setting the proper bids will move your account from just spending money to making money. Knowing where your dollars are being spent, watching the returns, and making adjustments as necessary are paramount to finding profit with AdWords.

However, a bid just tells Google how much you are willing to pay for a click. The ad copy and keywords allow you to reach the consumer with the proper message. The ad copy and keywords are governed by the campaign's reach, be it by time of day, day of the week, geographic location, or display versus search reach. The organization of your account will have as much to do with your success as the bid will.

In the next chapter, you will learn various ways of organizing your account based on the goals of your account and how you want to reach customers.

Successful Account Organization Strategies

Successful account organization consists of three levels of decisions. The first decision is determining how many accounts you need. The second requires you to look within an account at the number of campaigns you need based on your targeting and budgets and determine how to properly organize the campaign settings. Finally, you need to decide how to organize your campaign's ad groups so you have tightly themed ad copy and keywords.

Account organization is not difficult if you understand your marketing goals and the AdWords settings we have discussed throughout the book so far. Proper account organization is essential if you want to gain the most benefit from your AdWords marketing dollars.

Chapter Contents

What is an AdWords account?

Developing a successful campaign structure

Organizing an ad group to increase CTR and conversion rates

Best practices for account organization strategies

What Is an AdWords Account?

An AdWords account represents a business. Each business should have only one AdWords account. Only one ad from an account will ever show in any given search result.

If you manage accounts on behalf of clients, such as a PPC (pay-per-click) agency, each client should have its own account. If you are an internal marketer, even if you have multiple websites you should have a single Google account.

There are times when a business might be very large, or the business has sub-sidiaries with multiple websites that you feel are so separated that the business should be allowed to show two ads on a given search result page or have multiple AdWords accounts. In these cases, talk to a Google representative before enabling multiple accounts for the same business to make sure you are not violating the AdWords terms of service.

 Note: If you need multiple accounts because you are an agency managing accounts on behalf of third parties, then you do not need to talk to a Google representative.

In the early days of AdWords, a search for many keywords might have led to a page of ads for the same company. Often, these additional ads were affiliate ads that all led to the same website. When multiple ads lead to the same page, searchers often become frustrated over lack of options. In January 2005, Google made a policy change: Only one ad per website would be shown on a search results page. This expanded consumer choice on a search result has meant a much better search experience.

The "one account per company" policies are also based on consumer choice. If you are creating multiple accounts to get around policies designed to enhance the search experience, you could run into terms of service issues. This is why it is a good practice to talk to Google about why you need multiple accounts and let them help you.

What Are the Limits of an AdWords Account?

A basic Google account has maximum limits of:

- 500 campaigns (includes active and paused campaigns)
- 20,000 ad groups per campaign
- 5,000 keywords per ad group
- 300 display ads per ad group (includes image ads)
- 50 text ads per ad group
- 3 million keywords per account

Some older accounts still have the old limits (2,000 ad groups per campaign and 50,000 active keywords per account). If you see the message "Your account is nearing

an unmanageable size," that usually indicates you are reaching the keyword limits
for an account. If you have an older account and are under 50,000 keywords, talk to
Google and they can fix your limitation issues.

If you need more active campaigns or active keywords, your Google representative can link accounts together on the back-end. It is possible to have over 10 million
keywords active in Google at one time; however, doing so would require several accounts
being linked together. Just remember that you should always contact Google before creating a second account to make sure you will stay within their terms of service.

Unfortunately, there are no fixed guidelines defining a large spend or when an
account qualifies for a representative. Google assigns reps on a "need-analysis" basis.
If you spend more than $100,000 per year on AdWords, it can be worth your time to
contact Google and ask them if you have a representative or any additional support
options.

Not everyone will be allowed to link accounts together. Each keyword, campaign,
ad group, and ad copy takes up space in Google's database. Each time someone searches
for a keyword, Google must examine their entire database and perform an auction to
see which keywords and ad copy should be shown to the searcher. If you are spending a
low amount per month, it is not cost effective for Google to store all that data and use
the processing power required to continually look through all your keywords to see what
should be shown. It can be useful to talk to your Google representative about your keyword and campaign needs to see if you can link multiple accounts together.

Managing Multiple Accounts the Easy Way

If you need multiple accounts—either because your account is so large that you need
two linked accounts or because you are an agency and manage accounts on behalf of
multiple companies—the My Client Center (MCC) will be extremely useful to you.

A My Client Center account (Figure 14.1) allows you to link multiple accounts
together in a single interface. From within the interface, you can easily navigate
between the accounts, see account statistics in a single place, or run reports across all
the accounts in the MCC.

To navigate between the accounts, you can use the drop-down box at the top of
the screen, click on a client name from the MCC screen, or use the search box. If you
have thousands of clients, I recommend that you name them appropriately so that you
can easily use the search feature to find the account you want to view.

By default, one account in an MCC does not affect another. Therefore, items
like Quality Score are not shared, and each account can show an ad on a search result
(assuming they have different display and destination URLs).

If you are running a large account where Google linked the accounts together on
the back-end, you can also add all of these accounts to the MCC so that you can enjoy
the benefits of the MCC. In this case, the accounts can affect each other.

Figure 14.1 My Client Center overview screen

If you have a tremendous number of accounts, you can also nestle MCCs. For instance, if you manage clients, manage your own PPC spend, and have one large client that has five linked accounts, you would want to organize your MCCs accordingly:

- Top-level MCC to see everything
- Sub-MCC for your large client with five accounts
- Sub-MCC for your own spend
- Sub-MCC for the rest of your clients

 Note: Although you can have multiple levels of sub-MCCs, unless you are managing more than 10,000 accounts, you will rarely need more than four or five levels of MCCs.

The two reasons to have multiple levels of MCCs are either for organizational purposes or if you are on consolidated invoicing with Google. Manager Defined Spend (MDS) allows you to receive a single invoice for all clients either in all MCCs or for a specific MCC. Therefore, if you have one client paying their bill directly to Google and other clients who are paying you for their spend, you may also want to organize the clients based on billing options to make it easier for the accounting department.

My Client Center Benefits

The My Client Center (MCC) comes with many benefits that will save you time and make it easier to manage multiple accounts:

Access Levels As with AdWords accounts, there are also different access levels you can give an individual. The first is administrative access. Someone with this access level can add and delete any user—and that can include you. Be careful when assigning this access level. The second level is standard access. This user cannot add or remove users but can make changes to any account. The third level is report access. These users can see the data but cannot make changes in an account. When you give someone access through the MCC, they can see that MCC and any sub-MCCs. If you give someone access to a sub-MCC, they cannot see the MCCs above their level of access.

Linking Accounts If a user already has an existing AdWords account, you will need to send them an invitation to link their account to yours. Once you send them an invite, they will see a message in their AdWords account that they have to click on to give you permission to link to their account. Once the account is linked, you can enjoy the benefits of having an account linked to from the MCC.

Creating Accounts Linking accounts can be time consuming if you have hundreds or thousands of accounts. Instead of creating accounts outside of the MCC and then having to link them at a later date, you can create new accounts in the MCC so that they are already linked.

Budget Controls The Budget tab of the MCC allows you to see the spend of each account. In addition, if the accounts are on invoicing or other payment methods instead of credit card billing, you can change the monthly spends, see the percentage of their budget spent, and other options from this tab (Figure 14.2).

Client	Labels	Budget	% spent	Remaining budget	Start date	End date	Amount spent
☐	-	$6,100.00 Daily	N/A	N/A	Daily (GMT-06:00) Central Time	N/A	$43,906.46
☐	-	$5,945.81 Account manage	100.00%	$0.00	Jun 12, 2009 (GMT-05:00) Eastern Time	No end date	$0.00
☐	-	$1,000.00 Daily	N/A	N/A	Daily (GMT-08:00) Pacific Time	N/A	$0.00

Figure 14.2 Viewing and managing budgets from the MCC

Alerts If there are issues with your account, Google will show alerts at the account level. In the MCC, you can view the alerts for all the accounts in the MCC on a single screen, making it easier to troubleshoot issues.

Cross-Account Reporting Finally, you can run reports across all accounts in an MCC at a single time. If you are a large advertiser and therefore need five different accounts, this will be a huge timesaver. Instead of having to log into each account to run a report, you can run reports that include data from all your accounts at once. You can select various reports to run and which accounts to include with these cross-account reports.

To create a My Client Center account, go to www.google.com/adwords/myclient-center and use the wizard to create a new MCC. Once you have access to the MCC, you can also join the Google Advertising Professionals Program.

Becoming a Google Advertising Professional

Google has a professional certification program that offers certification for individuals and companies. To become individually certified, you must pass a fundamental exam and at least one other exam from several Google offers, such as search, display, or reporting. To become a Certified Partner, your company must have at least one certified individual and manage at least $10,000 in spend over 90 days.

Once you have met the requirements, your company can be considered a Google Certified Partner and gain the use of a logo that you can use in various means with your marketing materials (Figure 14.3).

Figure 14.3 AdWords
Certified Partner logo

 Note: To sign up for the Google Advertising Professionals, go to https://adwords.google.com/professionals/account/ and sign in with your Google account. You will walk through a wizard to create your professional account. Once you have an account, you will be able to invite new professionals, take the AdWords certification tests, and gain access to helpful materials (Figure 14.4).

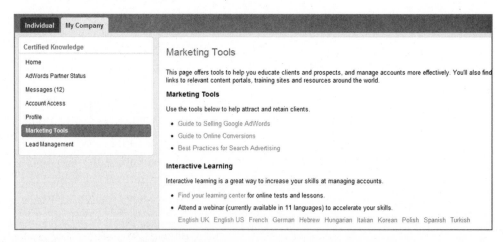

Figure 14.4 Google Certified Partner materials

You do not have to sign up for the Google Certified Partner program to gain access to an MCC account. It is an additional certification you can gain to help you sell your AdWords services to other companies or use as a nice bullet point on your résumé.

Since each AdWords account represents a business, items such as billing information, contact information, and access rights are stored at the account level. This is the basic information you need to open an AdWords account.

Developing a Successful Campaign Structure

A campaign is a collection of ad groups. Each ad group consists of keywords and ad copy. Google follows your campaign settings to determine where, when, and how you would like those ads displayed. If you would like keywords or ads displayed differently based on varying conditions, you need a different campaign for each of those conditions.

Every time you create a new campaign, you must set a budget for that campaign. If you spread your budget out across too many campaigns, your budget can become very thin and you could be limiting your ad display. In addition, every time you make a new campaign, you have more campaigns to manage. Therefore, the first question is: Why should you create a second campaign? This section first examines the reasons to separate campaigns, and then I will use sample company objectives to show you how a company should structure their campaigns based on their objectives.

Reasons to Create New Campaigns

The decision to create a new campaign is a big one. Most companies have finite budgets, and every campaign must have a budget. So if you try to spread that budget out across hundreds of campaigns, you could have an organizational nightmare on your hands. There are many reasons to have multiple campaigns; here is a list of the most common reasons to create new campaigns:

Daily Budget Every campaign must have a daily budget. As you add more campaigns, you have to decide how much you want to spend on each. One way of organizing campaigns is by business objectives or conversion types, and then by deciding how much you want to spend to reach those objectives. If you have multiple products, and each product has its own marketing budget, separating the campaigns by products will help you reach those goals.

Network Reach This is the most common reason to separate campaigns. Have one campaign for display, another for display with managed placements, and a third one for search. This organization was discussed in depth in Chapter 10, "Advanced Display Network Techniques."

Location Targeting The second most common reason to have multiple campaigns is when you want to use different keywords, ad copy, or landing pages in different geographies, as covered in Chapter 11, "Advanced Geographic Targeting."

Bidding Type In Chapter 13, "Profitable Bid Strategies," you saw the various bidding types: budget optimizer, conversion optimizer, and maximum CPC or CPM bidding. If you want an account to utilize multiple bidding strategies, each bidding type must have its own campaign.

Demographic Bidding If you find that you do well with certain demographics and receive a significant amount of volume on sites that support demographic bidding, as discussed in Chapter 10, you should have a demographic campaign. Since you can only increase your bids based on demographic characteristics, and you cannot decrease them, create a campaign that only contains placements that support demographic bidding. Then, at the ad group or placement level, set low bids. Use demographic bids to increase your bids based on the cost per conversion of each demographic combination.

Device Platforms You can choose if your ads are shown to desktops, tablets, mobile devices, or all three, as discussed in Chapter 8, "Beyond Text: Image, Video, and Mobile Ads." If you want to show different ads, keywords, or landing pages to desktop and tablet versus mobile users, you will want both a mobile and a desktop campaign.

Ad Scheduling By default, campaigns are set to show ads 24 hours a day, 7 days a week. As long as your budget is not limiting your ad delivery, your ad is eligible to be shown all the time. If you want one ad to be shown on a Monday and a different ad to be shown on Tuesday, you will need a different campaign for each time frame that you want different ads, keywords, or landing pages to be eligible for the auction, as discussed in Chapter 13.

Whenever you want your keywords, ad copy, or landing pages to be governed by a different campaign setting, you need a new campaign. The items earlier in this list are the most common reasons to create new campaigns, but even items such as ad delivery method or ad serving methodology can be reasons to create new campaigns if you want different keywords or ad copy to follow different campaign rules.

Structuring Campaigns to Achieve Business Goals

There are thousands of ways to structure your campaign settings based on your business goals. If you do not know your business goals, you cannot set bids appropriately or understand the best way to structure your campaigns. This is why it is so important to know what you would like your marketing to accomplish.

This section examines some common business goals and then shows you how the campaigns in an account should be organized.

Basic Campaign Structure: Maximize Returns

When you want to maximize returns for all your keywords, placements, and ads, there is a straightforward place to start that will use three campaigns:

Search Campaign Your first campaign will only be shown on search. In your campaign settings, choose only the search network. Then within your ad groups only choose keywords that you want to be triggered based on the searcher's query with appropriately written ad copy. This campaign will have a large percentage of your total budget, usually between 40 and 60 percent. For each keyword, you will use a profit-based bidding strategy, as discussed in Chapter 13.

Display Discovery Campaign Your second campaign will be a display-only campaign using automatic placements. The goal of this campaign is to find sites that meet your goals across the display network, as discussed in Chapter 10. When you find sites that meet your goals, you will exclude them from this campaign and add them to your managed placements campaign. As you find sites that do not meet your goals, you will block them from showing your ads in the future.

The keywords in these ad groups should form a theme. It is okay across the display network to use general keywords that you would not use for search but when combined with other keywords in the ad group create a theme. That way, Google can accurately place your ads on the proper types of display network pages.

As this campaign may or may not turn out not to be profitable, you will set the lowest daily budget for it, usually 10 to 20 percent of your total daily budget. When you first open a new account, since you will not have placement data, this campaign may consume as much as 30 to 40 percent of your daily budget. But as you fine-tune it, and move more traffic into your managed placement campaign, your budget should be reallocated from this discovery automatic placements campaign to the managed placements campaign.

If you are new to advertising on the display network, skip this campaign and start with the managed placements campaign until you are comfortable managing a display campaign.

Managed Placements Campaign When you find sites across the display network that are meeting your goals, you always want your ads to be shown on those sites. Therefore, add them to this placement campaign. Run the placement performance reports to see your cost per action for each placement, and then adjust the bids for each placement based on your goals. Follow the flow chart (Figure 10.10 in Chapter 10) to continuously refine your automatic and managed placements display campaigns. As this campaign should provide measurable returns for your AdWords account, this campaign's daily budget will be similar to your search campaign's budget. Eventually, this campaign should be spending 30 to 60 percent of your daily budget. As you add new placements, transition some of your budget from the automatic placements discovery campaign to the managed placements campaign.

This basic account organization (Figure 14.5) should get any account started. It combines the basic principles of using the search and the display network appropriately. However, it does assume that you are only choosing one geographic reach for all your campaigns. If you want to show different ads to different users, you may want to restructure your campaigns.

Meeting Location-Based Goals

There are times when you will want to create campaigns that showcase different ads to users based on the user's location. A common reason for this is if you find different response rates by location from the geographic performance reports discussed in Chapter 11.

The geographic performance reports give you the data to refine your campaigns over time. This example looks at a company that should start with multiple location-based campaigns.

Our fictional company, Illinois Insurance, is licensed in the state of Illinois to sell insurance; therefore, they only want users in Illinois to see their ads. After conducting some research, they find that people located in Chicago have different insurance concerns. Chicago is one of the largest cities in the world, and the residents want more information about car theft and home break-ins than the rest of the state. Illinois Insurance is headquartered in Rockford. They want to stress that customers in that city can come into their office and meet face to face with an insurance agent.

Figure 14.5 Basic account structure

This company has three different goals for three different locations (Illinois, Chicago, and Rockford), therefore, they will need three search-based campaigns (Figure 14.6).

Figure 14.6 Search-based campaigns for Illinois Insurance

Illinois Campaign This campaign will be shown throughout the state of Illinois, so it should use the location setting of Illinois only. However, because Illinois Insurance want different ads to show in Rockford and Chicago, the Excluded Regions feature (discussed in Chapter 11) should also be utilized to keep their ads from showing in those two cities. Since this campaign is only shown to users in the state of Illinois, the keywords will not need geo-qualifiers such as "Peoria home insurance" or "Illinois home insurance." These ads will go to a landing page that corresponds to the keywords being searched.

Chicago Campaign This campaign is for searchers who live in the city of Chicago; therefore, in the location settings this campaign should only be displayed in Chicago. Since the company found that Chicago users had different insurance concerns, those findings should be echoed in the ad copy. As with the Illinois campaign, the keywords should not use geographic modifiers. Finally, the searcher should be sent to a page on the website that reinforces both the Chicago location and the keywords that were searched.

Rockford Campaign The Rockford campaign should also use the location feature so its ads are just shown in Rockford. The keywords should not use geographic modifiers. The ad copy and landing pages should be focused on the benefit of sitting down face to face with an agent.

Geo-Keyword Campaign If you want to reach everyone regardless of Google's ability to understand a searcher's location, you will want to add a fourth campaign that utilizes geographically modified keywords.

In this campaign, your target area will be the entire country. Then, within each ad group, you will use geographic keywords, such as "Chicago home insurance" or "Peoria car insurance."

Each ad group should be a different city and insurance type combination. For the keywords that use the Chicago modifier, the searcher should be sent to the same landing page that is being used in the Chicago campaign. The same goes for Rockford-based keywords.

For other geographic keywords, such as "Peoria home insurance" or "Illinois home insurance," you would want to send someone to an appropriate landing page that reinforces the geography and insurance type.

 Note: If your budget is being stretched by the first three campaigns, you could skip the geo-keyword campaign.

Display and Discovery Placement Campaigns The big question this company needs to ask is how they want to treat the display network. There are a few options:

Option 1 Showcase the same ads to all of Illinois. If your budget is being stretched, creating multiple campaigns for each location can be an accounting nightmare. Use display and text ads to showcase your general offer to anyone on insurance content pages and send them to a page that showcases the rest of your offers. You could test a general benefit page against a segmentation page (discussed in Chapter 15, "Testing Techniques That Will Increase Profits"). In this case, turn on display only, use Illinois as your location target, and then refine your exposure by using a placement campaign for successful placements.

Option 2 Create three display campaigns using automatic placements. Each display campaign will be shown to a different location: Rockford, Chicago, Illinois (minus Rockford and Chicago). Then use managed placements campaigns as you refine your exposure. The benefit of this method is targeted display exposure that sends a user to the most appropriate geographic landing page on the company's website. However, it is a tremendous amount of work, and the results might not be worth the effort. In addition, you need to keep adding new daily budgets, which can start to reduce how much any one campaign is allowed to spend, essentially handicapping your best keywords and placements.

Option 3 Create a managed placements campaign only. Use the Ad Planner tool to find appropriate websites where your target audience spends time, and then put ads on those pages. As you are guessing at placements, some of your ads will work, and others will not. Use the placement performance report to remove websites or set appropriate bids. This method will not let you find random sites around the Web that would have been good placements for your ads, but it will let you test sites you feel are appropriate and keep greater control of your display network campaign budget.

Reaching users with custom ad text and keywords based on their geography must be thought out carefully as you can quickly overwhelm yourself with the number of campaigns and ad groups that you are managing. First create a strategy for search and display location campaigns. Then examine how many campaigns it will take to reach those goals. If you have exceeded the number of campaigns that you can manage well, or spread your budget too thinly across multiple campaigns, refine your strategy and once again look to see how many campaigns that strategy will employ.

In this scenario, the company might show mobile and desktop users the same ads. However, there are times when you want to segment your campaigns based on the device customers use to access your website.

Showcasing Different Ads to Desktop vs. Mobile Users

There are times when the user intent changes based on the device they use to access the Web. For instance, someone searching for a locksmith on a mobile phone is probably locked out of a house or car and needs immediate assistance. Someone searching for a locksmith on a desktop computer is more likely looking to duplicate keys or change the locks on their doors.

If someone searches for Best Buy on a desktop, they are probably looking for products and the main website. If someone searches for Best Buy on a phone, they are more likely looking for driving directions.

In these instances, you would want to show different ad copy to the searcher:

- Locked out of your car? We'll be there in less than 20 minutes.

- Want to change the locks on your house? Call us for a free evaluation.

- Find the nearest Best Buy.

- Free delivery on orders over $50.

In your campaign settings, you can specify on what types of devices you want your ads to be shown. This is known as the *device platform setting.* Your choices are:

- Desktop and laptop computers
- Mobile phones with full HTML browsers
- Tablet users
- All of the above

There are two ways that mobile users can see ads. If the user is on a device with a full HTML browser, such as an Android phone or Apple iPhone, you must enable your campaigns to be shown on mobile devices. For devices without full HTML browsers, such as a BlackBerry Curve, you need to use mobile ads. It is worth noting that mobile ads ignore the device platform setting in your campaign. As a result, if you only examine how to reach the search network, you have two campaigns:

Desktop and Tablet Campaign In the first campaign, set your ads only to be shown to desktop and tablet users. In this campaign, you will use text ads and keywords based on what you would normally use in a standard search campaign.

Mobile Campaign In the second campaign, choose to have your ads only shown to users on mobile devices with full HTML browsers. Most users on mobile devices use shorter search queries than on a desktop device. Therefore, you also might want to use more general keywords. For instance, on a desktop someone might search for "Coldplay ringtones for the iPhone." On a mobile phone, "Coldplay ringtones" is often specific enough. As usual, you should measure conversion rates and adjust keywords and bids based on returns.

Once you have created the keywords in your ad groups, write a standard text ad or two. These ads will be seen by those on iPhones and other HTML phone browsers. These ads can go to an HTML page on your website; however, send them to a page optimized for your mobile action, such as driving directions or a "call us for immediate assistance" web page.

Next, create a mobile ad for each ad group. The mobile ads will be shown to mobile users without full HTML support. With mobile ads you can decide if someone should go to your website (which is what Best Buy should do by sending the user to a driving direction page), initiate a call (which is what the locksmith should do), or choose which action to take. You must send those who click on a mobile ad to a mobile-compliant site.

With this mobile strategy, you can engage users based on the device type they are using to access the Web and assist searchers based on their intent. As mobile campaigns also obey items such as location settings, you can choose to only have your ads shown in a specific city.

The campaign organizations just discussed have been focused on having the ability to set bids based on ROI or profit. However, there are times when you want to expand consumers' awareness of your website.

Creating Awareness or Branding Search Campaigns

There will be times when you like keywords, and those keywords accurately describe your products or services. If those keywords also lead to brand interaction—such as page views, low bounce rates, or video watches—yet by themselves do not convert for your primary conversion actions, you have three options.

The first option is to delete the keywords. If you are running a campaign strictly around profits and ROI and these keywords are not performing, get rid of them.

Note: Please note that just because a keyword does not lead directly to ROI does not mean it is not profitable. Keep in mind the keyword attribution funnel discussed in Chapter 13.

The first option is not fantastic if you have a long sales cycle or want to introduce new people to your buying funnel. Searches from people in the early stages of the buying funnel have lower conversion rates. Therefore, the second option is to create some monetary value for a page view or video view, and then bid by returns for those alternate conversions.

The last option is to create a branding campaign. This can also be called an awareness campaign because that is one of the first steps in the buying funnel. Your best option is to also track if these individuals convert at a later date so that you can see the full keyword attribution funnel. However, before you can see if they convert, you need the searchers to find your website. For these keywords, you should not care which ones get clicks. Your goal is to introduce people to your website.

To create this branding campaign:

1. Move all the keywords that you want to gain exposure into a separate campaign with the appropriate ad group organization.

2. Set a daily budget for how much you are willing to pay for people to find your website and learn more about your company.

3. Use the budget optimizer bidding strategy:

   • The budget optimizer attempts to maximize the number of clicks that a campaign receives. It does not care which keyword received the click—which is why you should not move keywords into this campaign if you know the returns for any of them.

   • In addition, the budget optimizer's maximum CPC should be set lower than any of the keywords in your search campaigns. If you know the returns for a keyword, you want your search campaign's keywords to be triggered. Budget optimizer campaigns are for words that do not convert but for which you want exposure, and they are usually less valuable than your search keywords.

When you are done creating the branding campaign, you will still have your typical search and display campaigns (Figure 14.7).

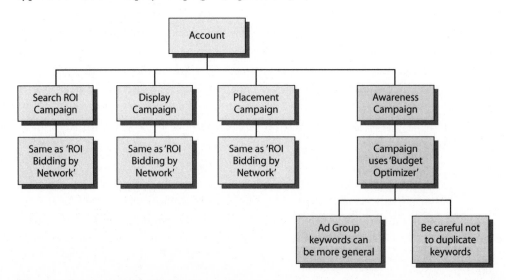

Figure 14.7 Campaign structure with a branding campaign

All of the organizations so far have been focused on showing the ads every day of the week and at all hours of the day. If you want your ads to show on different days of the week or at different times of the day, you need to utilize ad scheduling campaigns.

Showing Different Ads by Day of the Week

Marketing is about connecting with customers. With AdWords, the first connection point is with keywords. A second one can occur if you use the day of the week, or even the time of day, in an ad copy.

Most restaurants and bars have different specials each day of the week. If a restaurant wanted to put their daily special into their ad copy for the weekdays, and then highlight one weekend special, there is an easy way to accomplish this with ad scheduling (discussed in Chapter 13) by using a different campaign for each day of the week (Figure 14.8), as follows:

Figure 14.8 Ad scheduling campaign organization

1. Build your ad groups within a single campaign. If you are a restaurant, also set the location targeting based on the city in which you are located.

2. Duplicate your campaign six times using the AdWords Editor (featured in Chapter 12, "Save Time and Scale Accounts with the AdWords Editor"). Name each campaign for a day of the week or weekend. The naming convention is for your organizational purposes; a campaign's name does not affect any of its data points.

3. Choose what day of the week you want that campaign to be active. When using ad scheduling, always look at the time zone for your account. You can view your account's time zone on the ad scheduling interface. Assuming that the time zone for the account is in the same time zone as your target area, then the first campaign would be set to only run on Mondays, the Tuesday campaign would only run on Tuesdays, and so on.

Go back into the AdWords Editor and download your account. In each campaign, change the ads so that they showcase both the day of the week that the campaign is active and the specials for that day. Upload the changes, check those changes in the interface, and then you will have custom ads for each day of the week.

You can also use advanced ad scheduling to change your bids automatically throughout the day. If you run a restaurant, and you find that most people are looking for driving directions and the ability to reserve tables in the late afternoon, you may want to raise your bids at those times, and then leave them the same or lower at other times of the day. Using ad scheduling to reach consumers with time-sensitive ads, or changing bids by conversion rates, is a good method to help increase your profits.

Organizing Campaigns Based on Goals or Budgets

If you have different budgets for different goals on your website, organizing your campaigns based on how much you want to spend for each goal is a good way of controlling costs. In addition, you can use campaign negative keywords to help segment traffic so the searcher sees the proper ad.

For this example, we are going to examine a timeshare company. TS Inc. is our fictional company, which has a website based on buying and selling timeshares.

TS Inc. only makes money when they sell an ad to someone who is looking to sell their timeshare. If you want to sell your timeshare, you can connect with one of their sales reps, and they will walk you through the advertising options so you can get your timeshare listed on their site and hopefully sell it.

However, TS Inc. has found that they need to drive traffic to the listings sections of their timeshares for those who are looking to buy. The sales reps like to tell prospective advertisers how much traffic each section of their site receives, as it helps increase conversion rates of their ad sales. However, when TS Inc. drives traffic to the timeshare listings, they do not make any money. Although they need to drive traffic to their listings sections to help make sales, it's a loss leader; they have to pay for traffic but they do not directly make any money on these clicks.

TS Inc. wants to spend a lot of money when someone is looking to sell a timeshare and is bidding based on their sales close rates. They have a lower budget when someone is looking to buy a timeshare. They also have a budget for those who are not decisive in their search query and just use a keyword such as "Aruba timeshare; TS Inc." and TS Inc. does not know if that user wants to buy or sell a listing.

To accomplish their goals, and to send a user to the correct place on their website, they have devised three campaigns based on their budgets (Figure 14.9):

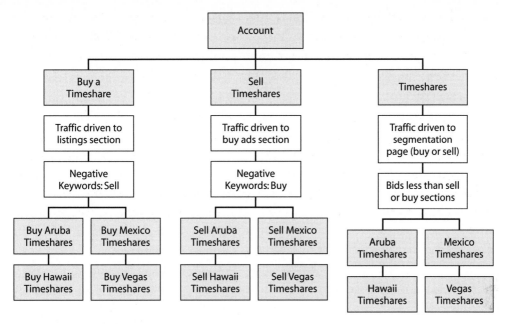

Figure 14.9 TS Inc. campaign strategy to separate campaigns by marketing objectives

Buy a Timeshare The first campaign is reaching consumers who want to buy a timeshare. Since TS Inc. does not make money on these keywords, they have the lowest of their daily budgets in this campaign. Each ad group is a combination of a city name with the word "timeshare" and the word "buy" (Buy Aruba Timeshares). The keywords inside the ad group all have buying descriptors such as buy, buying, purchase, and so on.

TS Inc. has found that they need to use broad match to reach all their prospects. However, since they do not make money on the keywords in this campaign, they want to make sure that the consumer searching is using the word "buy" and does not use the word "sell" because they can monetize someone looking to sell a timeshare by selling them an ad. At the campaign level, they use all the variations of the word "sell" in their negative keyword list (discussed in Chapter 2). By using negative keywords, they segment traffic based on their marketing goals.

Sell a Timeshare This is the campaign that makes TS Inc. the most money. When someone wants to sell their timeshare, TS Inc. wants to sell that person an ad on their website. The ad groups in this campaign are very similar to the first campaign, except the "buy"-based keyword qualifiers are changed to "sell" qualifiers. For instance, the keyword "Buy Aruba Timeshare" from the buy campaign would be "Sell Aruba Timeshare" in this campaign.

As the goal for this campaign is conversions through selling ads, all of the traffic is sent to a page that shows how TS Inc. can help you sell your timeshare and provides a quick form for you to fill out to get in contact with a sales representative. For higher conversion rates, each landing page features the location in the headline, such as "Contact Us to Sell Your Aruba Timeshare" along with a picture of the location.

Finally, to help segment traffic into selling versus buying intent, TS Inc. uses negative keywords such as "buy" and "buying" at the campaign level. This helps keep their lead quality higher, and gives their listings sections more page views for those with a buying intent.

Timeshares The third campaign is for those searchers who do not use either buying or selling qualifiers. These searchers just type in "Aruba timeshare." Since TS Inc. does not know if these searchers are looking to buy or sell a timeshare, the users are sent to a segmentation page where they are presented with two options of where to go next. If someone clicks on the "sell your timeshare" link, they are sent to the contact form used in the Sell a Timeshare campaign. If someone clicks on the "buy a timeshare" link, they are sent to the listings page from the Buy a Timeshare campaign.

TS Inc. finds they receive quite a bit of traffic from these listings, and since some of the traffic is monetizable from selling these consumers ads, this campaign is the second-highest daily budget, after the Sell a Timeshare campaign.

As the intent is ambiguous, and some users leave the segmentation page immediately, these searches are worthless to TS Inc. Therefore, all the keywords in this campaign have lower maximum CPCs than the keywords in either of the first two campaigns.

TS Inc. wants to make sure that users end up at the correct section of their website, so they use all of the campaign negatives from the first two campaigns for this campaign. It is worth noting that, with this structure, they would not have any ads that would show for a keyword query such as "buy and sell timeshares" due to their negative campaign keyword usage.

In this example, we used a website that is both the seller and distributor of their own ads. There should be two takeaways from this section. The first is that if you have various objectives for your website, and you want the various objectives to have different marketing dollars, you need to use your campaign organization to help you reach those goals. The second concerns user intent. Often you will find that you are willing to pay more if a user knows what they want or are more specific in their search query. If you can define the various intents of those who use your keywords, you can design campaigns and ad groups based on what the searcher is looking to find.

Defining Your Goals

A complex campaign structure is not difficult if you can define your goals. For the final example, we will examine the goals of a national e-commerce company that focuses on selling computers. As this is a larger company, their goals are diverse:

- Showcase offers to all of the United States and bids by ROI for both search and display

- Increase searchers finding their website for the first time
- Create demand for their goods on nonsearch sites

After examining their geographic performance reports (Chapter 11), they found they have low performance in Chicago. To increase performance in Chicago, they also want to test a B2B-focused ad on weekdays and a B2C-focused ad on weekends.

Showcase offers to all of the United States and bids by ROI for both search and display. This goal speaks to the basic campaign structure covered earlier in the section "Basic Campaign Structure: Maximize Returns." They start with search and managed placement campaigns. Since the second goal is to showcase a different offer to Chicago users, they will use the excluded regions feature in their search campaign so this campaign is not shown in Chicago.

Increase number of searchers finding their website for the first time. This company has found that the buying cycle for new computers can be quite long. However, if they can reach a searcher early in the buying funnel, often that consumer will stay focused with their company as they move down through the funnel to a purchase. Therefore, they have a large list of keywords that are relevant to their products but are in the interest or learning phase of the buying cycle; the company has had a difficult time determining bids because the words do not directly lead to sales. These keywords will be placed in an awareness campaign.

This awareness campaign will use the budget optimizer feature to maximize the clicks that the company receives for these keywords. The company will still try to get these consumers to subscribe to newsletters and learn more about their products; however, they are also measuring interaction with their website and will remove keywords that don't contribute to them. They will also measure how many of these consumers buy at a later date. If any keyword starts to receive a significant number of conversions, that keyword will be moved to the search campaign that uses maximum CPC bidding.

Create demand for their goods on nonsearch sites with highly targeted ads. This company would like to place ads on highly desirable review-based websites so that more people become aware of their brand. To accomplish this, they will use a placement targeted campaign with only image and video ads. In addition, as their goal is the ad view, the campaign will utilize CPM bidding (cost per thousand impressions) instead of CPC bidding.

The company will measure this campaign's success by examining the changes in branded queries, the number of people who watch a video, and changes to overall conversion rates on the website.

Test a B2B-focused ad on weekdays and a B2C-focused ad on weekends. To reach this goal, they are going to use both location targeting and ad scheduling. The company should create two new campaigns that only target Chicago.

The first campaign will use ad scheduling to only show their ads on weekdays. As weekdays often contain more B2B-focused searches, they are going to write ads that use a B2B benefit message. They will send those searchers to a B2B-focused page on how the company helps other businesses that are buying multiple computers save time and money with their enterprise services.

The second campaign will use ad scheduling to only show their ads on weekends. Because they are trying to reach more consumers who want to purchase new computers, these ads will focus on the consumer benefits of buying a new computer. These ads will lead to a consumer-focused landing page.

After the company has gone through the exercise of determining their goals and how to structure their campaigns to meet those goals, they create a chart (Figure 14.10) so they can visually understand their campaign's organization.

Figure 14.10 Complex campaign organization that meets the company's goals

Proper campaign organization can determine the success or failure of your marketing goals. List the goals you want your marketing to achieve. Then examine all the options that AdWords gives you to help you reach those goals. Once you understand all the features in AdWords, you can create complex campaign structures that will help you reach your goals.

A campaign tells Google where, how, and when to show your ads. It does not inform Google which keyword, ad copy, and landing page should be used. The next step to a successful campaign is properly organizing your ad groups in a campaign.

Organizing an Ad Group to Increase CTR and Conversion Rates

An ad group is a collection of keywords and ad copy. Any ad copy can show for any keyword in an ad group. It is essential that all ad copy properly reflect each keyword. This topic is covered in depth in Chapter 7, "Demystifying Quality Score."

You should always ask yourself a few questions for each keyword you use in a search campaign:

- Does the searcher think the page reached after clicking on your ad will answer their question?

- Can you write an ad that is more related to this keyword?

- If you look at the other ads, is there one that is more closely related to the keyword than yours?

A simple exercise to go through is to write a highly targeted ad, an ad so specific that if a searcher sees it, they assume you only offer one item. Then ask yourself, does that ad describe the keyword? If yes, the keyword is in the correct ad group. If no, the keyword needs to go to a new ad group.

Going through this exercise and applying it to your keywords should lead to higher Quality Scores, higher click-through rates, and higher conversion rates. The process is time consuming but essential.

Once you have created relevant ad groups and have accumulated some data, run the search query report. This report is indispensable if you use broad and phrase match. It will help you identify negative keywords, add new keywords, and even help organize your ad groups.

For instance, if a company sells various types of TVs, they would want ad groups for LCD, LED, and Plasma TV sets (among many other ad groups). Let's also assume that these ad groups are using broad-matched keywords to capture as much search volume as possible. As all of these ad groups just use big-screen TV type words, it is easy to imagine a scenario where the search query is "LED TV" and yet the "LCD TV" ad is triggered and shown to the searcher. This is not an ideal scenario, as you have the keyword "LED TV" in your account, accompanied by a LED TV ad copy, and a LED TV landing page. In this scenario, you would much rather your "LED TV" keyword be triggered by that search query, and not the incorrect TV type. When you have scenarios like this, use negative keywords to ensure the correct ad is being shown (Figure 14.11).

For the LED TV Ad Group, you would use the negative "-LCD" and "-Plasma" keywords. For the LCD TV Ad Group, you would use the negative "-LED TV" and "-Plasma" keywords.

Figure 14.11 Using negative keywords to control ad display

In this case, while you are ensuring the correct ad is being displayed, you will not show for comparison terms such as "LED vs. LCD TV." Therefore, you should create keywords and ad copy that is focused on comparing the items against each other. By using a combination of positive and negative keywords, you can ensure that the correct ad copy and keyword are triggered in your account when someone conducts a search that matches one of your keywords.

For organizing ad groups for display campaigns, please refer to Chapter 9, "Understanding the Display Network," in particular the section "Choosing the Correct Keywords for Your Display Network Ad Group."

The ideal scenario is to create ad copy and a landing page for each search query where the ad copy and landing page are specific to every single keyword query conducted. While that might be ideal, there is no way to accomplish that organization with a medium-sized account, let alone a large account.

To create effective ad groups, always think back to the search intent of any given query. If your keyword, ad copy, and landing page work together to answer the searcher's question, your organization is on the correct path.

Best Practices for Account Organization Strategies

Google AdWords gives you a tremendous amount of control in determining the conditions in which your ad is eligible for the auction. You have control over:

- Keywords
- Negative keywords
- Match types

- Geography
- Time of day
- Day of the week
- Google search
- Search partners
- General display network
- Specific placement in display
- Specific placement if the article contains your keywords
- Bidding type (budget optimizer, maximum CPC, conversion optimizer, CPM)
- Budget
- Device type

There are so many options that it can become overwhelming when you are trying to figure out all the combinations, where you would like your ad to be displayed, and how much you want to pay for each of those clicks or impressions. To ensure your account is organized properly, follow these best practice techniques:

- First determine your business goals. You cannot be successful if you do not understand what your marketing needs to accomplish.
- Next, learn all of the targeting options available through AdWords.
- Once you have a grasp of the first two points, create a map of your campaigns, keeping in mind that each campaign must have a budget, and that you do not want to make it too small so that it cannot get enough exposure.
- For each campaign, create ad groups that meet the campaign's objective.
- For search campaigns, all keywords and ad copy need to be closely related.
- Run a search query report to learn when to break an ad group into multiple ad groups or add negative keywords and positive keywords.
- If you manage more than one account, create a My Client Center account to link all of your accounts together.
- If you want to sell AdWords or add a bullet point to your résumé, become a Google Certified Partner.

Proper organization of your campaigns will help you reach the proper audience. Effective ad group organization will allow you to put the correct message in front of that audience.

However, creating ad copy and landing pages is just the first step in the process. You need to test different ad copy and landing pages to determine which message resonates best with searchers so you can continuously increase your account's profits.

In the next chapter, you will explore testing strategies for your ad copy and landing pages. First, we will look at different types of ad copy along with methodologies for testing those ads. Once you have obtained the click, you need the visitor to conduct an action on your website. We will then examine how to test where to send the traffic on your website along with how to test different landing pages so you can find ad copy and landing page combinations that lead to higher conversion rates.

Testing Techniques That Will Increase Profits

Testing is an essential component when optimizing any AdWords account. You should test both ads and landing pages to see what combinations improve the effectiveness of your account.

In this chapter, not only will you learn how to test ads, but you will also explore how to test landing pages, where to send traffic, and how to lay out different types of landing pages that can increase conversion rates.

Finally, this chapter will show you how to test ads and landing pages in conjunction with each other. Profit per impression *is a metric that will let you find the most profitable combination of ads and landing pages that you should use in your AdWords account.*

15

Chapter Contents
Testing is essential to increasing profits
Testing ad copy to increase conversions
Ad copy themes to spark your creativity
Testing landing pages to increase conversions
Testing profit per click and profit per impression
AdWords campaign experiments
Best practices for testing techniques that will increase profits

Testing Is Essential to Increasing Profits

Throughout this book, you have seen best practices for researching keywords, writing ads, and designing landing pages. But what if you have two or more ideas that seem as if they could be successful? That is where testing comes into play. You can test your ideas to see which ones lead to higher profits.

Testing is a crucial part of account optimization. Once you have created your AdWords account, it will start to accumulate metrics that will show you how successful your account currently is. You can improve these metrics over time by testing various ads and landing pages.

It is easy to impose your own will and designs when writing ads and creating landing pages. However, *you are not your target market*. Your target market will usually know less than you do about your products and your business. Therefore, whenever you say, "I think we should do it this way," when writing ads or designing your website, you need to test the ideas to see if consumers agree with you.

If marketing thinks a website should look one way, your IT department thinks it should look a different way, and the CEO wants to splatter the corporate logo all over the website, there is an easy solution. Create three landing pages and see which ones lead to higher profits. It is hard to argue with profits.

You should let consumers tell you what is best for them. The easiest way to do this is to test your ideas. The two major elements you can test are ads and landing pages. Let's begin by examining the various types of ads you can test.

Testing Ad Copy to Increase Conversions

There are two main ways to test ads: the unique approach and the methodical approach.

Unique Approach With the unique approach, you will write a few different ad types. For example, you may write one ad with prices, another that uses testimonials, and a third that answers a question. When you use this method, each ad will have completely different components than the other ads you are testing. This is a good way to determine which type of ad resonates best with your customers.

With this approach, it is also useful to see what types of ads your competitors are using, and then test both their ad type and a completely different one. This will let you see how consumers in your industry are responding to different messages.

Methodical Approach In this scenario, you will write two or three headlines, description line 1s, description line 2s, and then mix and match them. If you have three headlines, description line 1s, and description line 2s, once you mix and match those ad components you will have 27 combinations. This is not the place to start. You need a significant amount of traffic to test 27 combinations. You may move to this approach at a later date once you have determined what type of ads and messages work best for your consumers, but do not start with this approach.

Before you can run a test, you need at least two different ads. Next let's examine various ad copy messages so you can identify ones that resonate with your audience.

Ad Copy Messages You Should Test

There are various types of ads that will help you connect with your consumer base. Not all of these will resonate with your customers, which is why you need to test your ideas to see which ones increase profits. Chapter 4, "Writing Compelling Ads," discussed these ad formats:

- Numbers, prices, and discounts
- Calls-to-action
- Informational
- Question
- Testimonials and reviews
- Negative messages
- Display URLs

In this section I will introduce you to some more ads types you can test. Understanding message types is essential, not just for testing, but to know what your competitors are doing as well.

Ad Copy Themes to Spark Your Creativity

You can test ad copy themes to see which resonate best for people looking at your ads. You may find that certain types of ads perform differently depending on where someone is in the buying funnel.

> **Tip:** Ad copy is the only part of your account that a searcher ever sees. Your ad has only seconds to grab the searcher's attention, connect with them, and direct them to click on your ad to visit your website. If your ad fails to deliver visitors to your website, designing exceptional landing pages is a waste of time since they will never be seen.

For instance, for those who are in the early stages of the buying funnel, informational ads often do better than review-based ads. However, someone who is comparison shopping may like review-based ads more than informational ads.

You can also mix different themes within a single ad. For instance, you can use an informational description line 1 and a call-to-action for description line 2 in the same text ad.

Test Discounts Instead of Prices

In Chapter 4, we explored the psychology of numbers and how a new ad can influence consumers' perception of prices. However, if you are not price competitive for some reason, instead of adding prices to your ads, you could test discounts (Figure 15.1).

Bluetooth Headset Sale
Great selection. 25%-60% Off.
Free Shipping on All Orders
example.com/BluetoothHeadsets

Bluetooth Headset Sale
Great selection. 25% Off
Free Shipping on All Orders
example.com/BluetoothHeadsets

Figure 15.1 Ad copy using discounts

If your prices are constantly changing and requiring you to change your ads, you may want to use discounts instead of prices in the ad copy. The reason for this is that each time you modify an existing ad, you are actually deleting that ad and creating a new one; because all new ads must go through editorial approval before they are shown on search partners' or display network sites, this means that you are reducing your potential exposure.

 Note: Although discounts will often increase conversion rates, they may not increase profits. You should examine the dollars lost from giving a discount compared to the additional revenue gained from selling more items to determine if you want to use discounts in your ads.

There are other items you can test, such as using geographic components or dynamic keyword insertion in your ads.

Geographic Ad Copy Are your customers locals or nonlocals? Always consider how much information someone has about an area when using that area in your ad copy (Figure 15.2):

- When someone moves to Chicago, the first decision they make is if they want to live in North or South Chicago. The third ad does not help someone reach that decision. Therefore, if someone has just decided to move to Chicago, it is a bad ad. However, if someone has decided they want to live in North Chicago, then the ad copy has meaning for the searcher. Therefore, this is bad ad copy when someone is in the informational phase of the buying funnel, but good ad copy if they are further down in the funnel.

- The second ad related to the hotel has good ad copy for a nonlocal. A nonlocal wants to be reassured you are in the correct location. As most hotel bookings are for nonlocals, you can make some assumptions about your audience.

- The first ad uses good ad copy if you are a physical business trying to get people to walk into your store. A precise location, the Water Tower, is used in the copy. However, this is a bad nonlocal ad as most people outside of Chicago do not know where the Water Tower is located.

The more a user knows, the more precise your ad can be. Always consider the knowledge of your audience when writing any ads, especially location-based ads.

Figure 15.2 Geographic ad copy

Dynamic Keyword Insertion In Chapter 6, "Advanced Optimization Techniques," I discussed dynamic keyword insertion, which automatically changes your ad to include a keyword from your ad group based on the search query. Testing keyword insertion is simple. Write one or two ads. In the first group, do not use dynamic insertion. Duplicate the ads and use dynamic insertion in the second set (Figure 15.3).

Figure 15.3 Dynamic keyword insertion ads

The use of keyword insertion does not always increase both click-through rate and conversion rate. It commonly increases click-through rate, but not always; it may not affect conversion rates at all.

Be Creative in Writing Ad Copy

When choosing what type of messaging to use in your ad copy, you should always keep the landing page in mind as the ad copy sets the expectation for what will be found after the click. Creating synergies with the landing page is essential to writing successful ad copy. For instance, if you used a testimonial in your ad copy, you should echo that call-to-action on the landing page. By using the same elements in the ad and the landing page, you ensure that the ad copy and landing pages will work together to increase conversion rates. This same principle applies to testimonial or review ads (Figure 15.4).

Figure 15.4 Reinforcing testimonials on the landing page

As your ad copy initially connected with the searcher—it's why your ad was clicked—reinforcing that same message on the landing page will tell the consumer they are in the right place and the information presented is exactly what they were looking to find.

There are many additional items that you can test:

- Shipping method
- Customer benefits
- Unique selling propositions

- Product features

- Service features

- Title casing vs. sentence casing

- Guarantees

- Symbols: ©, ™, ®

- One-line vs. two-line ad copy

When working with AdWords, most of your time is spent in spreadsheets crunching numbers. Writing ad copy is a good time to use the right side of your brain. The left side of the brain is focused on logic and facts. The right side of the brain is much more creative and emotional. Ad copy should connect emotionally with individuals, so using the creative side of your brain to write ad copy can help you reach your target market.

Creating the Ad Copy Test

When starting with the unique ad approach, write a few different types of ads. For instance, write one informational ad, one with dynamic keyword insertion, and another ad that uses a discount. Do not forget to mix and match some of these concepts. For instance, you can use dynamic keyword insertion in an informational ad or a call-to-action in a geographic ad.

The next step in running a test is to specify how Google decides which ad from an ad group to display.

Ensure Your Ads Receive Equal Exposure

There are three ways that Google will display the ads in the ad groups for your campaigns: optimize for clicks, optimize for conversions, and rotate.

Optimize For Clicks When Optimize For Clicks is enabled, Google will determine which of your ads has the highest click-through rate. Over time, they will show the ad with the higher CTR more often than the other ads in that ad group. Eventually, you may see one ad receiving 95 percent of all impressions for an ad group.

Optimize For Conversions When Optimize For Conversions is enabled, Google will determine which of your ads has the highest conversion rate and start to show that ad more often. Although this might seem like a great setting, it does not care about your CTR. Therefore, you might have an ad with a very high conversion rate show often, but if its CTR is too low, you might rarely receive visitors from the ad to your site.

Rotate When you have the Rotate option enabled, Google will attempt to show your ads evenly and gives your ads equal distribution.

When you enable Rotate, you will find that the ads do not receive exactly equal impressions. This is due to the complexity of Google's system and how they serve ads across many geographies and time zones. It is not uncommon to see that ad 1 has 450 impressions, ad 2 has 350 impressions, and ad 3 has 475 impressions. The ads will have similar but not exact impression volume.

Ad Serving Considerations

The bidding method you choose sets the bid; it does not serve the ad. If you are using Conversion Optimizer, it will try to determine what a keyword's conversion rate and average CPA are for setting the bid, but it does not choose to show the ad with the highest conversion rate. If you are focused on just conversions, using both the bid system Conversion Optimizer and Optimize For Conversions is a good choice. If you are also taking into account average order value, profit per impression (discussed later in this chapter) or other metrics, you should still use Rotate or AdWords Campaign Experiments (also discussed later in this chapter) to serve your ads.

If your goal is to improve your conversion rate, increase your ROI, or find the ad with the highest profit, you do not want to use the Optimize For Clicks setting; doing so only maximizes CTR. In these cases, you want to enable the Rotate feature. To do so, navigate to your Campaign settings. Under Advanced Settings, open the Ad Delivery section and choose Rotate (Figure 15.5).

Figure 15.5 Choose Rotate in your Campaign settings.

Please note that since this is a Campaign setting, it will affect all the ad groups within that campaign. The next step of the testing process is entering the new ads in the test ad group.

Create the Test Ads

Navigate to the ad group where you would like to test your ads and enter them in the Ads tab of the ad group (Figure 15.6).

If you are testing ads across many ad groups at once, you may want to use the AdWords Editor import function to add the new ads to your account.

Now be patient as the ads run for a while so you can accumulate the necessary data to determine which of the test ads leads to the best results for your company.

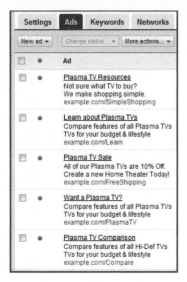

Figure 15.6 Multiple ads running in one ad group

General Guidelines for Statistical Significance

When testing, the most important concern is that you believe in the data before you make a decision. If a single person converting versus not converting makes a large difference in your conversion rate, you do not yet have statistical significance.

For example, if 100 people click on your ad and one converts, you have a 1 percent conversion rate. If the very next person, click 101, leads to a conversion, your conversion rate almost doubles. If your conversion rate doubles and you are using ROI-based bidding rules, your bid doubles as well. In this case, you do not have statistical significance.

There are two ways that Excel will help you calculate when you have enough data. You can use either chi-square distribution or analysis of variance (ANOVA). Using either of these two methods will give you very accurate data of when you can end a test and make decisions on the data. However, both methods take some work to understand and implement in Excel. If you want to learn about these methods, Microsoft has online tutorials about using these two mathematical functions.

For our purposes, I'll lay out some basic rules for how much data you need before you can end a test and measure the results.

There Is No "Best" Ad Copy

There is only a best ad copy as it relates to your marketing goals. If you are trying to bring more visitors to your website or raise your quality score, you will focus on click-through rate. If you are bidding to maximize your profits, you will examine how much profit you receive from each visitor. Testing ads without a goal in mind will leave you staring at a spreadsheet of data without any meaning.

How Long Should the Tests Run?

Search behavior is different on weekdays than on weekends. Often the search versus buy process changes over the course of a month, as with the high-end electronics sales example in Chapter 13, "Profitable Bid Strategies." In these cases, you want to make sure that you capture search data over the lifespan of the entire buying funnel.

If your sales cycle is short, or searchers come to your site and either buy or do not return again, you should run a test for at least a week. This captures the differences between weekday and weekend buyers. If your sales cycle is longer or you want more data (which is always useful), let the test run for at least a month.

If you have a good idea of your sales cycle length, run the test over the course of three sales cycles. In the case of the high-end electronics company, three months would net you sufficient data. If you sell used books, a week is long enough; however, waiting for a month is never a bad idea. In fact, for most of my personal testing I will use a month of data in the results even for accounts that spend millions each month. However, never use December's data or holiday peaks for your testing. The traffic that you receive during holidays generally converts much higher than the rest of the year. Feel free to use holiday traffic to test holiday ads that are only enabled during those peak times.

Even if you decide to use ANOVA or chi-square for your analysis, using these rules of thumb for making sure you capture searchers over the course of your entire sales cycle is a good idea. Neither of those systems will tell you that search behavior changes at different time periods. They will only examine the differences in the traffic and conversion numbers.

How Much Traffic Should Your Ads Receive?

The minimum amount of traffic each ad should receive is 300 clicks. That ensures that one person clicking versus not clicking will not change your CTR by a large amount.

I prefer 500 to 1,000 clicks for each ad before making decisions. This is where ANOVA and chi-square analysis can help significantly. If after the course of a month one ad has 200 clicks and one has 500 clicks and they both have similar impressions, you can make some assumptions about CTR, though you might not have enough data to make assumptions about conversion rate. In cases like this, utilizing higher-level Excel functions will let you know that you have enough data to end a test.

If these numbers seem too high for you—which is often the case with accounts that only receive 1,000 clicks a month and any one ad group might not receive more than 100 clicks—there is another way to test ad copy.

In the cases of low-traffic accounts, you can write two tag lines. Put each tagline in two ads across multiple ad groups. When you are ready to examine the data, combine the metrics for those ads across all of the ad groups where you conducted the test. This method is not perfect, but it will let you test aspects of ads even with low traffic, which is better than not testing at all.

How Many Conversions Should You Have?

If you are testing for conversion rate, ROI, or profit metrics, you need conversions to tell you which ad is leading to higher metrics. A good guideline is a minimum of 7 conversions per ad copy. A higher number, around 15, is better. If in doubt, let the test run longer.

Meeting All the Requirements

Each test should meet a minimum number of days being run, clicks per ad, and conversions per ad. If you have enough data according to ANOVA but the test has only run for a single day, let the test run for a longer time frame. Each of the variables can affect your metrics, so you want to make sure that your ads run under all of the conditions possible.

Finally, you want to separate these metrics by search and display. Do not combine the data from the two different distribution methods. If on the search network you have accumulated enough data to finish running a test, you can complete the test for search, but your display test must run longer.

Once your tests have met all the conditions I have described, it is time to run an ad performance report to examine the test results.

Measuring the Results of Your Ad Test

The ad performance report is one of many reports available in AdWords. This report shows you all your ad copy and associated metrics. For ease of showing metrics, let's assume that you are using the AdWords conversion tracker (discussed in Chapter 13) to show conversion information in your reports.

When you create the report, there are two important steps. First, choose the appropriate columns. Open the Customize Columns settings (Figure 15.7) and choose these inputs:

Performance Statistics

- Impressions
- Clicks
- CTR
- Cost
- Avg Position

Conversion Columns

- Conversions (1-per-click)
- Conversion rate (1-per-click)
- Cost / Conv (1-per-click)
- Value / Conv (1-per-click)
- Total conv. value

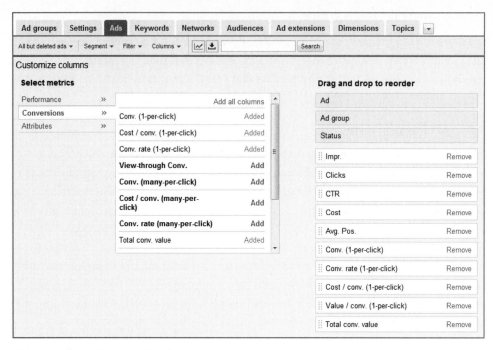

Figure 15.7 Advanced settings in ad performance reports

You Can Test Any Ad Type

In the Customize Columns data for the Ads tab, you can choose to view the type of ad such as text, image, mobile, or display ads so that you can segment your data to just view image ads or video ads. The principles for testing ads are the same. If you want to test image ads across the display network, create two to five images in an ad group. Wait for the images to collect enough data so you can make a decision. Then, run the exact same ad performance report as discussed earlier and decide which ad to keep based on your website's goals.

You may find that certain images do better or worse on various types of sites. When examining the reports, if you see patterns that suggest certain types of images or videos are doing better on one site than another, you may want to create placement targeted ad groups using your best images for that particular website.

If you are testing multiple conversion types, you may want to choose additional conversion columns or segment the data by conversion type. Once you run the report, you will have a large Excel file that you can manipulate to view the data, which will help you make a decision.

Finally, when you choose to download the data you can also segment the information. Segment the data by network so that you can see the difference between search and display. Never mix these two distribution methods together.

For ease of illustration, Figure 15.8 shows an Excel report with only a few data points selected.

	A	B	C	D	E	G	H	J	K
1		Impressions	Clicks	CTR	Cost	Conversion Rate	Cost/ Conversion	Value Per Click	ROI
2	Ad Copy 1	30529	899	2.94%	$1,060.82	12.35%	$9.56	$6.17	523.18%
3	Ad Copy 2	30585	754	2.47%	$889.72	11.41%	$10.35	$5.70	483.30%
4	Ad Copy 3	23942	751	3.14%	$863.65	12.52%	$9.19	$6.26	544.20%
5	Ad Copy 4	31097	759	2.44%	$903.21	11.20%	$10.63	$5.60	470.54%
6	Ad Copy 5	31184	1546	4.96%	$1,793.36	5.69%	$20.38	$2.85	245.35%
7	Ad Copy 6	23953	696	2.91%	$953.52	13.22%	$10.36	$6.61	482.42%
8	Ad Copy 7	35326	1018	2.88%	$1,099.44	8.25%	$13.09	$4.13	382.01%

Figure 15.8 Ad performance report

Once you have this report, you need to make a decision about which is the best ad for your account:

- If you are looking to maximize customers, Ad Copy 6 with the highest conversion rate is your best ad.

- If you are looking to lower lead costs, Ad Copy 3 with the lowest cost per conversion is your best ad.

- If you are looking to get the most visitors to your website, or to increase your quality score, Ad Copy 5 with the highest CTR is your best ad.

The first step is to save the ad that did the best for your company. Before you delete the losing ads, examine them to see what you can learn.

For instance, if your goal is to have the lowest cost per conversion, which is Ad Copy 3, but you want to increase total visitors to your website, your next goal is to increase CTR for a similar ad. Ad Copy 5 is by far the highest CTR of all the ads that were tested. Therefore, see if there are elements that you can combine from Ad Copy 3 and Ad Copy 5 to write some new test ads in the ad group and continue testing.

At this point, you could use the methodological approach. If you want to go this route, mix and match the elements of each ad. For instance, if you want to use the existing elements from Ad Copy 3 and 6, you can start to create new ads with these elements:

New Ad Copy 1

- Ad Copy 3 headline
- Ad Copy 5 description line 1
- Ad Copy 5 description line 2

New Ad Copy 2

- Ad Copy 5 headline
- Ad Copy 3 description line 1
- Ad Copy 5 description line 2

Keep repeating the process until you have created the new combinations. Then when you run an ad performance report, not only will you be examining each ad individually, but you can also break down the metrics of each copy element within that ad. For instance, you would examine the CTR of Ad Copy 3's headline against the CTR of Ad Copy 5's headline. By looking at the metrics for the headline, description line 1, description line 2, and the display URL individually, you will discern patterns that show which elements lead to higher conversion rates and higher CTRs.

Do not feel you need to use the methodical approach all the time, because it does take significantly more traffic than a unique ad approach before each ad will have enough data for you to choose a winner. In the earlier case, you could keep the winner, write a couple of new ads using variants from the two pieces of ad copy, and then test those new ads.

Once you have added the new ads to test, delete all the losing ads from the initial test. By using this methodology, you can continuously test new ads to see which ones are helping you reach your marketing goals.

Along with testing ads, you should also test landing pages. The ad transfers a visitor from a search page to your website and sets the expectations for what the searcher will find post-click. Once the ad has completed its job, the landing page must continue to move the visitor through your website so that you receive conversions. The first step in landing page testing is deciding where to send the traffic.

Testing Landing Pages to Increase Conversions

There are two aspects to landing page testing. The first is determining where you should send the traffic on your website. Once you have determined the best type of page to send your traffic, you need to test various layouts of the landing pages.

Testing Where to Send Traffic

In Chapter 5, "Landing Pages That Convert Searchers into Buyers," I discussed where you should send traffic on your website. The conventional wisdom says traffic should be sent to:

- The furthest logical point in the buying cycle
- A page dedicated to the search query

Although conventional wisdom is typically correct, there are definitely times when it is wrong. You should test your own traffic to make sure that you are sending the traffic to the correct pages before performing the more difficult work of testing different layouts on your website.

Let's examine some common queries to see where you should test sending traffic.

Informational Queries

Informational queries make up the majority of search queries on the Web. In Chapter 5, I illustrated the point that you must answer the searcher's question before attempting to monetize the query. In that example, you looked at the search query "candle burning times" and how that should not be sent to a shopping cart but instead to a comparison page that shows all the candles and how long each burns.

However, each time you add a click to the final conversion process your conversion rates will decrease. Therefore, it is worthwhile testing what leads to higher profits, attempting to monetize an informational query, or answering the searcher's question with a comparison chart.

This is especially true for lead-generation websites. If your goal is to gather a lead so you can call someone back with their information, it can be more profitable to send someone to the lead-generation form, or shopping cart page, instead of the comparison page.

Ambiguous Queries

The search query "merchant accounts" is both an informational and ambiguous search query. You do not know if someone is looking to sign up for a merchant account or if they are looking for information on a merchant account.

Search queries such as "merchant account," "Chicago mortgage," or "auto insurance" often go to a landing page with a small amount of information and a form to be completed. This is not necessarily a bad search experience if someone knows enough to finish filling out the form.

A common search experience is that the searcher conducts a search for "Chicago mortgage," sees the landing page, and then starts to fill out the form. Halfway through the form, there is a required field that asks, "What type of mortgage account do you want?" If the searcher does not know the difference between an ARM, fixed, reverse, or interest-only mortgage, they cannot finish filling out the form.

What happens next? The searcher returns to Google, searches for the different mortgage types, and finds a page that explains what all the different mortgage options are. If that page also has a form on it, they are more likely to finish filling out the form on the page that helped them understand the options than return to the initial form page.

To see which is more profitable for you, create a chart that explains the different mortgage types, the advantages and disadvantages of each, and that has a section where there is a call-to-action to apply for each specific mortgage type.

Test a form landing page against a comparison chart to see which one leads to higher total profits. Additionally, you can test a combination page that has both the comparison chart and a form embedded into the page.

Local Business Queries

If the search query is "Pittsburgh kitchen remodeling," conventional wisdom says to send the user to a page that shows before and after pictures of a kitchen. However, hiring a contractor is difficult. Everyone has heard horror stories about how they hired a contractor to remodel their house and three months later the job is over budget and still not completed.

Use the In-Page Analytics tool from Google Analytics to examine your website. This tool will show you where someone is clicking on your website and conversion information based on the searcher visiting specific pages.

In the case of a contracting business, their "about us" page might showcase how they have been in business for 25 years, say that they belong to the Better Business Bureau, and contain customer testimonials. If they use the site overlay tool, they may realize that when someone sees their "about us" page, their conversion rates go up. Therefore they have two options:

- Move some of the "about us" information to the kitchen remodeling page.
- Send traffic to the kitchen remodeling page and the "about us" page and see which leads to more business.

Narrow Theme Sites

If you conduct a search for "Washington DC nanny services," you expect to see a picture of the DC area, sample nanny résumés, and a form to sign up for access to their nanny résumés or schedule an appointment.

Hiring a nanny is a difficult decision. You are bringing a stranger into your house to care for your most prized possessions, your children. The question going through the searcher's mind is not just "Should I trust this site?" but "Where do these nannies come from?"

In cases like this, you want to increase the visitor's trust of your website. Using a segmentation page that shows a visitor two options might result in higher conversions. Option 1 is the "for families" link that goes into the family sign-up process. Option 2 is for nannies to apply for a job. Option 2 also shows that the nanny must pass a background check and meet minimum qualifications before they will be accepted.

What a page like this does is demonstrate to the families that nannies must meet certain qualifications before they are accepted, which can increase the level of trust. However, what is interesting about this example is that if you test the first example of the Washington, DC, sample résumés and a second segmentation page, you may see completely different conversion rates in search versus display networks for those two examples.

At this point, searchers are in the buying funnel, and therefore they have thought about hiring a nanny, background checks, and the issues of trust. But consumers clicking display ads might not have thought about those items yet. Therefore, in this example the segmentation page may mean higher conversions for search whereas the résumé page may mean higher conversions for the content network.

Testing segmentation pages is useful if your products have multiple uses (Figure 15.9) or if different types of searchers use the same keywords.

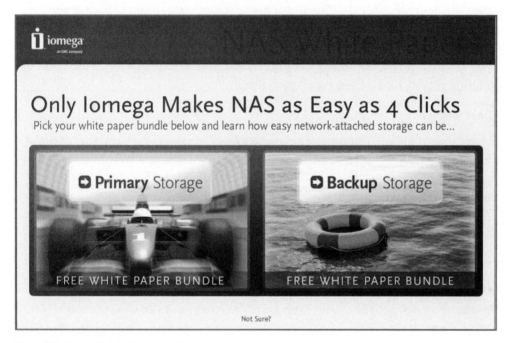

Figure 15.9 Iomega download segmentation page

In these cases, choose one product and send some traffic that way; often this will be the higher searched–for product or the higher margin product. Then send some traffic to a segmentation page. Measure results over time to see which leads to higher total profits.

Product Category Queries

If someone searches for "men's Seiko watches," the searcher expects to see a page full of Seiko watches for men. However, too many options can be just as detrimental to conversion rates as too few options. Most people can only hold five to seven items in short-term memory. One item is why you conducted a search in the first place. A second item might be that you have a meeting you need to attend in 15 minutes. That leaves only three to five open slots left for processing.

If you have a category page of 20 watches, searchers can become overwhelmed and confused over what to do next. In cases like these, the searcher may feel there is too much to process and decide to come back later when they have more time.

Instead of sending someone to a category page, choose three to five of your top-selling Seiko watches for men and feature them on a landing page. Many consumers will choose from these few items as they can easily process the difference between the designs and features of these watches. At the bottom of the page have a link such as "See all of our Seiko watches." You will have customers who want to look at every single watch, and this option allows them to see everything while keeping the total options limited.

Then test this limited product page against your typical category page. Does limiting options increase your conversion rates?

Brand Searches

Many companies use their own name as a keyword and then send the traffic to their homepage. While this is an example of a navigational query, it is also a waste of money. The company should rank number one organically for their company name, and consumers can find the company via multiple means.

However, if competitors are also buying your name, it is a good idea to buy it yourself so you do not lose out on traffic. But you may not want to send it to the homepage of your website.

It is difficult to launch new products on the Web. There is often little search volume for brand-new products, and you need to build awareness with your consumers that your new products exist. With branded terms, test by sending the traffic to a "what's new" page (Figure 15.10).

Then choose another action on your website, such as a newsletter subscription, and send some of the branded traffic in that direction. Measure whether creating awareness for your new products leads to more revenue than trying to increase your newsletter subscriber list.

Thank-You Pages

Many thank-you pages say, "Thank you for your purchase. We will process your order within 2–3 business days," which says to the customer, "Thank you for giving us your money. We will get to your order when it is convenient for us." Most thank-you pages do not continue to engage the customer. The thank-you pages essentially tell the customer to close the browser because there is nothing left to do on your website.

If someone reached a thank-you page, they gave you a level of trust. Do not send these visitors away. Test different thank-you pages to see which one leads to a higher customer engagement.

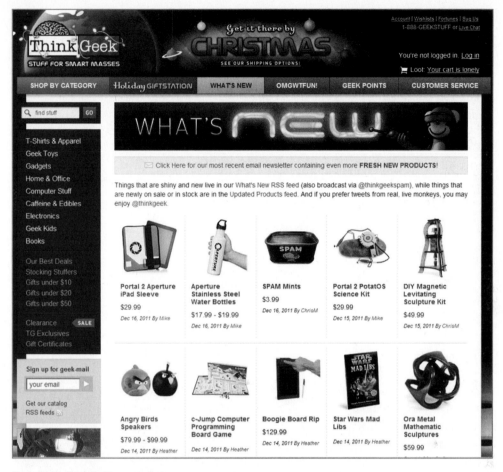

Figure 15.10 Think Geek's new products page

Depending on your business model, there are different types of thank-you pages you can create. Here are some examples to get you started:

- Learn more about our company by downloading this whitepaper.

- Create an account to track your order.

- Subscribe to our newsletter.

- Suggested products.

- Send a 10 percent off coupon to a friend.

- Get 10 percent off your next purchase by referring a friend.

Once you have determined which page on your website is the best place to send traffic for each keyword or ad group, the next step is to test the layout of the individual pages.

Landing Page Testing Factors

Landing page testing is both a science and an art form. There are entire books dedicated to testing single pages that go into much more depth than I can allocate in a single section. I will examine the big factors you should test and items to be aware of while you are creating pages and marketing campaigns. This will get you started in the right direction for creating landing pages and tests to help you improve your profits.

Start with Dramatic Changes

ArdenB.com uses very different pages for their top-level categories (Figure 15.11) compared to their sublevel categories (Figure 15.12).

These pages are dramatically different. Although these pages do appear as different categories on their website, it would be worthwhile to test their current subcategory page with a similar layout to their main category page to see the differences in conversion rates.

You want to start your testing with dramatic changes. If you cannot see the difference within a few seconds, neither can your visitors. Once you have a handle on the larger items that affect conversion rates, you can move to smaller changes.

Figure 15.11 Arden B. category page

Figure 15.12 Arden B. subcategory page

Should You Add Navigation?

The more choices you give someone, the more likely they are to become confused over what to do next. Navigation options are additional choices. That does not mean you should always restrict navigation. There are different types of shoppers. Some shoppers want to make quick decisions, and limited choice is good. Other shoppers want to research the details and see all the options; limited choice can isolate these shoppers.

In addition, one of the factors that makes a landing page relevant for quality score factors is navigation. Too little navigation can adversely affect whether your page is deemed relevant by Google.

There are often nice compromises you can use to engage both of these shoppers, as shown on the Certified Knowledge website (Figure 15.13).

The main call-to-action above the fold is to "Take the AdWords Challenge." The secondary items on the page are benefits, testimonials, and a video tour for the research-oriented audience. At the bottom of the page are secondary conversions, newsletter signup, consulting requests, and in-person training.

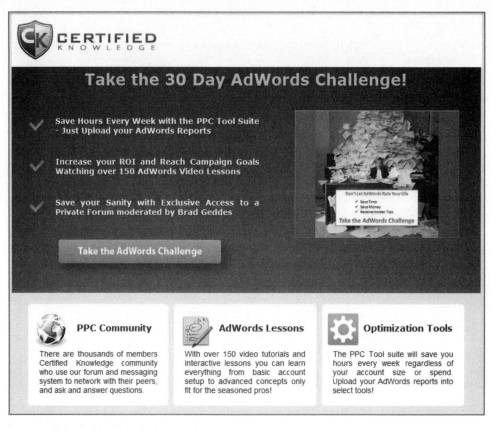

Figure 15.13 Certified Knowledge landing page that restricts navigation

Amazon takes a different approach to navigation. When you are in their main site, there are more navigational options than most people can comprehend. As soon as you enter the shopping cart, your choices become limited (Figure 15.14). You can change your shipping address, use a different payment method, and update quantities. What you cannot do is leave the shopping cart unless you click the Back button.

You most likely have a product or service page you are sending traffic to now that includes navigation. Create a second page with limited navigation and clear calls-to-action. Then test to see which of those pages increases conversion rates.

Are You Using Faces?

We are drawn to human faces. When a face appears on a page, the first thing most searchers do is look at it. Next, they follow the eyes to see where they are looking. If the face on your page is looking away from your content, so will the searcher.

Make sure that any face you have on a page is looking toward the main items on your page you want the user to see. For some sites, this will be the service benefits. For others, it will be the Submit button or the Add To Cart button.

Figure 15.14 Amazon limits shopping cart navigation

Create two pages, one where the eyes are looking into your product benefits and another where the eyes are looking toward your submit action. See which version raises your conversion rates the most.

English Speakers Read Left to Right

If there is not a face on the page, the next item that draws the consumer's attention is an image. Once our eyes are drawn to an image, we then start reading left to right. If your images are on the far-right side of a page, there is nothing left for the consumer to read and they can become distracted.

In Figure 15.15, the page on the right will perform worse in most cases. Since the page on the left also places the image on the left, as someone views the image their eyes will naturally be drawn back into the content of the page.

Figure 15.15 Identical pages with the image flipped

If you were advertising to a country where the population reads right to left, the exact opposite information would be true. Ensure that your images are strategically placed so that consumers' natural reading habit keeps bringing them back into your content.

Testing Video

Images and text allow you to show a product. However, video allows you to demonstrate a product or show real-life examples. When using video, you must first consider the searcher's environment to decide if you want the video to start playing or not. If someone is in a work cubicle and their computer starts to speak, they are likely to click the Back button very quickly. If someone is at home or in an enclosed office, they are less likely to click the Back button if their computer makes noise. There are four ways to test video:

- Autoplay with sound on
- Autoplay with sound off
- Do not autoplay
- No video

I work closely with Google to conduct the advanced sessions of the AdWords Seminars for Success program. The initial landing page did not use video (Figure 15.16).

Figure 15.16 AdWords Seminar for Success landing page

These pages worked quite well for a couple of years. As video hosting and bandwidth significantly increased, I decided to test three versions of the page. One version did not use the video (Figure 15.16), the second version only used video testimonials, and the third version used even more video testimonials (Figure 15.17) followed by other videos on the Web where I have been interviewed. As most of the audience is in a business environment, I decided not to autoplay any videos.

Figure 15.17 Video testimonials on the landing page

Table 1.1 shows a high-level set of metrics from the test pages. As the page without videos was the initial baseline page, there is no reason to include those statistics. Both versions of the page started with the same opening video, hence the same number of users who played a video.

▶ **Table 1.1** Conversion rate lift from using video

	Testimonial video	Testimonial and interview video
Number of videos	3	9
Length of all videos	2 minutes	28 minutes
Percentage of users who started watching	32%	32%
Total time watched	1 minute, 45 seconds	7 minutes, 16 seconds
Conversion rate lift	31%	38%

What was fascinating is that once someone started playing the testimonial videos, they watched almost all of them. Rarely did someone stop watching the video. Of course, if someone decided they were ready to buy and left the page to enter their credit card details before the videos finished playing, they would not have seen all of the videos in their entirety.

While this shows for my test that videos increased conversion rates, there are many more items to test, such as these:

- Opening video testimonial being a female
- Showcasing the seminar content in video before the testimonials
- Starting with a short interview before moving to testimonials

Any testing you do should evolve from what you have learned. This test first showed me that using video testimonial increased our company's conversion rates. The second thing it taught me was that consumers liked seeing who the speaker was by watching interviews. Much more can be learned by continuously evolving the video tests.

Making Ads and Landing Pages Work Together

Your landing page is only as good as the synergy it creates with your ad copy. If your ad copy is not compelling or does not set the proper expectations for the landing page, the perfect page may still produce disappointing results. This synergy should extend not just to text ads but to display ads as well.

Showcasing the Offer on the Landing Page

If your ad copy and landing page use different color layouts, themes, and calls-to-action, you can confuse visitors and they may think they have arrived at the wrong place. eTrade created a nice banner ad (Figure 15.18) with a simple call-to-action to open an account in minutes.

Figure 15.18 eTrade banner ad

The ad itself is clean and easy to read. The effectiveness of this ad increased dramatically when the user clicked on the ad and then saw the majority of the ad as part of the landing page (Figure 15.19).

The color scheme of the ad and the landing page are the same. The numbers are the same. The benefit messages are the same. The user knows they have arrived at the correct page and can easily continue the action from clicking on the ad to applying for a new account.

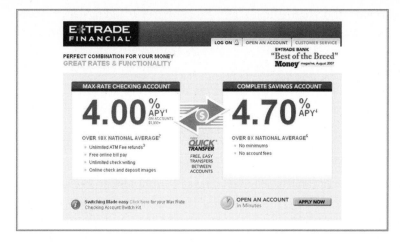

Figure 15.19 eTrade landing page

Ensure Relevance for Your Audience

The concepts of connecting ads and landing pages apply to all your marketing efforts, not just your AdWords ads. Your social, email, and other advertising outlets can take advantage of these same ideas.

Delivery.com delivers takeout food to your door so you do not have to leave the house. They came up with a fantastic marketing idea during the winter. Essentially, the offer is that the colder it is outside, the more bonus points you receive to your account (Figure 15.20) if you order from them.

Figure 15.20 Delivery.com email promotion

While the idea was good, there were two areas where they could have increased the effectiveness of this campaign. This email was sent to many people in the northeastern United States. There are large weather differences between Pittsburgh; Washington, DC; Boston; and New York. When you are deciding to stay in or go out, the weather outside your house is more important than the weather in a different city. However, the offer in the newsletter was based on the temperature of Central Park in New York City. If you lived in Boston, and it was cold in Boston but warm in New York, this promotion did not do you a lot of good.

Second, Delivery.com knows the zip code of everyone in their database, as they deliver to people's doors. The link in the email to "browse restaurants in your area" goes to the homepage of Delivery.com. I hope by now you realize that the homepage is rarely the best page to send traffic. In this case, they should have coded the links based on the zip code of the recipient so that when they visited Delivery.com's website they were directed to the restaurants that delivered to their address.

The overall idea for the marketing campaign was brilliant. The execution could have increased its effectiveness. Make sure you think through your campaigns as a consumer so that you are delivering effective messages.

Echo Special Offers on the Landing Page

Too often a consumer will see an ad that contains the text, "Use Discount Code EHCODE for 20% Off" and then they will visit the site and not see the code. They will navigate to the page where they enter their credit card information and not see the code. If the consumer looked around the site at all, odds are they have forgotten the code. Next, the consumer returns to the search results page and tries to find the ad again. If they cannot find the ad, they become frustrated and may not return to your site to complete the transaction.

If you add discount or special offer codes in either text or display ads, it is imperative that the exact same code and special can be found on the landing page (Figure 15.21).

Testing special offers and discounts is useful. The use of discounts will often increase conversion rates. However, your final profit on each sale is also less. Therefore, when testing discounts, what you should be testing to see if the use of a special offer increases conversion rates enough that it is worth taking a lower profit on each sale, or if the lower conversion rate without a discount is more profitable.

Convey the Proper Experience

If you sell used books at a $5 price point, a searcher does not want to spend 20 minutes attempting to find their next used book. The searcher wants a quick Add To Cart button and an even faster checkout experience, and does not want to take time out of their day to deliberate over a $5 investment.

Figure 15.21 eHarmony's special offer landing page

When a consumer goes into a physical store to buy a diamond, they are treated to gorgeous showcases, helpful sales staff, and the ability to touch and examine not only the diamonds, but the rings and necklaces that make the diamonds sparkle.

If you sell diamond jewelry online, that same consumer does not want the same shopping experience as one buying a used book. The monetary investment is different, and the time between examining the products and buying a piece of jewelry is much longer. An expensive jewelry shopper wants to be treated to an exquisite sales experience (Figure 15.22).

The Theologos House of Jewelry website (`www.theologos.gr/en.html`) would not make for a good site to demonstrate how most e-commerce sites selling low-end products should be crafted. The site is mostly Flash, takes a long time to navigate, and is full of high-resolution images, yet one feels they are entering a website full of luxurious products.

While these are two extreme examples, when thinking of redesigning your website or changing the sales experience, do not assume your marketing and design teams know best. Create a few design variations to see which one helps you reach your marketing goals.

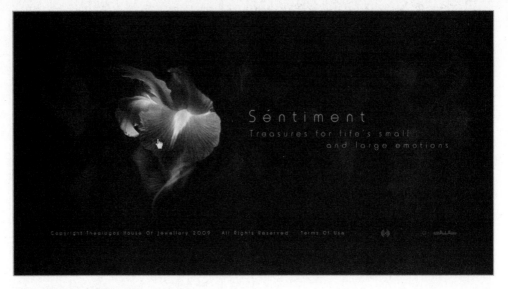

Figure 15.22 Theologos' English homepage

Ensuring Easy Information Retrieval, Not Perfection

Do not get caught up in creating landing pages that cost more to design than you can afford. You can spend thousands of dollars creating each landing page variation to test. For some companies, that price point fits into their marketing budget. For others, it does not. Your pages do not have to be perfect Flash pages that mimic the Theologos House of Jewelry site. Your landing pages need to quickly and easily convey the information necessary for someone to get the answer to their question and make a conversion decision (Figure 15.23).

This landing page, created by R.H. Donnelley for Royal Volkswagen, is not an expensive Flash-driven landing page. It is a clean landing page that tells a consumer what the company does, shows their service area, and offers several conversion options. In the case of this site, the dark-colored navigation bar is actually a conversion bar. The consumer's options are

- Send to friend
- Send to phone
- Add to address book
- Add to bookmarks
- Print the page

You would not accuse this page of being an expensive-looking landing page or one that is hard to create. However, it is an effective page as it quickly conveys information to the consumer in a friendly, easy-to-digest manner.

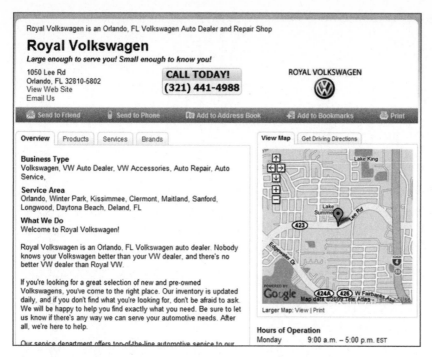

Figure 15.23 Logically organized landing page for Royal Volkswagen

Essential Items to Test First

When deciding which pages to test first, start with your landing pages that receive the most traffic. Even small gains in conversion rates for pages with high traffic will help increase your profits. The other pages you should start testing are ones that have the highest potential of profits. This might be a page of your top-selling products, your sales pages, or your high-margin products.

Once you have started testing the beginning part of the funnel, test the second step of the funnel. Do not start with the second or third steps. If someone does not make it from step 1 to step 2 of your funnel, it does not matter how good your secondary pages are.

The main items to start testing are:

- Headline
- Hero shot (the picture on your page, either a person or a product image)
- Page layout
- Call-to-action
- Custom benefit
- Navigation

When thinking about your layout, additional items to test would be:

- Color scheme
- Logo
- Authority and trust icons
- Product or service descriptions

Once you have decided what you are going to test, it is time to set up your test.

Creating a Landing Page Test

There are two ways to test landing pages: an A/B test and multivariate testing.

A/B Test This is where you have two versions of a page and you send some traffic to page A and some traffic to page B. This method is good for testing websites with low traffic or testing where to send the traffic before testing different page layouts.

Multivariate Testing This testing methodology allows you to test several variables at once. For instance, you may have two headlines, two hero shots, two customer benefits, and two calls to action. Testing two variations of four variables is 16 different tests. Multivariate testing requires a significant amount of traffic.

Google offers a calculator, available at www.google.com/analytics/siteopt/siteopt/help/calculator.html, to determine how long it will take to complete a multivariate test based on various inputs. In the multivariate example, if the page only received 100 visitors a day and has a 5 percent conversion rate, and we were expecting a 30 percent lift in conversions, it would take 651 days for the test to be completed (Figure 15.24).

Estimate Test Duration	
16	# Test combinations
100	# Page views per day
100	% Visitors in experiment
5	% Current conversion rate
30	% Expected improvement
Duration: 651.04 days.	

Figure 15.24 Website Optimizer Test duration calculator

Creating a test that will take almost two years before you can expect results is not the way to start testing. Instead, if that page had only two versions, such as found in A/B testing, it would only take 31 days (Figure 15.25) to see results from the experiment. Multivariate tests show confidence and lift factors by testing variable combinations. While this might sound complex, many systems such as Google's Website Optimizer do the page serving and the math for you.

Estimate Test Duration	
2	# Test combinations
100	# Page views per day
100	% Visitors in experiment
5	% Current conversion rate
30	% Expected improvement
Duration: 31.42 days.	

Figure 15.25 Duration calculator for two variables

An easy way to get started with multivariate testing is to use Google's free Website Optimizer. Google Website Optimizer is integrated into Google AdWords and allows for easy multivariate tests. For our purposes, I will illustrate setting up a straightforward A/B test in AdWords without going through the technical implementation of Website Optimizer to show how easy it is to start testing your website. Testing is not difficult—the hard part is determining what to test.

Creating A/B Landing Page Tests in AdWords

The first step, just like with ad testing, is to make sure that you are using the rotate campaign settings. You want each test to receive equal exposure. Next, choose two or three pages where you want to send traffic.

Finally, navigate to the ad group where you want to set up the test. Duplicate your existing ad a second or third time, depending on how many different pages you want to test. Then change the destination URLs of the new ads to send traffic to the new pages you want to test (Figure 15.26).

Figure 15.26 Use the same ad copy to send traffic to different pages.

Just as with ad testing, wait until you have enough data to obtain statistical significance by using chi-square or ANOVA in Excel, or the guidelines from the ad copy testing section earlier, "General Guidelines for Statistical Significance."

Make Sure Your Duplicate Pages Are Not Crawled

If you use the same content on multiple pages within your site, you can cause issues for your organic rankings. As Google will find two variations of the same content, they will choose which page to rank on your website. The focus of PPC landing pages should be conversions. If you also do SEO, you often need to change page elements based on search engine ranking factors that might not increase conversion rates. Therefore, you might have two sets of similar pages on your website: one set for PPC and the other for SEO. If this happens on your website, use your `robots.txt` file to block your testing pages from being crawled by the organic spiders.

Once you have enough data, run a Destination URL performance report (Figure 15.27), which is found under the Dimensions tab, using at a minimum these data points:

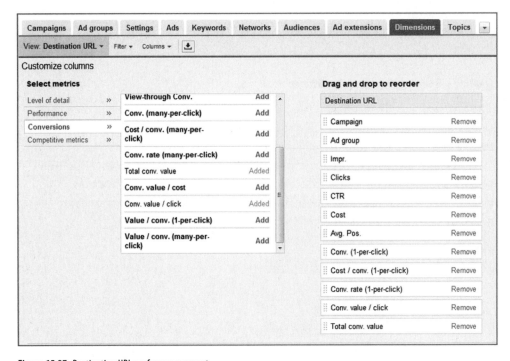

Figure 15.27 Destination URL performance report

Level of Detail

- Campaign
- Ad Group

Performance Statistics

- Impressions

- Clicks
- CTR
- Cost
- Avg Position

Conversion Columns

- Conversions (1-per-click)
- Conv. Rate (1-per-click)
- Cost/Conv. (1-per-click)
- Conv. Value/Click
- Total Conv. Value

If you have multiple conversion types, choose the various conversion actions for which you want to see performance data to determine how well the page converted.

Examine the landing page metrics and compare those metrics to the goals you are trying to reach. There is no best landing page. If you want the most conversions, the highest conversion rate is your best page. If you are looking for minimizing lead cost, examine your lowest cost per conversion.

It is essential when running either ad copy or landing pages tests that you do not combine search and display data. Figure 15.28 shows the results from a narrow theme site test.

	A	B	C	D	E	H	I	J	K	L
1		CPC	Impressions	Clicks	CTR	Conversion Rate	Cost Conversion	Revenue	Value Per Click	ROI
2	**All Networks**									
3	Home Page	$1.16	984,043	18,932	1.92%	8.73%	$13.34	$82,600	$4.36	375%
4	PPC Dedicated Page	$1.22	972,954	17,043	1.75%	10.70%	$11.42	$91,150	$5.35	438%
5										
6	**Search**									
7	Home Page	$2.23	43,565	4,065	9.33%	16.68%	$13.35	$33,900	$8.34	374%
8	PPC Dedicated Page	$1.90	40,785	4,251	10.42%	9.48%	$19.99	$20,150	$4.74	250%
9										
10	**Content**									
11	Home Page	$0.87	940,478	14,867	1.58%	6.55%	$13.34	$48,700	$3.28	375%
12	PPC Dedicated Page	$1.00	932,169	12,792	1.37%	11.10%	$8.99	$71,000	$5.55	556%

Figure 15.28 Narrow theme landing page test data

If you were to combine all data regardless of whether the metrics came from search or display, it would appear that the PPC dedicated page would be the best page, as its ROI, value per click, cost per conversion, and conversion rate are all better numbers than the homepage.

When someone is engaged in search, they have thought about the products or services associated with their search. They are somewhere within the buying funnel. In this case, you see that the homepage led to a higher conversion rate than the PPC dedicated landing page.

The PPC dedicated landing page was a page that showcased a specific offer to the user. It had fewer navigation elements than the homepage and did not explain multiple sides of the business. It had one call-to-action and explained only half the business. For the display network, the PPC dedicated landing page converted much better than the homepage, which converted better for search users.

 Note: I conducted an informal survey of PPC experts on this experiment. Almost all of them thought the PPC landing page would do better. This result is the reason you test. Conventional wisdom is not always correct. Ideas will get you started thinking about layouts that will increase conversions. However, the data will give you conclusive results on which test result is best for your company.

Testing Profit per Click and Profit per Impression

Which combination leads to higher profits?

- High CTR, many visitors, low conversion rate
- Low CTR, few visitors, high conversion rate

When you start to combine several metrics together, it can start to become overwhelming to determine which keyword, ad copy, and landing page combination leads to the highest profits for your company.

A searcher's query sets their expectations for the search results page. The ad copy on the search results page sets the expectation for the landing page. The landing page needs to be an extension of the ad copy and answer the searcher's initial question. Therefore, all of these elements affect each other. There is a way to boil down these various metrics to a single number that will tell you which combination is the most profitable.

This leads to my absolute favorite testing metrics: profit per click or profit per impression.

Every time your ad is shown on a search, you have a chance of a conversion. You chose a keyword. Someone searched for that keyword. Your ad was shown on a search page. You have a chance of converting that visitor. Therefore, you should measure how much profit you make on a search result every single time your ad is shown, even when it does not receive the click. This is known as profit per impression.

On the display network, you do not know the intent of the user. Some people are reading the articles, or the ad is well below the fold. In these cases, you should measure profit per click. However, when you use placement targeting on the display network, as you are choosing specific sites on which you want your ad shown, you should measure profit per impression.

When you measure profit per click/impression, what you want to know is how ad and landing page combinations affect your total profits. Therefore, you will combine a landing page and an ad test together. To set up this test, follow these simple steps (Figure 15.29):

1. Write two ads.

2. Choose two landing pages.

3. Send ad copy 1 to landing page 1.

4. Duplicate ad 1 and send it to landing page 2.

5. Write ad2 and send it to landing page 1.

6. Duplicate ad 2 and send it to landing page 2.

Figure 15.29 Profit per click ad group setup

Once the test is set up, let it accumulate the necessary data for you to make a decision. When you have enough data, run an ad performance report with the same data points as in the ad copy testing section earlier, "Measuring the Results of Your Ad Test."

Export the report to a spreadsheet and add these three columns (Figure 15.30):

- Profit = Revenue – Cost (or other calculations you complete with margins)

- Profit per Impression = Profit × Impressions

- Profit per Click = Profit × Clicks

	Test Name	CPC	Impressions	Clicks	CTR	Cost	Conversions	Conversion Rate	Cost Conversion	Revenue	Profit	Profit Per Impression	Profit Per Click
2	Ad Copy 1												
3	Test 1 Landing Page 1	$0.73	376,023	22,034	5.86%	$16,032	1511	6.86%	$10.61	$75,550	$59,518	$0.16	$2.70
4	Test 2 Landing Page 2	$0.92	378,094	24,955	6.60%	$23,034	1823	7.31%	$12.64	$91,150	$68,116	$0.18	$2.73
5													
6	Ad Copy 2												
7	Test 3 Landing Page 1	$0.62	312,918	26,013	8.31%	$16,023	1103	4.24%	$14.53	$55,150	$39,127	$0.13	$1.50
8	Test 4 Landing Page 2	$1.16	369,447	18,991	5.14%	$22,034	1701	8.96%	$12.95	$85,050	$63,016	$0.17	$3.32

Figure 15.30 Profit per Click/Impression spreadsheet

In Figure 15.30, you can see that Test 2 has the highest profit per impression. This test does not have the highest CTR, conversion rate, or lowest cost per conversion. However, all the metrics combined lead to the most profitable user experience for either search or site targeting.

If you take this report to the extreme and look at total profit as if each combination received all the possible impressions (Figure 15.31), you can see how much profit each test combination would have received.

	A	B	C	D	E	F	G	H	I	J	K	L	M	N
1	Test Name		CPC	Impressions	Clicks	CTR	Cost	Conversions	Conversion Rate	Cost Conversion	Revenue	Profit	Profit Per Impression	Profit Per Cilck
2		Ad Copy 1												
3	Test 1	Landing Page 1	$0.73	1,436,482	84,174	5.86%	$61,245	5772	6.86%	$10.61	$288,616	$227,370	$0.16	$2.70
4	Test 2	Landing Page 2	$0.92	1,436,482	94,811	6.60%	$87,512	6926	7.31%	$12.64	$346,304	$258,791	$0.18	$2.73
5														
6		Ad Copy 2												
7	Test 3	Landing Page 1	$0.62	1,436,482	119,415	8.31%	$73,555	5063	4.24%	$14.53	$253,172	$179,616	$0.13	$1.50
8	Test 4	Landing Page 2	$1.16	1,436,482	73,841	5.14%	$85,672	6614	8.96%	$12.95	$330,691	$245,018	$0.17	$3.32

Figure 15.31 Extrapolated profit if each test received all available impressions

Test 2 would have led to $258,791 in profit, which is $13,773 higher than the next most profitable combination, Test 4. Using profit per impression numbers is one of the best ways to understand which testing combination leads to the highest profits.

You do not have to follow the exact steps of creating two landing pages and two ads to do profit per impression and click testing. Whenever you run a test and you do not know which test is best for you, just divide the total impressions for each test by the profit for each test and see which is higher. This could be two ads and one landing page, one ad copy and five landing pages, or other combinations.

The testing methodologies you have seen so far require you to add new ads to an ad group and split your traffic in half. If you have profitable ad groups right now, you are taking a lot of risk that the new combinations will lead to similar or higher profit margins than you already have. There are ways to lower your risk threshold when testing new ads or landing pages.

AdWords Campaign Experiments

AdWords Campaign Experiments (ACE) allow you to test a subset of your traffic. This is a good way to test various settings such as bids, match types, ads, and landing pages—especially in high-traffic or high-profit ad groups.

The way ACE works is that you will define how often you want the test versus the control to run (Figure 15.32) in the Campaign settings. You can optionally set start and end dates.

Once you save the experiment, it will not be active until you launch it. You need to navigate through the campaign and choose what should be control only or experiment only.

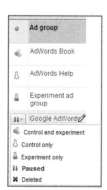

Figure 15.32 AdWords Experiment settings

By default, if something is paused, it will remain paused. All other enabled items will be set to control and experiment. If you want something to always be displayed, make sure it is set to both control and experiment.

What happens is that for every auction, Google looks at your control versus experiment settings to decide which to use. In Figure 15.32 we chose experiment 30 percent of the time and control 70 percent of the time. Therefore, at the beginning of an auction 70 percent of the time Google will treat only the items in our control data as being active; 30 percent of the time, Google will treat the items in our experiment as being active. When items are marked as experiment and control, they will always be considered active.

You can set control, experiment, or control and experiment settings by keyword, ad, or ad groups. Next to each data point, you will see additional options (Figure 15.33).

Figure 15.33 Choosing the control and experiment settings

In this instance, the ad group AdWords Book will run all of the time as it's listed as Control And Experiment. The ad group AdWords Help will be treated as active in

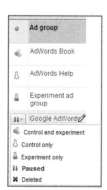

70 percent of the auctions. The ad group Experiment Ad Group will only be treated as active in 30 percent of the auctions.

If you wanted to test ad copy, you could either create an ad group that only contained your experimental ads or you could mark each ad you are testing as experimental. Either method would achieve the same results of mitigating risk and controlling how often your test data is displayed.

The Low-Tech Approach to Lowering Test Risks

ACE is a great way to test if you only want to test a few items at a time. However, the weakness of ACE is that you can have only one experiment running at a time. Therefore, if you are testing ads in ten ad groups, and you have enough data to end the test in four ad groups but not the other six, you cannot just end those four tests. You have to end all of them or leave them all running.

The low-tech approach to mitigating risk is to first duplicate the existing ad several times. Wait for the ads to be approved by Google, and then add just one new test ad.

For instance, if you duplicate an existing ad three times and then have only one test ad (as shown in the following illustration), the established ads will be served 75 percent of the time and the test ad 25 percent of the time (assuming you are using Rotate as your ad copy setting). This will create a scenario where you are only putting 25 percent of your existing revenue at risk.

Established Ad Copy

{KeyWord:Chicago AdWords Seminars}
Learn AdWords Success in just 1 day
Limited Seats. Reserve Yours Today!
bgTheory.com

{KeyWord:Chicago AdWords Seminars}
Learn AdWords Success in just 1 day
Limited Seats. Reserve Yours Today!
bgTheory.com

{KeyWord:Chicago AdWords Seminars}
Learn AdWords Success in just 1 day
Limited Seats. Reserve Yours Today!
bgTheory.com

Test Ad Copy

Chicago AdWords Seminars
Learn AdWords Success in just 1 day
Limited Seats. Reserve Yours Today!
bgTheory.com

You can do the same risk mitigation for landing page testing. Duplicate the established ad several times and send all of those ads to your existing landing page where you know your profits. Then duplicate the ad one last time and only send the traffic from that single ad to the test page. If you only wanted to test 10 percent of the traffic, you would have nine ads going to your established landing page and only one ad going to the test page.

Once you have defined all of your tests, navigate back to the Experiment section in your Campaign settings (Figure 15.34) and launch the experiment.

Figure 15.34 Launching the experiment

Now that you have collected enough data to make decisions, you can end the experiment and choose your winners, delete your losers, and create your next test.

Best Practices for Testing Techniques That Will Increase Profits

Testing ad copy and landing pages is essential to maximizing the potential of your AdWords account. The most important thing with testing is to just start doing it. It is not difficult to test. Search behavior changes over time. Your competition will be changing their ads, landing pages, and offers. If you do not test ad copy and landing pages, you will never realize the full potential of your AdWords account or website.

By following the instructions in this chapter, you will be able to create both ad and landing page tests that will increase your profits and show you which of your marketing elements resonate best with your customers.

- When testing, make sure your campaign is set to Rotate so all the ads receive equal exposure.

- Start by writing different types of ads, such as question, review, and informational ads.

- Always filter your reports to see search only or display only data.

- When you have statistical significance, run an ad performance report and examine the data. Keep the best ad in your ad group. Examine the data from the losing ads to see if you can learn anything. Delete the losing ads, and then create new ads to continue the cycle of testing.

- On the display network, if you find that certain ads only perform better on specific sites, use those ads in conjunction with managed placements.

- When testing landing pages, first test where on your site you should send the traffic.
- Once you are certain where to send visitors on your website, create different layouts for your landing pages and test which one performs better.
- Use the Destination URL performance report to see which page is best. You may see different pages perform best for the display network or search network.
- If you are testing multiple metrics at once or are focused on profits, use profit per impression/click testing.
- If you have established ad groups, test a smaller percentage of your traffic to lessen the risk of losing profits.

When you first start testing, it is not uncommon to see dramatic changes. This is often because it is the first time you may have thought about how searchers view and interact with your ads and landing pages. Over time, your improvements will be smaller, yet every improvement continues to increase your profits—so never stop testing.

In this chapter, you used the ad performance report and the URL performance report to examine data. AdWords offers many different reports. In the next chapter, you will delve deeper into the reports to learn what type of data can be extracted from AdWords and the best uses of that data.

AdWords Reports: Extracting Actionable Information

16

Your AdWords account will accumulate a variety of statistics that are available through the AdWords reporting interface. Creating a report consists of three steps: understanding what you need to know, extracting the data from AdWords, and analyzing the report. In this chapter, you will learn how to create a report, and then take an in-depth look into each of the reports and learn how to use them to improve your account's performance.

Chapter Contents

Choosing general AdWords report settings
Using reports to optimize your account
Custom alerts
Best practices for using AdWords reports

Choosing General AdWords Report Settings

Google allows you to extract a plethora of data about your AdWords account's performance. To download the data, you must take a few steps. You first need to customize the interface—a report will mimic the interface—choose your time frame, and then segment the data if necessary.

This section initially focuses on preparing the interface to include the data you wish to examine, and then looks at the most common reports in detail and discusses their best uses.

Customizing the Interface

The first choice you need to make is what type of data you wish to see. For example, if you want to see campaign data, navigate to the Campaign tab. And if you want to see keyword data, navigate to the Keywords tab.

If you do not see a tab listed, click on the silver arrow at the end of the tabs (Figure 16.1) to enable additional tabs to be displayed by default.

Figure 16.1 Viewing additional tabs

It may not be obvious where you'd find some reports, such as for geographic or demographic data. These additional reports are mostly stored under the Dimensions tab (Figure 16.2).

Figure 16.2 Dimensions tab reports

Some tabs offer secondary reports, such as the search query data for keywords or the automatic and managed placement reports for the display network. You will learn how to download these secondary reports in the "Using Reports to Optimize Your Account" section later in this chapter.

Finally, you will also want to choose a time frame for the data being displayed. The time frame dictates the range of data you are seeing. If you see a set of data that does not make sense, it is often related to the date range.

For instance, in the ad data you can see the percentage of an ad served. If you create a new ad and the next week log into your account and see that the new ad has never been served, you might be wondering why (assuming the ad has not been disapproved by Google). If the date range you are examining includes only data from the previous month when the ad was not in the account, it has to be served zero percent of the time because the ad was not live during that time frame.

To customize the time frame, click on the Custom Date Range box (Figure 16.3) and choose your time frame.

Once you have chosen your time frame and navigated to the proper tab for the data you wish to see, it is time to customize the data being displayed.

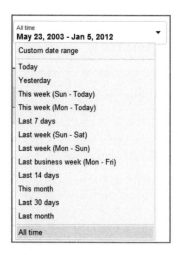

Figure 16.3 Customizing your time frame

Customizing Columns

To customize the data, you will need to select the column data necessary for you to analyze. To start, click the Columns button and choose Customize Columns, as shown in Figure 16.4.

Figure 16.4 Customizing the columns

The column options will vary for each tab, but two sets of columns are available in most reports: Performance and Conversions. Here are the most common column selections you will see:

Performance Basic data such as clicks, CTR, CPC, and cost.

Conversions All the data based on conversion tracking.

Call Details Phone call data if you are using any of the call options.

Competitive Metrics High-level data based on both your and your competitors' data.

Campaign Settings Only shown in the Settings tab. This is an easy way to see all the settings at once.

Ad Attributes Available only for the Ads tab. You can see the ad type, ad ID, and image ad URLs.

Level of Detail This option is mostly found within dimension reports where you might want to segment by campaign or ad group, and report specific data such as gender for demographic data, cities for geographic data, or match types for search term data.

Attributes Typically used for adding destination URL to various reports.

In the interface, select the columns you wish to see in the report and add them. As you add columns, you will also see a list of all the columns that will be displayed. You can drag and drop the columns to easily reorder them (Figure 16.5).

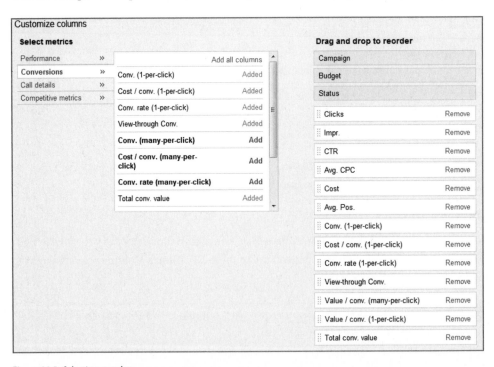

Figure 16.5 Selecting your data

If you have a set of columns you intend to use multiple times, you can save it. That way, when you click Customize Columns in the future, your selections will be available.

Finally, click Save and you will be presented with all the data you wish to see. However, working with large data sets within the interface can be overwhelming. Often you will want to download the data to easily manipulate it within a spreadsheet program.

Downloading Your Data

The next step to extracting data from AdWords is to click the Download Report icon, as shown in Figure 16.6.

Figure 16.6 Clicking Download Report

In the resulting Download And Schedule Report screen, you are presented with several more options. First, you can choose the report's format, such as PDF, CSV, or XLM. If you are working in Microsoft Excel, choose Excel CSV.

Next, you can segment the data. If you segmented the data within the interface, that segment will be displayed by default. However, the interface will only show one segment at a time. When you download the data, you can segment the data multiple times.

For instance, if you are running a test with AdWords Campaign Experiments on mobile devices to see the difference in clicks versus calls, you will want to segment by device (mobile, tablet, desktop), click type (call, click, direction, sitelink, etc.), and experiment (ACE), as shown in Figure 16.7.

Figure 16.7 Segmenting the report data

Be careful to avoid over-segmenting the data. Every time you segment the data, you are adding more rows to the output file. If you add too much data, you could be overwhelmed by the number of rows and not know where to start. In cases like that, run the report again with less segmentation until you start to become comfortable looking at multiple segments at once.

If you are going to create the same report multiple times, be sure to name the report. When you run a report, it will also be displayed in the Reports screen as the name you used with the option Run Now or Create Similar.

Finally, in the Email And Schedule Report section, you can choose who to notify when a report runs. You can also specify that you want to have the report automatically created and choose a Frequency setting, as shown in Figure 16.8.

Once you have specified the options, create the report and soon you will have a download file to work from. You can always visit the Reports screen (Figure 16.9) to change your report names, notifications, or frequency, and to run the same or a similar report again.

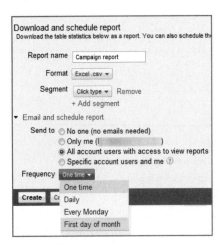

Figure 16.8 Email And Schedule Report options

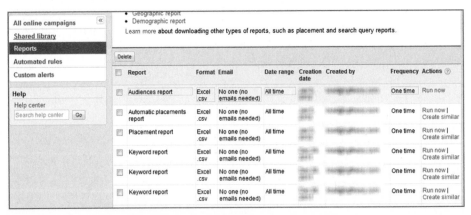

Figure 16.9 Created reports data

Next, we'll look at all the major reports and see various uses of the data to optimize your AdWords account.

Using Reports to Optimize Your Account

Now that you can download and extract data from AdWords, it is important to learn how to take advantage of the various reports so that you make the best use of your valuable time in analyzing your account.

With most of these reports, if you want to visualize the data utilizing conditional formatting, refer to Chapter 13, "Profitable Bid Strategies," in the section "Revenue per Click," to see how to color-code your data so you can easily see what is making—or losing—you money.

Campaign Reports

Campaign reports allow you to see quick snapshots of all your campaigns at once. This report is valuable if you have a large account and need quick access to high-level data.

However, since most of your decisions will be made at the ad group, placement, and keyword levels, these reports should not be used for making bid decisions. The purpose of running a Campaign report is to view performance statistics that are only shown at the campaign level. You will find these statistics in the Invalid Clicks and Impression Share reports.

Invalid Clicks Report

Under Performance in the Customize Columns section are two selections: Invalid Clicks and Invalid Clicks Rate. These statistics show you how many clicks you received for which you were not charged, as well as the percentage of total clicks that were not charged.

> **Note:** If you are trying to reconcile your analytics data with AdWords, this is a useful report to examine. Analytics systems include all visitors who made it to your website regardless of whether you were charged for that click. AdWords automatically discounts certain clicks from costing you money or accruing statistics within your account.

Impression Share Report

Under Competitive Metrics in the Customize Columns section are the following data points: Impr. [Impression] Share, Exact Match IS, Lost (IS) Budget, and Lost IS (Rank), as shown in Figure 16.10. If you choose all of these options and run a report, you will create an Impression Share report.

Figure 16.10 Impression share selections

The Impression Share report will show you how often your ads are being shown and reasons they are not being displayed:

Impression Share (IS) The percentage of times your ad was shown when it was eligible for the auction

Lost IS (Rank) The percentage of times your ad was not shown because your ad's position was below the number of ads displayed on a page

Lost IS (Budget) The percentage of times your ad was not shown because your budget was too low

Exact Match IS Your impression share if all your keywords were set to exact match

If you ever wonder how much an account could spend if you increased the budget, the Impression Share report is the place to look. This report is also a great place to determine what needs the most attention in an account: Quality Score or bids.

Ad rank is determined by both bid and Quality Score. If you examine your account and find that most of your impressions are lost due to rank, that means one of those numbers needs to improve. If you put your Quality Scores in a pivot table (refer to the section "Healthy Quality Score Accounts" in Chapter 7, "Demystifying Quality Score," for more information) and find that most of your Quality Scores are 7 or higher, you will need to increase bids to receive more exposure. If most of your Quality Scores are below 7, you need to spend more time on improving Quality Score.

If you are losing most of your impressions due to budget and you cannot increase your budget, then you are probably overbidding. If you have a $100 daily budget with $1 CPCs, that means you will receive roughly 100 clicks per day. If you were to decrease your CPC to $0.75, you could receive 133 clicks a day. Since ad position has little effect on conversion rates, those additional clicks should result in additional conversions. Of course, there does come a point where you can lower your bid too much to be on page one and you will not receive any clicks. There is a balancing act between CPC, clicks, and budget to find the best spots for you.

Ad Group Performance Report

Sometimes seeing keyword-level information is data intensive and you might want to see a higher level of information. The Ad Group Performance report is a good place to start.

Setting Ad Group Bids

If you are setting ad group–level bids instead of keyword-level bids for the search network, you can use the Ad Group Performance report to determine your max CPC calculations and then use the AdWords Editor to import the new bids into AdWords.

Setting Display Network Bids

You cannot set keyword-level bids for the display network; you can only set bids by placement or ad group. Therefore, when doing calculations for display network exposure (except for placement targeting), Ad Group Performance is a useful report to run to determine your max display CPC. You can do the same analysis under the Networks tab as well.

Ad Performance Report

The Ad Performance report allows you to see metrics for each of your ads. If you are testing ad copy, this is the report you will want to use. When you run an Ad Performance report, look in the Attributes section of the Customize Columns section to select ad types so that you can see the difference between text, image, Wireless Application Protocol (WAP), and other ad formats.

Be sure to segment the data by network so that you only examine search data or display data. Do not combine the metrics for search and display together.

If your account does not accrue enough clicks per month for you to be able to test individual ads at the ad group level, and instead you use a tagline in several ads across your account, follow these steps to create the report necessary for you to analyze the data:

1. Create an Ad Performance report that includes the following:
   Headline
   Description line 1
   Description line 2
   Display URL
   Impression
   Clicks
   Average CPC
   Cost
   Conversions
   Conversion rate
   Cost per conversion
2. Export the data to a spreadsheet.
3. Create a pivot table from the spreadsheet.

4. Choose your ad element (such as headline or description line 1) as your row element.

5. Add the metrics (impressions, clicks, etc.) as your values.

Follow these steps to create a pivot table that shows all of the metrics associated with an ad element (see Figure 16.11), so you can make decisions about which element of the ad copy is working best for your account.

Row Labels	Values Average of CTR	Average of Cost per Conversion	Average of Conversion Rate
AdWords Seminars for Success™	5.34%	$15.21	7.23%
Easy & Free Subscription Options	5.10%	$17.78	5.23%
Hosted by Brad 'eWhisper' Geddes	4.65%	$8.28	11.23%
Knowledge, Training, and Sales	2.12%	$16.90	9.23%
Learn AdWords Success	3.43%	$55.16	2.23%
Learn AdWords Success for Only $249	1.54%	$17.67	6.34%
Limited Seats. Reserve Yours Today!	4.45%	$25.11	2.23%
Limited space. Reserve seats now!	8.23%	$6.95	11.23%
Max your AdWords ROI for Only $249!	6.32%	$8.90	10.23%
Max your AdWords ROI.	2.23%	$7.78	17.23%
One Day Only. Register Online Now!	4.43%	$133.91	1.15%
Grand Total	**4.35%**	**$28.51**	**7.60%**

Figure 16.11 Pivot table for an Ad Performance report

Although making decisions based on combining the data from various ads into a single report is not nearly as useful as examining individual ad copy results within a single ad group, it is better than not testing at all.

Using this method without manipulating the data is useful if your ads have fairly similar impression, clicks, and conversion data in the different ad groups where they appear. If you find that the ads have large differences in CTR or conversion rates in various ad groups, you should use a weighted average for the data before examining it in a pivot table. You can use the same method discussed in Chapter 7 to create weighted averages. Just substitute the data columns from this report.

The Ad Performance report allows you to see how ads are doing by ad group or campaign. However, it will not tell you how an ad is doing on a specific placement. If there are placements where you are receiving a significant amount of high-quality traffic and you want to test different ads on those specific sites, put just those sites, or even a single placement, in an ad group along with your test ads. This approach will allow you to create an ad report that only includes that specific ad group so you can see how multiple ads are performing on an individual placement.

Find Underperforming Ads

Another use for the Ad Performance report is to identify underperforming ads. Run an Ad Performance report for only the search network. Each report will contain summary information where you can locate your account's click-through rate, conversion rate, and cost per conversion. Then look to see which individual ads are below your account's norm.

Before you assume that these ads are underperforming compared to your account, always examine the keywords that are causing these ads to show. You will find instances where an ad group had more general keywords than other ad groups, in which case it is normal to see the CTR and conversion rate lower than the account's norm.

However, if the keywords are as specific as other ad groups, and those ads have lower conversion rates, either the ad needs to be tested or the landing page should be changed. Always look at the keyword or placement, ad copy, and landing page together when determining performance.

Find All Disapproved or Paused Ads

On the Ads tab, you can filter to see only disapproved ads or paused ads (Figure 16.12). Ads can be disapproved for a variety of reasons. When an ad is disapproved, then it is not running. If an ad group only contains disapproved or paused ads, then you are currently not showing for those keywords. When you filter and then download the data, only the filtered data is included in the report. If you have seasonal or month-end sales-based ads that you pause and resume on a regular basis, this report makes it easy to find all of your ads in a paused or disapproved state.

Figure 16.12 Filtering ads by approval status

In addition, if you have had several ads disapproved, you can filter only for disapproved ads so you know which ad groups need new ads.

Keyword Report

If you want to see keyword information, start by downloading data from the Keywords tab. You can use this data to analyze your account in the following ways:

Set Keyword Level Bids If you set bids for each keyword based on its returns, run this report and include keyword, match type, cost per conversion, value per click, and total revenue stats. Next, use the formulas in Chapter 13 in the section "Calculating Your Max CPC" to determine your new CPCs. Finally, input this data into a spreadsheet and use the AdWords Editor to upload your new CPCs.

If you have a significant number of keywords where the bid would have to be $0.00 based on your conversion metrics, you will have to choose to delete those keywords, set your own bid not based on conversion metrics, or move it to a Budget Optimizer campaign (see "Understanding Attribution Management" in Chapter 13).

Improving Your Quality Score If your Quality Score is under 7, you should continue to optimize your score. Run a keyword report and include the Ad Group, Keyword, Cost, and Quality Score columns. Then input the data into a pivot table and look for ad groups with low Quality Scores and high spends. This will help you find pockets of high-opportunity areas to increase your Quality Score. For full details on this procedure, see the section "Increasing Your Quality Scores" in Chapter 7.

Determining What Keywords Are Not on Page 1 Some keywords may have limited impressions and low conversions because they are not on page 1. To quickly view what keywords are not on page 1, create a keyword report with the Keyword, Match Type, First Page Bid, and Max CPC columns. Then use conditional formatting to highlight keywords where the max CPC is below the first page bid. You may want to increase these CPCs so that the keywords receive enough impressions for you to make determinations about their effectiveness.

Top versus Other Data It is common to see vastly different click-through rates when your ads are on the top versus the side or bottom of the page. You can segment the keyword data to show the difference between top versus other data. When you run this report, it is also useful to include the estimated first page bid and the estimated top page bid so you can see the difference in estimated CPCs.

Search Query Report

If you use broad or phrase match keywords, your ads will show for a variety of words that are not in your account. The Search Query report will show you what someone actually searched for that caused your ads to be displayed. If you use AdWords conversion tracking, you can see the conversion rate and cost per conversion for all of these keyword variations.

To see this data, navigate to the Keywords tab and click See Search Terms, as shown in Figure 16.13. You can either click next to a word to see the search terms for that particular word, or you can view all the search terms at once.

Figure 16.13 Viewing search query data

You should run this report regularly and look for two specific pieces of information:

Search Queries That Cost You Money but Do Not Convert With broad and phase match keywords, your ads will be shown on a variety of queries. Some of those variations will convert and others will not.

When you find variations that are spending money and not converting, you should determine whether the keyword that is triggering the search query is appropriate to that ad copy and landing page. If the keyword is not appropriate to that ad group but is appropriate to another one, then add the keyword as a negative in the first ad group and as a positive keyword in the more appropriate ad group. Later, run a keyword report and either choose to keep that keyword in the more appropriate ad group or delete the keyword altogether once it accumulates more data. Because you still do not want this keyword shown in the first ad group, leave the negative keyword in place, or move the negative keyword to the campaign level so that none of the ad groups will show for that word.

If the search query is not appropriate to any ad group in your account, you can add it as an ad group–level or campaign-level negative keyword in whatever campaigns it may be triggered so that your ad will not be displayed for that search query again.

Search Queries That Convert but Are Not in the Ad Group If you find there are search queries that are converting but are nowhere to be found in your ad group, add these variations as positive keywords so you can track their performance and set appropriate bids for each keyword.

Whenever you are conducting positive or negative keyword research, start with the Search Query report. Viewing search queries can give you insight into your customers and trigger new ideas for keywords.

Network Reports

When you are working with the display network, you have several ways to extract data to determine how your automatic and managed placements are performing.

When you first navigate to the Networks tab, you can see how Google Search, search partners, managed placements, and automatic placements are performing (Figure 16.14).

Campaigns	Ad groups	Settings	Ads	Keywords	**Networks**	Dimensions

All but deleted managed placements ▾   Segment ▾   Filter ▾   Columns ▾

	Clicks ⑦	Impr.	CTR ⑦	Avg. CPC ⑦	Cost	Conv. (1-per-click) ⑦	Cost / conv. (1-per-click) ⑦	Conv. rate (1-per-click) ⑦	View-through Conv. ⑦
Search	5,171,674	294,043,653	1.76%	$0.78	$4,048,299.35	80,626	$41.88	2.57%	0
Google search	4,120,406	184,302,596	2.24%	$0.78	$3,215,110.86	58,974	$44.37	2.54%	0
Search partners ⑦	1,051,268	109,741,057	0.96%	$0.79	$833,188.49	21,652	$35.08	2.66%	0
Display Network	2,001,271	3,387,562,250	0.06%	$0.73	$1,457,785.09	37,769	$38.12	1.94%	2,289
▪ Managed placements ⑦ show details	145,626	267,964,573	0.05%	$0.89	$129,707.10	2,580	$50.27	1.77%	561
▪ Automatic placements ⑦ show details	1,855,645	3,119,597,677	0.06%	$0.72	$1,328,077.99	35,189	$37.22	1.96%	1,728
Total - All networks	7,172,945	3,681,605,903	0.19%	$0.77	$5,506,084.44	118,395	$40.68	2.33%	2,289

Figure 16.14 Networks tab data

To dig into the automatic or managed placement data, you need to click the Show Details link directly below the placement types. This will show you the full details for the automatic or managed placements, as shown in Figure 16.15.

Campaigns	Ad groups	Settings	Ads	Keywords	**Networks**	Dimensions

All but deleted managed placements ▾   Segment ▾   Filter ▾   Columns ▾

	Clicks ⑦	Impr.	CTR ⑦	Avg. CPC ⑦	Cost	Conv. (1-per-click) ⑦	Cost / conv. (1-per-click) ⑦	Conv. rate (1-per-click) ⑦	View-through Conv. ⑦
Search	5,171,674	294,043,653	1.76%	$0.78	$4,048,299.35	80,626	$41.88	2.57%	0
Google search	4,120,406	184,302,596	2.24%	$0.78	$3,215,110.86	58,974	$44.37	2.54%	0
Search partners ⑦	1,051,268	109,741,057	0.96%	$0.79	$833,188.49	21,652	$35.08	2.66%	0
Display Network	2,001,271	3,387,562,250	0.06%	$0.73	$1,457,785.09	37,769	$38.12	1.94%	2,289
▪ Managed placements ⑦ show details	145,626	267,964,573	0.05%	$0.89	$129,707.10	2,580	$50.27	1.77%	561
▪ Automatic placements ⑦ show details	1,855,645	3,119,597,677	0.06%	$0.72	$1,328,077.99	35,189	$37.22	1.96%	1,728
Total - All networks	7,172,945	3,681,605,903	0.19%	$0.77	$5,506,084.44	118,395	$40.68	2.33%	2,289

Figure 16.15 Automatic placement data

From here you can download the URL list to see each URL where your ad is being displayed, customize the columns to see additional data, exclude the placement, or make it a managed placement. The most common way to use this data to ensure you are receiving high-quality traffic from your automatic placements is to follow these two steps:

1. Make sure your ad is being displayed on the correct types of pages. Click on the URLs and look at the pages where Google is placing your ads.

   • If the pages are correct, regardless of the performance metrics, your keywords are creating appropriate themes and you do not need to adjust your keywords.

- If the pages where your ads are being shown are not correct, you need to adjust your keywords so that you receive better placement.

For more information on choosing display keywords, see the section "Choosing the Correct Keywords for Your Display Network Ad Groups" in Chapter 9, "Understanding the Display Network."

2. Look at the basic data at the domain level, or download the report, create a pivot table, and key the metrics off the domain:
- If you see domains that are not meeting your goals, block them.
- If you see domains that are meeting your goals, add them to a placements campaign and block them in the display only campaign.

Note: When adding sites to a placements campaign, always check to see if there are subsections of a website available for placement; if there are, look to see how your ads have done on the various subsections.

If you are seeing too many websites in this report and do not know where to start, use the filtering options to view only websites that have sent you over a minimum amount of traffic, such as 20 or more clicks. By removing sites with low traffic from the report, you can create a report that only includes websites that have enough data for you to make decisions about blocking the site or turning it into a managed placement.

After you examine the automatic placement data, you will want to study the managed placement information. With managed placements, since you are choosing exactly where your ads are being displayed, you can manage them similar to keywords. Make sure the placement is performing, and use your typical bid formulas to set bids for each placement.

Dimension Reports

Several reports are listed on the Dimensions tab. Some of them, such as Time, have multiple subsets of reports—you can see time data by day of the week, day, hour of day, month, and so forth. In addition, some reports that appear on other tabs are duplicated here, such as the automatic placements and search terms. Therefore, this section will not examine every single report on the Dimensions tab. Instead I will focus on the most common reports and ways of using that data.

Destination URL Report

The Destination URL report allows you to see metrics for every page you are sending traffic to within your AdWords account. If you are testing various landing pages, this report can show you which landing pages have the highest conversion rate.

Note that you will see metrics for every destination URL even if they are different only through tracking parameters, such as those found in the section "Step-by-Step

Guide to Building Destination URLs" in Chapter 5, "Landing Pages That Convert Searchers into Buyers." For instance, while these three links are the same page on a website, the URL Performance report will show three different lines of data in your report:

Example.com?src=4

Example.com

Example.com?matchtype=exact&{keyword}

In this case, it is useful to strip off the tracking parameters and combine the data for each URL. Follow these steps to easily strip off the tracking links:

1. Copy the Dest URL column.
2. Paste it into a new sheet.
3. Highlight the column, and select the Text To Column function on the Data tab.
4. Choose Delimited, and click Next.
5. Choose Other, and in the text box type a question mark.
6. Click Finish.
7. Copy that column and paste it into the original report.

Although this appears to be a complicated process, after you do it once or twice you will find it takes less than 10 seconds to accomplish. Since you will now have the same URL on different rows, it is time to combine the data across all the rows. The easiest way to do this is to create a pivot table. In your Row Labels, show the destination URLs. In your Value column, choose the metrics you want to see, such as cost per conversion and conversion rate.

 Note: If on your website the URL example.com?123 is a different page than example.com?1234, you may need to use a different delimiter than the question mark in the Text Import Wizard.

Another good use of the Destination URL report is identifying underperforming landing pages. You can create an average for your account and then use the same steps as you did for the ad copy analysis earlier; just substitute the destination URL for the ad copy information.

Destination URL is also the report you will want to use for checking your site for broken links. Websites change over time, so it is common to see URLs get broken. If you are sending traffic to broken pages, you are just wasting money. Run this report and then either use a tool like Certified Knowledge's Broken Link Checker or import the data into a crawler tool like Xenu and spider the URLs to see if any of your links are broken.

Viewing Conversion Rates by Time Frames

You can view your conversion rates by day of the week, day, week, month, quarter, year, or hour of the day. If you are doing analysis to determine whether you should use ad scheduling to change your bids on certain days or times of day, these reports are the best place to start that analysis.

If during your analysis you find that only a handful of ad groups change performance by time of day, you might move those ad groups to a new campaign and leave the others in the original campaign.

Demographic Report

The Demographic report on the Dimensions tab displays your performance metrics, such as click-through rate or cost per conversion by age range, gender, and website. Demographic information is currently only available for some websites in the display network.

If you run this report and see very little demographic information, do not fret—it just means your ad is on sites that do not collect or do not share demographic information with Google. Generally, only social media sites collect and share this anonymous demographic data.

> **Note:** If you run the Demographic report and see widely different conversion rates by demographics, you may want to use demographic bidding (see the section "Setting Different Bids by Demographics" in Chapter 10, "Advanced Display Network Techniques"). In addition, use the Google Ad Planner (see the section "DoubleClick Ad Planner: Free Access to Expensive Data," also in Chapter 10) to find other sites with similar demographics and content so you can use managed placements to target those similar websites.

Geographic Report

The Geographic report on the Dimensions tab allows you to see your metrics by country, region, metro, or city. You will want to segment the data by network so you can see search and display data separately.

Run this report and examine the differences in your clicks and conversions by geography. If you find there are certain geographies that are not converting, you may want to create a separate campaign to show different messages to those areas. If you find there are geographies that are converting at a much higher rate than normal, you may want to create a campaign with a higher daily budget to reach just those areas.

The Geographic report can also give you a point of investigation for your website analysis. It is not uncommon for American companies to advertise in both the United States and Canada, only to find that their Canadian conversion rates are much lower. This is because many sites do not ship to Canada or accept non-U.S. billing addresses, yet these same companies still serve ads to Canada. By using this report to find areas where your conversions are lower than normal, you can identify other errors that have nothing to do with AdWords.

One of the Quality Score factors is click-through rate in a specific geography. If you find that your CTR is much lower in a geographic region, your Quality Score for just that region may also be lower. In this case, you might want to exclude that geography or create a specific campaign with ad copy that speaks to that region to increase your CTR and visibility in that geography.

When you are trying to determine where people are clicking and buying, the Geographic report can give you insight into the performance of various geographies and help you decide whether you need to include, exclude, or change your geographic targeting options.

Reach and Frequency Report

The Reach and Frequency report is only shown for the display network. You can see the data by day, week, or month. *Reach* and *frequency* are two common metrics for media campaigns and display ads that determine how many people saw an ad and how often those people saw an ad.

If you are buying CPM, you are paying for impressions. Many CPM buys are on a set number of impressions. The lower your frequency cap, the less an individual person may see your message, but more total people will see your message for those impressions. Conversely, the more an individual person sees your message, the fewer total people will see your message.

There is a balance to be found in reinforcing your message with CPM or CPC display ads to an individual person by having them see your ad multiple times compared to the total number of people you want to see your ad.

When running remarketing campaigns, take a look at your frequency numbers to make sure you are not serving your ads too often to the same people. Remarketing can be a fantastic source for conversions. It can also be an easy way to annoy your customers if you show your ads too often to them.

There is no magic number for frequency capping. Some websites are full of distractions, and any one ad might not be noticed; in that case you would want a higher frequency. Some ads are prominent, such as interstitials or large banners on a mostly text-based page, and therefore the frequency number can be lower.

 Note: I recommend that you set a frequency cap on your ads, even if it is as high as five to seven per user per day. That will help distribute your ad to more individuals. For CPM ads, you will often set lower frequency caps than with remarketing or general display ads.

If you find that your frequency is higher than you desire, you can set or adjust the frequency cap in your Campaign settings.

Even More Reports

There are more reports to be found in AdWords, and the same data analysis applies to these additional reports. For instance, use your display bidding metrics for Audience and Topic reports. Use your keyword bidding methods for auto targets.

Between choosing the type of data you wish to see, customizing the columns, and segmenting the data, there are thousands of possible combinations of reports that you can create.

You should first determine what data you need to make sound decisions and create actionable items. Then, you should create the reports that will help you extract that data so you can analyze it and make changes that will further enhance your account's performance.

Custom Alerts

In AdWords you can create alerts to let you know when something has changed in your account. This is a useful way of getting notifications of changes so you do not have to constantly monitor your account.

You can create an alert in the Campaign, Ad Groups, Ads, and Keywords tabs. To create an alert, navigate to the appropriate tab, click the Alerts button, and choose Create A Custom Alert, as shown in Figure 16.16.

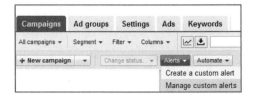

Figure 16.16 Creating a custom alert

The options you see will vary depending on the tab you choose. For instance, you can receive an alert if the percentage of daily spend has exceeded 80 percent (Figure 16.17). However, Spend is a Campaign setting so this alert is not available on the Ads tab.

You can create alerts for many different scenarios; however, receiving a plethora of emails might not be useful. It is best to identify what matters most to you and then create an alert.

For instance, here are some common custom alerts:

- Conversions increased more than 20 percent. In this case you might want to increase your budget to capture these additional conversions.

- Conversion rate decreased more than 20 percent. In this case, you might want to pause your ads and investigate.

- Percentage of spend has increased or decreased more than 20 percent. There is more or less interest in your ads and keywords and you might want to double-check your budgets.

- The number of impressions has increased or decreased more than 20 percent. Similar to your budgets, what is causing the change in impressions?

- Average CPC has increased more than 20 percent. In this case, it is likely that either your Quality Scores have dropped or your competition has increased their bids.

Figure 16.17 Custom budget alert

If you are a brand manager, you can create an alert for when your brand terms suddenly spike or drop. To do this, put all of your brand terms either in the same campaign or a set of ad groups, and then create alerts for that campaign or ad group. Once you have created alerts, you can manage all them in the Custom Alerts section, shown in Figure 16.18.

If there are certain metrics that you regularly log into your account to check on, that is the perfect opportunity to use an alert and save yourself time.

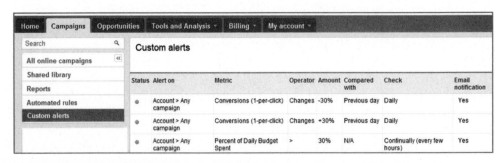

Figure 16.18 Managing custom alerts

Best Practices for Using AdWords Reports

Being able to extract actionable data from your account is essential to ongoing optimization. First determine the data you need, and then examine the available reports.

By following the practices in this chapter, you should be able to create reports that give you the data necessary to make optimization decisions for your AdWords account.

- When you find custom reports that help you make decisions, save those reports as templates so you can easily re-create the same report.
- Schedule your favorite reports to be automatically created and a notification email sent to you.
- Always segment the data so you are only viewing search data or display data. Never combine the two networks in your analysis.
- When examining managed placement and automatic placement data, you first have to show the data on the Networks tab before you can download it or make display network decisions.
- When running short on time, run an ad group report to find ad groups that are not meeting your goals. Then examine the keywords in just that ad group to determine new bid prices or move keywords into new ad groups with new ad copy.
- The URL report will show you weaknesses in your landing pages. Use this report to determine where you should be sending traffic and to check your account for broken links.
- When you want to expand your keyword list or add negative keywords, start by analyzing the Search Query report.
- If you have more data than you can analyze, try less segmentation of the data.
- If you need specific information that is not available, determine if there is another way to structure your account so you can retrieve that data. For example, if you want to see conversion rates by hour for a particular keyword, create an ad group with only that keyword. Now the hour-of-day conversion report will show you conversion rates by hour for that particular keyword since it is the only keyword in that ad group.
- If there are certain metrics that are very important to you, create an alert to be notified when those metrics have changed.

You should regularly extract and analyze AdWords data so that you understand how your account is performing and what optimization steps you need to take to increase your account's effectiveness.

However, with so many options available in AdWords, it can be difficult to prioritize how often you should run reports and make decisions. In the final chapter, I will discuss the best places to spend your time so that you can continuously increase the success of your AdWords account.

Step by Step: Create and Monitor Your AdWords Account

In the previous 16 chapters, we examined best practices, research, and optimization techniques. AdWords gives you a dizzying array of possibilities. In this chapter, I simplify the process of starting and managing AdWords by showing you how to create and optimize your account step by step.

Much of the information in this chapter is contained in other chapters. This chapter consolidates the various information into a single place that you can refer back to as you are optimizing your accounts.

17

Chapter Contents
Before you create your account
Creating campaigns
Optimizing ongoing campaigns
Best practices for creating and managing your AdWords account

Before You Create Your Account

It is easy with AdWords to start choosing keywords and writing ad copy, but do not start by getting caught up in the details. The time you spend doing keyword research can be wasted if you do not first lay out a plan based on your AdWords goals.

Follow this list of items you need to accomplish before working with your AdWords account:

List your marketing goals. The first step in creating a successful AdWords account is to determine your marketing goals. Goals are the reasons you are advertising. If you do not have goals, it is impossible to tell if you are reaching your goals or wasting money. For a full recap of setting goals, see the section "Setting Your Marketing Goals" in Chapter 13, "Profitable Bid Strategies."

Always be as specific as possible. To make more money or to get more leads is not a goal. To increase your ROI from 200 percent to 240 percent or to receive 17 new leads a day from Miami are examples of well-thought-out goals.

Set a priority for each goal. Do not list them as high, medium, and low. Instead, list them in order of importance. By making the hard choices of putting them in order to begin with, you will find it easier to determine budgets and account organization.

Keep in mind your AdWords Campaign settings as you create these goals, since you may want to tailor your goals based on your potential exposure. For example, if you are selling insurance in Florida, you might have one goal for the state of Florida and another goal for Miami.

Determine your budgets. Set a budget for every goal you listed. AdWords budgets are kept at the campaign level. The minimum campaign budget is $1 per day. Therefore, ensure that all of your goals can support a $30 per month spend.

Refine your starting goals based on your budget. If you find that your budget is not high enough to support all your goals, you have two choices. One is to combine some goals. For instance, instead of having one goal for Florida and another for Miami, combine them into a single goal when you start. However, you should still plan to separate out these goals in the future. Periodically review and refine your initial goals.

The second option is to set a budget for each goal in descending order of importance. Once you have hit your maximum allowed spend, each goal without a budget will not be used for now (Figure 17.1). Review these goals in the future to see if you can allocate them some portion of the budget.

Determine account organization. Once you have a list of goals and budgets, it is time to determine how to organize the campaigns in your account. See "Structuring Campaigns to Achieve Business Goals" in Chapter 14, "Successful Account Organization Strategies," for the in-depth details of account structure.

Total Budget: $1,000

Goal 1
• Max spend: $600
• Budget left: $400

Goal 2
• Max spend: $300
• Budget left: $100

Goal 3
• Max spend: $200
• Can only spend remaining: $100

Goal 4
• Next goal to receive additional budget

Figure 17.1 Allocating budget by goal importance

Install conversion tracking. For every goal you want to track, set up conversion tracking. The conversion tracking script is tied to the entire AdWords account—which means that when you change your account structure, add or remove ad groups, or make other changes, the conversion tracking script will continue to work. See "AdWords Conversion Tracking Code" in Chapter 13 for details on creating and installing conversion tracking.

By installing conversion tracking before creating the account's details, you can determine whether the site can support conversion tracking or whether new pages need to be created. In addition, you will become more familiar with the content management system (CMS) of your website, which is necessary when choosing landing pages and keywords and deciding on testing methods. By establishing whether any issues exist before creating the account, you will save yourself from having to change all the landing pages if a new CMS is installed or new pages are created.

Keep this in mind: If you are using alternate conversions such as phone calls, create a method for tracking these conversions.

Install an analytics system, such as Google Analytics. Finally, choose and install an analytics system. Google Analytics is a free analytics solution; however, based on your data needs you may require a more sophisticated system. The advantage of Google Analytics is that it is intimately tied to AdWords with a minimum amount of work.

After you have determined your goals, established budgets, and installed tracking scripts, it is time to build the AdWords account.

Creating Campaigns

Once you have determined your account structure, it is time to create the campaigns. The three types of campaigns we have discussed are as follows:

- Search only
- Keyword display campaign only (also called a discovery campaign)
- Managed placements campaign

Name each campaign appropriately so that you can quickly see its purpose. Adding items such as geographic targeting, time-of-day targeting, search, display, or mobile to the name helps identify your campaign. Some sample campaign names are:

- iPhone – California – Search Only – CPC
- Newsletter Subscriptions – Mobile – Search – CPA
- E-commerce Specials – USA – Display – Managed Placements – CPM

If You Are Using the AdWords Editor

If you are planning on using the AdWords Editor to upload most of your keywords and ad copy, it is quicker to create all of the campaigns, ad groups, and keywords in the AdWords Editor and then upload all the data at once.

If you want to use the interface to ensure that the Campaign settings are correct, create the new campaigns in the interface and adjust the settings, such as budget and geographic target. Next, download your account into the AdWords Editor. Then populate the ad groups, ad copy, and keywords into the editor using the bulk import functions. When you are done, upload the new data into your AdWords account.

Creating Search Campaigns

Search campaigns are only shown when someone does a search. These campaigns do not show up on the display network. Follow these steps to create your search campaigns:

Determine your Campaign settings. To create a search campaign, start by determining all of the campaign's settings. These include budget, location targeting, devices (mobile or desktop), bidding options, and ad scheduling. In the Network settings, choose Google Search and Search Partners. These initial settings determine when, where, and how any ads within that campaign can be viewed (Figure 17.2).

Conduct initial keyword research. The purpose of doing some initial keyword research is to determine all of your themes, or ad groups. You do not need to find all of your keywords yet. Determine the various ways that people are searching for your products or services. Make a list of all your themes.

Campaign settings

General

Campaign name   **Maryland - Search - CPC - Dekstops**   Edit

Locations and Languages

Locations ⑦   Targeted locations:
- **Maryland, United States (state)**
Edit

Languages ⑦   **English**   Edit

⊞ Advanced location options

Networks and devices

Networks ⑦   **Search**   Edit

Devices ⑦   **Computers; Tablets**   Edit

Bidding and budget

Bidding option ⑦   **Focus on clicks, manual maximum CPC bidding**   Edit

Budget ⑦   **$100.00/day**   Edit

⊞ Delivery method (advanced)

Ad extensions

Use this option to show relevant business information with your text ads. You can create and manage your extensions from the Ad extensions tab. Take a tour.

Advanced settings

⊟ Schedule: Start date, end date, ad scheduling
Start date   **May 23, 2003**

End date   **None**   Edit

Ad scheduling ⑦   **Only show ads at selected times**   Edit
Scheduled to run: 46%

⊟ Ad delivery: Ad rotation, frequency capping
Ad rotation ⑦   **Rotate: Show ads more evenly**   Edit

Frequency capping ⑦   **No cap on impressions**
Display Network only   Your campaign must be opted in to the Display Network to use this feature.

⊞ Demographic bidding
⊞ Social settings
⊞ Automatic campaign optimization (Display Network only)
⊞ Experiment[BETA]

Figure 17.2 Available Campaign settings

Focus on differentiating themes based on buying cycle, and wide, informational, transactional, explicit, problem, symptom, product names, and branded keywords.

List your ad groups. From your initial keyword research, make a list of all the ad groups you want to create within your new campaign. By starting with ad groups, you will find it easier to organize your keywords and ad copy. Your ad group name is only used for organizational purposes. Therefore, use an ad group name that lets you quickly identify the ad group's purpose.

Choose your landing pages. For each ad group, choose the most appropriate landing page on your website. If you have two good landing pages for an ad group, first ask yourself if your ad groups are granular enough. You may need more granular ad groups. If you still have multiple landing pages for an ad group, make note of them so you can start testing different landing pages immediately.

If you are using a different landing page for each keyword, you should move this step into the keyword research phase.

Write one targeted ad per ad group. For each ad group, write one highly targeted ad. When someone sees this ad, they should think that your specialty is selling the product or service that the keywords in this ad group provide. Ensure that the landing page you choose for the ad group shares the same intent as the ad copy. You may decide not to use this ad once your account goes live. The ad is for organizational purposes.

While the draft concept ad shown in Figure 17.3 is not a great search ad, it is an excellent organizational ad. It segments businesses from consumers, separates Peachtree software from all other accounting software types, and is only for businesses in Denver.

Denver Accounting Firm
We help businesses who only use
Peachtree accounting software.
bgTheory.com

Figure 17.3 Highly targeted draft ad copy

Start your keyword research. Conduct keyword research for every single ad group. As you choose a keyword for an ad group, look at the ad copy. If the ad copy accurately describes the keyword, it's in the correct ad group. If the ad copy does not describe the keyword, then put it in another ad group. You may find that you need to create additional ad groups.

Do not start with deep or long-tail keywords. Few accounts should start with these types. Adding deep keywords is an optimization technique to use once you determine what words are leading to conversions.

Find negative keywords. As you are conducting keyword research, take note of keywords that you do not want your ad to show for and add them as negative keywords. By starting with positive and negative keywords, you can refine your ad display. If you are unsure whether a keyword should be a negative, it can be useful to leave it out when you first start your account. Later on, you can use the Search Query report to see the metrics for these keywords and add them as negatives.

Determine match types. As you do your keyword research, keep in mind the match types you will want to use. If you have a small budget, you will want to start with mostly exact and either some phrase or modified broad matches. If you have a larger budget, start with more modified broad matches. If you are trying to gather research and your primary goal is not conversions, broad match can be useful. It is okay to have the same keyword with different match types inside the same search campaign.

Write ad copy. For each ad group, write at least two ads. By starting with at least two ads, you are beginning the ad copy testing phase immediately. Since a brand-new account does not have any metrics, there is no best or worst ad copy yet. If you have an established account, you should run an ad report to see what ads and taglines have been most effective so far and borrow those elements when writing your next ads. If you have multiple landing pages for your ad group, use the ad and landing page testing methodology found in "Testing Profit per Click and Profit per Impression" in Chapter 15, "Testing Techniques That Will Increase Profits." If you want, you can delete the draft concept ad you created for organizational purposes.

Set initial bids. Setting initial bids is difficult, since you have very few metrics to work from. The best way to set an initial bid is to estimate your conversion rate and profit per sale and then use one of the bidding methodologies found in Chapter 13 to determine your initial CPC. If there are certain keywords that you think will do well regardless of initial bids, you could use the first page bid estimate to set bids. Be careful of using first page bids in competitive areas. You can easily lose a lot of money by overbidding to page 1 if the landing page or keyword does not convert as expected.

While it is okay for a keyword to appear twice in a search campaign, using different match types, it is *not* okay for those keywords to have the same bid. The exact match version should have a higher bid than the phrase match. If you use broad match, that should be the lowest bid among the match types.

By following these steps, you should have a well-organized beginning to a search campaign. You will need to refine your keywords, test ad copy, add negative keywords, and change bids over time to continuously optimize your campaigns.

Creating Keyword-Based Display Campaigns

Keyword-based display campaigns are only shown across the display network. Because these campaigns are not triggered by individual keywords but by the theme of the ad group, the setup is different than for search-only campaigns. It is okay if the same word appears in multiple ad groups within a display campaign. Individual keywords matter less than the theme of an ad group, so you can have the same word in several ad groups.

In addition, you may have several ad groups with similar keywords within a display campaign. Sometimes, subtle variations of keywords make a difference in where AdWords places your ad. The first step in keyword display organization is finding what combinations of keywords are working. Therefore, feel free to have many closely related ad groups to see which one actually brings in returns. You can follow these steps to create your keyword-based display campaigns:

Determine Campaign settings. As with search campaigns, start by determining all of the campaign's settings. These include budget, location targeting, devices (desktop, tablet, mobile), bidding options, and ad scheduling. If you want to use the CPM bidding option, make sure that only Display Network is selected before you choose your bidding option; the CPM bidding option is not displayed if the campaign is also shown on Search. Also, set a frequency cap. In the Network settings, select Display Network and "Broad reach: Show ads on pages that match my primary targeting method," as shown in Figure 17.4. These initial settings determine when, where, and how any ads in that campaign can be viewed.

Figure 17.4 Campaign network settings

Find web pages where you want your ad displayed. Do some searches for your products or services and create a list of pages where you want your ad to be displayed. Examine the words used on those pages or use a keyword density analyzer. If you are having a difficult time finding sites, use DoubleClick Ad Planner to help with your research or skip to the next step, "Play the game Taboo."

If you find pages that closely resemble your products but you do not want your ad to appear on those pages, determine what words are appearing on the page that you would want to use as negative keywords and add them to your list.

Play the game Taboo. For each product or service, play the game Taboo (see the section "Choosing the Correct Keywords for Your Display Network Ad Groups" in Chapter 9, "Understanding the Display Network," for details) and make a list of words. If there are words that you do not want to trigger your ads, add these as negative words.

Create your ad groups. For each list you have created by finding web pages or playing the game Taboo, make an ad group. A display ad group should contain anywhere from 1 to 12 words. Rarely will more than 12 be necessary. Google only uses 50 words at most to determine your ad group's theme, so never have more than 50 words in any display-only ad group. Match types do not matter for placing your ads. All of your keywords can be listed in broad match. Negative keywords are used in determining where your ads are shown. Therefore, add any appropriate negative keywords to each ad group.

When creating your ad group, name it something appropriate that describes the words inside the ad group. In addition, if you are using video-only or image-only ads in an ad group, it is a good idea to end the ad group name with the ad type for organizational reasons. For instance, "Verizon Cell Phone Plan – Video Ads" is a descriptive ad group name.

Create your ads. There are more ad formats available with the display network than with search. First determine what types of ads you want the ad group to have. An ad group can contain a mixture of image, video, and text ads because keyword display bids are only set at the ad group level. Therefore, it can help to have ad groups that only show one ad type, since you may start bidding differently based on the ad that will be shown.

If you find that you want both image and text ads for the same keywords, you can duplicate the ad group and then have one ad group that is only image ads and another that contains only text ads.

When creating display ads, do not just think about your keywords; consider the pages that your ad will be shown on and that site's audience. As with search, start with two or more ads for each ad group.

Set initial bids. Many times your display campaign will reach individuals not yet in the buying cycle. In these instances, your first conversion option may not be a sale, but instead another action to introduce someone to the buying funnel, such as a newsletter subscription or whitepaper download. In this instance, evaluate what you are willing to pay for someone to enter your buying funnel and your current site conversion rate to determine your starting bid. If you are trying to convert display clicks into sales, use the same methodology as with search to determine your initial bids.

There are more than a million sites in the display network, so if in doubt about the initial bid, set a lower bid than you think is required. You can always raise your bid if you are not getting good placement, but you will never get your money back for clicks returned if you overbid.

Following these steps will get you started creating display-only campaigns. Over time, you will have to measure results to block sites, change keywords within an ad group, and test new ads. One of the steps to optimizing display is to determine what sites are sending you good traffic and move those sites into a managed placements campaign.

Creating Managed Placements Campaigns

With managed placements campaigns, keywords can be used to refine your placement on an individual site; however, keywords are optional. You must choose each site where you want your ad to appear. If you have a small budget or you are new to display advertising, start with a managed placements campaign before creating a keyword-based display campaign You can follow these steps to create your managed placement campaigns:

Determine campaign settings. Again, the first step is to choose your initial settings such as budget and geography. In the Network settings section, there are two options you want to choose. First, choose Display Network for your network reach. Under the Display section, choose "Specific reach: Show ads only on pages that match all my targeting methods" (Figure 17.5). This is the setting that tells Google not to place your ad across the entire display network but only on the specific sites, audiences, and so forth you have chosen. If you are using CPM bidding for your placements, make sure you have unchecked Google Search and Search Partners before choosing CPM as your bidding methodology.

```
Networks  ?
           ○ All available sites (Recommended for new advertisers)
           ⦿ Let me choose...
   Search  ☐ Google search
              ☐ Search partners (requires Google search)
   Display  ☑ Display Network  ?
              ○ Broad reach: Show ads on pages that match my primary targeting method  ?
                 Example: Show ads if keywords match
              ⦿ Specific reach: Show ads only on pages that match all my targeting methods  ?
                 Example: Show ads only if both keywords and placements match

              💡 Your ads won't show on Google Search or search partners.

   [ Save ]  [ Cancel ]
```

Figure 17.5 Only show ads on managed placements.

Organize your ad group. There are three reasons to create ad groups for placement campaigns. The first is if you are using enhanced campaigns that utilize both keywords and placements together. In this case, if a new placement needs to be refined with a set of keywords, you will only add placements to that ad group when you want those keywords to also control the ad's display.

For example, if you were Verizon attempting to market the Droid, you might have both ads in Figure 17.6 in your AdWords account. One of the ads compares the iPhone to the Droid. In this case, you would want iPhone-related keywords in the ad group so the ad shows up on pages that talk about the iPhone. The second ad talks mostly about Droid benefits; therefore, you would want a second ad group with more general keywords, such as "mobile phone" and "cell phone," to maximize the exposure of this ad on those placements. Both of these ad groups can have the same placements in them; it will be the keywords in the article that determine which ad is actually displayed.

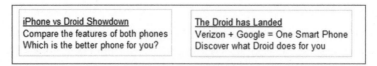

Figure 17.6 Display network ads with different purposes

The second reason to create new ad groups is if you want different ads to be shown on different placements. In this case, if an existing ad group contains an ad you want to be shown on that placement, add the placement to that ad group. If there is no ad group with an ad you want to be shown, add the placement to a new ad group with the appropriate ad copy.

The third reason is if you are using different types of ads and want to set different bids for a placement based on the ad shown. This generally only applies if you are using both text ads and rich media ads, such as video or image, to target the same site. Because you cannot set different bids for different ads, if you want to bid more for image or video ads than for text ads, you will have one ad group that contains text ads with a bid, and another ad group that has the same placements but uses rich media ads with a different bid.

Find placements via the Placement Performance report. If you are using the campaign organization discussed in the section "Organizing Your Display Campaigns" in Chapter 10, "Advanced Display Network Techniques," you will use the Placement Performance report to find sites doing well for you and add them to your managed placements campaign. If you do not have any data within your automatic placement campaign, skip this step since you will not yet have any placement data to work from.

Find new placements for your ads. If you want to find highly relevant sites on which to place your ad, you need to do research to find them. There are two tools for finding new placements. The most robust tool is DoubleClick Ad Planner, discussed in the section "DoubleClick Ad Planner: Free Access to Expensive Data" in Chapter 10. The second tool is the placement tool, discussed in Chapter 9 in the section "Placement Tool." Using these two tools, along with the Placement Performance report, is the easiest way to find sites where you want your ad to be shown.

Create ads. If you are using the placement performance report to find placements where you always want your ad to be shown, copy the existing ad that should be displayed on the corresponding website when you add the placement.

If you are finding new placements, you can either write new ads or use the ad report to find which ads have been successful in your display campaigns. With managed placements campaigns, it is still useful to create multiple ads and test which one performs better.

Set initial bids. If you are using the placement report to find placements for your managed placements campaign, you already know the corresponding metrics by placement, such as cost per acquisition, and can use the formulas from Chapter 13 to set your initial bids.

If you are adding new placements and have an automatic placements keyword-based display network campaign, choose starting bids based on the data from similar types of placements.

If you do not have access to either set of data, you will have to choose a starting bid with little information. The steps will be the same as with the display campaign initial bid information discussed earlier. It is easy to raise and lower bids. You should start with a lower bid, and if you are not receiving much exposure on a site, raise the bid to see how that affects your exposure.

Other Campaign Types

Search, keyword-display, and managed placements campaigns are where you will spend the bulk of your time with new accounts. However, there are other campaign types you can create.

One of the most useful is a retargeting campaign. You create retargeting campaigns much like the managed placements campaigns. However, instead of finding sites to advertise on, you will be breaking down your own site into various sections to create lists. Your campaign settings and bid options will be managed just like a managed placements campaign.

You can also have campaigns just for topic, interests, and other targeting options within AdWords. When considering whether you should create a new campaign, consider the reasons listed in Chapter 14, "Successful Account Organization Strategies," in the section "Reasons to Create New Campaigns."

Having a mobile and a desktop campaign for search is a good idea. The process of creating these two campaigns is identical except for the campaign setting about devices.

In general, the practices of creating these various campaigns are very similar. If you understand the overall workflow from creating these three main types of campaigns, you can easily create any campaign type based on your own business needs.

After you have created your initial campaigns, it is time to let the campaigns accumulate statistics. When the campaigns have data, it is time to optimize each campaign.

Optimizing Ongoing Campaigns

You will need to regularly run reports to determine how your campaigns are performing, and then make decisions based on that data. In this section, you will examine optimization steps for each campaign type. In the next section, I will show you how often to run reports to create a comprehensive reporting schedule.

Optimizing Search Campaigns

The first step in optimizing search campaigns is to determine whether you are going to bid at the keyword or ad group level. The most granular bid type, at the keyword level, gives you more control. However, it also takes more time to set keyword-level bids. You may use a combination of both. For keywords that receive a significant amount of traffic, set keyword bids. For a set of keywords that receive little traffic, use ad group bids.

Making Bid Changes

Based on if you are using ad group–level or keyword-level bids, you will want to run the corresponding report. Use conditional formatting, found in "Revenue per Click" in Chapter 13, to make a visual reference chart of your data (Figure 17.7). This will give you a high-level look at how profitable or unprofitable the various keywords and ad groups are. Next, use the formulas from Chapter 13 to adjust your bids.

Placement/ Keyword	Est. First Page Bid	Current Max CPC	Clicks	Avg CPC	Cost	Conversions	Value/ Click
Placement1		$0.35	8716	$0.32	$2,826.35	195	$1.96
Keyword1	$0.05	$0.50	8270	$0.65	$5,382.30	194	$1.37
Placement2		$0.35	6955	$0.31	$2,152.21	131	$0.51
Keyword2	$0.05	$0.50	3852	$0.95	$3,645.98	111	$0.49
Keyword3	$0.30	$0.35	3522	$0.27	$957.59	75	$0.31
Keyword4	$0.05	$0.50	1658	$0.53	$874.55	49	$0.29

Figure 17.7 Using conditional formatting to visualize the data

If you are making many bid changes, using the AdWords Editor's import function can save you a significant amount of time.

The frequency of bid changes will be constrained by your technology and resources. If you are using automated bid systems, you may change bids several times daily. If you are using manual systems and you have other responsibilities besides AdWords, you may want to change bids only weekly.

If you find keywords that are not profitable, first examine the ad copy and landing pages to make sure they are appropriate. Make any necessary adjustments. The second step is to examine the match type. If the unprofitable keywords are in broad or phrase match, you may want to look at the metrics in the Search Query report and change the match type to be more restrictive, such as exact match, to see how the keyword performs. If a keyword is not performing regardless of ad copy, landing page, and match type, delete the keyword.

The logic just described assumes that you have unlimited budget if your keywords are profitable. However, that is rarely the case. If you are reaching your budget early in the day and cannot raise it, then delete the keywords that are not receiving conversions or that have the highest cost per conversion. The other option is to lower your bids for all keywords. It is not uncommon to see an account that has a $100 daily budget and is spending $10 per click. This leads to only 10 clicks per day, and the budget is often depleted by noon. In this case, lowering your bids so that your average CPC drops to $5 might bring in 20 clicks at the same budget, or better yet, a $1 CPC for 100 clicks.

Conducting Additional Keyword Research

You will never find every keyword possible; there are just too many different ways that people search. However, you can continuously search for new words. There are three ways to keep conducting keyword research.

The first is by using the Search Query report. This report will show you what someone actually searched for that triggered your ad. If you are using AdWords conversion tracking, you will also see the conversion rate and cost per conversion by each search query variation. Run the Search Query report and look for search queries that are costing you money but do not exist as keywords in your account. If they look like they would be good keywords, then add them as positive keywords so you can set a bid on them explicitly. If the search query or keyword is not leading to conversions, there are two steps to take. The first is to examine the associated ad copy and landing page. If the ad copy or landing page is not appropriate for that keyword, you may want to add that keyword to a different ad group that has a more appropriate landing page and ad copy to see if that keyword will be profitable under a different combination. If the ad copy and landing page are appropriate and the keyword is just not profitable, then delete the keyword and consider making it a negative keyword so your ad is no longer shown for that search.

The exception to deleting the keyword from your search campaigns is if you are also using a Budget Optimizer campaign to increase your exposure on early buy cycle keywords, as discussed in the section "Understanding Attribution Management" in Chapter 13. In the case of words that are not profitable but are leading to interaction on your website, delete these keywords from your current search campaign and place any appropriate ones into a Budget Optimizer campaign.

The second way to continuously conduct keyword research is to use the AdWords Keyword Tool site-spidering capability discussed in the section "Website: Jumpstarting Your Keyword List" in Chapter 3, "Keyword Tools: Extracting Valuable Data from Google." If you are ever on a web page that discusses your products, use the site-spidering function to see if there are new keywords you do not have in your account yet.

The third method is to set aside time to conduct keyword research. Use the tools found in Chapter 3 and spend some time looking for new keywords.

Additional Optimization Techniques

Changing bids is the most common optimization. It is easy to become so focused on bidding that other types of optimization techniques are forgotten. Other types of account analysis should be performed on a regular basis, such as the following:

Improve your Quality Score. Quality Score is displayed at the keyword level. However, running a keyword report and examining all the data can be time consuming. To use your time well, run a keyword report and then put the data in a pivot table, as discussed in "Increasing Your Quality Scores" in Chapter 7, "Demystifying Quality Score." Look for ad groups with low Quality Scores and high spends. Then work on the Quality Score for that ad group. Increasing the Quality Score in high spend, low Quality Score ad groups will lead to the largest gains for your account.

Test your ad copy. If you create at least two ads when you initially build a campaign, you can start by measuring the results and refining your ad copy. To understand the metrics of your ad copy, run an ad performance report. Take the ad that performs the best and keep it. Examine the other ads to see if there are any outliers in the data where you can learn from other ads, and then delete the underperforming ads. Create new ads for the ad group and continue testing. If you have well-established ad groups, you may only want the test ad to run a small percentage of the time. Refer to "AdWords Campaign Experiments" in Chapter 15 to run limited tests.

Test your landing pages. You should continue testing landing page layouts and where you are sending traffic to increase conversion rates. Send traffic to different landing pages, and then run the Destination URL report to see which landing pages are leading to the most profits. Keep the winning test, create new test variables, and continue testing. Small changes in conversion rates can lead to large changes in profits.

Adjust your budget based on changes. The easiest way to determine what you could have spent is by using the Impression Share report. This report will tell you why your account did not accrue impressions. Combine this report with Google Trends or Google Insights for Search and you can learn to adjust your future budgets based on changes in search volume and lost impression share.

Analyze trends for ad scheduling. Analyze your data to determine if there are clear trends in your conversion rates or profit based on times of day or days of the week. If trends start to emerge, you can use ad scheduling (see "Ad Scheduling: Automatically Changing Bids by Time Periods" in Chapter 13) to adjust your bids, or turn your campaigns on and off based on performance metrics.

Before deciding there is a trend, ensure that you have enough data to see a clear pattern. First, run an Ad Group Performance report by hour of day. Next, run an Ad Group Performance report by day of the week. Examine these two reports to see if there are clear trends. If there are, use ad scheduling to adjust your bids.

Determine geographic performance. The Geographic report allows you to see your performance in different geographic regions. Use this report to find underperforming areas. If there are geographies where your conversion rates are lower than normal, you will either want to exclude the area or create a campaign specific to that area. If you have areas where the conversion rates are higher than normal, you may want to create dedicated campaigns for that area to maximize your spend.

If your advertising reach is too big—for instance, any company advertising in every country with a $100 daily budget—use Google Trends to find areas that are searching for your keywords, and limit your geography until you have the budget to start adding new areas.

Although these techniques will get you started optimizing search campaigns, you should always be creative when trying to reach your target market. Whether it is running different ads by time of day for different geographies or using a single high-value keyword in an ad group so you can test different ad copy with that keyword, there are many options available within AdWords if you know all the settings. These steps to optimization should get you started, but they are not an ending point. You are limited only by a combination of your creativity and knowledge of AdWords.

Managing Budget Optimizer Campaigns

When you use the Budget Optimizer—by choosing "Focus on clicks: AdWords will set my bids to help maximize clicks within my target budget"—AdWords takes over your bidding and tries to maximize the clicks you are receiving for your keywords.

You can use the Budget Optimizer (Figure 17.8) in a search-only or display-only campaign. Therefore, your initial campaign setup is the same as when you are creating search or display campaigns.

Figure 17.8 Choosing Focus On Clicks to enable the Budget Optimizer

When using the Budget Optimizer for search, ensure that each keyword is leading to page views, time on site, and low bounce rates. If a word in a Budget Optimizer campaign is not helping you reach your goals, that word should be deleted.

When using the Budget Optimizer for display campaigns, you will not see metrics by keyword, because all AdWords reports show display data at the ad group level. The success metrics for Budget Optimizer search and display campaigns are the same; however, for search you will examine keyword data and for display you will examine ad group data.

What Is a Low Bounce Rate?

A bounce within Google Analytics is when a visitor only views one page of your site. Typically when you see high bounce rates, the visitor is on your site for a short amount of time. This usually occurs because they did not find the content of the site useful. Your site's layout does affect bounce rates. If someone visits a single page of your site and calls you from that page, they could spend 20 minutes on the phone, place an order over the phone, and then leave your site. In this scenario, the visitor was still a bounce even though they are also a new customer.

The specificity of the search query, commercial nature of the term, and design of the landing page all contribute to typical bounce rates. For very broad terms such as "TV" that can have multiple meanings, a bounce rate under 60–70 percent is good. For a very specific term, such as a product name, your goal is to have bounce rates under 20–30 percent.

There are two ways of measuring Budget Optimizer campaign effectiveness. The first is to use the AdWords conversion tracking (Figure 17.9) and look at page views by keyword or ad group. However, keywords, ads, and landing pages share all conversion types within a campaign, so you might not want to use every page view as a conversion to measure these campaigns' effectiveness. In this case, using Google Analytics or another analytics program to view this information is crucial. If a word or ad group starts to lead to conversions, you can move it back to your conversion optimizer or max CPC bidding campaigns to regain control over the keyword's visibility.

		Conversion	Conversion location	Category
	●	Book Contact	Webpage	Lead
	●	Contact	Webpage	Lead
	●	Contact (Actual PPC Keywords)	Analytics	Lead
	●	Contact (Full Referral)	Analytics	Lead
	●	Feed Subscription (Actual PPC Keywords)	Analytics	Other
	●	Pageview	Webpage	View of a key page

Figure 17.9 Tracking page views as conversions

If the Budget Optimizer campaign is your only exposure campaign across all marketing channels, examining the changes to brand searches and direct type in traffic can also give you an idea of any additional lift that this campaign is creating.

Optimizing Display Campaigns

The most exposure you can receive with AdWords is to run display campaigns, because the reach of the display network far exceeds that of search. However, with display campaigns you must take certain steps, listed next, to ensure that your ads are being placed correctly, and then you need to make sure your ads are being shown on those sites.

Ensure your ads are being displayed appropriately. Once you have chosen keywords to create a theme for each ad group, your first optimization step is to make sure those ads are being shown on the correct sites. Run a Placement Performance report that shows the individual URLs where your ads are being displayed.

Click on the URLs in the report to see if the pages where your ads are being displayed are the types of pages where you want your ads. If they are not, change the keywords in your ad group and repeat this step.

If the pages where your ads are being displayed are correct, it is time to move on to the next step: blocking websites.

Block websites and types of content. Examine the Placement Performance report. When you see sites that are not meeting your goals, use the site and category exclusion tool or the interface blocking options to block your ads from being shown on those sites.

Change display bids. Your bids for automatic placements on the display network are set at the ad group level. You cannot choose different bids by keyword. Therefore, when deciding what to bid on the display network, start by running an Ad Group Performance report and segment the data to be display only. If your campaign is set to only display, you do not need to segment the data.

If you are using the display network to bring sales into your company, and you are not necessarily using it as a discovery mechanism for finding placements, you will want to set a bid based on your marketing goals. Take the data from the Ad Group Performance report, and apply the same math from Chapter 13 to set your ad group–level bids. The only difference is that you will not examine the bid for each keyword—you will examine the bid by ad group.

If you are using the display network as a discovery mechanism, you will still want to set a bid based on some performance metrics, but one of your goals will also be impressions and clicks for each ad group. If an ad group's bid is so low that it is not bringing in any impressions, you will never find new placements. Conversely, if your ad group is receiving so many clicks that you are quickly hitting your budget every day, lower your ad group bids to receive more clicks at the same total budget.

Use managed placements. When you see a site that is meeting your goals, and you always want your ad to show on that site, you have two options.

You can add that site as a placement within that ad group. If you add a site as a placement, you can set a bid for that placement. Placement bids override ad group bids. Set a bid for that placement based on its performance.

The second option is to use a managed placements campaign. The advantage of using a managed placements campaign is that you can set a higher daily budget for the websites that are meeting your goals. In this case, block the website from the automatic placement discovery campaign and add it to a managed placements campaign. The discovery campaign will be able to find new websites that meet your goals, and the managed placements campaign will be able to manage sites that are currently meeting your goals.

There will be times when you want to create a placement for a website, yet you cannot seem to add that site as a placement. A publisher can control if their website can be targeted specifically for placements. If the publisher does not allow this, the only way for your ad to be shown on that site is through using automatic placements targeted by your keywords.

Test your ad copy. The display network reaches a large audience and is a good place to test ad copy to see which is performing best for you. Since the display network supports text, video, and image ads, you can conduct tests across different ad formats. Testing rich media ads in this manner is also useful before doing large CPM buys with websites directly.

When testing ad copy on the display network, run the Ad Performance report. With this report, you can segment out each ad type individually so that you only see video or image ads.

The display network has many options available. You can choose to display your ads based on keywords, placements, topics, interests, placements and keywords, and more, and then segment each ad group with different ad formats. Always keep in mind that the display network obeys your other campaign settings, such as ad scheduling or location targeting.

These steps will help you refine and optimize your display campaigns. However, keep your business goals in mind as you may want to use the display in unique ways that will cause you to use different optimization techniques.

Optimizing Managed Placements Campaigns

Managed placements campaigns allow you to choose specific placements, either websites or sections of a website, where your ad will show. Because you are choosing a specific placement, your keywords are optional. Follow these steps to improve your managed placement campaigns:

Placements moved from discovery campaigns do not perform. If you run a Managed Placements report and learn that the placements you found in your discovery campaign are no longer meeting your goals, do not immediately assume that the placement is no longer valid. First, examine these possibilities to see if you can regain the previous targeting.

- Is different ad copy running on the new managed placement than what is in the discovery campaign? If yes, add the ad copy from the discovery display campaign. You may want to create a new ad group for just this placement and the new ad copy.

- Did you add the placement, but not the keywords?
  - While the site might be the same, you could be shown on different pages of a placement if you did not move the keywords. Add the keywords from the discovery display ad group that found success on this placement.
  - For narrow theme sites, you might not always move the keywords since the entire site could be relevant to your offer and using keywords may remove your ad from being shown to a targeted audience.

- Use the placement tool to see if you can target a smaller section of the site. If you found success on the *New York Times* and added the entire site as a placement, your ad could easily be shown on a completely different section of such a large site. Your ad will convert differently when placed in the leisure section versus the business section. In this case, see if you can target a smaller section of the website.

Placements added directly do not perform. If you use the placement tool or DoubleClick Ad Planner to find websites, before assuming the websites do not convert go through two steps. The first step is to test different ads. You might even test a couple of image ads as well as text ads to see how the different ad formats perform. The second step is to add keywords to the ad group. Adding keywords is more appropriate for placements on large sites, but doing so can help refine your exposure on smaller sites as well.

Your ad is not being shown on the placement. If your ad is not being displayed on a placement, there are two common reasons. The first is that your bid is too low. Raise your bid to see if your ad starts to be displayed. The second reason is publisher control. All website owners can filter certain ads from being shown on their sites. Just as advertisers have a category and site exclusion tool, the website owner has a similar tool. However, the advertisers are not notified if a publisher has rejected their ad or is not allowing your site to advertise on them directly.

When you combine placements, ad formats, keywords, ad scheduling, and geographic targeting, you have a lot of options for controlling exactly where and when your ads are displayed. Creating scenarios, as discussed in the section "Creating Scenarios to Understand and Reach Your Targeted Audience" in Chapter 10, can help you put the correct message in front of your ideal audience at the proper time.

Optimizing CPM Campaigns

CPM bidding, also known as *focus on impressions*, is a bid type where you pay for an impression, not for a click. This bidding option is only available for a campaign that is only targeting the display network.

To create a CPM campaign, follow the earlier steps for creating a placement campaign or a display campaign. Start with only managed placements so you can choose each placement and become comfortable with the metrics. Bidding CPM for an automatic placement display campaign is possible, but you may waste a lot of money having your ads shown on inappropriate sites. CPM keyword bidding is not recommended for a beginner or anyone with a small budget.

With CPM campaigns, you are paying for the impression. The goal is often higher brand awareness or to introduce a new product. Since you are paying for an impression, not a click, you want every impression to count. Therefore, only use image or video ads when bidding CPM. Follow these steps to optimize your CPM campaigns:

Run the Reach and Frequency Performance report. The Reach and Frequency Performance report will show you how many people saw your ad and how often they saw it over a certain time period. If your ad is being seen too often by the same people, change your frequency capping in the Campaign settings.

Run the Free Clicks report. If you are using video ads, your optimization goals should include how often a video is watched and how much of the video is being watched. In the Dimensions tab is a report called Free Clicks. The report will show you in 25 percent increments how much of your video is being watched. AdWords video ads do not autoplay, so the opening image is crucial to convince someone to watch your video. Testing the opening image to find which one leads to a higher play rate can drastically increase the success of a CPM campaign. It can be useful to test these images in a CPC campaign while you determine which image is best before moving to a CPM campaign.

Measure success for CPM campaigns. While you can get into complex measurements such as aided brand lift to measure your CPM campaigns, I will focus on some of the simpler ones to measure. The most common goals for online performance advertisers for CPM campaigns are to increase awareness and increase interaction with the website.

- Examine how many clicks you are receiving from the CPM ads.
- Examine the time on site and page views for those clicks.
- If using video, examine play rates and length of video viewed.
- While ads are running:
  - Examine changes in direct traffic.
  - Look for an increase in traffic from branded search keywords.
  - Analyze changes in CTR and conversion rates for your search ads.
  - Examine total conversions and sales.

You can create charts from the CPM data to easily view the performance differences when CPM is running. The charts do not have to be complex; you can build a simple spreadsheet (Figure 17.10) that allows you to compare two time frames against each other.

	AdWords Only	AdWords & Display
Branded Searches	1211	1545
Conversion Rate	2.12%	2.45%
AdWords CTR	1.70%	1.70%
Total Site Visitors	212,083	302,423
Site Visitors from Display	0	12,089
Total Conversions	3605	5141
Total Sale $$	$90,135.28	$128,529.78
Cost of Display	0	$11,000
Cost of AdWords	$22,565	$21,872
Total Profit	$67,570.28	$95,657.78

Figure 17.10 A simple comparison of two time frames

With CPM ad buying, you often need to measure more than just the ad's metrics to determine success. It is not uncommon for a company to buy CPM ads and have the ads appear to be a failure. However, perhaps you notice that while those ads were running, the conversion rates of the search ads increased by 8 percent. In this case, the CPM ads may be the catalyst for the higher performance on your search ads. If so, you may want to examine the cost of the CPM ads versus the increase in revenue from the conversion rate lift to see if the ads are profitable, based on the influence they had on your search campaigns.

Unless you have a sophisticated marketing department that understands how to measure success and failure of branding campaigns, judge the effectiveness of your CPM ads with metrics you can track.

Optimizing Other Campaign Types

Just as with building other campaign types, such as remarketing, topics, interests, and others, the steps you will use to optimize the campaigns are similar to the ones just covered.

You will manage remarketing campaigns similarly to placement campaigns. Examine your goals and the cost-per-action for your lists, and use a bidding type that fits your goals to set these bids.

The most important setting to understand with display campaigns is the Campaign setting for reach:

- **Broad Reach:** Show Ads On Pages That Match My Primary Targeting Method
- **Specific Reach:** Show Ads Only On Pages That Match All My Targeting Methods

With broad reach, since these ads can be shown on any site that matches your targeting methods, you will treat them similarly to the keyword display network. With specific reach, since you control how these ads are displayed, you will treat them similarly to the managed placements campaign.

Creating an Optimization Schedule

There are many ways to optimize campaigns based on your goals. With so many options available—from finding new exposure by expanding your placements to taking care of the money by setting bids—you need to create a structured process that will help you continuously optimize and grow your account without feeling overwhelmed by the options.

I will walk you through what a medium-sized account in a semi-competitive industry that is being run by an in-house person would do throughout the month to optimize their account.

If you manage a small business, or AdWords is not your full-time job, you may want to look at some of these reports less frequently. If you manage a large account, you might want to break down these reports further so that you are only looking at a subset of data instead of the entire account. For instance, instead of examining the entire account daily, you may look at five campaigns on Monday and a different set of five on Tuesday. If you advertise in a competitive arena, you may want to look at some of these reports more often. However, the first step is to put together a time frame and what you want to see by each time frame.

Status Check: Every Day Run a campaign report that includes every campaign in your account. Look for changes in spend, profit, conversion rate, cost per conversion, and total conversions. What you are looking for are significant changes from the norm. If you find changes, investigate the reason for them. This is your daily AdWords check-in. You can also view this information in the AdWords Editor or the AdWords interface.

This will let you quickly see that your conversions dropped significantly and that it's because you had several ads disapproved. Or your display spend went up dramatically because your products were mentioned on CNN and people started looking for the products (in which case you might want to raise your budget).

You can automate this check-in with alerts discussed in Chapter 16, "AdWords Reports: Extracting Actionable Information." However, there are messages that are only displayed in the interface, so logging into the interface on a regular basis is a good idea to see these alerts.

Keyword Bids: Every Day or Week Decide how often you want to change bids: daily, twice weekly, or weekly. If you want to set bids weekly, choose a day of the week, such as every Monday, to make these changes.

Run a keyword report that only includes search data. Use the formulas discussed in Chapter 13 to set your bids, add or remove keywords, or move them to a Budget Optimizer campaign.

Placement Bids: Every Day or Week As with keywords, choose how often you want to change placement bids. It is generally okay to change placement bids weekly and not to fret about them every single day unless it is a site that is spending a significant portion of your budget. Run a Managed Placements report and then change the bids for your existing placements based on the formulas in Chapter 13. If you are changing your keywords bids each Monday, run this report every Monday as well so you know that Mondays are bid change days.

> ### How Often Should You Change Bids?
>
> You will most likely not change every keyword, ad group, or placement bid every week. There will be some that need to be adjusted with new bids, and others will be fine with the current bid. Do not feel you constantly need to change bids if your account is doing well.
>
> Most advertisers find that they need to change bids often in new campaigns to find the nice middle ground between exposure and conversions, and once it is found, the bid changes become more incremental in nature.

Quality Score Tuesdays Every Tuesday, work on Quality Score by using keyword reports and pivot tables. Quality Score is not updated regularly in AdWords, so keep track of the ad groups you have optimized for Quality Score. Leave those ad groups alone from a Quality Score standpoint for at least a week; often, two weeks allows time for AdWords to catch up to all your changes before you need to optimize the same ad groups again. If you are making landing page changes, it may take several weeks for those Quality Score changes to be reflected in your AdWords account.

New Keyword Wednesdays Every Wednesday, start by running a Search Query report. If keywords are not meeting your goals, either make them negatives or put them in a new ad group with new ad copy.

If keywords are meeting your goals and are not in your account, add them as keywords. This is also the time to examine your match types. Technically the same keyword in broad and exact match is two different keywords. A unique keyword is both a keyword and match type combination.

Use the AdWords Keyword Tool to do some new keyword research. Another option is to bookmark pages throughout the week that discuss your products and services. On keyword Wednesday, use the site-spidering function of the AdWords Keyword Tool to spider those sites for new keywords.

If you have a small account, you may want to do keywords research every other week or monthly. However, set aside a specific time each month to conduct keyword research and look for negative keywords.

Display Network Thursdays Every Thursday, run a Placement Performance report. If placements are not meeting your goals, block them in your campaign settings. If placements are meeting your goals, add them to a placement-only campaign.

If you are using demographic bidding, run the demographic bidding report each Thursday as well to see if you need to adjust your bids. If you are waiting to see if you have enough demographic data to set demographic bids, schedule a report to be sent to you monthly. You can then quickly examine it and determine whether to use demographic bids or delete the report and wait until next month.

Use the placement tool and DoubleClick Ad Planner to find new placements. If you are doing a minimal amount of placements, you may want to run these reports every other Thursday or once per month.

Testing Fridays You should always be testing. If you set up your ad groups with at least two ads, you always have testing data to analyze. There are two types of tests you should be running: ad copy and landing pages.

The first and third week of the month, run an ad report. Examine your ads to see if you have enough data to draw a conclusion about which ad is best for your account. For those ads, keep the best ad, examine the losers for any outliers, delete the losing ads, and then write a new ad so you are always testing.

If you have a large account and you are testing for both the display and search network, you might just look at search ads on the first Friday and your display ads on the third Friday.

The second and fourth week of the month, run a Destination URL report to determine which landing pages are performing best for your goals. If you have conclusive data, then keep the best landing page and remove the other ones from your tests. If you do a limited amount of landing page testing, you might want to just look at a URL performance report the second week of the month, and then design new landing pages the fourth week of the month.

Trend Reporting: Monthly Each month, run a geographic performance report. Look for areas where you are not receiving good returns; then, either write custom ads for those regions in a new campaign or exclude those regions from your campaigns.

Each month, examine your ad scheduling data by looking at conversion data by hour and day in both AdWords reports and your analytics systems. If there are changes to your conversion rates or cost per conversions, modify your ad scheduling settings.

Run an Impression Share report to see why you are losing impressions. This report will give you a snapshot of your visibility for the previous month as well as ideas on how to increase your visibility.

AdWords Management Calendar

I am such a fan of a calendar for managing AdWords that I have created one that you can sub-scribe to at CertifiedKnowledge.org. All you need is a free membership to access it. Each of the optimization tasks listed in this chapter is there with instructions. Just change the calendar to fit your needs. Some companies will need to set bids more often. Others will need to spend more time on display. Add or remove items as you need them. Having a basic calendar to start with should save you a lot of time.

Examine your demographic performance statistics to see if you want to set demo-graphic bids or adjust your current demographic bids.

Use Google Trends and Google Insights for Search to see changes in your keyword trends so you can take advantage of seasonal behavior.

Creating a reporting schedule like this one for your account will help you keep track of what needs to be done each day or week, and it will ensure that you are con-tinuously optimizing the basics.

There are more metrics available in AdWords and analytics than I covered in this typical reporting schedule. For instance, the suggested schedule did not regularly examine conversion rates by position. Most companies' conversion rates do not vary by position, so you don't have to constantly monitor those metrics when you have more important items to change. You may want to examine some of these additional metrics on a quarterly basis.

If there are reports in this suggested schedule that are not applicable to you, just skip over them. If there are other metrics you do need to see on a regular basis, you can add them to your reporting schedule.

The best way to keep up with these reports is to put them in your calendar as recurring items. Then go into AdWords and set up the scheduling feature so these reports are run automatically.

It is also helpful to use a dedicated calendar for your AdWords account so you can keep track of notes, changes, and other reminders. For instance, if you are doing limited testing and do not want to look at test data every single week, instead of setting up recurring reports, add a note in your calendar that you started a test on this day. Then set a reminder to examine that data in one month so you do not forget to analyze the test results.

The more you customize your targeting, the more complex AdWords becomes to set up, monitor, and analyze. However, the system is flexible so that if you understand all the settings and your company's goals, you can target users with unique and creative methods that will ultimately make your business more successful.

Best Practices for Creating and Managing Your AdWords Account

When creating and managing your AdWords account, first refer to the steps in this chapter. While each step seems simple, there are a large number of options for each step. When any one step involves making decisions that you are not yet comfortable making, refer back to the chapter where the options behind each step are fully explained.

By using the practices laid out in this chapter, you should be able to successfully create, organize, and optimize your AdWords account:

- The most important step in advertising successfully is first to determine the goals for your campaign.
- Once you understand the goals, you need to find a way of tracking your goals.
- Next, determine your campaign organization based on your goals and budget. When organizing your campaign, make sure you have search-only and display-only campaigns. Do not have campaigns shown on both networks.
- For each campaign, determine your ad groups before spending extensive time on keyword research. By determining your ad groups first, keyword research and ad group organization become more manageable.
- For each ad group, create keywords and ads. Make sure you include at least two ads in every new ad group so you can test ad copy.
- For search campaigns, use exact and either modified broad match or phrase match keywords with small budgets for more control over ad serving. For larger budgets and for finding new keywords through the search query report, include

some modified broad, and possibly even broad match, keywords along with the other match types.

- When creating display campaigns, limit yourself to 1–12 keywords; 3–8 is generally a good number. Do not worry about match types; they are ignored for the display network. Include any appropriate negative keywords—AdWords does take these into account.

- For more control over the display network, use managed placements so you know what websites will show your ads.

- Using a combination of keyword display and managed display campaigns will help both maximize your exposure and control where your budget is being spent.

- Create profiles of your ideal customers and then use DoubleClick Ad Planner to find sites that house your target market.

- To properly optimize your campaigns, first create a reporting schedule. Set up a calendar with reminders for what you want to accomplish each day. Then schedule reports to be run and emailed to you automatically so you have data to work with each day and from which to make decisions.

AdWords allows you to be creative in reaching your target market. The system is flexible so that once you understand how ads are displayed, you can test the various variables discussed throughout this book to see which combination leads to the most profits for your account.

Following the advice in this book will help you create campaigns, choose keywords, write ad copy, design landing pages, and put your ad in front of your potential customers, which will help you succeed using Google AdWords.

The first ads were cave paintings created several millennia ago. The ancient Egyptians were the first to put ads on paper. The first ad to appear in a newspaper was in 1704. The first online clickable ad appeared in 1983. Google AdWords launched their first PPC product in 2002.

Google AdWords is still in its infancy. Many new features and targeting options will emerge over the coming years. By understanding how to use the advanced features of AdWords today, you will be able to take advantage of the new capabilities tomorrow.

Glossary

A

account report An AdWords report that displays metrics for the entire account.

ad extensions Expand ad copy with additional information such as business locations. This information is stored within the Campaign settings.

ad group A collection of one or more ads and one or more keywords and/or placements.

ad group report An AdWords report that displays metrics for each ad group.

Ad Performance report An AdWords report that displays metrics for each ad.

ad preview tool An AdWords tool that allows you to see search results as they would appear in various geographic locations.

ad rank The position of an ad in a search result or on a display network page. Ad rank is determined by the formula: ad rank = (max cost per click) × (Quality Score).

ad scheduling Controls when an ad is shown by time of day or day of the week. The advanced version allows you to automatically adjust your bids up or down by time of day and day of the week.

AdWords Campaign Experiments (ACE) A campaign feature that allows you to set up and run split tests for testing changes to bids, keywords, ad groups, and placements, and control how much of your traffic goes to the experiment (test) and how much goes to the control (control).

AdWords conversion tracking An AdWords feature that enables you to track conversion actions on your website and view those metrics in your account by placing a free script on your goal (conversion) pages.

AdWords Editor A free downloadable desktop program created by Google that allows you to view and make changes to your AdWords account.

AdWords Keyword Tool A tool offered by Google that allows you to conduct keyword research and view metrics for each of those keywords.

Audiences A targeting method that allows you to reach people based on topics, interest categories, or remarketing lists.

automatic placements The placements where your ad is shown across the display network based on the keywords in that ad group.

average cost per click Also known as average CPC, the average amount paid for your clicks. For example, if you spend $100 on keyword and receive 100 clicks, the average cost per click is $1.

average position The average of all the positions where your ad is displayed. If your ad appears once in positions 1, 3, and 5, then your average position is 3.

B

B2B An acronym meaning business to business. It generally refers to businesses selling to other businesses.

B2C An acronym meaning business to consumer. It generally refers to businesses selling to consumers.

benefit An ad copy element that showcases to a consumer a benefit of buying a product.

bid simulator A tool displayed for keywords that shows an estimate of impressions, clicks, and cost that the keyword would accrue if the maximum cost per click was changed.

broad match A keyword matching option that allows your keyword to show for misspellings and related words.

Budget Optimizer A bidding technique also known as "focus on clicks," where AdWords will bid for you in an attempt to maximize the number of clicks a campaign receives.

buying funnel The steps a consumer goes through before buying a product. The stages are awareness, interest, learn, shop, and buy.

C

call extension An ad extension that includes a phone number in the ad copy.

campaign A collection of ad groups. In AdWords, most of the options for controlling your ad's display are set at the campaign level and affect every ad group within that campaign.

campaign report An AdWords report that displays metrics for each campaign.

click A click occurs when someone sees your ad and then clicks on it.

click-through rate (CTR) A calculation of the number of times your ad is clicked divided by impressions (the number of times that ad is displayed). If your ad has 100 impressions and 2 clicks, it has a 2 percent click-through rate.

conditional formatting A tool found in many spreadsheets, including Excel, that allows you to apply formats to cells or a range of cells based on formulas or conditions in other cells.

content network The old name for the display network.

conversion A conversion occurs when a consumer conducts an action on your site that you deem valuable, such as subscribing to a newsletter, buying a product, or contacting your business.

Conversion Optimizer A bidding technique also known as "focus on conversions," where AdWords bids for you in an attempt to maximize the conversions a campaign receives.

conversion rate A formula derived from dividing the number of conversions a data point (keyword, placement, ad, etc.) receives by the number of clicks. If a keyword receives 100 clicks that lead to 2 conversions, that keyword has a 2 percent conversion rate.

cost per click (CPC) How much a click costs. Related to average cost per click.

cost per conversion Also known as cost per action (CPA), the average amount it costs to receive conversions. The formula is total cost divided by total number of conversions. If an account spends $100 and receives 20 conversions, the cost per conversion is $5.

CPA See *cost per conversion*.

CPM An acronym for cost per thousand impressions.

CPM bidding Also known as "focus on impressions," this bidding technique is only available for display network campaigns. With CPM bidding, you bid how much you are willing to pay each time your ad receives 1,000 impressions.

D

daily budget The amount you are willing to spend on a campaign each day. Each campaign must have its own daily budget.

demographic bidding Demographic bidding allows you to automatically raise your max cost per click based on gender and age characteristics of the person viewing your ad. Currently available only for the display network.

Demographic report An AdWords report that displays metrics based on demographic information, such as age and gender.

destination URL An aspect of an ad that defines what page the user is taken to after they click on an ad.

Destination URL report An AdWords report that displays metrics for each destination URL used within an account.

Display Ad Builder A tool found inside an AdWords account that allows you to build different types of ads, such as video and image ads.

display network A collection of sites that have partnered with Google to display AdWords ads. Display network ads are displayed based on the content of a page matching your keywords or chosen placements.

display URL An aspect of ad that allows the viewer to understand where they will be taken if they click on an ad.

DoubleClick Ad Planner A research tool offered by Google that lets you see detailed statistics for websites and search for websites based on a variety of criteria.

dynamic keyword insertion (DKI) A tool that allows you to automatically insert a keyword from your ad group into the ad copy.

E

enhanced display network A technique of using both placements and keywords in the same ad group to control where your ad is displayed on the display network. Now more commonly referred to as keyword managed placements.

exact match A keyword matching option that allows your keyword to show only when the search query matches your keyword exactly.

F

feature A term used in ad copy to explain an attribute or aspect of a product or service.

first page bid The minimum bid for a keyword to appear on page 1 for all geographies where the corresponding ad could be displayed.

frequency The average number of times a unique individual sees your ad in a certain time period. It is generally a measurement used for CPM ads.

frequency capping A campaign setting that allows you to cap the number of times an individual will see your ad in a given time frame. Frequency capping only applies to the display network.

G

Geographic report An AdWords report that displays performance metrics for the geographies where your ads were displayed.

geo-qualified keyword Keywords that include geographic modifiers, such as "Chicago dentist" or "Arizona insurance."

Google AdWords Google's advertising platform.

Google AdWords Certified Partner A certification offered by Google for those who meet certain requirements.

Google Analytics A Google tool that allows you to see detailed statistics for a website once you have installed a free script on your website pages.

Google Merchant Center A shopping website where merchants can add their products.

Google Places A website where you can input your local business information. This information can be connected to AdWords through ad extensions to display additional location information in the ad.

Google Plus Google's social network.

H

headline The top line of an ad.

I

image ad An ad made of a still or animated image ad type that can be shown across the display network.

impression The number of times a data point (keyword, ad, etc.) is displayed on search result or display network pages.

impression share The percentage of times an ad is shown when it is eligible to be shown.

Impression Share report A campaign report that includes impression share metrics.

interest targeting A method of targeting people across the display network based on their interests.

Invalid Clicks report A campaign report that includes information on the number of invalid clicks the campaign received.

K

keyword A single word or phrase inside an ad group that signals to AdWords that you would like an ad displayed when that word matches the search query. The match type is used in conjunction with a keyword to determine whether your ad should be displayed for any given search query.

keyword density analyzer A program that examines a page or set of pages and displays the frequency with which words and phrases appear on those pages.

keyword insertion See *dynamic keyword insertion (DKI)*.

keyword match type Signals to AdWords how closely your keyword needs to be related to the search query before your ad can be displayed. The three options are broad, phrase, and exact.

L

landing page The page that is displayed after an ad is clicked.

landing page load time The length of time it takes for the landing page to load. This is a factor of Quality Score.

location extension An ad extension that is specific to a geographic location. This additional location information may be appended to ad text.

location targeting A campaign setting that allows you to choose where an ad will be displayed.

M

managed placements Display network websites, specifically chosen and managed by an advertiser, on which to display ads.

match type See *keyword match type*.

max CPC Also known as maximum CPC, the bid set for a keyword, ad group, or placement and the most an advertiser will pay for a click.

max CPM Also known as maximum CPM, a bid set for a placement or ad group and the most an advertiser will pay for 1,000 impressions.

mobile ad See *WAP ad*.

modified broad match A variation of broad match where a plus sign has been added to one or more words in a keyword phrase to signify that the search query must contain the word, or a very close variant of that word, to which the plus sign is attached in order to qualify for the auction.

multivariate testing A testing method that simultaneously tests several variables to determine which combination of variables is the best.

My Change History tool An AdWords tool that allows you to see what changes were made in an AdWords account.

My Client Center (MCC) An administrative interface that allows you to connect, view, and manage multiple AdWords accounts from a single login.

N

navigational query A search query where the user's intent is to find a specific page on the Web. Examples include "Google," "Facebook," or "IMDB Sean Connery."

negative keyword A keyword matching option that allows you to stop an ad from being displayed if the search query contains a listed negative keyword.

P

pay per click (PPC) An advertising medium where the advertiser is only charged for each click that an ad accrues.

phrase match A keyword matching option that allows your keyword to show only when the search query contains that keyword. Phrase match will allow matches on search queries that contain additional words before and/or after the keyword within the search query.

pivot table A data summarization tool found in Microsoft Excel and other spreadsheet programs.

placement Locations on the display network where an ad is displayed. A placement can be a domain, section of a website, or an individual ad unit within a website.

Placement report An AdWords report that shows metrics for each placement where your ad is displayed. You can see individual URLs of the sites that display the ads.

premium ads Ads that show above the natural search results at the top of a page.

product extension An extension that includes product data from Google merchant center.

profit per click The average amount of profit a data point (ad , keyword, etc.) receives each time it receives a click. Profit per click is calculated as profit divided by clicks. If a keyword leads to $100 in profits on 50 clicks, then the average profit per click is $2.

profit per impression The average amount of profit a data point (ad, keyword, etc.) receives each time it is displayed. Profit per impression is calculated as profit divided by impressions. If an ad copy receives 1,000 impressions that lead to $100 in sales, on average each impression is worth $0.10.

Q

Quality Score A measure of how relevant an ad copy, landing page, or keyword is. Quality Score is used to determine your ad rank and whether an ad should be displayed.

R

reach The total number of unique users who see an ad over a given time period.

remarketing A method of showing display network ads exclusively to people after they have visited your site.

return on ad spend (ROAS) Similar to ROI, but it does not contain cost other than ad spend. It is calculated as (Revenue – Ad Spend) / Revenue, or alternatively as 1 –{(Revenue – Ad Spend) / Revenue}.

return on investment (ROI) A formula used to determine the efficiency of an investment. To calculate ROI, use this formula: ROI = (profit – investment) / investment.

revenue per page view (RPV) A measure of how much revenue each page view or 1,000 page views generate. Pertains to publishers who sell ad space on their sites.

rich media ads Ads that contain media types other than text, such as video or images.

S

search partners Websites that Google has partnered with to display Google search ads.

search query The words typed into a search engine by a user.

Search Query report An AdWords report that displays metrics based on the user search queries.

Search Terms report An alternate name for the Search Query report.

site and category exclusion tool An AdWords tool that allows you to exclude ads being shown on certain domains, subdomains, IP addresses, or certain types of content.

sitelinks extension An ad extension that shows links to specific pages on your site underneath the ad copy.

smart pricing The discounting system used by AdWords to determine what an advertiser should be charged for a click on the display network based on how likely a site is to lead to a conversion.

social extension An ad copy extension that includes Google+ information.

spider A program that crawls the Web indexing content.

split testing Testing two variables against each other at one time to determine which leads to better performance.

T

topic targeting A method of targeting based on the topics across the display network.

transactional query A search query where the user is looking for a site on which to conduct a transaction. Some examples are "buy LCD TV" or "plumber phone number."

V

value per click An AdWords reporting metric that displays the average revenue that a click generates.

video ad An ad type that can be shown across the display network that contains video.

W

WAP ad An ad type that shows on phones that do not have full HTML browsers.

Index

Note to the reader: Throughout this index **boldfaced** page numbers indicate primary discussions of a topic. *Italicized* page numbers indicate illustrations.

Symbols

- (negative sign), in search query, 211
& (ampersand), in URL, 124
! (exclamation point), in ad copy, 93
? (question mark), for query delimiter in URL, 123–124
~ (tilde) search command, for finding keywords, **211**
+ (plus) sign, for important keywords, 38–39
+1 button, 112

A

A/B test
   creating landing page for, **481–484**
   for landing pages, 480
Abandoned Cart Shoppers code, 298
About.com, 27
accessibility, for website, **143–144**
account. *See* AdWords account
account history, and Quality Score, 198
account visibility, 166
active cookies
   numbers of, **297**
   viewing in shared library, 294, *295*
ad copy, 85
   adding phone number, 110
   address display in, 344, *344*
   associating with user intent, 35
   "best," 457
   best practices for writing, 118
   calls-to-action in, **89–90**, 175, *175*
   display URL, **106–108**
distinguishing features and benefits, **94–98**
efforts to improve, **116–117**
and expectation of searcher, 12
format to start utilizing features and benefits, 97
Google editorial guidelines, **91–93**
   character length, 91
   editorial requirements, 92–93
informational, **103–105**
inserting address into, **341–344**
jargon in, 23
and landing page, 154, **474–478**
for locals vs. non-locals, **340–346**
negative, **105–106**
for new account, 519
numbers in, **99–102**
purpose, **10–12**
reflecting customer's question, 104
reflecting search query, **86–87**
regional lingo in, 339–340
relevance of keywords to, 196
screenshots, 86
for search queries, 446
"secret" in, 102
testimonials and reviews in, **104–105**
testing, 450–451, 455–456, 499, 527
   on display network, *531*
   in interest targeting, 307
writing, creativity in, **454–455**
writing effective, **88–90**
writing multiple, 370–371
writing that sells, **174–176**
writing thousands, 368–373

ad display
    based on day of week, **439–440**
    control of, **54–55**
    at top vs. side, 404
        click-through rates and, *502*
ad extensions, *108*, **108–113**
    call extensions, **110–112**, *111*
        with smartphones, *227*, **227**
        for tracking phone calls, **385–386**
    product extensions, *110*, **110**
    sitelink extensions, *108*, **108–109**,
        109
    social extension, **112–113**
Ad Group Performance report, **498–499**
ad groups, 26
    account limits, 424
    adding multiple match types to,
        52–53
    average Quality Score, 215
    bids
        Ad Group Performance report
            and, 499
        as default bids, 391
    brand-specific, 367
    code in URL, 127
    cost per action (CPA) for, 388
    creating, 366, **520–521**
        Excel for thousands, **364–368**
        ground rules for display network,
            251–252
        highly relevant, **209–212**
    importing into AdWords Editor, **368**
    keywords in, *278*
        number of, 88
        placements and keywords, 276
        refining by, 305
    labels, *420*, **420–421**
    listing for new campaign, 517
    managed placements, **271–273**, *272*,
        277, 522
    minimum number, 32
    moving keywords to, 218
    multiple ads running in, *457*
    negative keywords in, 46
    negative phrase match keywords in, *49*

organizing to increase CTR and
        conversion rates, **445–446**
    remarketing, **296**
    report organization, 418–420
    restricting match types by, **53**
    targeted ads for, 518
    theme, 207
ad ID, 125
Ad Performance report, **459–462**,
    499–501, 531
    advanced settings, *460*, *461*
    finding underperforming ads, **501**
    pivot table for, *500*
Ad Planner (DoubleClick), **312–319**,
    520, *523*, *537*
    conducting research, **312–319**
    detailed website information, 315,
        315
    filtering bar, 313, *314*
Ad Preview tool, *347*
ad rank, 43, 52, 498
    and Quality Score, **194–195**
    for search network, 192
ad scheduling, *406*, **406–415**
    copying from one day to another,
        408
    examples of success, **410–415**
    multiple campaigns and, 430
    trend analysis for, *527*
Ad Share, 70
add-to-cart buttons, 178
address, inserting into ad copy, **341–344**
administrative access, to My Client
    Center, **426–427**
Adobe Flash pages, 62
ads
    creating keyword insertion, **167–170**,
        168
    finding underperforming, **501**
    premium, 218–219, *219*
    ranked order of, 192
    strategies to increase display
        frequency, **162–166**
    testing types, 460
"Ads by Google," 247

Ads Preferences page, 306
Adsbot-Google, 177, 202
Adsbot-Google-Mobile, 202
adult content, 60
advertiser, transparency of data to, 7
advertising. *See also* landing pages
    goals, vs. Google vs. searcher, **15–16**
    vs. information, **13–15**
    intrusive vs. helpful, 14
    local belief systems and response
        rates, 345
    pay-per-click (PPC), 1
    performance-based, 3
    placement, auction process for
        keyword and, 4–5
advocacy phase, in buying cycle, 20
AdWords account
    basics, **424–429**
    campaign creation, **516–524**
    changes review before uploading, *362*
    combining Google Analytics with,
        385
    limits, 424–425
    linking with Google Analytics
        account, 127
    linking with Local Business Center
        account, 342
    management
        best practices, **539–540**
        of multiple accounts, **425–428**
    multiple people with access, **360–362**
    organization, 209, **365–367**, 423
        best practices, **446–448**
        granular, 87
        planning, 514
    planning for, **514–515**
    reports for optimizing, **497–509**
    scaling, **362–373**
AdWords Bid Simulator, **404–405**, *405*
AdWords Campaign Experiments
    (ACE), 305, **486–489**, *487*
AdWords Certified Partner, logo, *428*
AdWords conversion tracking code,
    380–383, *383*, 386, 416
    publisher use of, 398

on thank-you pages, 383, *383*
AdWords Discounter, 257
AdWords Editor, 71, 213, 353, 516
    advantages of using, **373**
    basics, **354–362**
    best practices, **374–375**
    bulk import feature, 368, 403
    downloading, 354
    to duplicate campaign, 439
    importing keywords and ad groups,
        368
    interface, **354–358**, *355*
    keyboard shortcuts, 356–357
    Keywords tab, 362–363, *363*
    optimizing display with, **373–374**
    posting changes online, 359, *359–360*
    syncing file before offline edits, 360
    tabs, *356*
    viewing account in, *358*, **358–362**
    viewing first page bids, *206*
    viewing Quality Scores in, 199, 201,
        201
    visual cues, 358
AdWords Keyword Tool, **58–72**, 536
    accessing, 58
    ad share, search share, and landing
        pages, **69–70**, *70*
    Advanced Options and FIlters, *59*,
        59–60
    browsing through categories, **64–65**,
        65
    campaign Device settings, *225*
    CPC data, 69
    customizing columns in, *67*
    finding new keywords, 58
    Global Monthly Searches in, 68
    input words or phrases, *61*, **61**
    interpreting data, **65–68**
    Local Monthly Searches in, 68
    main screen, *59*
    relative competition level, *68*, 68
    and relevant keywords, 202
    spidering capability, 526
    vs. third-party keyword tools, **71–72**
    trend data, **68–69**, *69*

AdWords preview tool, 227

AdWords reports. *See* reports

AdWords Seminar for Success, landing page, *472*

.aes file extension, 361

affiliate ads, 424

affiliates, 203

age group, bid based on, 287

Agency Land, 429

air cards, location targeting and, 324–325

airport codes, as keywords, 339

alerts
   custom, *509*, **509–510**
   in My Client Center, 427

Amazon.com, 33
   navigational options, 178, 470
      shopping cart, *471*

ambiguous query, testing landing page for, **463–464**

American Express, 182

ampersand (&), in URL, 124

analysis of variance (ANOVA), 457, 481

analytics system, installing, 515

Anderson, Chris, 33

Android devices, 436
   HTML browser on, 224–225

animation, in ads, 235

ANOVA (analysis of variance), 457, 481

AnyBrowser.com, 146

AOL dial-up users, location targeting and, 324

Apple iPhone, 436

ArdenB.com, *468*, *468*, *469*

area codes, 338–339

articles, breaking into multiple pages, 172

.aspx file extension, 381

associations, **152–154**

attribution management, **416–418**

auction process for keyword, and ad placement, 4–5

audience. *See also* target audience
   defining for remarketing, *293*, **293**
   segmenting, 95

authority sites, 27

auto-tagging AdWords data, 128–129

autoinstalling software, 204

automated bid system, 41
   rules, 389

automatic placements, 249
   managing, **265**
   report on, 504, *504*
   viewing data, 260, *260*

autoplay, for video ads, 473

average cost per click, 394

awareness, 25
   campaign for, **437–439**, 443
   CPM ads and, 271
   image ads to increase, 231

awareness phase in buying funnel, 21
   jargon and, 96
   keywords for, 25

B

back button, 121
   disabling, 204

BackRub, 5

below-the-fold inventory, blocking, **270**

benefits
   in ad copy, 95
   ad copy format to start utilizing, 97
   and buying funnel, **96–97**
   vs. features, **97–98**

best practices
   for account organization strategies, **446–448**
   for ad copy writing, 118
   for AdWords account management, **539–540**
   for AdWords Editor, **374–375**
   for bids, 421–422
   for display network, 273–274
      advanced usage, 319–320
   for keyword tools, **82–83**
   for landing pages, **158–159**
   location targeting, **350–352**
   for optimization techniques, **188–189**
   for reports, **511**

search theory, **17**
testing, **489–490**
bid cap, 387
bid per call, 111
Bid Simulator, **404–405**, *405*
bid strategies, 377
marketing goals, **378–379**
bids, 279
ad group-level as default, 391
and ad serving, 456
automatically changing by time
periods, *406*, **406–415**
based on ROAS, **402–403**
alternatives, 415–418
best practices, 421–422
budget optimizer strategy, 438
calculating max CPC, **401–405**
cost per thousand impressions
(CPM), 269–270
demographic, *289*, **289–290**
for display campaign, 521
display network, 499
for exposure, **403–405**, *404*
focus on impressions, **390**
frequency of change in, 535
Impression Share report and, 498
keyword-level, 524–525
keyword report and, 502
lowering, 162
making changes, **525–526**
making multiple changes, 403
and managed placement, 523
for match types, 43, 45
multiple campaigns and, 430
for multiple placements, 286, *287*
options, *386*, **386–390**
profitable strategies, **390–401**
revenue per click, **392–395**
ROAS vs. profit, **391–392**
setting by demographics, **287–292**
setting initial, 519
suggested from Contextual Targeting
tool, **256–257**
bitly.com, 173
BlackBerry Curve, 436

blind auction system, AdWords as, 195
blocking
below-the-fold inventory, **270**
demographic sites, from discovery
campaign, 291
websites, data for decision, **284**
blocking ad display
from domains, *262*, **262**
next to undesirable content, **263**
by page types, **264–265**
from specific website, 282
on websites not converting, **261–262**
blue, on websites, 156
bookmarks, options on web page,
172–173, 187
Booth, Danielle, 133
Bose, e-commerce landing page
example, 178, *179*
bot, 63. *See also* spider
bounce rate, low, 529
brackets, for exact match, 42
brand protection, 263
brand searches
testing landing page for, **466**
volume, 367
branding search campaigns, **437–439**
campaign structure with, *438*
breakeven point, 403
Brin, Sergey, 5
broad match, **36–45**
avoiding estimates with, 65–66
budget and, 43
for campaign settings, 278–280,
279
conversion rate, 44
modified, **38–39**
negative, **47–48**
reasons to use, 40
zip codes and, 339
broadband, 148
broken links, checking site for, 506
browsers, 143
compatibility, **144–146**
default version, 145
enhancing functionality, **146–147**

on mobile phones, **224–226**

w3schools.com on resolution statistics, 149, *150*

web page loading by, 382

browsing AdWords Keyword Tool categories, **64–65**, *65*

browsing the Web, search engines and, 8

budget, 308, 404, 514, *515*

and branding campaign, 438

for campaign, *54*, 429, 430

custom alert, *510*

daily, 162–163

and ad display, 165

managed placements vs. discovery campaign, 283

and match type choice, 43

Budget Optimizer, 387

Budget Optimizer account, 418, 419

budget optimizer bidding strategy, 438

Budget Optimizer campaign, 526, **528–529**

bulk changes, AdWords Editor for, 360

bulk importing, into AdWords Editor, 368

business-to-business

case study, *411*, **411–413**

testing ad on weekdays, 443–444

buttons

add-to-cart, 178

for conversion activities, **156–157**, *157*

buy phase, in buying funnel, 22

buying cycle, 20

buying funnel, *20*, **20–23**, *248*, 310–311

adding conversion actions to different segments, 185

benefits, features and, **96–97**

capturing search data over lifespan, 458

consumer flow through, **22–23**

early stages, conversion rate, 437

free information and entry, 233

and keywords in Budget Optimizer, 387

moving customer through, 311

phases, 21–22

and search behavior, 416

buying guides, 172

C

calculator (Google), for multivariate testing, 480, *480*, *481*

calendar, for AdWords management, 538, *538*, *539*

call extensions, **110–112**, *111*

with smartphones, *227*, **227**

for tracking phone calls, **385–386**

call-in search, 8

call report, 111, *112*

calls-to-action, 311

in ad copy, **89–90**, 175, *175*

for ad groups, 370

ad lacking, *233*

in image ads, 233–234, *234*

on landing page, 120–121, 454

strength of, **102–103**

in video ad, 238

campaign level

ad extensions for, 108

billing options in, 386

limits on ad groups within, 53

limits on match types by, **53–54**

negative keywords at, 47, 54

campaigns. *See also* display campaigns; search campaigns

account limits, 424

broad reach, 278–280, *279*

Budget Optimizer, *526*, **528–529**

creating, **516–524**

demographic, **290–292**

developing successful structure, **429–444**

display vs. search, *253*

duplicating, 226

location targeting set for, 326

multiple to reach all searchers, **336–337**

optimizing, **524–539**

reasons for multiple, **430–431**

reports, **497–498**
search- and display-only, **250**
separate for different countries,
  334–335
specific reach, 280
structure to achieve business goals,
  431–444
  awareness or branding search
    campaigns, **437–439**
  day of week ad variations,
    439–440
  defining goals, **442–444**
  desktop vs. mobile users, **435–437**
  location-based goals, **432–435**, *433*
  maximizing returns, **431–432**
  organizing based on goals or
    budgets, **440–442**, *441*
Canada, conversion rates and, 507–508
capitalization
  in ad copy, 92
  for keyword insertion, 168
card verification value (CVV), 140
case studies
  business-to-business, *411*, **411–413**
  high-end electronics, *413*, **413–415**
category, Ad Planner filtering by, *318*,
  318
cell cards, location targeting and,
  324–325
cell phones, **224–226**
  call extensions with, *227*, **227**
  speed of, 225
central point, reaching users around, 331
certification, by Google, **428–429**
Certified Knowledge
  Broken Link Checker, 506
  Google Analytics URL Builder, 127
  Mass Ad Copy Creator, 371
  website, 469, *470*
Certified Partner, 428
  materials, *428*
Change History report, 361
character length
  for ad copy, 91
  formula-based ads and, **372–373**

chi-square distribution, 457, 481
Chrome browser
  resizing text in, *144*
  translating speech into search
    queries, 8
cities
  crossing state lines, location targeting
    and, 325
  names as keywords, 338
  search engine accuracy in
    determining, 326
Click-Assisted Conversions, 417, *418*
click prices, for display network, 258
click-through rates (CTR), 162, *175*,
  192
  ad group organization to increase,
    445–446
  and ad placement, 6–7
  discounts and, 100
  on exact site, 207
  negative keywords and, 45
  and Quality Score, **195–196**, 217, 508
CMS (content management system), 515
code identifiers, collecting from callers,
  386
cognitive load, 174
color
  ad and landing page, 474, *475*
  for websites, **156**
color blindness, **155**
columns
  in AdWords Keyword Tool,
    customizing, 67
  in reports, customizing, *493*,
    493–495, *494*
comment icon, in AdWords Editor, 358,
  358
comparison shopping, benefits and, 97
competition
  ads, 102
  bids, 195
  and keyword research, 27
  and Quality Score formulas, 218
  theme use, 99
  with yourself, 389

comScore, 312
concepts, turning into words, **8–10**
conditional formatting in Excel, 206, *394*, **394–395**, 418
  for keyword profitability, *525*
confidence factors, 386
constraints, for search queries, 52
consumers. *See* customer
content management system (CMS), 515
content network, 247. *See also* display network
  hierarchy for destination URLs, 123
Contextual Targeting tool, *256*, **256–257**
Conv. Value/Click column, 393, *393*
conversion analysis, 143
conversion category, tracking, 380
conversion data, accessing in AdWords reports, **384–385**
conversion funnel, 186
  tracking long sales cycles with, **399–401**, *401*
Conversion Optimizer, **388–390**, 456
conversion rate
  ad group organization to increase, **445–446**
  discounts and, 452
  e-commerce, **178–179**
  increasing form-fill, **180–184**, *181*
  keyword insertion and, 169–170
  landing pages and, **131–142**, **176–185**, *505*
  negative keywords and, 45, 54
  optimization for, **174–187**
  and psychological factors, **151–158**
  by time of day, 410, *411*
  usability and, 142
  viewing by hour, *410*
  viewing by time frames, 507
conversion tracking, negative keywords and, 45
conversion tracking script for Google, 379, **380–383**, *383*
conversion value field, in AdWords reports, 381–382

conversions
  adding actions to different buying funnel segments, 185
  buttons or text links, **156–157**, *157*
  finding information by time frames, **408–410**
  minimum amount for testing, 459
  options, **186–187**
  testing landing pages to increase, **462–484**
  tracking, **398–399**, 515
converter cookie, 298
cookies, 382
  defining length, 293
  estimate, and actual population, 328
  from remarketing script, 292
  viewing active, in shared library, 294, *295*
copy and paste, in AdWords Editor, *356–357*
copying ad scheduling from one day to another, *408*
copyright symbol, in ad copy, 93
corporate VPNs, location targeting and, 324
cost per acquisition (CPA), 53
cost per action (CPA), 380
  for ad groups, 388
  target vs. max, **388–390**
cost per click (CPCs), 162, 380
  determining actual from Quality Score, **194–195**
  Enhanced bidding, **387–388**
  for image and rich media ads, 231
cost per conversion, 380
  for measuring success, **257–259**
  negative keywords and, 45
cost per thousand impressions (CPM), 3, 162, *508*
  ads, and search ads, 534
  bidding, **269–270**
  in management placements, 208
  optimizing campaigns, **533–534**
cost per view (CPV), 242

countries
  costs per click (CPCs) by, *59*
  names as keywords, 338
  optimization based on, 334
  of origin, search engine accuracy in
    determining, 325
  targeting multiple, **333–335**
coupons, **154–155**, 187
CPA (cost per action), 380
  for ad groups, 388
  target vs. max, **388–390**
CPCs (cost per click), 162, 380
  determining actual from Quality
    Score, 194–195
  Enhanced bidding, **387–388**
  for image and rich media ads, 231
CPM. *See* cost per thousand impressions
  (CPM)
CPP bidding, 111
credit cards
  CVV (card verification value), 140
  forms, vs. non-credit card form, 182
cross-account reporting, 427
CSV files, for website placements,
  268–269
curing searches, 24
custom alerts, *509*, **509–510**
Custom Search Engine (Google), 28
customer
  ad copy language and, 88–89
  ad copy reflecting question of, 104
  click location, 150
  contact options, 185
  conveying proper experience,
    476–477
  cost to acquire, 53
  flow through buying funnel, **22–23**
  forcing registration, 180
  image for focus, **155**
  interest determination, **81**
  moving through buying funnel, 311
  options for those not ready to buy,
    184–185
  reaching in specific location, **326–333**

relationships, thank-you pages and,
  141
remarketing to, **303–304**
  and "creeping out," **304–305**
respecting time of, 183
shopping cart access, 179
trust errors with, 381
unclear intent of keyword, 138, *138*
CVV (card verification value), 140

D

daily budget, 162–163
  and ad display, 165
data cards, location targeting and,
  324–325
data point, unique phone number per,
  385
day of month, conversion rates by, *413*
day-of-week
  ad display based on, **439–440**
  conversion information, *412*
    finding in AdWords reports,
      408–410
day parting, 406
December, avoiding for test data, 458
dedicated landing pages, **176–177**
deep keywords, vs. wide, 35–36
DEKE (Dynamic Keyword Insertion
  Simulator), 168
deleting
  keyboard shortcut for, 357
  keywords, 437, *526*
Delivery.com, 475, *475*
demand for goods, creating on
  nonsearch sites, 443
demographic bidding, **287–292**
  multiple campaigns and, 430
  report on, 537
  setting, *289*, **289–290**
    in current display campaigns, 291
  viewing statistics, **287–289**, *288*
demographic campaign, organizing,
  290–292

Demographic report, **507**

demographic research, Google Ad
 Planner for, 314, 315

density analysis, for keywords, *255*,
 255–256

description lines, in ad copy, 98

desktops
 ad copy for, **435–437**
 campaign for, 524
 fee for calls on, 111
 keyword research filtering by, 60

Destination URL report, *482*, 482–483,
 505–506, *527*

destination URLs, *122*, **122–131**
 for ad, 122
 adding custom parameters, **124–125**
 and display URL, 106–108
 editorial policies, 130–131
 gclid on, 128
 guide to building, **126–130**
 for tracking, **123–125**

device platforms
 multiple campaigns and, 430
 settings for, 436

DexKnows.com, 27

Digg, 8, 173

dimension reports, **505–509**

direct mail, keywords in, 27

disapproved ads, finding, *501*, **501**

discounts, **154–155**
 in ad copy, 99–100
 testing, 476
  vs. prices, **452–455**

Discover, 182

discovery campaign, 283, 286
 blocking demographic sites from, 291

Display Ad Builder, **239–243**, *240*
 accessing, *239*
 ad creation screen, *241*

display ads
 account limits, 424
 matching with pages in display
  network, **249–257**
 targeting, 308–309
 writing effective, **310–312**

display campaigns, 250, **431–432**
 Budget Optimizer for, 528
 Campaign setting for reach, 534
 enhancing, **276–287**
 keyword-based, **519–521**
 optimizing, **280–282**, **530–531**
 organizing, **282–287**
 vs. search campaigns, 253
 settings for, 520

display network, 193, **245–274**
 ad groups, ground rules for creating,
  251–252
 advantages, **247–248**
 basics, **246–249**
 best practices, **273–274**
  for advanced usage, **319–320**
 bids, 499
 bids for automatic placement, 530
 examining, **248–249**
 general keywords in, 431
 matching display ads with pages,
  249–257
 organization flowchart, 286, *287*
 performance, **259–265**
  network reports, **259–261**
 Quality Score, **207–209**
 reasons to use, 311
 reports, **503–505**, *504*
 schedule for assessing, 537
 testing ad copy on, 531
 writing ads for, **310–312**

display network CTRs, vs. search
 CTRs, 207

display reach, general, 308

display URL
 in ad copy, **106–108**
 click-through rate within ad group,
  196
 maximum length, 130

DKI (dynamic keyword insertion),
 166–170
 testing, 453

DMOZ.org, 27

Dogpile, 72

domains, blocking from ad display, **262**, *262*

Donnelley (R.H.), landing page for Royal Volkswagen, 478, *479*

DoubleClick Ad Planner, **312–319**, 520, 523, 537

conducting research, **312–319**

detailed website information, *315*, 315

filtering bar, 313, *314*

Download And Schedule Report screen, 495, *495*

downloading

AdWords Editor, 354

data for reports, *495*, **495–496**

Driving Directions, providing, 187

duplicate content penalty, 177, 203

duration of call, 111

duration of cookies, and active cookie count, 297

dynamic ads, 235

dynamic keyword insertion (DKI), **166–170**

testing, 453

Dynamic Keyword Insertion Simulator (DEKE), 168

E

e-commerce checkout, 140, 187

ego bidding, 403

eHarmony, special offers landing page, *477*

eligibility, to appear on specific display sites, 192–193

emotion, ad copy and, 90, *91*

Engage, 429

Enhanced CPC bidding, **387–388**

enhanced targeting, 249

error page, blocking ad display, 264, *264*

estimated first page bid, vs. value per click, 394

exact match, **42–43**

budget and, 43

conversion rate, 44

negative, **49**

Exact Match IS column, 165, 497, 498

exact number, in ad copy, 101

Excel

advantages of using, **373**

chi-square distribution or ANOVA, 457

conditional formatting, 206, *394*, **394–395**

for character limits, 372

creating ad copy in, 368–370, *369*

importing keywords from, **362–364**, *364*

mass-creating keywords and ad copy in, **364–368**, 372

pivot tables

from Ad Planner data, 316–317

creating, 215

geographic data in, 349, *349*

from keyword list, 318

report on keyword value per click data, *393*

for setting bids by ROAS, 403

Excel plug-in tool, Microsoft Advertising Intelligence as, 81

exclamation point (!), in ad copy, 93

expandable video ads, 242–243

expectations

for search landing page, 120

of search results, 10, 11

expert reviews, 105

explicit keywords, 24

Export Changes for Sharing (AES), *361*, 361–362

exposure, bids for, **403–405**, *404*

extension betas, 113

Extracted From Webpage data, 70

F

Facebook, 152, 173

faces on websites, 155

testing use, 470–471

fake reviews, 152

favicon, on Google Maps, 343

featured phones, 228

features
  in ad copy, **94–95**
  ad copy format to start utilizing, 97
  vs. benefits, **97–98**
  and buying funnel, **96–97**
feed placements, 268
feed readers, 268
file formats
  for image ads, 235
  for video ads, 238
files, syncing before offline edits in
  AdWords Editor, 360
filtering, *59*, **59–60**
  ad groups, *421*
  by computer type, 60
  in Google Ad Planner
    by ad size and type, **318–319**
    by category, *318*, **318**
    by other sites visited, 317, *317*
finding
  conversion information by time
    frames, **408–410**
  disapproved or paused ads, *501*, **501**
  locations for targeting, **327–331**,
    328
  sites to block, Google Analytics for,
    285
  underperforming ads, **501**
Firefox
  plug-ins, 147
    for browser appearance on mobile
      device, 230
  profile with default settings, 146
Firesizer, *150*
first impressions, 119
  from landing pages, 158
first page bid, 192
  estimating, **205–206**, **403–404**
Flash, 227
Flash pages (Adobe), 62, **146–147**
FlashBlock, 147
Focus on Clicks, option for bidding,
  386–387
focus on impressions, *533*
font size of website, **143–144**

forms
  credit card vs. non-credit card, 182
  ease of completing, 183
  increasing conversion rate, **180–184**,
    181
  as landing pages, **139–140**
  tracking abandoned, 184
formula-based ads, character limits and
  naming conventions, **372–373**
formulas, for multiple ad groups,
  371–372
forums, blocking ad display, 265
franchise companies, and trademarks,
  114
Free Clicks report, *533*
free listings, for searches, 15
free training offers, targeting users
  accepting, **301–302**
frequency capping, **272–273**, *508*
  and remarketing, 304

G

GAP (Google Advertising Professional),
  428–429
gclid, on destination URL, 128
gender, bid based on, 287
general display reach, 308
general keywords, for display network
  ad group, 252
general offers, 311
geographic ads
  displaying to searchers outside
    region, 330
  testing, **452–453**
Geographic Keyword Finder Tool, 338
geographic keywords, most popular,
  337–340
geographic regions
  account performance in, 198
  search campaigns for, **78–79**
Geographic report, *348*, **348–350**,
  507–508, *527*
geographic targeting, 321. *See also*
  location targeting

GeoTrust, 149
Global Monthly Searches, in AdWords
    Keyword Tool, 68
global web stats, from w3schools.com,
    144–145
goals
    for campaign, 378
    campaign structure to achieve,
        431–444
        awareness or branding search
            campaigns, **437–439**
        day of week ad variations,
            439–440
        defining goals, **442–444**
        desktop vs. mobile users, **435–437**
        location-based goals, **432–435**,
            433
        maximizing returns, **431–432**
        organizing based on goals or
            budgets, **440–442**, *441*
    Google, vs. advertiser vs. searcher,
        15–16
Goog-411, 8
Google, 5–6
    calculator, for multivariate testing,
        480, *480*, *481*
    data about search queries, 58
    data transfer by, 306
    editorial policy page, 236
    goals, vs. advertiser vs. searcher,
        15–16
    growth, 6
    profits, 16
    remarketing policies, 297
    unique queries, 38
    Website Optimizer, 481
    vs. Yahoo!, *5*
Google account, 31
    terms of service, 424
        multiple unlinked and, 31
Google Ad Planner
    adding sites to AdWords, **319**
    for demographic research, 314, *315*
    filtering
        by ad size and type, **318–319**

by category, *318*, **318**
    by other sites visited, *317*, 317
    finding related websites, **316–317**
Google Advertising Professional (GAP),
    428–429
Google AdWords, 7
    account limits, 30–31
    Ad Extensions tab, Location
        Extensions, 342
    adding Ad Planner sites to, **319**
    adjust network settings, *250*
    Audiences tab, 296, *296*
        Interests, *306*
    Campaigns tab, 492
        Competitive Metrics category, 163
    Dimensions tab, 287, *288*, *492*
        call report in, 111, *112*
    impression share report, **163–166**,
        164
    Keywords tab, 492
    management calendar, *538*, *538*, *539*
    Networks tab, *259*, *259*, *504*
        excluding categories using, 261
        Managed Placement section, 266
    origins, *2*, **2–7**
    Settings tab, Location And
        Languages section, 326, *327*
    Tools & Analysis tab
        Conversions section, 417
        Placement tool, 266
    Topics tab, 307, *307*
Google AdWords conversion tracker,
    259
Google AdWords Select, **6–7**
Google Analytics, 27, 515
    account setup, 128
    auto-tagging AdWords data for, *129*
    bounce within, *529*
    to find sites to block, **285**
    goal tracking, **385**
    goals associated with last entrance to
        website, 416
    linking account with AdWords
        account, 127
    URL Builder tool, *126*, **126–128**

Google display network, 193
Google editorial guidelines for ad copy, **91–93**
  character length, 91
  editorial requirements, 92–93
Google Engage, 429
Google Insights for Search, **76–81**, *78*, 538
Google Maps
  ads on, 344
  icons on, 343
Google Merchant Account, 110
Google Mobile, 230
Google mobile ads, **228–230**, *239*
Google network, 193
Google Places account, 342, 343
Google Plus, 173
Google representative, and multiple accounts for same business, 424
Google search engine, country extension of, 322
Google search network, 193
Google Trends, **74–76**, *75*, *76*, 538
Google Webmaster Central account, 202
Googlebot, 202
GoTo.com, 2, 3
  ad placement, 7
  patent, *5*
grammar, in ad copy, 92
granular account organization, 87
green circle, in AdWords Editor, *358*
green, on websites, 156
Gross, Bill, 2
grouping keywords, two-word rule for, 26

H

headlines for ad, 11, 98
  character length, 91
Herder, Eelco, *Off the Beaten Tracks*, 150
high-end electronics case study, *413*, **413–415**
high-quality sites, 281, 284

Hitwise, 312
holidays
  avoiding for test data, 458
  shopping trends and remarketing, 303
hotel, location campaigns for, 333
hour, viewing conversion rates by, *410*
hover items, on landing page, 204
HTTP script, 295
HTTPS script, 295
hub sites, 27
human faces, testing use on website, 470–471

I

icons, on Google Maps, 343
Idealab, 2
IDN (Internationalized Domain Name) converter, 131
ifcontent variable, 125
ifsearch variable, 125
iGoogle, 8
image ads
  ad group for, 521
  best practices, 243–244
  and bidding CPM, 270
  calls-to-action in, 233–234, *234*
  creating, **231–236**
    guidelines for, 232–235
    technical and editorial requirements, **235–236**
  file formats for, 235
image-sharing pages, blocking ad display, 265
images
  consumer focus and, **155**
  left-to-right reading and position of, *471*, 471–472
  mobile ads, 227
  opening for video ads, 237
important keywords, plus (+) sign for, 38–39
importing keywords
  into AdWords Editor, **368**
  from Excel, **362–364**, *364*

Impr. Share (IS) column, 165, 497, 498
Impression Share report, **163–166**, *164*,
    497–498, 527
impressions, 2
    bid focus on, **390**
    paying for, **3**
impulse purchase, 171
In-Page Analytics tool, 464
in-stream video ads, 242
in-video static image, 243
"inbox," 103
industry, Google policies on, 93
information
    vs. advertising, **13–15**
    gathering in buying funnel, 21
    retrieval from landing pages, **478**
informational ad copy, 89, **103–105**
informational query, 25, 132, **133–134**
    leveraging, **134–136**
    testing landing page for, **463**
inserting address into ad copy, **341–344**
interest phase in buying funnel, 21
    jargon and, 96
interest targeting, 299–302, 305–307,
    306
Internationalized Domain Name (IDN)
    converter, 131
Internet Advertising Bureau (IAB),
    standard ad sizes, 235
Internet connection, speed of, 148
Internet Explorer, default conditions,
    145, 146
Invalid Clicks report, 497
IP address, and location-based ads, 323
IP campaign, 336
iPhone device, HTML browser on,
    224–225

J

Jansen, Bernard, 133
jargon, 89
    as keywords, 23
Java, 146–147

K

keyboard shortcuts, in AdWords Editor,
    356–357
keyword-based display campaigns,
    creating, **519–521**
keyword density analyzer, 277
keyword level
    bids, **524–525**
    destination URLs at, 128
        setting, **122–123**
keyword lists, 29
    creating, **31–32**
    website for jumpstarting, **62–64**
keyword performance report, 317–318
keyword report, **502**
    pivot table from, 214–216, *216*
keyword tools, best practices for, **82–83**
keywords, **23–36**
    account limits, 424
    ad rank score for, 194
    best practices for research, **55**
    conversion data for, *384*, 384–385
    density analysis, *255*, 255–256
    for display network ad group,
        252–255
    dynamic insertion, **166–170**
    Excel for creating thousands,
        364–368
    finding ideas, **26**
    for general display reach, 308
    generating ideas, **60–64**
    importance, 19
    importing
        into AdWords Editor, **368**
        from Excel, **362–364**, *364*
    jargon as, 23
    knowledge of, **28–29**
    location for saving data, **70–71**, *71*
    and location targeting, 335–336
    long-tail, **33–35**
    match types, **36–45**
        broad match, **36–38**
        exact match, **42–43**
        modified broad match, **38–39**

phrase match, 40–41
selecting best, 43–45
mixer tools, 32
most popular geographic, 337–340
moving to new ad groups, 218
negative, 45–52. *See also* negative
 keywords
negative and positive together, 50–51
number in account, 29–31
organizational techniques, 52–54
place in buying cycle, 20
refining ad group by, 305
for refining display exposure,
 276–278, *277*
research
 for ad group, 518
 for starting campaign, 516
resuming after pause, 218
saving, and Quality Score, 218
starting research, 27–28
tilde (~) search command for finding
 relevant, 211
two-word rule for grouping, 26
types, 24–25
unclear consumer intent, 138, *138*
unprofitable, *525*
wide vs. deep, 35–36

L

landing page quality factor, 197
landing pages, **12–13**, 35, **119–159**
 ad copy and, 92, 454, **474–478**
 for ad group, 211
 and AdWord Keyword Tool, *62*
 and answer to searcher's question,
  120–122
 best practices for, **158–159**
 crafting perfect, **142**
 creating for A/B test, **481–484**
 creating to increase conversions,
  176–185
 first impressions from, 158
 forms as, **139–140**
 Google spider site for, 70

identifying underperforming, 506
impact on conversion rate, *505*
to increase conversion rates, **131–142**
 based on query type, **132–136**
information retrieval from, **478**
for keywords, 23
keywords based on, 62
load time, and Quality Score,
 197–198
in mobile campaign, 226
for mobile search vs. desktop, 224
navigation on, 204–205, **469–470**
quality, **202–205**
 for display network, 208
relevance of, **202–205**
for search queries, 446
segmentation pages, **138–139**
selecting during account creation,
 517–518
special offers on, **476**
testimonials on, 454, *454*
testing, **462–484**, 527
 factors for, **468–474**
 risk mitigation, 488
Lands' End, organizing remarketing
 campaigns, 302, *303*
language, costs per click (CPCs) by, *59*
laptop devices, keyword research
 filtering by, 60
lead, cost to acquire, 53
lead-generation site, 463
 max CPA for, 388
learning phase in buying funnel,
 21, *96*
left-to-right reading, image position
 and, *471*, 471–472
length of video ad, 238
lifetime RPV, 398
linking accounts, 425, 427
load time, of landing page, and Quality
 Score, **197–198**
local ads, optimizing, 350
local audience, vs. nonlocal, 137–138
 ad copy for, **340–346**
local belief systems, **345–346**

Local Business Center account, linking with AdWords account, 342
local business queries
  differentiating, **136–138**
  testing landing page for, **464**
Local Monthly Searches, in AdWords Keyword Tool, 68
location-based goals, campaigns with, **432–435**, *433*
location targeting, 321
  advanced options, **332–333**, *333*
  basics, **322–326**
    technology of, **322–324**
  best practices, **350–352**
  considerations, **333–340**
  excluding location, **328–330**, *329*
  finding locations, **327–331**, *328*
  most popular geographic keywords, **337–340**
  multiple campaigns and, 430
  performance reports, *348*, **348–350**
  radius targeting, **331–333**, *332*
  reaching users in specific, **326–333**
  users in area smaller than country, **335–340**
  viewing results, **346–348**, *347*
locations of business, showing in ad copy, 342
logic ad copy, 89
long-tail keywords, **33–35**
Lost IS (Budget) column, 165, 497, 498
Lost IS (Rank) column, 165, 497, 498
low bounce rate, *529*
low-quality sites, 281
low-traffic accounts, testing, 458
low-traffic sites, 281, 284
loyalty, coupons and, 155

M

Macintosh, keyboard shortcuts, 357
managed placement ad groups, ongoing management of, **271–273**, *272*
managed placement targeting, 265
managed placements, 193, 249
  in ad groups, *277*

creating demographic campaign with, **290–291**
  for display campaign, **530–531**
  flowchart diagram, 286, *287*
  for general display reach, 308
  Quality Score for, **208–209**
  report on, 504
managed placements campaign, 283, 432, **521–524**
  ad group for, 522
  optimizing, **531–532**
  settings for, 522
management time, and number of keywords, 30
Manager Defined Spend (MDS), 426
margin data, creating reports including, 396, *397*
marketing
  ad copy language and, **88–89**
  vs. sales, and information collection, **182–183**
marketing goals, 514
  bid strategies and, **378–379**
markup language, for conversion tracking script, 381
Mass Ad Copy Creator, 371
MasterCard, 182
match types for keywords, **36–45**, 251
  for account setup, 518
  adding multiple to ad group, **52–53**
  broad match, **36–45**
  competition and, 68
  exact match, **42–43**
  modified broad match, **38–39**
  negative keywords, **47–49**
  phrase match, **40–41**
  reach for, 44
  restricting by ad group, 53
  selecting best, **43–45**
max cost per action (CPA), target vs., **388–390**
maximum CPC
  for budget optimizer, 438
  calculating, **401–405**
  projected changes by, *405*

Mayer, Matthias, *Off the Beaten Tracks*, 150
MCC. *See* My Client Center (MCC)
media plan, creating, 312, *313*
medium-quality sites, 281, 284
messaging, determining, **80**
meta-search engines, Wordtracker and, 72
methodical approach, to testing ads, *450–451*
metrics, **379–386**
metropolitan level
    names as keywords, 338
    search engine accuracy in determining, 325–326
microsites, 177, *178*
Microsoft, *5*
    tutorials on mathematical functions, 457
Microsoft adCenter account, 81
Microsoft Advertising Intelligence, **81–82**, *82*
Microsoft Atlas Solutions, 410
misspellings
    negative keywords and, 48
    phrase match and, 41
mobile ads, **228–230**, *239*, **435–437**
    best practices, 243–244
    creating, **224–231**
    images, 227
    phone number in, 227–228
mobile audience, 223
mobile campaign, 524
    landing pages in, 226
mobile devices. *See also* cell phones
    Call-only Format for ads, 111
    keyword research filtering by, 60
    sending information to, 187
modified broad match
    budget and, 43
    estimating, **67**
multinational companies, campaign in multiple countries, 335
multivariate testing, for landing pages, 480
My Change History tool, *213*, 361

My Client Center (MCC), **425–428**, *426*
    account, 31
        creating, 427, 428
    benefits, **426–428**
    Budget tab, 427, *427*
    nesting, 426

N

names
    for campaign, 516
    formula-based ads and conventions, 372–373
    for reports, 496
narrow theme sites, testing landing page for, **464–465**
navigation, on landing pages, 204–205, 469–470
navigational query, 132, **136**
negative ad copy, **105–106**
negative broad match, **47–48**
negative exact match, **49**
negative information, in reviews, 152
negative keywords, **45–52**, 71, *445*, *446*
    in campaign level, 54, 520
    and display network ad groups, 251
    formatting, 46
    implementing, **46–47**
    for new account, 518
    with positive, **50–51**
    researching, **51–52**
    and total conversions, 54
negative lists, in ad group, 296, *297*
negative phrase match, **48–49**
negative sign (-), in search query, 211
neighborhoods, as keywords, 339
Netflix, 33
network reach, and separate campaigns, 430
network reports, **259–261**, **503–505**, *504*
New Jersey, 345
new products pages, testing, 466
New York Times, 276
    placements, 268

newsletters, signing up users for, 204
no override tag, 128
nonconverter cookie, 298
nonlocals, ad copy for, 452
numbers, in ad copy, 99–102

O

Obendorf, Hartmut, *Off the Beaten Tracks*, 150
Off the Beaten Tracks (Weinreich, Obendorf, Herder and Mayer), 150
offers
    on landing pages, **476**
    time-sensitive, **415**
Ogilvy, David, 13
one-word queries, search volume skew to, 34
opening image, for video ads, 237
optimization techniques, 161
    best practices, **188–189**
    for campaigns, **524–539**
        search campaigns, **524–528**
    for conversion rate, **174–187**
    country-based, 334
    for CPM campaigns, **533–534**
    creating schedule, **535–539**
    for display campaign, **280–282, 530–531**
    display with AdWords Editor, **373–374**
    local ads, 350
    managed placements campaign, **531–532**
    reports and, **497–509**
    testing and, 450
    for traffic, **162–173**
        impression share report, **163–166,** *164*
        page views per visit, **170–173**
        strategies to increase display frequency ads, **162–166**
Optimize for Clicks, 455
Optimize for Conversions, 455

options, for optimizing for page views, 171
options on web page, and cognitive overload, 174
organic listings, for searches, 15
organic rankings, duplicate pages crawled and, 482
originality of website, 203
Overture, 5

P

Page, Larry, 5
page security level, for conversion tracking script, 381
page views
    revenue from, 397
    tracking as conversions, *529*
page views per visit, 135
    increasing, **170–173**
parameters, for URL tracking, 124
parked domains, blocking ad display, 264, *264*
part numbers, as keywords, 25
paused ads, finding, **501,** *501*
paused keyword, resuming, 218
pay-per-click (PPC) advertising, 1, 2
paycheck schedule, and conversion rates, **413–415,** *414*
Pennsylvania, 345–346
performance-based advertising, 3
performance, viewing demographic stats, **287–289,** *288*
personal information, collecting, 204
Pew Internet, 247
Philadelphia, CTR difference with rest of state, 346
phone calls
    providing option for, 187
    tracking, call extension for, **385–386**
phone number
    adding to ads, 110
    for customer support, 185
    in mobile ad copy, **227–228**
.php file extension, 381

phrase match, **40–41**, 66
  budget and, 43
  conversion rate, *54*
  negative, **48–49**
physical store, vs. website, 477
pivot table
  for Ad Performance report, *500*
  from Ad Planner data, 316–317
  for day-of-week conversion
    information, 408–409, *409*
  demographic data, *288*, 288
  Destination URL report and, *506*
  geographic data in, *349*, 349
  from keyword list, 318
  from keyword report, 214–216, *216*
placement ads, controlling display,
  278–280
placement bids, 391
  change in, *536*
Placement Performance report, 260,
  284, 435, 523, 530
placement targeting, 248–249, 266, 282
  destination URL for, 123
Placement tool (Google), 266, 285, *286*
placements, 248. *See also* managed
  placements
  organizing, **269**
  reason for adding demographic sites
    as, 291
Places account (Google), 342, 343
play button, for video ads, 237
play rate, for video ad, 236
plug-ins, 146–147
  for WordPress, 229
plurals, phrase match and, 41
plus (+) sign, for important keywords,
  38–39
pop-ups, avoiding on landing page, 204
poster images, 242
precise matches, and Quality Score, 198
premium ads, 218–219, *219*
prices
  in ad copy, 99–100
  vs. discounts, testing, 452–455
pricing model, 3

printer-friendly pages, 173, 187
priority, for goals, 514, *515*
privacy policies, **157**, 204
  page for visitor information on
    remarketing, 295–296
problem-based keywords, 24
product category queries, testing
  landing page for, **465–466**
product extensions, *110*, **110**
product names, as keywords, 25
profit per click
  testing, **484–486**, *485*
  vs. value per click, 395
profit per impression, testing, **484–486**,
  485
profits
  formula for setting bids based on,
    402
  increasing, 180
  vs. return on ad spend (ROAS),
    391–392
progress, in checkout process, 183
psychology
  and conversion rates, **151–158**
  of search, **7–15**
    ad copy purpose, **10–12**
    landing page, **12–13**
    turning concepts into words, **8–10**
publishers
  blocking individual advertiser, 282
  determining revenue per click,
    397–399
  tracking of subscriptions, 398
  traffic from international queries, 135
punctuation marks, in ad copy, 93
purchase decisions, research and
  learning before, 133
purple, on websites, 156

Q

quality call, length of, 111
quality control team, at Google, 16
Quality Score, 92, **191–221**
  and ad rank, **194–195**

basics, **192–199**
best practices for optimizing, 220–221
click-through rate and, 508
determining actual CPC from, 194–195
development of, 197
display network, **207–209**
factors for search, **195–199**
FAQs, **218–220**
fixing drops in, **212–217**
frequency of updates, 219
healthy accounts, **217**
Impression Share report and, 498
improving, 526–527
increasing, **214–217**
keyword insertion and, 170
keyword report and, 502
for managed placements, **208–209**
schedule for assessing, 536
testing display URLs and, 108
tracking and archiving, 212
viewing, **199–201**, *200*
weighted, 215
Quality Score Analyzer, 216
queries
geographic qualifier, 322–323
landing page choice based on query type, **132–136**
search volume skew to one-word, 34
testing landing pages for types, 463
in URL, question mark for delimiter, 123–124
query string in URL, 123–124
question mark (?), for query delimiter in URL, 123–124
questions, testing in ad copy, 104
quotation marks, for phrase match, 40

R

radius targeting, **331–333**, *332*
Reach and Frequency Performance report, 533
reach for match types, 44

Really Simple Syndication (RSS) feeds, 268
recommended products, on websites, 172
red circle, in AdWords Editor, 358
red, on websites, 156
redirect, and landing page load time, 197–198
region, search engine accuracy in determining, 325
regional lingo
as keywords, 339–340
nonlocals and, 340–341
registration of users
forcing, 180
option for, 179
relevance, 2–3, 16, 192, **209–212**, 311, 475–476
of ads to particular website, 207–208
factors in Quality Score, 199
of keywords, 30
to ad copy within ad group, 196
of landing page, 202–205
remarketing, 275, **292–305**, 534
500 cookie rule, **297**
creating ad group, **296**
custom combinations, **294**, *294*
defining audience, **293**, *293*
frequency numbers in, 508
Google policies on, 297
strategies, **298–304**
targeting by interest, 299–302
visitors, abandons, and nonconverters, 298
visitors and converters, 298
tag code, *295*
topic targeting for, 308
by trends, **303–304**
repeating words in ad copy, 93
reports, 491
access to My Client Center, 427
for account optimization, **497–509**
Ad Group Performance, **498–499**
Ad Performance, **459–462**, *461*, **499–501**, 531
pivot table for, *500*

best practices, **511**
campaigns, **497–498**
Change History, 361
cross-account, 427
customizing columns, *493*, **493–495**,
    494
   to include conversion data, *384*
Demographic, 507
Destination URL, *482*, **482–483**,
    505–506, *527*
dimension, **505–509**
downloading data, *495*, **495–496**
finding day-of-week conversion
   information, **408–410**
Free Clicks, 533
general settings, **492–496**
   customizing interface, *492*,
    492–495
Geographic, *348*, **348–350**, **507–508**
impression share, **163–166**, *164*
Impression Share, **497–498**, *527*
Invalid Clicks, 497
keyword, 317–318, **502**
on keyword value per click data, *393*
network, **259–261**, **503–505**, *504*
Placement Performance, 260, 284,
   435, 523, 530
Reach and Frequency Performance,
   533
scheduling in Google, 212, *213*
Search Funnel, 417
Search Query, 44, **502–503**, *503*,
   526, 536
   negative keywords in, 51–52
for video ads, 237
research sessions, 304
research, with DoubleClick Ad Planner,
   312–319
resizing text, in Chrome browser, *144*
Resolution Test Chrome plug-in, 150
restaurants, specials ads for day of
   week, 439
retargeting campaign, *524*
retention phase, in buying cycle, 20

return on ad spend (ROAS), 100
   alternatives to bid based on, 415–418
   bid decisions, AdWords reports and,
    418–421
   vs. profit, 391–392
   setting bids based on, **402–403**
return on investment (ROI), 171, 391
   ad groups with high, learning from,
    420
returns, campaign structure to
   maximize, **431–432**
revenue per click, 392–395
   determining for publishers, **397–399**
   and max CPC, 402–403
revenue per search (RPS), 6
revenue per visitor (RPV), 397
   combining with subscription revenue,
    398
reviews
   in ad copy, **104–105**
   sociability and, **151–152**
R.H. Donnelley, landing page for Royal
   Volkswagen, 478, *479*
rich media, 223
rich media ads, **231–239**
   best practices, 243–244
   bids, 523
risks in testing, low-tech approach to
   lowering, **488**
ROAS. *See* return on ad spend (ROAS)
robot, 63. *See also* spider
robots.txt file, 63, 177, 202, 203
   blocking testing pages with, 482
ROI (return on investment), 171, 391
   ad groups with high, learning from,
    420
root word list, 35–36
Rotate option for ads, 455–456
   for landing page testing, 481
Royal Volkswagen, landing page, 478,
   479
RPS (revenue per search), 6
RSS (Really Simple Syndication) feeds,
   268

S

sales cycles, tracking long with conversion funnel, **399–401**, *401*

sales, vs. marketing, and information collection, 182–183

saving keywords, and Quality Score, 218

scaling AdWords account, 362–373

scenarios, creating for target audience, 308–310

schedule. *See also* ad scheduling for optimization techniques, 535–539

scheduling campaigns, 439

scripts, and web page loading, 382

search
psychology, **7–15**
turning concepts into words, **8–10**
Quality Score factors for, **195–199**

Search Alliance, 5

search behavior, and buying funnel, 416

search box, on websites, 172

search campaigns, 250, 431
creating, **516–519**
vs. display campaigns, 253
optimizing, **524–528**
settings for, *517*

search CTRs, vs. display network CTRs, 207

search engine optimization (SEO), 64
dedicated landing pages and, 177

search engine results page (SERP), 7

search engines, 27

Search Funnel report, 417

search hierarchy, for destination URLs, 123

search history, geographic qualifiers, 323

search network, ad rank for, 192

search page views, 247

search partners, 193

search queries
ad copy reflecting, 86–87
change over time, 74
cost without conversions, 503

number of words used, 33–34

relevance of keyword and ad copy, 196

Search Query report, 44, **502–503**, *503*, 526, 536
negative keywords in, 51–52

search results, **10**
ads on page, 2
user time on page, 15

search sessions, 304

Search Share, 70

search theory, best practices, **17**

searchers
as focus for ad, 11
goal of increasing first-timers, 443
keyword research and, 23
landing page to answer question, 120–122
multiple campaigns to reach all, 336–337

"secret," in ad copy, 102

security, **148–149**, *149*
error warning, *148*
web technology for, **143–150**

Security Sockets Layer (SSL), 149

segmentation pages, **138–139**, 442
testing, 465

segmenting audience, 95

segmenting data by network, for testing, 461

self-serve ad model, **3–4**, *4*

selling propositions, unique, **93–94**

Send to Friend option, 187

SEO (search engine optimization), 64
dedicated landing pages and, 177

SERP (search engine results page), 7

services, offering, **77–80**

sharing web page, encouraging, 173

shipping prices, 179

shopping cart
progress in checkout process, 183
targeting abandoners, 302
user access to, 179

shopping, coupons to track, 154

shopping phase, in buying funnel, 22
short-term memory, 174
signup process, 3
Silverstein, Craig, 6
Site and Category Exclusion tool, 261, 270
sitelink extensions, *108*, **108–109**, *109*
size of ad images, 227, 235
smart pricing, for display network, 257
smartphone, call extensions with, **227**, 227
smartphone users, **224–226**
SMS, sending information to, 187
sociability, testimonials and reviews and, **151–152**
social extension, **112–113**
social media sites, options on web page, 172–173
social network share, 187
social networks, 282
  blocking ad display, 265
software, autoinstalling, 204
spaces, avoiding in destination URL, 124
spam, 157
special offers, on landing pages, **476**
specific reach, for campaign settings, 280
speech to text, 8
spelling, in ad copy, 92
spider
  Flash and JavaScript as limitation, 147
  landing page and, 202
  role in web, 63
  to start wide keyword research, 63–64
Spink, Amanda, 133
split testing, 88
spreadsheets. *See* Excel
SSL certificates, **148–149**, *149*
standard access, to My Client Center, 427
states
  abbreviations as keywords, 337
  names as keywords, 337

search engine accuracy in determining, 325
statistical significance, 481
  guidelines for, **457**
statistics, viewing demographic performance, **287–289**, *288*
status check, daily, 535
StumbleUpon, 8
subdomains, blocking ad display, 262
subscriptions, 135, 187
  combining revenue with RPV, **398**
  publishers' tracking of, 398
success, cost per conversion for measuring, **257–259**
suggested bid, from Contextual Targeting tool, **256–257**
superlatives, in ad copy, 93
supporting products, 171
symbols, in ad copy, 93
symptoms, as keywords, 25
syncing file before offline edits, in AdWords Editor, 360

T

tablets
  campaign for, 436–437
  targeting, 226
tags, for remarketing, 293
target audience
  creating scenarios for, **308–310**
  local or nonlocal, 137
targeting
  interest, **305–307**, *306*
  topic, *307*, **307–308**
telephone. *See* cell phones; phone number
templates, from AdWords, 240
terms of service (TOS) issues, multiple unlinked accounts and, 31, 424
testimonials
  in ad copy, **104–105**
  on landing page, *454*, 454
  sociability and, **151–152**
testing, 449
  ad copy, **450–451**, 499, 527

on display network, 531
in interest targeting, 307
B2B-focused ad on weekdays,
443–444
best practices, **489–490**
dynamic keyword insertion (DKI), 453
faces' use on website, 470–471
guidelines for statistical significance,
457–459
importance to increasing profits, **450**
landing pages, **462–484**, 527
factors for, **468–474**
low-tech approach to lowering risks,
488
measuring results, **459–462**
new products pages, 466
priority items for, **479–480**
profit per click, **484–486**, *485*
profit per impression, **484–486**, *485*
revising ads based on, 461–462
schedule for, *537*
segmentation pages, 465
segmenting data by network for, 461
statistical significance and, **457**
thank-you pages, **466–467**
themes for ad copy, **451–462**
ad copy, **455–456**
discounts vs. prices, **452–455**
time length for data collection, **458**
video ads, **472–474**
websites, 121
text
resizing in Chrome browser, *144*
viewing keywords as, 71
text ads. *See also* ad copy
account limits, 424
ad group for, 521
bids, 523
text links, for conversion activities,
156–157, *157*
Textanz, keyword density analyzer, *255*
thank-you pages, **140–141**
AdWords conversion tracking code
on, 383, *383*
testing, **466–467**

theme, 26, 98–108, 431
of ad groups, 207, 251
Theologos House of Jewelry website,
477, *478*
tilde (~) search command, for finding
keywords, **211**
time frames
comparison, *534*
for data displayed in report, 493, *493*
finding conversion information by,
408–410
for test data collection, **458**
viewing conversion rates by, 507
time of day, conversion rate by, 410, *411*
time periods, automatically changing
bids by, *406*, **406–415**
time-sensitive offers, **415**
time zone, and ad scheduling, 407, 439
timeshare company, campaign based on
goals or budget, **440–442**, *441*
TLS (Transport Layer Security), 149
Tools menu, 261
Edit Negative Campaign Keywords,
47
topic targeting, *307*, **307–308**
touch points, multiple to move through
buying funnel, 399
tracking
abandoned forms, 184
conversions in AdWords, **398–399**
destination URLs for, **123–125**
long sales cycles with conversion
funnel, **399–401**, *401*
page views as conversions, *529*
phone calls, call extension for, **385–
386**
website changes, 212
tracking indicator, 382
tracking parameters, for URLs, 109
trademarks, **113–115**
exceptions, **115**
symbol in ad copy, 93
traffic
estimating for keywords, 71
minimum amount for testing, **458**

optimization techniques for, 162–173

    impression share report, 163–166, *164*

    strategies to increase display frequency ads, 162–166

Traffic Estimator, 72, 72–74, *74*

transactional queries, 132–133

transparency, 203–204

    of data to advertiser, 7

Transport Layer Security (TLS), 149

trends

    remarketing by, 303–304

    schedule for assessing, 537

trust, 120, 143

    errors with customers and, 381

    increasing, 464, 465

tutorials, targeting consumers who examined, 300–301

Twitter, 173

two-word rule, for grouping keywords, 26

U

umlauts, in URLs, 131

unique approach, to testing ads, 450

unique selling propositions, 93–94

United States, 157

U.S. Patent and Trademark Office, 114

URL parameters, 123–124

URLs. *See also* destination URLs; display URL

    broken, 212

    tracking parameters for, 109, 124

usability, 142–143

    goals for website, 157–158

    web technology for, 143–150

user-generated content sites, 265

user intent, 442

    associating ad copy with, 35

    exact match and, 42

    long-tail queries and, 34

user login, for AdWords account access, 360

users. *See also* customer

limiting ad view by single, 272

targeting based on interests, 305–307, *306*

V

value per click

    conditional formatting on report, 394

    vs. profit per click, 395

vCard download, 187

VeriSign, 149

video ads, 236–239, *237*

    autoplay for, 473

    best practices, 243–244

    and bidding CPM, 270

    creating, 237–238

    expandable, 242–243

    formats, 241–243

    in-stream, 242

    measuring effectiveness of, 236

    technical and editorial requirements, 238–239

    testing, 472–474

video sites, keeping ad off, 263–264, *264, 265*

view-through conversion window, 382

Visa credit cards, 182

visitors. *See* customer

volume, of video ad, 238

VPNs (virtual private networks), location targeting and, 324

W

w3schools.com

    browser resolutions, 149, *150*

    global web stats, 144–145

Wagner, Matt Van, 168

WAP Image Ad button, 228

web analytics system, 27

Web Developer toolbar, 147

web pages. *See also* landing pages

    browser loading of, 382

web technology, for usability and user security, 143–150

webbot, 63. *See also* spider
webinar, 187
Website Optimizer, 481
websites. *See also* landing pages
    accessibility for, **143–144**
    blocking ad display, 530
        on those not converting, **261–262**
    checking for broken links, 506
    choosing which to show ads, **265–273**
    color for, **156**
    content management system, 515
    conversion funnels on, 141
    with demographic bidding, 287
    detailed information in DoubleClick Ad Planner, *315*, 315
    difficulty judging own, 121
    faces on, 155
    finding related with Google Ad Planner, **316–317**
    information above the fold, **149–150**
    and jumpstarting keyword list, **62–64**
    markup language for, 381
    max CPA for lead generation, 388
    mobile-compatible, creating, **229**
    originality of, 203
    vs. physical store, 477
    placing cookie script on, **295–296**
    quality, **281**
    recommended products on, 172
    same content on multiple pages, 203
    search box on, 172
    speed of, 148
    testing, 121
    thank-you pages, **140–141**
    tracking changes, 212

usability goals, **157–158**
    user-generated content, 265
    viewing mobile usage, 226
weighted Quality Score, 215
Weinreich, Harald, *Off the Beaten Tracks*, 150
white, on websites, 156
whitepaper download, 187
wide keywords
    vs. deep, 35–36
    spider to start research, 63–64
Wikipedia.org, 27
Windows (Microsoft), keyboard shortcuts, 357
Wired, 33
wish list, 187
Wojcicki, Susan, 5
WordPress, 229
WordPress Mobile Edition, 229
words
    change in meaning, 28
    turning concepts into, **8–10**
WordStream, 72
Wordtracker, 71–72

Y

Yahoo!
    vs. Google, 5
    revenue per visitor, 6
Yahoo! Clues, 29
yellow circle, in AdWords Editor, 358
YouTube video ads, 241–242

Z

zip codes, as keywords, 338–339